EDUCATIONAL
AND
PSYCHOLOGICAL
MEASUREMENT
AND
EVALUATION

SIXTH EDITION
EDUCATIONAL AND PSYCHOLOGICAL MEASUREMENT AND EVALUATION

KENNETH D. HOPKINS

Laboratory of Educational Research
University of Colorado

JULIAN C. STANLEY

Department of Psychology
The Johns Hopkins University

Prentice-Hall, Inc., Englewood Cliffs, New Jersey 07632

Library of Congress Cataloging in Publication Data

Hopkins, Kenneth D
    Educational and psychological measurement and evaluation.

    (Prentice-Hall series in educational measurement, research, and statistics)
    In the 1972 ed. J. C. Stanley's name appeared first on t.p.
    Bibliography: p.
    Includes index.
    1. Educational tests and measurements. 2. Psychological tests.
I. Stanley, Julian C., joint author. II. Title.
LB1131.S698   1981   371.2′6   80-25015
ISBN 0-13-236273-2

Prentice-Hall Series in Educational Measurement, Research, and Statistics
Gene V Glass, Editor

Educational and Psychological Measurement and Evaluation, 6/e, *Kenneth D. Hopkins*
and Julian C. Stanley is the sixth edition of the book formerly titled
Measurement in Today's Schools, *Julian C. Stanley and Kenneth D. Hopkins.*

Printed in the United States of America

10 9 8 7

Editorial/production supervision and interior design by Fred Bernardi
Cover design by Jorge Hernandez
Manufacturing buyer: Edmund W. Leone

PRENTICE-HALL INTERNATIONAL, INC., *London*
PRENTICE-HALL OF AUSTRALIA PTY. LIMITED, *Sydney*
PRENTICE-HALL OF CANADA, LTD., *Toronto*
PRENTICE-HALL OF INDIA PRIVATED LIMITED, *New Delhi*
PRENTICE-HALL OF JAPAN, INC., *Tokyo*
PRENTICE-HALL OF SOUTHEAST ASIA PTE. LTD., *Singapore*
WHITEHALL BOOKS LIMITED, *Wellington, New Zealand*

To
Colleen
Jonathan
Beata

Contents

What is Measurement? How Much Precision Is Needed?
What About Variables That Are Not Directly Observable?
Observation and Quantification. The Paradox of Testing.
Measurement and Evaluation in the Educational Process.
Educational Decisions Founded on Evaluation. Essential Knowledge and Skills.
The Goals and Functions of Testing. Instructional Functions. Administrative Functions.
Guidance Functions. Summary. Important Terms and Concepts. Chapter Test.
Answers to Chapter Test. For Additional Reading.

Preface

For three decades (1941–72) *Measurement in Today's Schools,* in its four successive editions, was a standard textbook in educational measurement. The revision of the fourth edition included modifications that were so basic and extensive that it would have been inaccurate to describe that volume as a fifth edition of *Measurement in Today's Schools.* Therefore, in 1972 it was given the more descriptive title *Educational and Psychological Measurement and Evaluation.* This sixth edition, although changed considerably, is a true revision, not a new book. As in the previous edition, the selection and treatment of topics were guided by two general considerations: (1) knowledge and skills that are necessary for the *development* of valid evaluation measures and (2) knowledge and competences that are required for a proper *interpretation* of informal and standardized tests.

The book is divided into three major parts: (I) Basic Concepts, (II) The Development of Educational Measures, and (III) Standardized Measures. To afford flexibility in the selection of chapters to fit various curricular objectives, several chapters are essentially self-contained. Part III can be ignored when the course's emphasis is entirely on test development. The chapter on grading and reporting is a "cul-de-sac" option branching off from the thoroughfare of the other chapters. For certain courses in classroom and educational testing, Chapter 15 (Standard Interest, Personality, and Social Measures) may be skipped without disruption.

The sixth edition differs from the fifth in several respects. The content has been updated in terms of recent research and assessment trends. It has also been reorganized. The number of chapters has been reduced from 17 to 15 by integrating into other chapters the most important portions of the chapters on the history of educational measurement and the testing program.

The single chapter on statistics has been broken down into smaller, and more digestible, "bite-sized" units. These topics and concepts have been integrated with norms and criterion-related validity and are now spaced over three chapters. Because of the positive feedback we received, we have continued to use the innovation (among measurement texts) of interspersing self-instruction reinforcement into the usual narrative treatment of statistical concepts that was introduced in the fifth edition. The purpose of this strategy is to reduce the inordinate amount of time frequently devoted to statistics in introductory measurement courses so that the course does not become a watered-down statistics course. The primary objective of the statistics is conceptual, not computational, although of course the two interact.

The bibliography documents the fact that extensive use has been made of research from the past ten years to enhance and update topics of current interest such as the "achievement decline" and "ethnic bias." The treatment of criterion-referenced, mastery, and minimum competency testing has been expanded considerably. The treatment of test development represents a more balanced view, reflecting both norm-referenced and criterion-referenced aspects. Other topics that were not included or emphasized in earlier editions include cloze testing, readability, and the measurement of study habits and other school-related attitudes.

The chapter on test reliability has been completely rewritten, and most of the other chapters have been substantially revised.

Another change in the sixth edition is the addition of mastery tests following each chapter. These are designed to be of diagnostic value to students as well as to reinforce their understanding.

During the two years we spent developing this edition, numerous individuals contributed in many ways to our efforts. We cannot name them all here, but several colleagues deserve special thanks. Gene V. Glass, Lorrie Shepard, Mary Lee Smith, Steve Jurs, Dick Bennet, George Kretke, Carey Nelson, Marilyn Averill, Linda Sasser, La Prelle Martin, Carol Vojir, and Lynn Daggett contributed helpful suggestions and insights. The instructor's manual and author and subject indexes were prepared by Bob Hopkins.

We are indebted to Viki Bergquist, Karen O'Grady, Gwen Decino, Mary Ann Gard, and Lisa Johnson for the tedious task of deciphering, typing, and correcting the various drafts of the manuscript.

KENNETH D. HOPKINS
JULIAN C. STANLEY

Tables

Figures

EDUCATIONAL
AND
PSYCHOLOGICAL
MEASUREMENT
AND
EVALUATION

I

BASIC CONCEPTS

1

Measurement: Its Nature and Function

What Is Measurement?

Many people have erroneous notions about the nature of measurement. *Measurement is the process by which things are differentiated.* It is not limited to the use of highly developed and refined instruments. Certainly, thermometers, yardsticks, and stopwatches can be used to measure temperature, distance, and time. But these variables can also be measured informally by observation—by the "trained eye." Skilled printers using only sight and touch are said to be able to assess (measure) the thickness of a film of ink to an incredible degree of precision—millionths of an inch! Our senses are our yardsticks for measuring the environment around us.

We do not need a thermometer to tell whether it is "hot" or "cold" today, even though the thermometer can measure more accurately and purely (i.e., without the confounding effects of humidity, wind, etc.) than our impressionistic assessment. The point is that any differentiation among members of a class of things involves a process of measurement, be the things objects, days, schools, dogs, or persons. "To exist is to measure." Of course, the validity of the differentiation is a direct reflection of the quality of the measuring instrument. Indeed, there is a close correspondence between the scientific maturity of a discipline and the degree to which the relevant variables in that discipline can be measured objectively and accurately.

How Much Precision Is Needed?

If you estimate (measure by observation) how much each of your classmates weighs, the resulting "measurements" would have some validity, but not as much as they would if a bathroom scale had been used. The weights (measurements) yielded by the scale would contain some degree of measurement error, because no manmade measuring instrument is perfect. This need not discourage us; the degree of precision needed in a measurement depends on its purpose. Physicists and chemists need to measure temperature to hundredths of a degree, but do you care whether it reaches 82.6° or 82.3° today? Or whether you are not actually 67 1/2″ tall but only 67.47″? Or whether you can correctly spell 43.76%, and not 44%, of the words in *Webster's College Dictionary*? *The degree of precision needed in a measurement is related to the purpose served by the measurement.* The appropriate degree of precision of measures in education and the behavioral sciences is usually less than that required in engineering and the physical sciences.

What About Variables That Are Not Directly Observable?

If *personological* (person) *variables* cannot be observed directly but instead must be inferred from indirect indications, the measurements will contain a greater degree of error. Musical aptitude, scholastic aptitude, and self-concept cannot be measured with the same validity as height, weight, and age. Such variables as reading ability, writing ability, and penmanship can be observed behaviorally but nevertheless lack the common "yardsticks" possessed by height, weight, and age. Variables like these are, and must be, assessed continually by teachers during the process of education. The more accurate the measurements are, the more valid decisions based on those measurements can be. A goal of this book is to enable you to understand better the degree of accuracy in various measures in order to estimate and improve the reliability and validity of important educational and psychological measures.

Observation and Quantification

How do first-graders know that the "blue birds" are the best readers and the "yellow birds" are the poorest readers even before any formal reading test has been administered? They do so because observation itself is a process of measurement. Even now, as you read this chapter, you are implicitly or explicitly monitoring (measuring) many variables—how long you have been reading (time), how well the material is written, the level of vocabulary being used, the degree of interest you have in the material, your fatigue, and so forth. If the situation required it, you could quantify these measurements on, for example, a scale from 1 to 5.

But *the process of measurement does not necessarily involve the use of numbers* (quantification). As you study a classmate, you assess, consciously or thoughtlessly, the age, sex, attractiveness, friendliness, and many other variables of that person. Perhaps the result of this measurement process is that the person is, to you, a "young, attractive, friendly female." Although we have a pretty clear notion of the meaning of "female," what is "young," "attractive," and "friendly"? These variables do not have a precise, uniform meaning from one observer to another—they are to some extent dependent on "the eye of the beholder." By your yardstick "young" might mean less than 25 years of age, but by my yardstick "young" could include persons in their 40s. In other words, words contain much ambiguity—there is uneven calibration from one person to another. Indeed, a speaker and a listener often do not realize that the meaning of the information sent is not identical with the meaning of the information received. "We're having a cold winter day" means one thing in Florida but something else in North Dakota.

But when the results of measurement can be quantified and expressed in numbers, this source of error—semantic ambiguity—can be reduced greatly. "I'm tall and skinny" means something; "I'm 6'4" tall and weigh 160 pounds" means much more. Is the latter expression dehumanizing because it uses numbers? You are too wise to be taken in by such fatuous, "knee jerk" associations.

Quantification is not an end in itself; it is employed because it allows information to be communicated and interpreted with less ambiguity and less subjectivity than would otherwise be the case. Educational and psychological tests and inventories are simply attempts to obtain information and personological variables in a systematic manner and to express these results with a minimum of ambiguity, a point that has eluded many critics of educational and psychological tests.

The Paradox of Testing

There is a paradox in educational measurement today. While assessments of achievement and competence are being more urgently called for and more widely employed than ever before, tests are, at the same time, being more sharply criticized and more strongly opposed. [Ebel, 1976]

Glass (1975) discusses the paradox: Many people are opposed to measurement and evaluation, yet at the same time favor excellence, which is facilitated by and can be identified only through measurement and evaluation. Glass poses two questions to illustrate the paradox: (1) "Would you show a judgmental-evaluative attitude toward a person you were counseling?" (2) "Would you show a judgmental-evaluative attitude toward a person if you sought to improve his or her performance as a professional or an employee?"

Many people answer no to the first question but yes to the second. When Glass asked his colleagues if they sensed an inconsistency, they admitted that they did. We hope you will agree with us that measurement and evaluation are in the best interests of students in particular and society in general—that educational decisions are only as good as the quality of the measurement information on which they are based.

Anti-testing crusades have often been ignited by first- or secondhand contact with a poor test, poor test items, or tests that have been inappropriately used and interpreted. These "straw men" are not defended by reputable measurement specialists. Indeed, the testing profession has a tradition of pulling-no-punches critiques of every published test via the *Mental Measurements Yearbooks,* begun in 1936 by the late O. K. Buros. Journalistic exposés can make a cogent case on the evils of testing, especially standardized testing, if the audience lacks an understanding of the fundamentals of measurement.

Particularly unfortunate were two 1975 issues of *National Elementary Principal* that carried several unfair and naive articles, which appeared in 1977 as a book, *The Myth of Measurability,* in which tests and those who develop them are vilified. Here are some quotes from the book: "I feel emotionally toward the testing industry as I would toward any other merchants of death." "[Tests] are polluting the whole atmosphere of education." "One serious disadvantage of the present use of tests is that they let the wrong sort of people take control of testing." Such outlandish and emotionally charged language may make interesting reading, but it does not serve the best interests of education; it is not professionally responsible. The choice is not between current tests (many of which are excellent) and superior alternatives kept back by people who are bent on subverting education. Most test publishers are private-enterprise operations that offer their wares in a competitive marketplace; they are not sinister organizations. The substance of various anti-testing criticisms will be considered in the appropriate contexts in later chapters of this book.

The attacks on testing represent misunderstandings about the nature and purposes of tests; how they are developed; what *norms, reliability,* and *validity* mean; how tests should be used and interpreted; and the emotional effects they have on examinees. Of course, the fact that a test is standardized and published is no guarantee of quality or professional endorsement—"there is much chaff amongst the wheat."

Providing an understanding of these and related issues is the basic objective of this book. Some of the basic issues in the anti-testing movement are addressed in a position paper (APGA, 1972) developed by the American Personnel and Guidance Association (APGA), the Association for Measurement and Evaluation in Guidance (MEG), and the National Council on Measurement in Education (NCME):

WHAT TESTING IS[1]

Testing is not a policy nor a set of beliefs or principles. Testing is a technique for obtaining information. Its special virtue is that this information is provided in organized form, and that the technology of testing also provides methods for determining how dependable or undependable the information is.

As a technique, testing itself is neutral. It is a tool that serves the ends of the user. The better he understands the technology of testing, the better it meets his needs. The less well he grasps this technology, the greater the risk that inadvertently (and perhaps unknowingly) he may work at cross-purposes to his own goals.

In schools and colleges, the principal needs served by testing include the pro-

[1] Copyright 1972, American Personnel and Guidance Association. Reprinted by permission.

viding of information (a) to teachers, as an aid to the improvement of instruction; (b) to students and, in the case of younger students, to their parents, as an aid to self-understanding and to both educational and vocational planning; and (c) to administrators, as a basis for planning, decision-making, and evaluating the effectiveness of programs and operations.

In business, industry, government service, and other walks of life, the general goal of testing is that of improving the match between persons and jobs, whether they be manual or managerial, personal contact or professional. Tests serve either to verify claimed knowledge or competence (e.g., a typing test) or to appraise readiness to master the training needed in order to perform the job. They may be used either competitively (to aid in selecting the best qualified and to avoid political or racial favoritisms), or as a standard (to avoid placing on the job persons whose work would likely be unsafe or uneconomic). Not every job nor every selection situation is equally likely to benefit from the use of tests, of course.

In these terms, testing as such would seem hard to criticize and quite unlikely to arouse antagonism or draw complaints from anyone. Yet it has been the target of bitter attacks, by members of some minority groups and by others in their behalf. The attacks usually result from one, or from a combination of two, of these three factors:

1. The use of tests, more or less competently, by administrators and others with whose goals and values the attackers disagree.

2. Side effects of testing, unintended results obtained when tests are used incompetently or without due regard for their technological strengths and limitations.

3. Misunderstandings of the role played by testing—the tendency to attribute to the tool shortcomings of its user, often accompanied by the simplistic assumption that if use of the tool is forbidden, things will somehow get better if not be entirely all right. . . .

THE RESPECTFUL USE OF TESTS

. . . Good testing is marked by

I. Respect for the Individual

In educational and clinical testing, all the work is undertaken for the benefit ultimately of those who are tested, not of the institutions and agencies doing the testing.

In employment testing, the primary benefit may be the employer's—but in the long run no selection program can be of genuine value to the employer if it is not so designed and conducted as to benefit also the employees and the applicants.

II. Respect for the Instrument

It is an abuse of the instrument, as well as disrespectful of the individual's needs and rights, to use a test for a purpose inappropriate to those characteristics and limits that make it a test. Test directions, stimulus material, verbal or other content, time limit, and supporting data, all must be considered in the decision to use a particular measure with particular individuals for a particular purpose under particular circumstances. . . .

Decisions of this kind may be quite clear and easy to make, but often are neither; frequently the *purpose* is the crucial consideration. It may, for example, be both fair and useful to give an individual examination in English to a child or adult whose native language is another, when the purpose is simply to appraise his readiness to profit from lectures given in English; yet the same activity clearly is indefensible if the test score is to be used as an estimate of his all-round intellectual capability. . . .

Fix the tools? It is very tempting to think that if only better, "fairer," more nearly perfect tests were made, all will be well. But better tests will not solve the social ills they reflect. Indeed, as John W. Gardner pointed out ten years ago in *Excellence,* the more adequately tests do what they are supposed to do, the *more, not the less,* will they provide disturbing information when the underlying social, economic, and educational conditions are not those of equality.

Better tests can and will be made—but while seeking perfection, we cannot wait for its realization. Even though imperfect and incomplete, the information tests provide is essential to realistic handling of our educational and personnel problems—whether they be those of learning or of teaching, of hiring a worker or of getting a job.

Ban testing? The role of measurement is too central, too fundamental to the conduct and improvement of education and to sound personnel practices in business and industry for this to be a realistic alternative. For some years it was illegal to request information as to race on applications for admission or employment; forbidding the recording of such information was thought to work toward the abolition of discrimination. Now the trend is reversed; organizations are required by law to obtain and report the very information that they once were forbidden to ask. What vanished under the ban was not discrimination, but the ability to tell whether and to what extent colleges or employers were doing what nearly all now agree they should do. The same cycle may be predicted if we try to deal with the present problem by doing away with tests; the ostrich approach does not lead to the effective solution of problems. Organizations and persons committed to changing educational or social systems, no less than those seeking to preserve a system, will need the information that measurement provides.

Measurement and Evaluation in the Educational Process

Are you aware of how widely various *measures*—such as tests of achievement, intelligence, interest, and aptitude—are used? More than 200 million standardized tests are administered each year, in addition to many times that number of classroom tests. The process of education depends extensively on measurement and on a related procedure—*evaluation.* The word *evaluation* designates a summing-up process in which value judgments play a large part, as in grading and promoting students, whereas the development, administration, and scoring of tests constitutes the *measurement* process. Interpreting such scores is part of the process of evaluation.

A simple illustration may clarify the distinction. Miss Pelz gives her class a standardized spelling test consisting of 25 difficult words. She finds that the number of words spelled correctly ranges from 6 to 25, and that the average number correct is 15. Will Miss Pelz stop here? The mother of one of her pupils may ask, "How *well* is David doing in spelling?" Miss Pelz may show her his test and explain that he spelled 16 words correctly out of 25 on the test. David's mother may press for an evaluation of the measurement (i.e., the score of 16) by replying, "Nine words wrong, 64 percent right; is that as terrible as it sounds?"

If Miss Pelz answers, "More than half of the pupils missed a greater number than he did," she is confining her remarks to the distribution of scores on the test, that is, staying within the area we call measurement. If, however, she agrees that 16 is indeed a "poor" score, or if she insists that in view of his aptitude David is spelling about as well as can be expected, then Miss Pelz is evaluating the score.

We consider the conversion of test scores to grades such as A, B, C, D, F, "Excellent," "Good," "Fair," "Poor," or "High," "Average," "Low" as evaluation rather than measurement, because value judgments are implicit in such conversions. Important value judgments are made in selecting the items and the time and method of giving the test and scoring it, but the process of attaching value judgments to *performance* on the measure is uniquely evaluation. Whether a student's score is good or bad for a given purpose cannot be determined solely from the score itself. An interpretation must be made. The test score is often interpreted in terms of fixed standards, such as 80–89 percent receives a grade of B, or in terms of the student's rank on the test in his class or the student's score in relation to his or her academic aptitude. Throughout this book the distinctions between measurement and evaluation that we emphasize are not always sharp or meaningful—their colors run together. But an evaluation is subjective to the extent that the results depend on *who* is evaluating rather than on *what* is being evaluated. Little subjectivity is involved in determining the fastest runner in Mr. Smith's fourth-grade class, but considerable subjectivity is involved in *deciding* who should receive the best citizenship award. If a rating remains constant irrespective of the rater, the rating is said to be objective. The extent to which a measurement or evaluation is subjective is the degree to which personal bias and prejudice can influence scores. It is desirable to increase the objectivity of testing, interviewing, rating, and similar enterprises that often are pursued quite subjectively. *Increasing the objectivity of the assessment and evaluation of human behavior is a chief aim of this book.*

We are interested in increasing objectivity not for its own sake but because, as later chapters will make clear, the validity of a measure or evaluation is usually enhanced as it becomes less subjective.

Educational Decisions Founded on Evaluation

If we view "tests and measurements" narrowly as the preparing, administering, scoring, and norming of objective tests, we are likely to overlook important ways in which evaluation supports the entire educational system. Why do we have schools? Obviously, society has decided that without them many people would probably not acquire essential knowledge, understanding, skills, and attitudes. Schools are organized the way they are because, on the basis of much experience, current patterns appear to "work best"—at least in the eyes of those who make educational decisions. Why is a particular school built where it is, as large as it is, and with certain facilities? Why are some teachers hired to staff it and others not? What determines salaries, the choice of textbooks and other instructional aids, grades, promotions, reports to parents, grouping patterns, the community's reactions to the school and its products, recommendations for college and jobs? All of these decisions involve evaluations. Objective measurement is usually an essential prerequisite for sound evaluation, but it is by no means sufficient.

Most educators consider that a school's main business is promoting "growth" toward desirable individual and societal objectives; fewer agree on who should judge the desirability of these objectives. However, since all schools focus on pupil progress as the ultimate criterion, it is important to evaluate the status and gains of pupils expertly. How well are Mary and Paul doing? Should they be doing better?

Measurement and evaluation encompass such subjective aspects as the judgments made by teachers and administrators. Let us not fall into the trap of asking whether we should use teacher judgments *or* test scores. Faced by complex problems of measurement and evaluation of pupil growth and influences affecting it, we cannot reject any promising resource. Various sorts of information *supplement* each other.

Are today's educators being equipped adequately for the performance of their evaluation responsibilities? One study (Mayo, 1967) found that graduating seniors in 86 teacher-training institutions did not demonstrate a very high level of measurement competence. A study of the social consequences of testing and the development of talent (Goslin, 1967) found that about 60 percent of all teachers had only minimal exposure to training in test and measurement techniques. The unsatisfactory quality of the majority of teacher-made tests no doubt reflects this inadequacy in training. Not surprisingly, teachers who have had little preparation in tests and measurements tend to make little use of the information obtained from standardized tests (Goslin, 1967). We are in complete sympathy with the concluding statement from Goslin's comprehensive study (1967b, p. 140): "The role of teachers in testing is too important to be left to chance."

Essential Knowledge and Skills

What should school personnel know about measurement and evaluation, and what abilities do they need in this area? Figure 1–1 presents the three primary components of the educational process—a process for changing the behavior and attitudes of students. First, educational goals are established either explicitly or (more often) implicitly. Learning experiences are then designed to promote the attainment of those goals. Finally, an evaluation is conducted to determine the extent to which the objectives have been attained. The results of the evaluation may affect the objectives and the instruction. The double-

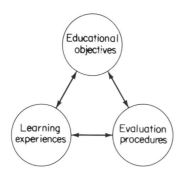

FIGURE 1-1 A graphic representation of the three interacting components of the educational process.

directed vectors of Figure 1–1 indicate the interacting nature of the entire process. If evaluation procedures are poor, then the quality of the information on which judgments must be based cannot be adequate.

The measurement and evaluation skills needed depend partly on the position one holds. The skills needed for kindergarten and primary-school teachers differ from those needed by high school physics and English teachers. Principals, counselors, and school psychologists need certain competencies besides those that are essential for teachers.

Fortunately, *certain concepts, principles, and skills are useful at all levels* and in nearly all positions. Even parents and others who are not professionally concerned with individual appraisal would benefit from a clear understanding of such concepts as "validity," "reliability," "IQ," and "norms." By concentrating on fundamental concepts and skills, we present in one textbook the basic measurement and evaluation *essentials* for most test users. Ebel (1961a, p. 68) has outlined six requisites for testing competence:

1. Know the uses, as well as the limitations, of tests.
2. Know the criteria by which the quality of a test should be judged and how to secure evidence relating to these criteria.
3. Know how to plan a test and write the test questions to be included in it.
4. Know how to select a standardized test that will be effective in a particular situation.
5. Know how to administer a test properly, efficiently, and fairly.
6. Know how to interpret test scores correctly and fully, but with recognition of their limitations.

Throughout this book these fundamentals are carefully illustrated with examples from various age and grade levels. No single book can present all of the specialized phases of measurement and evaluation, but it should at least refer the reader to good supplemental sources. This book does so at the end of each chapter.

Test users must know how to perform certain aspects of measurement and evaluation, such as constructing tests, giving grades, assessing potentialities, and interpreting standardized intelligence and achievement tests, themselves. They should know how to select from the many available tests, inventories, questionnaires, rating scales, checklists, and the like those that are most suitable for a particular purpose. Besides being able to understand directions for administering, scoring, and interpreting tests, test users should possess the ability to compare the most promising ones before the choice itself is made (Ebel, 1961c). This requires attaining the various concepts necessary to understand test publishers' literature, reviews, and articles reporting test research. *Educational and Psychological Measurement and Evaluation* is designed to help you achieve these important objectives.

The Goals and Functions of Testing

Tests serve a variety of functions. The purpose for which a test is given determines not only the appropriate *type* of test but also the test's *characteristics* (e.g., difficulty and reliability). A measure designed for accurate assessment of individual differences in arithmetic fundamentals requires very high test reliability, whereas a much shorter (and, hence, less reliable) test might suffice for program evaluation. Findley (1963b) classified the purposes served by tests in education under three *interrelated* categories: (1) instructional, (2) administrative, and (3) guidance. Standardized measures provide the basis for most of the guidance and administrative test roles, whereas teacher-made tests are used principally for instructional functions. In the sections that follow we discuss each of these three categories.

Instructional Functions

The Process of Constructing a Test Stimulates Teachers to Clarify and Refine Meaningful Course Objectives. If teachers are continually reminded of their destination, they are more apt to stay on course. Bloom (1961, p. 60) observed that

> participation of the teaching staff in selecting as well as constructing evaluation instruments has resulted in improved instruments on one hand, and on the other hand it has resulted in clarifying the objectives of instruction and in making them real and meaningful to teachers. . . . When teachers have actively participated in defining objectives and in selecting or constructing evaluation instruments they return to the learning problems with great vigor and remarkable creativity. . . . Teachers who have become committed to a set of educational objectives which they thoroughly understand respond by developing a variety of learning experiences which are as diverse and as complex as the situation requires.

Tests Provide a Means of Feedback to the Teacher. Feedback from tests helps the teacher provide more appropriate instructional guidance for individual students as well as for the class as a whole. Well-designed tests may also be of value for pupil self-diagnosis, since they help students identify specific weaknesses.

Properly Constructed Tests Can Motivate Learning. As a general rule, students pursue mastery of objectives more diligently if they expect to be evaluated. In the intense competition for a student's time, courses without examinations are often "squeezed" out of high-priority positions. When queried, students have consistently reported greater study and learning with periodic testing (Feldhusen, 1964). The anticipation of a forthcoming test may also affect pupils' "intention to remember" instructional set. Fifty years ago, a study (White, 1932) found that students expecting a final examination performed much better than comparable students in the same classes who thought they had been exempted from the final. More recently, Williams and Ware (1976) confirmed that students who expected to be tested following a videotaped lecture learned more from the lecture than a control group of students who were not told that they would be tested immediately following the lecture.

Examinations Are a Useful Means of Overlearning. When we review, interact with, or practice skills and concepts even after they have been

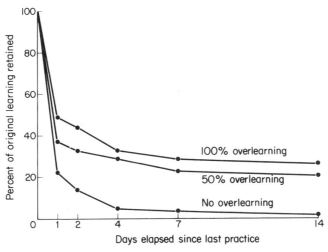

FIGURE 1-2 Forgetting following various degrees of overlearning.

mastered, we are engaging in what psychologists call *overlearning*. Even if a student correctly answers every question on a test, he or she may be engaging in behavior that is instructionally valuable *apart from the evaluation function being served* by the test. Scheduled examinations not only stimulate review (relearning and overlearning) but also foster overlearning through the process of reacting to test questions that assess content that has already been mastered. The value of overlearning for long-term retention is apparent in Figure 1-2, which presents the results of the classic study by Krueger (1929). The degree of retention of the meaning of a learned set of nouns was very slight for the no-overlearning group (bottom line), whereas the overlearning groups had a much superior degree of retention. Underwood (1964, p. 140) stated, "The evidence that such continued repetition does influence retention performance is so strong that it cannot be dismissed."

Although most of the research on overlearning has been based on the learning of mazes and nonsense syllables, it is probable that the forgetting curves for meaningful materials follow a similar but less dramatic pattern. "The best way of mitigating forgetting is to give immediate feedback of results" (Wood, 1977, p. 201). Many studies have shown that immediate knowledge of results enhances learning (Berglund, 1969; Zontine, Richards & Strang, 1972; Beeson, 1973; Strang & Rust, 1973; McMillan, 1977).

Administrative Functions

Tests Provide a Mechanism of "Quality Control" for a School or School System. National or local norms can provide a basis for assessing certain curricular strengths and weaknesses. If a school district does not have a means for periodic self-evaluation, instructional inadequacies may go unnoticed. This function is illustrated in Figure 3-3 (p. 63) and Figure 14-14 (p. 411). Also, the much-discussed national "achievement decline" (Harnischfeger & Wiley, 1976; Beaton, Hilton & Schrader, 1977; CEEB, 1977; Munday, 1979; see also Figure 3-3) illustrates the quality control function of tests and is a major purpose of the National Assessment of Educational Progress (NAEP, 1975), which monitors the educational achievement of American students in most curricular areas in three- to five-year cycles (see Table 14-2, p. 404).

Tests Are Useful for Program Evaluation and Research. Outcome measures are necessary to determine whether an innovative program is better or poorer than the conventional one in facilitating the attainment of specific curricular objectives. Standardized achievement tests have been the key sources of data for evaluating the success of federally funded programs (Jacobs and Felix, 1968, p. 19), although several other criteria are required for any comprehensive evaluation.

Much of teaching consists of searching for better ways to help students learn. For example, if three different methods for aiding seventh-graders to solve arithmetic reasoning problems are readily available to the teacher, which one or ones should be used? Is one of the methods superior to the other two for all seventh-graders, or is one of them better for slow learners and another better for fast learners? This question suggests an experiment in which nine groups are used, representing all combinations of three levels of ability (low, medium, and high) with the three methods. Tests would play a prominent part in such a study, but experimentation involves much more than testing.

More generally, how does one evaluate the effects of new curricula and various "social reforms"? (See Campbell, 1969.) An innovation such as "open education," computer-assisted instruction, compensatory preschool education, an eleven-month school year, or a radically different physics course may seem obviously promising to those who propose it, but skeptics will demand more evidence of its effectiveness than mere enthusiasm.

Tests Facilitate Better Classification and Placement Decisions. Grouping children by their ability levels is an example of classification for which tests can be of value. Reading readiness tests can be helpful for placing first-grade pupils in the proper classes, sections, or groups.

Tests Can Increase the Quality of Selection Decisions. Scholastic aptitude and achievement test scores have repeatedly demonstrated their value in identifying students who are or are not likely to succeed in various colleges. Certain jobs require special skills that are best assessed by well-designed tests. Tests are the primary criteria for identifying gifted or retarded children.

A test designed especially for a particular selection purpose may have quite different characteristics than one to be used for classification. For example, selection of the sixth-grade pupils who are proper candidates for a special remedial reading program would not require a test that would reliably detect differences between average and superior readers. However, *classification* of all pupils into high, average, and low reading groups would require a test that reliably differentiated among students along the entire reading ability continuum. Classification is the process of deciding which "treatment" a person should receive, whereas the selection decision is concerned with whether the person should be treated, employed, admitted, or the like. The distinguishing feature of selection decisions is that some persons are rejected. A test that identifies kindergarten pupils who will have difficulty reading (selection) may not be helpful in deciding which instructional strategy is best for a given pupil (classification).

Tests Can Be a Useful Means of Accreditation, Mastery, or Certification. Tests on which standards of performance have been established allow the demonstration of competence or knowledge that may have been acquired in an unconventional way. The examinee may thereby receive some deserved credit or authorization. As Harcleroad (1974, p. 5) observed, "measurement can help reduce some artificial barriers to the degree or credential." For example, the Tests of General Educational Development (GED tests) were designed to allow men returning from military service to receive formal credit for demonstrated proficiency in various areas of academic achievement. This provision expedited the acquisition of a high school diploma for thousands of World War II veterans (Dressel and Schmidt, 1951; Lindquist, 1944). Students who have taken college-level courses in secondary schools can receive advanced placement in college if they demonstrate adequate competence on the Advanced Placement Examinations of the College Board (CB). In 1966 the CB began an extensive College Level Examination Program (CLEP) based on the principle of credit by examination (Flaugher, Mahoney, and Messing, 1967); its goal was to provide a national program of general and subject examinations so that people who have reached a college level of achievement outside the classroom can receive college credit or placement. Tests on which there is an established standard for acceptable performance are often referred to as *criterion-referenced tests.*

Perhaps the most common example of a test that serves as a means for demonstrating mastery or proficiency is the test one must pass to obtain a driver's license. Additional examples are the state board examinations for physicians, dentists, lawyers, and psychologists.

Guidance Functions

Tests Can Be of Value in Diagnosing an Individual's Special Aptitudes and Abilities. Obtaining measures of scholastic aptitude, achievement, interests, and personality is often an important aspect of the counseling process. The use of information from standardized tests and inventories can be helpful for guiding the selection of a college, the choosing of an appropriate course of study, the discovering of unrecognized abilities, and so on. Of course, there are poor tests just as there are good ones—they can be misused and misinterpreted, and in the wrong circumstances a test can become a weapon rather than a tool. If we achieve our objectives in this book, the chances that you will misinterpret or misuse tests and their results will be greatly reduced. As the president of the American Federation of Teachers has written,

> Tests are not perfect, they are subject to error and misinterpretation. We will seek to improve our methods of testing and measurement. But we cannot wait until there are perfect and infallible tests—there never will be. As professionals we will use the best measurements we have available to us. . . . The worst possible approach is to suggest prohibition of any standardized tests. Such a position only convinces the public that teachers are merely trying to cover their own shortcomings. [Shanker, 1977]

Summary

Tests play an important role in today's schools and other aspects of life. Thus, test users must know how to use and interpret them correctly.

Tests provide objective measurements on which educational decisions are based. From the standpoint of *instruction*, tests provide for feedback, motivation, and overlearning. From that of *administration*, they facilitate "quality control," program evaluation and research, classification and placement, selection, accreditation, mastery, and certification. From that of *guidance*, they serve to diagnose special aptitudes or abilities.

The aim of this book is to provide the necessary tools for proper selection and use of these various types of tests. However, it is up to you to make competence in educational measurement a reality.

We hope that this book will contribute to your thinking and actions. You should finish it with more *knowledge* about the special concepts and principles of measurement and evaluation than you may now possess. You will learn to *apply* your knowledge to new problems that confront you, to *analyze* situations efficiently, to *synthesize* (put ideas together creatively), and to *evaluate* soundly on the basis of internal evidence (e.g., within a test itself) and outside information (e.g., published standards for tests).

This book is important only to the extent that you permit it to *change* you. A continuous increase in your measurement competence in future years is the ultimate criterion.

In this chapter you have glimpsed a few of the ways in which measurement and evaluation figure in the educative process. The ideas and operations that we have mentioned will receive detailed treatment in the chapters that follow.

Educational and Psychological Measurement and Evaluation contains three main sections: The first five chapters deal with fundamental principles and concepts of measurement and evaluation; the next seven chapters are concerned with the construction, evaluation, and use of measuring instruments; and the final three chapters pertain to the use of various types of standardized tests and other measures. The appendix offers resources for the development and selection of measuring instruments for many personological variables.

evaluation   classification   personological variable
measurement   selection   quantification
subjectivity   criterion-referenced test
objectivity
overlearning

1. What is the process by which the members of a class of things are differentiated?

    a) counting

    b) measurement

    c) quantification

    d) evaluation

2. Which one of the following terms *least* belongs with the other two?

    a) assessment

    b) measurement

    c) evaluation

3. Which one of the following adjectives *least* belongs with the other two?

    a) objective

    b) impressionistic

    c) subjective

4. Place the following processes in the temporal order in which they normally should occur: evaluation, quantification, assessment.

5. Which one of the following variables is not directly observable but instead is a psychological construct that must be inferred from indirect behavioral indications?

    a) age

    b) intelligence

    c) strength

    d) high-jumping ability

    e) height

6. The measurements of which one of the variables listed in question 5 would be expected to contain the *most* measurement error?

7. The principal function of quantification is best summarized as

    a) an essential in the measurement process

    b) an essential in the evaluation process

    c) reducing inefficiency

    d) reducing ambiguity

8. Which one of the following statements represents evaluation?

    a) "Jim's score on the test was 98."

b) "JoAnn's score was at the 98th percentile of national norms."
c) "Lori's IQ is very high."
d) "Sherry answered 100% of the questions correctly."
e) "Dale did well on the test."

9. Which one of the following is *not* one of the three principal components of the educational process itself?
    a) evaluating learning
    b) setting objectives
    c) developing learning experiences
    d) providing transportation

10. Which of the following are major functions served by tests?
    a) administrative uses
    b) guidance uses
    c) instructional uses
    d) two of the above
    e) all of the above

11. Which one of the following is *not* a direct *instructional* function served by tests and testing?
    a) motivating learning
    b) quality control
    c) clarifying course objectives
    d) overlearning

12. Which one of the following is *not* considered a principal function of tests and testing in education?
    a) to help evaluate students
    b) to help evaluate teachers
    c) to help in curriculum evaluation
    d) to help in selection and classification decisions
    e) to help identify an individual's special aptitudes

ANSWERS TO CHAPTER TEST

1. b	5. b	9. d
2. c	6. b	10. e
3. a	7. d	11. b
4. assessment,	8. e	12. b
quantification, evaluation		

FOR ADDITIONAL READING

AMERICAN PERSONNEL AND GUIDANCE ASSOCIATION. The responsible use of tests: A position paper of AMEG, APGA, and NCME. *Measurement and Evaluation in Guidance,* 5 (1972), 385–88.

COFFMAN, W. E. A moratorium? What kind? *NCME Measurement in Education,* 5 (2) (1974).

DYER, H. S. Criticisms of testing: How mean is the median? *NCME*

Measurement in Education, 8 (3)(1977).

GLASS, G. V. A paradox about excellence of schools and the people in them. *Educational Researcher,* 4 (1975) 9–12.

EBEL, R. L. The paradox of educational testing. *NCME Measurement in Education,* 7 (4) (1976).

KIRKLAND, M. D. The effects of tests on students and schools. *Review of Educational Research,* 41 (1971), 303–50.

MEHRENS, W. A. Evaluators, educators, and the publics: a détente? *NCME Measurement in Education,* 5 (3)(1974).

NATIONAL INSTITUTE OF EDUCATION. *Testing, teaching and learning.* Washington, D.C., 1979.

SHANKER, A. AFT position paper on testing. *American Education,* 62 (1977), 15.

THORNDIKE, R. L., and E. P. HAGEN. Social and political issues in testing. In *Measurement and evaluation in Psychology and Education,* 4th ed. New York: Wiley, 1977. Chap. 16.

2

Communicating Information: Quantitative Description and Interpretation

Measurement and evaluation information should be communicated as accurately as possible. For this reason, the use of numbers is very common in test reporting and interpretation. In most situations performance can be described more precisely using numbers than using words alone.[1]

Nearly all of today's test manuals refer to central tendency, variability, percentiles, standard scores, reliability, and validity. It is usually assumed that the reader is familiar with commonly used statistical terms and concepts. Some understanding of these concepts is essential for proper use and interpretation of classroom and standardized tests. In addition, at least a rudimentary grasp of basic statistical concepts is required for comprehending much of the current educational literature. All fields of education and psychology can expect increased use of statistical concepts and measures in the future.

The view emphasized years ago by a renowned teacher of educational statistics (Walker, 1950, p. 31) is even broader: "The conclusion seems inescapable that some aspects of statistical thinking which were once assumed to belong in rather specialized technical courses must now be considered part of general cultural education." Even to be an intelligent reader of newspapers and newsmagazines one frequently needs knowledge of certain statistical con-

---

[1] Unfortunately, some persons appear to equate the use of numbers with the dehumanization of individuals. Such a view imputes virtue to ignorance. Categories of performance, whether reported in terms of numbers, letters, or words, have precisely the same function—to describe as accurately as possible.

cepts, such as mean, median, percentile, and range. Most elementary measurement and general psychology textbooks include a terse treatment of statistics designed to teach in a few weeks material that is usually covered in an entire course. But it is neither appropriate nor practical to devote a *major* portion of a measurement course to statistics.

We have tried to solve this problem in several ways. We have interspersed sequences of programmed material throughout our sections on statistics. This type of material lends itself especially well to self-instructional methods. We also present the concepts in the usual narrative manner. This dual presentation, which approaches the concepts using two different instructional strategies, should reduce the amount of classroom time required for mastery of these concepts. We emphasize concepts more than computations, and have omitted several "shortcut" computational procedures that have been rendered obsolete by hand calculators.

The mastery test at the end of this chapter will help you assess your grasp of basic principles and assist you in identifying topics that need further study. A summary of common statistical terms and symbols and a selected list of statistical textbooks appear at the end of the chapter for students who wish to study these topics further.

Despite these aids, you will probably find that you cannot read this chapter quickly and easily. It will require the same sort of careful study that you would use in studying mathematics or physics. This effort will be rewarded by increased confidence and ability to understand and communicate information that is expressed quantitatively.

Numbers can communicate certain kinds of information accurately and succinctly. In describing a distribution of scores, the two most informative characteristics are summarized by measures of central tendency and variability.

Frequency Distributions, Central Tendency, and Skewness[2]

1. Many people have the mistaken notion that one must have a good mathematical background and high quantitative ability to learn and use statistics. Whether we are aware of it or not, we all use statistics frequently. Most fields of study use certain statistical concepts. When discussing topics such as average rainfall, temperature, and income, we are dealing with information that is expressed statistically by using the mean, median, or mode. When weathermen report a new high or low temperature for a given day of the year, they are conveying statistical information about the range, another statistical concept. When students' reading achievement is evaluated in relation to their IQ scores, the statistical concept of correlation is implicit. So although we may not be statisticians, we all use _____ to communicate quantitative information in our work and daily activities.

   statistics

[2] To obtain the maximum benefit from the programmed instruction, cover the answer, which appears in the right-hand margin, with a card and view it only after you have responded.

2. Statistics have many functions. They summarize and simplify kinds and quantities of data that would otherwise be unwieldy. They help to bring order out of chaos. For example, suppose you obtained a raw score of 15 on a 20-word spelling test. Of course, we can determine that your score was 75%; that gives us some information. But we can evaluate your performance much better if we know something about the difficulty of the test. If the test was composed of words like *occasion, parallel, vacuum,* or *misspell,* your score of 75% would mean something quite different from what it would if the words were *travel, measure,* or *interpretation.* Your score of 15 may have been the best or even the poorest score in the class. When we examine the scores of a class of 30 students, your score begins to acquire more meaning. Suppose those 30 scores were 13, 12, 15, 13, 14, 18, 13, 13, 12, 14, 16, 17, 14, 15, 11, 16, 15, 14, 19, 14, 16, 17, 11, 9, 18, 12, 17, 16, 15, and 20. It can be sensed that your score of 15 is somewhere near the middle of the group. Your score can be interpreted more accurately if these raw scores are tallied into a frequency distribution. A *frequency distribution* shows the number of persons (frequency) who obtained each score. If we list each score with the number of times it was obtained, we are constructing a _____.

frequency distribution

3. The spelling scores from the preceding frame are partially tallied in the following frequency distribution. Complete the distribution.

Score	Frequency
20	/
19	/
18	//
17	///
16	////
15	////
14	~~////~~
13	////
12	
11	
10	
9	

12–///
11–//
10–
9–/

4. The frequency distribution facilitates a more meaningful interpretation of your score. We can see at a glance that the lowest score was 9 and the highest was __, for a difference or *range* of __ points. (To obtain the range, simply subtract the lowest score from the highest score.)

20, 11

5. The range gives us some idea of the variability of a set of scores, but information regarding the point around which the scores tend to cluster is also useful. This information is a measure of average or *central tendency.* There are three common measures of central tendency: *mean, median,*

and *mode*. The score that occurs most frequently is called the mode. From the frequency distribution of the spelling scores, we can see that more students earned the score of __ than any other single score; therefore, the ____ of this distribution is __.

14

mode, 14

---

6. We can determine the mode of a distribution by finding the score that has the greatest _____. The mode of the distribution in frame 3 is __.

frequency, 14

---

7. The mode of the following set of scores [1, 3, 4, 4, 4, 5, 6] is __.

4

---

8. Another measure of central tendency is the *median*. The median is the point that divides the scores of the examinees into two halves. It is another name for the fiftieth percentile (50th %ile) because 50 percent of the scores fall below it. The median of the following set of scores [11, 12, 12, 13, 14, 15, 17] is __, but the mode is __.

13, 12

---

9. The simplest way to determine the median is to arrange the raw scores from low to high and then count up to the middle "score"—that is, to the point at which one-half of the scores are exceeded. The median for the following distribution of scores [52, 59, 61, 66, 68, 75, 77, 84, 88] is __. (Frequencies at the median are considered to be half above and half below the median; hence, 4 1/2 or 50% of the scores fall below the median.)

68

---

10. In the distribution in frame 9, were there an equal number of scores above and below the median? ____. Another name for the median is the ____ percentile.

Yes, 50th

---

11. When there are an even number (*N*) of examinees, the median is halfway between the two middlemost scores. For example, the median of the following scores [21, 23, 24, 25] is __. The median of the distribution in frame 3 is __.

23.5 (or 23½)
14.5

---

12. If one additional score, 30, were added to the distribution in frame 11, the median would become ____.

24

---

13. If one additional score, 50, were added to the distribution in frame 9, the median would become ____.

67

---

14. In the following frequency distribution the mode is __. How many of the examinees earned the score of 6? __ From the frequency column we can

7
2

determine that N, the number of scores in the distribution, is ___. The ⟶ 9

median of the distribution is ___. ⟶ 7

Score	Frequency
X	f
9	1
8	2
7	3
6	2
5	1

15. You have demonstrated your understanding of the mode and median of certain simple distributions, but the most widely used measure of central tendency is the mean. The *mean* is simply the sum of the scores divided by the number of scores. The procedure for computing the mean is defined by the formula

$$\overline{X} = \frac{\Sigma X}{N},$$

where $\overline{X}$ is the symbol for mean,
Σ is a symbol meaning "the sum of,"
X represents scores, and
N is the number of scores.
This formula is simply a shorthand way of saying that the mean equals the _____ of the scores divided by the _____ of scores. ⟶ sum, number

16. Let's try an example. Find the mean of these scores: 2, 3, 5, 7, 8, 9. $\Sigma X = 2 + 3 + 5 + 7 + 8 + 9 =$ ___, and $N =$ ___; therefore, $\overline{X} =$ ⟶ 34, 6
34/6 or 5.67. For the following set of scores [3, 2, 5, 8, 2] $\Sigma X =$ ___, ⟶ 20
$N =$ ___, and $\overline{X} =$ ___. ⟶ 5, 4

17. When the term *average* is used, it usually refers to the mean. This mean is the most stable or reliable measure of central tendency; the crude mode is the least stable. In other words, if a group is divided randomly into halves and the three measures of central tendency are computed separately for each half, the difference between the modes will tend to be greater than the differences between the medians or means. Since modes are highly unstable, large samples are usually required before they become very meaningful. If a choice were available, one generally would prefer the mean or the median to the ___. ⟶ mode

18. Let's review. There are three commonly used measures of central tendency. Usually the scores will cluster around the most frequently occurring score, which is called the ___. The point that separates the frequency ⟶ mode

24

distribution into two equal-sized groups (i.e., halves) is called the _____.   median
The most dependable or stable measure of central tendency tends to be
the ___.   mean

---

19. The mean is sensitive to the value of every score in the distribution; this is
not true of the mode or the median. To illustrate this characteristic, consider the distribution given in frame 14. If, for example, a score of 6 was
changed to a score of 3, the values of the ___ and ___ would not   median, mode
change, whereas the value of the ___ would decrease.   mean

---

20. Many distributions are symmetrical and "bell shaped." The distributions
of many human traits, such as height, weight, IQ score, and reaction
time, tend to show this pattern. Distributions that are symmetrical and
have a certain mathematically specified "bell shape" are termed *normal
distributions.* In a true normal distribution the mode, median, and mean
have the same value. Since IQ scores tend to be approximately normally
distributed with a mean IQ of 100, the median and the mode of IQ scores
are also approximately ___.   100

---

21. If the mean and the median of a distribution differ considerably, the
shape of the distribution is not symmetrical and therefore cannot be
_____. (All normal distributions are symmetrical, but many symmetrical   normal
distributions are not _____.)   normal

---

22. The shape of a distribution can provide some useful clues about the adequacy of a test. Such asymmetrical distributions as the one in the following diagram are said to be *skewed* (it appears as if a normal curve has
been pushed to one side). When the "tail" points to the left, the curve is
said to be skewed negatively or skewed to the left. In this distribution
there were many rather ___ scores but relatively few ___ scores; the   high, low
distribution would be described as being _____ negatively. Scores on   skewed
"mastery" or "criterion-referenced" tests are often negatively skewed.

Low   High
 −   +
      Scores

---

23. A test may be so difficult that there are many low scores and few high
ones. Such a distribution would be described as being skewed _____.   positively
Draw a distribution with positive skewing. (Low scores are always plotted

184811

to the left and high scores to the right, just as in the preceding frame.)

---

24. When skewing is present and the samples are large enough to make the measures of central tendency stable, the three measures will differ systematically. As shown in the following diagrams, the mean is always "pulled" most toward the tail and the mode the least; the median is between the mean and the mode. Since the height of the curve represents frequency, the highest point in the curve indicates the ____ of the distribution. On a very easy test like the one represented in frame 22, the median will be greater than the ____ but less than the ____.

mode

mean, mode

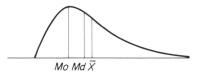

---

25. If the mean is considerably greater than the median, the distribution is probably skewed _____. If the mean has the lowest value of the three measures of central tendency, the distribution is probably skewed _____; if the mean, median, and mode have the same value, the shape of the distribution is probably _____.

positively

negatively
normal

---

26. Which of the following four terms least belongs with the other three?
normal   *skewed*   *bell shaped*   *symmetrical*

skewed

---

27. Let's return to the common situation in which a test was too easy for a given group of examinees. The actual shape of the curve for the group of test scores will be skewed _____. The measure of central tendency with the largest value is the ____; the measure of central tendency with the smallest value is the ____.

negatively
mode
mean

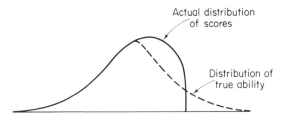

Actual distribution of scores

Distribution of true ability

---

28. The measurement of ability differences with the easy test in frame 27 was adequate for examinees of low ability, but true differences in ability were obscured for the more capable examinees since an adequate test ceiling was lacking. A test with an inadequate ceiling is like a high-jump apparatus that does not allow the crossbar to go beyond a certain height, a height that is below the jumping ability of many participants. (The psychological effect on the talented *may* be similar in both situations; that is, challenge and motivation for improvement are decreased.) The validity of the test is related to the extent to which the distribution of observed scores and the distribution of the examinees' true abilities are similar. Distributions of true abilities are rarely substantially skewed unless one is assessing knowledge of recently studied content that is primarily factual rather than conceptual or process oriented.

A rough indication of skewness can be obtained by comparing the measures of central tendency, especially the mean and the median. (The mode is quite unreliable unless the sample is very large; consequently, it is not very useful for indicating skewness.) If the mean and the median are close in value, the distribution is probably not seriously skewed. For example, if the mean IQ for a class is found to be 110 and the median 100, the distribution is probably skewed _____.   positively
If a class had a mean of 89.3 and a median of 90.1, does it appear that skewing is negligible?   Yes

---

29. Sketch a distribution that has a mean of 70, a median of 65, and a mode of 55. (The median is usually closer to the mean than to the mode.)
The distribution is skewed _____.   positively

---

30. If the mean of a large distribution is 40 and the median is 50, the mode is probably _____ than 50.   greater

---

The concepts of central tendency and skewness and other related concepts will now be developed in narrative style.

Classification and Tabulation

Test scores and other quantitative data can be understood and interpreted more clearly if they are organized and summarized in some orderly manner. Table 2-1 shows the results of a test administered to a class of 20 students. However, the scores are difficult to interpret in this form. For example, we can tell only with some difficulty whether Carrie, with a score of 80, is a very superior pupil or just average when compared with her peers. Knowing that the maximum score was 100 is of some value, but less than people often assume since test difficulty is arbitrary—it is easy to ask simple or difficult questions about the same material.

TABLE 2-1

TEST SCORES FOR TWENTY STUDENTS

Name	Score	Name	Score	Name	Score	Name	Score
Carrie	80	Nora	95	Jim	75	Stacey	75
Maxine	66	Bob	78	Zane	91	Jonathan	81
Robert	87	Barbara	70	Christy	81	Ann	71
Ila	84	Jeanne	83	Sherry	89	Beata	85
Dale	85	Linda	96	Kinda	89	Cynthia	85

The Ungrouped Frequency Distribution

An "ungrouped" frequency distribution can be a useful way of presenting test data. If we start with the lowest score and list every *possible* score with its frequency (if any) until we have included the highest score, we will construct an ungrouped *frequency distribution.*[3] (See Table 2-2.) The various scores are arranged in order of size (here, from 66 to 96), and to the right of each score the number of times it occurs is tallied. The total of the frequency column is N, the number of scores (here, 20).

If marks or other categorizations of the scores are to be assigned, it is preferable (if there is no fixed standard of performance, such as 70–79 percent = C) to establish the cutoff scores for the groupings at a point where there will be a "gap" between the lowest score in one category and the highest score in the next-lower category.

Central Tendency and Variability

Two of the most important statistical measures that apply to various kinds of test data are central tendency and variability. These concepts are useful in summarizing the main features of a bewildering mass of data. It is possible to understand them fairly well at a conceptual level apart from the computational details. The computations do, however, serve to enrich one's understanding of the statistical concepts.

A tendency for the scores to concentrate in density about some "center" is characteristic of most frequency distributions, as is typified to some extent by the data shown in Table 2-2. An important statistic is, therefore, the point on the scale around which the scores tend to be grouped or centered. This is a measure of *central tendency;* it is the value that typifies and best represents the whole distribution.

We might want to compare the performances of several schools or classes on a certain test. To determine this, we would compute an average for each school and then note which had the highest average and which the

---

[3] In the past, considerable attention has been given to the mechanics of grouping into fewer and larger-sized intervals for "computational convenience." With the limited numbers of scores that confront most teachers, together with the widespread availability of hand calculators, the student no longer need be burdened with rote computational mechanics, which obscure the logical meaning of various statistical measures.

TABLE 2-2

TWENTY SCORES FROM TABLE 2-1
TABULATED INTO AN UNGROUPED
FREQUENCY DISTRIBUTION

Score	Frequency
96	/
95	/
94	
93	
92	
91	/
90	
89	//
88	
87	/
86	
85	///
84	/
83	/
82	
81	//
80	/
79	
78	/
77	
76	
75	//
74	
73	
72	
71	/
70	/
69	
68	
67	
66	/
	N = 20

lowest. Statisticians use several different "averages." Three of the most useful are the median, the mean (more precisely, the arithmetic mean), and the mode.

The Median

A widely used average in educational measurement is the *median. The median is the point that divides the distribution into halves.* Of the 20 frequencies in Table 2-2, half (10) are for scores 66 through 83; the other half are for scores of 84 through 96. Thus, the midpoint of the frequencies is between 83 and 84, or 83.5. This is the point that we would arrive at by arranging the 20 test papers in decreasing order by score (96, 95, 91, . . . , 70, 66) and then counting halfway down the pile. The average of the score on the tenth test paper (83) and the score on the eleventh test paper (84) is 83.5, the point in the test score distribution above and below which half of the scores lie. This point is called the *median*.

In an ungrouped distribution, when *N* is an odd number the middlemost score is the median. For example, if 31 students took a test, the sixteenth-highest score would be the median—15 scores would be above it and 15 scores below it. Strictly speaking, when *N* is an even number there is no midscore. In that case it is customary to average the middle pairs of scores, as we did in the example given in Table 2-2. The median of the distribution of the 20 scores shown in Table 2-2 is 83.5, the average of the middle pair of scores. Since the median is the point that divides a distribution into two equal-sized groups, 50 percent of the scores are below the median; therefore, *the median is always the fiftieth percentile* (to be discussed later).

The median is often used as a reference point for describing the location of individual pupils in a distribution. A pupil in the higher half is said to be "above the median," one in the lower half "below the median." If John received a score of 29 on a test with a median of 26, he scored in the upper half of the class.

If scores are ranked or in an ungrouped frequency distribution, the median is easier to obtain than is the mean, which, for the data in Table 2-2, is found by adding together all 20 scores and dividing by 20. For most of the classroom teacher's purposes, the median provides a sufficient indication of the *central tendency* of the test scores.

The Mean

The most familiar average is the *mean*. This measure is in such common use that many people regard it as *the* average because it is the one they are familiar with. When the term *average* is used in ordinary conversation or in newspapers in such statements as "average temperature," "average rainfall," "average height for a given weight," and "average income," it is likely (but not certain) that the mean is meant.

If one took a 12-inch ruler and put dimes at 1, 3, and 8 inches, it would balance if a fulcrum were placed at 4. The "weight" on one side of the mean is equal to that on the other side. By thinking of frequencies as weights, we see immediately that any score distribution balances at its mean ("center of gravity") but not at its median or mode—except, of course, when they are equal to the mean.

The mean can be computed by simply obtaining the sum of the measures and dividing by their number. The measure so obtained is the value that each individual would have if all shared equally. Unlike the median, the mean is affected by the *magnitude* of every score in the distribution. Increase any score by 10 points and you increase the mean by $10/N$ points, where *N* is the number of scores in the distribution. Decrease any score by 20 points and you lower the mean by $20/N$ points. Increase the highest score in a distribution and decrease the lowest score all you please; the *median* will not be changed. When *N* includes all persons in the population, the symbol, μ, is used for the population mean; more often N represents only a sample and the symbol, $\overline{X}$, denotes the sample mean.

If scores are not grouped into a distribution and one has access to an adding machine or a hand calculator, computing the mean of 25 or more scores may require less time than computing the median. *On well-constructed tests designed to measure individual differences, the mean will usually differ little from the median.* The formula for the mean is in Equation 2.1:

$$\overline{X} = \frac{\Sigma X}{N} , \qquad (2.1)$$

where
$\overline{X}$ = the mean,
X = a score,
Σ = a symbol meaning "the sum of," hence,
ΣX = the sum of all scores, and
N = the number of scores.

The symbol Σ means "the sum of." The symbol X is consistently used to represent scores.

Using the data given in Table 2–2, we find that ΣX, the sum of all 20 scores, is 1,646. Substituting these values into the formula for the mean, we find that

$$\overline{X} = \frac{\Sigma X}{N} = \frac{1,646}{20} = 82.30.$$

You will notice that here the mean (82.3) and median (83.5) are quite close in value. This will be the case in any approximately symmetrical distribution. One of the most important symmetrical distributions is the *normal distribution,* often called the *normal curve.* This type of distribution describes many human characteristics and abilities. Characteristics of the normal distribution will be discussed later in this chapter and in Chapter 3.

The Mode

The most frequently occurring score is called the *mode.* It is determined by inspection. In Table 2–2 the mode of the scores is 85 because more pupils (3) obtained this score than any other score. The mode is not a very reliable average, especially with small groups. In our example, the changing of two scores could shift the mode considerably. If one of the pupils who made 85 had made 75, the mode would decrease from 85 to 75. Largely because of its fickleness, the mode is not a very useful measure of central tendency on quantitative variables for small groups.

Comparisons of the Mean, Median, and Mode

Which average is best? Overall, *the mean is the most reliable measure of central tendency. Reliable* means stable. If you gave two equivalent tests to a class, as a general rule the two means would differ less than the two medians, which in turn would differ less than the two modes. The mean, however, is greatly influenced by skewness (see frame 24, p. 26). Whenever we wish to minimize this influence, the median is best. Since such situations often arise in educational measurement, the median is widely used. For example, if a test is very difficult, there may be several zero or chance scores; if a test is very easy, there may be several perfect scores. But in neither case are individual differences among the pupils at the extremes measured accurately. In such situations the median is usually the best or most descriptive average to use. The median income of families in the United States is more informative than the mean, owing to the extreme influence of the rich.

An illustration may help indicate appropriate uses of these measures of central tendency. Suppose that a school district employs 1,000 persons, all of whom earn between $10,000 and $25,000 per year except for the 50 administrators, who each earn more than $30,000. The *mean* salary for the district is likely to be misleadingly high, since it does not adequately characterize the 950 nonadministrators. However, the *median* will not be sensitive to the great discrepancy represented by the few high salaries. In fact, we can determine the median without even knowing the actual salaries of the administrators by just having a top category of "more than $25,000" whose frequency is 50. In most instances it is desirable to report both the median and the mean. It would probably be even more meaningful to exclude the administrators from the distribution and to report their salaries separately. The 950 teachers represent a more homogeneous group, yet even here there would probably be skewing in the distribution, with new teachers near the bottom of the salary schedule far outnumbering old-timers receiving the maximum. A dishonest superintendent might use the mean as the "average" salary at professional meetings or when negotiating with teachers, but would use the mode as the "average" when trying to obtain public support for an increase in teachers' salaries. In skewed distributions the median is usually the best single measure, although each average conveys some complementary information. A church, for example, might find that in a given year the average contribution per member was $0 or $1,500, depending on whether the mode or the mean was used.

An improbable anecdote will illustrate further the unique aspects of each average. Five men sat together on a park bench. Two were vagrants, each with total worldly assets of 25 cents. The third was a workman whose bank account and other assets totaled $2,000. The fourth man had $15,000 in various forms. The fifth was a millionaire with a net worth of $5 million. Therefore, the mode cash worth of the group was 25 cents. This figure describes two of the persons perfectly but is grossly inaccurate for the other three. The median figure of $2,000 does little justice to anyone except the workman. The mean, $1,003,400.10, is not very satisfactory even for the millionaire. If we *had* to choose one measure of central tendency, perhaps it would be the mode, which describes 40 percent of this group accurately. But if we were told that "the modal assets of five persons sitting on a park bench are 25 cents," we would be likely to conclude that the total assets of the groups are approximately $1.25, which is more than $5 million lower than the correct figure. Obviously, no measure of central tendency whatsoever is adequate for these "strange benchfellows," who simply do not "tend centrally." Fortunately, in such situations we need not choose one, but can report two or three different measures of central tendency as needed to summarize the distribution accurately. Or, as in this instance, we can simply report all the scores when N is small.

Measures of Variability

31. Although measures of central tendency indicate the values about which the scores tend to cluster, they provide no information on the degree of individual differences or variability that exists among students. We have already been introduced to one measure of variability, the difference between the highest score and the lowest score, which is called the _____.

range

32. The range, however, is a crude measure of variability or dispersion. The two distributions shown in the following figure have the same mean and median and the same _____, yet they represent very different types of distributions.

range

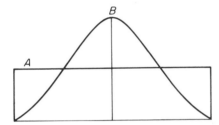

33. Curve A in frame 32 is a *rectangular distribution* and might represent the distribution of the ages of a large group of kindergarten pupils (excluding early and late entrants). Curve B appears to be a _____ distribution.

symmetrical or normal

34. To emphasize the need for measures of variability as well as measures of central tendency, consider the following normal distributions, which depict IQ scores from two classes of students, both of which have identical means, modes, and _____. Although their averages are the same, they differ greatly in their degree of dispersion or _____.

medians
variability

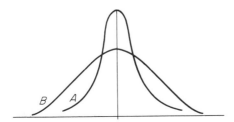

35. In the preceding frame, the more heterogeneous class (the one with the greater degree of individual differences) is class_____. The more homogeneous class (the one with the lesser variability in scores) is class _____.

B

A

36. Since the range is a crude, undependable indicator of variability, more refined measures of dispersion have been devised. The most widely used is the *standard deviation,* which is symbolized for a population by the Greek letter σ (sigma), or for a sample by *s*. We know now that the mean, median, and mode are measures of _____, while the range and standard deviation are measures of _____.

central
tendency
variability
(dispersion,
scatter,
hetero-
geneity)

37. A simple example will illustrate the direct computation of the standard deviation from its definitional formula. The formula for the standard deviation[4] is

$$s = \sqrt{\frac{\Sigma x^2}{N}},$$

where s = the standard deviation,
N = the number of scores, and
Σx^2 = the sum of the squared deviation of the scores from the mean, with $x = X - \overline{X}$.

The scores of five examinees on a test are 40, 35, 30, 25, 20.

X	x	x^2
40	___	___
35	___	___
30	___	___
25	___	___
20	___	___
$\Sigma X =$ ___	$\Sigma x^2 =$ ___	

You recall that to compute the mean one finds the sum of the raw scores and divides by the number of scores.

[4] A note to the statistically trained reader: For purposes of this course no computational distinction will be made between the sample standard deviation, *s*, and the population value, σ. When a class of students includes all persons about whom we want to make inferences, it is then the *population* in a statistical sense. In all computations the maximum-likelihood variance estimate is employed; that is, Σx^2 is divided by N and not by $N - 1$. Contrary to popular opinion, even when $N - 1$ is used in computing the standard deviation, the resulting *s* is a biased underestimate of the standard deviation in the population (see Hopkins and Glass, 1978, pp. 81–82), although the bias is trivial. Unless N is very small (10 or less), the computed values using N and $N - 1$ will not differ meaningfully. We will divide by N throughout and designate all computed standard deviations with the symbol, *s*.

$$\overline{X} = \frac{\Sigma X}{N}, \text{ or } \overline{X} = \frac{(\quad)}{(\quad)}, \text{ or } \overline{X} = \underline{\quad}.$$

$\dfrac{150}{5}$, 30

---

38. Since x is the difference between X and $\overline{X}$, we simply subtract $\overline{X}$ from every raw score; that is, $x = X - \overline{X}$. For the score of 40, $x = (\underline{\quad}) - (\underline{\quad}) = \underline{\quad}$.

40, 30, 10

---

39. For the score of 20, $x = 20 - (\underline{\quad}) = \underline{\quad}$.

30, -10

---

40. Enter the x values for 40 and 20 in the x column of frame 37. The x values for the three other scores (25, 30, and 35) are $\underline{\quad}$, $\underline{\quad}$, and $\underline{\quad}$, respectively.

$-5, 0, 5$

---

41. The column x^2 represents the square of the deviation from the mean, x, for each score. (When a number is *squared*, it is multiplied by itself.) For example, three squared (3^2) means 3 times 3, which equals 9. The x-value for the score of 40 was found to be 10; therefore, the square of 10 will be entered in the corresponding row of the x^2 column; $(10)^2 = \underline{\quad}$. The x-value for the score of 20 was -10; the square of which, $(-10)^2$, is $\underline{\quad}$. (Recall that the square of a negative number is always positive; hence, values in the x^2 column are always positive.)

100
100

---

42. The corresponding x^2 values for scores 35, 30, 25, and 20 are 25, $\underline{\quad}$, $\underline{\quad}$, and $\underline{\quad}$.

0, 25
100

---

43. The formula calls for Σx^2 and N; in this problem, $N = \underline{\quad}$. We remember that the symbol Σ means " $\underline{\qquad}$."

5
the sum of

---

44. The sum of x^2 is the total of the x^2 column; for this problem, $\Sigma x^2 = \underline{\quad}$.

250

---

45. Let's "plug in" our numerical values for N and Σx^2 into the formula

$$s = \sqrt{\frac{(\quad)}{(\quad)}} = \sqrt{}.$$

$\sqrt{\dfrac{250}{5}}, \sqrt{50}$

---

46. We will not review here the process of extracting a square root.[5] For our

[5] You probably once learned, and then mercifully forgot, the barbarous, tedious procedure for calculating the square root of a number. The computations are so time-consuming that in our opinion it is an unwarranted expenditure of your time to relearn the computational mechanics. In 1965, a calculator with the square root feature cost about $1,400. Today, hand calculators that give square roots silently and more quickly have been advertised for as little as $10! Stop squandering your riches on things of lesser value and get yourself one.

purposes an approximation is satisfactory. Our present problem is to estimate the square root of 50. We know that the square root of 49 is ___ (that is, $7 \times 7 = 49$); therefore, we conclude that the square root of 50 is slightly more than ___.

7

7

---

47. To summarize: The mean of the distribution with which we have been working (40, 35, 30, 25, 20) is ___, and its standard deviation is approximately ___.

30

7

---

48. Let's review the steps we have taken to compute the standard deviation.

    1. First, the mean is computed.
    2. Next, the deviation (x) of each score from the mean is found by subtracting the mean from each of the scores.
    3. Finally, these deviations are squared and placed in the x^2 column. When this column is totaled we have the value indicated by the symbols ___, which is then divided by the number of scores (N). The square root of the resulting value is the _____ of the distribution.

Σx^2

standard deviation

---

49. In frames 49–53 you will compute the standard deviation for the following distribution of scores:

X	x	x^2
7	___	___
4	___	___
3	___	___
3	___	___
2	___	___
2	___	___
0	___	___

$\Sigma X =$ _____

21

---

50. The mean of the distribution is _____. The values for the x column from top to bottom are 4, 1, 0, 0, -1, _____, and _____.

3

$-1, -3$

---

51. The corresponding x^2 values from top to bottom are 16, 1, 0, 0, 1, _____, and _____. The value for $\Sigma x^2 =$ _____.

1

9, 28

---

52. The standard deviation is the positive square root of the following:

$$s = \sqrt{\frac{(\ )}{(\ )}} \text{ or } \sqrt{(\ )}.$$

$\sqrt{\dfrac{28}{7}}, \sqrt{4}$

---

53. The square root of 4 (and the standard deviation for the distribution) is _____ points.

2

Now that we have found the standard deviation, you might ask, "So what?" You will soon see how the standard deviation is of great value in interpreting performance, especially on standardized tests. This will become clear when you are more familiar with the normal distribution and its relationship to the standard deviation.

Knowledge of central tendency and variability convey important information about the quality of a test. Central tendency depicts a test's level of difficulty and variability indicates the degree of individual *differences* among the scores.

You are now ready to overlearn these and related concepts.

The Meaning of Variability

No distribution is adequately described by a measure of central tendency. The mean intelligence in two classes may be the same, and yet the classes may be very dissimilar. Whereas the ability level in one class may vary all the way from borderline mental retardation to mentally gifted, the individual differences among members of another (homogeneously grouped) class will be much less. Obviously, these two classes, with equal means, present very different instructional problems because they differ in variability. *Variability* is the extent to which the scores of a group tend to scatter (or disperse or spread) above and below a central point in the distribution. Clearly, it is important to have some convenient method of determining the variability of a group. Two common measures of variability are the range and the standard deviation. Whereas measures of central tendency are points, these measures of variability are expressed as distances; the larger their values, the greater the variability (scatter, spread, heterogeneity, dispersion) in the distribution of scores.

The Range

The *range* is simply the distance between the highest score and the lowest score. From the data given in Table 2-2 (p. 29) the range can readily be determined:

Range = the highest score (96) minus the lowest score (66) = 30 points

Since the range depends solely on the two most extreme scores, it is a very untrustworthy, unreliable measure of variability. A shift in a single score may greatly alter the range. In addition, the range is highly dependent on the number of scores in the set. As the size of the group increases, the range will tend to increase; therefore, the ranges of groups of unequal size cannot be meaningfully compared. For example, if scores are normally distributed, we would expect the range for a random sample of 50 of the infinite population of scores to be twice that of a set of 5 scores (see Hopkins & Glass, 1978, p. 85). Nevertheless, the range can serve as a rough measure of the degree of dispersion.

The Standard Deviation

A second measure of variability, which has many uses in educational and psychological measurement, is the *standard deviation,* represented by the letter *s* for samples and σ (the Greek letter *sigma*) for populations. It is defined as the square root of the mean of the squares of the deviations of the scores from their mean.

Let us illustrate the computation of the standard deviation of a set of test scores directly, following the definition just given. Formula 2.2 shows the standard deviation to be the square root of the average squared deviation of each score from the mean:[6]

$$s = \sqrt{\frac{\Sigma x^2}{N}} \text{ or } \sqrt{\frac{\Sigma (X - \overline{X})^2}{N}}. \tag{2.2}$$

Using the 20 scores of Table 2-2, whose mean we already know to be 82.3, the standard deviation is[7]

$$s = \sqrt{\frac{(96 - 82.3)^2 + (95 - 82.3)^2 + \ldots + (66 - 82.3)^2}{20}}$$

$$= \sqrt{\frac{(13.7)^2 + (12.7)^2 + \ldots + (-16.3)^2}{20}}$$

$$= \sqrt{\frac{187.69 + 161.29 + \ldots + 265.69}{20}}$$

$$= \sqrt{\frac{1240.2}{20}} = \sqrt{62.01} = 7.87.$$

It is easier to work directly with raw scores, instead of with deviations from means, to obtain Σx^2, using the following formula:

$$\Sigma x^2 = \Sigma X^2 - N\overline{X}^2$$
$$= 136,706 - 20(82.3)^2 = 136,706 - 20(6773.29)$$
$$= 136,706 - 135,465.8$$
$$\Sigma x^2 = 1240.2$$

(Will σ computed by these two methods always be identical? Yes, except possibly for a slight difference due to rounding-off errors. The two formulas are algebraically equivalent.)

Use a hand calculator when you need to compute a standard deviation; otherwise, the procedure is too fraught with error and too time-consuming to be practical. (Many calculators have a square root key.) If a calculator is not available, there is a shortcut procedure for computing σ that has been shown to be very accurate (Jurs & Hopkins, 1971; McMorris, 1971; Mason & Odeh, 1968; Sabers & Klausmeier, 1971). Diederich (1964, p. 19) proposed a quick

[6] See footnote 4, p. 34, for the distinction between σ and *s*. Many hand calculators are designed to compute the standard deviation of a distribution automatically.

[7] See footnote 5, p. 35, for comment on square root computation.

estimate of the standard deviation for classroom use by teachers.[8] It is simply the *difference* between the sums of the top and bottom sixths of the scores, divided by $N/2$. His formula is

$$s' = \frac{\Sigma \text{ (upper } N/6 \text{ scores)} - \Sigma \text{ (lower } N/6 \text{ scores)}}{N/2}$$

In the sample data given in Table 2-2, $20/6 = 20/6 = 3\frac{1}{3}$, so the three highest and three lowest scores will be used.[9]

$$\Sigma \rightarrow \text{(upper 3 scores)} = 96 + 95 + 91 = 282$$
$$\Sigma \rightarrow \text{(lower 3 scores)} = 66 + 70 + 71 = 207$$

Therefore,

$$s' = \frac{282 - 207}{N/2} = \frac{75}{10} = 7.5.$$

The value of s' (7.5) is a reasonably good approximation of s (whose value as computed earlier is 7.9). The values of s' and s will usually differ by less than 2 percent on classroom tests (Sabers, 1970).[10]

When high precision is required, one should find a calculator and use the raw-score-formula computations for s. Be sure, however, that you actually need the standard deviation. Unless you wish to estimate test reliability or validity, you probably do not. The greatest use of the standard deviation is in the interpretation of norms that use the standard deviation as a unit (i.e., standard scores), which are considered in the next chapter. In a normal distribution approximately two-thirds of the scores fall within one standard deviation of the mean. On most intelligence tests the standard deviation is about 16 points. Since the mean IQ is 100, approximately two-thirds of the IQs fall between 84 and 116. Obviously, the remaining one-third is split evenly below 84 and above 116; one-sixth of the IQ scores exceed 116 and one-sixth fall below 84.

Which Measure Is Best?

The standard deviation is an important measure of the variability of test scores. A small standard deviation indicates that the group has small variability—that is, it is relatively homogeneous with respect to the characteristic in question—whereas a large standard deviation indicates the opposite condi-

---

[8] Diederich's method is a slight simplification of a method originally proposed by Jenkins (1946). The rationale for these shortcut methods is given by Lathrop (1961). The derivation assumes that scores are normally distributed, although it appears to work well on nonnormal distributions (Jurs & Hopkins, 1971).

[9] If $N/6$ is not a whole number, Ebel (1979) recommends that the number of scores in the upper and lower sixths be rounded to the nearest whole number. This procedure appears to be sufficiently accurate for classroom use (Sabers & Klausmeier, 1971).

[10] If instead of the three highest and lowest scores we had used the three highest scores plus one-third of 89, the fourth-highest score ($N/6 = 3\frac{1}{3}$), and likewise added one-third of 75, the fourth-lowest score, then $s' = (311.7 - 232)/10 = 7.97$, which is a more accurate estimate of $\sigma = 7.87$. The difference really is not worth the extra trouble.

tion, heterogeneity. As a rule, the standard deviation is considered the best and most reliable measure of variability; the range is undoubtedly the poorest. The range is subject to many of the limitations of the mode as a measure of central tendency. Similarly, when the mean is used, s is the companion measure of variability, because like the mean it is a function of all the scores in the distribution.

The standard deviation has certain other important uses besides serving as a measure of the dispersion of scores within a group. For example, on standardized tests the position of a pupil in a distribution is often expressed in terms of standard-deviation units, as we will see in Chapter 3.

The standard deviation is of interest chiefly because it is used a great deal by test publishers and educational researchers. You need to understand what it means far more than how to compute it. Part of the next chapter is devoted to a study of test manuals in order to reveal what statistics are mentioned there and how such statistics help you understand the tests better.

Summary

The following is an outline of some concepts that are useful in connection with test scores and other quantitative data:

1. Central tendency and skewness
   a. The *mean, $\overline{X}$*, usually called the average in everyday life, is obtained by adding all the scores and dividing their sum, ΣX, by the number of scores, N. It is the most reliable and, for many purposes, the most useful measure of central tendency.
   b. The *median* (Md) is the point above which half of the scores lie and below which the other half lie; it is the 50th percentile. The median is easier to interpret than the mean, especially with skewed distributions.
   c. The *mode* (Mo) is the most frequent score and is a rather crude measure of central tendency unless the number of scores is very large.
   d. In normal distributions, the mean, median, and mode are equal.
   e. In skewed distributions, the mean is "pulled" toward the "tail" and the median falls between the mode and the mean. The mean will have the lowest value in negatively skewed distributions ($\smile\frown$) and the highest value in positively skewed distributions ($\frown\smile$).

2. Variability
   a. Like the mean, the *standard deviation, s,* is influenced by the value of every measure in the distribution. Approximately two-thirds of all scores in a "normal" distribution lie within plus or minus one standard deviation from the mean.
   b. The *range* is the distance between the highest score and the lowest score. It is a crude measure of variability and should be used primarily as a supplement to s.

frequency distribution
　symmetrical distribution
　normal distribution
　skewness (positive and
　　negative)

central tendency
　mean ($\overline{X}$, μ)
　median (Md)
　50th percentile
　mode

variability
　range
　standard deviation (s, σ)

Question 1 refers to the following distribution of observations:

1, 1, 1, 2, 2, 3, 5, 8, 12

1. Determine: A. the mode; B. the median; C. the value of *N;* D. the value of ΣX; E. the mean; and F. describe the shape of the distribution.

2. In a negatively skewed distribution, which measure of central tendency tends to have the smallest value? the largest value?

3. In skewed distributions, which one of the three measures of central tendency tends to fall between the other two?

4. Which measure of central tendency is the most reliable? the least reliable?

5. Which term *least* belongs with the others?
　a) mode
　b) median
　c) most popular score
　d) most frequent score

6. In a distribution of scores for which $\overline{X}$ = 65.5, Md = 64, and Mo = 60, it was found that a mistake had been made on one score. Instead of 70, the score should have been 90. Consequently, which of these measures of central tendency would certainly be incorrect?
　a) the mean
　b) the mode
　c) the median
　d) more than one of these measures

In questions 7–11, match the verbal and graphic descriptions:

7. rectangular distribution

8. normal distribution

9. positively skewed distribution

10. negatively skewed distribution

11. Of curves a–d, which two are symmetrical?

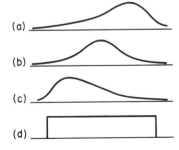

(a)

(b)

(c)

(d)

In questions 12 and 13, indicate whether the skewing in the distributions tends to be positive or negative.

12. U.S. family income in dollars per year

13. age at graduation from college

14. If most students in your statistics class had read this chapter so carefully that they knew the answers to almost all questions on this test, the scores would probably be
   a) normally distributed
   b) skewed negatively
   c) skewed positively
   d) rectangular

Answer questions 15–18 regarding these two measures of variability: (a) range and (b) standard deviation.

15. Which one is less reliable (stable)?

16. Which one becomes much larger as sample size increases?

17. Which one is easier to calculate?

18. For a given distribution, which one will never be the smaller of the two?

In a sixth-grade class of 30 students, a "guess who" sociometric technique was administered to assess the degree of positive peer relationships for each of the students. Construct a frequency distribution for the scores for the 30 students.

0, 1, 1, 1, 1, 1, 2, 2, 2, 2, 3, 3, 3, 4, 4, 5, 5, 7, 8, 8, 9, 10, 11, 12, 13, 15, 17, 28, 33, 41

19. The distribution is a) normal, b) skewed positively, c) skewed negatively.

20. Determine: A. the range; B. the mode; and C. the median.

21. On the basis of the answers to questions 19–20, the mean would be expected to be
   a) greater than 4.5
   b) less than 4.5
   c) less than 1
   d) between 1 and 4.5

22. Which of these is *not* characteristic of a true normal distribution?
   a) symmetrical
   b) unimodal (having one mode)
   c) skewed
   d) bell shaped
   e) two or more of the above are not characteristic of a normal distribution

1. A. 1; B. 2; C. $N = 9$;
   D. $\Sigma X = 35$; E. $\overline{X} =$
   3.89; F. skewed positively
2. mean; mode
3. median
4. mean; mode
5. b
6. a

7. d
8. b
9. c
10. a
11. b and d
12. positive
13. positive
14. b

15. a
16. a
17. a
18. a
19. b
20. A. 41; B. 1; C. 4.5
21. a
22. c

FOR ADDITIONAL READING

GLASS, G. V., and K. D. HOPKINS. *Statistical methods in education and psychology,* 2nd ed. Englewood Cliffs, N.J.: Prentice-Hall, 1982. Chaps. 4–7.

HOPKINS, K. D., and G. V. GLASS. *Basic statistics for the behavioral sciences.* Englewood Cliffs, N.J.: Prentice-Hall, 1978. Chaps. 3–5.

3

The Meaning and Application of Norms

Testing and measurement are performed to achieve certain aims; these purposes are not well served if the findings are interpreted incorrectly. The interpretation of educational and psychological tests is less clear-cut than that of measurements in the physical sciences. Knowing that a child's score on a math test is 82 points is less informative than knowing that the child's weight is 82 pounds. Measures of length, weight, and time are very refined; they represent *absolute* scales—scales with an absolute zero and equal units. The weight of 82 pounds is twice the weight of 41 pounds, but does a math score of 82 represent twice the knowledge of a score of 41? Obviously not.

Expressing test scores as percentages helps somewhat, but not nearly as much as the layman assumes. Suppose the score of 82, converted to a percentage, is 90%. Does this high percentage ensure excellent performance? Perhaps it means that the test was made up of very easy questions. If you correctly read the time on a clock 90% of the time, are you an excellent time teller? Test scores are interpreted most meaningfully when they are viewed in relation to the performance of a suitable *reference group*. When Mary tells her father that she got a score of 19 on a test, what is his response? "Out of how many?" His next question is likely to be "How did the class as a whole do?" The question illustrates the usefulness of data on a reference group to serve as a backdrop to enrich the meaning of test scores.

Norms are nothing more than information regarding the performance of a particular reference group to which an examinee's score can be compared. Norms can be useful even with measures of height, weight, speed, and strength, which have direct meaning in an absolute sense. For example, suppose Henry, a 10-year-old boy, is 50 inches tall and weighs 80 pounds. Is his weight "about right" for his height? Who knows without norms (or at least informal "norms" based on experience)? If we use norms based on a national sample of 10-year-old boys, we will find that Henry appears to have a serious weight problem; he is at the 5th percentile in height but at the 75th percentile in weight. Data on a relevant reference group (i.e., norms) enrich the meaning of a measurement or score even when measurements are on an absolute scale. But norms are especially useful with measurements of educational and psychological performance resulting from measures that have neither an absolute zero point nor equal units.

Norms Are Not Standards

It is important to distinguish clearly between a *norm* and a *standard,* because these terms are frequently misused. The confusion doubtless arises because norms are used with *standardized* tests and the development of norms is part of the process of standardization. Test norms are based solely on actual performance of a group of persons, not on predetermined levels or standards of performance. If most adults in America are overweight, the ideal weight (the standard) could be well below the median weight—the norm would differ from the standard.

Standardized tests are objective tests that have undergone the stringent process of standardization. First, the content has been refined. Each item has been carefully scrutinized and evaluated by both editorial and statistical processes that have eliminated poorer items. Second, the method of administration has been standardized and explicit directions have been formulated, with fixed time limits and instructions. Third, the method of scoring has been standardized. Finally, tables of norms have been provided to facilitate interpretation of the scores on the test. These norms are merely transformations of the raw scores into a more meaningful scale derived from the performance of a large sample of persons representative of one or more specified groups. Thus, norms are not standards but instead, are descriptions of typical performance.

The word *standard* implies a goal or objective to be reached. Thus, a norm is not necessarily a measure of what ought to be—that is, it is not a goal—but a measure of what is (i.e., the status quo). If the median score for a school or class is at the national median on a standardized test, is there cause for rejoicing? Whether this performance level is satisfactory cannot be determined from the norms themselves. The fact that the class median corresponds to the 50th percentile in the norm group does not of itself establish anything other than that the performance is like that of the norm group. It is obvious that a group of students with superior opportunities and capacities should be expected to perform better than a representative group (the norm group), whereas it would be exceptional for a group of students with low ability and opportunity to do as well as a typical group of students.

Most current standardized tests give age or grade norms based on a composite reference group. Others give norms by sex, geographical region, type of school (e.g., large-city schools, public vs. private schools, Title I schools, etc.), or for other subsets of the population. The objective of a meaningful reference group is facilitated by the dual standardization of scholastic aptitude and achievement tests. When the tests are normed on the same group of students, there is a sounder basis for evaluating achievement in relation to measured scholastic aptitude. (The evaluation of achievement in relation to aptitude is considered more extensively in Chapter 14.)

Definitive standards, or goals of attainment, are almost altogether lacking in education. An adequate method for establishing meaningful standards has yet to be worked out. It is conceivable that such standards might be established and expressed in numerical units on existing tests, or on tests yet to be devised, but such a process is inherently difficult (Shepard, 1980). The process of building norms, although time-consuming and expensive, is technically simple and straightforward. An understanding of the way norms are determined should make it obvious that norms are not, and should not be, goals of performance.

The point that norms should not be viewed as standards does not preclude such use when the standards have been established on some other basis. For example, persons who did not graduate from high school can obtain a certificate of equivalency, which is generally accepted as a high school diploma, if proficiency equivalent to the average of a representative group of high school graduates is demonstrated on the General Educational Development Tests (GED) (Graff, 1965). In this instance a certain predetermined *norm* value is a minimal *standard* of performance. The validity of the standard has been supported by studies showing that people who receive high school accreditation via GED tests perform as well as regular high school graduates in industrial and public employment and almost as well in college work (Peters, 1956; L. E. Tyler, 1956, Farley, Wienhold & Crabtree, 1967). Without norms of some sort, there would have been no definitive way of establishing the equivalent level of proficiency acquired outside the school setting.

The current "minimal competency" testing efforts which have used arbitrary, "logical" standards have not met the challenge of criticisms very successfully (Glass, 1978a, 1978b).

Many colleges and universities participate in the College-Level Examination Program (CLEP), whereby students have an opportunity to obtain college credit by examination. Examinations are available in any of approximately fifty subjects. The examinee's performance is reported in terms of norms, but each institution establishes its own standard—the level of performance required to receive credit. The more reputable "external-college degree programs" (college credit without residence) use the CLEP tests extensively in awarding college credit.

Another example of the use of norms to define standards is illustrated in a bill passed by the New Jersey Senate in 1978. The bill requires a minimum standard of a ninth-grade achievement level (defined by national norms) in reading, math, and writing in order to receive a state-approved high-school diploma. Obviously, norms and standards are arrived at in very different ways and serve different purposes.

We now need to become more familiar with the normal distribution and how it is related to the concepts of central tendency and variability introduced in Chapter 2. These concepts are needed to interpret properly the norms provided by standardized tests.

The Normal Distribution

The so-called normal distribution is defined by a mathematical formula.[1] The formula is a stern taskmaster, so few distributions of scores meet its requirements fully. Sheerly random, chance events tend to follow its form most closely, but so do certain physical characteristics such as height and general intelligence that depend on a variety of genetic and environmental factors.

All "normal curves" have just one mode, located in the middle, and are symmetrical. But, *most* unimodal symmetrical distributions are not precisely normal. Nevertheless, quite a few distributions obtained by administration of carefully devised tests approximate the normal distribution sufficiently well to make it a useful way to simplify interpretation of all but the most extreme parts of the curve.

---

1. The scores on many standardized tests (and many other human traits) are approximately normally distributed. To properly interpret many types of norms it is necessary to become acquainted with characteristics of the normal curve. Look at the normal curve below. It is unimodal (the scores cluster around a single point) and symmetrical (if the portion to the left of the mean were folded over on the right half, there would be an exact "fit"). Notice that the "tails" never quite touch the baseline, although they continue to approach it more closely as one moves _____ from   farther the mean.

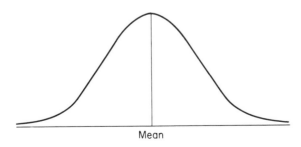

Mean

[1] For that formula and detailed explanations about its use, see Chapter 6 (The Normal Distribution), Glass & Stanley (1970), Glass & Hopkins (1982), or Hopkins and Glass (1978).

2. We learned previously that in normal distributions the mode, _____, and _____ are identical in value.

median
mean

---

3. If we begin at the mean and mark to the left and to the right in units of one standard deviation, we find that a normal distribution spans approximately ____ standard deviations (see curve below). That is, very few scores lie more than ____ standard deviations above or below the mean.

6
3

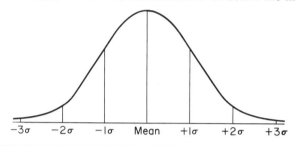

---

4. Since the curve is symmetrical, the area to the left of the mean equals the area to the _____ of the mean. Therefore, the area between the mean and one standard deviation above the mean is the same as that between the _____ and one standard deviation below the mean.

right

mean

---

5. Remembering that the height of the curve at a given point denotes the frequency of scores at that point, we can say that in a normal distribution there are as many scores that are one standard deviation above the mean as there are scores that are _____ standard deviation below the mean.

one

---

6. It should be clear that the area under the curve between two points represents the number or frequency of scores falling between those two points. In a normal distribution 34 percent of the scores fall between the mean and one standard deviation above the mean; therefore, between the mean and one standard deviation below the mean fall _____ percent of the scores.

34

---

7. In the following normal curve the percent of the area (or the percent of the cases) falling in the shaded area between one σ below the mean *and* one σ above the mean is _____ percent + _____ percent, or _____ percent.

34, 34, 68

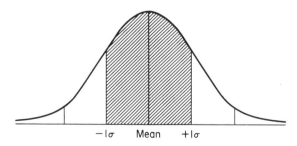

8. The area under the curve from the mean -1σ to the mean $+1\sigma$ includes approximately two-thirds of the scores; therefore, about one-_____ of the scores fall outside this range, that is, below -1σ or above $+1\sigma$.

third

---

9. We have seen that approximately one-third of the scores lie more than one standard deviation from the mean. Consequently, one-_____ of the scores fall above mean $+1\sigma$, and one-sixth fall more than _____ standard deviation below the _____.

sixth
one
mean

---

10. The mean IQ on intelligence tests is 100, and the standard deviation is 15 (on Wechsler tests) or 16 (on the Stanford-Binet, see Figure 3–1, p. 58) points. Assuming a normal distribution and $\sigma = 15$, from what we have just learned about the normal curve we can say that about two-thirds of all IQ scores fall between 85 and _____; one-sixth of the IQ scores are above _____; one-_____ have IQs below 85.

115
115, sixth

---

11. In frame 10 we described the distribution of IQs in terms of approximate fractions. To be more precise, assuming the IQ scores to be normally distributed, we would say that _____ percent of the examinees obtain IQs between 85 and 115; _____ percent have IQs above 115; and 16 percent have IQs below _____. Eighty-four percent have IQs above _____.

68
16
85, 85

---

12. A common method of reporting test scores is in terms of percentile norms. An IQ score of 85 exceeds the scores of 16 percent of the population—that is, the score is at the 16th percentile; the percentile *rank* of 85 is 16. An individual who obtains an IQ score of 100 exceeds _____ percent of the population and therefore is said to be at the _____ percentile. An IQ score of 115 is one standard deviation above the mean, and since the percent of the IQs that fall between the mean and one standard deviation from it is _____, that score exceeds _____ percent more scores than are exceeded by an IQ of 100. Therefore, the percentile rank of this IQ score is _____.

50
50th

34, 34

84

---

13. Complete the fractions that approximate the portion of the curve in the corresponding segments shown in the following diagram. Only 2 percent of the cases in a normal distribution fall below the point -2σ, two standard deviations below the mean. The corresponding percentile equivalent of -2σ to be inserted in the appropriate blank below this point on the curve is 2. Since the curve is symmetrical, can you determine the corresponding percentile value for $+2\sigma$? If 2 percent of the population fall below -2σ, then _____ percent fall above $+2\sigma$. Consequently, $+2\sigma$ exceeds 98 percent of the scores and is at the _____ percentile.

2
98th

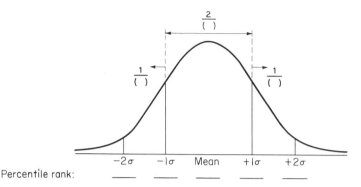

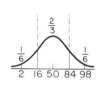

Percentile rank: ____ ____ ____ ____ ____

---

14. One criterion for mental retardation is an IQ score below 70 on an individual intelligence test. If the IQ distribution exactly followed the normal curve, about _____ percent of the population would meet this criterion for mental retardation.

2

---

15. Remembering that for a representative sample of children on the Wechsler intelligence tests the mean IQ score is _____ and the standard deviation is _____, insert the missing percentile ranks and corresponding IQs in the rows provided below the normal curve.

100

15

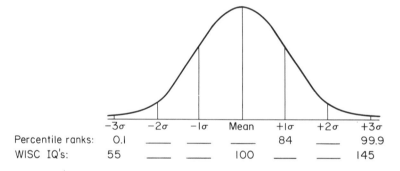

	−3σ	−2σ	−1σ	Mean	+1σ	+2σ	+3σ
Percentile ranks:	0.1	___	___	___	84	___	99.9
WISC IQ's:	55	___	___	100	___	___	145

2, 16, 50, 98

70, 85, 115, 130

---

16. Assuming that IQ scores are normally distributed, for 100 randomly selected children we would expect approximately

_50_ percent to have IQ scores above 100	
_____ percent to have IQ scores above 115	16
_____ percent to have IQ scores below 115	84
_____ percent to have IQ scores below 85	16
_____ percent to have IQ scores below 130	98
_____ percent to have IQ scores above 70	98
_____ percent to have IQ scores between 85 and 115	68
_____ percent to have IQ scores between 100 and 130	48
_____ percent to have IQ scores between 70 and 130	96

_____ percent to have IQ scores above 130   2
_____ percent to have IQ scores between 85 and 130   82
_____ percent to have IQ scores below 145   99.9

---

17. On a certain standardized reading test, the mean grade-equivalent (GE) score at the beginning of the third grade is 3.0. The corresponding standard deviation of the GE scores on this reading test is 1.0. Assuming a normal distribution, what are the GE scores that correspond to the points one and two standard deviations above, and below, the mean?

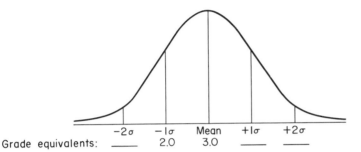

Grade equivalents: _____ 2.0 3.0 _____ _____

(below the curve: -2σ -1σ Mean $+1\sigma$ $+2\sigma$)

---

18. The curve in frame 17 shows that at the beginning of grade 3, 50 percent of the pupils obtain a grade-equivalent score of _____ or better. Bob's GE score on the test is 3.0, which has a percentile rank of _____. Approximately one-sixth of the children receive scores above _____. About 1 pupil in 6 obtains a score below _____. A score of 4.0 is the _____ percentile; a score of 2.0 is the _____ percentile. In a typical class of 30 students, approximately 5 will have GE scores above _____ and another 5 will score below _____. A grade-equivalent score of _____ places a pupil at the 98th percentile. This score means that the pupil scored higher than _____ of every 100 students across the nation who are entering grade 3. The middle two-thirds of a typical class will probably receive grade-equivalent scores between _____ and _____.

3.0
50
4.0
2.0, 84th
16th
4.0
2.0, 5.0
98

2.0, 4.0

---

19. On the standardized reading test just described, the average beginning fourth-grade student would be expected to receive a score of _____. Approximately _____ percent of beginning third-grade pupils obtain higher scores than the average score of the beginning fourth-grade student.

4.0
16

---

20. If the standard deviation at grade 4 were the same as that for grade 3 (it is actually slightly larger), the *average* entering third-grade student would score higher than what percent of the students in grade 4? _____

16

---

21. If the top, middle, and lower thirds of typical students in grades 3 and 4

51

form reading groups, as a group, which students are probably the better readers?

a) the third-grade students in the high reading group
b) the fourth-grade students in the middle reading group   a

---

22. Suppose a pupil received a score of 72 on a 100-item test. Does this really give a good indication of the quality of his or her performance? This could be the highest or the lowest score for the group of examinees. What additional information is needed to give the score of 72 more meaning? You are probably thinking that knowledge of the mean or median would help, and of course it would. Suppose the mean on the test was 62. You now know that a score of 72 is a better-than-average score; but how much better? It is probably between the 51st and 99.9th percentiles, but at what point within this interval? It is evident that in addition to information on central tendency we also need data on _____ .   variability

---

23. You remember that the mean is a common measure of central tendency; its companion measure of variability is the _____ . If we   standard
know these two measures, we can evaluate the score of 72 more accu-   deviation
rately. Assume that the distribution of test scores was approximately normal in form (which is common on well-constructed tests) and that the
standard deviation was 5. Since the mean was 62 and the student's score
was 72, the score is _____ standard deviations above the mean. This is   2
equivalent to a percentile rank of _____. Now the score of 72 has taken   98
on more meaning.

---

24. Fortunately, statisticians and psychometricians have devised a system of reporting test scores on standardized tests so that the interpreter always knows the mean and the standard deviation. Scores of this type are called *standard scores*. Regardless of what the raw score mean and standard deviation on a given test happen to be, they are converted to a fixed mean and a fixed standard deviation. The raw scores are then expressed in terms of a standard-score scale; hence, they are called standard scores. Since the standard-score mean and the standard deviation are known and fixed, any given score automatically takes on meaning. Standard scores are especially useful for standardized tests. It is impractical for a teacher to refer back continually to a test manual for the values of the mean and the standard deviation. Scores expressed in terms of a standard, constant mean and a standard, constant standard deviation are called _____ .   standard scores

---

25. Look at Figure 3–1 (p. 58), which shows the normal curve. Notice the section illustrating typical standard scores. The z-scale is simply a standard score in which a raw score is expressed in terms of the number of standard deviations it deviates from the mean. A raw score one standard deviation

above the mean is equivalent to a z-score of +1; that is, the raw score is +1σ above the mean raw score. If, for example, a score is one-half of a standard deviation below the mean, the corresponding z-score is − .5. A minus value for a z-score indicates that the score falls below the _____.

mean

A z-score of +2 is two _____ above the mean.

standard
deviations

---

26. A score of 72 on a test with a mean of 62 and a standard deviation of 5 is _____ standard deviations above the mean. Expressed as a z-score, the score of 72 is _____ .

2
+2

---

27. Obviously, the mean deviates not at all from itself; therefore, the mean z-score is _____ .

0

---

28. By definition, the standard deviation of the z-score distribution is _____ . If the mean of a raw-score distribution is 80 and the standard deviation is 12, a score of 68 expressed as a z-score will be _____ .

1

− 1

---

29. The z-score system itself is not widely used in reporting test results, but it does enable us to understand better the standard scores that are. Notice the T-score row of Figure 3–1 (p. 58). The T-score type of standard score has a mean of _____ . If we move to a point one standard deviation above the mean, we can see that the standard deviation of the T-score system is _____ , since we move up ten units in going from the mean (50) to one standard deviation above the mean (60).

50

10

---

30. Recall that a score at the second percentile is about _____ standard deviations below the mean. Expressed in T-score units, this would be _____ , since it is two standard deviations (or 2 × 10 = 20) below the T-score mean of _____ .

2
30

50

---

31. If two tests report results using T-scores, an examinee's relative level of performance can be compared directly without any additional information, since the mean and the _____ for both sets of scores will be the same.

standard
deviation

---

32. Consider the following example, which illustrates the advantages of standard-score norms: Miss Martin teaches sixth grade. Suppose one of her pupils, Tommy, obtained an IQ of 130 on a group intelligence test and a grade-equivalent score of 7.6 on a reading test. Is his reading relatively better or poorer than his performance on the intelligence test? Miss Martin no doubt knows that an IQ of 130 is a high score and that 7.6 is a good

reading score, but are they equally good? Is a grade placement score of 7.6 relatively better or poorer than an IQ of 130? Are their percentile ranks equivalent? As it stands, Miss Martin has no way of knowing without obtaining information on the central tendency and variability of the respective tests. Suppose she obtains the following information from the test manuals:

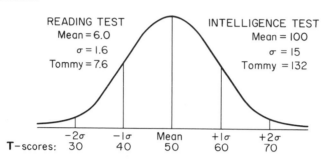

READING TEST
Mean = 6.0
$\sigma = 1.6$
Tommy = 7.6

INTELLIGENCE TEST
Mean = 100
$\sigma = 15$
Tommy = 132

	-2σ	-1σ	Mean	$+1\sigma$	$+2\sigma$
T-scores:	30	40	50	60	70

Tommy is _____ standard deviations above the mean on the intelligence test, which would be equivalent to a *T*-score of _____. On the reading test, he is only _____ standard deviation above the mean, which is equivalent to a *T*-score of _____. Now, it is obvious that his reading performance is not nearly as outstanding as his performance on the intelligence test, although he is well above average on both measures.

2
70
1
60

33. Notice that the teacher needed to go to the test manuals to determine the relative status of 130 and 7.6. If both tests had used the same standard-score system, such as *T*-scores, the relative status would have been apparent at a glance. Since the standard deviation for the *T*-score type of standard score is 10, the *T*-score of _____ on the intelligence test would exceed the *T*-score on the reading test of _____ by 10 points or 1σ.

70
60

34. It is evident that Miss Martin's task of comparing scores would be much easier and more accurate if the results on all the tests were expressed in _____ scores.

standard (or *T*-)

35. Assume in a distribution with a mean of 33 and a standard deviation of 12 that a given raw score was 45. The score of 45 would be _____ standard deviation above the mean, which would place it at the _____ percentile. This would be equivalent to a *z*-score of _____ and a *T*-score of _____.

1
84th
1, 60

36. Most, but not all, intelligence tests report IQs that are also a type of standard score called deviation IQs. Referring again to the normal curve in Figure 3–1 (p. 58), we can see that the mean IQ on the Wechsler Intelligence Scale is _____ and the standard deviation is _____. From Figure 3–1 we see

100, 15

that the mean IQ on the Stanford-Binet Intelligence Scale is 100 and its standard deviation is _____. If a person scores one standard deviation below the mean of his or her age group, that person's Wechsler IQ is _____, and his or her Stanford-Binet IQ is _____. If one is three standard deviations above the mean on the Wechsler, one's IQ score is _____, whereas a score three standard deviations above the mean on the Stanford-Binet results in an IQ score of _____.

16
85
84
145

148

---

37. Let's review some of the characteristics of standard scores. A given standard score has a fixed mean and a fixed _____. Because of this, individual scores on different tests can be compared directly and interpreted easily. A disadvantage of standard scores is that many users have not been introduced to them and consequently do not understand them, which is unfortunate since they are used in virtually all standardized tests.

standard
deviation

---

38. Suppose Jon had the following percentile ranks (*PR*) on five standardized tests:

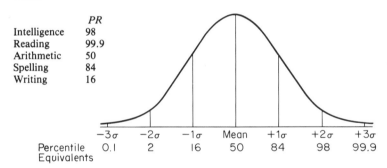

	PR
Intelligence	98
Reading	99.9
Arithmetic	50
Spelling	84
Writing	16

Look at the normal curve with the accompanying percentile equivalents marked off in standard deviation units from the mean. From Jon's percentile ranks it might appear that he performed at about the same relative level on the intelligence and reading tests, whereas the difference is actually as great as the difference between the intelligence and spelling tests. In both instances there was a difference of _____ standard deviation; yet in percentile units the difference was only 1.9 in the first comparison, but _____ in the second—again illustrating that equal differences in standard scores (or raw scores) do not yield equal differences in the corresponding percentile ranks.

1
14

---

39. Consider another example: If Jon improved his writing score by 2 standard deviations his percentile rank would increase _____ percentile units; the same improvement in spelling would cause an increase of only _____ percentile units.

68
15.9

184811

40. If, on the other hand, the scores had been expressed in standard-score norms, no such problem of interpretation would have been present. Using *T*-scores, Jon's test scores would have been as follows:

	PR	T-*score*	
Intelligence	98	70	
Reading	99.9	_____	80
Arithmetic	50	_____	50
Spelling	84	_____	60
Writing	16	_____	40

41. We have mentioned two specific types of standard scores: *z*-scores and *T*-scores. Even though we are not among the proponents of a third type, *stanines,* we will mention them briefly since they are used on several standardized tests. Notice from Figure 3–1 (p. 58) that the stanine is a standard score in which the mean is 5 and the standard deviation is 2. If a person scores at the 84th percentile (one standard deviation above the mean), his or her stanine score is _____ .

7

42. Notice from Figure 3–1 that the stanine units are .5σ in width except in stanines 1 and _____ . Referring to Figure 3–1, indicate Jon's test performance using the stanine scale. Notice that information is lost in exchange for the simplicity of a single digit for reporting results.

9

	PR	Stanine	
Intelligence	98	_____	9
Reading	99.9	_____	9
Arithmetic	50	_____	5
Spelling	84	_____	7
Writing	16	_____	3

43. To convert a raw score (*X*) to a *z*-score, we express the distance from the mean to *X* in standard-deviation units:

$$z = \frac{X - \overline{X}}{s}$$

If $\overline{X} = 32, s = 5,$ and $X = 30,$

$$z = \frac{(\quad) - (\quad)}{5} = \underline{\quad} = \underline{\quad}.$$

(30) (32), $\dfrac{-2}{5}$,

$- .4$

44. To transform a *z*-score to a *T*-score, multiply the *z*-score by 10 and add 50:

$$T = 50 + 10z$$

The raw score of 30 in frame 43 was equivalent to a z-score of $-.4$.
Hence, in T-score units,

$$T = 50 + 10(\ \ ) = 50 - \underline{\hspace{1cm}} = \underline{\hspace{1cm}}.$$

$-.4, 4, 46$

The concept and use of standard scores will now be developed in conventional narrative style.

Many Norms Are Based on the Normal Curve

If a test is neither too easy nor too difficult for the group tested, the scores will usually be distributed approximately "normally" (Lord, 1955), that is, in a pattern resembling the bell-shaped pattern shown in Figure 3–1. Notice that the curve is symmetrical (the left half is the mirror image of the right half) and unimodal (there is just one mode). In any symmetrical unimodal distribution, the mean, median, and mode are equal. The "normal curve" is a special kind of symmetrical unimodal distribution in which the relationship of height to width at every score is mathematically specified. (If you are curious, you can find the mathematical formula in most statistics books—e.g., Glass and Stanley, 1970, p. 97.)

In a normally distributed set of scores, the 16th percentile lies one standard deviation below the mean and the 84th percentile lies one standard deviation above the mean—you can readily see this in Figure 3–1. Similarly, a score two standard deviations above the mean has a percentile rank of approximately 98. The corresponding PRs for -3σ and $+3\sigma$ are .13 and 99.87, respectively. The areas under various portions of the normal curve have been tabled in detail by Hopkins and Glass (1978, pp. 401–5) from -6σ to $+6\sigma$. From these tables we can readily ascertain the distance from the mean in standard-deviation units that corresponds to any percentile rank, from no deviation, which corresponds to a PR of 50, or -4σ and $+4\sigma$, which are at the .003th and 99.997th percentiles, respectively. It should be borne in mind that the distribution in Figure 3–1 is a true normal curve. Actual test scores never conform exactly to this distribution, although the approximation between -2σ and $+2\sigma$ is often very good. For example, the highest IQ score possible on most intelligence tests is less than 160 $(+4\sigma)$; so, the .003% of IQ scores exceeding 160 "predicted" by the normal curve obviously cannot agree with the observed distribution of IQs.

Standard Scores Are a Useful Form of Test Feedback

We have already wrestled with the problem of giving meaning to a student's raw test score. One way is to express the score as a deviation from the mean of the group tested, such as -12 points if the score is 12 points below the mean.

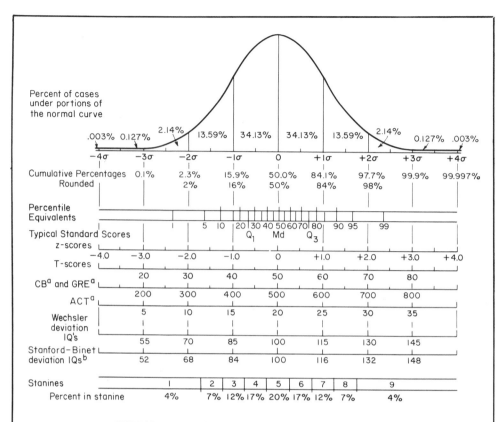

THE NORMAL CURVE, PERCENTILES AND STANDARD SCORES

Distribution of scores of many standardized educational and psychological tests approximate the form of the NORMAL CURVE shown at the top of this chart. Below it are shown some of the systems that have been developed to facilitate the interpretation of scores by converting them into numbers which indicate the examinee's relative status in a group.

The zero (0) at the center of the baseline shows the location of the mean (average) raw score on a test, and the symbol σ (sigma) marks off the scale of raw scores in STANDARD DEVIATION units.

Cumulative percentages are the basis of the PERCENTILE EQUIVALENT scale.

Several systems are based on the standard deviation unit. Among these STANDARD SCORE scales, the z-score, the T-score and the stanine are general systems which have been applied to a variety of tests. The others are special variants used in connection with tests of the College Entrance Examination Board, the Graduate Records Examination, and other intelligence and ability scales.

Tables of NORMS, whether in percentile or standard score form, have meaning only with reference to a specified test applied to a specified population. The chart does not permit one to conclude, for instance, that a percentile rank of 84 on one test necessarily is equivalent to a z-score of +1.0 on another; this is true only when each test yields essentially a normal distribution of scores and when both scales are based on identical or very similar groups of people.

Most of the scales on this chart are discussed in greater detail in Test Service Bulletin No. 48, copies of which are available on request from the Psychological Corporation, 304 East 45th St., New York, N.Y. 10017.

[a] Score points (norms) on the scales refer to university students and not to general populations.

[b] Standard-score "IQ's" with $\sigma = 16$ are also used on several other current intelligence tests, e.g., California Test of Mental Maturity, Kuhlmann-Anderson Intelligence Test, and Lorge Thorndike Intelligence Test.

FIGURE 3-1 Types of standard-score scales. Adapted from Test Service Bulletin no. 48, The Psychological Corporation, New York, by permission of The Psychological Corporation.

How low is the score? Twelve points below the mean might be the lowest score among 1,000 persons tested if the standard deviation were small (3 or 4). On the other hand, it would be the 16th percentile if the standard deviation were 12 and the scores normally distributed. Sixteen percent of the students would score more than 12 points below the mean if the scores were distributed approximately normally. Therefore, it is desirable to divide the deviation of -12 points by the standard deviation to obtain a "standard score," a score that indicates how many standard deviations above or below the mean it falls.

z-Scores

The basic standard score, a z-score, is defined as follows:

$$z = \frac{\text{raw score} - \text{mean}}{\text{standard deviation}};$$

that is,

$$z = \frac{X - \overline{X}}{s} \tag{3.1}$$

The mean of a full set of z-scores is zero because, of course, the mean does not deviate from itself. If a test had a mean of 62 and a standard deviation of 9, a raw score of 71 would be equivalent to a z-score of 1, since it is one standard deviation above the mean. In other words, z-scores are simply raw scores expressed in standard-deviation units from the mean. Therefore, the standard deviation of a full set of z-scores is 1. If we plot the distribution of z-scores, we find that it has exactly the same shape as the distribution of the original raw scores. Computing z-scores does *not* change the shape of the distribution. Skewed distributions—tailing off in one direction or the other—remain skewed; symmetrical distributions remain symmetrical.

Of course, z-scores below the mean are negative. In order to get enough precision when using z-scores, we must use at least one decimal place. This makes z-scores such as -2.3 unpalatable—the scores are decimal fractions, and approximately half of them are negative. We can avoid negative scores and decimals by simply setting up a standard score scale with a mean sufficiently greater than 0 to avoid minuses, and a standard deviation sufficiently greater than 1 to make decimals unnecessary.

The general formula for any computed standard score is as follows:

$$\text{Standard score} = M + S(z)$$

$$= M + S \left(\frac{\text{raw score} - \text{mean of raw scores}}{\text{standard deviation of raw scores}} \right); \tag{3.2}$$

where M = the standard-score mean,
S = the desired standard deviation of the standard scores, and
z = the z-score.

Wechsler's intelligence tests use this standard-score form: IQ score = $100 + 15z$. The 1960 Stanford-Binet Intelligence Scale has this standard-score form: IQ score = $100 + 16z$.

Is a score of 145 on the Wechsler Adult Intelligence Scale (WAIS) as rare as a score of 145 on the Stanford-Binet? It should be rarer, because $(145 - 100)/15 = 3$ is greater than $(145 - 100)/16 = 2.81$.[2] Certain tests, such as the Graduate Record Examination (GRE) and the College Board, report results on a scale in which $M = 500$, $S = 100$, which is not likely to be confused with percentage or percentile scales.

The *T*-Scale

The *T*-scale employs a mean of 50 and a standard deviation of 10. This scale has all the properties of the *z*-scale without the awkwardness resulting from negative scores and decimal fractions. Any score can be converted to a *T*-score by using the formula

$$T = 50 + 10z \qquad (3.3)$$

Scores from skewed and other nonnormal distributions can be forced into an approximate normal distribution by a process of *normalizing*. Normalized *T*-scores can be obtained by converting raw scores to percentile ranks and the PRs to the corresponding *z*-scores that those percentiles have in a normal distribution, and then applying the formula just given.[3] On well-constructed standardized cognitive tests, normalized and nonnormalized *T*-scores will differ little. The *T*-scale is used for several standardized tests, for example, the Differential Aptitude Tests.

A dramatic advantage of using standard scores for reporting results is that the mean and the standard deviation are the same for all tests, so that the pupil's relative performance on various tests can be directly compared. The percentile scale also has this advantage, but the marked inequality of percentile units makes the comparison of performance less precise (cf. Figure 3–1). The raw-score difference that corresponds to a difference of 14 percentile units (e.g., between the 84th and 98th percentiles) at one location in the distribution may be as large as a difference of 34 percentile points at another location in the distribution (e.g., between the 50th and 84th percentiles).

Stanines

Another standard score system that is widely used on standardized tests is the *stanine scale* (standard scores with nine categories), which was developed and used extensively by the U.S. Air Force during World War II. Stanines are

---

[2] Small differences in σ become very significant at the extremes. For example, if scores are normally distributed, we would expect 0.13% of the scores to exceed 145 on the Wechsler ($z = 3.00$), whereas on the Stanford-Binet we would expect almost twice as many (0.25%, $z = 2.81$) IQ scores to exceed 145.

[3] As originally proposed, the *T*-score scale was a *normalized* standard score. Some writers denote nonnormalized *T*-scores as *Z*-scores. Since on standardized tests and in several statistics and measurement textbooks the use of "*T*-score" is not limited to normalized standard scores, we have not adhered to the original definition. When scores are normalized, the resulting scores will approximate the normal distribution as closely as possible. There are differences of opinion as to whether distribution of scores on standardized tests should be normalized or not (Angoff, 1971). Scores on most standardized tests are not normalized.

normalized standard scores with a mean of 5 and a standard deviation of 2.[4] Consequently, all stanines except 1 and 9 are one-half a standard deviation in width. The nine stanines (1, 2, 3, 4, 5, 6, 7, 8, and 9) are shown in Figure 3-2 in relation to the normal curve. Corresponding z-score and T-score limits are also given in Figure 3-2.

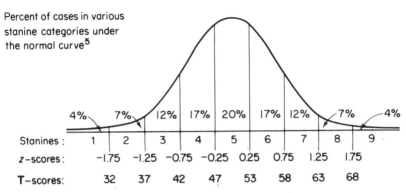

Percent of cases in various stanine categories under the normal curve[5]

Stanines :	1	2	3	4	5	6	7	8	9
	4%	7%	12%	17%	20%	17%	12%	7%	4%
z-scores :		-1.75	-1.25	-0.75	-0.25	0.25	0.75	1.25	1.75
T-scores :		32	37	42	47	53	58	63	68

FIGURE 3-2 The stanine scale related to T-scores, z-scores, and the normal distribution.

To convert raw scores into stanine scores, one arranges the scores in rank order from the highest to the lowest. The top 4 percent are assigned a stanine score of 9. The next 7 percent (see Figure 3-1 for the percents falling in each stanine) receive a stanine score of 8; the next 12 percent fall in stanine 7, the next 17 percent in stanine 6, the next 20 percent in stanine 5, and so on. Does this sound simple? With a little practice, it is. Any conscientious clerk can obtain stanine scores in this way, and at the same time the scores are being *normalized*. Normalizing occurs when we "force" the raw scores to fit the normal curve as closely as possible. Normalization is justified when the deviation from normality results from defects in the measure itself, but it is not appropriate when the distribution of the underlying ability of the sample is nonnormal in form (cf. Anastasi, 1976, p. 84).

Some people advocate the stanine scale as the standard general system of reporting results from all standardized tests. Although the stanine scale offers the advantage of a one-digit index, its user pays a price for this convenience, namely, some loss of information. If intelligence test results were reported in stanines, we would not be able to distinguish among people with IQs above 127, and among persons with scores below 73—a significant shortcoming,[6]

---

[4] The standard deviation of normalized stanine scores is not exactly 2.0 but 1.96, as shown by Kaiser (1958), who suggested a slight modification that would yield a standard deviation of precisely 2.0. For practical purposes the difference in the resulting scores is inconsequential.

[5] When the number of scores is very large or when greater accuracy is needed, the percentages of scores assigned to each stanine are 4.01, 6.55, 12.10, 17.47, 19.74, 17.47, 12.10, 6.55, and 4.01 for stanines 1 through 9, respectively.

[6] For greater differentiation at the extremes, the sta-eleven scale breaks stanine 1 into sta-elevens 0 and 1, and stanine 9 into sta-elevens 9 and 10. Approximately 1 percent of scores in a normal distribution will fall into each of the lowest and highest sta-eleven (0 and 10).

since the identification of gifted, educable, and trainable pupils is an important function of standardized intelligence tests.

It is true that the stanine scale helps convey the important concept that scores on a test should be viewed as *bands* rather than *points,* but the fixed bands of the stanine scale are the best band width only for those examinees who scored near the middle of the stanine. Some examinees will earn scores that differ by 2 stanines when their performance on two tests varies only slightly more than .5 standard deviations, whereas other students whose performance differs by .9 standard deviations (or even much more if stanines 1 or 9 are involved) will have stanine scores that differ by only 1. Although the stanine scale is the most widely used standard score and even appears to be increasing in popularity, we feel that its disadvantages are such that it is a second choice to the *T*-scale for most educational uses. Two-digit accuracy seems needed.

There are two important things to keep in mind regarding standard scores: (1) The mean and the standard deviation of the standard-score scale may have any value one chooses, without any resemblance to the mean and standard deviation of the raw scores themselves; and (2) standard scores are no more or less normally distributed than the raw scores from which they were obtained, unless they were normalized.

Norms Provide a Means of Comparison with a Reference Group

The instructional strengths and weaknesses of an examinee, school, or school district are illuminated when the performance is viewed in terms of a larger, representative reference group. Figure 3–3 depicts the results of students in a large high school who took the Scholastic Aptitude Test (SAT) of the College Entrance Examination Board over a sixteen-year period.

The widely publicized decline is evident in the national norms on both the Verbal and Math SAT tests; the decline is greater on the Verbal (48 points, $.5\sigma$) than on the Math (31 points, $.3\sigma$). The pattern for Fairview High School is less consistent; there is a trend for the Math scores to increase up to 1973 and to decrease very slightly thereafter. The Verbal scores show a larger decline beginning in 1975, even though both scores remain much above the national averages.

The identification of an individual pupil's instructional accomplishments and needs likewise can be expedited via appropriate, properly used standardized tests, as we will see later in the chapter.

A Representative Sample Is Needed for Accurate Norms

The size of the group on which norms are established is much less important than the degree to which it is representative of the relevant population. On measures of scholastic aptitude and achievement, there are marked differences across geographic region, socioeconomic status, urban-rural residence, and other factors. Norms based on 1 million persons from a "grab" sample are

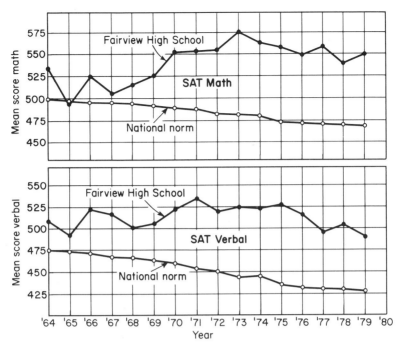

FIGURE 3-3 Performance of Fairview High School on the verbal and math sections of the Scholastic Aptitude Test (SAT) contrasted with the national norms over a 16-year period. (The authors are grateful to George Kretke for providing these data.)

much less useful than norms based on 1,000 representative pupils.[7] Samples for standardization purposes are often selected to correspond to the total population with respect to geographic region, sex, age, urban–rural residence, community size, father's occupational and educational level, and/or ethnic-group membership. One of the most carefully selected norm samples was used in the standardization of the widely used Wechsler Intelligence Scale for Children—Revised (WISC-R). The data in Table 3-1 were abstracted from the WISC-R (Wechsler, 1974); they illustrate the comparability of the WISC-R standardization sample with the national population as described in the most recent census data. Although only 200 persons were used at each age level, the sample was carefully selected to be representative; note the close correspondence between the norm sample and the population with respect to geographic region, ethnicity, urban–rural residence, and occupational level of head of household. Norms from tests that have been carefully standardized can be interpreted with much greater confidence than norms based on a group of uncertain representativeness.

Most standardized group tests (tests on which several examinees can be tested at the same time) have norms based on more than 5,000 students at each grade level, yet the norms are less accurate than those on the WISC-R, which are based on only 5–10% as many students. For example, the mean IQ score

[7] Most of Gallup's surveys are based on a *representative* sample of 1,500 persons, which is less than .001% of the population.

TABLE 3-1

COMPARISON OF THE STANDARDIZATION SAMPLE FOR THE
WECHSLER INTELLIGENCE SCALE FOR CHILDREN (WISC-R)
AND THE U.S. POPULATION[a]

By Geographic Region and Ethnicity

	White		Nonwhite		Total	
	U.S.	WISC	U.S.	WISC	U.S.	WISC
Northeast	20.3%	19.0%	2.6%	2.8%	22.9%	21.8%
North Central	25.7	26.1	2.9	3.0	28.6	29.1
South	23.7	24.0	7.6	7.6	31.3	31.6
West	15.3	15.9	1.9	1.6	17.2	17.5
Total sample	85.0%	85.0%	15.0%	15.0%	100.0%	100.0%

By Ethnicity and Urban–Rural Residence

	White		Nonwhite		Total	
	U.S.	WISC	U.S.	WISC	U.S.	WISC
Urban	59.3%	59.1%	11.7%	11.7%	71.0%	70.8%
Rural	25.7	25.9	3.3	3.3	29.0	29.2
Total sample	85.0%	85.0%	15.0%	15.0%	100.0%	100.0%

By Occupational Group of Head of Household and Ethnicity

	White		Nonwhite		Total	
	U.S.	WISC	U.S.	WISC	U.S.	WISC
I. Professionals, etc.	15.5%	16.5%	7.9%	6.4%	14.6%	15.0%
II. Managers, officials, etc.	28.0	28.8	14.8	17.0	26.5	27.0
III. Craftsmen, foremen, etc.	23.9	24.0	14.2	14.8	22.8	22.6
IV. Machine operators, service workers, etc.	27.6	26.7	46.9	42.4	29.7	29.0
V. Unskilled laborers, etc.	5.0	4.1	16.2	19.4	6.3	6.4

[a] From U.S. Bureau of the Census, *General Population Characteristics* (Washington, D.C.: U.S. Government Printing Office, 1972).

SOURCE: Wechsler, 1974, pp. 19–22.

from the WISC-R norm sample of 400 will almost certainly (95% confidence) be not more than 1.5 points from the mean for the entire population.[8] We are much less certain of the accuracy of the norms on most other standardized achievement and intelligence tests, even though they have much larger standardization samples. The size of the standardization sample is much less critical than its representativeness.[9]

[8] If you take an elementary statistics course, you will learn that the 95% confidence interval is approximately $\bar{X} \pm 2\sigma_{\bar{X}}$ ($\sigma_{\bar{X}}$ is the standard error of the mean). For the WISC-R, $\sigma_{\bar{X}} = \sigma/\sqrt{n} = 15/\sqrt{400}$, or .75 of an IQ point. The .95 confidence interval is based on the assumption that the sample was selected completely at random. The stratification illustrated in Table 3–1 would further reduce the value of $\sigma_{\bar{X}}$, which makes it *very improbable* that the mean of the norm sample ($\bar{X}$) is as much as 1 point from the mean that would have resulted if the entire national population of children had been tested.

[9] In the future, test norms may be established by item-sampling methods such as the Rasch model (Hambleton et al., 1978, 1979; Rentz & Rentz, 1979) or Lord's (1962a) method, rather than by examinee sampling. Each person in the norm sample will answer only a few items while other persons are attempting different items. Empirical studies indicate that norms developed using Lord's method are essentially equivalent to the more time-consuming and expensive examinee-sampling approach (Cook & Stufflebeam, 1967; Owens & Stufflebeam, 1969; Plumlee, 1964). Results from the Rasch model are less clear (Whitely & Dawis, 1974; Wood, 1977; Slinde & Linn, 1978, 1979).

Kinds of Norms

National norms are the most common type used in education and psychological testing. Some states and provinces, however, have established norms on various achievement tests for their particular domains. Many school districts use their local achievement norms in addition to national norms. Figure 3–4 shows the test performance of Roger Adams, a beginning sixth-grader, using national grade-equivalent and percentile norms as well as local percentile norms.

Notice that although Roger's reading score is better than those of 2 out of 3 beginning sixth-graders in his school district (i.e., local percentile rank of 65), it is just at the U.S. median (50th percentile). Although Roger's performance in mathematics was outstanding (94%ile), he is very poor (4%ile) in use of sources (e.g., dictionary, index, library). Roger's mental ability (STEA) appears to be good but not outstanding—his IQ score of 111 places him at the 74th percentile nationally. The xxxxx confidence bands to the right of the national percentiles help us attach the appropriate degree of precision to our interpretation. Notice that the composite 3R score is more precise (i.e., has a smaller xxx confidence band) than any of the three test components—the length of a test is an important determiner of its precision and reliability, as will be seen in greater detail in Chapter 5.

Norms Should Be Relevant

A score on a standardized test can be referenced to any number of different norm groups. In Figure 3–4 Roger Adams' achievement is compared to that of two norm groups, his local and national grade-level peers. We see that his performance is somewhat higher relative to that of his local peers than relative to that of his national peers. The two sets of norms complement each other and, used together, contribute to a better evaluation of Roger's achievement—both sets of norms are relevant but allow his performance to be viewed from different perspectives. Another relevant norm group could be the norms for Roger's state or region, which are available on certain tests. On the tests Roger took, norms are also available for large-city schools, Title I schools, affluent suburban schools, small-city and rural schools, and church-related schools. Are all of these norms relevant for evaluating Roger's performance? Some probably are, but only if Roger is a member of that particular subgroup or needs to be compared to that subgroup. If Roger attends a rural school, then the small-city/rural norms could be useful in addition to the national norms.

The relevant norm group is sometimes a highly select group of persons. Scaled score norms on the Graduate Record Examination (GRE) are based not on the performance of a representative sample of the nation's population but on that of graduating seniors at certain colleges (Schultz & Angoff, 1956). Hence, a mean score of 500 on the GRE represent greater abilities than does the mean on a college admission test, which in turn represent considerably higher abilities than an IQ score of 100 on general intelligence tests such as the

Grade equivalent.   Growth scale value.   Local norm percentile rank.   National percentile rank.   Percentile confidence bands. Show range of scores student would likely get if he took the test many times.

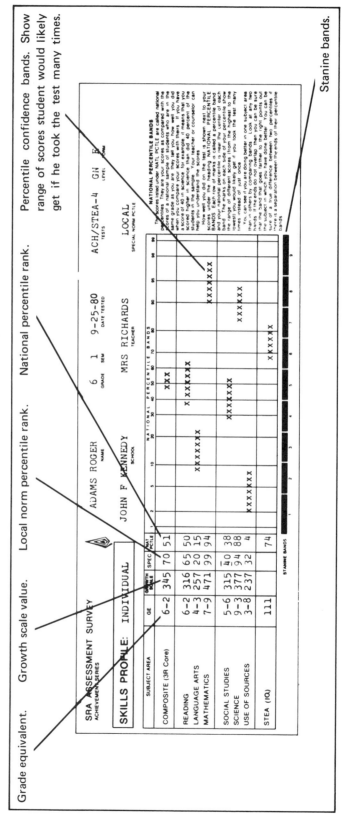

Stanine bands.

FIGURE 3-4 Individual report on Roger Adams, a beginning sixth-grade student at John F. Kennedy Elementary School on the *SRA Assessment Survey*. (From *SRA Test and Guidance Catalog*, © 1974. Science Research Associates, Inc. Reproduced by permission.)

Stanford-Binet Intelligence Scale or the Wechsler Adult Intelligence Scale (WAIS). Do you see why Fig. 3-1 cannot be used to estimate your IQ score from scores on CB, ACT, or GRE tests?

In addition to the total-group norms, standardized tests sometimes offer separate norms for special subgroups, for example, by sex, race, year, or region. The critical importance of the nature of the reference group is illustrated by the GRE data in Tables 3-2 and 3-3. Table 3-2 gives percentile norms for each of the three GRE subtests. Table 3-3 gives the identical data for the Verbal and Quantitative subtests for 1965-68. (The table also gives separate norms for each sex.) Using Table 3-2 and the "Total" norms in Table 3-3, can you determine whether there has been a change in average performance between 1965-68 and 1977-78? A scaled score[10] of 500 on the Verbal section exceeded the scores of 43 percent of the examinees in 1965-68 but those of 54 percent in 1977-78, reflecting an "achievement decline." That is, if your scaled score is 500, your percentile rank changes from 43 to 54, depending on whether the 1965-68 or the 1977-78 reference group (norms) is employed. Note that on the Quantitative subtest there is little change in the norms between 1965-68 and 1977-78. The percentile rank of a scaled score of 500 increased trivially, from 43 to 45, during this interval.

Note in Table 3-3 that, instead of the "Total" group norms, a different reference group can be employed. If your scaled score of 500 on the Quantitative subtest was compared to those of other people of the same sex, the percentile rank would be 34 or 60, depending on whether you reference the "Men" or "Women" norm group. From Table 3-3, can you estimate the median scores for men and women graduate students on the Verbal subtest? (The men's median is 520; the women's is almost 540.) Repeat the task on the Quantitative subtest. (The medians approach 570 and 470 for men and women, respectively.)

Even more relevant for decisions pertaining to graduate study are norms by major field of study, as illustrated in Table 3-4. (See Khoury, 1978 for more complete normative data.) Note that a scaled score of 600 on the Verbal test would be quite good relative to that of most of the reference groups represented in Table 3-4, but would be well below average for the classical-languages subgroup. Similarly, a Quantitative score of 700 would be excellent in relation to almost all reference groups, but only about average for the fields of computer science, mathematics, physics, and statistics. The implications of these normative data for vocational and academic counseling are obvious.

In addition to showing the large differences among major-field means, the data illustrate how extremely variable examinees are in verbal and quantitative ability *within* each major field of study. This fact should reduce our penchant for stereotyping by field of study. There are extremely able people in every field.

---

[10] The GRE scaled-score norms are based on the performance of 2,095 graduating seniors in the spring of 1952 at eleven colleges that were generally representative of schools that normally administer the GRE to their students. Test content is continuously revised by the inclusion of approximately one-sixth new and unscored items among the scored items in each GRE testing. Thus, normative data is obtained on the new items so that they may replace older items with the same statistical characteristics (difficulty and reliability).

TABLE 3-2

1977–78 PERCENTILE NORMS ON THE APTITUDE
TESTS OF THE GRADUATE RECORD EXAMINATIONS
(BASED ON THE PERFORMANCE OF EXAMINEES
TESTED AT NATIONAL ADMINISTRATIONS BETWEEN
OCTOBER 1, 1977, AND JUNE 30, 1978)

Scaled Score	Percent of Examinees Scoring Lower Than Selected Scaled Scores		
	Verbal Ability	Quantitative Ability	Analytical Ability [a]
820		99	
800		98	
780	99	97	
760	98	96	
740	97	94	99
720	96	92	98
700	94	90	96
680	93	87	93
660	90	83	89
640	87	80	84
620	84	75	79
600	80	72	75
580	76	66	69
560	71	61	63
540	65	55	58
520	60	49	52
500	54	45	47
480	48	38	42
460	41	33	36
440	37	27	32
420	30	23	28
400	26	18	23
380	20	15	20
360	16	11	17
340	14	9	14
320	10	7	11
300	8	5	9
280	5	4	6
260	4	3	5
240	2	2	3
220	1	1	2

[a] In 1977, the GRE subtests were restructured to include a measure of "analytical ability" (ability to recognize logical relationships, draw conclusions from information, etc.). Performance on the Analytical Ability section correlates substantially with performance on the two original Verbal and Quantitative sections ($r_{VA} = .72$, $r_{QA} = .69$, whereas $r_{VQ} = .51$—Khoury, 1978).

SOURCE: From *Guide to the Use of the Graduate Record Examinations,* copyright © 1972, 1975, 1977, 1978 by Educational Testing Service. All rights reserved. Reprinted by permission.

TABLE 3-3

1965-68 PERCENTILE NORMS ON THE APTITUDE TESTS
OF THE GRADUATE RECORD EXAMINATIONS[a]

| Scaled Score | Percent of Students Scoring Lower than Selected Scaled Scores | | | | | |
| | Verbal | | | Quantitative | | |
	Men	Women	Total	Men	Women	Total
800				99		99
780	99	99	99	96		97
760	98	97	98	94	99	96
740	96	96	96	90	98	93
720	94	94	94	86	97	90
700	92	91	91	81	96	87
680	89	87	88	78	94	84
660	86	83	85	73	92	80
640	82	79	81	68	90	76
620	77	74	76	63	87	72
600	73	69	71	58	84	67
580	67	63	66	53	80	63
560	62	57	60	48	76	58
540	56	51	54	43	70	53
520	50	45	48	38	65	47
500	44	40	43	34	60	43
480	38	34	37	29	54	38
460	33	29	31	24	48	33
440	27	24	26	20	41	27
420	22	19	21	16	35	23
400	18	15	17	12	28	18
380	14	12	13	9	22	14
360	10	9	10	6	17	10
340	8	7	7	5	13	8
320	6	5	5	3	9	5
300	4	4	4	2	6	3
280	2	2	2	1	4	2
260	2	2	2		2	1
240	1	1	1		1	

[a] Scaled scores on the aptitude tests can range from 200 to 900. The data are based on the performance of a group consisting of graduate students and applicants for admission to graduate school tested from May 1965 through April 1968.

Note also that the *numbers* of persons vary greatly among the various fields. Although the classical-language group and philosophy had the largest percents (36.7% and 22.4%) of extremely able persons on the verbal test (scaled scores of 700 or above), the field of education/teaching still contained more persons with extremely high verbal ability (.021 x 31,770 = 667) than either philosophy (.224 x 2,761 = 618) or classical languages (.367 x 645 = 237). It is obvious that for a correct interpretation of any test, the precise nature of the reference group and the kinds of norm used must always be borne in mind.

TABLE 3-4

MEANS, STANDARD DEVIATIONS, AND PERCENT OF SCORES OF
700 OR MORE OF GRADUATE RECORD EXAMINATION VERBAL
AND QUANTITATIVE APTITUDE TEST SCORES OF SENIORS
AND NONENROLLED COLLEGE GRADUATES[a] BY INTENDED
GRADUATE MAJOR FIELD OF STUDY

		Verbal			Quantitative		
	N	*Mean*	*σ*	*% ≥ 700*	*Mean*	*σ*	*% ≥ 700*
All fields	518,530	507	120	5.0%	529	133	10.0%
Anthropology	3,846	571	106	12.3%	519	115	6.7%
Architecture	4,400	512	117	6.1%	586	107	15.8%
Biology	6,867	519	113	5.7%	572	114	12.7%
Business/commerce	11,052	478	112	2.6%	554	123	12.5%
Chemistry	7,159	525	117	6.5%	649	100	35.9%
Classical language	543	645	107	36.7%	564	112	13.3%
Computer science	5,809	523	129	8.7%	669	102	45.5%
Dentistry	657	476	102	.8%	563	113	10.5%
Education/teaching	31,770	469	108	2.1%	472	117	3.3%
Educational administration	3,660	454	109	1.5%	473	112	3.7%
Educational psychology	3,353	507	106	3.8%	500	115	4.4%
English	13,057	592	110	18.3%	504	116	5.2%
Economics	6,962	527	130	9.2%	607	121	25.2%
Forestry	1,559	512	97	3.4%	592	99	15.4%
German	729	567	107	10.4%	530	111	7.0%
Guidance and counseling	9,905	474	107	1.8%	465	117	2.7%
History	9,405	555	118	12.2%	502	124	6.3%
Home economics	2,139	446	99	.4%	464	106	.8%
Industrial engineering	1,249	433	125	1.6%	633	104	29.9%
Journalism	4,265	547	112	9.2%	497	118	4.7%
Law	3,188	518	124	7.2%	521	136	9.7%
Mathematics	4,833	530	130	10.6%	678	104	47.7%
Mechanical engineering	2,706	463	129	2.7%	668	94	37.6%
Medicine	3,149	541	109	6.9%	607	113	22.8%
Music	7,325	514	114	5.7%	507	121	6.3%
Nursing	9,740	506	97	2.5%	482	102	1.7%
Pharmacy	909	466	113	1.7%	574	108	11.1%
Philosophy	2,761	605	110	22.4%	567	124	16.3%
Physics	4,426	562	123	12.7%	702	86	59.3%
Psychology	37,295	533	109	6.6%	523	118	7.4%
Social work	11,465	483	111	2.5%	456	117	1.8%
Sociology	5,266	494	121	4.6%	476	129	4.4%
Spanish	1,680	474	101	4.4%	454	107	1.8%
Speech	4,598	474	101	1.8%	454	107	1.5%
Statistics	911	516	119	6.5%	677	100	49.0%

[a] Limited to persons who earned their college degree within five years of the test date: October 1, 1974, through June 30, 1977.

Norms Should be Current

Society in general and education in particular are continually undergoing change. The norms in Table 3–3 are quite old. Can we be sure the pattern of sex differences that existed in the mid-1960s is still true today? Certainly not. There have been significant changes in sex roles in our culture since those norms were obtained. For norms to be representative of current populations, they must be continually updated.[11] The Wechsler Intelligence Scale for Children (WISC) was originally normed in 1949. The question of interest is not how intelligent a child is in relation to children of the same age in 1949, but in relation to his or her contemporaries. That is why the test was renormed in 1974. The older the norms are, the more caution must accompany their interpretation.

The National Assessment of Educational Progress and state assessment programs such as the California Assessment Program consistently find substantial differences in achievement between whites and Spanish-surnamed or black students. Does this mean that national or state norms based on a representative sample are irrelevant? Should special subgroup norms be used for these groups? Some people maintain that separate ethnic-group norms should be used on all intelligence tests (i.e., that the mean IQ be defined as 100 for each ethnic group). A better alternative would be to have supplementary percentile norms for the relevant subgroups, similar to the separate sex norms illustrated in Table 3–3.

Summary

Raw scores and percentage scores are greatly influenced by the difficulty of the items, which is arbitrary. Therefore, "percent correct" scores cannot be rigorously interpreted as an absolute scale such as "percent of mastery."

Standardized tests are tests in which the content and conditions of administration (e.g., directions, allotted time) are held constant.

The meaning of test scores is enhanced if the scores are expressed in relation to a *reference* or *norm group.*

The *norms* on standardized tests describe the performance of the reference group (norm sample). The reference group should be a representative sample of the current relevant population.

Norms are not standards or goals, but represent the status quo. They provide a means for comparing an examinee with a reference group. *Percentile norms* are widely used and relatively easy to understand, but have the disadvantage of very unequal units.

Most standardized tests make use of the normal distribution and standard-score norms to describe an examinee's level of performance. All standard scores express performance in terms of standard-deviation units from the mean. The most "basic" standard score is the *z-scale,* which has a mean of 0 and a standard deviation of 1.

T-scores have a mean of 50 and a standard deviation of 10, thereby avoiding the negative scores and decimal fractions that occur with *z*-scores. The *stanine scale* is a standard score with a mean of 5 and a standard devia-

---

[11] Some tests, such as the College Boards and the GRE, serve an important function in the assessment of trends or changes in student ability or aptitude; hence, it is necessary to keep the scaled-score norms based on the same reference group even though the percentile norms are updated. This fixed meaning of the scaled scores on the college board tests quantify the "achievement decline" noted in Figure 3–3.

tion of 2. It has the advantage of single-digit reporting, but the disadvantage of being less precise, especially at the extremes.

There are many different kinds of norm groups: age, grade, sex, national, state, local. The relevant reference (norm) groups are those with which an examinee's score can be compared meaningfully. To remain accurate, norms need to be updated periodically.

IMPORTANT TERMS AND CONCEPTS

absolute scale
norm
standard
standardized test
reference group (norm group,
  standardization sample)

national norms
local norms
percentile norms
standard scores

z-score: $z = \dfrac{X - \overline{X}}{s}$

T-score: $T = 50 + 10z$

stanine

CHAPTER TEST

Suppose Mary obtained the following percentile ranks on five subtests of the *McCarthy Scales of Children's Abilities:*

Subtest	Percentile
Verbal	98
Perceptual	99.9
Quantitative	50
Memory	84
Motor	16

Use Figure 3–1 to answer questions 1–4, assuming the scores are normally distributed.

1. If Mary's Motor performance improved by 1σ, the percentile equivalent would increase from 16 to _____, or _____ percentile units.

2. If the Verbal score improved by 1σ, the percentile equivalent on the Verbal tests would increase from 98 to _____, or _____ percentile units.

3. In *standard-deviation* units, is the size of the *difference* between Mary's Verbal and Perceptual tests the same as the difference between her Motor and Quantitative scores?

4. If expressed in *T*-scores, would the change in percentile units of 34 and 1.9 in questions 1 and 2 be equal?

5. "Grading on the normal curve" was popular in some circles a few decades ago. The most common method used the following conversion:

Grade	z-Score
A	above 1.5
B	.5 to 1.5
C	−.5 to .5
D	−1.5 to −.5
F	below −1.5

Using this system, estimate the percent of A's, B's, C's, D's, and F's expected with a normal distribution of scores. (Use Figure 3–1.)

6. Occasionally you may encounter another measure of variability, the *quartile deviation* (also known as the semi-interquartile range), *Q*, which is one-half the distance between the first quartile (the 25th %ile), Q_1, and the third quartile (the 75th %ile), Q_3. In other words,

$$Q = \frac{Q_3 - Q_1}{2}.$$

Using Figure 3–1, estimate the value of Q for the Wechsler IQ scale.

7. Small changes in z-scores near the mean (e.g., from 0 to .5) correspond to (large or small) changes in percentile equivalents; but large z-score changes near the extremes (e.g., 2.0 to 2.5) correspond to (large or small) changes in percentile equivalents.

Information on certain standardized intelligence and achievement tests is given in the following table. When answering questions 8–17, assume that the scores are normally distributed.

	Wechsler IQ	Iowa Test of Basic Skills Grade-Equivalent Scores			
		Reading			Arithmetic
		Grade 3	Grade 5	Grade 8	Grade 5
Mean	100	3.0	5.0	8.0	5.0
σ	15	1.0	1.4	1.9	1.1

8. An IQ score above 115 is obtained by what percent of the population?

9. If a fifth-grade pupil obtains a percentile rank of 84 in reading, what is the pupil's grade-equivalent score?

10. What is the grade-equivalent (GE) score for the same relative performance (84%ile) in arithmetic at grade 5?

11. Jack obtained a GE score in reading of 6.1 when he entered grade 8. If his Wechsler IQ is equivalent to the same percentile rank, what is it?

12. If Jack's score in question 11 is valid, he reads better than about what percentage of the children in his grade?

13. Upon entering grade 3, what fraction of third-grade children
   a) obtain a reading grade-equivalent score of 4.0 or better?
   b) obtain a score of 5.0 or better?

14. On the reading test, what percent of beginning third-grade students (3.0) score at least as high as the *average* beginning fourth-grade students (4.0)?

15. At grade 5, is a grade-equivalent score of 6.0 relatively better (i.e., does it have a higher percentile rank) in arithmetic than in reading?

16. In reading, what percentages of third-grade students score below grade-equivalent scores of 2.0, 3.0, 4.0, and 5.0, respectively?

17. How much reading "growth" in grade-equivalent units is required during the five years between grades 3.0 and 8.0 to
a) maintain a percentile equivalent of 50?
b) maintain a percentile rank of 84?

18. If X is 176, $\overline{X} = 163$, and $s = 26$, express X as:
a) a z-score
b) a T-score
c) a percentile rank

19. In a typical school district of 100,000 students, how many could be expected to qualify for a gifted program that required an IQ score of at least 130 on the Wechsler tests, assuming a normal distribution. (*Hint:* obtain proportion from Table 3–1 by adding proportion above $+ 2\sigma$ and $+ 3\sigma$.)

20. Estimate the percentage of IQ scores that fall between 90 and 110.

21. Which of these is *not* characteristic of a normal distribution?
a) symmetrical   c) skewed
b) unimodal   d) bell-shaped

22. Which of these represents the poorest performance on a test?
a) 10th percentile   c) $T = 30$
b) $z = -1.5$ d) stanine 2

23. The heights of current U.S. men have been found (1978 norms) to closely approximate the normal distribution with a mean of 69.5 inches and a standard deviation of approximately 2.5 inches; estimate the percent of men over six feet tall.

24. The national percentiles for Roger Adams are given in Figure 3–4 (p. 66). Express his reading score as: A. a z-score; B. a T-score; C. a stanine.

25. Remedial work for Roger appears to be least needed in _____ and

26. and most needed in _____ and _____.

27. Roger's school district is achieving at a level _____ (above or below) that of the national reference group. (Compare national and local norms).

28. Which of these scores represents the highest level of performance?
a) $z = +1.0$ c) stanine 5
b) $T = 55$ d) 35%ile

29. In question 28, which score represents the lowest level of performance?

Here are four generalizations pertaining to norms:

a. Norms are not standards.
b. Raw scores and percentage scores do not represent an absolute scale.
c. *Percentile* refers to percent of the reference group, not percent of items.
d. The reference group should be relevant.

Each of the statements in the following questions shows a misunderstanding of one of these generalizations. Identify the generalization in each case.

30. "No first-grade child who is reading below the national grade equivalent should be promoted to the second grade."

31. "Using the chimpanzee norms, I have an IQ of 200!"

32. "I guess I did pretty badly on the test; I scored at the 65th percentile —don't all scores below 70% get an F?"

33. "I guess I know all there is to know about standard scores—I got 100% on the test."

34. "Jerry got a score of 40% whereas Mary got a score of 80%; that makes Mary twice as smart as Jerry."

ANSWERS TO CHAPTER TEST

1. 50, 34
2. 99.9, 1.9
3. yes, 1σ in each instance
4. yes, *T*-score increase of 10 in each instance
5. A: 7%; B: 24%; C: 38%; D: 24%; F: 7% (your answers may differ slightly, since precise values cannot be obtained from Figure 3–1)
6. $Q = (110 - 90)/2 = 10$
7. large, small
8. 16%
9. 6.4

10. 6.1
11. 85
12. 16%
13. a) 1/6, b) 1/50
14. 16%
15. Yes
16. 16%, 50%, 84%, 98%
17. a) 5.0; b) 5.9
18. a) $z = .50$, b) T = 55, c) approximately 69%ile
19. 2.14% + .13% = 2.27%; .0227 x 100,000 = 2,270.
20. 50%
21. c

22. c
23. 16%
24. a) 0; b) 50; c) 5
25. math and science
26. Use of Sources and Language Arts
27. below
28. a
29. d
30. a
31. d
32. c (also a)
33. b
34. b

FOR ADDITIONAL READING

HOPKINS, K. D. and G. V. GLASS. The normal distribution and standard scores. *Basic Statistics for the behavioral sciences.* Englewood Cliffs: Prentice-Hall, 1978. Chap. 6.

LYMAN, H. B. Derived scores. In *Test scores and what they mean,* 3rd ed. Englewood Cliffs: Prentice-Hall, 1978. Chap 6.

Test
Validity

The *validity* of a measure is how well it fulfills the function for which it is being used. Regardless of the other merits of a test, if it lacks validity the information it provides is useless. The validity of a test can be viewed as the accuracy of specified inferences made from its scores. These inferences will pertain to (1) performance on a "universe" of items (content validity), (2) performance on some criterion (criterion-related validity), or (3) the degree to which certain psychological traits or constructs are actually represented by test performance (construct validity). During the process of test validation one examines the relationships between test scores and other empirical data and logical considerations.

It should be evident that validity is a multifaceted concept. In Chapter 1 several different uses of tests were described. The extent to which a test improves the accuracy of decisions is the extent to which it provides useful information and, hence, has practical validity.

The common question, "Is the test valid?" is not directly answerable. A test possesses many validities—it may be highly valid for one purpose but not for others. The question of test validity is always particularized; it can be answered only in relation to a given specific task for a given population of examinees.

A joint committee of the American Psychological Association, American Educational Research Association, and National Council on Measurement in Education has prepared a set of recommendations to improve the quality of validity data and other information on published tests (APA, 1974). In this chapter validity is classified into three subtypes: content, criterion related, and construct, as outlined in the APA-AERA-NCME recommendations. The three types subsume the three principal purposes for which tests are used.

Content Validity

The relevant type of validity in the measurement of academic achievement is *content validity*. In assessing the content validity of an achievement test one asks, "To what extent does the test require demonstration by the student of the achievements which constitute the objectives of instruction in this area?" (Ebel, 1956, p. 269). For a test to have high content validity, it should be a representative sample of both the *topics* and the *cognitive processes* of a given course or unit; that is, as Cureton (1969, p. 798) suggests, the test should possess topic validity and process validity. Test publishers are increasingly providing such information on their tests. Figure 4-1, from the handbook accompanying the Sequential Tests of Educational Progress (STEP), illustrates both the content and the skill required for the STEP Science test. Even more explicit information on a test's content validity is illustrated in Figure 4-2, in which specific instructional objectives/topics are referenced to test items across the various levels of the Metropolitan Achievement Tests. Only a small portion of the math objectives are given in Figure 4-2; the teacher's manual delineates 47 "numeration," 45 "geometry and measurement," 28 "problem-solving," 64 "operations," and 12 "graphs and statistics" objectives. This kind of information is very helpful in assessing the test's content validity for a given curriculum.

An achievement test should *re-present* the content universe about which one wishes to make an assessment. It is axiomatic that the content validity of a test must always be viewed in relation to the particular objectives to be assessed.

How does one determine the content validity of a measure? Content validation is primarily a process of logical analysis. By means of a careful and critical examination of the test items in relation to the objectives and instruction, one must make the following professional judgments:

1. Does the test content parallel the curricular objectives in content and processes?
2. Are the test and curricular emphases in proper balance?
3. Is the test free from prerequisites that are irrelevant or incidental to the present measurement task? (For example, are the reading and vocabulary levels of the science test appropriate for the examinees?)

It is crucial that each of the points in question be studied carefully before selecting a standardized test. School districts too often make only a cursory examination of published tests before formulating their district-wide testing programs. Small wonder, then, that teachers complain, "The test

ITEM CLASSIFICATION

SCIENCE, FORM 3A

Item Number	Right Answer	Grade 7 % Right	Grade 8 % Right	Grade 9 % Right	Knowledge Biology	Knowledge Chemistry	Knowledge Physics	Knowledge Earth Sciences	Comprehension Biology	Comprehension Chemistry	Comprehension Physics	Comprehension Earth Sciences	Application Biology	Application Chemistry	Application Physics	Application Earth Sciences	Higher Biology	Higher Chemistry	Higher Physics	Higher Earth Sciences	Item Number
1	D	88	91	94												X					1
2	C	75	86	92	X																2
3	A	66	76	88										X							3
4	C	88	89	92												X					4
5	D	74	79	86						X											5
6	C	77	83	86				X													6
7	D	72	79	88						X											7
8	B	94	94	95					X												8
9	A	55	65	72					X												9
10	D	87	91	94								X									10
11	A	53	60	58								X									11
12	D	62	68	74												X					12
13	C	58	67	73									X								13
14	C	55	63	68						X											14
15	A	61	72	77	X																15
16	D	48	58	63									X								16
17	B	35	49	65		X															17
18	C	40	54	66	X																18
19	C	54	59	60												X					19
20	C	45	55	64													X				20
21	B	58	63	72					X												21
22	D	40	49	58					X												22
23	B	54	62	67										X							23
24	B	49	53	63											X						24
25	C	32	45	58												X					25
26	A	48	55	61											X						26
27	A	42	54	63	X																27
28	C	46	57	66														X			28
29	B	65	70	76														X			29
30	D	31	37	39						X											30
31	C	49	54	60									X								31
32	C	46	50	54										X							32
33	D	39	52	57		X															33
34	D	48	56	60									X								34
35	D	32	36	43										X							35
36	C	34	38	38																X	36
37	A	28	41	44									X								37
38	A	25	32	40														X			38
39	C	31	39	51														X			39
40	A	31	36	40									X								40
41	D	29	34	39	X																41
42	A	34	41	43									X								42
43	D	32	34	40												X					43
44	A	25	33	50										X							44
45	D	53	62	69				X													45
46	C	38	45	49										X							46
47	B	33	38	43										X							47
48	B	66	73	81	X																48
49	A	59	67	73									X								49
50	D	52	63	69								X									50

SCIENCE ITEM CLASSIFICATION CATEGORIES

Skill

Knowledge, the ability to recall ideas, material, or phenomena. (22% of the items)

Comprehension, the ability to translate ideas or material from one method of expression to another; to interpret material presented or to extrapolate from it. (20% of the items)

Application, the ability to use learned information in answering an unfamiliar question or solving a new problem. (46% of the items)

Higher level skills, analysis, the ability to break down material into its constituent parts and to detect the relationships among them and the way they are organized; synthesis, the ability to combine parts to produce a new pattern or structure; evaluation, the ability to make purposeful judgments of ideas and solutions. (12% of the items)

Content

Biology, includes development, ecology, evolution, heredity, morphology, physiology, and taxonomy. (40% of the items)

Chemistry, includes atomic structure and bonding, kinetic-molecular theory, the chemistry of particular substances, energy considerations, and fundamental terms and calculations. Some questions are laboratory oriented. (16% of the items)

Physics, includes atomic and nuclear physics, electricity and magnetism, heat and kinetic theory, mechanics, optics, and waves. (24% of the items)

Earth Sciences, includes astronomy, geology, and meteorology. (20% of the items)

FIGURE 4-1 An illustration of topic and process grid on a standardized achievement test. (Reprinted from the Haris book for the *Sequential Tests of Educational Progress,* STEP Series II Science Test, Form A, Level 3, p. 104, by permission of Educational Testing Service. Copyright © 1971 by Educational Testing Service. All rights reserved.)

doesn't measure what we're teaching." The teachers feel that the test does not "mirror" the curriculum. This is not to suggest that such objections be taken at face value. Some teachers think it is unfair to include any item that has not been covered in the course of study for the class—a very narrow view of an appropriate content universe for a standardized test. Nevertheless, those who select standardized tests for a district testing program are often much too casual. A systematic study of the available standardized tests will not usually identify a test that is a perfect "fit" for a district's curriculum; only tests constructed carefully by a team of curriculum and test experts (an expensive task) can approach this objective. However, some of the published tests will be more relevant for the district's objectives than others—even though none will measure all of the cognitive objectives, not to mention the affective objectives. This and related problems are considered more extensively in Chapter 14.

Besides providing norms, standardized achievement tests differ from locally constructed tests in at least two important respects: (1) Standardized tests measure larger blocks of content because they are administered at intervals of a year or more, and (2) standardized achievement tests attempt to measure general, broad objectives and to minimize any special local, state, or regional emphases. Consequently, standardized tests are more process oriented and less topic oriented than teacher-made tests. Standardized achievement tests are not substitutes for teacher-developed tests—they complement each other.

It is impractical to conduct an *extensive* content validity analysis on all or even most teacher-constructed tests, but the teacher should systematically examine each classroom test before its administration to ensure a good representative sampling from the content universe. The teacher should ask, "Are all the important instructional topics represented in about the correct proportions on the test?" "Is there a proper balance of cognitive processes required or is there an overemphasis on rote knowledge?" and "Are all of the questions relevant—are there trivial items that should be eliminated?" Such elementary questions as these, if raised systematically by teachers at all educational levels, would greatly improve the quality of educational measurement.

Content validity should not be confused with "face" validity, which lacks the systematic logical analysis required by content validation. A test is said to have face validity if on first impression it appears to measure the intended content or trait. It is important that tests have face validity; otherwise, students may feel that they are being unfairly assessed. Typically, a content-valid test will also have face validity, but it is possible to have one without the other. Essay tests usually have high face validity, especially for people who are unfamiliar with related research, but they may lack reliability, an indispensable prerequisite for valid measurement of individual differences. Conversely, a test item that is not presented in a practical context may actually measure an important concept or ability, but it may lack face validity for some examinees. For example, consider the following item:

Which of these least belongs with the other three?
(a) 84%ile, (b) T = 60, (c) stanine 8, (d) $z = 1.0$

MATHEMATICS OBJECTIVES

For the following Mathematics objectives, item numbers on the Survey and Instructional tests are combined within the same chart, but are separated by a slash mark (⬭). For example, Numeration Objective 01 is tested by items 1, 2, and 3 on the Primer Numeration Test (Mathematics Instructional Test), and by item 1 on the Mathematics Test of the Survey Battery. Preprimer and Advanced 2 are Survey only.

Key: Instructional (above slash) / Survey (below slash)

Objective	Preprimer	Primer	Primary 1	Primary 2	Elementary	Intermediate	Advanced 1	Advanced 2
NUMERATION								
01 Can count groups of objects to 10	/ 12	1,2,3 / 1						
03 Can associate the numerals 1-10 with the correct number of objects	/ 13	7,8,9 / 3						
11 Can determine ordinal position through 10		19,20,21 / 6	7,8,9 / 3					
18 Can count by 2's, 5's, and 10's			16,17,18 / 6	16,17,18 / 6	7,8,9 / 3			
28 Can associate the correct number-words with numerals (through millions)					25,26,27 / 9	19,20,21 / 14		
30 Can complete a simple number sequence when pattern must be discovered						13,14,15 / 12	1,2,3 / 7	
34 Can convert between standard and exponential notation						13,14,15 /		31
GEOMETRY & MEASUREMENT								
08 Can tell time to the hour		25,26,27 / 23	10,11,12 / 14					
19 Can determine the amount of change due on purchases of one dollar or less				28,29,30 / 20	25,26,27 / 18	1,2,3 / 18		
22 Can determine the perimeter of squares, rectangles, and triangles					16,17,18 / 16	13,14,15 / 21		
PROBLEM SOLVING								
1SD Can solve a simple problem, dictated by the teacher, involving addition (Basic Facts: Sums to 10)	/ 25	13,14,15 / 25,26	1,2,3 / 20					
9SR Can solve a word problem, read by the pupil, involving one of the four basic operations, with no limit on the computation involved						16,17,18 / 6	13,14,15 / 3	16,18
OPERATIONS: WHOLE NUMBERS								
A4 Can find sums of two-digit numbers, and sums of two-digit and one-digit numbers, where *no regrouping* is required			10,11,12 / 33,34	16,17,18 / 36,37	1,2,3 / 40			
M5 Can multiply two-digit and one-digit numbers where *regrouping* is required					25,26,27 / 48	10,11,12 / 36	10,11,12 / 36	
D5 Can divide a two-digit number by a one-digit number, with remainder						19,20,21 / 39	19,20,21 / 39	
OPERATIONS: LAWS & PROPERTIES								
12 Knows the *Associative Properties of Addition and Multiplication* and can use them						13,14,15 / 28	1,2,3 / 15	
13 Recognizes multiplication and division as inverses						22,23,24 / 29	4,5,6 /	
14 Knows the rules for *order of operations* in algebraic sentences and can use them						7,8,9 / 16		

FIGURE 4-2 Illustrative mathematics objectives for the Metropolitan Achievement Tests classified by test level. (Abridged from *Metropolitan Achievement Tests: Teacher's Manual for Administering and Interpreting*, pp. 107–116, by permission of the Psychological Corporation, copyright © 1978.)

Objective | Test Level
OPERATIONS: FRACTIONS & DECIMALS

		Intermediate	Advanced 1	Advanced 2
01	Can add fractions with like denominators where *no reducing* is required	1,2,3 46		
04	Can subtract fractions with like denominators, with *reducing*	10,11, 12	7,8,9	
05	Can multiply two fractions where *no reducing* is required	19,20, 21	25,26, 27 46	
06	Can draw inferences from tabled data	7,8,9	4,5,6 26	
07	Can determine the average (mean) of data from a table		7,8,9 27	
08	Can interpret a frequency distribution		10,11, 12	
16	Can compute with percents		43,44, 45 50	12,13
17	Can multiply fractions and mixed numbers			8
GRAPHS & STATISTICS				
09	Can determine the probability of an independent event *not* occurring and the combined probability of independent events		22,23, 24	
10	Can determine a linear equation in two unknowns from a graph			47
11	Can determine slopes and intercepts for graphs of linear equations in two unknowns			48
12	Can determine graphs for quadratic equations			50

FIGURE 4-2 Illustrative mathematics objectives for the Metropolitan Achievement Tests classified by test level. (*Continued*)

The item requires knowledge of the normal curve in relation to percentiles and some understanding of standard scores of the *T, z,* and stanine types as well. Options (a), (b), and (d) describe the identical point in a normal distribution, whereas stanine 8 is above this point. Some students might respond, "If that's what you wanted to know, why didn't you ask?" If the item were recast into the form, "Which one of the following is not one standard deviation above the mean in a normal distribution?" much of the cognitive synthesis and induction of the item would be destroyed, and hence its potential for measuring higher levels of understanding would be attenuated.

When properly used, the kind of item that requires the student to find the concept being assessed as well as the answer *can* measure a high level of conceptual comprehension and application. Such items may lack face validity for examinees who are unsophisticated in measurement. Face validity is important for the test's clientele, be they students or job applicants. Examinees should feel they are being treated fairly. Tests with good content validity *usually* have face validity; the reverse, however, is much less likely to be true.

Content validity is relevant not only for achievement tests but for psychological, psychomotor, and behavioral measures as well. Are the items on the instrument a representative sample of the domain of content to which an inference is being made? If a performance measure in tennis required no use of a backhand stroke, its content validity would not be high—the sample of tasks assessed would not be representative of the content universe. A teaching proficiency measure that pertains exclusively to interpersonal relationships with staff and students would be a nonrepresentative sample of tasks within the job description of a teacher. Some general intelligence tests are composed entirely of vocabulary and verbal stimuli; the content validity of such tests is weaker than that of intelligence tests that also include pictorial, numerical, spatial, and abstract-reasoning items. *The content validity of a test is the degree to which the items of that test are a representative sample of the universe of content and/or behavior of the domain being assessed.* The generalization from test scores to the domain of intelligence behavior is only as good as the representativeness of the sample of tasks (items) employed. The concept of content validity will be further discussed in Chapter 7 (course-oriented achievement tests) and Chapter 14 (standardized achievement tests).

Criterion-Related Validity

In contrast to content validity, which is based almost entirely on logical considerations, *criterion-related validity* is an empirical matter. There are two subclasses of criterion-related validity, predictive and concurrent. The more common is *predictive-validity,* in which the test has the task of predicting some subsequent measure of performance. For example, an employer wishes to identify which applicants are most likely to be productive workers. The employer is not concerned primarily with whether the test is a representative sample of some universe (content validity) or with whether the test is a good indicator of some psychological trait (construct validity); he or she wishes to select the applicants who are good risks and reject those who are poor risks. Although unlikely, if people who indicate that they prefer strawberry to vanilla ice cream become more successful salespeople, then that would be a relevant item for inclusion in the screening test for salespeople. It is relevant because it contributes to a more accurate decision for the selection task at hand, regardless of whether the items appear to be logically related to the job. In most instances, however, predictors are related logically as well as empirically to the criterion.

A measure's predictive validity, then, is how well its predictions agree with subsequent outcomes. The type of validity that is relevant for the Scholastic Aptitude Test (SAT) of the College Board entrance examinations is predictive validity. The extent to which scores on the tests are related to success in college is the extent to which the test fulfills its predictive function. The accuracy of the predictions is usually represented by the *correlation coefficient* between test scores and the criterion. This coefficient is a validity coefficient, since it defines the degree of criterion-related validity of the test. Decisions involving selection (e.g., to admit or hire an applicant or not) are predictive in nature. The extent to which the use of tests can improve the accuracy of the decision is the extent to which the tests are of value. We will now take a break from the general concepts of validity and explore the meaning of correlation and correlation coefficient.

Correlation and Prediction

1. Most people have a general understanding of the meaning of correlation (that is, co-relationship or co-variation). Two traits are correlated if they tend to "go together." If high scores on variable X tend to be accompanied by high scores on variable Y, then the variables X and Y are correlated, since the scores "co-vary." For example, there is a tendency for tall people to weigh more than short people. Since height and weight tend to co-vary, they are said to be _____ .

correlated

2. We can describe the degree of correlation between variables by such terms as *strong, low,* or *moderate,* but these terms are not sufficiently explicit. A more precise method is to compute a coefficient of correlation between the sets of scores. A coefficient of correlation is a statistical summary of the degree of relationship or "going-togetherness" between two variables. Correlation coefficients range in magnitude from $+1.0$ to -1.0. A positive correlation coefficient means that high scores on one measure tend to be associated with high scores on another measure, and low scores on one tend to be associated with low scores on the other. For example, there is a tendency for individuals who score high on a scholastic aptitude test to receive better marks than those who score low on it. The correlation coefficient for this example would be _____ (positive or negative).

positive

3. On the other hand, for adults age correlates negatively with certain psychomotor abilities. The sign ($+$ or $-$) of the correlation coefficient indicates the *direction* of the relationship. When low scores on variable A are accompanied by low scores on variable B, and high scores on A by high scores on B, r_{AB} (the coefficient of correlation between A and B) is _____ ; if high scores on A are associated with low scores on C, and vice versa, r_{AC} would be _____ .

positive
negative

4. The sign of r does not indicate the strength of a relationship. For example, if test scores correlate $-.3$ with number of days absent for a group of third-grade pupils, then the correlation between tests scores and days present would be _____ .

$+.3$

5. The numerical value of r denotes the degree of the relationship; the higher the absolute value (the value irrespective of the sign), the stronger is the relationship. If $r_{AB} = +.55$ and $r_{AC} = -.70$, there is a stronger relation between A and _____ than there is between A and _____ .

C, B

6. When $r = +1.0$ or -1.0, there is a perfect relationship between the two variables. In both cases a knowledge of one of the variables makes it pos-

sible to predict the second variable without error. With $r = +1.0$, the z-scores of each individual would be the same on both measures. With $r = -1.0$, the highest score on one measure would be associated with the lowest score on the second measure, and so on. Any pair of z-scores would be identical in value but opposite in sign, perhaps $+2.3$ and -2.3. If two tests intercorrelated $+1.0$ and John ranked third on test A, he would rank _____ on test B. If his z-score on test A was $+1.8$, his z-score on test B would be _____ .

third

$+1.8$

---

7. Although a correlation coefficient cannot be interpreted as the percent of agreement, it does reflect the expected percentage of deviation from the mean of the second variable. For example, in the general population, fathers' IQs (or mothers') tend to correlate about .5 with offspring's IQs. The .5 correlation indicates that the best prediction we can make of a child's IQ score is that it will be only 50 percent as far from the population mean as the father's. If one selected from a representative sample 100 fathers scoring 130 on an intelligence test, and then tested one child of each father, the children's mean would be expected to be only one-half (.5) as far from the population mean (100) as were the fathers'. The mean of the children would be expected to be about _____ .[1]

115

---

8. On the other hand, if we selected a group of fathers with IQ scores of 80, and then examined their fathers, we would expect the mean IQ score of the fathers to be about _____ .

90

---

9. It is important to bear in mind that a correlation coefficient expresses the ratio of the average or *expected* deviation from the mean on the predicted variable (y) to the *known* deviation from the mean on the predictor variable (x) in standard-deviation units. The following regression equation makes this clear:

$$z_y' = rz_x,$$

where z_y' = expected or predicted z-score on variable Y
   r = the correlation between variables X and Y, and
   z_x = the known z-score on variable X.

If the distances that a group of children can high-jump and long-jump correlate .6, then we can say that, on the average, those who are two standard deviations from the mean in long-jumping are only _____ standard

1.2

[1] An erroneous conclusion, often drawn when one is first introduced to this "regression toward the mean" (be it illustrated with IQ scores, height, or any other variable), is that successive generations become less variable. This is not the case. There are enough individual exceptions to the general trend to preserve the equality of the standard deviations for the two groups. In our example you will note that $\sigma = 15$ for both fathers and children; hence, the children are not more homogeneous in IQ scores than their fathers. The regression operates both ways; for example, had we selected 100 children with IQs of 130 and then tested their fathers, the mean IQ of the fathers would be expected to be 115.

deviation(s) above the mean in high-jumping. If a child has a z-score of -1.0 in high-jumping, that child would be predicted to have a z-score of _____ in long-jumping.

$-.6$

---

10. Grade point average (GPA) at most colleges correlates about .5 with the Verbal portion of the Scholastic Aptitude Test (SAT-V). For College A, suppose you have the following information about this year's freshman class:

	SAT-V	GPA
Mean	500	2.5
s	100	.7

$r = .5$

In this class, a certain freshman has an SAT-V score of 660, which is 1.6 standard deviations above the mean of the class; $z_x = 1.6$. We predict her GPA to be $(.5)$ (____) = ____ standard deviations above the mean GPA of the class. Therefore, her predicted GPA is $2.5 + ($____$)($____$)$ = 3.06.

1.6, .8
.8, .7

---

11. In any elementary statistics course you will learn how to compute r, the Pearson product–moment coefficient of correlation.[2] The rank difference correlation coefficient is a very close relative. It is easy to compute, and its computation helps us understand the meaning of correlation. The rank-difference correlation coefficient (r_{Ranks}), also known as Spearman's rank difference correlation, will be approximately the same as the Pearson r for the same data.

Correlation can be viewed simply as the degree to which persons maintain the same relative positions or ranks on two variables. If there is much change, the correlation coefficient will be low; if there is little change, the coefficient will be high. A correlation coefficient can be obtained between any two variables if scores or ranks are available on both.

Example: Two of the tests from the Primary Mental Abilities (PMA) battery, the Verbal Meaning (VM) and the Word Fluency (WF) tests, were given to the students in a measurement class. To simplify our illustration, only 11 of the pairs of scores are used to illustrate the computation of the rank difference correlation coefficient, _____.

r_{Ranks}

---

12. To compute a rank difference coefficient correlation, follow the procedure outlined here:

1. Rank the individuals on the first variable (VM) from the highest score (1) to the lowest score (N). N is the number of pairs of scores (in this example

[2] There are many relatively inexpensive hand calculators on the market that compute r on command.

184811

$N = 11$). The VM score of 50 (see the following table) is the highest score and receives a rank of 1; 49 is the next-highest score and receives a rank of 2, and so on; 35 is the lowest VM score and hence ranks 11th.

2. Rank the individuals on the second variable in the same way. The highest WF score is 67, which receives a rank of 1, and so on; the lowest WF score is 25, which ranks 11.
3. Take the difference between ranks for each individual, putting this value in the column headed "Rank Difference" (D). (The sign of the difference is unnecessary, since all values will be squared.)
4. Square each rank difference (D) value and place the result in column "D^2."
5. Total the D^2 column to get ΣD^2. (Recall that Σ means "the sum of.")
6. Compute the coefficient (r_{Ranks}) using this formula:

$$r_{Ranks} = 1 - \frac{6\Sigma D^2}{N(N^2 - 1)}.$$

	Score		Rank		Rank Difference (D)	D^2
Person	VM	WF	VM	WF		
A	50	51	1	5	4	16
B	49	56	2	4	2	4
C	48	59	3	2	1	1
D	47	48	4	6	2	4
E	46	37	5	9	4	16
F	45	25	6	11	5	25
G	44	58	7	3	4	16
H	43	44	8	8	0	0
I	42	34	9	10	1	1
J	41	67	10	1	9	81
K	35	46	11	7	4	16

$$\Sigma D^2 = 180$$

$$r_{Ranks} = 1 - \frac{6\Sigma D^2}{N(N^2 - 1)}$$

$$= 1 - \frac{6(180)}{11[(11)^2 - 1]} = 1 - \frac{1080}{11(121 - 1)}$$

$$= 1 - \frac{1080}{11(120)} = \frac{1080}{1320}$$

$$= 1 - \underline{\qquad} \hspace{3cm} .82$$

$$r_{Ranks} = \underline{\qquad} \hspace{3cm} .18$$

13. The low relationship (.18) between the VM and WF scores can be illustrated graphically by a *scatterplot*—a plot that shows the performance on both variables. To complete the following scatterplot, first find the person's rank on the horizontal axis (VM in this example) and then move up vertically from that point until you coincide with the rank on the vertical variable (WF in this example). Those persons with ranks of 1, 2, and 3 on VM have already been entered. Complete the plot of the corresponding ranks.

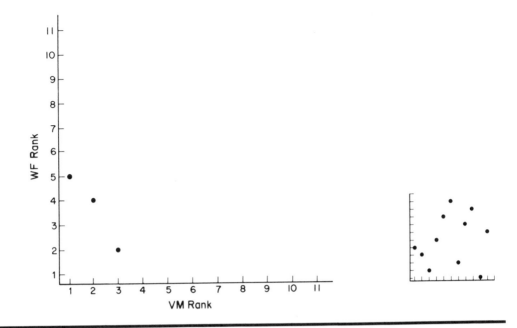

---

14. Compute the rank difference correlation coefficient between arithmetic and IQ scores using the 15 pairs of scores given in the following table:

Person	Score Arith.	Score IQ	Rank[3] Arith.	Rank[3] IQ	D	D²
A	30	105	8			
B	38	120		4		
C	16	83				
D	37	137				
E	32	114		7		
F	25	96				
G	19	107				
H	45	117	1			
I	33	108	6			
J	29	130				
K	26	88				
L	24	129		3		
M	13	76				
N	41	118				
O	36	112	5			

$$\Sigma D^2 = \underline{\hspace{2em}} \qquad 220$$

$$r_{\text{Ranks}} = 1 - \frac{6 \Sigma D^2}{N(N^2 - 1)}$$

$$= 1 - \frac{6(220)}{(\ \ )[(15)^2 - 1]} \qquad 15$$

$$= 1 - \underline{\hspace{2em}} \qquad .4$$

$$r_{\text{Ranks}} = \underline{\hspace{2em}} \qquad .6$$

---

[3] Actually, the computation of r_{Ranks} in this example was simplified by the exclusion of tied scores. Suppose two persons tied for the highest arithmetic score (45) and three had earned the

87

The following narrative treatment of correlation should enhance and extend your knowledge of the basic concept of correlation and its quantification, the coefficient of correlation.

The Concept of Correlation

During the latter part of the nineteenth century, Sir Francis Galton and the pioneer English statistician Karl Pearson succeeded in developing the theory and mathematical basis for what is now known as *correlation* (Walker, 1929). They were concerned with relationships between two variables, for example, height and weight. It is obvious that above-average height tends to go with above-average weight. Height and weight vary together (i.e., correlate positively), though certainly not perfectly; "beanpole" and "fats" explain why the relationship is not higher than it is.

Let's examine some other variables that usually "go together." There is a substantial, but again by no means perfect, positive correlation between scholastic aptitude test scores in high school and grades earned during the freshman year of college. The higher the test score obtained by a student, the higher the grades are *likely* to be. The lower the score is, the lower the grades the student will *probably* obtain. This relationship has been found with all sorts of intelligence tests used in a great number of colleges ever since such tests first became available commercially, shortly after the end of World War I (Lavin, 1967).

Husbands and wives *tend* to be more like each other with respect to age, amount of education, and many other factors than like people in general. The sons of tall fathers tend to be taller than average, and the sons of short fathers tend to be shorter than average. Children resemble their own parents in intelligence more closely than they resemble other adults. Some degree of positive correlation between members of families is usually found for almost any characteristic—such as personality, attitude, interest, or ability (Anastasi, 1958, pp. 266–316).

To quantify Galton's concept of co-relationships among traits, Pearson devised as a measure of relationship the *product–moment coefficient of correlation, r*. Since about 1900, *r* has been a widely employed statistic—virtually all test manuals are sprinkled plentifully with *r*'s, as is most research literature.

Pearson's original *r* (and several related measures of correlation) summarizes the magnitude and direction of the relationship between two sets of measurements, such as height and weight based on the *same* persons, or between the same measurement on *pairs* of persons like the fathers and sons just mentioned. A *correlation coefficient* can be obtained for any set of paired observations (e.g., history grades and geography grades, speed of running the 100-yard dash and skill in playing the violin, school attitude and IQ, etc.). The

---

next-highest score (41). The ranks for these five scores would have been 1.5, 1.5, 4, 4, 4. When ties occur, all scores receive the average of the associated ranks; in this case, $(1 + 2)/2 = 1.5$ and $(3 + 4 + 5)/3 = 4$.

correlation coefficient, r, can have values that range from -1 for a perfect inverse (negative) relationship, through 0 for no systematic correlation, to $+1$ for perfect direct relationship. The r's between radically different kinds of variables can be compared. For example, it is meaningful to say that, for the pupils of a certain group, reading ability and intelligence are more closely related than height and weight. Or, more interesting, whereas the IQ scores of identical twins reared apart are more highly correlated than the IQ scores of fraternal twins reared together, the relationship for scholastic achievement is reversed—the r for fraternal twins reared together is much higher than the r for identical twins reared apart. Although r's are concise statistical summaries of relationships, their meaning is more evident when it is depicted graphically using scatterplots.

Correlation and Scatterplots

The scatterplot enables us to study the nature of the relationship between two variables. Each ''dot'' of the scatterplot indicates the intersection of the X and Y points for one pair of scores. The scatterplot enables us to determine whether or not the relationship between the two variables is linear. The relationship between two variables is *linear* if a straight line more closely fits the dots of the scatterplot than any curved line does. A perfect positive linear relationship ($r = 1.00$) is shown in Figure 4-3, in which the dots move in a straight line from low–low to high–high, with no dots in the low–high and high–low quadrants. A perfect negative relationship ($r = -1.00$) is illustrated in the scatterplot in Figure 4-4. Actual r's of 1 and -1 are very rare; nevertheless, they help us understand the meaning of perfect linear correlation.

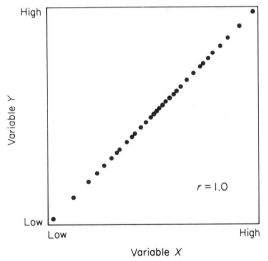

FIGURE 4-3 An illustration of a perfect positive correlation, $r = 1.00$.

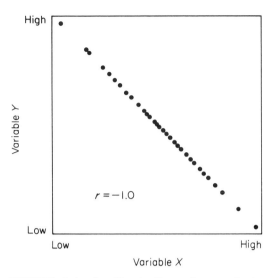

FIGURE 4-4 An illustration of a perfect negative relationship, $r = -1.00$.

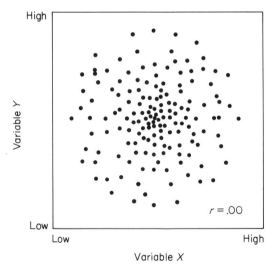

FIGURE 4-5 An illustration of no correlation, $r = 0.00$.

Figure 4–5 depicts no relationship between two variables, which results in an r of zero. Knowledge of a student's score on one test does not help predict his or her score on the other test. No matter how the student scored on one test, our best prediction is that he or she would score at the mean of the group on the other test. Intermediate values for $r = .30, .60,$ and $.90$ are illustrated in Figures 4–6, 4–7, and 4–8.

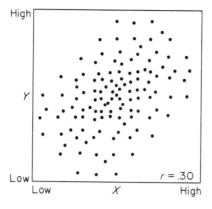

FIGURE 4-6 An illustration of $r = .30$.

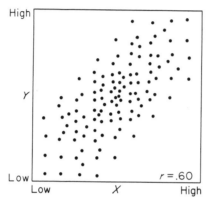

FIGURE 4-7 An illustration of $r = .60$.

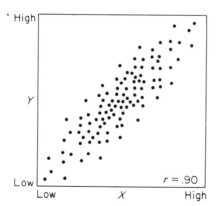

FIGURE 4-8 An illustration of $r = .90$.

A curvilinear relationship is shown in Figure 4–9. If one score of an individual is known, it is possible to predict his or her other score with considerable accuracy despite the r of 0. For scatterplots of this sort, r will greatly underestimate the relationship between the two sets of scores and therefore is not an appropriate measure of relationship.

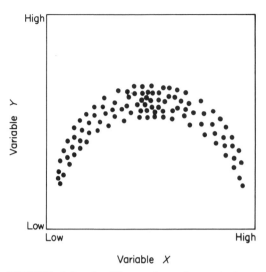

FIGURE 4-9 An illustration of a substantial curvilinear relationship.

Interpreting r

In interpreting a coefficient of correlation, several factors must be considered. The first is the *sign* of the coefficient; the second is the coefficient's *magnitude* or size. The sign indicates the *direction* of the relationship. Positive coefficients indicate direct relationship, that is, the tendency for the two scores to vary in the same direction. High values in one column are associated with high values in the other column; low values in one column are associated with low values in the other column; and so on. Negative coefficients indicate inverse relationship, which is a tendency for the two scores to vary in opposite directions—high values in one column are associated with low values in the other column, and vice versa.

More difficult to interpret is the coefficient's *size,* which indicates the *degree* or closeness of the relationship, just as the sign indicates the direction of the relationship. The minimum coefficient is .00, which indicates no consistent relationship whatsoever. From this minimum value the coefficients increase in both directions until −1.00 is reached for one limit and 1.00 for the other. It should be noted that −1.00 and 1.00 indicate equally close relationships, for both are perfect. Their one important difference is in direction, the former being inverse and the latter direct. Similarly, all other values of the same size, such as −.50 and .50, indicate equally close relationships. The size, not the sign, of the coefficient indicates the closeness or degree of relationship.

Two cautions should be observed. First, *r cannot be interpreted directly as a percentage in the usual sense.* An *r* of 0 represents no linear relationship at all, but an *r* of .66 does *not* usually indicate a 66 percent relationship. For large *r*'s, a small gain in the value of *r* indicates a considerable increase in the degree of association. An *r* of .66 usually indicates more than twice the relationship shown by an *r* of .33. Suppose traits A and B correlate .66, and A and C correlate .33. On the average, a person will be 66 percent as far from the B mean as from the A mean (in standard-score units); that person will be expected to be only 33 percent as far from the C mean as from the A mean (in standard-score units). The *accuracy* of our prediction of B from A, however, will be considerably greater than that of our prediction of C from A.

It is critical to understand that correlation does not necessarily mean causation. Often variables other than the two under consideration are responsible for the association. Furthermore, problems in the social sciences, the field in which correlation is most often employed, are usually too complex to be explained in terms of a single cause. The fact that people who have taken driver training have fewer automobile accidents than those without such training is a far cry from establishing a causal relationship between accidents and lack of driver training.

Let us take several examples. It is probably true that in the United States there is some positive correlation between the average salaries of teachers in various high schools and the percentages of the schools' graduates who go on to college, but to say that these students attend college *because* their teachers are well paid is as inaccurate as to say that their teachers are well paid *because* many of the graduates attend college.

It has been found that the percentage of pupil dropouts occurring in high schools varies inversely with the number of books per pupil in the libraries of those schools. But common sense tells us that merely piling more books into the library will no more affect the dropout rate than hiring a better attendance officer will bring about a magical increase in the number of books. If only common sense always served us so well!

Failure to recognize that correlation may not mean causation is, in its broadest sense, a widespread logical error, for the fundamental notions of corelationship affect our lives at many points. Going to church is generally believed to be valuable from many standpoints, but a positive relationship between the rate of attendance and a characteristic such as honesty does not *prove* that people are honest because they attend church. Underlying and causing both attendance and honesty may be another factor, such as home training.

For most testing purposes, causation is not the issue. "Is Bob's low score on the social studies test indicative of his true level of understanding of the content universe" is the validity question, even though the cause may be lack of study, lack of ability, or several other factors. If students who obtain low scores on the SAT or ACT subsequently obtain low grade point averages in college, the tests have predictive validity irrespective of the causes of the poor showing on either or both variables. The degree of criterion-related validity is denoted by a correlation coefficient.

The relationship between 43 college students' scores on an arithmetic pretest and their subsequent scores on a midterm examination is graphically depicted in the scatterplot in Figure 4–10. Notice that although there is a definite relationship ($r = .52$), it is far from perfect—the student with the

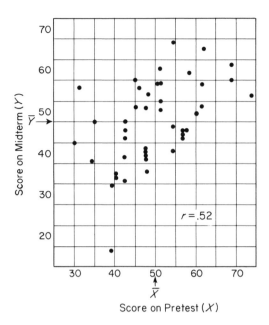

FIGURE 4-10 Scatterplot of 43 students for pretest and midterm examination scores.

highest score on the midterm (*Y*) was only slightly above the mean on the pretest ($\overline{X}$).

Influence of *N*

Another important factor in interpreting correlation coefficients pertains to the size of the sample on which the correlation coefficient was determined. For example, consider the correlation between IQ and height with $N = 2$. The computed *r* must be either $+1.0$ or -1.0 (unless it is a rare case in which the two persons would be precisely the same height or have identical IQ scores). The higher-ranking person in IQ will be either the taller of the two (hence, $r = 1.0$) or the shorter of the two (hence, $r = -1.0$).

To keep us from being misled by high correlation coefficients resulting from small samples, statisticians have developed procedures to assist in determining whether a given correlation coefficient can be attributed to chance (sampling error) or whether a genuine relationship exists. If a correlation is *statistically significant,* we can be confident that there is some degree of true relationship between the two variables. For example, if you encountered in your reading of professional literature a statement such as "For first-grade boys the correlation between height and IQ was statistically significant at the .01 level," it would mean that it is very unlikely that the true correlation is zero. Hence, we can be quite confident that some genuine relationship exists between the two variables. A common error in interpreting such *statistically significant* relationships is to assume that they are therefore *large* relationships. "Statistically significant" indicates only that it is unlikely that the true correlation in the population (that is, the parameter, ϱ) is 0.00. A relationship may be statistically significant and yet be very small if it is based on a very large sample. For example, the relationship between height and IQ, though statistically significant, is too low to be of value for practical purposes.

To guard against the error of interpreting statistically significant relationships as large relationships, researchers are increasingly using *confidence intervals*. These give the upper and lower limits of the range within which the true correlation coefficient in the population can be expected to fall. For example, a highly significant correlation of .32 was observed between study habits and scholastic aptitude for 172 ninth-grade boys (Bennett et al., 1974). How much error is there in the value of .32? The confidence interval around r gives a reasonable estimate as to how high or how low the value of r might be if the entire population in question were included. Consequently, the confidence interval gives us some assurance (e.g., "95 percent confidence") that, in spite of the N of only 172, we can expect the true correlation coefficient in the population to be somewhere in the .16 to .44 range. If our sample is representative and if we repeatedly use this strategy, we will be correct 95 percent of the time; that is, in the long run the true correlation, ϱ, will fall outside the .95 confidence interval only on one occasion in twenty.

Since high values for r are much more likely to occur by chance with small N's, high values of r are required for statistical significance when N is small. Table 4-1 shows that correlation coefficients based on small samples are not very reliable and that very low relationships can be statistically significant with a very large N. Table 4-2 was constructed to illustrate the influence of sample size on the precision of the r's. Since height is a variable that we can observe directly, it serves as a good illustration. We know that tall parents are more likely to have children who are taller than average. The correlation coef-

TABLE 4-1

MINIMUM VALUES OF r^a REQUIRED
TO BE STATISTICALLY SIGNIFICANT
AT THE .05 LEVEL FOR VARIOUS
SAMPLE SIZES (N)

N	Minimum r for Statistical Significance
5	.878
10	.632
25	.396
100	.197
1000	.062

[a] These values are from Hopkins and Glass (1978, p. 409). The corresponding values of the rank correlation r_{Ranks} required for statistical significance are very similar. (See Glass & Stanley, 1970, pp. 536, 539.)

TABLE 4-2

TYPICAL CORRELATION COEFFICIENTS AND CONFIDENCE
INTERVALS, USING HEIGHT AS AN ILLUSTRATION

	r	N	.95 Confidence Interval for ϱ
Identical twins reared together	.96	83	.93–.97
Identical twins reared apart	.94	30	.88–.97
Height at age 3 vs. height at maturity (males)	.75	66	.62–.84
Height at age 3 vs. height at maturity (females)	.70	70	.56–.77
Fraternal twins	.58	235	.49–.66
Siblings	.50	853	.45–.55
Parent and child	.51	374	.43–.59
Husband and wife	.34	320	.24–.43
Grandparent and grandchild	.32	132	.18–.47
First cousins	.24	215	.11–.36
Height and IQ	.20	4061	.17–.23

ficient quantifies this relationship. The confidence interval makes allowances for sampling error (chance); it is the "band" of values within which we can expect the true correlation—that is, the parameter, ϱ—to lie. Since the sample on which the value of .51 is based was quite large ($N = 374$), the confidence interval is quite narrow (.43–.59). As you recall, the .51 value indicates that, on the average, a child tends to be only about half as far from the mean height as his or her mother or father.

Validity Coefficients

One of the most important uses of the coefficient of correlation is in determining the validity of a test. As we will see later in this chapter, *predictive validity* is determined by identifying a criterion to be predicted and then computing the coefficient of correlation between the predictor scores and the scores on the criterion, for example, rank in high-school graduating class correlated with college freshman gradepoint average. The *r* so obtained is called a *predictive validity coefficient* and is interpreted in the same way as other coefficients of correlation.

Some Examples of Criterion-Related Validity

What can validity coefficients tell us about the usefulness of tests for selection purposes? Colleges that use the SAT or ACT are particularly interested in the average grades that selected students will attain. Figure 4–11 illustrates the average grades that would be expected at a typical college. Figure 4–11 is a composite illustration based on the typical distributions of SAT test scores and grades found at 159 colleges in 1974 (ETS, 1980). Figure 4–11 indicates that the relationship of SAT scores to grades is substantial; those students with higher SAT scores are typically those who go on to earn higher grades in

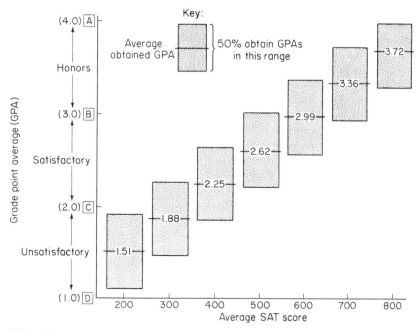

FIGURE 4-11 Average college grades for students with different SAT scores. (Typical SAT score—college GPA correlation = .40, based on data from 159 validity studies in 1974. From *Test Use and Validity*. Copyright © 1980 by Educational Testing Service. All rights reserved. Reproduced by permission).

college. As shown in the figure, there is also variation in the grades obtained by students with any given score. The bands in Figure 4–11 show grades for the middle 50 percent of the students at each score level. Other students will obtain scores outside these ranges.

Most universities in the United States require graduate students from non–English-speaking countries to take an English proficiency test, the Test of English as a Foreign Language (TOEFL), to demonstrate competence in English. But do scores on the TOEFL have anything to do with academic success as a graduate student? Are minimum scores for admission being set too low or too high? Figure 4–12 displays the relationship between TOEFL scores and subsequent grades in the first semester of graduate work for 110 foreign graduate students. Note that the relationship is substantial ($r = .631$); for example, of the 29 students with TOEFL scores below 475, 20 achieved a GPA of 2.5 or less and only 3 achieved a GPA above 3.0. On the other hand, note that for the 25 students with TOEFL scores of 600 or above, only 5 had a GPA below 3.0. Stated differently, the mean GPA for students scoring below 475 was 2.60, whereas students with TOEFL scores above 600 had a mean GPA of 3.76. The implications of these data for the selection of graduate students as well as academic counseling are obvious.

97

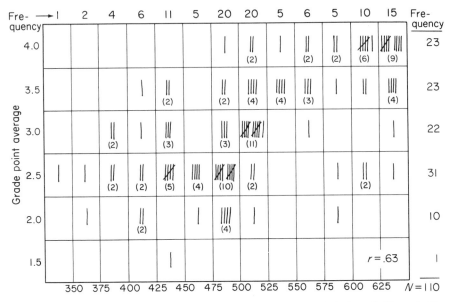

FIGURE 4-12 Scatterplot depicting the criterion-related validity of the Test of English as a Foreign Language (TOEFL) for predicting grade point averages of 110 first-semester foreign graduate students. (Data courtesy of Vera Santos and David Williams.)

Another Example of Predictive Validity

The principal function of the reading readiness tests administered in kindergarten or early in grade 1 is to identify (predict) those pupils who are likely to perform well, or not so well, in reading in the first grade. The purpose of the test is to assist the teacher in deciding which children are ready to begin reading and which should continue to engage in readiness activities for some time. Figure 4-13 shows the validity of scores on a reading readiness test given at the beginning of grade 1 for predicting subsequent reading performance on a standardized reading test ($r = .61$, data from Hopkins and Sitkie, 1969). Notice that, as a general rule, high scores on the readiness test (the predictor) are associated with good performance on the reading test (the criterion) administered several months later.

Figure 4-14 also shows the predictive validity of the reading readiness test, but it uses a different criterion for reading success: teachers' marks. Figure 4-14 shows that the pupils with low scores on the reading readiness test did not read well at the end of grade 1, as judged by their teachers. Only one of the 28 pupils with scores below 40 received a grade of B. The pupils with high scores generally read well, but there were some pupils with good readiness scores who subsequently did not perform well in reading. Of the 76 pupils with readiness scores between 50 and 60, there were 22 (29 percent) who received A's, 25 (33 percent) who received B's, 27 (36 percent) who received C's, and 2 (3 percent) who received a grade of D in reading. From Figure

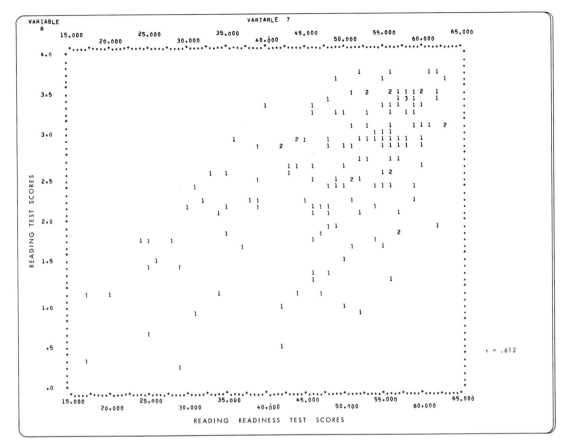

FIGURE 4-13 A scatterplot of the criterion-related validity of a reading readiness test for predicting subsequent scores on an end-of-year standardized reading test.

4-13, it is evident that failure was more predictable than success, a fact that is not evident from the correlation coefficient alone.

The predictive validity of a test is always in relation to a *particular* criterion. Teachers' marks may be influenced by factors that are not associated with performance on the standardized reading test (such as deportment and effort); thus, to some extent marks may represent different factors. The two criteria depicted in Figures 4-13 and 4-14 correlated substantially ($r = .75$), but they are not interchangeable.[4] By looking at both criteria we get a more complete picture than we could by considering only one.

How Large Does a Validity Coefficient Need To Be?

Obviously, the higher the validity coefficient is, the better; but how large must the coefficient be before it provides useful information? Tests with relatively

---

[4] Some of the lack of correlation between the two criteria is due to errors of measurement (unreliability). If the reliabilities of both criteria were known, one could estimate the extent to which the two criteria measure different factors, apart from measurement error (see p. 358).

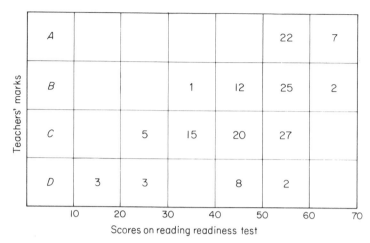

	10	20	30	40	50	60	70

FIGURE 4-14 Scatterplot showing the criterion-related validity of reading readiness test scores at the beginning of grade 1 for predicting teachers' marks at the end of grade 1 (*N* = 157). (Data from Hopkins and Sitkie, 1969.)

low validity coefficients can be extremely useful in certain situations. Figure 4-15 portrays the results of a study (Creager, 1965) of the validity of the GRE Advanced Test (special achievement tests in students' majors) for predicting attainment of the Ph.D. degree. Note, for example, that in spite of the rather low validity coefficient of the advanced test in psychology (*r* = .34), whereas approximately 50 percent of students with stanine scores of 8 or 9 attain the Ph.D., virtually none of those in stanines 1 or 2 do so. A recent study found the GRE tests to have considerable validity for predicting quality criteria in doctoral programs in education—much more than the other widely used test for admission to graduate programs, the Miller Analogies Test (Furst & Roelfs, 1979).

Expectancy Tables

For most people, predictive validity can be represented most meaningfully by an expectancy table. If in Figure 4-14 we convert the frequencies within each score interval to proportions, we obtain probabilities for various levels of performance on the criterion for any test score. For example, if a pupil earned a score of 45 on the reading readiness test, it is extremely unlikely that he or she would receive an end-of-year grade of A; the probabilities of receiving grades of B, C, and D, respectively, would be .30 (12 of 40), .50 (20 of 40), and .20 (8 of 40). A similar expectancy table is found in Chapter 13 (p. 371), in which success in a vocational training is predicted from a special aptitude test.

Concurrent Validity

Criterion-related validity is not always predictive over time. Occasionally our purpose is to predict one measurement from another. In this situation little or no interval is desired between the administration of the new test and the estab-

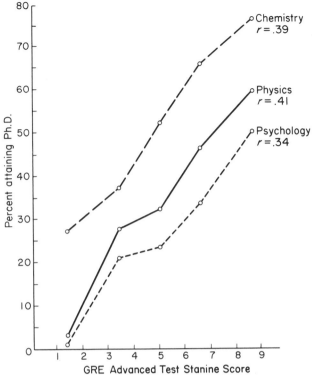

FIGURE 4-15 The validity of the Graduate Record Examination (Advanced Tests) for predicting attainment of the Ph.D. in chemistry, physics, and psychology (from Willingham, 1974). From *GRE Technical Manual.* Copyright © 1977 by Educational Testing Service. All rights reserved. Reprinted by permission of ETS, W. W. Willingham, and the American Association for the Advancement of Science: © 1974 by AAAS.

lished test or criterion. It would be quite useful to find a short, inexpensive reading test that would correlate highly with experts' ratings or with a valid individual (and, hence, expensive to use) test. The new test would be said to have *concurrent* validity to the extent that it correlates with the established test or some other concurrently obtained criterion. For example, the Wide Range Reading Test requires only a few minutes to administer and correlates highly (about .8) with teachers' ratings of reading ability (Hopkins, Dobson, & Oldridge, 1962) and with other standard individual reading tests (Garlock, Dollarhide, & Hopkins, 1965).

Concurrent validity is often the initial step for establishing predictive validity. In the early development of the Strong Vocational Interest Blank, studies of concurrent validity demonstrated that the interest scores could, for example, differentiate physicians from men in general. Only after twenty years of additional research could Strong provide evidence that interest scores of college freshmen did correlate with their adult occupations (Campbell, 1968b).

In determining criterion-related validity we are usually most concerned with the test, but it is equally important to consider the qualities of the criterion. *To be predictable, a criterion must be reliable;* even highly relevant and reliable tests cannot predict a criterion that lacks reliability. If a criterion does not predict itself—that is, lacks self-correlation—it cannot be predicted by any other variable. This is probably the principal reason that the many attempts to predict teacher success have been so fruitless. The common measures of teacher success are quite unreliable and, hence, essentially unpredictable. For example, Walberg (1967) found only a .21 correlation between supervisor and principal ratings of the teaching success of 280 teacher trainees. Other studies have reported comparable results (Quirk, Witten, & Weinberg, 1973). This is no doubt an important reason why logically relevant factors such as GPA and intelligence have yielded such low correlations with ratings of teacher effectiveness.

The present predictability of grades in college is probably about as high as it can be without an improvement in the reliability of the criterion. Walberg (1967) found a .6 correlation between the grade point averages (GPAs) obtained during a student's first and seventh academic terms in college. The reliability of a grade in a single course is less; one study (Etaugh, Etaugh, & Hurd, 1972) estimated single-grade reliability for freshman-level courses to be only .44. Goldman and Slaughter (1976) studied the predictive validity of tests for predicting GPA and concluded, "In sum, we believe that the validity problem in GPA prediction is a result of shortcomings of the GPA criterion rather than the tests that are used as predictors" (p. 14).

It is a statistical fact that the *maximum* criterion-related validity that any test can have is the square root of the reliability coefficient of the test. This maximum value will be obtained only if the test is itself perfectly relevant (i.e., except for random measurement error, the test and the criterion are measuring the same factors) and the criterion is perfectly reliable. It should be obvious that in practice this maximum value is rarely approached.

One final point should be made regarding criterion-related validity. When a test is used for selection purposes, such as admission to graduate school, much of its predictive value is used at that point. To correlate scores only for the selected group with a subsequent criterion will underestimate the test's predictive validity, that is, its value as a selection measure. For example, suppose that no pupil with a readiness score below 40 was admitted to grade 1; instead, all of them had to repeat kindergarten. When all scores below 40 in Figure 4–14 are covered, the resulting figure is much "fatter"; hence, the correlation coefficient for those with scores of 40 and above would be much less than the coefficient for the total group. In fact, the validity coefficient of .61 for the entire group drops to only .44 if the examinees scoring below 40 are excluded.

Figure 4–16 is an extreme illustration of the common phenomenon of "range restriction" and its effects on validity coefficients. There is little relationship between the criterion and test scores within the selected group

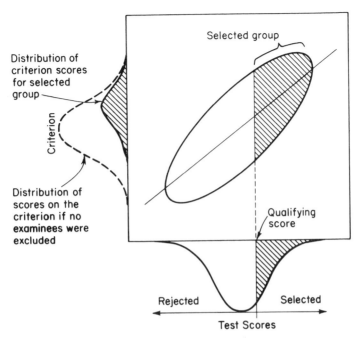

FIGURE 4-16 An illustration of the effect of selection on the correlation between test scores and a criterion. The validity coefficient *within* the selected group underestimates the actual predictive value of the test.

(shaded area), yet there is a substantial relationship for the entire group. For example, Roemer (1965) substantially underestimated the value of the Medical College Admission Test (MCAT), and Thacker and Williams (1974) underestimated the predictive validity of the Graduate Record Examination (GRE) because they failed to recognize this important point. If test scores correlate, say, only .3 with subsequent GPAs for the admitted group, they may still be of great value for admission purposes (especially when the limited reliability of the criterion is borne in mind).

For example, Figure 4-17 depicts the relationship ($r = .68$) between scores on the Graduate Record Examination—Quantitative Aptitude Test and test scores in an introductory statistics class for a heterogeneous group ($\overline{X} = 495$, $s = 91$) of 20 graduate students. But what would the correlation have been if a minimum score of 450 on the GRE-Q had been required for admission to graduate work? The predictive validity coefficient of the GRE-Q would have dropped from .68 to .18! Indeed, the r would have dropped to .52 if the one extremely low scorer (280) had not been admitted. Obviously, one obtains an extremely conservative value of a test's criterion-related validity if some portion of the examinees are excluded on the basis of their performance on the test. The full predictive value of a test can be assessed only if no applicants are eliminated on the basis of their test performance.

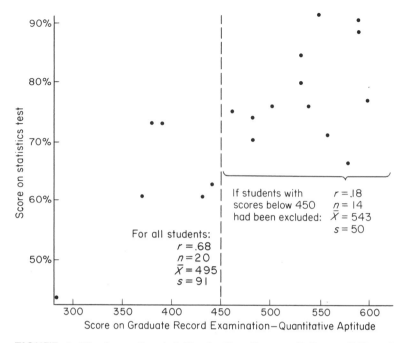

FIGURE 4-17 A scatterplot illustrating the predictive validity of the Graduate Record Examination-Quantitative Aptitude for predicting test performance in an introductory statistics class. Notice that *r* for the entire group is .68, but only .18 for the group scoring above 450. (Figure courtesy of Rick Kroc.)

The effect that restricting the range of scores has on the validity coefficient obtained is further illustrated by R. L. Thorndike (1949), who compared the validity coefficient for a total group (N = 1,031) of aspiring pilots to the coefficient for the group that was successful (N = 136). The validity coefficient for the composite score on the predictors was .64 for the total group, but a correlation of only .18 remained for those who qualified.[5]

Research on the National Merit Scholarship Program also illustrates the strong effect that the range of scores or talent has on validity coefficients. Among scholarship winners, a highly select group, there is little relationship between scores on the National Merit examinations and whether or not the recipients completed college (the criterion). Nevertheless, the strong relationship between ability and obtaining a college degree is illustrated by the fact that the mortality in the Merit group was only 8 percent compared to 50 percent in an unselected population (Stalnaker, 1961).

Construct Validity

When a test is used to describe the degree to which an individual manifests an abstract psychological trait or ability, the *construct validity* of the measure is the relevant concern. Psychological constructs are unobservable, postulated

---

[5] There are procedures to estimate the correlation for the entire group from the correlation within the selected group (Hopkins & Glass, 1978, pp. 139–44), but these estimates are often quite imprecise unless N is very large (Gullickson & Hopkins, 1976).

variables that have evolved either informally or from psychological theory. Intelligence, anxiety, mechanical aptitude, critical thinking, ego strength, dominance, and achievement motivation are examples of commonly used constructs. *Construct validation* is the analysis of test scores in terms of psychological constructs (Cronbach and Meehl, 1955). If a test is designed to measure emotional stability, what kinds of evidence are necessary before we can be confident that the information provided by the test reflects this variable? We make certain predictions or statements that should be correct if, indeed, the test does measure the construct in question. For example, if the scale actually measures emotional stability, one would expect: (1) some correlation between inventory scores and psychologists' ratings, (2) some difference between scores of people who are in mental hospitals and people who are not, (3) some relationship between peer ratings and inventory scores, and so on. However, we might expect little or no relationship between inventory scores and sex, IQ, GPA, and the like. In a true sense every bit of information about a test has relevance for construct validity, that is, in establishing what it does and does not measure. In construct validation there is no single criterion, as there is with criterion-related validity; many criteria are required to confirm what the test does and does not measure.

The measurement of intelligence provides a classic example of construct validation. Early attempts to measure "intelligence" using reaction time, auditory memory, and other psychomotor and psychophysical measures were discarded because performance on these measures did not correlate with other behavioral evidence of intelligence, such as school grades. The expected and logical relationships between relevant variables were not confirmed. Later, the French physician Alfred Binet constructed tasks that were logically related to intelligence; they required complex cognitive abilities. Many of Binet's tasks were found to be related to other variables in a manner expected of a measure of intelligence and, hence, to possess a degree of construct validity.

Gradually, through a continual process of research and revision, these scales yielded scores that agreed substantially with logical and theoretical expectations: (1) The scores correlated with age until maturity and then leveled off, in the manner of other directly measurable human abilities; (2) the scores had a substantial relationship with academic achievement; (3) children who repeated grades scored much lower on these measures than those who were promoted; (4) the IQ scores yielded by these tests showed some stability over a period of years; (5) persons with clinical types of mental subnormality (e.g., mongolism) performed poorly on the tasks; and (6) the correlation of identical twins was extremely high—much higher than for fraternal twins, even when they were reared separately. Such information illustrates the incremental procedure inherent in construct validation.

Certain tests such as the Stanford-Binet Intelligence Scale became accepted as highly valid measures of intelligence (except for persons having atypical environmental backgrounds) because persons who obtained high scores on the test tended to behave intelligently in situations in which such behavior was required. Although certain predictions can be made regarding future performance from tests designed to measure psychological constructs, their primary function is to assess the degree of some variable or trait that is present within the individual at a given point in time.

If two pupils are achieving at the same level but one has an IQ score of 90 and the other a score of 130, we may be relatively satisfied with the educational success of the one but quite concerned about that of the other, who appears to have more scholastic aptitude. However, if our sole task is to predict subsequent performance, there would be no point in administering intelligence tests; achievement tests usually predict subsequent achievement better than intelligence tests (Bracht & Hopkins, 1970b; Churchill & Smith, 1966). Intelligence or scholastic aptitude tests are the only type of test taken by virtually all Americans for which validation rests primarily in the construct validity domain.

The process of developing a measure of a psychological construct and establishing its validity can be summarized as follows:

1. Develop a set of tasks or items based on theory and a rational analysis of the construct.
2. Deduce testable predictions regarding the relationship between the construct and other empirical measures; for example, if the test measures anxiety, we should expect to find some relationship between test scores and clinical ratings of anxiety level, and so on.
3. Conduct studies of these predicted relationships.
4. Eliminate items or tasks that operate contrary to theory (or revise the theory) and proceed again with steps 2 and 3.[6]

Summary

The need for an objective and precise measure to describe the degree of relationship between two variables is obvious. The Pearson product–moment correlation (r or ϱ) and the Spearman rank correlation (r_{Ranks} or ϱ_{Ranks}) are such measures.

The degree of relationship can vary from -1.0 through 0 to $+1.0$. The magnitude of the relationship is indicated by the absolute value of the correlation coefficient. The sign ($+$ or $-$) of a coefficient only indicates the *direction* of the relationship. A coefficient of 0.0 indicates *no correlation* between two variables.

A positive correlation indicates that "high numbers on X are associated with high numbers on Y" and that "low numbers on Y are associated with low numbers on X."

[6] The interested reader should be informed of the more elaborate scheme for construct validation using a *multitrait–multimethod matrix* proposed by Campbell and Fiske (1959). From a matrix of correlation coefficients that describe the relationships among the same and different traits using a variety of assessment methods, certain criteria are suggested for establishing the validity of a construct and its measurement.

The correlation coefficients, r and r_{Ranks}, are accurately described by the degree of association between X and Y when X and Y are linearly related; the true association is underestimated if a curvilinear relationship exists between X and Y. Scatterplots allow visual checks of linearity.

The values for r_{Ranks} and r will usually be quite comparable, especially if N is large.

We have discussed three rather distinct classes of validity. *Content* validation is relevant for achievement testing; it consists of a logical study of the relationship of the topics and processes included on a test to the corresponding curricular objectives and instruction. *Predictive* validation is basic to selection and classification decisions and results from an empirical study of the extent to which performances on a test (or some other measure) and a criterion are related. *Construct* validity refers to the extent to which a test reflects an abstract psychological trait or ability. Both logical and empirical means are used to establish the validities of a test. All three types of validity are crucial for certain, although different, purposes. In a real sense content and criterion-related validity are subsumed by construct validity; everything that is known about a test—its content, its correlations with other relevant (and irrelevant) variables—helps establish what the test does, and does not, measure.

IMPORTANT TERMS AND CONCEPTS

correlation	statistically significant	validity coefficient
linear relationship	correlation coefficient	content validity
curvilinear relationship	confidence interval	construct validity
correlation coefficient:	criterion-related validity	expectancy table
r, ϱ, r_{Ranks} (+ and −)	predictive validity	range restriction
scatterplot	concurrent validity	

CHAPTER TEST

1. Which of these correlation coefficients indicates the strongest relationship?

   a) .55
   b) .09
   c) −.77
   d) .1

2. Using the options given in question 1, which coefficient shows that the scores below the mean on one variable tend to be associated with scores that are above the mean of the other variable?

In questions 3–7, select the scatter diagram that best matches the relationships described.

Value of r	Description of Linear Relationship	Scatter Diagram
3. +1.00	Perfect direct relationship	(a)
4. About +.50	Moderate direct relationship	(b)
5. .00	No relationship	(c)
6. About −.50	Moderate inverse relationship	(d)
7. −1.00	Perfect inverse relationship	(e)

8. Indicate whether the expected correlation of the two designated variables would be positive, negative, or zero. (Assume that the population for items a–d is all persons in grade 10 in the United States.)

    a) *X*, height in inches; *Y*, weight in pounds

    b) *X*, reading achievement in grade placement units; *Y*, arithmetic achievement in grade placement units

    c) *X*, shoe size; *Y*, "citizenship" rating of students on a 10-point scale by their teachers

    d) *X*, social security numbers; *Y*, IQs (ignore persons without Social Security numbers)

e) *X*, total miles traveled by a car; *Y*, year in which the car was manufactured

f) *X*, maximum daily temperature; *Y*, amount of water used per day by residents

9. If you obtained a Pearson *r* of $+1.3$, you would know for certain that

a) the relationship is extremely strong
b) the relationship is positive
c) both of the above
d) a computational error has been made

10. One study reported the importance of eight morale factors for employees and employers as indicated in the following table:

	Rank	
Factor	*Employers*	*Employees*
A. Credit for work done	1	7
B. Interesting work	2	3
C. Fair pay	3	1
D. Understanding and appreciation	4	5
E. Counseling on personal problems	5	8
F. Promotion based on merit	6	4
G. Good working conditions	7	6
H. Job security	8	2

A. Compute r_{Ranks} between the rankings.

B. Which two factors contributed most to the negative correlation?

The data given in the following table show the relationship between verbal and nonverbal IQs from the Lorge-Thorndike Intelligence Test (LT) and reading and arithmetic achievement as measured by the Iowa Test of Basic Skills (ITBS). At each grade level, each correlation is based on approximately 2,500 nationally representative pupils.

	Verbal IQ			*Nonverbal IQ*		
	Grade			*Grade*		
	3	*5*	*7*	*3*	*5*	*7*
Reading	.68	.76	.81	.53	.65	.67
Arithmetic	.66	.72	.74	.61	.68	.71

On the basis of this information, indicate whether each of the following statements is true or false.

11. The correlation between the intelligence and achievement measures appears to increase with grade level.

12. The nonverbal IQs correlate as highly with achievement as verbal IQs do.

13. Verbal and nonverbal IQs tend to correlate slightly higher with reading than with arithmetic.

14. The correlation between both measures of achievement and both measures of intelligence is substantial at each of the three grade levels.

15. In the content/skill grid of the STEP II Science Test depicted in Figure 4-1, (p. 78), which science content is represented most heavily?
   a) biology
   b) chemistry
   c) physics
   d) earth sciences

16. If a school district's science curriculum deals primarily with the physical sciences at the grade level for which Form 3A of STEP II is designed,
   a) the STEP II content validity does not appear to be strong
   b) the item norms (percent passing) would be especially important for evaluating a school district's performance
   c) no useful information could be obtained from this test
   d) more than one of the above

17. From Figures 4-1 and 4-2 (pp. 78, 80):
   A. Which test allows a more explicit study of the test content validity in terms of topics covered?
   a) STEP II
   b) Metropolitan Achievement Test
   B. Which test provides more information on the type of cognitive process required by the items?
   a) STEP II
   b) Metropolitan Achievement Test

18. Which type of test is able to reflect the specific content and objectives of a particular course?
   a) standardized tests
   b) teacher-made tests

The following applies to questions 19–26: Which type of validity is most important for the following measures?
   a) content validity
   b) criterion-related validity
   c) construct validity

19. an algebra test

20. a test to select job applicants for employment

21. a test of ideational flexibility

22. the GRE, SAT, or ACT

23. a self-concept test

24. a final examination based on this book

25. a new, short, "cheapie" test designed to replace a long, expensive test

26. the extent to which this test measures the topics/objectives of this chapter

27. Among items 19–26, which best represents concurrent validation?

28. Suppose that for a sample of 25 people you obtained a correlation of .30 between a measure of obnoxiousness and a measure of garrulity. Is an *r* of .30 large enough to be statistically significant? (See Table 4–1, p. 95.) If you increased your sample to 100, would the *r* of .30 be greater than you would expect from chance alone if the true correlation is .00?

29. If colleges represented in Figure 4–11 began to require all foreign students to have a TOEFL score of at least 500, what effect would you expect this to have on the TOEFL's validity coefficient in subsequent studies? (See Figure 4–12, p. 98.)

    a) It would probably increase substantially.
    b) It would probably increase slightly.
    c) It would probably remain about .63.
    d) It would probably decrease slightly.
    e) It would probably decrease substantially.

30. Suppose that a new practice of assigning grades was instituted at the universities represented in Figure 4–11 that required more frequent testing, more careful evaluation, greater use of the full range of grades (A–F), etc., such that the reliability of GPA was increased. Other things being equal, what effect would this have on the TOEFL's predictive-validity coefficient?

    a) *r* would increase.
    b) *r* would remain unchanged.
    c) *r* would decrease.

31. Refer to the expectancy table in Figure 4–14 (p. 100). For beginning first-grade pupils obtaining a score of 35, what is the most probable grade they will receive in reading?

    a) A
    b) B
    c) C
    d) D

32. If in Figure 4–16 (p. 103) the test scores represent scores on a college admission test (SAT or ACT) and the criterion is performance on the Graduate Record Examination, the criterion-related validity coefficient of the SAT or ACT would be least at

    a) highly select institutions (minimum score of one standard deviation above the mean required for admission)
    b) a moderately select institution (minimum score is the mean)
    c) an "open door" university

33. From Figure 4–11, determine: A. the average GPA for persons scoring 600 on the SAT; B. the percent of students with scores of 500 who earn a B-average or better; C. the percent of examinees with SAT scores of 200 who fail to achieve a C-average.

1. c
2. c
3. c
4. d
5. e
6. a
7. b
8. a) positive
   b) positive
   c) zero
   d) zero
   e) negative
   f) positive
9. d

10. A. $r_{Ranks} = -.095$;
    B. A and H
11. true
12. false
13. false (with verbal IQ, true; with nonverbal IQ, false)
14. true
15. a
16. d
17. A. b; B. a
18. b
19. a
20. b
21. c

22. b
23. c
24. a
25. b
26. a
27. 25
28. no; yes
29. e
30. a
31. c
32. a
33. A. 2.99 (or 3.0);
    B. approximately 25%;
    C. approximately 80%

FOR ADDITIONAL READING

AMERICAN PSYCHOLOGICAL ASSOCIATION. *Standards for educational and psychological tests and manuals.* Washington, D.C.: American Psychological Association, 1974. Contains recommendations regarding test validity (also found in Buros, 1974, pp. 759–800).

ASTIN, A. W. *Predicting academic performance in college.* New York: Free Press, 1970.

BENNETT, G. K., H. G. SEASHORE, and A. G. WESMAN. *A rich source of validity data and illustrations.* New York: Psychological Corporation, 1974.

CAMPBELL, D. T., and D. W. FISKE. Convergent and discriminant validation by the multitrait–multimethod matrix. *Psychological Bulletin,* 56 (1959), 81–105.

CRONBACH, L. J. Test validation. In R. L. Thorndike, ed., *Educational measurement,* 2nd ed. Washington, D.C.: American Council on Education, 1971. Chap. 14.

———, and P. E. MEEHL. Construct validation in psychological tests. *Psychological Bulletin,* 52 (1955), 281–302.

EBEL, R. L. Obtaining and reporting evidence on content validity. *Educational and Psychological Measurement,* 16 (1956), 294–304.

———. Must all tests be valid? *American Psychologist,* 16 (1961), 640–47. Reprinted in G. H. Bracht, K. D. Hopkins, and J. C. Stanley, eds., *Perspectives in educational and psychological measurement.* Englewood Cliffs, N.J.: Prentice-Hall, 1961. Selection 8.

———. Content standard test scores. *Educational and Psychological Measurement,* 22 (1962), 15–25.

HOPKINS, K. D., and G. V. GLASS. *Basic statistics in the social sciences.* Englewood Cliffs, N.J.: Prentice-Hall, 1978. Chapters 7–9 treat the concepts, computation, interpretation of correlation, and prediction.

SECHREST, L. Incremental validity: A recommendation. *Educational and Psychological Measurement,* 23 (1963), 153–58.

5

Test
Reliability

To do its job well, a measure must yield accurate results. A test has little value if the score it yields for Bill today is quite different from the score it would yield for him under similar conditions tomorrow. It is theoretically possible, however, for a test to yield highly consistent results from day to day without having any practical value. A highly reliable measure of reaction time may be useful in predicting the quickness with which one applies an automobile brake, but it is useless for indicating how well one reads or solves arithmetic problems. The Foolproof Emotional Adjustment Test (FEAT) may have high reliability but no validity whatsoever. Reliability is the extent to which the FEAT measures consistently, whatever it does measure. What is measured may not be what is desired. In other words, a test can be reliable without being valid.

The concepts of reliability and validity (Chapter 4) are central to the theory and practice of educational and psychological testing. This chapter offers an overview of the theory of test reliability. Methods of estimating the reliability of a test or inventory are also considered together with the implications for test interpretation. This chapter is the most conceptually challenging in the entire book; expect to read and reread it two or three times before the material will be properly assimilated.

Suppose we wish to develop a simple inventory to measure the trait of honesty. Let's call it the Honesty Inventory (HI). We will write a series of questions that appear to sample honesty behavior, such as "Do you ever deliberately distort the truth?" "If you have the opportunity, do you ever cheat on a test?" "If a clerk makes a mistake and gives you too much change, do you ignore the error?" Suppose the HI was administered to 100 persons; are the HI scores reliable and valid? If we readministered the HI to the same group a week later, do you think the two sets of scores would correlate highly? The correlation coefficient between the two sets of HI scores (first score vs. second score) is a *reliability coefficient*. It will be between 0 and 1. One might obtain a coefficient of .90 or even higher. If each person answered all the questions exactly the same way both times, would we be sure that the answers were truthful? The reliability coefficient could be 1.0, but the HI's validity is the extent that the reported answers are truthful answers. It is possible that the least honest person has the best HI score. The least honest person may conceal his imperfections, thus, validity can be poor even when the reliability coefficient is very high. If the examinees took the HI anonymously, the HI's validity would probably increase greatly—people are unlikely to distort the truth unless a dishonest answer is perceived to be self-serving.

The point is that *reliability* (measurement precision) *is necessary, but not sufficient for validity*. If repeated measurement yields disparate scores, we cannot have confidence in their validity. We work for reliability as an essential prerequisite, but we check further to ascertain validity.

If the HI contained a representative sample of honest behavior, it would be viewed as having good content validity; but if the conditions under which the HI was administered did not disarm examinees of all incentive to "fake it," it would lack construct validity (i.e., the extent to which scores on the test represent the examinees' standing on the trait or construct of honesty). The criterion-related validity of the HI is the extent to which HI scores correlate with some observed criterion measure (e.g., anonymous honesty ratings given by peers, teachers, or supervisors) or more direct behavioral measures (e.g., "cash shortages" for clerks).

But the HI does not have norms; does that make its validity or reliability suspect? Norms have no necessary relationship with either validity or reliability. A normed test may have high reliability and validity or none at all. Norms simply enable us to interpret scores more meaningfully, by allowing us to compare the score to the distribution of scores from the norm group.

A psychomotor measure, such as a handwriting scale (see Figure 8–1) or a measure of reaction time can be made quite reliable (perhaps .95). The scores, however, may not correlate with variables that we wish to predict, such as college grades, job success, or high-jumping ability. The test may be fine for predicting this psychomotor ability at some other time (i.e., it may possess reliability), but it may not be useful for predicting other criteria. Thus, a certain psychomotor test can have very high reliability but low predictive validity for the criteria of interest. And validity of some sort is the real aim of testing; but reliability is a prerequisite for validity.

An Example of Reliability without Validity

At the turn of the century Wissler (1901) conducted the first statistical study designed to predict success in college. Using a test of reaction time (which can be measured very reliably), he obtained a validity coefficient of only − .02! Obviously, reliability does not guarantee validity, although validity does guarantee some degree of reliability.

Zero Reliability

Assume that form I of a 100-item multiple-choice reading vocabulary test of Chinese is given to your class. All students are required to attempt all 100 items, each of which has five options. Theoretically, scores can range anywhere from 0 to 100, but (assuming that no student has any reading vocabulary in Chinese) the class mean will probably be about 20 (1/5 of 100) with a standard deviation of about four points. Suppose your score is 28, a very high score for this group of Chinese language illiterates. If you were asked to take form II of the test, would you expect your score on form II to be 28? Not if you know much about the laws of chance and the reliability of random guessing. In this example all deviations from a score of 20 are random events. The best estimate of your score on form II (and the score of each of your Chinese-illiterate classmates) is 20, regardless of the score obtained on form I. Your "luck" score on form I was 8 (28–20) and is technically termed the *error of measurement*.

Errors of measurement can be positive or negative; they have a mean of 0 and they are normally distributed. The best bet is that your error of measurement on form II will be 0 and that your score will be 20.

For a fairly large class, the correlation between the scores on forms I and II will not differ significantly from 0, i.e., the test scores will have zero reliability. Are the scores useful for predicting students' ages? IQs? Knowledge of English grammar? Anything at all? Most assuredly not. If scores on form I will not predict scores on form II, they cannot possibly predict anything else. A test whose reliability is nil cannot predict anything more accurately than chance alone. Thus, the lowest possible reliability is zero and the highest possible reliability coefficient is 1.0. Between these two points lie the reliability indices for all test scores.

Reliability and True Scores

"An investigator asks about the precision or reliability of a measure because he wishes to generalize from the observation in hand to some class of observations to which it belongs" (Cronbach, Rajaratnam, and Gleser, 1963, p. 144). Rarely is our primary interest in the test scores themselves. A test should or-

TABLE 5-1

TWO FORMS OF THE WEBSTER VOCABULARY TEST (WVT)

Form A	Form B
1. *accouchement*	1. *amphiaster*
2. *aim*	2. *appeasable*
3. *assume*	3. *baggle*
4. *beat*	4. *congruity*
5. *camera*	5. *digestive*
6. *checkers*	6. *elevate*
7. *colostomy*	7. *exhibit*
8. *dementia*	8. *forsworn*
9. *epitomize*	9. *hacienda*
10. *heather*	10. *informational*
11. *impetus*	11. *keepsake*
12. *inviolability*	12. *manageable*
13. *layerage*	13. *microgroove*
14. *mayonnaise*	14. *mustard*
15. *nibs*	15. *nymph*
16. *opulence*	16. *perk*
17. *quamash*	17. *remarkable*
18. *round*	18. *rhizomatous*
19. *sanatory*	19. *slate*
20. *scream*	20. *sporadically*
21. *somnific*	21. *theanthropism*
22. *titulary*	22. *trapezohedron*
23. *turbogenerator*	23. *unhallow*
24. *valvulitis*	24. *virtual*
25. *water*	25. *whorish*

dinarily be viewed as a *sample* from a *population* or *universe* of items. Many other items similar to those that appear on a test could have been employed. Suppose we randomly select 25 words from *Webster's New World Dictionary of the American Language* (NWDAL) for a vocabulary test. Our principal interest is not in the percent of the *sample* of 25 words that you know; rather, it is in the percent of words in the *universe* of content (the dictionary) that you know. If we randomly selected another 25 words from the dictionary for a second form of the test, few (if any) examinees would receive scores identical to the scores they obtained on the initial form, since both forms contain measurement error.

Table 5-1 gives two representative samples of 25 words from the content universe of 86,000 words in the NWDAL. Look over the words in form A of the test, checking all the words you are familiar with. Since there are 25 words, multiply your score by 4 to convert it to a percent. This percent is an *estimate* of the percent of words you would check (your *"true"* or *universe*[1] percent score) if you similarly reviewed all 86,000 words in the content universe. But how closely does your observed score agree with your universe or true score? This is the central concern of reliability—*the correlation of*

---

[1] The term *true score* is conventionally used in classical test theory. We will follow Cronbach's nomenclature, *universe score,* which is more descriptive and less apt to be misinterpreted. The term *true score* encourages mental slippage from reliability to validity—*true* and *valid* are similar in meaning in common parlance but are not necessarily related in classical test theory.

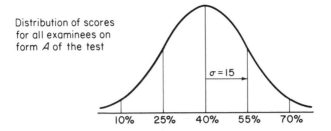

Distribution of scores
for all examinees on
form *A* of the test

$\sigma = 15$

10%   25%   40%   55%   70%

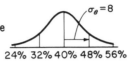

Hypothetical distribution
of scores for one examinee
on many parallel forms
of the test of 25 items
each (reliability index
= .85)

$\sigma_e = 8$

24% 32% 40% 48% 56%

FIGURE 5-1 A distribution of scores for all examinees on one form of a test contrasted to a hypothetical distribution of scores of one examinee on many parallel forms of the test, assuming that the examinee has a universe score of 40%.

observed scores on a test with corresponding universe scores is the test's index of reliability.

Most examinees will, by chance, be familiar with a few more words on one form than on the other. Our greatest interest is in what an examinee's mean percent score would be on many (theoretically, an infinite number) forms containing 25 randomly selected words each; this average is known technically as his universe percent score—the percent score in the universe of content. Universe scores are free from the good or bad "luck" (measurement error) associated with chance factors in the sample of the items that appear on a given form, as well as from other random sources of variation. In classical test theory a person's obtained score is said to be composed of two independent parts: the universe (or true) score and an error of measurement; the mean of the latter is 0 and its standard deviation is denoted by σ_e or s_e. Suppose form *A* was given to a large representative sample of the U.S. adult population and the mean and standard deviation were found to be 40% and 15%, respectively.[2] The upper graph in Figure 5-1 depicts this distribution. The lower graph represents the hypothetical distribution of observed scores on many parallel forms from one repeatedly tested examinee, Jane, whose universe score is 40%.

Occasionally Jane was "lucky"—the form included more words that she knew, and she scored 56% or more; sometimes she knew only 32% or less of the words on the test. Obviously, our principal interest is not in the idiosyncrasies of a particular form of the test but in Jane's general word knowledge (i.e., her universe score). In Figure 5-1 we see that the mean of Jane's obtained scores (her universe score) is 40%, and all deviations from this score

[2] Is 40% a poor score? Not at all; 40% of 85,000 is 34,000 words!

are called *errors of measurement. Other things being equal,* the smaller the errors of measurement, the greater the reliability of the measure.

Universe Scores

Figure 5–2 depicts the interrelationship among universe scores, obtained scores, and errors of measurement, using IQ scores as an example. Recall that a person's universe IQ score is a theoretical construct; it is the *average* IQ score that would result if that person were tested an infinite number of times on an infinite number of parallel forms of the test. Universe scores are given along the horizontal axis (*X*-axis) and obtained scores along the vertical axis (*Y*-axis). The correlation between true and obtained scores is termed the *index of reliability.*

Figure 5–2 shows that on this hypothetical intelligence test the obtained IQ scores for examinees with universe IQ scores of 100 have a mean of 100 but some variation above and below 100. What is the standard error of measure-

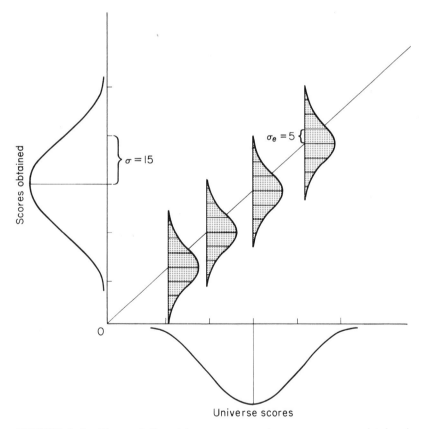

FIGURE 5-2 The relationship among universe scores, obtained scores, and standard error of measurement, illustrated using an IQ test with a reliability of .90.

ment, that is, the standard deviation of obtained scores for a given universe score? In this example it is 5 points. This σ_e of 5 indicates that about two out of three examinees (68 percent) will obtain IQ scores that fall within 5 points of their universe IQ score. Approximately half of the examinees will have an obtained score above their universe score, and vice versa. About 95 percent received IQ scores that were within 10 points ($\pm 2\sigma_e$) of their universe scores. The σ_e helps us know how much elasticity should accompany our interpretations of test scores.

It is important to remember that a universe (or true) score is *not* necessarily a perfectly valid score. Universe scores represent the average score a person would obtain on an infinite number of parallel forms of a test, assuming that he or she is unchanged by taking the tests (i.e., assuming no practice effect).

The Standard Error of Measurement

The standard deviation of these errors of measurement is called the *standard error of measurement* (σ_e). Because it is a measure of the discrepancies between obtained scores and true scores, it is very useful in test interpretation. Approximately two-thirds of the examinees on any test will have obtained scores that differ by one σ_e or less from their universe scores; only 5 percent of the examinees will obtain scores that deviate by $2\sigma_e$ or more from their universe scores.

The concepts of reliability and the standard error of measurement are closely associated, as Figure 5–3 illustrates. The figure shows that when the standard deviation of a test is held constant (by the use of standard-score IQs), the value of the standard error of measurement is completely determined by the test's reliability index, and vice versa. The figure also illustrates that this relationship is not linear. A change of .1 in a test's reliability index has a much greater effect on the standard error of measurement when the coefficient is large than when it is small. An increase in the index of reliability from .8 to .9 decreases σ_e from 9 to 6.5 (2.5 points, or $\frac{1}{6}\sigma$), but an increase from .1 to .2 decreases σ_e only .16 points (or $\frac{1}{100}\sigma$).

The Standard Deviation and the Standard Error of Measurement

Figure 5–3 also indirectly depicts the relationship among a test's standard deviation (σ), standard error of measurement (σ_e), and reliability index. If a measure has no reliability, then σ and σ_e are equal; that is, individual differences on the test are totally the result of errors of measurement (as on the Chinese vocabulary test). When reliability is perfect, all differences in scores are due entirely to differences in universe scores. Between these extremes are found all tests and other empirical measures.

The reliability index of a test indicates how nearly the distribution of obtained scores coincides with the distribution of universe scores. If the measure has a reliability index of 1.0, the obtained scores that it yields are the universe

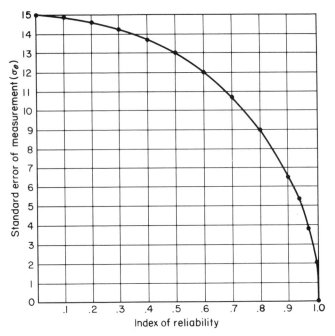

FIGURE 5-3 A graphic illustration of the relationship between the index of reliability of an intelligence test ($\sigma = 15$) and its standard error of measurement.

scores. If the reliability is 0, there is only a chance relationship between the examinees' universe scores and the obtained scores.

Some Test Theory

In classical test theory an observed score is viewed as being composed of two independent parts, the universe score and the measurement error:

$$\text{Observed score} = \text{universe score} + \text{measurement error} \qquad (4.1)$$
$$X = U + e$$

Rearranging the equation, we see that $U = X - e$. Notice that the smaller the measurement error, e, the less the values of U and X differ. The mean error over the set of examinees is zero. For half of the examinees, X will be higher than U (they had good "luck"—a positive error of measurement); for the other half, the obtained scores are less than the universe scores (they had bad "luck"—a negative error of measurement). In other words, the odds that $X > U$ and $U > X$ are equal. (The symbol ">" means "greater than.")

The index of reliability, r_{UX}, quantifies and describes the closeness of the relationship between the U's and X's—it is the correlation between the U's and X's for the set of examinees. If r_{UX} is 1.0, all X's and U's are equal.

The measurement of the weights of a group of students on a given day using a good scale would have a reliability index that approaches 1.0, perhaps

.99. Why wouldn't it be 1.0? Why is there any measurement error at all? If a $10.00 bathroom scale were used, the reliability would probably drop to perhaps .97 because there would be more measurement error—the effects of standing in a different location on the scale, errors in reading the register (e.g., different angles, rounding errors). If one person is weighed repeatedly many times (see Figure 5-1), the measurement errors balance out (the mean of the e's is 0); hence, the mean observed score would equal the universe score. Likewise, for a group of persons the measurement errors balance out so that the mean observed score equals the mean universe score. The formula for the standard error of measurement for a sample of persons is denoted by s_e, in contrast to σ_e for the entire population:

$$s_e = s\sqrt{1 - r_{XX}^2} = s\sqrt{1 - r_{XX}}. \qquad (4.2)$$

Thus, for 10-year-old students we can estimate s_e from the standard deviation of weights (approximately 10 pounds) and the reliability coefficient (e.g., $r_{XX} = .99$):

$$s_e = 10\sqrt{1 - .99} = 10(\sqrt{.01}) \doteqdot 10(.1) = 1.$$

We would expect the recorded weight to be within ± 1 pound of the true weight for most (68 percent) of the students, because the errors are normally distributed and have a mean of 0 and a standard deviation of 1.

Applying the same theory to test results, we can say that 68 percent of the obtained scores are within one standard error of measurement (σ_e) of the corresponding universe scores and that 95 percent are within $2\sigma_e$ of their respective universe scores. In interpreting test results, the value of σ_e should be used as a margin for error so that no unwarranted precision is ascribed to test scores. Thus, for students who obtain an IQ score of 105 on a test with a standard error of measurement of 5 points, we infer that the corresponding universe IQ scores for most (68%) fall somewhere between 100 and 110. Only one student in six with an obtained score of 105 will have a universe IQ below 100. Conversely, one student in six will have a universe score above 110. In other words, a much safer and more appropriate interpretation of test performance is possible when a confidence band of $\pm \sigma_e$ is set around the obtained score.[3]

Index of Reliability vs. Reliability Coefficient

Although the *index of reliability* describes the correlation of observed scores with universe scores, the *reliability coefficient* is more commonly reported. The reliability coefficient is the correlation between two sets of observed scores. For example, the correlation between scores on form A with scores on form B of the WVT (see Table 5-1) is termed a *reliability coefficient*. Although the reliability coefficient is less interesting than the index of reliability,

[3] Confidence bands or intervals have the same meaning and interpretation here as they do in statistics. Here, the universe score is the parameter; $X \pm s_e$ yields the .68 confidence interval for U; $X \pm 2 s_e$ approximates the .95 confidence interval.

both convey the same information, expressed in different ways. If forms *A* and *B* of the WVT are parallel, an examinee's universe score is the same on both forms. Stated differently, what is the correlation between universe scores on form *A* and universe scores on form *B*? Obviously, the correlation is 1.0. If, on the other hand, the scores on one form contain measurement error, the resulting correlation (the index of reliability) will be less than 1.0. If both scores contain measurement error, the correlation (the reliability coefficient) decreases further. Stated more precisely, the square root of a test's reliability coefficient equals the test's index of reliability.

The relationship between a test's reliability index and coefficient is graphically depicted in Figure 5–4. Note that the index of reliability is numerically larger than the corresponding reliability coefficient (except at 0 and 1.0). It is obviously a simple matter to convert a reliability coefficient (r_{xx}) into a reliability index (r_{UX}): $r_{UX}^2 = r_{XX}$ or $\sqrt{r_{XX}} = r_{UX}$.

Regression toward the Mean

In classical test theory, an individual's test score is considered to be composed of two independent parts, a universe or "true" score and a random measurement error component. An obtained test score is used to estimate the universe score. A difficulty arises, however, because high obtained scores tend to have positive errors of measurement (*e*'s) and low scores tend to have negative *e*'s. In addition, high obtained scores tend to have larger *e*'s than scores near the center of the distribution. These two facts lead to a phenomenon called *regression toward the mean*. When a group of examinees is retested with a comparable form of the same test, the very high scorers on the first form will tend, on the average, to be not quite as high (though still high) on the retest. The initially low scorers will tend to "improve" their scores on the retest because

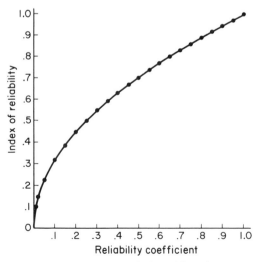

FIGURE 5-4 The relationship between reliability coefficients and reliability indices.

their errors the first time were negative. These results occur because errors of measurement on the first test are uncorrelated with errors of measurement on the second. Therefore, obtained scores tend to underestimate universe scores for the bottom half of the distribution and overestimate universe scores for the top half of the distribution. By how much? That depends on the reliability index of the test. If scores on form X were perfectly reliable ($r_{UX} = 1.0$), there would be no regressing toward the mean at all on form Y because the scores would contain no error. Perfectly unreliable test scores would be expected to regress all the way to the mean on the retest; that is, the expected score obtained on form Y is the same for all examinees, irrespective of standing on form X. (In this case σ_e would equal σ.)

In other words, the obtained score of an examinee is the best estimate of the corresponding universe score only when $r_{UX} = 1.0$ or $X = \overline{X}$. If Mary obtained an IQ score of 140, her universe IQ score is probably less than 140, perhaps 136. Conversely, Billy's universe score is probably higher than his obtained IQ score of 80. There is a tendency for universe scores to be closer to the mean than the corresponding obtained scores.

Is this regression toward the mean just an abstract theoretical possibility, or does it really occur in practice? Figure 5-5 gives a scatterplot of IQ scores for 354 students on two forms of an intelligence test. The shaded boxes denote the areas in which scores on both forms fall within the same score interval. If there was no tendency for scores to regress toward the mean, the scores in each column would have a central tendency falling in the shaded boxes. But note that most examinees whose scores are above the mean (100) on form 1 obtain scores on form 2 that fall below the shaded boxes. This trend becomes more pronounced for scores deviating substantially from the mean. For example, notice that for the 32 examinees scoring 120 or above on form 1, only 2 scored higher on form 2. At the other (lower) end, the trend is reversed: 24 of the 29 students scoring below 80 on form 1 improved their scores on form 2 (i.e., their scores fell above the shaded boxes).

Estimating U's from X's

The universe score, U, for a given obtained score, X, can be estimated from the reliability coefficient, r_{XX} (the square of the index of reliability). The reliability coefficient is the average ratio of deviation of the universe score from the mean ($U - \overline{X}$) to the deviation of the obtained score from the mean ($X - \overline{X}$). Thus, for a test with a reliability coefficient of .9, the universe scores tend to deviate from the mean only 90 percent as far as the corresponding obtained scores. Thus, we estimate Mary's universe IQ score to be 136, even though her obtained IQ score was 140 [90% of ($X - \overline{X}$) = (.90)(40) = 36].

Figure 5-6 illustrates this phenomenon graphically using IQ scores. The graph allows us to estimate the universe IQ score corresponding to any obtained IQ score for tests with reliability coefficients of 1.0, .9, .75, .5, .2, and 0. If Mary obtained an IQ score of 140 on a test with a reliability coefficient of .9, her expected universe IQ score is 136. If r_{XX} is not .9 but .75, the ex-

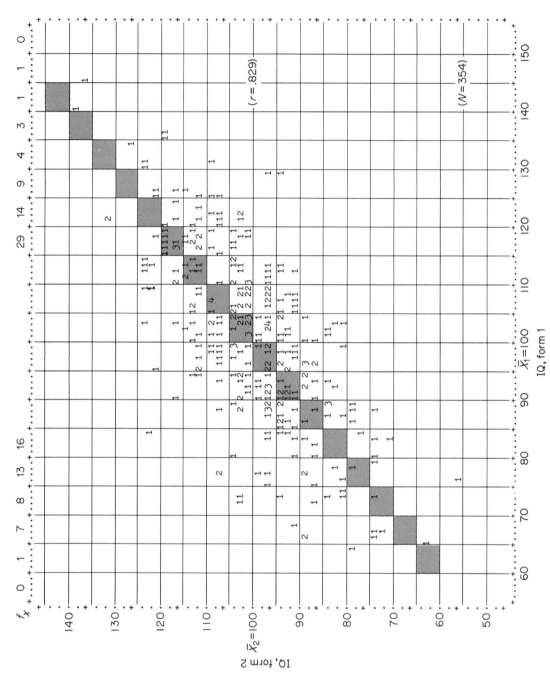

FIGURE 5-5 Scatterplot of IQ scores, for 354 pupils on two forms of an IQ test. (Data from Hopkins and Bibel-heimer, 1971.)

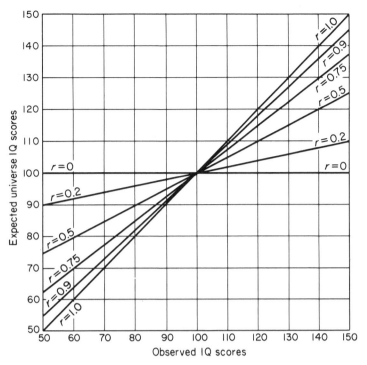

FIGURE 5-6 Expected universe IQ scores for observed IQ scores as influenced by test reliability, for tests having reliability coefficients (*r*) of .0, .2, . . ., .9, 1.0.

pected universe IQ score is 130—the universe score would be expected to deviate only 75 percent as far from the mean (100) as the obtained score. Likewise, the expected universe IQ score for an obtained IQ score of 80 is 82, 85, or 90, depending on whether the test's reliability coefficient is .9, .75, or .5.

Expected universe scores are closer to the mean than obtained scores because all tests contain some measurement error. But the differences between obtained and universe scores are relatively small for tests with high reliability coefficients. Indeed, on well-constructed standardized tests with reliability coefficients of .9 or higher, there is little need to estimate *U* because it differs inconsequentially from *X*. But the concept of regression toward the mean needs to be kept in mind; otherwise, school administrators will wonder what's wrong with the gifted program—their performance declined when the group was retested (see Figure 5-5). At the same time, the program for slow learners will appear very successful, since most of these students will earn higher scores on the retest (see lower scores on form 1 of Figure 5-5); gains in obtained scores will result even without any true improvement in universe scores because, as a group, low scorers (on form 1) tend to have had bad "luck" (*X*'s tend to be below *U*'s—*e*'s tend to be negative) whereas high scorers tend to have had good "luck" (*X*'s tend to be above *U*'s). Since luck at time 1 will not be correlated with luck at time 2, our best prediction of obtained scores on test 2 are universe scores.

Test Length, Reliability, and σ_e

The Spearman-Brown Formula

Test length has a very significant effect on both reliability and standard error of measurement.

The effect of changing the length of a test on a test's reliability can be predicted quite accurately using the Spearman-Brown formula (4.3), where r_{xx} denotes the reliability coefficient of the original test and r'_{xx} is the reliability coefficient of the "new" test, which is L times as long as the original test (i.e., L is the ratio of the "new" length to "old" length). (It is assumed that the additional items and the original items are parallel.)

$$r'_{xx} = \frac{Lr_{xx}}{1 + (L - 1)r_{xx}} \tag{4.3}$$

If a test is doubled in length ($L = 2$), the Spearman-Brown formula becomes

$$r'_{xx} = \frac{2r_{xx}}{1 + r_{xx}}. \tag{4.4}$$

Thus, if a test with a reliability of .50 is doubled in length, using Eq. 4.4, the new reliability coefficient is predicted to be

$$r'_{xx} = \frac{2(.50)}{1.50} = .67.$$

Test length and σ_e

Lord (1959b) and Kleinke (1979) have shown that a reasonably accurate estimate of the standard error of measurement of a test is given by equation 4.5.

$$s_e \doteq .43\sqrt{k} \tag{4.5}$$

where k is the number of items on a test and s is expressed in raw score units.

Thus, if $k = 25$, $\sigma_e \doteq .43\sqrt{25} = .43(5) = 2.15$, but if $k = 100$, $\sigma_e \doteq 4.3$.

Does it surprise you that σ_e increases as the length of a test increases? Note that this is true only in raw-score units. When scores are expressed as standard scores or percent scores, σ_e decreases as k increases. (See Figure 5-7.) When raw scores are converted into percents, the standard error of measurement of the percent scores, $s_{e\%}$, is given by Equation 4.6.

$$\sigma_{e\%} \doteq \frac{43}{\sqrt{k}}. \tag{4.6}$$

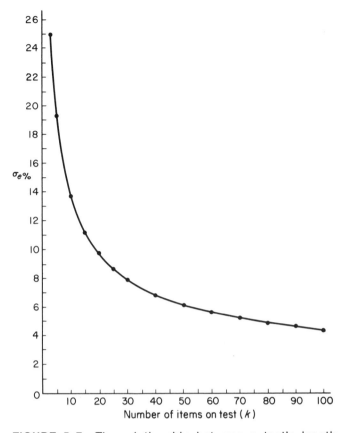

FIGURE 5-7 The relationship between a test's length and its standard error of measurement of the scores expressed as percents.

Thus, if $k = 25$, $\sigma_{e\%} \doteq 43/5 = 8.6\%$, but if $k = 100$, $\sigma_{e\%} = 4.3\%$.

Note in Figure 5-7 that on a typical 20-item test, $\sigma_{e\%}$ will be approximately 10%, but if $k = 50$, $\sigma_{e\%} \doteq 6\%$.

How long would a typical test need to be to yield a $\sigma_{e\%}$ of 5%? About 75 items. It is evident that the percent scores on very short achievement tests will be crude estimates of universe percent scores.

Estimating Reliability

The Test–Retest Method

Different methods of estimating the reliability of a test (or other measuring instrument) take into account different sources of measurement error. The *test–retest reliability coefficient* is the correlation between scores on a test with scores on the same test administered at a later time. Test–retest reliability coefficients are often termed *coefficients of stability:* How stable are the individuals' scores between the testing and retesting when the same questions or the same apparatus is used.

If the test–retest method were used to estimate the reliability of form *A* of the WVT (Table 5–1), the chance factors (sampling errors) involved in the particular set of 25 items would be constant on both occasions. Perhaps 40 percent of the words in the dictionary are scientific terms. On a given form of a test of 25 words, the percent of scientific words might vary from 20% to 60%.[4] If form *A* has 45% scientific terms, examinees whose scientific vocabulary is greater than their general vocabulary would be overrated; "Lady Luck" was good to them as she assembled form *A*. If form *A* is given a second time, the test content is fixed; hence, the consistency between scores is higher than it would be if different forms were administered. Therefore, the stability coefficient tells only the test–retest stability of performance *on different administrations of this particular test,* which may be much less interesting and relevant than the stability of performance on other parallel tests. Test–retest reliability coefficients are usually higher than parallel-form reliability coefficients because the latter permit a fresh sample from the same content universe.

Figure 5–8 shows two equally representative parallel forms of a test, *A* and *B,* from the same universe of content. The test–retest method of estimating reliability does not permit a new sample of items to be used in the second testing. Therefore, the test–retest reliability coefficients, r_{AA} and r_{BB}, will be higher, but usually less meaningful, than the parallel-form reliability estimate (r_{AB} or r_{BA}), in which different random samples of items have been selected from the same item universe. Forms *A* and *B* are both random samples from the universe of content, yet r_{AA} will be greater than r_{AB} because the sample of test content is not allowed to vary in the test–retest method.

An important point in evaluating reliability coefficients is illustrated in Figure 5–8. If the procedure used to estimate reliability does not allow certain factors to vary (e.g., sampling error in item selection), then, of course, they are constant and cannot be categorized as measurement error, even though they may logically belong in that category. Figure 5–8 also demonstrates that the term *reliability coefficient* is ambiguous when the method used to estimate it is not reported. (For further discussion see Stanley, 1971a, 1971b.)

Parallel-Form Reliability

Since 1910 the parallel-form reliability coefficients have been preferred for estimating the reliability of a test. It is simply the correlation coefficient between the obtained scores on two forms of the test. (See Figure 5–8.)

---

[4] The standard deviation, σ_P, of the percent of scientific words that would be found on 25-item tests, assuming that the words were selected randomly from a large unabridged dictionary in which technical words represented 40 percent (*P*) of the entries, would be

$$\sigma_P = \sqrt{\frac{P(1-P)}{n}} = \sqrt{\frac{40(60)}{25}} = 9.8,$$

or approximately 10%. Notice that on a longer test there would be less difference among forms: If $n = 100$, $\sigma_P \doteq 5\%$.

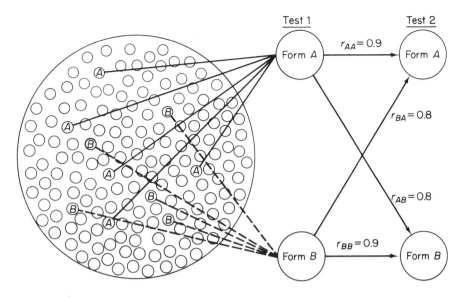

Item universe
(e.g., all words in Webster's dictionary)

FIGURE 5-8 Graphic illustration of test-retest reliability (r_{AA} and r_{BB}) and parallel-form (r_{BA} and r_{AB}) reliability estimates.

Examinees' universe scores are the same on the parallel forms. The standard errors of measurement for the two forms are also the same. Determining the parallel-form reliability coefficient of a test requires two forms of the test be administered to the same examinees. For many purposes this is impracticable, for example, when the user needs just one form or does not have the financial resources to develop alternate forms. Since both the test–retest and parallel-form methods require two test administrations, hence the testing time is doubled. Examinee cooperation, motivation, fatigue, and boredom also present additional practical obstacles. Methods of estimating a test's reliability that require only one administration are more commonly employed, especially for teacher-made tests, because of the practical difficulties associated with developing two forms of a test and/or the problems of two test administrations.

The Split-Half Method

To avoid two test administrations, a power (unspeeded) test can be split into two parts. For example, one might put the odd-numbered items (1, 3, 5, . . .) into half *a* and the even-numbered items (2, 4, 6, . . .) into half *b*. From a single test administration a score for each half can be obtained for each examinee, and the half-scores can be correlated to secure a coefficient that could be labeled r_{xx}, that is, the "parallel-form reliability" of a test *half as long*. Fortunately, one can estimate the r'_{XX} of the full test from r_{XX} via the Spearman-Brown formula (4.4):

$$r'_{XX} = \frac{2r_{XX}}{1 + r_{XX}}$$

For example, if the Pearson correlation between the odd and even items is r_{XX} = .5, then the estimated reliability of the full-length test is predicted to be, r'_{XX} = 2(.5)/1 + .5 = .67. The halving procedure is called the *odd–even* or *split-half method,* and the stepped-up coefficient is usually referred to as a "corrected" split-half reliability coefficient. Thorndike and Hagen (1969, p. 193) note that split-half estimates tend to exceed parallel-form estimates .03–.11 on selected standardized tests.

Although the split-half correlation with Spearman-Brown correction has been the most commonly used procedure for estimating reliability and has been shown empirically to yield accurate results when its assumptions are satisfied, the method proposed by Flanagan (1937) is computationally simpler because it does not require either the computation of a correlation coefficient or the use of the Spearman-Brown formula. In addition, it is preferable because it does not assume that the two halves have equal standard deviations which is assumed by the Spearman-Brown formula. Flanagan's formula is

$$r_{XX} = 2 \left(1 - \frac{s_a^2 + s_b^2}{s^2} \right), \tag{4.7}$$

where s_a^2 and s_b^2 are the variances of halves a and $b,$ and s^2 is the variance of total scores on the test. For example, if s_a = 5, s_b = 6, and s = 10,

$$r_{XX} = 2 \left(1 - \frac{(5)^2 + (6)^2}{(10)^2} \right) = 2 \left(1 - \frac{61}{100} \right) = 2(.39) = .78.$$

The Flanagan and odd–even correlation with the Spearman-Brown correction method usually yield reliability estimates that agree very closely. Indeed, they will yield identical coefficients when $s_a^2 = s_b^2$; otherwise, the Flanagan[5] method yields a slightly lower value.

Reliability via Internal Consistency

Many years ago Kuder and Richardson (1937) devised a procedure for estimating the reliability of a test without splitting it into halves. The rationale for

---

[5] The Flanagan formula is algebraically equivalent to a formula devised by Rulon (1939),

$$r_{XX} = 1 - \frac{s_d^2}{s^2},$$

where s_d^2 is the variance of the *difference* in scores on the two halves and is also a direct estimate of σ_e^2. The ratio is s_d^2/s^2 is an estimate of the proportion of the total variance that is due to error, and r_{XX} is the proportion of the variance that is not due to error (i.e., is true variance). Thus, we see that the reliability coefficient of a test is said to be the portion of the total variance (σ^2) that is "true" (or universe) variance (σ_u^2) that is,

$$r_{XX} = 1 - \frac{s_e^2}{s^2} = \frac{s_u^2}{s^2}$$

Kuder and Richardson's most commonly used procedure, KR formula 20, is roughly equivalent to (1) securing the mean intercorrelation of the k items in the test, (2) considering this to be the reliability coefficient of the typical *item* in the test, and (3) stepping up this average r with the Spearman-Brown formula to estimate the reliability coefficient of a test consisting of k items (see Stanley, 1957).[6] Since there are 300 unique item intercorrelations even for a 25-item test, it is fortunate that we do not actually have to compute these r's but can estimate the reliability coefficient fairly easily from data on the items and the variance of the scores.

Kuder-Richardson Formula 20. Even when the average intercorrelation ($\bar{r}$) of items is rather small, the internal consistency of the test in the Kuder-Richardson sense will be *much* higher than this $\bar{r}$ if the test is composed of a fairly large number of items. When the average intercorrelation of the 25 items in a test is .10, the KR20 coefficient for the test will be approximately .74 as estimated by the Spearman-Brown formula[7] (4.3). For 50 items that intercorrelate .10, it is .85. The more items of a given quality, the higher the KR20 coefficient. Therefore, other things being equal, *longer tests are more reliable than shorter tests.*

A desirable feature of the KR20 reliability estimate is that it is the mean of all possible Flanagan split-half reliability estimates (see Cronbach, 1951, and Novick and Lewis, 1967). It also tends to provide a good estimate of parallel-form reliability on unspeeded tests (Cronbach and Azuma, 1962). Its computation is straightforward; the formula is

$$r_{KR20} = \frac{k}{k-1}\left(1 - \frac{\Sigma pq}{s^2}\right), \qquad (4.8)$$

where p = the proportion passing a given item and q = the proportion not passing that item ($q = 1 - p$), and these pq values are summed over all k items to obtain Σpq.

To keep the computation simple, suppose that for a three-item test the proportions of correct answers were .8, .7, and .5 and the standard deviation of the total scores, s, is .9. The value of Σ_{pq} is $(.8)(.2) + (.7)(.3) + (.5)(.5) = .62$; hence,

$$r_{KR20} = \frac{3}{3-1}\left(1 - \frac{.62}{(.9)^2}\right) = \frac{3}{2}\left(1 - \frac{.62}{.81}\right) =$$

$$1.5(1 - .765) = 1.5(.235) = .35.$$

[6] Stanley (1957) showed that if $\bar{r}$ is the average intercorrelation of the k items, then the reliability coefficient estimated via the Kuder-Richardson formula is very nearly that yielded by the general Spearman-Brown formula (4.3).

[7] Thus, for a 25-item test, if the reliability of a single item (average r between items) is .1, the reliability of the 25-item test is:

$$r'_{XX} = \frac{25(.1)}{1 + (25-1)(.1)} = \frac{2.5}{1 + 2.4} = \frac{3.5}{3.4} = .74.$$

The r_{KR20} is a special case of a more general reliability coefficient, "alpha," developed by Cronbach (1951):

$$r_\alpha = \frac{I}{I-1}\left(1 - \frac{\Sigma s_i^2}{s^2}\right), \qquad (4.9)$$

where s_i^2 is the variance of scores on part i of the test, which is composed of I parts. When the parts are individual items, $r_\alpha = r_{KR20}$. When the parts are halves, r_α is the split-half reliability coefficient yielded by the Flanagan formula.

Suppose the standard deviations for five 10-item quizzes are $s_1 = 2$, $s_2 = 3$, $s_3 = 2$, $s_4 = 1$, $s_5 = 2$; the sum of the variances of the parts, Σs_i^2, is $2^2 + 3^2 + 2^2 + 1^2 + 2^2 = 22$. The standard deviation of the total scores (the sum of the scores on the five quizzes), σ, is 8; hence, $\sigma^2 = 64$. The reliability estimate (coefficient alpha) of the composite scores is then

$$r_\alpha = \frac{5}{5-1}\left(1 - \frac{22}{64}\right) = 1.25(1 - .344) = 1.25(.656) = .82.$$

An important point for classroom evaluation is illustrated in this example. The reliability of a composite score can be high even if the component parts do not possess high reliability.[8]

Kuder-Richardson Formula 21. Because computing r_{KR20} by hand is tedious, Kuder and Richardson (1937) proposed a second formula, Kuder-Richardson formula 21, that is somewhat less accurate but is simple to compute. It requires only the test mean ($\overline{X}$), the variance (s^2), and the number of items (k) on the test; it assumes that all items are of equal difficulty, $\overline{p} = \overline{X}/k$:

$$r_{KR21} = \frac{k}{k-1}\left(1 - \frac{k\overline{p}\overline{q}}{s^2}\right) \qquad (4.10)$$

For example, on a 50-item test where $\overline{X} = 30$ and $s = 10$, $\overline{p} = 30/50 = .6$ and $\overline{q} = 1 - \overline{p} = .4$; hence,

$$\frac{50}{49}\left(1 - \frac{50(.6)(.4)}{100}\right) = \frac{50}{49}(1 - .12) = .90$$

The value of r_{KR21} is always less than (and less accurate than) the corresponding value of r_{KR20}, but the differences are usually not great on *well-constructed* tests (Lord, 1959a; Cronbach and Azuma, 1962; Payne, 1963). Figure 5-9 depicts the high relationship between r_{KR20} and r_{KR21} on 58 carefully developed tests; r_{KR20} consistently exceeds r_{KR21}, but usually by .05 units or less if r_{KR21} is .70 or greater. The higher the reliability, the less r_{KR21} and r_{KR20} differ. Kuder-Richardson formula 21 assumes that the items on the test are equally difficult; it is lower than r_{KR20} to the extent that item difficulty varies

---

[8] Using the Spearman-Brown formula (4.3) "in reverse," we can estimate the average reliability of a single quiz (a 10-item "test") from the reliability of the composite score: $L = 10/50 = .2$ and $r_{XX} = .82$; hence,

$$r'_{XX} = \frac{.2(.82)}{1 + (.2-1)(.82)} = \frac{.164}{1 + (-.8)(.82)} = \frac{.164}{1 - .656} = \frac{.164}{.344} = .48.$$

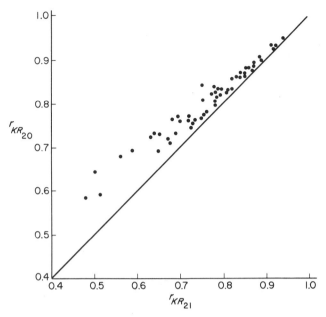

FIGURE 5-9 Relation between Kuder-Richardson formulas 20 and 21 reliability coefficients for 58 standardized tests. (Data from Lord, 1959b.)

within a test. (See Stanley, 1968.) On mastery criterion-referenced[9] or teacher-made tests that have many very easy items, r_{KR21} becomes quite conservative and may underestimate r_{KR20} by as much as .15 (Cronbach and Azuma, 1962). On unspeeded tests, the Kuder-Richardson formulas are often given as a lower-bound (minimal) estimate of reliability. Using Figure 5-9, one can make a reasonable estimate of r_{KR20} from r_{KR21}. For example, if $r_{KR21} = .8$, r_{KR20} can be expected to be .83; if $r_{KR21} = .5$, r_{KR20} may be .6.

Internal-consistency reliability methods are not useful in situations, such as the measurement of height, in which the items are not viewed as comprising a representative sample from a universe of behavior. The ruler is a near-perfect scale for measuring height. To find the error of measurement we need a second, *independent* measurement of height. Physical measurement is usually more reliable than educational and psychological measurement, because the units and scales of psychological measurement—the items themselves—are subject to much larger errors of measurement.

Speeded Tests

Split-half and internal consistency procedures are appropriate only for *power tests,* tests in which every student has adequate time to complete each item. These procedures are not proper for speeded tests—tests in which not all the

---

[9] Criterion-referenced tests are treated in Chapters 7 and 8. Livingston (1972) has shown that the classical concepts of reliability can be refined in a more general form that will apply to criterion-referenced measures. (See Stanley, 1971.)

examinees have enough time to respond to all questions. If a test begins with items that are so easy that nearly everyone marks them correctly, and ends with items that are so difficult that nearly everyone misses them, it may not be speeded even though not all students attempt all the items. When questions are ordered by degree of difficulty, a student may run out of ability long before completing the test.

Most standardized ability tests are not heavily speeded. But rarely is a standardized educational test strictly a pure "power" test. Educational tests usually contain elements of both speed and power. Some students do not have time to answer (or even to read) some of the items that they could answer correctly.

Tests will yield spuriously high reliability coefficients when split-half or internal consistency methods are employed if they contain a significant speed component. To assess the reliability of speeded tests, one should administer separately timed comparable halves and use the Flanagan or another split-half procedure. Of course, the test-retest and parallel-form methods of estimating reliability are also legitimate for speeded tests.

What Is a High Reliability Coefficient?

Obviously, we want tests to be highly reliable. Standardized tests need to be more reliable than classroom tests, since standardized test results must stand alone whereas scores from quizzes and classroom tests are usually aggregated into a composite "score" that will typically have much higher reliability than the individual components. Standardized tests such as those used for college admission or special-education placement should have reliability coefficients of at least .90 (or reliability indexes of $\sqrt{.90} = .95$). But for most purposes the standard error of measurement is a more meaningful indication of measurement precision. It is useful on both norm-referenced and criterion-referenced tests (CRT).[10] Recall that $s_e = \sigma\sqrt{1 - r_{XU}{}^2}$; hence, since $r_{XU}{}^2 = r_{XX}$, $\sigma_e = \sigma\sqrt{1 - r_{XX}}$.

Reliability coefficients for CRT measures and other tests on which individual differences among examinees can be low, even if the standard error of measurement is small. For example, the reliability of standardized achievement tests for a high-ability class will ordinarily be much lower than the reliability of the same test for a more heterogeneous class of students, even though the σ_e is the same in both instances.[11]

On criterion-referenced tests or other minimum-competency measures, the standard error of measurement conveys the degree of measurement preci-

---

[10] Norm-referenced tests are designed to measure *individual differences* as reliably as possible; most standardized tests are examples of norm-referenced tests. Criterion-referenced tests are used to certify some level of mastery of certain skills. They are treated in Chapter 7.

[11] Note in the Rulon (1939) reliability formula below that r_{XX} will decrease when s^2 decreases even if s_e^2 remains constant:

$$r_{XX} = 1 - \frac{s_e^2}{s^2}$$

sion far more meaningfully than the reliability coefficient does. To take an extreme example, suppose a 20-item mastery test for telling time was given to groups of first-graders, with these results: $\overline{X} = 18$, $s^2 = 2$, and $s_e^2 = 1$. The reliability coefficient (Rulon formula) is only .50, even though observed scores differ little from corresponding universe scores. In other words, virtually all students are answering 80% or more of the items correctly. If $s_{e\%}$ is 5% or less of the items, the test will ordinarily have very high measurement precisions regardless of r_{XX}, i.e., the universe scores are within 5% of the obtained scores for most (68%) of the students.

Summary

What are the earmarks of a good measuring instrument? The two most important qualities are *validity* and *reliability*. The first consideration in educational and psychological testing is always validity. Measurement precision (reliability in some sense) is a crucial prerequisite for validity, but it is only a means toward that end.

When a test is administered to an examinee a score is obtained. If the examinee had been tested on some other test or occasion, the exact same score probably would not have been earned. The score that would be earned, on the average, if the examinee had been tested at various times under exactly the same testing conditions is called the true or universe score. Although we can never actually know universe scores, we can be aware of the magnitude of the discrepancies between obtained scores (which we know) and universe scores (which we do not know). This difference, the obtained score minus the true score, is called *error of measurement*.

The standard deviation of the errors of measurement is the *standard error of measurement* (σ_e or s_e). About two-thirds of the examinees will have obtained scores that are within one σ_e of their universe scores. Only about one person in twenty will obtain a score that varies from his or her universe score by as much as $2\sigma_e$.

The *reliability index* of a test is the correlation between universe scores and obtained scores. The index of reliability is the square root of the test's reliability coefficient, i.e., $r_{UX}^2 = r_{XX}$. Observed scores tend to deviate from the mean more than corresponding universe scores, which accounts for the phenomenon of regression toward the mean.

There are several methods for estimating the reliability of a test. The test–retest and parallel-form methods have the practical disadvantage of requiring two administrations, and the latter requires the construction of two forms. Although the parallel-form method is theoretically preferable, the split-half and internal-consistency methods are more common because only one test and one administration are required. These one-form methods are inappropriate for speeded tests; they give inflated reliability estimates to the extent that speed rather than power influences test scores. Split-half (usually odd–even) reliability estimates tend to be slightly higher than those yielded by the Kuder-Richardson formulas. Kuder-Richardson formula 20 yields the average of all possible split-half coefficients and is usually a good estimate of parallel-form reliability when the interval between forms is short. Kuder-Richardson formula 21 yields conservative reliability estimates, but its computation requires only the number of items on a test, the mean, and the variance. If r_{KR21} is .70 or above, r_{KR20} tends to be .05 or less higher. The higher the r_{KR21} value, the less it tends to differ from the corresponding r_{KR20} value.

Even though a test produces valid and reliable scores, it may not be functional because of some practical problem. If the test is too expensive, requires too much time to administer or score, or is difficult to interpret, its real value is reduced accordingly.

IMPORTANT TERMS AND CONCEPTS

sample	index of reliability (r_{UX})	split-half method
universe of content	universe (true) score	Spearman-Brown formula
errors of measurement	variance (σ^2)	Flanagan formula
standard error of measurement	regression toward the mean	Coefficient alpha (r_α)
(σ_e and $\sigma_{e\%}$)	parallel-form reliability	Kuder-Richardson formulas
reliability coefficient (r_{XX})	test–retest reliability	20 and 21

CHAPTER TEST

1. Can a test be highly reliable and yet have no validity?

2. Can a highly valid test lack measurement precision?

3. If on forms A and B of a handwriting test your penmanship ratings were very good, but otherwise your handwriting is poor, does the handwriting test appear to possess reliability?

4. Does the handwriting test just described appear to have validity?

5. Which of these is the classical term for universe score?
a) real score
b) valid score
c) true score
d) correct score

6. If σ_e is less than σ, the test
a) is perfectly reliable.
b) has a reliability index of 1.0.
c) has a reliability index greater than 0.0.
d) has a reliability index of 0.0.
e) has a negative reliability index.

Suppose that there were many parallel forms of this mastery test. You took them all; assume no practice effect from the test. The distribution of your scores had a mean of 84% and a standard deviation of 6%.

7. Estimate your universe score.

8. You obtained scores between 78% and 90% on approximately two out of _____ tests.

9. How frequently did your score exceed 90%?

10. How frequently did your score fall below 78%?

11. How frequently did your scores fall within the 72–96% interval?

12. The $\overline{X}$ and s of your class on this mastery test were 80% and 10%, respectively. Using this and other given information, estimate the reliability coefficient of the test using the formula:

$$r_{XX} = 1 - \frac{S_e^{\,2}}{s^2}$$

13. From the reliability coefficient, r_{XX}, estimate the index of reliability, r_{UX}.

14. What is the correlation between the obtained scores and the corresponding universe scores on the test?

15. If a second, parallel form were given to the class, estimate the correlation between the two sets of obtained scores.

16. Except when r_{XX} = 0.0 and 1.0, r_{UX} will have a _____ (larger, smaller) value than r_{XX}.

17. If the mastery test were doubled in length
   a) r_{XX} would increase.
   b) r_{UX} would increase.
   c) $\sigma_{e\%}$ would decrease.
   d) two of the above.
   e) all of the above.

18. Suppose Mark scored 60% on this mastery test (recall that $\overline{X}$ = 80%, s = 10%, and r_{XX} = .64); his universe score would be expected to
   a) be less than 60%.
   b) be 60%.
   c) be greater than 60%.

19. Estimate Mark's universe score. [(Recall that the universe score is expected to deviate less from the mean than the obtained score; expected deviation = (r_{XX})(observed deviation).]

20. Does Mark appear to have one of the lowest scores in the class?

21. Jill obtained an IQ score of 120; estimate her universe IQ score using Figure 5–6 (p. 125)
   a) if the test had a reliability coefficient of .9
   b) if the test had a reliability coefficient of .75
   c) if the test had a reliability coefficient of .5

22. On highly reliable tests X's will differ (little, greatly) from estimated universe scores.

23. Where will an obtained score equal the estimated universe score?
  a) when $X = \overline{X}$
  b) when $r_{XX} = 0$
  c) when $r_{XX} = 1.0$
  d) both (a) and (b)
  e) both (a) and (c)

24. What is the primary disadvantage of the parallel-form method as compared to the test–retest method of estimating reliability?

25. Practical considerations aside, which method of estimating reliability is generally preferable?
  a) parallel-form
  b) test–retest
  c) split-half
  d) internal-consistency

26. Which statistical measure describes the test–retest and parallel-form reliability?
  a) $\overline{X}$
  b) σ
  c) r

27. Which formula is used to estimate the reliability of a test if its length is increased or decreased?
  a) Flanagan formula
  b) Spearman-Brown formula
  c) r_{α}
  d) r_{KR20}
  e) r_{KR21}

28. Which of these tends to yield the lowest reliability coefficient for power tests?
  a) r_{α}
  b) corrected split-half
  c) r_{KR20}
  d) r_{KR21}
  e) test–retest

29. Which of these methods of estimating reliability requires the computation of a correlation coefficient?
  a) Flanagan formula
  b) Kuder-Richardson formula
  c) coefficient alpha
  d) all of the above
  e) none of the above

30. Which of the procedures in question 29 are appropriate for a speeded test?

31. When would r_{KR20} and r_{KR21} be identical?

32. When the "parts" of a test are items, are r_α and r_{KR20} identical?

33. Which of these r_{KR21} values will be the best estimate of the corresponding r_{KR20} value?

    a) .40
    b) .50
    c) .60
    d) .70
    e) .9

34. Using Figure 5-9 (p. 133), if r_{KR21} is .75, which of these is probably a good estimate of the corresponding r_{KR20} value?

    a) .70
    b) .75
    c) .80
    d) .85
    e) .90

35. For interpreting an individual's score, which is more informative:

    a) r_{XX}
    b) σ_e
    c) σ

36. If σ_e remains constant but σ increases, r_{XX} and r_{UX} will:
    a) increase
    b) remain unchanged
    c) decrease

37. Most intelligence tests have a standard error of measurement of approximately five IQ points. For a very homogeneous class [e.g., $\sigma = 7.1$ ($\sigma^2 = 50$)], estimate the test's reliability coefficient. (*Hint:* See formula in question 12.)

38. For a typical class ($s = 15$), the same test would be expected to yield a reliability coefficient of _____ .

39. If a test has a reliability of .60, estimate its reliability if the test is doubled in length using the Spearman-Brown formula 4.4 (p. 126).

40. Estimate σ_e of the raw score for (a) a test of 25 items and (b) a test of 100 items (see Equation 4.5, p. 126).

41. If raw scores are expressed as percents, does $\sigma_{e\%}$ decrease as test length increases? What is the value of $\sigma_{e\%}$ for (a) $k = 25$ and (b) $k = 100$ (see Equation 4.6 and Figure 5-7, pp. 126-127).

42. If a test of 80 items had a $\sigma_{e\%}$ of 5%, estimate $\sigma_{e\%}$ if the test is reduced to 20 items. (Note the relationship between length and $\sigma_{e\%}$ in question 41.)

43. What is L (as defined in Spearman-Brown formula 4.3), if the number of items is increased from 25 to 100?

44. Given the 25-item test with $r_{XX} = .50$, estimate the reliability of the 100-item test.

Other things being equal, as test length is increased, the standard error of measurement decreases (T or F):

45. when raw scores are used.

46. when percent scores are used.

47. when standard scores are used.

ANSWERS TO CHAPTER TEST

1. yes
2. no
3. yes
4. no
5. c
6. c
7. 84%
8. three
9. on about 1 test in 6 (or 16%)
10. on about 1 test in 6 (or 16%)
11. on about 19 tests in 20 (95% or 96%)
12. $r_{XX} = 1 - \dfrac{\sigma_e^2}{\sigma^2} = 1 - \dfrac{6^2}{10^2}$

    $= .64$
13. $r_{UX} = \sqrt{r_{XX}} = \sqrt{.64} = .80$
14. .80
15. .64
16. larger

17. e
18. c
19. .64 × 20 = 12.8; 80 − 12.8 = 67.2 or 67%
20. Yes, since he is 20% below the mean, which ordinarily will be at about the second percentile.
21. a) 118, b) 115, c) 110
22. little
23. e
24. Two forms of the test are required.
25. a
26. c
27. b
28. d
29. e
30. None, unless the halves are separately timed, in which case a, (and c if "parts" are halves) are appropriate

31. only if all items were exactly equal in difficulty
32. yes
33. e
34. c
35. b
36. a
37. $r_{XX} = 1 - \dfrac{5^2}{50} = .50$
38. $r_{XX} = 1 - \dfrac{5^2}{15^2} = 1 - .111$

    $= .89$
39. .75
40. a) 2.15, b) 4.3
41. yes, a) 8.6%, b) 4.3%
42. 10%
43. 4
44. $r'_{XX} = .80$
45. F
46. T
47. T

FOR ADDITIONAL READING

AMERICAN PSYCHOLOGICAL ASSOCIATION. *Standards for educational and psychological tests and manuals.* Washington, D.C., 1974. Sect. D (Reliability).

BAUER, D. H. Error sources in aptitude and achievement test scores: A review and recommendation. *Measurement and Evaluation in Guidance,* 1973, 6, 28–34.

STANLEY, J. C. Reliability. In R. L. Thorndike, ed., *Educational measurement,* 2nd ed. Washington, D.C.: American Council on Education, 1971. Chap. 13.

———. Reliability of test scores and other measurements. In L. C. Deighton, ed., *The encyclopedia of education.* New York: Macmillan, 1971. Reprinted in G. H. Bracht, K. D. Hopkins, and J. C. Stanley, eds., *Perspectives in educational and psychological measurement.* Englewood Cliffs, N.J.: Prentice-Hall, 1972. Selection 6.

THORNDIKE, R. L. Reliability. In E. F. Lindquist, ed., *Educational measurement.* Washington, D.C.: American Council on Education, 1951. Chap. 13.

6

Extraneous Factors that Influence Performance on Cognitive Tests

Cronbach (1970) distinguished between measures of *maximum performance* (achievement, intelligence, and aptitude tests) and measures of *typical performance* (attitude, interest, and personality inventories). The goal of cognitive measurement is to obtain an examinee's best, maximum, and highest level of performance. The purpose of affective measurement is to assess an examinee's usual, representative, and typical behavior. The measurement problems are very similar among measures within each of the two categories, but are quite different between the classes. In this chapter we discuss the influences of certain irrelevant factors on the measurement of maximum performance.

In addition to the trait, knowledge, or proficiency that is to be measured, many other factors may affect an examinee's performance on a test. To evaluate test results properly, one should not only be aware of the existence of extraneous variables but also be able to make appropriate allowances for such factors in interpreting the results.

Test Sophistication, Practice, and Coaching

Test Sophistication

A general "know-how" of test taking can affect test performance. *Test-wiseness* has been defined as an examinee's ability to use the characteristics and formats of the test and/or the test-taking situation to increase his score

(Millman, Bishop, & Ebel, 1965). People who are unfamiliar with objective or essay tests usually perform somewhat more poorly than people who have considerable experience with such tests.

The basic principles of test-wiseness (Millman et al., 1965; Millman & Pauk, 1969; American College, 1978) for objective tests are summarized in Table 6-1. Test-wiseness as it applies to essay tests is treated in Chapter 8. It has been shown (Slakter, Koehler, & Hampton, 1970) that test-wiseness increases progressively in grades 5 through 11. It has been demonstrated (Moore, Schutz & Baker, 1966; Wahlstrom and Boersma, 1968; Nilsson, 1975; Bajtelsmit, 1977) that pupils can be taught principles of "test-wiseness." Such test-taking skill usually improves the scores of "test-naive" examinees on poorly constructed test items, although little effect is typically found on well-constructed items (Bajtelsmit, 1977; Keysor & Williams, 1977; Pike, 1978) unless examinees are in the primary grades (Callenbach, 1973).

Since poor items are found on almost all teacher-made tests and on many standardized tests, test sophistication is probably a factor on most tests. It apparently is a major factor only with naive examinees on poor tests or on tests given under conditions in which certain response styles play a significant role. A recent study by the College Board (Powers & Alderman, 1979) found that an orientation booklet, *Taking the SAT*—which provides students with detailed information about the test, including sample items—did not influence SAT test performance.

TABLE 6-1

COMMON BEHAVIORS OF TEST-WISE EXAMINEES

On objective tests, test-wise examinees tend to

1. pay careful attention to directions and ask examiner for clarification when necessary.
2. have more than one pencil ready in case one breaks.
3. work as quickly as possible without being reckless; pace their test-taking rate in relation to the allotted time; be sure that they have time to attempt every item.
4. guess at items that will require a disproportionate amount of testing time; place a check-mark by these items so that they can be returned to if time permits.
5. use any time remaining to double-check answers, especially to doubtful answers.
6. guess on all items if only right answers are scored or if the "penalty for guessing" is simply a "correction for chance" (it almost always is.)
7. use deductive reasoning—the process of elimination; eliminate incorrect and implausible options; choose from among the remaining options.
8. reject options that imply the correctness of each other.
9. utilize relevant information from other items on the test.
10. put themselves in the shoes of the test constructor; consider the intent of the test and test constructor; adopt the level of sophistication that is intended.
11. use relevant and extraneous clues to help identify the correct option (the correct answer is more likely to be qualified more carefully or longer, represent a different degree of generalization, or be composed of textbook or stereotyped phraseology).
12. learn the test constructor's tendencies to use certain response positions more (or less) frequently, such as the middle position, or to include a disproportionate percentage of "false" (or "true") items.
13. recognize the use of specific determiners and clues from grammatical construction (e.g., subject–verb agreement, parallelism).

SOURCE: Adapted from Millman et al., 1965, and American College, 1978.

Practice

Several studies provide data on the effects of taking a test on the examinee's subsequent performance on that test or its parallel form. Almost all studies consistently show a general "improvement" in score on the retest. Most such studies have used intelligence tests; the gains are usually reported in IQ units. Rodger (1936) gave six different intelligence tests to the same group of children and found an average gain of 8 points (about $.5\sigma$) from the first to the sixth test. A mean gain of 2.5 IQ points (about $.2\sigma$) was observed on the Stanford-Binet when the forms were counterbalanced (Terman & Merrill, 1937). Kreit (1968) observed a practice factor of 7 IQ points (about $.4\sigma$) when third-grade pupils were administered four intelligence tests over a five-month interval.

A one-week practice effect of only 1.1 IQ points was found for verbal IQ scores on the Lorge-Thorndike Intelligence Tests; the corresponding value for nonverbal IQs (3.3 points) was only slightly larger ($.2\sigma$) (Thorndike & Hagen, 1974).

The practice factor on tests used for admission to college or graduate school is important to note. Levine and Angoff (1958) investigated the effect of repetition on the College Board (CB) Scholastic Aptitude Test for high school juniors and seniors. The authors found an average gain of only 10 points ($.1\sigma$) for the first retest after a two-month interval and an additional gain of 10 points for the second retest, but no further gain for a third retest. (Angoff, 1971, provides detailed information about changes in Scholastic Aptitude Test scores over longer periods.) Campbell, Hilton, and Pitcher (1967) compared the performance of a large group who had repeated the aptitude sections of the Graduate Record Examination after a three-month interval. Unlike the sample in Levine and Angoff's (1958) study, these examinees had repeated the test on their own initiative; some apparently felt that the first test score did not accurately reflect their abilities. An average gain of only approximately 20 points ($.2\sigma$) was observed on both the verbal and quantitative aptitude sections. Thus, it appears that the practice effect is a very minor factor on these important tests. A similar gain of 25 points ($.25\sigma$) was observed for medical school applicants on the Medical College Admission Test (MCAT) (Schumacher & Gee, 1961).

A study by Knapp (1960) illuminates several factors pertaining to the practice effect and its ally, test-wiseness. Knapp found a greater practice effect for Mexicans than for Americans on the Cattell Culture Free Intelligence Test. The practice effects were much larger when speed was a factor, especially for the Mexicans, who were less experienced in taking tests.

The review of these and related studies of the practice effect on cognitive tests supports the following generalizations:

1. Practice effects are more pronounced with people of limited educational background or experience with tests.
2. The effects are greater on speeded tests (Tuinman, Farr, & Blanton, 1972).
3. The effects are greater on a repeated test than on a parallel form of the test. There is little or no practice effect after the second retest.

144

*Extraneous
Factors that
Influence
Performance on
Cognitive Tests*

4. The greater the interval between tests, the smaller the effect. There appears to be little practice effect for an interval greater than three months.
5. Other things being equal, the effects appear to be slightly greater for examinees of high mental ability (Weiss, 1961).
6. For a group of typical examinees, the average practice effect is usually $.2\sigma$ or less in magnitude.

Coaching

The topic of coaching is difficult to treat because it may mean anything from drill on items that were missed on a test to a general remedial course. In addition to the kind of coaching given, the amount of time spent varies considerably in the published studies. Consequently, the results of "coaching" studies are quite varied. Greene (1928) reported the following results on the Stanford-Binet for three groups of schoolchildren. The control group, which received no coaching (practice effect only), gained on the average 2–3 IQ points (about $.2\sigma$) on the retest. A second group received two hours of training on material that was similar but not identical to that appearing on the test; this group had an average gain of 7–8 IQ points (about $.4–.5\sigma$). A third group, which was coached on identical material, reflected a mean gain of about 30 points (about 2σ)! These differences declined with time for three years, at which time no coaching advantage remained. When the term *coaching* as used by Yates and colleagues (1953, 1954) is interpreted properly, the results are remarkably consistent with those of Greene. Vernon (1954) observed an average gain of 2–3 IQ points (about $.2\sigma$) for a control group on the second testing, a mean gain of about 6 points ($.4\sigma$) on the third testing, and no additional gain thereafter. When coached examinees had numerous similar items explained, they gained 5–6 IQ points (about $.4\sigma$) on the first retest. This increased progressively to 8–10 points (about $.6\sigma$) for the third retest, and there was no additional gain thereafter.

Several studies have been conducted on the effect of coaching on the Scholastic Aptitude Test (CB, 1968; Alderman & Powers, 1979). The studies reveal a small 5–20 point ($.05–.2\sigma$) gain from special coaching. Frankel (1960) compared students who took a commercial coaching course with a group matched on initial SAT score who merely repeated the test. The coached students gained less than 10 points ($.1\sigma$) more than the matched group. Special secondary-school programs designed specifically to improve student performance on the SAT-Verbal averaged only 7 points (less than $.1\sigma$) gain (Alderman & Powers, 1980).

From the results of these and related studies, we can make the following generalizations pertinent to the effects of coaching on test performance:

1. Coaching usually results in small (often negligible) gains in test performance, over and above the practice effect.
2. The magnitude of the gain rarely exceeds $.2\sigma$ unless the examinees have been coached on the actual test items. Somewhat larger gains (often $.3\sigma$) may result on achievement tests for those examinees who have not had recent association with the content area.

As long as the objective questions are reasonably straightforward, the amount of improvement typically brought about by coaching and/or practice is not great (Wood, 1977).

Anxiety and Motivation

A poorly motivated pupil cannot be expected to give maximum effort on a test. Most examinees are intrinsically motivated to succeed in test situations, although the degree of motivation varies widely among ethnic and socio-economic groups (Anastasi, 1958, p. 551). Incentives like cash, grades, and special urging have little or no effect on normal students who are already motivated to do well (Klugman, 1944; Sinick, 1956). When the test content is not intrinsically interesting or examinees are not ego-involved with their performance, effects can be moderate (Tuinman et al., 1972) to sizable (Duncan, 1947; Yamamota and Dizney, 1965). If examinees are too ego-involved with their performance on a test, they may become anxious. There have been dozens of research studies relating anxiety and test performance. (See Ruebush, 1963.) Almost all of this research is consistent in showing a small negative $(-.1$ to $-.3)$ correlation between paper-and-pencil self-report test anxiety measures and performance on intelligence and achievement tests. Too often these findings have been interpreted incorrectly; that is, they have been assumed to show that "test anxiety depresses ability test performance." Correlation may reflect causation, but it does not *necessarily* do so. One would be equally unjustified in concluding from the negative correlation that "poor performance on ability tests generates high test anxiety." A brief look at some of the items used on the self-report scales designed to measure test anxiety (Sarason et al., 1960) will show that both explanations are logically plausible:

> When the teacher says she is going to find out how much you have learned, does your heart begin to beat faster?
> While you are taking a test, do you usually think you are not doing well?

As French (1962, p. 555) stated, "Evidence that anxiety is usually found to accompany low test scores proves nothing about the part that anxiety plays in bringing about the low scores."

In a few studies, researchers have attempted to ascertain experimentally whether high anxiety impairs test performance. In these studies subjects were randomly assigned to various anxiety-inducing or anxiety-reducing treatments. The evidence obtained thus far has failed to support the common contention that such experimentally induced "anxiety" depresses test performance (Allison, 1970; Chambers, Hopkins, and Hopkins, 1972; French, 1962; Silverstein et al., 1964). However, in tests requiring psychomotor performance in addition to cognitive performance (such as mazes), anxiety-inducing instructions did cause more errors to be made by high-anxiety examinees (Sarason, Mandler, and Craighill, 1952).

145

146

Extraneous
Factors that
Influence
Performance on
Cognitive Tests

It can be concluded that *although measured test anxiety is inversely associated with cognitive test performance, the available research fails to establish a causative relationship with the usual kind of cognitive test of maximum performance.* This generalization does not necessarily apply to degrees of anxiety beyond those which can be investigated experimentally, to psychomotor measures, or even to individual tests in which the examiner plays a more active role in the testing process. Anxiety may influence performance on affective measures more than on cognitive tests (Jensen & Schmitt, 1970; Phillips, 1971; Chandler & Hunter, 1976).

Response Styles

Cronbach (1946, 1950, 1970) defined *response sets* or *styles* as test-taking habits that cause people of equal ability to earn different scores on a test or inventory. An examinee may bring to a test some patterns of test-taking behavior that influence performance but are unrelated to ability.

The Speed-vs.-Accuracy Set

Some examinees have a test-taking set that causes them to work slowly and carefully; others have a tendency to work quickly and with less caution (Guilford & Lacey, 1947). The correlation between ability and working rate on tests have been shown to be very low (Tate, 1948; Ebel, 1954; Hopkins, 1964b). Some examinees respond more slowly than others irrespective of item difficulty or test content (Bennett & Doppelt, 1956; Davidson & Carroll, 1945; Tate, 1948).

Little or no relationship has been found between order of finishing and scores on a test (Barch, 1957; Michael & Michael, 1969). When tests are pure power tests, the effects from this response style are negligible. (*Power tests* are tests given with ample time for all examinees to demonstrate how well they can perform.) Speeded achievement tests tend to be less valid (Traub & Hambleton, 1972).

Teacher-made and standardized tests (Boag & Neild, 1962; Kahn, 1968; Knapp, 1960) frequently have inadequate time limits; this allows the irrelevant effects from the speed-vs.-accuracy response set to contaminate the validity of test scores. Several studies have found that tests may measure different mental functions when administered under power and speed conditions (Lord, 1956; Myers, 1960; Mollenkopf, 1960). Older people tend to work more slowly, a factor that led to a gross overestimation of the degree of intellectual decline with age in some early studies (Lorge, 1952).

Except for those educational objectives for which speed of response is an important objective (e.g., typing, reading), tests should be constructed and administered so that virtually all examinees (perhaps 90%) complete the examination. Special directions or periodic announcements during the test may help pace the examinees and reduce the contamination resulting from the speed-vs.-accuracy set. Every standardized cognitive test should report the ex-

147

*Extraneous
Factors that
Influence
Performance on
Cognitive Tests*

tent to which speed is a factor on the test (APA, 1974; Stafford, 1971; Myers, 1960).

The Acquiescence Set

If one is uncertain about a true–false item, there is a significant tendency to choose the "true" option (Cronbach, 1942, 1950). Gustav (1963) found that 62 percent of a group of college students had marked more items "true" than there were true items on the test. This is particularly interesting since some instructors have a tendency to include more true than false items on their tests (Metfessel and Sax, 1957). The acquiescence set allows more people to get undeserved credit for true items than for false items; thus, true items tend to be easier and less discriminating (Ebel, 1960; Storey, 1968).

The Positional-Preference Set

Guilford (1965, p. 490) stated that

> when examinees are ignorant of the answer to an item, their habits of taking tests are such that they do not choose among the alternatives entirely at random. Certain positions in a list of five responses may be favored by habits of reading or attention.

The research on the positional-preference response set has not yielded consistent findings. A few studies have found it to be a small factor on certain tests (Gustav, 1963; McNamara & Weitzman, 1945; Ace & Dawis, 1973), but most studies have failed to find any significant preference for certain response positions (Wevrick, 1962; Marcus, 1963; Hopkins & Hopkins, 1964; Wilbur, 1970; Jessell & Sullins, 1975).

There does appear to be a tendency for examinees not to respond in a random manner (Wood, 1977). They tend to avoid repeating the same response position on consecutive items (e.g., BB or CCC). They also tend to use backward-series response sequences (for example, EDC) more often than would be expected by chance; there does not appear to be a corresponding phenomenon for forward series (Rabinowitz, 1970).

The response position of the correct answer has reflected a keying bias toward certain positions on certain standardized tests (Metfessel & Sax, 1957). The bias most often results in fewer correct answers for the initial and, to a lesser extent, final response options. More recently standardized tests are less likely to have keying biases (Jacobs, 1968).

The Option Length Set

Chase (1964) and Strang (1977) found a set favoring the longest option on difficult multiple-choice tests. The set can easily be removed by inserting some long incorrect options on easy items early in the test. Examinees tend to select nontechnical options more frequently than technical options, irrespective of length (Strang, 1977).

The Set to Gamble

The topic of examinee guessing has received extensive attention during the past several decades. There would be no serious problem if all pupils of equal ability guessed with equal frequency, but it is well established that there are great individual differences in the tendency to guess on test items, that these differences are reliable within a test, and that they are generally consistent from one test to another (Granich, 1931; Jackson, 1955; Slakter, 1967, 1969; Swineford, 1938, 1941). The tendency to gamble varies from the person who will not guess even when told that he or she must answer every question to the "gambler" who attempts almost every item regardless of penalties or directions (Waters, 1967). This response style is particularly evident when students are told that there is a "penalty for guessing." There are those, however, who omit some items even when they are assured of no penalty.

Most standardized tests do not employ correction for chance (Womer and Wahi, 1969); hence, the "gambler" is given a special advantage over the more deliberate student. In one study (Davis, 1951, p. 277) that illustrates the potential magnitude of this factor, a standardized reading test was administered to approximately 400 high school students. Those examinees who obtained scores below the twelfth percentile ($N = 47$) were told that they might have done better if they had marked an answer for every item, whether they knew the answer or not. When they were then given an alternate form of the same test, their mean score increased from 25.53 on the first test to 46.32 on the second test, with an average grade-placement gain of 2.7 grades according to the published norms![1]

The gambling set has been found to have little or no relationship to ability (Swineford & Miller, 1953; Crocker & Benson, 1976) and to be related to certain personality traits that are irrelevant on ability tests (Hamilton, 1950; Sherriffs & Boomer, 1954; Votaw, 1936; Ziller, 1957; Cross & Frary, 1977).

Examinees with personality scores indicating introversion and low self-esteem tend to omit more items, and to omit more items for which they know the answers. On most tests examinees can "guess" better than chance (Cross & Frary, 1977; Wood, 1976) because (1) they may have partial information on several items and (2) on many items not all the distracters are plausible. Little and Creaser (1966) asked examinees to indicate whether they guessed, were uncertain of their answers, or were certain on each item of a test containing three-option questions; the percentages of correct answers were 55, 67, and 93, respectively, for the three categories. If the examinees possessed no partial information and guessed randomly, they would have been expected to have answered correctly only 33 percent rather than 55 percent for items in the "guessed" category. Jackson (1955) similarly found that students correctly answered one-third of the five-option items on which they reported guessing rather than the one-fifth expected solely from chance. More able examinees tend to heed "Do not guess" instructions more than those of lesser ability (Wood, 1976, 1977).

[1] Although some portion of this difference can be attributed to the regression effect (see Campbell and Stanley, 1966; Hopkins, 1969; Shepard & Hopkins, 1977), the increase is substantially greater than the regression effect alone.

149

*Extraneous
Factors that
Influence
Performance on
Cognitive Tests*

Corrective Measures for the Gambling Set. The most widely used method to reduce the effects of guessing is the "correction for chance," often erroneously referred to as the "penalty for guessing." The correction-for-chance formula actually corrects for omissions rather than for guessing as such. If the students omit no items or all omit the same number of items, their relative scores (i.e., the *z*-scores or percentile ranks) will be the same, whether or not the formula is applied (Stanley, 1954). The most commonly used formula is

$$S = R - \frac{W}{I},$$

where S = the examinee's score corrected for chance,

R = the number of **R**ight responses marked by the examinee,

W = the number of **W**rong responses, *not* including omitted items, and

I = the number of **I**ncorrect options (distracters) per item.

For two-option items, including true–false, this becomes

$$S = R - \frac{W}{1} = R - W.$$

For three-option items, the formula is

$$S = R - \frac{W}{2}.$$

For four-option items, the formula is

$$S = R - \frac{W}{3}.$$

For five-option items, it is

$$S = R - \frac{W}{4}.$$

It should be evident that the greater the number of options per item, the less likely it is that one will select the correct option by chance and, hence, the less the magnitude of the weighting of an incorrect response.[2]

These formulas theoretically reduce to zero the scores of students who, totally ignorant of the material presented in the test, guess with a chance degree of success that depends only on the number of options each item has. If a test contains 100 true–false items and a student ("Larry") guesses an answer to each of these, he should, by chance, answer about 50 items "correctly." Thus, we expect the typical totally uninformed person to score 50 wrong. However, since Larry richly deserves a final score of zero, which by

---

[2] If not all items on a test have the same number of options, each subset of items with the same number of options should be treated separately with the appropriate formula. For example, a test composed of 25 true–false items and 30 four-option multiple-choice questions would use $S = R - W$ for the true–false items and $S = R - W/3$ for the multiple-choice questions. The corrected scores for the two subtests would sum to the corrected-for-chance score for the entire test.

our definition represents his true knowledge of the material, the 50 wrongs are subtracted from the 50 rights: $R - W = 50 - 50 = 0$.

If Larry answers 50 items correctly and *omits* the other 50, his score will be $50 - 0 = 50$. Had he tried the 50 omitted items he would, on the average, by chance have answered half of them (25) correctly and missed the other 25; his "rights score" would be 50 known + 25 guessed = 75, and his "wrongs score" would be 25. He would therefore receive $75 - 25 = 50$, the same score he would have obtained without any guessing. The possible fallacy in this procedure has already been discussed. Because of poor distracters in some items and the partial information possessed by examinees, they can usually do better than chance when forced to guess at items that they have omitted (Ebel, 1968; Jackson, 1955; Little & Creaser, 1966; Wiley, Collins, & Glass, 1970; Cureton, 1971; Wood, 1976, 1977; Cross & Frary, 1977). Consequently, even when the correction formula is used, the gambler usually obtains a higher score than an equally knowledgeable but more cautious person.

One study (Traub, Hambleton, & Singh, 1968) reported slightly better results obtained from using a positive rather than a negative correction approach. Even though the formulas yield scores that correlate 1.0, they appear to have different psychological effects on examinees. The following formula was used:

$$S = R + \frac{O}{A} ,$$

where S and R are defined as before, A is the number of alternatives (options) per item, and O is the number of omitted items. This procedure yields scores that lack the logical meaning of the usual procedure; for example, a person who omitted all 100 T–F items on a test would nevertheless receive a score of 50.

The consequences of correction formulas are not consistent across tests, although perhaps a majority of the studies show a negligible decrease in reliability (Glass & Wiley, 1964; Frary, Cross, & Lowry, 1977). The evidence on validity is also inconclusive, although the evidence slightly favors the corrected scores (Cureton, 1969; Lord, 1963; Sax and Collet, 1968; Lord, 1975; Cross & Frary, 1977).

It should be reemphasized that the correction formula is needed *only* when some students omit a fairly large number of items and others omit few. When this does not occur, the student ranking will be virtually unchanged whether or not the scores are corrected for "chance." For psychological reasons, the teacher may wish to return corrected scores to the students even though few items have been omitted. This may be especially advisable with two-option tests, since the poorest students may not realize the extent of their ignorance and may protest if they are given low grades on the basis of uncorrected test scores that to them seem to indicate considerable knowledge (Stanley, 1954). For example, 60 correct of 100 two-option items marked may represent only 20 percent knowledge of content, but the student may think that he or she knew 60 percent.

If every student tested answers every item, the standard deviation of

151

*Extraneous
Factors that
Influence
Performance on
Cognitive Tests*

scores corrected for chance is A/I times the standard deviation of the right scores. From this relationship it is apparent that correcting scores for a test with no omissions composed of two-option items will double their standard deviation:

$$\frac{A}{I} = \frac{2}{1} = 2. \qquad \text{(See Figure 6–1.)}$$

If there are no omissions, the standard deviation of corrected-for-chance five-option-item test scores is $\frac{5}{4} = 1.25$ times the standard deviation of the uncorrected scores. The correction formula with true-false and two- and three-option multiple-choice test scores more accurately emphasizes the range of knowledge within the group tested, even when omissions are negligible.

The Educational Testing Service uses the $R - W/4$ formula to obtain raw scores on the Preliminary Scholastic Aptitude Test (PSAT), Scholastic Aptitude Test (SAT), and Graduate Record Examination (GRE), which are all composed of five-option multiple-choice items. Theoretically, negative SAT scores can result if an examinee's "true" ability on the SAT is near 0; the score obtained may (if the examinee marks many items) depart by chance from 0 in either direction.

Most students grossly overestimate the role of chance on multiple-choice tests. Unless a test contains very few items, it is virtually impossible to receive a satisfactory score by chance alone. Suppose many students have *absolutely no knowledge* of the material on a 100-item test on which each item contains only two options (perhaps T–F). They choose one option for each item entirely by chance. The righthand distribution, curve 2 of Figure 6–1, shows various scores that would result. The average score is 50 out of 100 (i.e., 50%) correct by chance alone, because one-half of 100 is 50 (the mean chance score). The standard deviation of the scores is approximately 5. About two-thirds of the scores group themselves in a rather narrow (50 ± 5) range on both sides of this most likely score of 50. A score above 60 correct could be expected to occur by chance about as frequently as a score below 40 correct— for about 2 percent of the examinees' trials. For 98 students in 100 the scores will occur in the range of 40 to 60 correct answers, as shown. The most probable individual score is 50, which would be obtained by 8 percent of random guessers. There is less than one chance in 3 million that an examinee would select the correct answer on 75 or more of the 100 items by chance alone! Only about one examinee in 1,000 would score 65 or higher by chance alone.

Notice what happens to the range of chance scores when the correction-for-guessing formula (in this case $R - W$) is applied (curve 1). The most probable no-information score appropriately becomes 0. Also possible, though less probable, are scores lower than -20 or higher than $+20$; each of these has a probability of approximately .01 (1 in 100). Ninety-eight times in 100 the student's score will occur within the range of -23 to $+23$, with a most probable individual score of 0. The figure shows graphically two important results of applying the correction for guessing to chance scores even when no omissions occur: (1) The average chance score is reduced to 0, and (2) the variability of possible scores is increased. The standard deviation of the

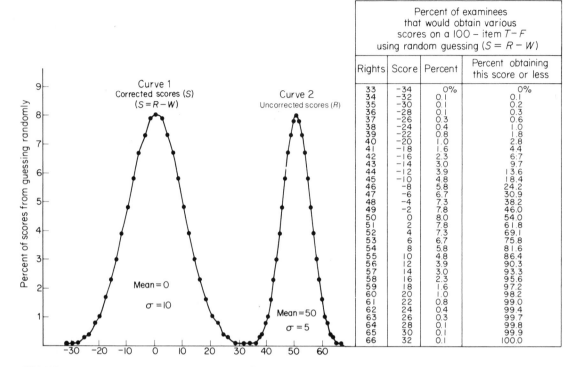

FIGURE 6-1 Frequency distributions of corrected-for-chance scores ($S = R - W$) (curve 1) and of number-right scores (curve 2) resulting from guessing answers to test of 100 two-choice items.

"number-right" distribution when there are no omissions is $\sigma = 5$. The standard deviation of a corrected-for-chance distribution is $(A/I)\sigma$ or, in this illustration, 2σ or 10.

Although guessing may produce variations among the scores, one should not pay serious attention to the beaming student who insists that she "guessed her way" to a high score on a long test (even on one composed of two-option items). The probability is great that she approached the items with considerable knowledge or test-wiseness, although she may not have been aware of it (unless the test was poorly constructed, in which case test-wiseness could be an important factor).

In summary, the correction for chance may have some slight advantage over "rights only" scoring. The correction is especially useful when tests are difficult or speeded, situations in which the speed-vs.-accuracy and gambling response sets are operative. However, as Mollenkopf (1960) suggested, it is only fair to inform the examinees that *such a correction is not a penalty* because, as we documented earlier, it usually undercorrects. As Cureton (1971) suggests, if an examinee has a hunch he or she should play it because hunches are right more frequently than chance. Of course, if an examinee is more *mis*informed than partially knowledgeable, his or her score may be unduly lowered by the correction. For example, a person who believes that

153

*Extraneous
Factors that
Influence
Performance on
Cognitive Tests*

separate is spelled *seperate* will choose that distracter deliberately but be penalized $-1/I$ points for "guessing."

Elimination Scoring and Answer-Until-Correct Procedures. Instead of having examinees select the correct or best answer, some investigators have directed examinees to eliminate all the incorrect options that they can (elimination scoring) or to continue selecting options until the correct alternative is selected (answer-until-correct or self-scoring). Several investigators (Collet, 1971; Gilman & Ferry, 1972; Hanna, 1975), but not all (Kane & Maloney, 1978), have found slight gains in reliability from these procedures. In spite of the gain in reliability, one study (Hanna, 1975) found that a decrease in validity accompanies their use. At present it appears that these procedures may not be worth the extra testing time and special answer forms required (Wood, 1977; Hakstian & Kansup, 1975).

Confidence Scoring. Another approach designed to remove the consequences of guessing (first proposed by Soderquist, 1936) asks students to indicate how certain they were of the correctness of their answers. Students received more credit for answers given with confidence than for those of which they were uncertain. The penalty for an incorrect response rated as highly confident was greater than for one rated as uncertain. Soderquist found that confidence scoring yielded slightly higher test reliability than conventional scoring. Interest in Soderquist's approach has been revived by several investigators who have also found higher test reliability with confidence scoring (Armstrong and Mooney, 1969; Ebel, 1965a; Michael, 1968a). The effects of confidence scoring on test validity are much less certain, although the available evidence is disappointing (Hopkins, Hakstian & Hopkins, 1973; Koehler, 1971, 1974; Hanna & Owens, 1973; Diamond, 1975; Hakstian & Kansup, 1975), especially when test length is defined in terms of testing time, not number of items (confidence weighting requires more testing time per item).

It seems likely that the increase in reliability that results from confidence scoring may be due to its encouraging a reliable response style of gambling or "bravado" (i.e., examinee rates choices with high confidence). Consequently, the procedure offers no clear advantages at present.[3]

Some Conclusions Regarding Response Sets

1. Response styles are reliable. They tend to show consistency from test to test and from item to item, which may allow their effects to contribute to increased test reliability even though validity may be decreased.
2. Knowledge of response sets can be used to improve teacher-constructed tests. For example, the tendency to use too many "true" items can be eliminated in order to increase test validity. Liberal or generous time limits can be estab-

[3] See Stanley and Wang (1970) and Wang and Stanley (1970) for a review of research on other scoring strategies.

lished to minimize effects from the speed-vs.-accuracy set. Special directions can reduce the role of the gambling set.

3. Response sets, if unchecked, can reduce the validity of test scores. An ability assessment should be as free as possible from personality factors.

Administrative Factors

A number of miscellaneous variables associated with the administration of a test have been explored.

Mode of Administration

Several studies have shown that tests administered via television (Burr, 1963; Curtis & Kropp, 1961; Fargo et al., 1967) or overhead projector (Schwarz, 1967) yield results comparable to those obtained on conventionally administered tests, provided that speed is not a factor and other conditions are held constant.[4]

Examiner

Masling (1959) found only slight effects of a hostile tester and a congenial tester on the results obtained from an individual adult intelligence test. Under certain conditions the sex or race of the examiner has resulted in some small differences (Abramson, 1969; Stevenson, 1961). The teacher can be a significant variable in the administration of standardized tests (Hopkins, Lefever, & Hopkins, 1967); when teachers administered standardized achievement tests, the grade equivalents of pupils averaged .2 years higher than when the test administration was controlled via TV. Goodwin (1966) also found that classes in which the teacher administered the test averaged .2 grade placements higher than when an outsider administered the tests.

To reduce possible contamination from administration error, some current tests offer recorded directions that control time and other relevant factors; these should reduce the effects of errors in test administration. In many instances the validity of scores on standardized tests has been reduced by errors in administration such as extending the time limits, giving nonstandardized directions about guessing, or even more flagrant deviations from the standard procedure.

Preannouncement

Little is known about the potential effects of informing students of a forthcoming *standardized* test. A study conducted in Japan showed that the an-

[4] Individualized or "tailored" testing such as Lord's (1971a,b) "flexilevel" testing, in which items of appropriate difficulty are matched with the ability level of the examinee, appears to have promise, especially for low-ability examinees who are continually faced with many guessing/omission decisions. Without computer-assisted testing, the logistic problems are considerable, however (Weiss, 1976; Wood, 1977).

155

*Extraneous
Factors that
Influence
Performance on
Cognitive Tests*

nouncement resulted in slightly higher scores (Hashimoto, 1959). Goodwin (1966), however, found no significant difference between groups that received a preannouncement and groups that did not. If the scores are to be interpreted unambiguously, the procedures that are used in obtaining test norms should also be followed when the tests are administered in the schools.

Answer Sheet Format

Although many test publishers give the user the option of marking in the test booklet or on a separate answer sheet, the separate answer sheets cause more difficulty on timed tests (Whitcomb, 1958), especially for younger and low-ability students (Clark, 1968; Muller, Calhoun, & Orling, 1972; Gaffney & Maguire, 1971; Beck, 1974). In several studies it has been found that college students perform equally well on the new 1230, 85, and mark-sense cards and answer sheets (Dizney, Merrifield & Davis, 1966; Hayward, 1967; Slater, 1964). Differences among three answer sheet formats (805, 1230, and Digitek) were found, however, for fourth-grade children, especially boys (Hayward, 1967).

Scoring

Unless examinees are given explicit directions and follow them carefully, substantial errors in machine-scored tests can result (Burack, 1961; Durost, 1954). Teacher scoring is likely to result in even more errors. Phillips and Weathers (1958) found that 28 percent of approximately 5,000 Stanford Achievement Tests scored by fifty-one teachers contained errors. The most frequent errors were incorrect counting of marks (45%) and failure to follow directions (26%). Goodwin (1966) did not find that clerks were significantly more accurate in test scoring than teachers. Whenever practical, tests should be machine scored, and they should be administered only after special directions about marking and erasures.

Disturbance

An interesting study (Super, Braasch & Shay, 1947) explored the effects of a combination of various disruptions on test performance. One random group of graduate students took a standardized intelligence test under normal conditions. While another random group took the same test, the following sequence of prearranged events occurred:

1. While marking the answer to the third question, one student deliberately broke her pencil point with a loud snap. She made a mild exclamation as she dropped the pencil, slid her chair back with a scraping noise, got up and walked ostentatiously to the examiner to get another pencil.
2. At the end of the fourth minute, two people walked down the stairs from the fourth floor; they were arguing loudly about a suggested ban of the Communist party. The discussion near the door lasted for about one minute. The examiner had placed himself on the far side of the room so that he would arrive at the door at about the time the two people were ready to walk away.

156

*Extraneous
Factors that
Influence
Performance on
Cognitive Tests*

3. At the end of ten minutes, a trumpeter played six bars of "Home Sweet Home," faltered, recovered, and then finished the melody. The trumpeter gave the impression that the melody was being played by a novice. The inclusion of musical distractions was not incongruent because music students used nearby rooms for practice.
4. At the beginning of the test, the examiner set the timer to ring at fifteen instead of twenty minutes. When the bell rang, the examiner picked up the timer, looked at it, looked at his stopwatch, and announced "Go on with the test."

Despite these irregularities, the disrupted group's mean score was not significantly lower than that of the control group. Similar findings with college students have been reported (Ingle & de Amino, 1969). It appears that younger examinees do not possess the powers of concentration necessary to maintain their best performance under such circumstances (Trentham, 1975).

Several factors, such as time of day, physical conditions (lighting, temperature, etc.) and number of tests per day, are essentially unexplored. The safest procedure for administering standardized tests it to approximate norming conditions as closely as possible (although often, unfortunately, many details concerning the norming procedure are not reported in test manuals). These administrative factors are much less important on teacher-made tests because norms are not involved.

Answer Changing

Perhaps the most widely disseminated finding "based on educational research" is that examinees tend to obtain higher scores if they stay with their first impression and do not change their answers. On the contrary, the research on this point speaks with one consistent voice: answer changes are much more often from "wrong" to "right" than from "right" to "wrong" for all types of examinees, bright or dull, test-wise or naive (Jacobs, 1972; Reiling & Taylor, 1972; Pippert, 1966; Copeland, 1972; Foote & Belinky, 1972; Ramos & Stern, 1973; Pascale, 1974; Lynch & Smith, 1975; Mueller & Shwedel, 1975; Mueller & Wasser, 1977; Smith & Moore, 1976). The "changed-answer myth" should be dispelled once and for all, and examinees should not stick with their first response when on second thought they prefer a different one. The net consequences from answer changing are usually very small (Mueller & Shwedel, 1975) but are consistent for both factual and more complex items (Smith, White & Coop, 1979).

Cheating

The heart is deceitful above all things. [Jeremiah 17:9]

Cheating on examinations is an extremely widespread and serious cause of test invalidity. During the civil service examinations in ancient China, tests were given in individual cubicles to prevent examinees from looking at the test papers of others (Brickman, 1961). Examinees were also searched for notes before they entered the cubicles. The death penalty was imposed on anyone found guilty of cheating. Contemporary attitudes toward cheating are much more tolerant; indeed, Cornehlsen (1965) found that among high school seniors more than one-third of the girls and more than one-half of the boys felt that cheating was justified when success or survival was in jeopardy. Even among graduate students, Zastrow (1970) found a 40% incidence of cheating.

The instructor or test administrator and the testing conditions have a great influence on the extent to which cheating will occur during an examination (Bushway & Nash, 1977). To protect the innocent, the conditions of test administration must be carefully and continually monitored. In an unpublished study, the authors found less cheating when examinees were required to sit in alternate seats. As might be expected, there is more cheating on unproctored tests (Steininger, Johnson & Kirts, 1964). Many people rationalize cheating behavior by appealing to Aristotle's *ad populum* fallacy (i.e., "Everybody's doing it so it must be OK"). Page (1963) found that candid discussion with students about the immorality of cheating and its effects on students affected their attitudes regarding cheating as well as the amount of cheating behavior in the class. Responsible test administration requires that the opportunities for cheating be reduced as much as possible through conscientious monitoring, seating arrangements, and test design.

Summary

Many irrelevant factors can influence test performance. Test-wiseness can be a factor; it is especially influential on poorly constructed tests and for examinees who are unfamiliar with objective tests. The practice effect is greatest on speeded tests; however, it seldom accounts for more than $.2\sigma$ improvement. Coaching produces small gains in performance (usually less than $.2\sigma$); larger gains may result if the examinee has not had recent contact with the test content. Most effects of practice and coaching are temporary; they dissipate after a few months.

The response styles of gambling and speed-vs.-accuracy can have a major effect on test scores, especially on speeded tests or very difficult tests. Response sets tend to be stable personality characteristics. The correction for chance can be useful when the nature of the correction is carefully explained. Administrative factors usually have only a minor influence on test performance. Standardized instructions and procedures must be followed explicitly if results are to be interpreted in terms of the published norms.

IMPORTANT TERMS AND CONCEPTS

maximum performance
typical performance
test sophistication

response styles
  speed-vs.-accuracy
  acquiescence
  positional preference

correction for guessing
confidence scoring
elimination scoring

1. Which of these factors that influence test performance is *not* classified as a response style or set?
  a) Practice
  b) A tendency to work quickly vs. carefully
  c) Guessing
  d) Acquiescence

2. Among these factors, which typically would be expected to influence
performance on a standardized cognitive test *least*?
  a) Test-wiseness
  b) Practice on a parallel form of the test
  c) The gambling response style
  d) The positional-preference response set

3. Which of these is *not* an example of test-wise behavior?
  a) Using the process of elimination in selecting correct answers
  b) Working carefully, double-checking each item before going on to
     the next item
  c) Guessing at all times even when the standard correction-for-
     chance formula is used
  d) Using specific determiners as clues to correct answers

4. Test–retest practice effects on cognitive tests are
  a) greater for inexperienced examinees.
  b) greater on power tests than on speeded tests.
  c) less when the time interval between the tests is short.
  d) Usually greater than $.2\sigma$.

5. The effects of coaching on cognitive test performance usually improves subsequent performance
  a) greatly ($.75\sigma$ or more).
  b) greatly ($.5-.75\sigma$).
  c) moderately ($.25-.5\sigma$).
  d) slightly ($.25\sigma$ or less).

6. The research on anxiety and test performance suggests that
  a) it depresses cognitive test performance.
  b) it enhances cognitive test performance.
  c) it is negatively correlated with cognitive test performance.
  d) its effects are greater on cognitive tests than on affective tests.
  e) More than one of the above

7. The validity of a cognitive test is usually reduced when
  a) it is given as a power test.
  b) test-taking speed is a significant factor in test performance.
  c) all students are allowed to attempt all items.
  d) the correction for chance is employed.
  e) More than one of the above

159

*Extraneous
Factors that
Influence
Performance on
Cognitive Tests*

I. M. Wise attempted only 80 of the 100 items on a true–false achievement test; 60 of his answers were correct.

8. What is his uncorrected raw score?

9. What is his corrected-for-chance score ($S = R - W$)?

10. If I. M. is a typical examinee and if he had attempted all 100 questions, his uncorrected raw score would probably be
   a) greater than 90.
   b) 90.
   c) 80.
   d) 70.

11. If I. M. had answered 10 of the 20 unattempted items correctly, and the other ten incorrectly, his corrected-for-chance score would have been ____.

12. On a five-option multiple-choice test, what is the appropriate form for the correction-for-chance formula?
   a) $S = R - W$
   b) $S = R - W/2$
   c) $S = R - W/3$
   d) $S = R - W/4$
   e) $S = R - W/5$

13. A test consists of 10 five-option multiple-choice items. If you answered all 10 correctly, what is your corrected-for-chance score?

14. On multiple-choice tests, the standard deviation for corrected-for-chance scores, S, compared to uncorrected scores, R, is
   a) greater.
   b) the same.
   c) less.

15. If no examinee omitted any items and if your score was at the 90th percentile in the uncorrected (R) distribution, in the corrected-for-chance (S) distribution
   a) your percentile rank would not change.
   b) the T-score of your performance would change.
   c) your percentile rank score would decrease.
   d) your percentile rank would increase.

16. Elimination scoring
   a) usually increases the test's computed reliability coefficient.
   b) usually increases the test's validity.
   c) Both of the above
   d) None of the above

17. Confidence scoring
   a) requires more testing time per item.
   b) tends to increase test's reliability coefficient.
   c) tends to increase the test's validity.
   d) Two of the above
   e) All of the above

18. Which of these is *not* true regarding the effects of response styles on test performance?

   a) They tend to decrease test reliability.

   b) They tend to decrease the validity of tests.

   c) They have greater influence on difficult tests.

   d) They have greater influence on speeded tests.

19. Very young examinees tend to achieve higher raw scores on a standardized achievement test if they

   a) mark in the test booklet.

   b) use a separate answer sheet.

   c) none of the above.

20. Disturbance during a standardized test is likely to affect the test scores of college students less than the scores of less experienced examinees (T or F).

ANSWERS TO CHAPTER TEST

1. a	8. 60	15. a
2. d	9. $S = 60 - 20 = 40$	16. a
3. b	10. d	17. d
4. a	11. $70 - 30 = 40$	18. a
5. d	12. d	19. a
6. c	13. 10	20. T
7. b	14. a	

FOR FURTHER READING

AMERICAN COLLEGE, THE. *Test wiseness: Test-taking skills for adults.* New York: McGraw-Hill, 1978.

ANASTASI, A. Social and ethical implications of testing. In *Psychological testing,* 4th ed. New York: Macmillan, 1976. Chap. 3.

CLEMANS, W. V. Test administration. In R. L. Thorndike, ed., *Educational measurement,* 2nd ed. Washington, D.C.: American Council on Education, 1971. Chap. 6.

COLLEGE ENTRANCE EXAMINATION BOARD. *Effects of coaching on Scholastic Aptitude Test scores.* New York, 1968.

CRONBACH, L. J. Response sets and test validity. *Educational and Psychological Measurement,* 6 (1946), 475–94.

——. Further evidence on response sets and test design. *Educational and Psychological Measurement,* 10 (1950), 3–31.

DIAMOND, J. J., and W. J. EVANS. The correction for guessing. *Review of Educational Research,* 43 (1973), 181–92.

FRENCH, J. W. Effect of anxiety on verbal and mathematical examination scores. *Educational and Psychological Measurement,* 22 (1963), 553–64.

FRENCH, J. W., and R. E. DEAR. Effect of coaching on an aptitude test. *Educational and Psychological Measurement,* 19, no. 3 (1959), 319–30.

HOPKINS, K. D. Extrinsic reliability: Estimating and attenuating variance from response styles, chance, and

161

*Extraneous
Factors that
Influence
Performance on
Cognitive Tests*

other irrelevant sources. *Educational and Psychological Measurement,* 24 (1964), 271–81. Reprinted in G. H. Bracht, K. D. Hopkins, and J. C. Stanley. *Perspectives in educational and psychological measurement.* Englewood Cliffs, N.J.: Prentice-Hall, 1972. Selection 10.

KREIT, L. H. The effects of test-taking practice on pupil test performance. *American Educational Research Journal,* 5 (1968), 616–25.

LYMAN, H. B. *How to take a test.* New York: McGraw-Hill, 1968. Tape recording (#75488, 21 minutes).

MILLMAN, J., C. H. BISHOP, and R. EBEL. An analysis of test-wiseness. *Educational and Psychological Measurement,* 25 (1965), 707–26.

MILLMAN, J., and W. PAUK. *How to take tests.* New York: McGraw-Hill, 1969. 176 pp.

NUNNALLY, J. C. Contingent variables. In *Psychometric theory,* 2nd ed. New York: McGraw-Hill, 1978. Chap. 16.

SARNACKI, R. E. An examination of test-wiseness in the cognitive test domain. *Review of Educational Research,* 49 (1979), 252–79.

II

THE
DEVELOPMENT
OF
EDUCATIONAL
MEASURES

7

General Principles of Construction: Achievement Measures

There are important reasons why instructors need to become proficient in constructing classroom tests. They must develop most of the tests they use. If developed by a teacher without special training, essay and objective tests are frequently of poor quality. The research on essay examinations has repeatedly demonstrated this fact. Novice test developers fare even more poorly with an objective test than with an essay examination; some objective tests have even lower reliability than most essay examinations (Stalnaker, 1951).

Research has shown that skillfully constructed achievement tests can be as precise as some standardized tests and are usually more valid for a more limited and carefully defined set of objectives and content. Standardized tests rarely assess the objectives of a particular unit of instruction. Standardized tests tend to (1) focus on broad, commonly accepted objectives and (2) cover a wide range of curricular content because they are usually designed to assess a full year or more of instruction. Frequent evaluation is necessary for teachers so that they can monitor the progress of individual children and of the class as a whole. Periodic testing provides a more reliable and valid evaluation of student progress (see Chapter 9). In this chapter we consider the general principles of constructing achievement tests designed to measure cognitive objectives.

Constructing a satisfactory test is one of a teacher's most challenging tasks. Good tests do not just happen. Indeed, most teacher-made tests are rather crude measures that are thrown together without much care and forethought. Test construction is in one sense more of an art than a science, but this "art form" can be dramatically improved with special instruction and systematic practice and feedback. There are well-established, proven principles of test development that are often unknown or ignored. Constructing a *good* test item is a deliberate process; it demands an understanding of the objectives and content being assessed, the reading and vocabulary level of the examinees, and test-taking factors such as response styles and test sophistication.

A good test must be planned; careful planning must precede its construction. One must consider the topics and objectives to be measured, the purpose the scores are to serve, and the conditions under which testing will occur. The following general guidelines should be followed in developing educational achievement tests:

1. The test should make provisions for evaluating the important objectives of instruction that are immediately measurable.
2. The test should reflect the content and process objectives in proportion to their importance and emphasis in the course.
3. The nature of the test should reflect its purpose (e.g., to assess individual differences or to certify mastery).
4. The test should be appropriate in length and readability level.

Instructional Objectives

Adequate provision should be made for evaluating the important cognitive outcomes of instruction that are immediately measurable.

In Figure 1-1 we illustrated the interrelationships among three aspects—objectives, instruction, and evaluation—in the total educational process. The objectives should give direction to the instructional methods and curricular content. Evaluation seeks to ascertain the degree to which the objectives have been attained, both collectively for the individual students and the class as a whole. The results of the evaluation thus provide feedback that may suggest modification of either the objectives or the instruction, or both. For example, for a group taking a communications skills course, Bird (1953) found no significant improvement in listening comprehension, which was one of the important objectives of the course. With careful assessment, a course's unfulfilled "promises" can be discovered. Perhaps the objectives are unrealistic; even so, the "unrealism" needs to be demonstrated. For example, many of the objectives of certain educational programs (e.g., bilingual and compensatory educational programs) appear unrealistic—there is a tendency to overstate the case (perhaps for political reasons) in order to marshal support for special programs. But without realistic objectives and fair evaluation of students' progress, special programs can lead to frustration and disillusionment.

Historically, objectives have been stated as broad, ultimate goals. One of the earliest statements of educational objectives is the Yale report of 1830, which emphasized the importance of exercising the mental functions of "reasoning," "imagination," "taste," and "memory" (Ammons, 1969). The "Seven Cardinal Principles of Secondary Education" from 1918 are generally accepted today: good health, command of fundamental processes, worthy home membership, vocational efficiency, good citizenship, worthy use of leisure time, and ethical character. The same can be said of the four objectives of education formulated in 1938 by the Educational Policies Commission (EPC) of the National Education Association: self-realization, human relationship, economic efficiency, and civic responsibility.

The Educational Policies Commission (1961) stresses "the central role of the rational powers" and devises its own categories:

> The cultivated powers of the free mind have always been basic in achieving freedom. The powers of the free mind are many. In addition to the rational powers, there are those which relate to the aesthetic, the moral, and the religious. There is a unique, central role for the rational powers of an individual, however, for upon them depends his ability to achieve his personal goals and to fulfill his obligations to society.
>
> These powers involve the processes of recalling and imagining, classifying and generalizing, comparing and evaluating, analyzing and synthesizing, and deducing and inferring. These processes enable one to apply logic and the available evidence to his ideas, attitudes, and actions, and to pursue better whatever goals he may have. [pp. 4, 5]

Specificity of Objectives. These ultimate educational objectives are obviously important but are not defined explicitly enough to give explicit direction to curriculum development. In addition, they cannot possibly be realized or assessed until long after formal education has been concluded. It is therefore necessary to establish intermediate instructional objectives that are logically derived from and related to these accepted ultimate objectives.

The most thorough, sensitive, and useful treatment of educational objectives is found in Clark (1972). Clark illustrates that from any "parent" objective many "offspring" objectives can be derived at various levels of specificity. (See Figure 7-1.)

Notice that in Figure 7-1 each objective is a subset of all the objectives appearing above it. During the past two decades or so, the emphasis on behavioral objectives in education has exerted strong pressure for expressing educational objectives at a greater level of specificity. But for an objective to be *truly* behavioral it must be stated at such a microscopic level that the number of objectives in any course or unit is overwhelming. In addition, objectives stated at a molecular level are dysfunctional in that they lose their value as general targets that help the teacher keep the instruction "on course." Neither very general nor highly atomistic objectives are very functional. Determining the proper level of specificity is difficult, and this is an issue on which there is wide disagreement.

Each school district should have a statement of its educational purposes. Instructional objectives for particular courses and curricular areas should be

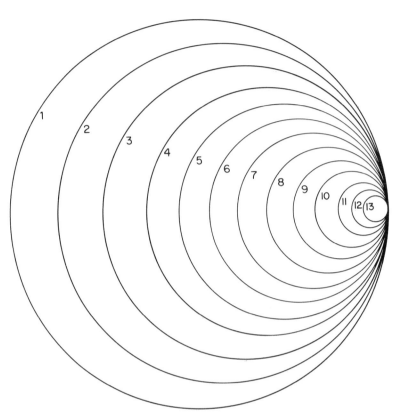

1. The student will be able to achieve personal goals and fulfill his or her obligations to society.

2. The student will be able to demonstrate functional literacy.

3. The student will be able to perform mathematical operations.

4. The student will be able to perform simple addition, subtraction, multiplication, and division operations.

5. The student will be able to perform simple addition operations.

6. The student will be able to add any two single-digit numbers.

7. The student will be able to add 3 and 2.

8. The student will be able to add 3 objects and 2 objects.

9. The student will be able to add 3 apples and 2 apples.

10. The student will be able to add 3 apples and 2 apples when words (not objects) are used.

11. The student will be able to add 3 apples and 2 apples when words are present in writing.

12. The student will be able to add 3 apples and 2 apples 90% of the time, when the problem is posed in written form.

13. The student will be able to add 3 apples and 2 apples 90% of the time when the problem is phrased, "If you had 3 apples and I gave you 2 more, how many would you have?"

FIGURE 7-1 A graphic illustration of the various levels of specificity in statements of educational objectives. (The authors are indebted to Cecil Clark for providing the basis for this example.)

available at each grade level. Most courses of study contain some statement of objectives, but to be helpful in teaching and testing, they cannot be sweeping generalities. The topics to be mastered or the expected *pupil behaviors* that exemplify the sought-after objectives must be stated. Such commonly offered objectives as "good citizenship," "an integrated personality," and "mathematical literacy" are not very helpful in giving direction to instruction or assessment. Instructional goals need to be stated in more precise and observable form to give direction to the important tasks of curriculum development and evaluation. A list of specific topic and concepts is often an implicit statement of objectives.

Teachers at all levels of education too often instruct and evaluate without giving careful thought to the educational objectives. The objectives are frequently undefined and vague (Ammons, 1969). Without critical, periodic reexamination, a course is likely to drift "off target." Boersma (1967) found that teachers who were systematically involved in applying evaluative criteria had a clearer perception of the curriculum. Bloom (1961) noted that when teachers participated in the construction of tests in a systematic way, not only were the objectives clarified, but also more relevant instruction was provided.

Armed with a clear and specific list of content and process objectives, a teacher can develop appropriate procedures for evaluating instruction, and the progress made toward the objectives.

A Taxonomy of Objectives. An important influence in providing a framework within which educational objectives could be organized and measured was the publication of *The Taxonomy of Educational Objectives,* (Bloom, Engelhart, Furst, Hill & Krathwohl, 1956). Instructional objectives are classified into three major "domains"—*cognitive, affective,* and *psychomotor.* Handbooks for the classification of the first two domains have been produced (Bloom et al., 1956; Krathwohl et al., 1964).

The cognitive domain includes those objectives that deal with the recall or recognition of learned material and the development of intellectual abilities and skills. The largest proportion of educational objectives fall into the cognitive domain (Krathwohl et al., 1964, p. 6). This domain is the core of most curriculum and test development. The clearest definitions of objectives for the cognitive domain are phrased as descriptions of desired student behavior, that is, in terms of knowledge, understanding, and abilities that can be demonstrated.

The affective domain includes objectives that emphasize interests, attitudes, and values, and the development of appreciations and adequate adjustment."Objectives in this domain are not stated very precisely; and, in fact, teachers do not appear to be very clear about the learning experiences which are appropriate to these objectives" (Bloom et al., 1956, p. 7). Chapter 11 deals with the evaluation of objectives in this domain. The psychomotor domain is concerned with physical, motor, or manipulative skills. Handwriting and many physical education objectives are examples of skills in the psychomotor domain.

The taxonomy of objectives in the cognitive domain has had a major impact on the development of educational curricula and on the methods by which they are assessed. The taxonomy categorizes behavior into six hierarchical categories from simple to complex, as illustrated in Figure 7–2. These six ascending levels are *knowledge, comprehension, application, analysis, synthesis,* and *evaluation.*

The rationale for the hierarchy is based on the assumption that each level is an extension of all previous levels. For example, attaining an objective in the *application* category requires (in theory, at least) that certain comprehension goals are achieved, which in turn can be achieved only if certain information in the knowledge category is acquired. *A rather sharp line is suggested in the taxonomy between "knowledge" and the five higher levels,* which involve "intellectual abilities and skills" in addition to knowledge. We will discuss and illustrate each of the six levels briefly.

knowledge-level items

Knowledge involves "the recall of specifics and universals, the recall of methods and procedures, or the recall of a pattern, structure, or setting. For measurement purposes, *the recall situation involves little more than bringing to mind the appropriate material.* . . . The knowledge objectives emphasize most the psychological processes of *remembering.* . . . To use an analogy, if one thinks of the mind as a file, the problem in a knowledge test situation is that of finding in the problem or task the signals, cues, and clues that will most effectively bring out whatever knowledge is filed or stored." People may

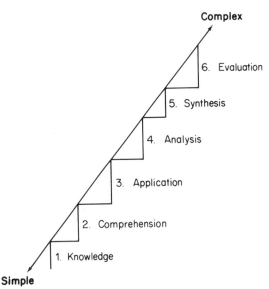

FIGURE 7–2 An illustration of the six hierarchical levels of Bloom's taxonomy. (Adapted from B. S. Bloom et al., 1956.)

have various kinds and levels of knowledge, from "knowledge of terminology," such as "familiarity with a large number of words in their common range of meanings," to "knowledge of theories and structures," such as "knowledge of a relatively complete formulation of the theory of evolution" (Bloom et al., 1956, pp. 201–4).

Examples of objectives within the knowledge category are the knowledge of specific facts, terminology, dates, persons. Below are two of many examples given by Bloom and colleagues (1956) and Hedges (1966) of test items designed to measure an objective in the knowledge category.

1. The Monroe Doctrine was announced about ten years after the
   a) Revolutionary War.
   *b) War of 1812.
   c) Civil War.
   d) Spanish-American War.

Answering this question requires no reasoning, only a simple knowledge of the date 1823 or knowledge that the event occurred after (b) but before (c).[1]

2. In physics, the term *acceleration* is defined as
   a) mass/force.
   *b) change in velocity/time.
   c) mass/velocity.
   d) distance/time.
   e) resistance/effort.

This item requires only a knowledge of acceleration in contradistinction to velocity. Here is another example (from Chapter 2):

3. Another name for the 50th percentile is
   a) the mean.
   *b) the median.
   c) the mode.
   d) the score that is equal to one-half the maximum score.

comprehension- and application-level items

Although it is basic and essential, knowledge is not sufficient for *comprehension*. Translation, interpretation, and extrapolation are common processes at this taxonomy level. Comprehension is evidenced by "the care and accuracy with which the communication is paraphrased or rendered from one language or form of communication to another." Some instructional objectives at the comprehension level are "the ability to understand non-literal statements (metaphors, symbolism, irony, exaggeration)"; "skill in translating mathematical verbal material into symbolic statements and vice versa"; "the ability to grasp the thought of the work as a whole at any desired level of generality"; and "skill in predicting continuation of trends" (Bloom et al., 1956, pp. 204–5).

---

[1] Additional examples of knowledge-level items (and higher-level items) can be found in Table 7–2 (p. 178) which classifies the items in the chapter test for Chapter 5.

Here are three examples of items from the comprehension level (pp. 100, 104):

1. Which of the following represents the *best* definition of the term "proto-plasm"?
   a) A complex colloidal system made up of water, proteins, and fats.
   b) Anything capable of growth by a regular progressive series of changes into a more complex unit.
   c) A complex mixture of proteins, fats, and carbohydrates, capable of responding to changes in its environment.
   *d) A complex colloidal system of proteins, fats, carbohydrates, inorganic salts, and enzymes which manifests life.

The exercise requires the examinee to judge the "best" of the four definitions which vary in correctness and completeness. Had three of the choices been totally incorrect, the item would be functioning only at the knowledge level of Bloom's taxonomy.

2. List all the verbs in the stem and options of item 1 above.

The examinee must comprehend what a verb is in order to identify *represents* as the only verb among the 70 words in item 1.

3. "Milton! thou shouldst be living at this hour: England hath need of thee; she is a fen of stagnant waters"—Wordsworth.
   The metaphor, "She is a fen of stagnant waters," indicates that Words-worth felt that England was
   a) largely swampy land.
   b) in a state of turmoil and unrest.
   *c) making no progress.
   d) in a generally corrupt condition.

The correct answer requires the *translation* of one verbal form into another.

If these questions were used directly in instruction, they would of course represent knowledge rather than comprehension objectives.

The third taxonomy level is *application,* which theoretically requires more than comprehension (knowing an abstraction well enough to use it correctly when required). Given an unfamiliar problem, the student must select and apply the appropriate abstraction. "The fact that most of what we learn is intended for application to problem situations in real life is an indication of the importance of application objectives in the curriculum." (Bloom et al., 1956, p. 122). It has been said that "transferability is the real test of educational attainment." The effectiveness of a large part of the school program is therefore dependent on how well the students' skills generalize to situations that the students never faced in the learning process.

Three illustrative objectives at the application level are "the ability to relate principles of civil liberties and civil rights to current events"; "the ability to apply the laws of trigonometry to practical situations"; and "the ability to apply Mendel's laws of inheritance to experimental findings on plant genetic problems.'' Two illustrative test items[2] at this level follow:

1. A candy bar was divided among three people. Lorrie had 1/3 of the bar, Gene had 1/2; what fraction of the bar was left for Ken? *a) 1/6, b) 1/2, c) 2/3, d) 5/6.

This item requires a greater degree of extrapolation and "transfer" from instruction than the related comprehension-level item: $1 - 1/3 - 1/2 = ?$

2. Below are four sentences expressing the same general thought. Mark the sentence which expresses the thought MOST EFFECTIVELY! a) She spoke to me in a very cool manner when we met each other yesterday. b) When we met yesterday, I was spoken to in a very cool manner by her. c) Her manner was very cool when meeting and speaking to me yesterday. *d) Yesterday she greeted me coolly.

The examples illustrate that the "parroting" of textbook definitions and the like is not sufficient to enable the student to select the correct answer to application questions offered in a fresh setting.

analysis, synthesis, and evaluation levels

Analysis is defined as "the breakdown of a communication into its constituent elements or parts such that the relative hierarchy of ideas is made clear and/or the relations between the ideas expressed are made explicit.'' Typical objectives at this level are "skill in distinguishing facts from hypotheses"; "ability to recognize unstated assumptions"; and "ability to recognize the point of view or bias of a writer in a historical account" (Bloom et al., 1956, pp. 146–48). Illustrative analysis items are the following:

1. Analyze the implicit philosophical presupposition in the statement, "If anything exists, it exists in some quantity, hence is measurable.''
2. In 300 words or less, write a summary of Chapter 5 ("Test Reliability").

Question 2 asks for a translation of information to a different level of generality. (For item 2 to be a true analysis item, the chapter summary could not be included in the book; otherwise, only a knowledge or comprehension level would be represented.)

Synthesis involves "the putting together of elements and parts to form a whole . . . not clearly there before." Sample instructional objectives at this level are "skill in writing, using an excellent organization of ideas and statements"; "ability to plan a unit of instruction for a particular teaching situation"; and "ability to formulate a theory of learning applicable to

---

[2] Items 1 and 2 were used in the 1976–77 California Assessment Program. Item 1 was answered correctly by 76% of twelfth-grade students and by 46% of sixth-grade students. More than 75% of the twelfth-graders also selected the best answer to item 2 (California State Department of Education, 1977).

classroom teaching" (Bloom et al., 1956, pp. 169–72). Examples of synthesis exercises follow (p. 179):

1. Add three lines to complete this verse:
   "I saw old autumn in the misty morn."
2. Write a position paper on closed-shop unionism. For example, should a steel-worker be required to join a union in order to be employed? Attend to the following facts in your answer . . .
3. Here are some general findings comparing babies who have colic and those who do not. Formulate a theoretical explanation and at least one testable hypothesis derived from the theory.

Evaluation includes "the making of judgments about the value, for some purpose, of ideas, works, solutions, methods, materials, etc." Examples of this, the highest level of cognitive ability in the taxonomy, are "the ability to indicate logical fallacies in arguments"; "the ability to evaluate health beliefs critically"; and "skills in recognizing and weighing values involved in alternative courses of action" (Bloom et al., 1956, pp. 189–92).

The taxonomy levels of analysis, synthesis, and evaluation have been of much less value for curriculum development and educational evaluation than the knowledge, comprehension, and application levels. There is nothing in the taxonomy per se to suggest that all good tests or evaluation measures will include items from every taxonomy level. The logic of the unitary underlying hierarchical continuum of complexity also is less compelling (Michael, 1968b) above the application level.

Research on the Taxonomy Hierarchy. Krathwohl and Payne (1971) summarized the available research on the taxonomy of the cognitive domain and concluded that the rationale has generally supported the differentiation of the knowledge level from the other levels, and to some extent the separation of the comprehension and application levels. However, support for the hierarchy of more complex categories—analysis, synthesis, and evaluation—has largely failed to develop (DeLansheere, 1977). Experience with the taxonomy has demonstrated that it is very difficult to reliably distinguish many application items from items in the higher levels. Several investigators (McGuire, 1963; Kropp, Stoker, & Bashaw, 1966; Stanley & Bolton, 1957) have reported that judges frequently disagree on the taxonomy level represented by items at levels other than the knowledge level. Among the higher categories, agreement is the exception rather than the rule (Poole, 1972; Fairbrother, 1975; Wood, 1977).

The principal contribution of the taxonomy has been its impact on the quality of educational measures. A teacher who has been exposed to the taxonomy, with illustrations of how higher mental processes can be measured (often objectively), can no longer be satisfied with a test that measures only rote learning of isolated facts. Much of the criticism of objective tests has arisen because many objective tests are of a very low quality and too often emphasize the knowledge level exclusively.

The *instructional value* that can result from examinations composed of items from the higher taxonomy levels was shown in a study by Hunkins

(1969). The experimental group was continually exposed to questions from the higher levels of the taxonomy during the course. The control group encountered fewer questions above the knowledge level during instruction. On the final examination, the experimental group performed significantly better on items that measured higher-level instructional objectives, yet did equally well on the knowledge-level questions.

For any course, a description of the particular content, principles, concepts, and skills of the course is needed. These concepts can usually be measured at the knowledge, comprehension, and/or application levels. The higher taxonomy levels more closely approach the broader educational objectives discussed earlier. In questioning students to see whether *comprehension* has actually occurred, teachers must try to avoid using both the wording of the textbook and that of earlier class discussion. Otherwise, the test may assess rote memory, not genuine understanding. Opportunities should be provided in the test to apply the concept to new problems and situations. The teacher must not confuse ends and means. Many years ago a leading psychometrician, E. F. Lindquist (1944, p. 366), stated this point well: "The real ends of instruction are the *lasting* concepts, attitudes, skills, abilities and habits of thought, and the improved judgment or sense of values acquired; the detailed materials of instruction—the specific factual content—are to a large extent only a means toward these ends."

Some curricular areas, such as mathematics, lend themselves to measurement at higher taxonomy levels (comprehension and above); in others, such as social studies, considerable ingenuity is often required to develop items at the comprehension and application levels.

Other Classifications. Bloom's taxonomy of the cognitive domain is not the only useful scheme available to us, though it is the most extensive attempt thus far. Ebel (1956) offered six ascending levels and attached to them "ideal" percentages for a good achievement test: content details, 0 percent; vocabulary, less than 20 percent; facts, less than 20 percent; generalizations, more than 10 percent; understanding, more than 10 percent; and applications, more than 10 percent. These percentages would usually vary from test to test and course to course.

Why bother to use a classification system in constructing an achievement test? The chief reasons are to ensure the measurement of the important cognitive objectives and to ensure that items represent higher (above the knowledge level) taxonomy levels that involve not only content but cognitive processing as well.

The "specifications" for the Mathematics section of the College Entrance Examination Board's Scholastic Aptitude Test illustrate a systematic approach to test construction. They consist of seven dimensions, each containing two to six classifications:

1. Content: (a) arithmetic or algebra, (b) geometry, (c) other
2. Context of presentation: (a) unusual, (b) familiar
3. Process for solution: (a) novel, (b) straightforward
4. Type of thinking: (a) computational, (b) numerical judgment, (c) relational thinking, (d) other

5. Characteristics of data: (a) adequate, (b) excessive, (c) insufficient
6. Form of presentation: (a) verbal, (b) tabular or graphic
7. Difficulty (six classifications from "easy" to "hard")

If just one question of each kind were used, there would be $3 \times 2 \times 2 \times 4 \times 3 \times 2 \times 6 = 1,728$ items on the test. Actually, the SAT quantitative test usually has less than 4 percent of that number, so only some kinds can be represented. For example, the committee might decide to include two questions dealing with geometry in an unusual context, requiring a straightforward process for solution, evoking a relational type of thinking, involving excess data, presented in graphic form, and classified as "easy."

How, according to the seven-point scheme just presented, would you classify the following item (Educational Testing Service, 1960, p. 47, problem no. 60)?

In which one of the following ways could 168 pencils be packaged for shipping?
(A) 11 boxes with 18 pencils in each
(B) 14 boxes with 12 pencils in each
(C) 17 boxes with 14 pencils in each
(D) 24 boxes with 12 pencils in each
(E) 28 boxes with 11 pencils in each

[The item represents category (a) in all classifications except 3, which represents category (b).]

One can readily see that there are many ways to classify and evaluate educational objectives and test items (Page & Breen, 1973); each has its advantages and disadvantages. A plan is needed, but more elaborate plans like that used for the SAT math test are usually too complex to be used extensively for classroom purposes. Perhaps a reasonable compromise between completeness and utility is to use a "table of specifications" (a topic–process grid) in which the major content topics (rows) are cross-classified by two (or three) taxonomy levels. Figure 4–1 (p. 78) contains a table of specifications for a standardized science test. Note the percentages of items for each content and process stratum given below the grid. Table 7–1 illustrates specifications for an examination in this course covering Chapters 1–5.

Another example is provided in Table 7–2, which corresponds to the chapter test (p. 178) for the chapter on test reliability. Notice that more items are needed for more complex and more important topics. Note that topics are defined at a finer level of specificity than they are in Table 7–1. Note also that the "fuzzy" distinction between comprehension and application levels was not attempted on this test.

Content and Process Objectives

The test should reflect the content and process objectives in proportion to their importance in the course.

A table of specifications ensures that the test has a proper balance of emphases; this will guide the test developer as blueprints and specifications guide the building contractor. It is valuable to indicate not only the various

TABLE 7-1

AN ILLUSTRATION OF TABLE OF SPECIFICATIONS OR A CONTENT-PROCESS GRID REPRESENTING THE TEST DESIGN FOR AN ACHIEVEMENT TEST COVERING CHAPTERS 1–5 OF THIS BOOK

Major Content Strata	Taxonomy Level			
	Knowledge	Comprehension	Application, Synthesis, etc.	Total
1. The functions of measurement in education	3	2	0	5 (10%)
2. Basic statistical concepts, central tendency and variability	1	2	2	5 (10%)
3. Norms: types, meaning, interpretation	3	3	4	10 (20%)
4. Validity: content, construction, criterion-related validity and correlation	4	6	5	15 (30%)
5. Reliability: concepts, theory and methods of estimation	4	7	4	15 (30%)
Totals	15 (30%)	20 (40%)	15 (30%)	50

objectives in mind but also, at least roughly, the relative amount of emphasis on each objective. The test should be a faithful mirror of the instructional objectives. The amount of time devoted to the different phases of the course is usually a rough indication of their relative importance. The content of the test should show similar proportions. The time devoted to a topic can indicate only the *proportion* of test items to be included and not the *type* of item (e.g., essay, multiple-choice, or matching). The type of item will depend on the nature of the content or objective to be measured. The empty cells in Table 7–2 (see strata 2) are not unexpected—certain objectives, by their very nature, may fall exclusively into the knowledge category.

Working from a list of instructional objectives or a topic outline (an implicit representation of objectives), each objective or topic should be weighted in percentage units according to its importance. This is to ensure that the test content does not overemphasize certain content strata at the expense of others. At times, one will wish to have an equal number of items from each chapter or section of a curriculum guide. At other times, certain areas will deserve more emphasis than others, as in Table 7–1, where the reliability and validity chapters are more heavily weighted because of their greater importance.

When objectives have been stated at a high level of specificity, there may not be time to assess each specific objective. For example, notice that there are 41 items in Table 7–2, which deals with a test covering only one chapter. Ob-

TABLE 7-2

A TABLE OF SPECIFICATIONS FOR CHAPTER TEST (P. 136) ON CHAPTER 5, "TEST RELIABILITY" (NUMERALS IN PARENTHESIS REFER TO SPECIFIC ITEMS ON THE TEST)

Content Strata (Objectives/Topics)	Taxonomy Level		
	Knowledge	Higher	Total
1. Interrelationships between reliability and validity	2 (1, 2)	2 (3, 4)	4 (10%)
2. Knowledge of reliability "vocabulary"	2 (5, 14)	0	2 (5%)
3. Interrelationships among s, s_e, r_{XX}	1 (39)	4 (6, 4, 20, 40, 41)	5 (12%)
Understanding of reliability concepts: 3. Universe scores	0	2 (7, 23)	2 (5%)
4. Standard error of measurement	1 (22)	5 (8–11, 38)	6 (15%)
5. Reliability index and coefficient	1 (13)	2 (15, 16)	3 (7%)
6. Estimating true scores, regression toward mean	0	3 (18, 19, 21)	3 (7%)
7. Effect of length, Spearman-Brown	1 (27)	1 (17)	2 (5%)
8. Split-half	1 (30)	1 (12)	2 (5%)
9. Parallel form, test–retest	2 (24, 25)	0	2 (5%)
10. Internal-consistency (r_{KR} and r_α)	2 (32, 33)	4 (34–37)	6 (15%)
Totals	14 (34%)	27 (66%)	41

viously, it will not be possible to give a midterm test on Chapters 1–5 at the same level of specificity: 5 × 40 = 200 items are not practicable for a single test. Nevertheless, all "parent" or broad objectives need to be represented. If you turn to the table of contents, you will find a topic outline within each of the first five chapters. But several more detailed offspring objectives could be generated from each topic. Ideally, we would like to have at least one question per objective at the knowledge and higher taxonomy levels. The testing time would be insufficient to do this (one should allow about one minute per item for items above the knowledge level). One might be able to include at least one question per topic for those that represent only information (knowledge level), and additional items above the knowledge level, for the more important concepts. Of course, tests on individual chapters could map the content universe more closely, as indicated in Table 7-2. Frequent testing covering smaller content strata is highly desirable and recommended for situations in which classes meet daily. But examinations at the college level with more mature examinees often can and must span larger units of instruction.

It is of fundamental importance to view test items as a sample from the content universe.

The reliability index and/or the standard error of measurement will indicate how adequately the content universe has been sampled, not objective by objective or topic by topic, but overall. Evaluating how adequately each student has achieved highly detailed behavioral objectives usually is not feasible—there simply isn't enough time. It may seem paradoxical, but nevertheless is true, that a test may yield obtained scores that are very good estimates of universe or true scores, yet at the same time may not be adequate for diagnostic purposes, that is for indicating whether or not individual students have achieved specific objectives on which the test is based.

An analogy may help clarify this principle. A test given to a nationally representative sample of 1,000 students in grade 6 can estimate with extreme precision the mean score on that test for the entire population of 4 million sixth-graders. The results on the 1,000 students can be generalized to the 4 million students with very little error. However, just because we have a precise estimate of the national average, it does not follow that we then have highly accurate results for subdivisions of the nation, such as states. The state averages in the larger states such as California and New York, which would each be based on approximately 100 individuals, would be reasonably accurate estimates; but several states have less than 1% of the nation's population—obviously, a random sample of 10 students in a given state does not provide a very precise estimate of that state's average score on the test. It is clearly absurd to subdivide the data into even narrower strata and estimate school district averages on the basis of 1 or 2 students.

This situation is an exact parallel to breaking down the total test score into detailed strata, each based on very few items. Total obtained scores may be accurate estimates of universe scores, but subtest (part) scores will be accurate to the extent that they are based on several items. A single item simply is not adequate to represent a higher-level objective. *At the very most,* the test described in Table 7–1 would yield only five meaningful scores per examinee, one for each broad content stratum, and even then the estimates of universe scores on content strata 1 and 2 (Chapters 1 and 2) will be crude, since each is based on only five items. (Class averages, however, can be meaningful even on individual items since several observations are involved, hence chance and other extraneous factors have an opportunity to be balanced out.)

Suppose the test described in Table 7–1 is very well constructed and yields the following results: $\overline{X}$ = 80%, s = 10%, r_{XX} = .80. Assuming that the scores are used to evaluate individual student performance on each content stratum (broad objective) and that the group's performance is uniform across the five strata, what will be the degree of measurement precision (how closely will observed percent scores estimate the corresponding universe percent scores)? The Spearman-Brown formula can be used to estimate the reliability of each of the five content strata (subtests):

$$r'_{XX} = \frac{Lr_{XX}}{1 + (L - 1)r_{XX}},$$

where $L = 5/50 = .1$ for content strata 1 and 2, $L = .2$ for stratum 3, and $L = .3$ for strata 4 and 5.

We find that r'_{XX_1} and r'_{XX_2} (reliability coefficients for strata 1 and 2) would be approximately .29; r'_{XX_3} approximately .44, and r'_{XX_4} and r'_{XX_5} approximately .55. We can also estimate the corresponding standard errors of measurement for the five strata (subtests) using the formula $s_e = s\sqrt{1 - r_{XX}}$. Although s_e for the total test is only 4.5% ($s_e = 10\sqrt{1 - .80} = 4.5$), s_{e_1} and s_{e_2} are 8.4%, s_{e_3} is 7.4%, and s_{e_4} and s_{e_5} are 6.7%. Breaking down the level of reporting further into even smaller units (as in Table 7–2) would, of course, make the extrapolation from observed scores to universe scores much cruder.

Diagnostic Testing

The example above illustrates the very complex problem of diagnostic testing. By its very nature, diagnostic testing must break down a content domain into fairly specific strata. Figure 7–3 (after Clark, 1972) illustrates how reading skill can be broken down into "parent" and "offspring" strata and substrata. Several items at each substrata are needed to compare performance among substrata. One might have a good general (survey) reading test with 50 or 60 items, but a diagnostic test based on Figure 7–3 would require 160 items even if there were only five items per each substratum (of course, a diagnostic test might be limited to a subset of the skills indicated in Figure 7–3). Notice in Figure 4–2 (p. 80) that the number of items per objective (below "slash" mark in each cell is usually one or two items for the "survey" test, but usually three for the "instructional" [more nearly diagnostic] tests.) Notice also that the greater the level of specificity at which the objectives are stated, the greater the number of items required to measure each objective.

For educational purposes it is important to emphasize that test data are only one component in student evaluation. Good teachers are continually observing, evaluating, and assessing by informal means the degree to which the class and individual students are achieving instructional objectives.[3]

The Nature of the Test

The nature of the test should reflect its purpose. If the purpose of the test is to provide a basis for grouping or selection, it should rank the pupils in order of overall achievement level. But if its purpose is diagnostic or "criterion referenced," it must be designed to reveal specific weaknesses in individual achievement. Diagnostic tests tend to cover a limited content domain, but in much greater detail than survey achievement tests; they are designed to yield scores on several separate parts. The range of item difficulty and the discrimination indexes of the items are relatively less important in diagnostic

---

[3] It is important to distinguish between individual and class assessment. Performance on a single item is based on a single response when $n = 1$ (individual assessment) but on perhaps 25 responses when class assessment is involved. Class assessment involves item analysis techniques treated in chapter 10.

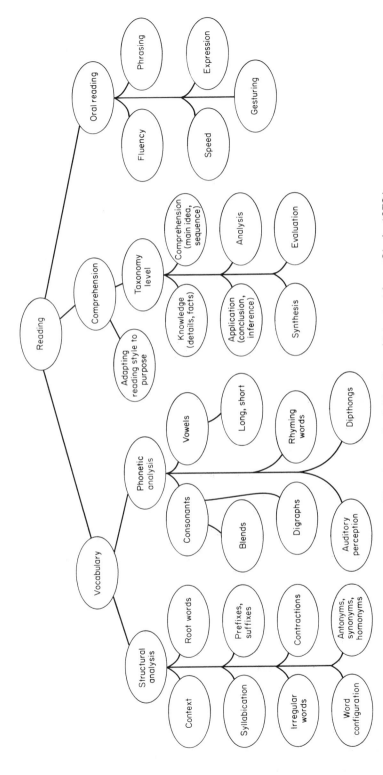

FIGURE 7-3 An example of parent and offspring topics/objectives. (Adapted from Clark, 1972.)

tests. This is also true of mastery, criterion-referenced, and minimum-competency tests—diagnostic tests administered to determine whether certain minimum standards of performance have been achieved.

Criterion-Referenced Testing

In recent years there has been renewed interest in the concept of minimum competency, mastery, and criterion-referenced tests (CRT), that is, measuring instruments constructed to yield measures that are directly interpretable in terms of "prespecified performance criteria" (Glaser & Nitko, 1971; Glaser, 1963; Mayo, 1970; Popham & Husek, 1969). These tests are given to identify individuals who have, or have not, acquired certain basal competencies. Differential consequences for instruction, such as remediation, may result. The rationale underlying most computer-assisted instruction, programmed instruction, and behavioral-objectives–oriented approaches to education is based largely on CRT.

Is criterion-referenced testing a new concept? "It could be argued that teachers have always employed implicit, but nonetheless criterion-referenced, standards in their evaluations of pupils" (Tyler & Wolf, 1974, p. 77).

What Is Mastery? The Problem of Setting a Criterion. There are a few competencies for which complete mastery is possible; for example, everyone should *know* the multiplication table through 10 × 10 perfectly. Perhaps everyone should be able to identify the major parts of speech of a simple sentence and to write legibly, know the laws pertaining to motor vehicles, tell time, be able to tie shoes, and so on. It is possible on logical grounds to set absolute standards for performance in these areas, for example, to assess whether an examinee has reached the particular level of performance required by the criterion. But is a criterion for mastery of 100% realistic? Do you ever make thoughtless mistakes like 8 × 7 = 42? Are 100% of the words you write legible to others? Do you know all the motor vehicle laws? Do your shoes ever come untied? Even though a 100% criterion is logically defensible, in practice the criterion is usually lower, such as 80%. But why not 90% or 95%? This arbitrariness coupled with the arbitrariness in a test's difficulty are impediments to the CRT and mastery learning strategies (Shepard, 1980). Note that the examples almost always represent training or knowledge-level objectives; standards are much more difficult to establish at the higher taxonomy levels, which represent more important educational objectives such as reading comprehension or arithmetic problem solving. In some contexts these standards can be established on definitive empirical grounds. We discussed earlier the General Educational Development (GED) tests, which use the actual achievement of high school graduates to establish the minimum *standard* that must be reached for one to obtain the GED high school equivalency certificate. The same principle is used on the advanced-placement tests administered by the Educational Testing Service to many high school seniors, and accepted in lieu of certain courses at many colleges and universities.

Norm-Referenced vs. Criterion-Referenced Testing. Individual differences are the major emphasis of norm-referenced testing (NRT); but they are of no concern in mastery or criterion-referenced testing (CRT)—if everyone scores 100% on the test, so much the better. CRT assessment should reveal what competencies students do and do not possess, not how one student compares with norms or peers (NRT). A succinct illustration of this distinction is percentile (NRT) versus percentage (CRT) scores. The percentage grades that were used almost universally in schools and colleges until about 1920 represent a primitive type of CRT. Most standardized tests represent NRT. There has been much heated controversy on the pros and cons of CRT and NRT (Ebel, 1972, 1978; Popham, 1978, Glass, 1978, Shepard, 1979b, 1979c, 1980).

NRT Misapplied

The CRT movement is in part a reaction to the misuse of psychometric methods (especially reliability theory) which were developed for assessing aptitudes and abilities. In measuring aptitudes, the intent is to maximize discrimination (individual differences) among the examinees; the greater the discrimination (variance), the greater the reliability.

In the past, *inadequate attention was given to the standard error of measurement* (σ_e) *as an indicator of measurement precision for achievement tests.* NRT-oriented persons were often inordinately interested in achievement tests with high reliability coefficients. Items were eliminated or retained for future use solely on the basis of their discrimination and difficulty. Since items that are answered correctly (or incorrectly) by a large percent of the examinees tend to have lower discrimination indexes, they were often eliminated solely on these grounds. If the standard error of measurement of percentage scores[4] (i.e., $\sigma_{e\%}$) had been used as the primary indication of measurement, this abuse might have been reduced. In other words, many achievement test developers lost sight of content validity—that the *items must first and foremost be representative of the domain (content) and process objectives to be assessed.*

Certainly, when there is a difference (and there almost always is), we want to be able to differentiate between individuals who have more nearly mastered the content universe from those who have less understanding of it. But *discrimination*[5] *per se is not a purpose of teacher-made achievement testing.* As illustrated in Chapter 5, theoretically a test may have a small σ_e

---

[4] Perhaps one reason σ_e has not been used more was the failure to use percent scores in reporting test results. If raw scores are used, σ_e increases as test length is increased, even though reliability increases. But if scores are expressed as percents, $\sigma_{e\%}$ decreases as test length increases. Percentage score reporting was prematurely abandoned as an unfortunate and unnecessary side effect of the norm-referenced testing movement (Buros, 1977).

[5] If an item is marked correctly more often by pupils with high total scores on a test than by pupils with low total scores, we say that the item discriminates between high scorers and low scorers, or simply that it has discriminating value or power. See Chapter 10 for a treatment of item analysis.

even if it has zero reliability (e.g., if $r_{XX} = 0$, and $s = 5$, then $s_{e\%} = s\sqrt{1 - r_{XX}} = 5\%$). Although a large variance among scores should not be, in and of itself, a goal of classroom achievement testing, *individual differences are a fact of life, especially whenever we are dealing with concepts* rather than with training or knowledge-level objectives. We can be delighted when all first-graders can tie their shoes (and have them remain tied for the entire school day)—all students achieve the objective and individual differences are minimal. But when we are concerned with higher-level cognitive or psychomotor competencies, such as written and oral expression, reading comprehension, arithmetic problem solving, or typing speed, there is no meaningful 100% mastery point. Who has 100% reading comprehension? If test scores suggest uniformity among unselected students in areas like written expression and reading comprehension, the progress of the more able is either being neglected or (more likely) the measuring instrument is like a high-jump stand that only goes up to 3 feet—individual differences beyond that point are there but are ignored because the measurement emphasis is geared to a primitive level of mastery (Shepard, 1980).

Several serious problems limit the utility of criterion-referenced tests in most curricular areas. Rarely is there a definitive logical basis for establishing the performance criterion standard. The standard of 70 percent for a passing grade that was common early in this century has been discarded as completely arbitary by thoughtful instructors. Even when a table of specifications is used, it is a simple task to write two sets of items on identical content strata or objectives, one set being composed of very easy items and another of very difficult items. A score of 70 percent on the easy test may reflect extremely poor achievement, whereas on the difficult items a 70 percent score may represent superior mastery. Consider the following two items, both designed to measure a sixth-grade science objective.

1. Dark colors absorb heat faster than lighter colors. (True or False)
2. Suppose we have two identical balloons except that one is white and one is black. Both are filled with the same amount of air and are tied so that no air can get in or out. What will happen if both balloons are put in direct sunlight?
   *(a) The black balloon will become larger than the white balloon.
   (b) The white balloon will become larger than the black balloon.
   (c) Both balloons will get smaller.
   (d) Both balloons will stay the same size.
   (e) Both balloons will burst.

Both items are designed to measure the same concept, yet item 2 requires much greater understanding than item 1. Item 2 is in the application taxonomy level, whereas item 1 is only a knowledge-level question. Obviously, such criteria for mastery as 90 percent of the items on the criterion test are arbitrary, since item difficulty is arbitrary.

As another illustration, consider the following two questions, which are designed to measure the concept of reliability.

1. If scores on two forms of a test correlate .00, what is the test's reliability coefficient? a) 1.0, b) .5, *c) 0.0, d) −.5, e) −1.0.

2. Other things being equal, which one of the following will *not* tend to increase the estimate of the reliability coefficient of a test?
   (a) Increasing the test's standard deviation
   (b) Increasing the correlation among items
   *(c) Increasing the number of examinees
   (d) Using the split-half rather than the parallel-form method of estimation
   (e) Giving the test to a more heterogeneous group

This example is deliberately exaggerated to make the following point: Many examinees would correctly answer the first question that measures the concept of reliability; but many of you probably would not, at this point, be able to select the correct answer to the second question, which is also designed to measure the concept of reliability.

What is mastery? How does one logically establish an absolute standard or criterion of mastery? How does one justify a criterion of, say, 80 percent as the cutoff score for mastery of some concept or domain? When does one have a proper understanding? How does one establish a minimum level of competence in reading, spelling, speaking, writing, listening, or even test construction or interpretation?[6] When concepts are involved, we are usually in a continual state of growth in understanding and never "arrive" at total mastery. Anderson (1970) showed that even the phrasing and format of the items employed in the measurement of a given concept can influence the examinee's performance. Thus, although the concept of mastery testing or criterion-referenced testing has strong logical appeal, at least initially, its practicability for most educational purposes is greatly restricted because of the unavailability of definitive means of establishing performance standards.

An even more dramatic illustration of the problem is given by Glass (1978). A grade 7 state assessment found an average of 86% on a "vertical" addition problem, but an average of only 46% when the same problem was presented with the numbers arranged horizontally! Other studies (Dudycha & Carpenter, 1973; Choppin, 1974) have also found that the difficulty of items can be altered considerably by logically irrelevant format changes.

CRT has considerably more relevance when training and knowledge objectives are involved, in areas such as developmental tasks, driver training, and industrial arts, in which a minimal level of satisfactory performance can often be established on logical or empirical grounds.

Ebel (1970b) has pointed out that the rationale for criterion-referenced testing is not new (Thorndike, 1918, p. 18; see Airasian and Madaus, 1972); CRT is a combination of more carefully defined objectives used together with prespecified performance standards. More than a century ago Chadwick (1864) described a "scale book" prepared by the Reverend George Fisher "which contains the numbers assigned to each degree of proficiency in various

---

[6] One large federally funded ($350,000 per year) experimental educational program with which the authors are familiar set a prespecified criterion performance standard of 80% correct on a CRT to denote the point at which the curricular objectives would be said to have been achieved. After year 1, when most pupils failed to achieve the desired criterion, it was "readjusted" to 60%; thus, after year 2 it was concluded that 83% of the students achieved the curricular objectives of the project. Obviously, such meaningless "bootstrapping" is not an appropriate use of CRT, but it does illustrate the problem of an arbitrary criterion.

subjects of examinations." That system was abandoned because examinees' scores were a function of two rather arbitrary factors—whether the test was easy or difficult, and the generosity (or lack of it) of the scorer.

Obviously, a criterion for mastery lacks credibility if it cannot be based on strong logical or empirical grounds. A criterion is more meaningful if it is empirically based; criterion-referenced tests should be used when a nonarbitrary criterion is available, as with the GED and CEEB advanced-placement tests, or perhaps in a carefully developed instructional program in which a performance criterion (e.g., 90%) has been shown empirically to be necessary in order to progress sequentially through the program in a satisfactory manner. Most classroom testing, however, should not only be geared to determining whether students meet the minimum, basal levels of achievement, but also should assess the individual differences that inevitably are present among the students. CRT should not result in an inordinate preoccupation with slow learners at the expense of average and above-average learners (Shepard, 1976; Madaus, 1979).

The arbitrariness of the criterion in CRT has caused many people to abandon the notion of a meaningful prespecified criterion for mastery[7] and to use instead more appropriate descriptions such as "domain-referenced tests" (Millman, 1974) or "objective-reference tests." But all good achievement tests should be based on either explicit or implicit objectives or topics in a table of specifications. Except for the prespecified performance standard in CRT and minimum competency tests, the distinction between them and *appropriately* developed diagnostic tests (or even many survey and teacher-made achievement tests) is not clear-cut. As Wood (1977, p. 262) observed, "In practice the differences between these kinds of tests may be more apparent than real." In practice domain-referenced and diagnostic tests are more likely to have been developed around a set of stated objectives or table of specifications so that the item content is a better representation of the content universe. But this is just practicing good test development procedures. NRT and CRT do differ in the method of reporting results; CRT is apt to employ "percent correct" scores, whereas NRT often employs percentiles or standard scores. However, reporting both percent scores and standard scores for classroom tests is more informative than either alone. There has not been enough emphasis on items above the knowledge level in the cognitive taxonomy in all types of classroom achievement tests.

Minimum Competency Testing

In recent years there has been much controversy about minimum competency testing (MCT). MCT is a special application of the rationale underlying CRT and mastery testing. Students in more than 30 states are now legally obliged to

---

[7] It has been recently suggested (Hambleton, 1978; Popham, 1978) that CRT had been misunderstood and that only a domain of behavior, not a minimum proficiency or performance standard, was implied by CRT proponents. That a prespecified performance criterion *was* suggested is obvious from Glaser and Nitko (1971, p. 647) and Popham and Husek (1969, p. 2). "Criterion-referenced measures are those which are used to ascertain an individual's status with respect to some criterion, i.e., performance standard."

demonstrate "minimum competency" in order to receive a high school diploma.[8] The impetus for MCT came largely from the continuing stream of studies that suggest a decline in academic achievement during the past decade or two. Minimum competency is not new: It was tried in Britain more than a century ago and abandoned after twenty years (Glass, 1978b).

MCT has all the difficulties of CRT in specifying a meaningful criterion. In addition, the consequences to the examinee of failing to achieve the criterion are often quite significant. But exactly what is minimum competency? Competency in what? For what purpose? The minimum competencies for a lumberjack are far different from those for a clerk. The MCT notion is very appealing until one begins to confront the difficulties of implementation.

In MCT "survival" skills are often emphasized. But what seems essential apparently is not always so. Consider the two sample items used in the National Assessment of Educational Progress. (See Figure 7-4.) Defining survival skills is no less difficult than defining minimum competencies (Shepard, 1976). As Burton (1978) has observed, "No single skill is so essential that it can be defined as necessary for survival" (p. 271). If minimum competency standards are to be employed, they should be based on normative data, not arbitrary judgments (Burton, 1978; Glass, 1978; Shepard, 1976). In Florida, for example, it was decided that a score of 70% was required for passing a MCT, causing nearly 40% of the students to fail. Why 70%? Why not 80%, 90%, or 95%? (See Glass, 1978; *Time,* 1979.)

The GED tests and the California High School Proficiency Examination (CHSPE), which allows 16- or 17-year-old students who pass to leave school immediately, are based on the normative approach to setting minimal standards—on the CHSPE, students must achieve the median of second-semester seniors (Abramowitz and Law, 1978). Normative criteria are much less hazardous than arbitrary standards.

Preparing the Test

The following suggestions are helpful in the actual preparation of the test. Many of these suggestions are amplified and illustrated in Chapters 8 and 9.

1. Prepare a preliminary draft of the test based on the table of specifications. In this way important points and topics are less likely to be overlooked or underemphasized on the test. Experienced teachers often develop large item pools that can be of great value when used properly. Increasingly test items are accompanying curricular materials, allowing the instructor to select some portion of the items for the test. This can be particularly helpful since developing comprehension and application items is very time-consuming.

2. It is usually desirable to include more items in the first draft of the

---

[8] A bill was recently introduced in Colorado that requires school districts to "develop and administer to all pupils in a district, a comprehensive educational examination as a prerequisite for advancement from one grade level to the next."

A new automobile can be bought for cash for $2,850 or on credit with a down payment of $400 and $80 a month for three years. How much MORE would a person pay by buying on credit rather than by buying the car for cash?

ANSWER

This math exercise was administered in 1973 to 17-year-olds and adults. The correct response is "$430." 56% at age 17 and 68% of the adults answered correctly.

Below is a sample application blank. Ones like it are used to get information from people who are applying for driver's licenses, credit cards, passports and other identification cards. Fill out the application below. Do not use your own name. For this application blank, each male should call himself Adam Baker Carson. Each female should call herself Alice Baker Carson. Make up the rest of the information. Be sure to fill in the entire form.

Please PRINT the information requested below

1. _____
   last name   first   middle initial

2. _____
          street address

3. _____
  city or town   county   state   zip code

4. DATE OF BIRTH: _____ 5. SEX: _____
        month day year M or F

6. HT: _____ WT: _____ HAIR: _____ EYES: _____

TODAY'S DATE: _____

This writing exercise was administered in 1969 to ages 9, 13, 17 and adults. To be considered acceptable, all lines had to be filled in and at least the first three had to be printed. 12% at age 9, 26% at age 13, 61% at age 17 and 50% of the adults were able to do this.

FIGURE 7-4 Sample item to measure writing and math skills from National Assessment Exercises (from NAEP, 1976).

test than will be needed in the final form. This permits a later culling of the items that appear weak or are not needed to provide proper balance. For each section of the test, 25% or so more items should be prepared than are likely to be required.

3. After some time has elapsed, the test should be critically reviewed. The items should be checked with the original outline to see that the test places the desired amount of emphasis on the various topics. A careful reading of the

test at this time will usually reveal some ambiguities and objectionable items. It is wise to have the test reviewed by another teacher of the same subject; that person may discover some test items of doubtful importance and others that are unclearly stated. A common and serious error results when items contain "intrinsic ambiguity"—one answer is correct under one interpretation but under another interpretation a different answer is correct.

4. The items should be phrased so that the content rather than the form of the statement will determine the answer. A common flaw is inclusion of a "specific determiner" that provides an unwarranted clue to the answer. Specific determiners are especially common in true–false items. Statements that contain such words as *always, never, entirely, absolutely,* and *exclusively* are much more likely to be false than to be true. On the other hand, items containing expressions that weaken a statement, such as "may," "sometimes," "as a rule," and "in general," are much more likely to be true. These expressions should be used judiciously. Avoiding the exact wording found in the textbook will prevent pupils with good rote memories from getting credit for items that they do not really understand. Such defects, however, are not inherent in objective testing and may be avoided by the careful test maker.

Double negatives, figurative language, needlessly abstruse vocabulary, or complicated sentence structure should be avoided; the meaning of an item can be so obscured that it may be answered incorrectly by students who understand the concept being assessed. Care should also be taken to see that one item does not give away the answer to another.

5. The difficulty level of the items should be appropriate to the group of examinees. Maximum test reliability requires questions that are so difficult that only about half of the group responds correctly. Lord (1952) has demonstrated that reliability will be at a maximum when item difficulty is approximately midway between chance success and 100 percent. Optimal difficulty for true–false items is about 75%, for five-option multiple-choice questions about 60 percent, and for completion items approximately 50 percent. But, as stated previously, difficulty is not an end in itself. The items should reflect several levels of mastery. The instructor should not be beguiled into thinking he or she is the world's greatest teacher just because the class average is 95%. Perhaps only easy questions were asked, or perhaps instruction was unconsciously or consciously oriented toward the specific test items (i.e., the instructor taught to the test). Items that are similar to the *types* of items used in instruction are quite appropriate for assessment, but when teaching is done with specific items in mind, the items can no longer be viewed as representative of the content universe to which we wish to generalize, and hence, success on these items says little about the success students would have on similar items.

One of the worst and most common defects of teacher-constructed tests is the lack of items beyond the knowledge taxonomy level. Such items tend to be more difficult than relevant knowledge-level items. Instructors too often fail to realize that on very easy tests the few difficult items do all the "work" in assessing individual differences. Sax and Reade (1964) found that college students who were given difficult tests learned more than students in the same class who took easier tests. Hunkins (1969) also found that when higher-taxonomy-level questions were used regularly, objectives were mastered at a higher level.

Difficult items are not necessarily good items. It is simple to ask trivial questions that are difficult. Difficulty is not an end in itself. For classroom achievement tests, the item content should be determined by the *importance* of the subject matter, with questions being asked at a difficulty level appropriate to the group. An adequate diagnostic test in basic arithmetic for prospective elementary school teachers might yield many nearly perfect scores and still perform its function.

6. Classroom tests should be power tests, not speed tests. One of the most common and serious problems results when a test is too long for the time allowed. Proficient students are not necessarily fast test takers—the correlation between ability and working rate on the tests has been shown to be very low (Tate, 1948; Ebel, 1954; Hopkins, 1964b; Barch, 1957; Michael & Michael, 1969). A test is speeded to the extent that it contains items that are known by some examinees yet are not answered because of inadequate time. For most curricular areas high response speed is not an important objective.

In practice it frequently happens that a test is too long for the time allowed; hence, the speed-vs.-accuracy response style becomes a factor. If more than 10% or 15% of the examinees fail to complete the test in the allotted time, speed is probably a factor for some examinees and the test should be shortened before it is used again. In addition, the scores should be corrected for chance to help prevent the slow workers from receiving an undue penalty. But if possible, all examinees should be allowed to finish the test. Test-taking speed has been shown to have little relationship to amount of understanding of the content universe. For fairly short factual items, two items per minute may be reasonable for pupils above the third grade. For items above the knowledge level, the time allotment should be increased. Younger pupils and longer and higher-taxonomy-level items require more time. To prevent disturbance and discipline problems, assigned readings or other work should be required for students who complete the test early. Keep tests short enough so that all students can finish.

7. Keep the reading level low. Unless measurement of reading ability is your objective, use simple vocabulary and sentence structure. This is especially important at the elementary and junior high school levels. For example, if an assessment of science or arithmetic reasoning is the object, an unnecessary reading ability hurdle should not block a student from demonstrating mastery. (Methods of quantifying the reading level [readability] of written material is treated in a later section of this chapter.)

8. The test may include more than one type of item. A test with a variety of item types is less likely to be monotonous, especially with long tests. The requirement that the question types be suited to the material covered may necessitate that a number of item types be used. These varied objective items are frequently included with one or more essay questions.

9. All the items of a particular kind should ordinarily be placed together in the test. Completion, true-false, and multiple-choice items arranged haphazardly can be distracting, especially for younger examinees. The

grouping of similar item-types together not only facilitates scoring and evaluation but also enables examinees to take full advantage of the "mind set" induced by a particular item form.

10. To the extent that it is feasible, items of a particular type should be arranged in ascending order of difficulty. It is good practice to have the easiest items at the beginning of the test and the hardest ones at the end. The psychological justification for this is the wholesome effect it has on the morale of the students. Placing very difficult items at the beginning may produce needless discouragement, particularly in pupils of average or below-average ability.

Before the test is given, it is impossible to accurately estimate the difficulty of the items. Teacher opinion is likely to have some validity. It is usually possible to identify those items that will be at the extremes of the scale, and fortunately, this is what is needed most.

Although most researchers (e.g., Brenner, 1964; Marso, 1970b; Sax & Cromack, 1966) have failed to demonstrate that any significant difference results from various item arrangements on power tests, Tollefson (1978) found that highly anxious students obtained higher scores on tests following the easy-to-difficult item order. The use of the difficulty gradient in item ordering is especially desirable because many teacher-made tests are not pure power tests. The undesirable effects of a speeded test are even more serious if an item difficulty gradient is not employed. If speed is a factor, order becomes significant (Hambleton & Traub, 1974; Sax & Carr, 1962). Even when the order in which the items are arranged is of no psychometric consequence, the easy-to-difficult order has no disadvantages.

11. The directions to the pupil should be as clear, complete, and concise as possible. The teacher's aim should be to make the instructions so clear that the least able examinees in the group have no doubt about what they are expected to do, even if they may not be able to do it. Examinees should know how and where to mark the items, how much time they have to do so, and the extent to which they should "guess." The amount of detail necessary will depend on the age of the students and their experience with that kind of test. It is better, for example, to tell very young children to "draw a line under" rather than to "underline" and to "draw a circle around the right answer" rather than to "encircle the correct response." In the lower grades the teacher should read the directions aloud while the pupils silently follow the written directions on their test papers. Where the form of the test is unfamiliar or complicated, generous use of correctly marked samples and practice exercises (or even practice tests) is recommended. Sometimes a blackboard demonstration is useful. When the examinees become familiar with the various kinds of items, the directions may be abridged greatly.

The following directions may be considered reasonably satisfactory for a class that is unfamiliar with objective tests:

DIRECTIONS TO THE PUPIL: Write your name in the space provided in the upper right-hand corner. Here are thirty statements. Read each one carefully and decide whether it is true or false. In the ( ) before each statement, put + if you think the statement is true, but 0 in the ( ) before each statement you think is false. Your score will be the number right. You should answer all questions. There is no penalty for guessing. You will have 20 minutes to finish the test; do not waste time. If you change an answer, please erase clearly and completely. Study the following samples. They are answered correctly.

SAMPLES:
    (0) A. Beef is especially high in carbohydrates.
    (+) B. Vitamins themselves have few calories.

After the pupils have become familiar with this type of test, the directions may be shortened to a form somewhat as follows:

DIRECTIONS: In the ( ) before each item put + if it is true and 0 if it is false. You will have ten minutes for the test.

12. Before the actual scoring begins, prepare answer keys and scoring procedures. Satisfactory scoring keys for teacher-made objective tests can often be prepared simply by filling in the correct responses on an unused answer sheet or copy of the test. Scoring then consists of comparing the pupil's responses with those on the key, which is placed beside his or her paper. Scoring rules for objective tests are typically one point for each correct response, with no fractional credits allowed, also indicating whether or not a correction formula is to be used. Ordinarily pupils will remain in nearly the same rank order regardless of whether the individual items are weighted equally or quite differently (Stanley & Wang, 1970; Wang & Stanley, 1970). Variable credit for items complicates hand scoring but is sometimes needed to allow appropriate weighting of the various topics or content strata when the number of items is not commensurate with their importance or emphasis.

In essay examinations, the scoring key would be a model answer for each question. The scoring procedure for essay examinations, besides giving the weight for each question, should indicate whether deductions are to be made for errors in spelling, grammar, and usage. In mathematics tests, the rules should cover such points as whether the answers to problems must be reduced to their lowest terms and whether credit will be allowed for solutions that are correct in principle but have the wrong answer.

A regular sequence in the pattern of correct responses should be avoided. The position of correct responses should not be in a regular pattern (S. B. Anderson, 1952). If, for example, items are arranged so that true and false alternate, or two true follow two false, some students may discover the arrangement. In a desire to make hand scoring easier, some educators have suggested that the correct responses to multiple-choice items be arranged in an easily remembered "datelike" pattern such as 1342. But there is still the risk that the pupil will recognize the pattern and be able to answer without even considering the content of the item. Metfessel and Sax (1958) found several standardized tests that had systematic keying biases; on several tests, the correct answer did not appear in the extreme positions as often as would be expected on a theoretical basis.

The availability of optical test-scoring equipment such as the IBM 1230 series and the DIGITEK 100 greatly facilitate not only the scoring of tests but also item analyses, which are critical for evaluating the quality of tests and test items. Such equipment is currently being used at most universities and in many large school districts. Its availability for classroom teachers below the college level remains quite limited, but should increase considerably, at least for large high schools, within the next few years.

13. Every reasonable precaution should be taken to ensure excellent testing conditions. The responses to any test are not only determined by the test itself but can be influenced by surrounding conditions. It is usually best to administer the test to examinees in the familiar environment of their own classroom. Any tendency to cheat should be forestalled by careful supervision. Careful proctoring is needed to minimize cheating. When cheating is likely to be a special problem, students should be spread out as much as possible. But careless proctoring invites abuse and invalid results.

Measuring the Difficulty of Reading Material

In order to measure, quantify, and describe the *readability* (reading difficulty) of books, tests, and other reading material, many different readability formulas have been devised. The subjective judgments of teachers of the grade level for which reading selections are intended have been found to be quite unreliable (Jorgensen, 1975). Readability formulas use such factors as percent of common words, average word length, average sentence length, average number of syllables per word, percent of words that are prepositions, and more recently, syntactic complexity (DiStefano & Valencia, 1980).

Research (Klare, 1975) suggests that the highly complex formulas add little to the use of the two factors that most highly correlate with reading difficulty: (1) a word or semantic factor, and (2) a sentence or syntactic factor. The semantic factor seems to be the single most significant determinant of readability.

The most popular method of assessing readability is described in Figure 7-5. Fry's "Readability Graph" uses two factors: (1) average number of syllables per 100 words (word complexity) and (2) average number of sentences per 100 words (sentence complexity). For example, a 100-word sample from *Tom Sawyer* contains 4.5 sentences and 126 syllables. The intersection of these points in Fry's readability graph indicates a seventh-grade level. On a specific topic (Mexico), the selection in the *World Book* was written at the eighth-grade level whereas the *Encyclopedia Britannica*'s selection was written at the eleventh-grade level.[9]

[9] Two other widely used readability formulas are the Dale-Chall and Flesh (1948) "reading ease" (RE) formulas. Flesh's RE formula uses the same two factors as Fry's, but combined and weighted differently:

$$RE = 206.84 - 84.6X_{sl/w} - 1.015X_{w/s}$$

where $X_{sl/w}$ is the average number of syllables per word and $X_{w/s}$ is the average number of words per sentence. RE values are scaled such that they range from 30 or below for very difficult material to 90 or above for very easy reading matter such as comics.

The Dale-Chall readability formula is one of the most accurate for reading material intended for grades 3–8 (Klare, 1975). It predicts the grade level, G, of the pupils who will be able to answer 50% of the comprehension test questions on the reading passage correctly: $G = .116X_{\%}$ $+ .060X_{w/s} + 3.27$, where $X_{\%}$ is the percent of words that are not on a list of the most common 3,000 words (the Dale list) and $X_{w/s}$ is defined as in the Flesh RE formula.

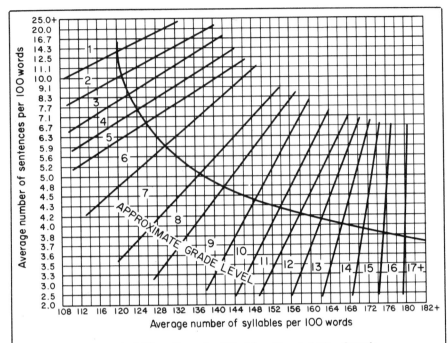

Expanded Directions for Working Readability Graph

1. Randomly select three (3) sample passages and count out exactly 100 words each, beginning with the beginning of a sentence. Do count proper nouns, initializations, and numerals.
2. Count the number of sentences in the hundred words, estimating length of the fraction of the last sentence to the nearest one-tenth.
3. Count the total number of syllables in the 100-word passage. If you don't have a hand counter available, an easy way is to simply put a mark above every syllable over one in each word, then when you get to the end of the passage, count the number of marks and add 100. Small calculators can also be used as counters by pushing numeral 1, then push the + sign for each word or syllable when counting.
4. Enter graph with *average* sentence length and *average* number of syllables; plot dot where the two lines intersect. Area where dot is plotted will give you the approximate grade level.
5. If a great deal of variability is found in syllable count or sentence count, putting more samples into the average is desirable.
6. A word is defined as a group of symbols with a space on either side; thus, *Joe, IRA, 1945,* and & are each one word.
7. A syllable is defined as a phonetic syllable. Generally, there are as many syllables as vowel sounds. For example, *stopped* is one syllable and *wanted* is two syllables. When counting syllables for numerals and initializations, count one syllable for each symbol. For example, *1945* is four syllables, *IRA* is three syllables, and & is one syllable.

Note: This "extended graph" does not outmode or render the earlier (1968) version inoperative or inaccurate; it is an extension.

FIGURE 7-5 Graph for estimating readability–extended. (By Edward Fry, Rutgers University Reading Center, New Brunswick, N.J. 08904)

In addition to their obvious curricular use, measures of reading difficulty can be useful in describing the "reading load" of standardized achievement tests in subjects other than reading. Except when measuring reading ability, the readability of test content should be kept as simple as possible so that the students who are, for example, good in math and science but whose reading skills are lagging are not penalized unfairly. As Gardner (1978, p. 2) has observed, "A test designed to measure achievement in elementary science, and in which the items are presented in language and syntax far above the level of the pupils tested, is biased, especially against the poor readers." The reading level needed to "decipher" non-reading standardized achievement tests varies considerably among tests, and often reduces the validity of those tests (Hopkins, 1965).

Summary

General educational goals are not specific enough to give clear direction to curriculum development and evaluation.

Instructional goals can be established, and more specific "offspring" objectives can be deduced from the "parent" objectives. Educational objectives can become dysfunctional if they are stated too atomistically. A carefully prepared topic outline is an implicit expression of certain instructional goals.

Bloom's taxonomy differentiates among six levels of cognitive complexity. The first two or three (knowledge, comprehension, and application) are distinct, but the higher levels are not clearly differentiated.

A table of specifications with a grid of content strata with two taxonomy levels appears to be a functional blueprint for classroom test development.

The number of separate subscores to be reported influences the length of a good measuring instrument. Diagnostic, criterion-referenced (CRT) and objective-referenced tests need a *minimum* of five or ten items per objective or topic. A good survey test is not usually adequate for detailed diagnostic conclusions pertaining to specific skills and objectives.

The movement toward criterion-referenced, domain-referenced, objective-referenced tests is, in part, a reaction to inappropriate and undesirable procedures for developing and selecting achievement test items primarily on the statistical characteristics of the items—procedures that are desirable for norm-referenced testing but which can result in sacrificing content validity for increased reliability.

A major problem with the CRT and minimum competency testing approaches is the arbitrariness of the criterion. Item difficulty is arbitrary; hence, the meaning of criteria such as 80% correct is often uncertain. When criteria are established on empirical grounds, the criteria are not arbitrary, and can become useful for decision making.

In preparing a test, the following procedures are recommended:

1. Use a table of specifications (e.g., a content-stratum-by-taxonomy-level grid).
2. Draft a surplus of items.

3. Have another person review the items for clarity, relevance, and appropriateness.
4. Construct items at low reading levels, ordinarily with half or more of the items being above the knowledge taxonomy level.
5. Control the test length so that the test is a power, not a speeded, test.
6. Test frequently over smaller units of content.
7. Develop clear instructions to examinees.
8. Provide a scoring guide.
9. Perform an item analysis to evaluate individual items and assess the test's measurement precision. (See Chapter 10.)

IMPORTANT TERMS AND CONCEPTS

cognitive
affective
psychomotor
parent objectives
offspring objectives
behavioral objectives
Bloom's taxonomy
content universe

content strata
domain-referenced tests
mastery tests
diagnostic tests
criterion-referenced test
  (CRT)
objective-referenced test
specific determiners

item difficulty gradient
power test
speed test
table of specifications
minimum competency test
  (MCT)
norm-referenced test (NRT)
readability

CHAPTER TEST

1. Which is the broadest, most inclusive term?
   a) Educational goals
   b) Behavioral objectives
   c) Instructional objectives

2. Which is the lowest level of Bloom's taxonomy?
   a) Synthesis
   b) Application
   c) Knowledge
   d) Comprehension
   e) Analysis

3. Has research supported the contention that all six levels of the taxonomy are clearly distinguishable?

4. Is it desirable to state instructional objectives at extremely specific levels (e.g., "Can add the numbers 9, 5, and 3 when vertically aligned")?

5. If a test is an excellent survey test, can we be certain that it will be useful for appraising the degree to which individual examinees have achieved specific objectives?

6. A major problem with the CRT approach is
   a) its emphasis on item discrimination and difficulty.
   b) the difficulty of developing good test items.
   c) the arbitrariness of the criteria.

7. A practical difficulty with CRT, objective-referenced, and diagnostic testing is that

a) it is difficult to develop items to measure behavioral objectives.
b) several items are needed to adequately assess each objective.
c) there is much public opposition to these approaches to student assessment.

8. If achievement tests include only those items that have characteristics that are desirable for norm-referenced tests, the net result will be

a) to sacrifice reliability at the expense of validity.
b) to sacrifice validity at the expense of reliability.
c) to sacrifice both reliability and validity for usability.

Are the following considered good test construction practices?

9. Arrange the items in a random order.

10. Group all items of the same type together.

11. Draft more items than will be used.

12. Keep the reading level simple.

13. Make the test length such that few examinees will not be able to finish in the time allowed.

14. Have a set pattern of correct answers to facilitate scoring.

15. Include many items above the knowledge taxonomy level.

16. Have the test reviewed by another person to detect ambiguity, triviality, and inappropriateness.

17. Include only a few difficult items.

18. Use only one type of item on any given test.

19. Devise a scoring plan before scoring the test.

20. Inform students of the time allowed and what to do about "guessing."

21. Which of these is least useful as an indicator of readability?

a) Ratio of consonants to vowels
b) Average number of syllables per word
c) Percent of common words
d) Average number of words per sentence

ANSWERS TO CHAPTER TEST

1. a	8. b	15. yes
2. c	9. no	16. yes
3. no	10. yes	17. no
4. no	11. yes	18. no
5. no	12. yes	19. yes
6. c	13. no	20. yes
7. b	14. no	21. a

BLOOM, B. S., et al. *Taxonomy of educational objectives: Handbook I, Cognitive domain.* New York: David McKay, 1956.

BLOOM, B. S., J. T. HASTINGS, and G. F. MADAUS. *Handbook on formative and summative evaluation of student learning.* New York: McGraw-Hill, 1971. See esp. chap. 2, Defining educational objectives; chap. 7, Evaluation techniques for *knowledge* and *comprehension* objectives; chap. 8, Evaluation techniques for *application* and *analysis* objectives; chap. 9, Evaluation techniques for *synthesis* and *evaluation* objectives.

CLARK, D. C. *Using instructional objectives in teaching.* Glenview, Ill.: Scott, Foresman, 1972.

EBEL, R. L. Some limitations of criterion-referenced measurement. In G. H. Bracht, K. D. Hopkins, and J. C. Stanley, eds., *Perspectives in educational and psychological measurement.* Englewood Cliffs, N.J.: Prentice-Hall, 1972. Selection 14.

———. The case for norm-referenced measurements. *Educational Researcher,* 7 (1978), 3–5.

GLASER, R., and A. J. NITKO. Measurement in learning and instruction. In R. L. Thorndike, ed., *Educational measurement,* 2nd ed. Washington, D.C.: American Council on Education, 1971. Chap. 17.

GLASS, G. V. Standards and criteria. *Journal of Educational Measurement,* 15 (1978), 237–62.

———. Mathew Arnold and minimal competency. *The Educational Forum,* January 1978.

HAMBLETON, R. K., and D. R. EIGNOR. Guidelines for evaluating criterion-referenced tests and test manuals. *Journal of Educational Measurement,* 15 (1978), 321–27.

HAMBLETON, R. K., H. SWAMINATHAN, J. ALGINA, and D. B. COULSON. Criterion-referenced testing and measurement: A review of technical issues and developments. *Review of Educational Research,* 48 (1978), 1–48.

HEDGES, WILLIAM D. *Testing and evaluation for the sciences in the secondary school.* Belmont, Calif.: Wadsworth, 1966.

HEYWOOD, J. *Assessment in higher education.* New York: Wiley, 1977. Chaps. 4–6.

HILL, W. H., and P. L. DRESSEL. The objectives of instruction. In P. L. Dressel, ed., *Evaluation in higher education.* Boston: Houghton Mifflin, 1961. Chap. 2.

JAEGER, R. M., and C. K. TITTLE. *Minimum Competency Achievement Testing.* Washington, D. C.: American Educational Research Association. 1979.

KRATHWOHL, D., and D. A. PAYNE. Defining and assessing educational objectives. In R. L. Thorndike, ed., *Educational measurement,* 2nd ed. Washington, D.C.: American Council on Education, 1971. Chap. 2.

MEHRENS, W. A., and R. L. EBEL. Some comments on criterion-referenced and norm-referenced achievement tests. *NCME Measurement in Education,* 10, no. 1 (1979).

MORRIS, L. L., and C. T. FITZ-GIBBON. *How to measure achievement.* Beverly Hills, Calif.: Sage Publications, 1978.

POPHAM, W. J. The case for criterion-referenced measurement. *Educational Researcher,* 7 (1978), 6–10.

———. *Criterion-referenced measurement.* Englewood Cliffs, N.J.: Prentice-Hall, 1978.

POPHAM, W. J., and T. R. HUSEK. Implications of criterion-referenced measurement. *Journal of Educational Measurement,* 6 (1969), 1–10. Reprinted in G. H. Bracht, K. D. Hopkins, and J. C. Stanley, eds., *Perspectives in educational and psychological measurement.* Englewood Cliffs, N.J.: Prentice-Hall, 1972. Selection 13.

SANDERS, N. M. *Classroom questions: What kinds?* New York: Harper & Row, 1966.

SHEPARD, L. A. Setting standards. In M. A. Bunda and J. R. Sanders, eds., *Practices and problems in competency-based measurement.* National Council on Measurement in Education, 1979.

———. Technical issues in minimum competency testing. *Review of Research in Education,* in press.

SHOEMAKER, D. M. Toward a framework for achievement testing. *Review of Educational Research,* 45 (1975), 127–47.

TINKELMAN, S. N. Planning the objective test. In R. L. Thorndike, ed., *Educational measurement,* 2nd ed. New York: American Council on Education, 1971. Chap. 3.

8

Constructing and Using Essay Tests

A Little History

Some historical background will serve as an aid in understanding current practices.

Measurement and evaluation have played a far more prominent role in human history than is generally recognized. The historical origins of testing and measurement are lost in antiquity. There was an elaborate system of civil service examinations in China several centuries before Christ (DuBois, 1966; Miyazaki, 1976).[1] Testing was a normal part of the education of the ancient Greeks (Chauncey & Dobbin, 1963). The Socratic method involves the skillful interspersing of instruction with oral testing. Some of the earliest records of the use of various testing devices are found in the Bible.

> And the Gileadites took the passages of Jordan before the Ephraimites: and it was so, that when those Ephraimites which were escaped said, Let me go over; that the men of Gilead said unto him, Art thou an Ephraimite? If he said, Nay; then said they unto him, Say now *Shi*bboleth: and he said *Si*bboleth: for he could not frame to pronounce it right.[2]

---

[1] It is interesting to note that after a decade of cultural revolution (1966–76) in which systematic examination and marks were virtually eliminated ("they create classes and elitism among the masses"), China reinstituted admission examinations for universities and other more traditional uses of testing and evaluation of students (Kraft, 1978).

[2] Judges, 12:5–6, King James Version.

The sole test of a man's being a Gileadite was the ability to use the *h* sound in the word *Shibboleth*.

In education, some form of measurement is inevitable; it is inherent in the teaching–learning process. Consider the constant evaluative role of the classroom teacher as he or she attempts to determine the degree of scholastic achievement and growth of students. Measuring devices are indispensable to the teacher, the guidance counselor, the school administrator, the curriculum planner, and the evaluator.

Oral questioning dates back to the beginnings of human language. Four centuries before Christ, Socrates used oral questions to "draw out" his students, as many good teachers do today. Indeed Christ himself, continually used oral questions as steppingstones to lead his "students" to Truth. But it is important to distinguish between the instructional value of an activity and its appropriateness for general assessment. A spelling "bee" may be useful as a motivation technique, but its measurement merits are few. Until the availability of inexpensive pencils and paper after the middle of the nineteenth century, oral examinations were standard in American schools. Some countries by law still require oral final examinations (Stanley, 1960a). Universities harbor vestiges of this in the form of "thesis orals."

A job interview often is nothing more than an oral test that assesses an applicant's cognitive and affective characteristics. From time to time, oral quiz programs appear on radio and television, though the contestants are often chosen in advance for their proficiency on written tests. Not until the second half of the past century did writing instruments largely replace glib or faltering tongues as a basis for educational decisions. Oral examinations were used for every subject except writing.

In the nineteenth century annual public oral tests of teachers were common. Teachers would be assembled in the town hall for the examination and questioned by the superintendent. All teachers who fell below the minimal standard of 75% were dismissed (Cureton, 1971). Who said "minimum competency teaching" was new? In a similar vein, "performance contracts" was decreed in England in 1862 (and continued until about 1900) and teachers were paid largely according to the results of their students on the annual examinations given by Her Majesty's inspectors (Cureton, 1971).

Important prerequisites for written testing were developed early in the nineteenth century: the "blackboard" in 1809 and the metal pen (replacing the goose quill) in 1828 (Cureton, 1971).

The first important steps toward the scientific use of measurement in education were taken by Horace Mann (1845) more than a century ago. This prominent New England educator, famous for his doctrine of free, compulsory, and universal education, had a remarkable understanding of the importance of examinations and of the limitations of the ones then being used. His penetrating analysis of the weaknesses of the oral examination then in vogue and of the superiority of written examinations for classroom purposes can hardly be improved upon today. Mann showed clearly where oral examinations were lacking; he used the concepts that have become the cornerstones of today's theories and are now known as validity, reliability, and usability.

Another American educator who understood both the value and the limitations of examinations was Emerson E. White, an educational writer and school administrator. He wrote, "It may be stated as a general fact that school instruction and study are never much wider or better than the tests by which they are measured" (E. E. White, 1886). In the same volume he enumerated several "special advantages" of the written test:

> It is more impartial than the oral test, since it gives all the pupils the same tests and an equal opportunity to meet them; its results are more tangible and reliable; it discloses more accurately the comparative progress of the different pupils, information of value to the teacher; it reveals more clearly defects in teaching and study, and thus assists in their correction; it emphasizes more distinctly the importance of accuracy and fullness in the expression of knowledge . . . ; it is at least an equal test of the thought-power or intelligence of pupils. [pp. 197–98]

Mann and White realized that the oral test can be unfair, since some questions are more difficult than others. It is also quite inefficient, since only one student is responding to one question at a time. The views of Mann and White seem surprisingly current. These pioneers understood the need for good assessment more than many educators do today. Measurement specialists now realize that some of the early enthusiasm for the ordinary essay test was unwarranted, pointing out that some of the limitations of oral tests also hold in some degree for certain written tests.

The improvement of existing tests and other measuring instruments has always lagged far behind theory, and educational practice has been farthest behind of all. Despite the marked superiority of written examinations over oral ones, which Mann pointed out in 1845, in many cases teachers have not moved either to adopt the former or to improve the latter. It is interesting to note, however, that in 1864 an enterprising English schoolmaster, the Rev. George Fisher, proposed the widespread use of objective and standardized measures of academic attainment. Fisher outlined the practice of the new system in his school as follows:

> A book, called the "Scale-Book," has been established, which contains the numbers assigned to each degree of proficiency in the various subjects of examination: For instance, if it be required to determine the numerical equivalent corresponding to any specimen of "writing," a comparison is made with various standard specimens, which are arranged in this book in order to merit; the highest being represented by the number 1, and the lowest by 5, and the intermediate values by affixing to these numbers the fractions 1/4, 1/2, or 3/4. So long as these standard specimens are preserved in the institution, so long will constant numerical values for proficiency in "writing" be maintained. And since facsimiles can be multiplied without limit, the same principle might be generally adopted.
>
> The numeral values for "spelling" follow the same order, and are made to depend upon the percentage of mistakes in writing from dictation sentences from works selected for the purpose, examples of which are contained in the "Scale-Book," in order to preserve the same standard of difficulty.
>
> By a similar process, values are assigned for proficiency in mathematics, navigation, Scripture knowledge, grammar, and composition, French, general history,

drawing, and practical science, respectively. Questions in each of these subjects are contained in the "Scale-Book," to serve as types, not only of the difficulty, but of the nature of the question, for the sake of future reference. [Chadwick, 1864]

Apparently, Fisher was too far advanced for his times, since his incisive work seems not to have attracted a widespread audience. As Ayres (1918) expressed it, "Progress in the scientific study of education was not possible until people could be brought to realize that human behavior was susceptible of quantitative study, and until they had statistical methods with which to carry on their investigations."

In 1910 the Thorndike Handwriting Scale (E. L. Thorndike, 1910) was published—the first of its kind. It consisted of formal writing samples of children in grades 5 through 8; the samples were arranged in a 15-category scale of increasing quality in essentially the manner suggested forty-six years earlier by Fisher (Chadwick, 1864). Figure 8-1 gives an abridged version of the Ayres Handwriting Scale, a refinement of Thorndike's scale. This is an example of "a wheel that was subsequently reinvented" (Lyman, 1978) and is now termed *criterion-referenced measurement* (see Chapter 7). A sample of a person's handwriting can be scaled according to the eight calibration "anchor" points provided. How would a sample of your typical handwriting rate? The median ratings on the Ayres scale for grades 2–8 are 38, 42, 46, 50, 54, 58, and 62, respectively.

Essay Tests for Measuring Achievement

It is important to distinguish between the two principal uses of essay tests: (1) as an achievement test, and (2) as a measure of writing ability. Examples of the first type of use include teacher-made tests in social studies, science, and other curricular areas; it will be considered first. The use of an essay test as a measure of writing ability will be considered later in the chapter.

Essay tests are used frequently by more than half of the teachers in public schools (Goslin, 1967). Essay tests have an advantage over oral questions in that all examinees respond to the same questions, but essay tests require subjective scoring, because each examinee's response will be unique. "What were the principal political considerations that led to the War Between the States?" "Write an essay of approximately 1,000 words about the cinema as an art form." "Distinguish between 'connotation' and 'denotation.'" "Is logic a branch of mathematics, or is mathematics a branch of logic? Why?" "Discuss the relative influence of heredity and environment on the development of verbal intelligence. Support your points by citing relevant studies." Such questions or assessment exercises are referred to as essay questions.

One or more essay questions will constitute an *essay test* if the answers are graded. An essay test differs from a short-answer test, in which the grader expects a precise set of answers. "Name the inert gases" permits an answer of only one set of names; it allows no display of individuality, although the student may vary the order in which he or she writes the names. Essay questions

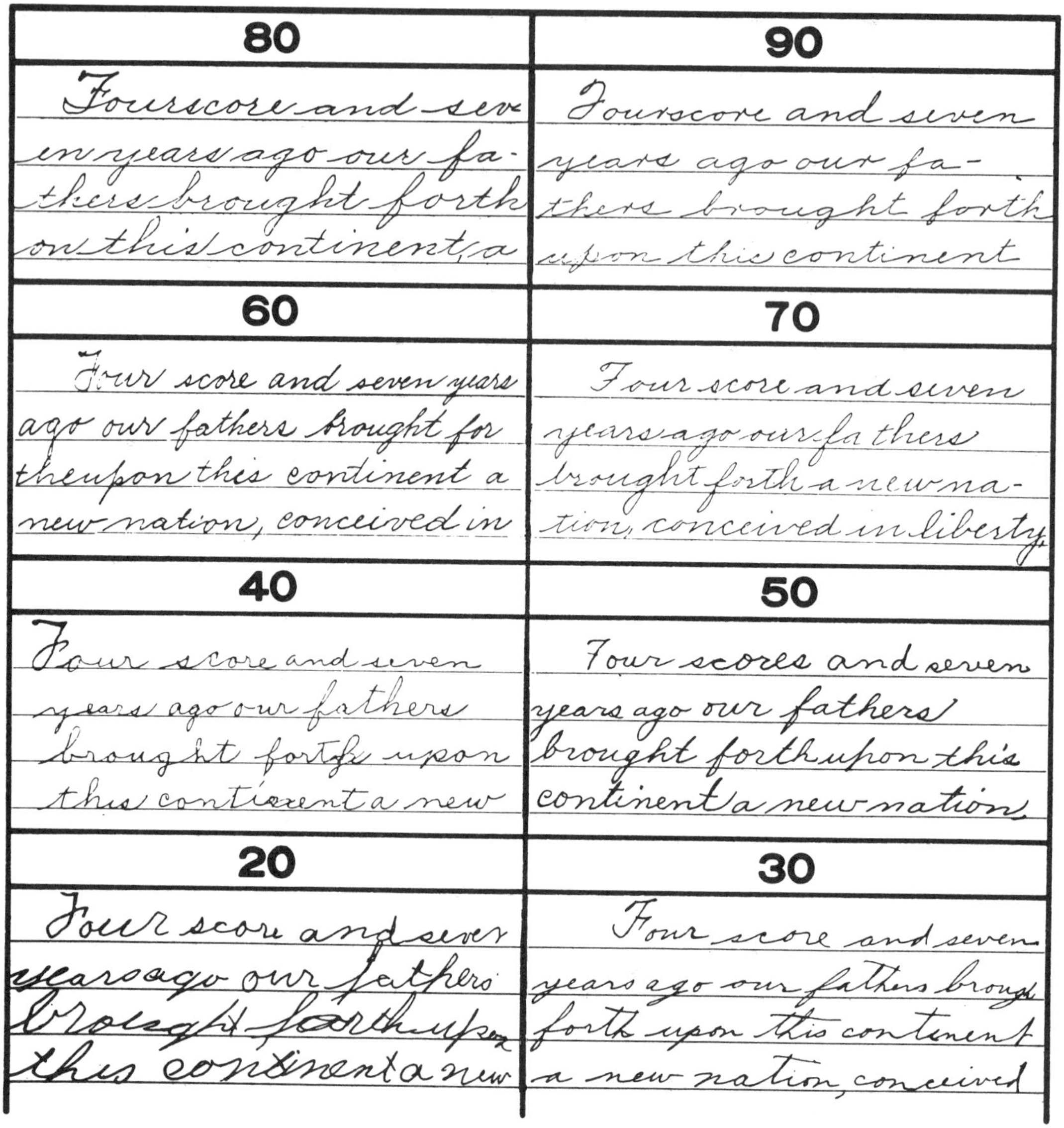

80	90
Fourscore and seven years ago our fathers brought forth on this continent, a	*Fourscore and seven years ago our fathers brought forth upon this continent*

60	70
Four score and seven years ago our fathers brought for theupon this continent a new nation, conceived in	*Four score and seven years ago our fathers brought forth a new nation, conceived in liberty*

40	50
Four score and seven years ago our fathers brought forth upon this continent a new	*Four scores and seven years ago our fathers brought forth upon this continent a new nation*

20	30
Four score and seven years ago our fathers brought forth upon this continent a new	*Four score and seven years ago our fathers brought forth upon this continent a new nation, conceived*

FIGURE 8-1 An abridged version of the Ayres Handwriting Scale. (Reproduced by permission of the University of Iowa.)

limit the student's responses less than other written-item forms do. The teacher does not merely say, "Write something," but neither is the form of the answer completely specified.

The grading of essay questions calls for expert judgment; unlike objective items, they cannot be graded by clerks. Nor can they be graded quickly or without bias. Even when skilled teachers expend their best efforts in grading them, the reliability of most essay tests is not high. For many years major efforts have been made to obtain adequate reliability in grading essay tests, particularly English compositions written by high school juniors and seniors applying for entrance to select colleges. Two "camps" have developed in recent years, one decrying objective testing and the other insisting that most important mental processes, including the composing of essays, can be measured well by objective test items.

Hoffman (1962, 1967a,b) contends that objective tests are not concerned with the quality of the examinee's reasoning or his or her ability to conceive, design, or carry out a complex undertaking in an individual way. He feels that multiple-choice tests discriminate against the bright, discerning student. The empirical research on this issue, however, contradicts the purported "Hoffman effect" (Dunnette, 1963; Chauncey & Hilton, 1965; Alker, Carlson & Hermann, 1969; Jensen, 1980). The comparative evaluation of the two types of test was summarized by Chauncey and Dobbin (1963, pp. 79–80):

> Given two examiners fully trained in the arts of achievement testing, one building essay examinations and the other objective tests, the examiner with the essay tests probably can do a better job of estimating a student's present skill in creative writing, but the examiner who builds objective tests can provide more valid and reliable estimates of just about every other kind of school achievement.

Some critics (Hoffman, 1962; La Fave, 1964, 1966) have argued that the objective test can measure only knowledge of facts but that the essay test can measure more complex, higher levels of understanding. One study, after correcting for the unreliability of the tests, found that performance on objective and essay tests over the same content measured essentially the same factors (Bracht & Hopkins, 1970a). Similar results have been observed in most, but not all, content areas (Cook, 1955; Coffman, 1971; Godshalk, Swineford, Coffman, and ETS, 1966; Horn, 1966; Stake & Sjogren, 1964; Vernon, 1962; Breland & Gaynor, 1979; Ward, Frederiksen & Carlson, 1980). Of course, the fact that in ordinary use the two kinds of test may not measure different factors should not be construed to mean that they cannot have unique measurement values *when used appropriately*. Whether objective or essay, tests used to assess learning are frequently of extremely poor quality.

Some teachers in many curricular areas use essay tests almost exclusively. Limiting the use of teacher-made tests to those that are classified as objective would be an unwarranted restriction. It is important not to confuse the educational and evaluation uses of essays. The essay exercise probably has important instructional merits apart from any evaluative weakness it possesses. The traditional essay still has a legitimate place in the modern school. In this chapter we consider some of the limitations and advantages of the essay test and offer suggestions for its improvement and use. The wise admonition offered many years ago by Hawkes, Lindquist, and Mann (1936, p. 20) is just as timely today:

> The intelligent point of view is that which recognizes that whatever advantages either type may have are *specific* advantages in *specific* situations; that while cer-

tain purposes may be best served by one type, other purposes are best served by another; and, above all, that the adequacy of either type in any specific situation is much more dependent upon the ingenuity and intelligence with which the test is *used* than upon any *inherent* characteristic or limitation of the *type* employed.

Limitations of the Essay Test

As it is ordinarily employed, the essay test has several serious limitations as a measuring instrument. It suffers in comparison with most forms of objective tests on the three important criteria for a satisfactory measuring instrument: reliability, validity, and usability.

Reader Unreliability. A major problem with essay examinations is the lack of consistency in judgments among competent raters, that is, the lack of scorer or reader reliability. The Educational Testing Service (1961) reported a study of 300 essays written by college freshmen and rated by 53 "outstanding representatives" from several fields. Each judge used a nine-point rating scale to indicate quality. *More than one-third (34 percent) of the essays received all possible ratings!* Another 37 percent received eight ratings, and 23 percent received seven. No essay received fewer than five of the nine possible ratings. Obviously, a highly valid rating must be a function of what is written, not of which person happens to evaluate the response.

In a study (Coffman & Kurfman, 1968) involving the Advanced Placement Test in American History, it was found that some readers were much more lenient in their grading than others and that this trend was consistent irrespective of whether the scoring was global-holistic or analytical (point-by-point).

Raters differ not only in their standards but also in how they distribute grades throughout the scale (Coffman, 1971). Some raters tend to spread scores more widely than others, even though the average scores may be equal. Good papers will receive lower scores and poor papers higher scores than they would from raters who cluster scores more closely around an average value. Thus, the scores of different raters differ in variability as well as central tendency.

In a study conducted at the University of West Virginia, Ashburn (1938) concluded that "the passing or failing of about 40 percent [of students] depends, not on what they know or do not know, but on *who* reads the papers" and that "the passing or failing of about 10 percent depends . . . on *when* the papers are read."

Unfortunately, scorer reliability tends to decrease when one attempts to capitalize on the essay test's unique characteristics—flexibility and freedom of choice (Coffman, 1971). This factor no doubt accounts for the great disparity among the reader reliability coefficients reported in the literature; the correlations between readers range from as low as .32 to as high as .98 (Coffman, 1969, p. 10). It is not difficult to obtain high scorer reliability if essay questions are narrowly focused and carefully structured. For example, "List the four principal causes of the Civil War identified by your textbook" and "Name the countries of South America and the chief export of each," are questions that could present only minor difficulty in scoring reliability. These questions, however, could be cast more efficiently in objective form. Broader, open-ended questions designed to assess more complex concepts in the higher levels of Bloom's taxonomy are precisely the kind of questions that tend to possess the least scorer reliability. The following essay question would probably have low reader reliability: "Defend or refute the following proposition: 'Liberty can be achieved only by an extension of governmental regulation of competitive business enterprise.'" This degree-of-structure factor is probably a principal reason that essay tests in mathematics tend to be more reliable than those in history, which in turn tend to have greater reliability than those in literature (Coffman, 1971; Burton, 1980).

The Halo Effect. The halo effect is the tendency, in evaluating one characteristic of a person, to be influenced by another characteristic or by one's general impression of that person. For example, in rating intelligence on the basis of observation, psychologists overrated men with introverted personality characteristics. The halo effect can seriously impair the validity of marks assigned by teachers to essay tests. If Mary Dogood is a well-behaved student who loves her teacher and tries very hard to please her, these characteristics can influence the teacher's judgment of the quality of Mary's essay test. When essay tests are not read anonymously, the halo effect can seriously contaminate the results (Chase, 1979a).

Item-to-Item Carryover Effects. A common contaminant in scoring essay tests is the item-to-item carryover effect. The rater acquires an impression of the student's knowledge on the initial item that "colors" his or her judgment of the second item. Bracht (1967) found that the carryover factor had a strong influence on the marks given to questions on an essay test. When the responses to each essay question were scored for all students before the next question was marked, the correlation between the marks on the questions was much lower than when the student's response to the first question was allowed to influence the rater's judgment of the response to the second question. Obviously, the response to an essay question should be evaluated on its own merits and should not be influenced by preceding questions on the test.

Test-to-Test Carryover Effects. It has been observed that the grade assigned to a paper tends to be greatly influenced by the grade given to the immediately preceding paper. Stalnaker's (1936) assertion that "A C paper may be graded B if it is read after an illiterate theme, but if it follows an A paper, if such can be found, it seems to be of D caliber" (p. 41) may be somewhat overstated, but only in degree. Hales and Tokar (1975) found that essays of average quality were rated about 1.5 points higher on a five-point scale when preceded by two poor essays than when preceded by two very good papers. Similar results were found using 25 experienced teachers (Hughes, Keeling & Tuck, 1980), irrespective of whether scoring was analytic or global.

Order Effects. The order in which a paper appears also affects scores. In several studies (Bracht, 1967; Coffman & Kurfman, 1968; Godshalk, Swineford, Coffman, and ETS, 1966), a "slide effect" was observed in the scores awarded by raters. Papers that were read earlier tended to receive higher ratings than those read nearer the end of the sequence. Perhaps readers become weary, and in this physical and mental condition nothing looks quite as good as it otherwise might.

Even when essays are reread by the same rater, there is considerable variation in the score a given paper receives. Bracht (1967) found that the first and second scores on a single brief essay question correlated .50 when reread by the same instructor and .47 when read by a different instructor. It is clear that there is considerable intrarater (within-rater) as well as interrater (between-rater) inconsistency.

Language Mechanics Effects. Investigators have found that teachers were unable to rate essay responses to social-studies questions on content alone, independent of errors in spelling, punctuation, and grammar (Scannell & Marshall, 1966; Marshall, 1967; Marshall & Powers, 1969). Several investigators (Chase, 1968; Markham, 1976; Chase, 1979a; Shepherd, 1929) also found that handwriting quality was related to the scores awarded to essays. Shepherd's (1929) early study showed dramatic differences in the scores received by identical essay responses presented in good and poor handwriting. More recent studies show real but small effects on essay rating for penmanship and general appearance.

Several investigators (Bracht and Hopkins, 1968; Klein and Hart, 1968; Garber, 1967) have found that the length of an essay response has a substantial relationship (*r*'s of .32–.56) to the rating assigned. Bracht and Hopkins (1968) noted that there was no relationship between the length of the essay response and the score received on an objective test over the same instructional unit, which suggests that those who wrote more did not necessarily know more. Even when grade point average and scholastic aptitude were held constant, the (partial) correlation between the length of the response and the assigned mark was almost .5. This pattern was consistent across several raters. If this finding is typical, it seems that there is considerable support for the common notion among test-wise students that instructors often assign marks on the basis of the "weight" of student products. It has been suggested that the essay overrates the importance of knowing how to say a thing and underrates the importance of having something to say.

In an extensive study in England, Pidgeon and Yates (1957, p. 47) concluded that

> the results of the experiments that we have outlined, however, show that even in ideal conditions, which cannot in practice be contrived—that is, with a faultless system of marking—papers of this kind [essay] do not achieve the level of reliability that is maintained by objective tests, nor do they achieve the same degree of validity.

The essay test also ranks low in usability unless the number of examinees is small. It is inevitable that the valid scoring of essay tests will be time-consuming. The additional expenditure of time and energy beyond that needed for objective tests is so serious a limitation that the exclusive use of essay tests as an evaluation tool can be justified only if it can be shown that the values realized are commensurate with the investment. From a practical perspective, one important advantage of the essay test is its high face validity —written exercises seem to be a rich way to measure important educational objectives.

Computer Scoring

Ellis Page and his associates (Garber, 1967; Page, 1966) have done some interesting work on the incongruous task of grading essays by computer. After studying Table 8-1 you will see that such a feat is not as preposterous as it initially appears to be. The computer ("judge *C*") is indistinguishable from the other four judges.

Page has shown that computer scoring can yield scores that are *superior* to a single judge's rating on each of the following factors: (1) ideas or content, (2) organization, (3) style, (4) mechanics, and (5) creativity. (See Coffman, 1971.) Although the information used by the computer often lacks face validity and even logical validity (scoring is based on number of words in the essay, average word length, number of commas, and so on), there is strong evidence that, when the criterion is the average rating given by several experts, the computer's "marks" are as valid as those of a judge. For the present, Page's research is more of a graphic illustration of the deficiencies in subjectively scored examinations than a practical "teacher's aid" for scoring essay tests.

Reader reliability is improved when essay questions are carefully delimited and explicitly framed. Agreements are further increased when the

TABLE 8-1

WHICH ONE IS THE COMPUTER?

Below is the intercorrelation matrix generated by the cross-validation of PEG I in the following fashion:

All "judges" graded the overall quality of a set of 138 essays written by high school students in grades 8-12. One "judge" was a computer, the other four were independent human experts. The correlations in this table show the extent to which each "judge" tended to agree with each other in grading essays. The computer-assigned grades were based upon beta weightings generated from the multiple prediction of human judgments on 138 essays by other students randomly drawn from the same population. Which one, A, B, C, D, or E, is the computer vector?

	Judges				
	A	*B*	*C*	*D*	*E*
A		.51	.51	.44	.57
B	.51		.53	.56	.61
C	.51	.53		.48	.49
D	.44	.56	.48		.59
E	.57	.61	.49	.59	

SOURCE: Reprinted from E. B. Page, The imminence of grading essays by computer, *Phi Delta Kappan*, 47 (1966), 238–43, by permission of the publisher.

raters are provided with a *model answer* that gives major points or concepts and their corresponding credit allocations. Even greater reliability can be attained when a set of "representative" essays for anchoring the grading scale (such as A–F) is used. When such carefully developed analytical scoring methods are allowed with clearly focused questions, it is possible to achieve high reader reliability. As Coffman (1971) has cautioned, however, these methods are expensive—they require large amounts of professional time to obtain the required number of independent ratings. In an extensive study Godshalk, Swineford, Coffman, and ETS (1966, pp. 39–40) found that

> if one can include as many as five different topics [of 20–40 minutes each] and have each topic read by five different readers, the reading reliability of the total score may be approximately .92 and the score [test] reliability approximately .84. . . . In contrast, for one topic reader, the corresponding figures are .40 and .25, respectively.

To achieve satisfactory essay test reliability, then, several questions, each graded by more than one reader, are desirable.

Essay Test Reliability

It is significant that most studies on the reliability of essay tests deal with between- or within-rater agreement in marking a particular examination—not with the reliability of the examination itself. Note in the quoted passage from the ETS study that the reader reliability for a single topic essay test of 20–40 minutes with a single reader was .40, but that test reliability was only .25. Reader unreliability limits test reliability, but it is theoretically possible to have perfect reader reliability without any test reliability. A few studies (see Coffman, 1971) have been reported on the correlation between two forms of an essay test designed for a particular purpose that were given to the same pupils and carefully marked by experienced examiners. One study used this procedure to study tests in 16 subjects taken by 952 eighth-grade pupils in 11 states. Each paper in the two sets of examinations was marked independently by two experienced teachers. This study made it possible to compare the reliability of the test with agreement in marking the test (reader reliability). The two independent markings of the *same* papers correlated .62, but the two different sets of examinations marked by the same teacher correlated only .43. In a similar study of the New York Regents' Examinations, comparable results were obtained. The average agreement of the two independent markings of the same paper was .72, but the average agreement of the two sets of tests marked by the same teacher was only .42. Of course, if the two sets were marked by different teachers, the agreement would be expected to be even lower.

In another study, two independent sets of marks assigned by two "experienced readers of essay examinations" correlated .94 on form *A* and .84 on form *B,* but the correlation between scores on form A and form B was only .60. Coffman (1971) found that correlations between two different 45-minute essay questions with two different readers on an advanced-placement test in American history were .28–.48, depending on the two questions involved, whereas correlations between readers on the same questions were .54–.67. These and other studies (Michael, Cooper, Shaffer & Wallis, 1980) illustrate an important point: *Agreement in marking the essay test is higher than the true reliability of the test itself.* It is important to have scorer reliability, but it is more important that the obtained scores are generalizable to the content universe of which the examination exercises are samples.

The reliability coefficient of an essay test is the correlation between two different forms of the essay test, scored independently. In simplest form, it is the correlation between teacher 1's grades for the form *A* essays with teacher 2's grades for the form *B* essays of the same students. If two teachers would grade the form *A* essays and two other teachers would grade the form *B* essays, the reliability would improve. Then for each student the total score would be found on form *A* for the two teachers who graded the form *A* papers, and the total score on form *B* for the two teachers (different from the form *A* graders) who graded the form *B* papers. The total scores of the pupils on form *A* would then be correlated with their total scores on form *B*. In other words, test reliability is improved when reader reliability is increased.

Notice, however, that a student's total score on the two forms combined would be more reliable than his or her total score on form *A* or form *B* alone. If r_{AB} is the reliability coefficient for either form *A* or form *B*, then the reliability coefficient of $(A + B)$ is estimated by the Spearman-Brown formula (4.3). For example, if $r_{AB} = .50$, then

$$r_{(A + B)} = \frac{2r_{AB}}{1 + r_{AB}} = \frac{2(.50)}{1 + .50} = .67.$$

If there were three comparable forms, *A, B,* and *C,* each with a reliability coefficient of .50, the reliability of total scores on all three forms combined, $A + B + C$, would be even higher as estimated by the Spearman-Brown formula (4.3):

$$r_{(A + B + C)} = \frac{3(.50)}{1 + (3 - 1)(.50)} = .75$$

Therefore, *to increase the reliability of essay test scores, increase the number of questions on the test.* If the number of competent readers were increased, an additional increase in reliability would result. It is crucial that the essay questions be prepared carefully so the r_{AB} for teacher 1 grading form *A* with teacher 2 grading form *B* will be as high as possible.

One study found that the correlation of less than .60 between a carefully developed and scored single-question 20-minute essay exercise designed to measure writing ability and an objective test of writing ability [the Test of Standard Written English (TSWE), a 30-minute test] is increased to more than .70 if three 20-minute essay exercises are used. When both measures were extended to one-hour tests, the correlation exceeded .75 (Breland & Gaynor, 1979).

Essay Test Validity

Since measurement precision is a necessary condition for validity and since reader reliability is a prerequisite for test reliability, all of the factors that we have been considering are also relevant to the validity of essay tests. There are additional concerns as well. Since the usual classroom essay examination has only a few questions, it tends to have low content validity as an achievement test. The limited subject matter sampling of the essay test means that a large chance factor (sampling error) is operative in the selection of the questions that appear on the test. Suppose there are a large number of possible questions that might appear on a three-question test. The test might be an essay test in social studies or three problems on a math or physics test. Suppose that you know the answers to only one-half of the questions that could conceivably appear on the test. Assuming a random selection of the questions, there is one chance in eight that you will know the answers to all three questions that appear on the test; there is the same probability that the test will contain none of the problems that you can solve. This is a simplistic example because one probably knows something about most of the questions; nevertheless, it illustrates the large role that chance plays when tests consist of only a few questions. If objective tests are very short, they are subject to the same problem. Since short tests are usually less reliable than long ones, the limited sampling—that is, the small number of questions—tends to restrict the reliability of an essay test. Accurate inferences about a population cannot be made by polling only a very small sample; in like manner, an examinee's general level of mastery or understanding of a universe of content cannot be accurately estimated from a very few questions.

Coffman (1971) reported that a well-constructed 45-minute objective test provided as much information as three 45-minute essay questions, each read by a different reader. The essay scorer is also confronted with many irrelevant factors, such as the quality of the spelling, handwriting, and English used, as well as bluffing, for which no correction formula exists. A recent study involving four colleges found that writing performance in a course in freshman English was predicted more accurately from a multiple-choice writing test (the TSWE) than from an actual sample of the student's writing (Breland & Gaynor, 1979).

Advantages of Essay Tests as Achievement Measures

Even the most enthusiastic advocate of essay tests would scarcely claim they are superior to objective tests in reliability or usability. The best that can be hoped is that by constructing a long test of several carefully focused questions and by using at least two readers who have model answers and sample responses at various anchor points as guides, we can make the reliability of essay tests satisfactory even though it will still be below that of well-developed objective tests. That the questions on an essay test can be written on the blackboard is no longer an advantage, since few of today's schools lack duplicating facilities. The savings in time required to prepare essay tests is more than offset by the extra time required to score them, which is extensive if the scores are to have much validity.

It is apparent that if the use of essay tests is to be justified, it must be for their superior value for certain purposes. What are the unique functions of these tests? If you want novel responses to divergent questions such as "List in two minutes' time all the possible uses you can devise for a book," it seems necessary to seek free responses rather than to provide a large number of uses to be checked in some manner. Conversely, if you want to determine whether pupils can reason ingeniously to arrive at the "best" or "correct" solution, the multiple-choice format can be excellent. As noted earlier, research studies have generally failed to reveal much support for the popular contention that essay and objective tests measure different abilities. Coffman (1969, p. 10), the leading authority on essay testing, summarized the research on this point:

> It seems safe to conclude that the decision to use a particular type of question ought to be made on the basis of efficiency of the type for the particular situation and the skills of the test writer rather than in terms of a supposed uniqueness of the data to be obtained.

In several studies (see Coffman, 1972, p. 2; Hakstian, 1971), students have reported that the kind of test they anticipate influences the study procedures they use. An opponent of objective tests (La Fave, 1964, p. 171) contended that "when preparing for multiple-choice tests the students probably spend more of their time memorizing facts; when preparing for essay exams, they will spend a considerably higher proportion of their time thinking about relations between facts, and with a problem-solving attitude." Hakstian (1971), in two separate experiments, failed to find that the kind of examination anticipated (essay, objective, or a combination) had a bearing on performance on either carefully developed and scored essay tests or objective tests, even though the students reported some differences in study emphasis. Similar findings were reported by Vallance (1947), although more research is needed on this topic, especially for middle and high school students. There is no reason for a teacher not to use a combination of essay and objective questions; this seems to be preferred by a majority of students and teachers (Hensley and Davis, 1952; Bracht, 1967). When the essay exercises can be evaluated fairly, perhaps 20–25% of the testing time should be allocated to essay tasks in order to reap any accompanying instructional gain.

There has been little empirical research on the kind of examination preferred by students. Bracht (1967) found that only 13 percent of college students preferred essay examinations exclusively; twice that number (26 percent) preferred entirely objective tests; and most (61 percent) preferred that the test format be part objective and part essay. Not surprisingly, there was a very high relationship between test preference and the kind of examination on which the student perceived his or her performance to be better. However, Bracht (1967) found that those who preferred essay examinations and those who preferred objective examinations performed equally well on both kinds of test.

Stanley and Beeman (1956) found that college students from most curricular areas did equally well on the objective and essay portions of a final examination in educational psychology. However, mathematics and science majors performed slightly better on the objective part, whereas English majors did slightly better on the essay portion.

Improving the Construction and Use of Essay Tests

Although the essay test has existed for hundreds of years, far less research has been devoted to it than to the objective test. Furthermore, much of the research relating to essay tests has been conducted with poor, unimproved versions. However, a study of the meager experimental literature available does yield several positive suggestions that, if employed, would substantially increase the validity and reliability of essay examinations.

It is just as important to know *when* to use the essay test as it is to know *how* to use it. It is wise to restrict the use of the essay test to the measurement of those organizing and expressive abilities for which it is best adapted. There seems to be no good reason for employing subjective measurement when objective tests measure the same abilities as validly.

Weidemann (1933, 1941) distinguished among eleven definable types of test item. Arranged in a series from simple to complex, these are as follows: (1) what, who, when, which, and where; (2) list; (3) outline; (4) describe; (5) contrast; (6) compare; (7) explain; (8) discuss; (9) develop; (10) summarize; and (11) evaluate. Items of the first two types are in the knowledge level of Bloom's taxonomy; the others require either an essay question or skillfully developed objective questions.

Years ago Monroe and Carter (1923) divided essay questions into twenty-one types. These types, together with sample questions from the field of measurement and some discussion, are as follows:

1. *Selective recall—basis given*
   Name three important developments in psychological measurement that occurred during the first decade of the twentieth century.
2. *Evaluation recall—basis given*
   Name the three persons who have had the greatest influence on the development of intelligence testing.
3. *Comparison of two things on a single designated basis*
   Compare essay tests and objective tests from the standpoint of their effect on the study procedures used by the learner.
4. *Comparison of two things, in general*
   Compare standardized and nonstandardized tests in terms of their proper educational uses.
5. *Decision—for or against*
   In your opinion which are better for educational evaluation, oral or written examinations?

Sometimes this kind of question appears as "What is your favorite *X* and why?" In this case nothing is scorable but the mechanics of composition.

Notice that "why" is ambiguous because it may call either for an account of the student's psychological development or for a list of qualities of X that have special appeal for him or her. There is no justification for scoring the *opinion,* since it was asked for and given.

6. *Cause or effects*

   How do you account for the increased popularity of objective tests during the last 50 years?

7. *Explanation of the use or exact meaning of some word, phrase, or statement in a passage*

   What is the meaning of *objective* in the preceding question?

8. *Summary of some unit of the textbook or of some article read*

   Summarize in not more than one page the advantages and limitations of essay tests.

A comment on the meaning of *summary* may be helpful. If a pupil responds with a mass of detail but omits the main ideas that the details support, he or she has not responded adequately; the ability to summarize is a manifestation of a high order of thinking, and a properly scored summary item should have considerable discriminating power as to degree of understanding of the matters involved.

Here is an example of a summary question:

Discuss X in not less than 300 and not more than 500 words.

In my opinion, for whatever it may be worth, which probably is not very much in view of the fact that I was not present at the time and have no direct knowledge of the central issue involved in the controversy between the contending parties . . .

This means no more than "I have no justification for thinking that. . . ," but it achieves 45 of the desired 300 words instead of just 7.

9. *Analysis (the word itself seldom appears in the question)*

   Why are many so-called intellectuals suspicious of standardized tests?

10. *Statement of relationships*

    Why do nearly all essay tests, regardless of the school subject, tend to a considerable extent to be measures of the learner's mastery of English?

11. *Illustrations or examples (the pupils's own) of principles in science, construction in language*

    Give two common examples of the Bernoulli effect.

12. *Classification*

    What type of error appears in the following test item? "With what country did the United States fight during World War II?"

13. *Application of rules, laws, or principles to new situations*

    In the light of experience in the United States with examinations for selecting college students, what public-relations problem would you expect to arise in developing nations as they begin to use selection tests for college admission?

14. *Discussion*

    Discuss the role of Sir Francis Galton in the development of the Pearson product–moment coefficient of correlation, r.

15. *Statement of an author's purpose in the selection or organization of material*

Why are individual mental tests not treated in greater detail in this book?

16. *Criticism—as to the adequacy, correctness, or relevance of a printed statement, or a classmate's answer to a question on the lesson*

Criticize or defend the statement, "The essay test overrates the importance of knowing *how* to say a thing and underrates the importance of having something to say." ("To criticize" assumes a set of standards, given or known.)

17. *Outline*

Outline the principal steps in the construction of an informal teacher-made test.

18. *Reorganization of facts (a good type of review question to provide training in organization)*

Name five practical suggestions from this book that are particularly applicable in evaluating the subject you teach or plan to teach.

19. *Formulation of new questions—problems and questions raised*

What are some problems relating to the use of essay tests that require further study?

20. *New methods of procedure*

Suggest a plan for proving the truth or falsity of the contention that exemption from semester examinations for the ablest students is good policy in high school.

21. *Inferential thinking*

Are the authors of this book likely to use essay tests frequently in their measurement classes?

Notice that the classifications by Weidemann and by Monroe and Carter distinguish several rather distinct abilities that *can* potentially be measured by essay tests that are carefully prepared and scored. Measuring these abilities by objective items requires skill and careful effort in item construction.

A more representative and valid sampling of the content universe can be obtained by increasing the number of questions and reducing the length of the discussion expected on each. In many cases a well-constructed paragraph is a sufficient answer. Few discussions need exceed one or two pages. In any case, the question should be so worded as to restrict the responses toward the objective that is to be measured. For example, the question, "Explain the reasons for the strike at Consolidated Electronics in 1972," is too general and would be improved if it were restricted by the addition of the phrases "to show (1) the grievances of the employees; (2) the practices of the employer; (3) related national, social, and economic factors; (4) the rival labor unions; and (5) the method of striking." Although such suggestions take away some of the "freedom" of the traditional essay examination, they will improve its validity and reliability. They make it less subjective and less susceptible to bluffing by test-wise examinees.

Many teachers, especially beginning teachers, believe that the essay test is the easiest kind to construct. *It is difficult to construct essay tests of high quality*. Much care and thought must be given to their construction if they are to measure anything but mere memory for factual knowledge. Many of the general principles of testing outlines in Chapters 7 and 9 are as applicable to essay tests as they are to objective tests. The special suggestions of this chapter should help you devise essay questions above the rote-knowledge level. Finally, it is quite possible that, in attempting to phrase essay questions so that they can be answered more specifically and scored more objectively, the results may not be as good as those of an objective test. In any case, it is especially important that the test be reviewed by a colleague if possible.

Preparing Students to Take Essay Tests

Several writers have emphasized the importance of *training* students to take examinations of all kinds. This training can be done well by teachers in classrooms. Wider experience and training in preparing for and taking tests of all kinds is likely to increase accuracy of measurement and, therefore, the fairness of scores for the students tested. For essay tests, pupils should be taught the meanings of the words used in the various types of thought question. They should be taught that "compare" requires a statement of similarities *and* differences and that the answer to such an item is not complete if it omits either. "Contrast" requires only a statement of differences.

Examinees should be taught to apportion their testing time wisely so as to avoid spending most of it on one or two questions. A thorough and excellent response to one question will almost never receive as much credit as good, but less elaborate, responses to two questions. Students should be cautioned about penmanship and the general appearance of their "product." They should be aware that teachers apparently cannot ignore spelling and grammatical errors in their grading (Marshall, 1967; Marshall and Powers, 1969). They should be told to do their best to respond to every question because if they do not, the "bluffer" will be rewarded even more than would otherwise be the case. As indicated previously, the length of an essay response tends to have an important relationship to its rated merit. There probably is at least as much "test-wiseness" in taking an essay test as in taking an objective test. If students are told the "tricks of the trade," the magnitude of irrelevant effects will be minimized, particularly if the scorers also are acquainted with these factors.

The Essay as a Measure of Writing Ability

Many of the problems in using essay tests as measures of achievement can also contaminate their use as measures of writing or composition ability. The problems of reader and test unreliability, the halo effect, penmanship, and item-to-item and test-to-test carryover effects can (and usually do) confound evaluations of students' abilities in written expression.

Questions designed to measure writing ability should not depend on knowledge of facts or prescribed information; otherwise, a student who writes well but has nothing to say will receive a low rating. Questions oriented toward opinions, short stories, or descriptions of a past event are especially useful. A sample 30-minute essay from a standardized test (the Primary Essay Tests, Veal & Biesbrock, 1971) is typical:

> We all do many different things when there is no school. When you are not in school—like in the afternoon or on the weekend or during the summer—what do you like to do best? Tell what you like to do best when there is no school and why it is so much fun.

A second example, used in the National Assessment of Educational Progress (NAEP, 1977b), is given in Figure 8-2, together with two illustrative responses by 17-year-olds. How would you rate each essay using the categories of "inadequate," "competent," and "excellent"? (If you rated response I as "competent" and response II as "excellent," you agreed with the NAEP evaluators.)

When judging writing ability on controversial issues such as the NAEP examples, it is important that the raters do not let their own points of view in-

Task:

Some people believe that a woman's place is in the home. Others do not. Take *one* side of this issue. Write an essay in which you state your position and defend it.

Response I:

One should not generalize about "a woman's place" because like men, a woman should have the choice of her profession. Being a housewife is like any other full time job which should be chosen by the individual. Keeping women in one profession is like telling all men to do the same job. In this way, our society would not be well rounded or prosper because of the imbalance. Women are human beings like men and should be given the full right of choice.

Response II:

A woman's place is not in the home. Woman (sic) are human beings, it is their God given right to pursue whatever career they desire. Life, liberty and the pursuit of happiness have been mentioned in the Declaration of Independence yet woman (sic) have been denied their rights in this sexist society. Not everyone wants to do the same job or pursue the same goals, must women be limited to a narrowly defined sphere of activity? No, a resounding no! We are people, human beings with as complex mental, emotional, physical needs as men, a fact ignored. We are regarded as the second sex, the incomplete sex, satisfied and made whole only by a family. And it is this false assumption shared by many men and women too, fostered by the society we live in that has destroyed many lives because people were not allowed to express the full range of their Godgiven gifts and creativity.

FIGURE 8-2 A sample question designed to measure writing ability and used in the National Assessment of Educational Progress (NAEP, 1977b), with two illustrative responses.

fluence their ratings. Otherwise, the ratings represent factors other than writing ability.

The purpose of essay exercises dictates how they will be evaluated. A global or holistic rating may be satisfactory for college admission, program evaluation, and quality control purposes, but its effective use in the curriculum requires more diagnostic feedback. "C," "average," or "not bad, Jimmy, but you can do better," do not help students improve their writing skills—they need specific, focused suggestions. Diagnostic statements help students deal with aspects of their writing such as style, organization, length, sentence fragments and run-ons, capitalization, spelling, word choice, sentence structure and length, grammar, appearance, and penmanship (Page, 1958).

The Decline in Writing Ability

Along with an achievement decline in most other curricular areas, the NAEP writing assessment revealed that the writing performance of middle and high school students declined between 1969 and 1974, rated both holistically and diagnostically (NAEP, 1976, p. 7). These findings stimulated interest in more systematic assessments of writing ability at the state and local levels, assessments that are often lacking because of the associated difficulties and costs.

The NAEP findings and the public allegations[3] that "most high school graduates can't write" have resulted in the addition of writing tests to the College Board tests.

Essay Tests in College Admissions

Until recently the College Board offered only an unscored writing sample to interested colleges—it did not mark or grade the sample in any way. An essay task is now offered as part of College Board's English Composition test. The essays are scored holistically on a four-point scale by three carefully trained high school and college teachers.

The following description, used by the College Board, illustrates good practice in assessing writing ability. The explicit directions and expectations reduce the influence of test-wiseness on essay tasks.

The Writing Sample, as its name suggests, is an essay-writing exercise which provides colleges with direct evidence of your competence in written expression. You are given one hour to write an essay on a single assigned topic, and copies of your essay, exactly as written, are sent to your school and to the colleges you specify at the time you write the essay.

Here is an example of the kind of topic you will be asked to write on if you are requested by a college to take the Writing Sample:

"Loyalty is a quality which, in the abstract, we delight to honor. In practice, however, it is something that may vary with circumstances and conditions. There is 'loyalty among thieves,' 'loyalty to an ideal, to country, or to cause.'"
Define your concept of loyalty and arrive at a principle regarding its use or abuse.

[3] See, e.g., "Why Johnny Can't Write," *Newsweek*, December 8, 1975.

DIRECTIONS: Express your ideas in a well-planned essay of 300 to 500 words, using several paragraphs to organize your discussion. Your point of view should be supported by and illustrated from your own experience, or by appropriate references to your reading, study, or observation. Be specific. You are expected to express your best thought in your best natural manner. After you have written your essay, *underline the sentence which you think comes closest to summarizing your central idea.*

Objective Measurement of Writing Ability

English composition is the only subject in which subjectively graded tests are used by CEEB. Many people would be surprised to learn that writing ability can be measured reasonably well with objective writing tests. These tests give narrative passages followed by alternative wordings of various portions, requiring the examinee to make judgments as to how the passages could be improved. Godshalk, Swineford, Coffman, and ETS (1966) were able to develop a one-hour objective measure of English composition skill that produced scores that correlated about .75 with a 2⅓-hour criterion essay test that had a reliability of .84. A one-hour "parallel" essay test could not be expected to do appreciably better.[4] Similar results have been found for elementary school students (Hogan & Mishler, 1980). The Test of Standard Written English (TSWE) is now offered as one of the College Board tests. There is also some indication (Bailey, 1977) that the SAT verbal score predicts course grades in English I at least as well as the TSWE. These predictive validity coefficients were not high, however, because of the low reliability of a grade in a single course [estimated by Etaugh, Etaugh, and Hurd (1972) to be .44 for freshmen]. The validity of the TSWE for predicting performance essay tests has been found to be much higher than its validity for predicting a student's grade in a composition course (Osterlund & Cheney, 1978). Other researchers (Hoffman & Ziegler, 1978) have found objective language tests to be an effective and efficient means of identifying college students with deficient writing skills. But the fact that many users will take results more seriously when written compositions are used cannot be dismissed lightly. Face validity is important—the value of medicine may not be realized if the patient does not have faith in it and, hence, does not use it. Another possible beneficial side effect of using essay tasks rather than, or in addition to, objective tests of writing is that their use could encourage more curricular emphasis on composition. Writing is often the neglected "R" because of the time-consuming processes of reading and providing diagnostic feedback to students.

First-Draft Versus Final-Draft Skills

The curricular objectives in writing skills are complex. We want students to be able to write clearly, but is it "first-draft" or "final-draft" excellence that

---

[4] Using the Spearman-Brown formula (see p. 126) to estimate the reliability of the 2⅓-hour essay test, the reliability of a one-hour essay test would be expected to be about .70. The observed score would then be expected to correlate with universe scores about $\sqrt{.70} = .84$. The correlation between the observed scores from the one-hour objective examination with universe scores on the essay test is estimated to be .82, employing a "correction for attenuation" in the criterion ($.75/\sqrt{.84} = .82$).

should be emphasized? Important writing skills such as those required for reports and business are not first-draft competencies. Some great novelists have reported that their efforts are polished through extensive revision before they achieve any special literary merit. This being the case, we will get closer to our ultimate objectives if, when measuring writing ability, we allow students the opportunity to revise and refine their initial efforts—to correct their punctuation, spelling, and sentence structure. In other words "rewriting" and editing skills should not be ignored when assessing writing ability. First-draft writing ability is important, but final-draft writing skills are more important.

Constructing Good Essay Tests

Suggestions for the construction and use of essay examinations include the following:

1. *Make definite provisions for preparing students for taking essay examinations.* Specific training in preparing for and taking examinations of the kinds that are commonly encountered is a legitimate objective of instruction. Perhaps the best way is to find or devise good practice tests, administer them, and discuss the results with the students.

2. *Make sure that questions are carefully focused.* The following questions present freedom not only to students but also to graders: "What are the advantages of individualized instruction?" "Discuss collective bargaining." Structure is needed or the student may miss the intent of the question (Coffman, 1971). A common ploy of the test-wise student is to appear to have "misunderstood" the intent of the question and to emphasize those aspects with which one is thoroughly familiar.

3. *The content and length of questions need to be structured.* Structure can increase the number of questions and reduce the amount of discussion required on each. Such a plan permits a better sampling of the content and, at the same time, allows the responses to be read with greater reliability; both of these increase the validity of the examination.

4. *Have a colleague critique the test.* The composer of a question is in a particular frame of reference that often prevents one from seeing the intrinsic ambiguity and potential misinterpretations that are readily apparent to another person. In addition, an opinion should be sought about (a) the emphases and breadth of coverage, (b) the appropriateness or difficulty of the questions, and (c) the adequacy of the model answers. The small amount of effort required will reap disproportionately large dividends.

5. *The use of optional questions should ordinarily be avoided.* All students should take the same test if their scores are to be compared. On the advanced-placement examination in American history, students write on 3 of 12 possible topics. Even though the questions were devised to be of approximately equal difficulty, the means and σ's on the questions vary considerably (Coffman, 1971, pp. 289-91). When students who were taking the 11+ ex-

aminations in England were offered a choice among five questions, more able children tended to choose three of the questions, while the duller children tended to choose the other two (Wiseman and Wrigley, 1958). Questions are intrinsically different in difficulty. One's score should not depend on which questions one elects to answer. However, if the intent is to measure writing ability, the tasks should be free of subject matter, since content mastery is incidental to the purpose at hand.

6. *Except for writing ability, restrict the use of the essay as an achievement test to those objectives to which it is best adapted.* The time required for students to write answers to a representative sample of questions and the time required to obtain satisfactory reader and test reliability are extensive. Nevertheless, the essay examination remains the preferred method of obtaining evidence of the candidate's ability in some contexts. When it is not clear that an essay test is required for measuring the desired instructional objective, use an objective test. This does not abrogate the use of ungraded essay *exercises* for instructional purposes. In fact, Pidgeon and Yates (1957, p. 38) reported that students in some primary schools in England that had eliminated essay examinations *because of their weaknesses as evaluation measures* frequently needed remedial instruction in written expression in the secondary schools. It is logical that one cannot learn to write well without writing.

7. *Several shorter questions are generally preferable to fewer longer questions for general achievement testing.* One of the greatest limitations of essay tests is the small number of samples of the content universe they provide. More, shorter tasks have greater reliability than fewer, longer tasks for the same amount of testing time (Coffman, 1972). When a test contains few questions a significant chance factor is injected. A small "gap" in a student's knowledge may carry undue weight. This difficulty is also common in math and physical sciences, where tests tend to have few problems or questions. Even though tests in math and the like tend to have high scorer reliability (objectively), they may not be an adequate sample of the content universe (i.e., have high reliability) if they contain only a few questions or exercises.

Improving the Grading or Rating of Essay Tests

Strictly speaking, it is more correct to speak of grading or rating essay examinations than it is to speak of scoring them; *grading* is interpreting quality subjectively in terms of a criterion.

All claims regarding the value of the essay test as a measuring instrument are based on the assumption that the test papers can be read accurately. For example, not only must the essay test elicit from more able students responses that are consistently superior, but the teachers marking the papers must be able to *recognize* consistently that their responses are better.

Cochran and Weidemann (1934, 1937) outlined a procedure for evaluating essay examinations; the essentials of their procedure can be taught in ten minutes. It is noteworthy that the majority of the consistency coefficients of two series of scoring made five weeks apart on highly structured essay tests were between .80 and .90 for teachers with ten minutes of training. Independent scores by experienced readers showed high agreement when the following procedure (given here in a slightly modified and abridged form) was used:

1. *Before scoring any papers, review the material in the textbook that covers the questions, and also the lecture notes on the subject.*

2. *Make a list of the main points that should be discussed in every answer.* Each of these points must be weighed and assigned a certain value if the scoring is to approach accuracy. This value assigned to the main points needed for a reasonably adequate answer is designated the *minimum score*. If examinees discuss points that are not required yet pertinent to the question, an additional value is awarded, called the *extra score*. This extra score may vary for different pupils, but it may not exceed a certain maximum.

3. *Read over a sampling of the papers to obtain a general idea of the quality of answer that may be expected.*

4. *Score one question through all of the papers before evaluating another question.* There are two outstanding advantages to this procedure. First, the comparison of answers appears to make the ratings more exact and fair. Second, having to keep only one model answer or list of points in mind saves time and improves accuracy.

5. *Read the answer through once and then check over it for factual details.* Attempt to mark every historical mistake on the paper and write in the correction briefly. As the answer is read, make a mental note of the points that were omitted and the value of each point, so that at the end of the question you have the minimum grade figured. If there is any additional or extra percentage to be given, it is added to the minimum score, and then the value of the question is written in terms of the percent deducted rather than the positive percent. Then, when every question on a paper has been scored, it is a simple matter to add the negative quantities and obtain the final grade. The use of illustrative answers to various anchor points is often a useful calibration activity (see the following section) that decreases the "slide effect" and increases agreement among raters. (This is especially useful when using essays to measure writing ability.)

6. More than one reader is always desirable and should be employed when practicable. Two ratings, even if they are made rapidly in order to allow time for rating more papers, are generally preferable to a single rating (Coffman, 1972, p. 7).

One cannot overemphasize the importance of three essential steps: (1) preparing in advance a list of points that are desirable in terms of the objectives of the test; (2) assigning a specific value to each essential part of each answer; and (3) grading one question through all the papers before going on to another question.

Attempt to distinguish among several degrees of merit in an answer. When examinations are read carefully, reliability can be increased by using a 10- or 15-point scale. In one study the reliability was .77 when a 5-point scale was used but .85 when a 15-point scale was employed on the same essays (Coffman, 1971, p. 295; 1972).

The Use of Anchor Points in Scoring

This procedure is similar to that used in evaluating handwriting (see Figure 8–1) in relation to illustrated samples along a continuum of proficiency within which there are illustrative examples to "calibrate" the scale at various anchor points. The reader can then judge each essay against these five products rather than a less clearly defined A-to-F scale or some other grading scale. The procedure is as follows:

1. Read quickly through question 1 on many, if not all, of the papers and sort them into five groups as follows: (a) very superior papers, (b) superior papers, (c) average papers, (d) inferior papers, (e) very inferior papers.
2. Reread the papers in each group and select one that is typical of each.
3. Read the papers and compare them to the five anchor point papers. Through the use of + and − markings, a 15-point scale can be developed even though only five anchor points are used.
4. Repeat the procedure for each essay question.

Bear in mind that an equal number of papers in each category is not to be expected. Flanagan (1952) showed that when the ability being measured is normally distributed, the percentages for five groups are 9, 20, 42, 20, and 9. Therefore, about 10 percent of the papers might be called "very superior" and 10 percent "very inferior." Twenty percent would be "superior" and a like percentage "inferior." The remaining 40 percent are "average." These are rough approximations, of course, depending on the ability level of the particular student group being graded. The assumption of a normal distribution often is not appropriate; the reader should not feel obligated to "normalize" the ratings. Perhaps there are few or no papers in category F.

Anonymity

The simple precaution of having the pupil write his or her name inconspicuously either on the back or at the end of the paper, rather than at the top of each page, will also decrease the bias with which the paper is graded. When teachers know the handwriting of their students, this problem cannot easily be avoided. If two teachers have common assignments, perhaps they could "swap" papers for essay grading if only one reading is feasible.

Style

Each teacher should adopt a policy regarding what factors shall be considered, and what factors not considered, in evaluating a written examination. *Only those factors should be taken into account that afford evidence of the degree to which the pupil has attained the objectives set for that particular course.* Except in English classes, this may rule out or reduce the influence of reductions for such things as faulty sentence structure, poor paragraphing, bad handwriting, and misspelling of nontechnical words. These factors will be considered only when they affect the clarity of the pupil's discussion. It is always legitimate to hold the pupil responsible for the spelling, as well as the meaning, of terms that are part of the curricular objectives.

This does not mean that the quality of the written English used in examinations is unimportant and should therefore be disregarded. On the contrary, it is always very important. But it should be considered in determining the student's mark in English, not how well he or she understands physics or economics.

Proper Use of Essay Exercises

Despite the valid objections to essay tests as they are often used, they can be employed wisely as an essential *part* of instructional activities; to a lesser extent, they can be useful for measuring and evaluating objectives in most curricular areas. Do not avoid using objective testing because of the attacks on such tests that have been published by well-intentioned people in professional and popular magazines and in books. Such attacks confuse testing with teaching. The two are related, of course, but not completely. Compositions, essays, and discussion questions that prove to be poor *tests* may nevertheless be worthwhile instructional activities. If the teacher goes through an essay carefully and makes constructive remarks, perhaps followed by oral discussion, the student may benefit greatly even if no grade is assigned. If, however, teachers merely mark the paper "A," "B," or the like without commenting, the grading may be highly unreliable and the students probably will not learn how to improve their skills. It is possible to do both—that is, grade and comment—in which event the comments may be helpful even if the grading is unreliable (Page, 1958).

Summary

Even though essay tests, as typically used in education, have face validity, they tend to be characterized by low scorer reliability and low test reliability, both of which are essential for test validity. Scoring is often contaminated by penmanship, length of response, lack of anonymity, and item-to-item and test-to-test carryover effects in grading.

The quality of essay tests can be improved if questions are carefully structured in content and length and if all students write on identical sets of questions. If possible, scoring should be done with the examinee remaining anonymous, with one question being evaluated on all papers before the next question is graded, and by more than one rater. Essays may be important instructional experiences apart from their use as evaluation devices.

IMPORTANT TERMS AND CONCEPTS

reader (scorer) reliability	model answer	test-wiseness
test reliability	slide effect	face validity
halo effect	objective tests	anchor (calibration) points
carryover effect	bluffing	

1. What is the order in which these types of tests appear to have been used for the first time in educational evaluation?
   a) Essay, oral, multiple-choice
   b) Oral, multiple-choice, essay
   c) Multiple-choice, oral, essay
   d) Essay, multiple-choice, oral
   e) Oral, essay, multiple-choice

In the following questions, match the test characteristic with the type(s) of test for which it is typical. More than one option is needed for some items.

a) Oral   b) Essay   c) Objective   d) both (a) and (b)   e) (a), (b), and (c)

2. The scoring of students' response is quite subjective.

3. The halo effect can easily influence scoring.

4. Students' questions are of unequal difficulty.

5. The effect of guessing (not bluffing) is greatest.

6. Bluffing can influence the results.

7. It is difficult to obtain satisfactory test reliability.

8. The potential for measuring originality and creativity is very limited.

9. Evaluations are not contaminated by language fluency.

10. The test is easy to score accurately.

11. The test can measure the ability to solve problems.

12. Scoring is influenced by penmanship.

13. Scoring is influenced by spelling ability.

14. The test requires the most time to develop.

15. The test can be scored quickly.

16. In which one of the following ways are essay tests superior to objective tests?
   a) Better samples the universe of content
   b) Higher face validity
   c) Higher test reliability
   d) Less influenced by test-wiseness

17. On essay tests, which of these two characteristics tends to be higher?
   a) Reader (scorer) reliability
   b) Test reliability

18. On objective tests, scorer reliability is approximately
   a) 0.0   b) 0.5   c) 1.0

19. Is it possible to have high test reliability without high scorer reliability?

20. Is it possible to have high reader reliability with low test reliability?

For questions 21–28, dealing with the grading of essay tests, select the appropriate option (a–d). Options may be used more than once or not at all.

a) Halo effect b) Carryover effect c) Slide effect d) None of these

21. The tendency for tests that are read early to be given higher marks than those read later.

22. The tendency for performance on question 1 to influence the grading of question 2.

23. The tendency for longer responses to be given higher grades.

24. A problem with computer scoring of essay tests.

25. The tendency for grades to be influenced by nontest characteristics of the examinee.

26. Can be prevented if questions are graded independently.

27. Can be prevented if essays are graded anonymously.

28. Which two can be reduced if essays are scored in a different order for each question?

29. Which one of the following essay tests would probably have the highest reliability?
  a) 500 words on one question
  b) 250 words on each of two questions
  c) 100 words on each of 5 questions

30. Research indicates that teachers often evaluate essays on content alone and are not influenced by errors in grammar, spelling, or punctuation. (T or F)

31. Research indicates that
  a) more students prefer essay tests than objective tests.
  b) students prefer the type of test on which they think they do best.
  c) students who prefer essay tests do relatively better on such tests than they do on objective tests.
  d) students report that they prepare similarly for both essay and objective tests.

32. Many essay tests measure only at the knowledge level, not at the higher levels of Bloom's taxonomy. (T or F)

33. An essay question such as "Write a summary of this chapter in 300 words or less" is an example of a question that requires mastery only at the knowledge level in terms of Bloom's taxonomy. (T or F)

34. If the parallel-form reliability of a two-question essay test is .40, estimate the reliability if forms A and B are combined into a single four-question test.

$$r_{(A + B)} = \frac{2(r_{AB})}{1 + r_{AB}}$$

35. If the test length is increased to eight questions, estimate its reliability.

36. The authors feel that test-wiseness skills for essay tests should be taught to students. (T or F)

Which of these are generally desirable practices in essay testing?

37. Provide optional questions.

38. Frame questions so as to allow examinees freedom in interpretation.

39. Use several shorter questions rather than one or two longer ones.

40. Use essay tests to measure facts.

41. Use model answers in scoring.

42. Grade by sorting into not more than three groups.

43. Reread questions after preliminary sorting.

44. More than one reader should grade the papers.

45. Keep identity of student in mind while grading the paper.

46. Give extra credit for good penmanship and neatness.

ANSWERS TO CHAPTER TEST

1. e	16. b	32. T
2. d	17. a	33. F
3. d	18. c	34. .57
4. a (b also if student has choice of questions)	19. no	35. .73
	20. yes	36. T
5. c	21. c	37. no
6. d	22. b	38. no
7. d	23. d	39. yes
8. c	24. d	40. no
9. c	25. a	41. yes
10. c	26. b	42. no
11. e	27. a	43. yes
12. b	28. b, c	44. yes
13. b	29. c	45. no
14. c	30. F	46. no
15. c	31. b	

FOR ADDITIONAL READING

COFFMAN, W. E. On the validity of essay tests of achievement. *Journal of Educational Measurement,* 3, no. 2 (1966), 151–56. Reprinted in G. H. Bracht, K. D. Hopkins, and J. C. Stanley. *Perspectives in educational and psychological measurement.* Englewood Cliffs, N.J.: Prentice-Hall, 1972. Selection 16.

———. Achievement tests. In R. L. Ebel, ed., *Encyclopedia of Educational Research,* 4th ed. New York: Macmillan, 1969.

———. Essay examinations. In R. L. Thorndike, ed., *Educational measurement,* 2nd ed. Washington, D.C.: American Council on Education, 1971. Chap. 10.

CURETON, L. W. The history of grading practices. *NCME Measurement in Education,* 2 (1971), 1–8.

GODSHALK, R., F. SWINEFORD, and W. E. COFFMAN. *The measurement of writing ability.* Princeton, N.J.: College Entrance Examination Board, 1966.

HAKSTIAN, A. R. The effect on study methods and test performance of objective and essay examinations. *Journal of Educational Research,* 64, no. 7 (1971), 319–24.

MARSHALL, J. C. Composition errors and essay examination grades re-examined. *American Educational Research Journal,* 4, no. 4 (1967), 375–85.

PAGE, E. B. The imminence of grading essays by computer. *Phi Delta Kappan,* 47 (1966), 238–43.

PIDGEON, D. A., and A. YATES. Experimental inquiries into the use of essay-type English papers. *British Journal of Educational Psychology,* 27 (1957), 37–47.

SHEPARD, L. A. Setting standards and living with them. *Florida Journal of Educational Research,* 18 (1976), 28–32.

SOLOMON, R. J. Improving the essay test in the social studies. In H. D. Berg, ed., *Evaluation in social studies.* Washington, D.C.: National Council for Social Studies, 1965. Pp. 137–53.

VERNON, P. E., and G. D. MILLICAN. A further study of the reliability of English essays. *British Journal of Statistical Psychology,* 7, pt. 2 (1954), 65–74.

Constructing Objective Tests

In Chapter 7 we considered general principles for constructing items to measure cognitive objectives. Now we develop specific guidelines and procedures for writing good items of several types. For classroom purposes this chapter can be one of the most important in the book; if test items are prepared insightfully and skillfully, a high-quality assessment will result.

No amount of statistical manipulation will transform poorly written items into good ones, but techniques such as item analysis (see Chapter 10) can help identify items that should be eliminated or revised.

The two main classes of objective test items are short-answer items and fixed-response items. Fixed-response items include multiple-choice, true-false, and matching questions.

Fixed-Response Items

Fixed-response items offer only a limited number of response options. Advantages of the fixed-response test are its applicability to a wide range of subject matter, objectivity of scoring, and efficiency (wide sampling of the content universe per unit of working time). The most common type of fixed-response item is the multiple-choice question used in most published tests. Here is an example from a social-studies test:

1. The House of Representatives has the authority, within limits, to determine who shall become President in case
   a) no candidate receives a majority of the popular votes.
   b) no candidate receives a majority of the electoral votes.
   c) no candidate receives a majority of both the popular and electoral votes.
   d) the elected candidate dies before he can be inaugurated.

Only one of the four options correctly completes the *stem* (the part of the item that precedes the options). The other incorrect options are designed to seduce the uninformed and are known as *distractors*. For an item to be effective, distractors must be plausible and tempting to examinees who do not know the correct answer. Indeed, *the single most important skill in constructing good multiple-choice items is the ability to devise plausible, attractive distractors.*

Multiple-choice items are sometimes viewed simply as "recognition" items capable of testing only rote knowledge. But they can measure higher taxonomy levels, as will be illustrated in this chapter. Even straightforward arithmetical reasoning items such as "How many minutes will it take you to jog to school if you live one mile from school and jog at a speed of 10 miles per hour?" involves application-level skills. A blank can be left at the end of such a question (short-answer format), or several options from which the examinee must choose can be provided. In neither case is recall alone involved, as it might be if we asked the year England entered World War I.

Multiple-Choice Items

A *multiple-choice item* presents two or more responses, only one of which is correct or definitely better than the others. It is also possible to have several correct options and one incorrect or least desirable option, which must be chosen. Item stems may be in the form of direct questions, incomplete statements, or words or phrases.

Rationale for the Multiple-Choice Item. Many persons assume that multiple-choice tests are popular because they are easy to score. Their major virtues, however, are that they (1) require the examinee to *discriminate* among alternatives and (2) remove ambiguity and subjectivity in scoring. The "best-answer" type of multiple-choice item can measure the degree of understanding of abstract concepts. Consider the following item:

2. Which one of the following changes would be expected to *reduce* the test–retest reliability coefficient of a pure power test of 50 items by the greatest amount?
   a) Eliminate the ten items that were answered correctly by all examinees.
   b) Eliminate the ten most difficult items.
   c) Eliminate the ten items that correlated negatively with the total score.
   d) Use the correction-for-chance in scoring.
   e) Base the test–retest correlation only on examinees who scored above the median on the initial test.

If one thoroughly understands the concept of reliability and the factors that influence it, one should be able to determine that option e is clearly the *best* answer.

Option a has virtually no effect on reliability. These ten items serve only to add a constant to all scores.

Option b would be expected to lower reliability somewhat.

Option c would be expected to improve reliability.

Option d would have no effect, since everyone attempted all items.

Option e would lower the reliability coefficient substantially.

Such an item can determine whether a concept is mastered or whether the examinee's understanding is incomplete. The item will seem ambiguous to "fuzzy-thinking" students because of inadequacies in the student's knowledge—this is termed *extrinsic ambiguity* (Ebel, 1979, pp. 118–20). The extrinsically ambiguous item will function well if many naive students select a distractor and hence do not receive credit. Extrinsic ambiguity is a desirable characteristic of a test—comprehension and application items should appear ambiguous to those who have a faulty grasp of the concept being tested.

Ambiguous Versus Trick Questions. It is important to distinguish between ambiguous and "tricky" questions. Knowledgeable examinees may miss trick questions because they fail to perceive a trivial detail. Examinees will typically respond quickly and thoughtfully to trick questions—missing them does not usually result from the compelling attractiveness of two or more options (i.e., ambiguity). Consider the following trick question:

3. If you bought 3 candy bars each costing 15 cents, how much change should you get back from $1.00?
a) .65¢ b) .55¢ c) .45¢ d) none of these

Some examinees who have mastered the relevant skills will miss the item because they failed to attend to the decimal point. Other examples of trick questions include trivial misspelling of names or forms, and confusing use of negatives.

Intrinsic Versus Extrinsic Ambiguity. Test makers may introduce irrelevant ambiguities by attempting to make too fine a distinction, thus making valid discrimination among options impossible. Such items illustrate *intrinsic* ambiguity, a highly undesirable characteristic. For example, suppose option e were excluded and "pure power test" were deleted from the stem of item 2. The knowledgeable student would be at a loss to choose between options b and d—the item would possess intrinsic ambiguity. Fortunately, intrinsic ambiguity can usually be identified when an item analysis is conducted (see Chapter 10).

In other words, there are two possible types of ambiguity in test items. Extrinsic ambiguity is a result of faulty understanding on the part of the examinee. Intrinsic ambiguity results from either imprecise wording, inadequate framing of the items, distinctions that cannot be validly made from the information available. Intrinsically ambiguous items should be revised or eliminated because they reduce the reliability and validity of tests. Extrinsically ambiguous questions increase reliability and validity.

In attempting to avoid intrinsic ambiguity, test makers often construct multiple-choice items that are so easy that little understanding is needed to identify the correct answer.

Comprehension- and application-level items are more vulnerable to intrinsic ambiguity. Consider the following item:

4. What is the most important characteristic of a test?
a) high validity b) large number of items c) large number of difficult items.

This item requires only a primitive level of understanding to select the correct answer, a. Distractors b and c are not very plausible. Distractors must be plausible to examinees with an inadequate grasp of the concepts being tested if the item is to serve its purpose. But if two more options—d) good norms, and e) high reliability—were added, the item could help identify examinees with greater levels of understanding, such as an understanding of the difference between validity and reliability. In short, a skillful test constructor must be able to develop attractive distractors.

One can also use the multiple-choice item to require the student to select the poorest or least accurate option. Suppose, for example, that on a vocabulary test examinees are asked,

5. Which of the following terms is least synonymous with the others?
a) contemplate   d) ponder
b) cogitate   e) cerebrate
c) comprehend

Option c, "comprehend," has the least semantic overlap with the others and would be identified by examinees who correctly understand the meanings of the various words.

Of course, if "comprehend" were replaced by "disseminate" or "irritate," the item would function at a more primitive level, since "disseminate" and "irritate" have no semantic overlap with the other terms.

What if the stem of item 5 were changed to "Which one of the following terms is most similar in meaning to *ruminate*?" The item would then be intrinsically ambiguous because there is not a definitive "best answer."

The multiple-choice item is usually regarded as the most valuable and most generally applicable test form. Years ago the measurement authority E. F. Lindquist (Hawkes, Lindquist, and Mann, 1936, p. 138) asserted that the multiple-choice item is "definitely superior to all other types" for measuring such educational objectives as "inferential reasoning, reasoned understanding, or sound judgment and discrimination on the part of the pupil." It remains so today. Another leading psychometrician (Cronbach, 1950) demonstrated that multiple-choice items are less vulnerable to response sets than other types of item.

It is the quality of the items, not the type of item employed, that determines a good test. Some multiple-choice items are so poor that they can be answered correctly by attending to irrelevant clues; others measure only isolated or trivial facts. *The measurement value of multiple-choice tests depends more on the skillful selection of distractors than on any other factor* (Weitzman & McNamara, 1946).

illustrations of multiple-choice items[1]

The following items, most of which are taken from standardized tests, illustrate several different arrangements of multiple-choice tests in a variety of subjects. The multiple choice test is widely used in all school subjects and on all educational levels for measuring a variety of teaching objectives.

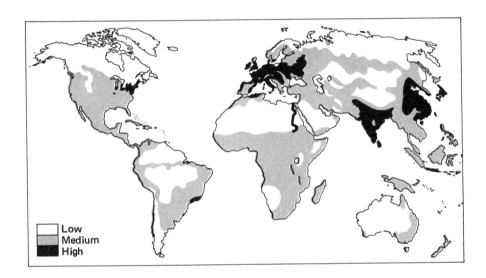

Low
Medium
High

6. The shading on the above map is used to indicate
  (A) population density
  (B) percentage of total labor force in agriculture
  (C) per capita income
  (D) death rate per thousand of population

In many of the multiple-choice questions included in social-science tests, an attempt is made to require the student to make use of general knowledge in the interpretation of materials. Thus, this question does not simply ask, What areas of the world have the highest population densities? Rather, it presents a novel situation in which the student must infer that, of the choices offered, only population density provides a plausible explanation of the shadings on the map.

[1] The first three of the illustrative items that follow are from *Multiple-choice questions: A close look.* Copyright © 1963 by Educational Testing Service. All rights reserved. Reproduced by permission.

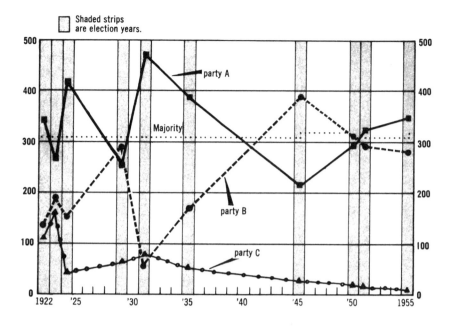

Shaded strips are election years.

7. The graph above represents the political composition from 1922 to 1955 of which of the following?
(A) German Bundestag
(B) French National Assembly
(C) Italian Chamber of Deputies
(D) British House of Commons

To answer this question correctly students must be able to do several things. First, they must be able to read the graph. Then, using the information they can infer from it, they must interpret it in the light of their knowledge of European history and government from 1922 to 1955 and draw a conclusion concerning which legislative body may properly be depicted thus. In such a process it is possible for different students to make use of different information to arrive at the correct answer.

8. One method of obtaining "artificial gravity" in a space station is to have the station rotating about axis AA' as it revolves around Earth.

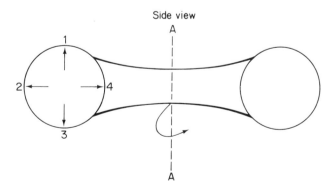

Side view

The inhabitants of the space station would call which direction "down"?
(A) Direction 1
(B) Direction 2
(C) Direction 3
(D) Direction 4
(E) Any one of the four, depending on speed of rotation

This was part of a set of questions administered to students who were completing a year of high school physics. The question illustrates the kind of response that can be expected of well-trained students of high school age when they are presented with a relatively novel situation based on fundamental concepts from the field of mechanics.

This question requires that the student consider the nature of a possible mechanism for providing a "down" direction in a space station to simulate the gravitational "down" that is so important in our normal activities on Earth. Choice (C) is the direction normally considered down in diagrams. Although this direction is not significant in the space station, a sizable number of the poorer physics students chose it. Other students assumed that the "down" direction would be toward the center of rotation of the station, choice (D). However, objects that are free to move in the space station behave like particles in a centrifuge and "fall" to the outer edge. This direction, (B), then, is the "down" direction in the rotating station. The other choices, (A), "up" as it is usually represented in diagrams, and (E), a direction that depends on the speed of rotation, were not selected by many students.

*sequential tests of educational progress,
social studies[2]*

"In these disputes, I find myself in an unfortunate position!"
Crosby Washington Star

[2] From *Sequential Tests of Educational Progress—Series II*. Copyright © 1969 by Educational Testing Service. All rights reserved. Reprinted by permission.

9. What is the main point of the cartoon?
A. Labor-management disputes often lead to violence.
B. The government is powerless to stop strikes.
C. Farmers lack a sufficient voice in national politics.
D. The public often suffers in labor-management conflicts.

metropolitan achievement tests, language[3]

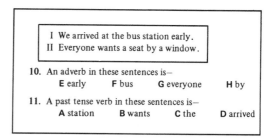

I We arrived at the bus station early.
II Everyone wants a seat by a window.

10. An adverb in these sentences is—
   E early   **F** bus   **G** everyone   **H** by

11. A past tense verb in these sentences is—
   A station   **B** wants   **C** the   **D** arrived

the modern school achievement tests, language usage[4]

          1. **off**
12. I borrowed a pen 2. **off of** my brother.   . . . . . .
          3. **from**

          1. **your**
13. Every student must do 2. **his**   best.   . . . . . .
          3. **their**

    1. **has got**
14. He 2. **has**   his violin with him.   . . . . . .
    3. **has gotten**

the barrett-ryan literature test: silas marner[5]

15. ( ) An episode that advances the plot is the—1. murdering of a man. 2. kidnapping of a child. 3. stealing of money. 4. fighting of a duel.

16. ( ) A chief characteristic of the novel is—1. humorous passages. 2. portrayal of character. 3. historical facts. 4. fairy element.

wesley test in political terms[6]

17. An embargo is
   1. a law or regulation
   2. a kind of boat
   3. an explorer
   4. a foolish adventure
   5. an embankment

[3] Published by Psychological Corp.
[4] Published by Teachers College Press.
[5] Published by Kansas State Teachers College, Emporia.
[6] Published by Charles Scribner's Sons, New York.

unit scales of attainment in foods and household management[7]

18. We get the most calories per pound from
   1. proteins
   2. carbohydrates
   3. fats
   4. mineral matter
   5. vitamins

college board, foreign-language items[8]

19. C'est la fin de l'entracte, et la pièce est très amusante. Vous dites à votre comarade:
   (A) La pièce va commencer tout de suite.
   (B) Qu'allons-nous faire maintenant?
   (C) Allons reprendre nos places.
   (D) Voulez-vous aller fumer une cigarette?

college board, english items

DIRECTIONS: The following sentences contain problems in grammar, usage, word choice, and idiom.

Some sentences are correct.

No sentence contains more than one error.

You will find that the error, if any, will be underlined and lettered, and that all other elements of the sentence are correct and cannot be changed.

If there is an error, select the *one underlined part* that must be changed in order to make the sentence correct, and blacken the corresponding space on your answer sheet.

If there is no error, mark answer space E.

EXAMPLE: He spoke <u>bluntly</u> and <u>angrily</u> to <u>we</u> <u>spectators.</u> <u>No error</u>
      A   B C D   E

SAMPLE ANSWER: A B C D E
          ☐ ☐ ■ ☐ ☐

---

20. Had we <u>known</u> of your desire to go with us, we <u>most</u> certainly <u>would of</u> in-
    A   B   C
vited you to <u>join</u> our party. <u>No error</u>
    D   E

21. Big Konrad's new helper, though somewhat <u>slighter</u> of build than <u>him,</u>
               A   B

---

[7] Published by Educational Test Bureau.

[8] From *A description of the College Board achievement tests* (Princeton, N.J.: College Entrance Examination Board, 1963).

set out <u>to prove that</u> skill <u>may</u> compensate for lack of brute strength.
C   D

<u>No error</u>
E

DIRECTIONS: Each group of sentences in this section is actually a paragraph presented in scrambled order. Each sentence in the group has a place in that paragraph; no sentence is to be left out. You are to read each group of sentences and decide the best order in which to put the sentences so as to form a well-organized paragraph.

Before trying to answer the questions which follow each group of sentences, jot down the correct order of the sentences in the margin of the test book. Then answer each of the questions by blackening the appropriate space on the answer sheet. Remember that you will receive credit only for answers marked on the answer sheet. . . .

sample paragraph

P. The Empire State Express, loaded with passengers, left New York.

Q. Unlike the businessmen, however, a few reporters on board had been told that this run would be newsworthy and were eagerly waiting for something unusual to occur.

R. At last the big day, May 10, arrived.

S. If some of the important businessmen on board had known what was going to happen, they might have found an excuse to leave the train at Albany.

T. Her secret had been carefully kept.

U. Only a few officials knew that a record was to be tried for.

CORRECT
ORDER
OF
SENTENCES

R
P
T
U
S
Q

sample questions

i. Which sentence did you put first?
 (A) P
 (B) R
 (C) S
 (D) T
 (E) U

ii. Which sentence did you put after Sentence P?
 (A) Q
 (B) R
 (C) S
 (D) T
 (E) U

cooperative test of social studies abilities, experimental form Q[9]

DIRECTIONS: The exercises in this part consist of a series of paragraphs each followed by several statements about the paragraph. In the parentheses after each statement, put the number

1. if the statement is a reasonable interpretation, fully supported by the facts given in the paragraph.

[9] Originally published by Cooperative Test Service.

2. if the statement goes beyond and cannot be proved by the facts given in the paragraph.

3. if the statement contradicts the facts given in the paragraph.

22. The nineteenth century witnessed a rapid growth in Germany's industrial power. Like England, Germany came to have a fairly satisfactory balance between the amounts of its export and import trade. Heavy exports of coke supplied full cargoes for ships to foreign ports and helped to balance heavy importations of raw materials. The imports especially provided a means for distributing freight rates to the advantage of the German trader competing overseas. By these means Germany was constantly obtaining larger portions of world trade. German wares were carried into every trading realm, and trade meant political as well as commercial power in foreign lands.

4. England was unable to balance the tonnage of her import and export shipments .... 4 ( )

5. By reducing freight rates Germany was constantly gaining a greater percentage of world trade .... 5 ( )

6. The sale of German wares in every part of the world resulted in added political influence and commercial growth .... 6 ( )

sequential tests of educational progress (STEP), science[10]

Level 4 (Grades 4-6)

23. SITUATION: Tom wanted to learn which of three types of soil—clay, sand, or loam—would be best for growing lima beans. He found three flowerpots, put a different type of soil in each pot, and planted lima beans in each. He placed them side by side on the window sill and gave each pot the same amount of water.

LOAM   CLAY   SAND

The lima beans grew best in the loam. Why did Mr. Jackson say Tom's experiment was NOT a good experiment and did not prove that loam was the best soil for plant growth?

A. The plants in one pot got more sunlight than the plants in the other pots.

B. The amount of soil in each pot was not the same.

C. One pot should have been placed in the dark.

D. Tom should have used three kinds of seeds.

Level 3 (Grades 7-9)

24. SITUATION: Tom planned to become a farmer and his father encouraged this interest by giving Tom a part of the garden to use for studying plant life.

Tom wanted to find out what effect fertilizer has on garden plants. He put some good soil in two different boxes. To box A he added fertilizer contain-

---

[10] Published by Cooperative Test Division, Educational Testing Service, Princeton, N.J.

ing a large amount of nitrogen. To box B he added fertilizer containing a large amount of phosphorus. In each box he planted 12 bean seeds. He watered each box with the same amount of water. One thing missing from Tom's experiment was a box of soil with

A. both fertilizers added
B. neither nitrogen nor phosphorus fertilizers added
C. several kinds of seed planted
D. no seeds planted

The following test items are from the Colorado Needs Assessment Program, Grade 5 Math. The percent of students giving correct answers for each of four ethnic groups is given in parentheses in this order: blacks, Chicanos, Indians, and whites.

25. What is the temperature shown by this thermometer?

A) 88°
B) 93°
C) 96°
D) 102°
E) 104°
(30%, 33%, 44%, 58%)

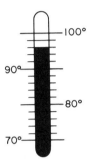

26. If the thermometer shown above is correct, and in Colorado, the season of the year is probably:

A) spring B) summer C) fall D) winter
(66%, 71%, 83%, 86%)

27. The time on the clock below is *NOT*

A) 45 minutes after three.
B) 15 minutes until 3.
C) 2:45.
D) forty-five minutes past two.
E) quarter until three.
(41%, 42%, 54%, 61%)

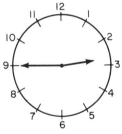

28. Which one of these is the longest period of time?

A) 600 minutes B) 100 hours C) 20 days D) 2 weeks E) 1/2 month
(33%, 31%, 38%, 51%)

29. If you are calling your grandmother on the phone, and the operator says, "Sixty-five cents, please," which set of coins would *NOT* total 65¢?

A) 6 dimes, and 1 nickel
B) 2 quarters, 1 dime, and 1 nickel
C) 1 quarter, 3 nickels, and 3 dimes
D) 13 nickels
E) 3 dimes and 7 nickels
(52%, 54%, 44%, 63%)

30. Twenty minutes is what part of an hour?

A) 1/2 B) 1/3 C) 1/4 D) 2/5 E) 1/5
(25%, 30%, 44%, 48%)

31. The shaded portions of the diagram below represent what part of the figure?

A) 1/2 B) 5/10 C) 5/9 D) 5/12 E) 4/9
(52%, 52%, 65%, 67%)

32. Which one of these is the greatest distance?
A) 1 yard B) 5 feet C) 1 ⅓ yards D) 50 inches E) 4 ½ feet
(36%, 33%, 44%, 48%)

33. The greatest number using the digits 3, 9, 7, 6 only once is:
A) 3679 B) 9376 C) 7963 D) 9763 E) 6739
(44%, 48%, 60%, 69%)

Guidelines for Constructing Multiple-Choice Items. Testing specialists Harry Berg (1958, 1961) and Jason Millman (1961) have given suggestions for increasing the quality of objective test items in the social studies. Many of the suggestions appear to be just good "common sense," but evidently the sense is not common, because virtually all teacher-made tests contain violations of these rules. These suggestions deal primarily with item form and format. It is presumed that the test constructor has used a table of specifications or some other procedure to ensure content validity and has attended to the need to have higher-taxonomy-level items.

1. *The stem should contain the central problem and all qualifications,* including words that would otherwise be repeated in each alternative. The pupil should not be required to construct the question by consulting the options. In two of his examples Berg illustrates such flaws:

   I. "The study of the price system narrows down to an analysis of these two sets of prices and the interrelationships between them." The two sets of prices referred to are
   (A) those for consumption goods and those for capital goods.
   (B) those for consumption goods and those for productive services.
   (C) those for labor and those for the other productive factors.
   (D) those for economic and those for noneconomic goods.

Obviously, "those for" should have been included in the second sentence of the stem because "those for" occurs as the first two words of every option. If the incomplete stem is used, it must include all the language that is exactly applicable in every option in order to avoid wasting the pupil's time.

   II. Consumer cooperatives
   (A) are to consumers what labor unions are to laborers.
   (B) have recently been declared illegal.
   (C) originated in the United States and later spread to Europe.
   (D) have been criticized as not paying their equitable share of taxes.

Here there are actually four true–false questions; each concerns consumer cooperatives, but only one is keyed as true. The stem, "Consumer cooperatives," does not constitute a statement of a central problem. Questions that lend themselves naturally to a true–false item form should not be forced into a multiple-choice style.

2. *Each item should be as short as possible,* consistent with clarity. Otherwise, valuable testing time is wasted.

3. *Negatively stated stems must be used with care.* Negatively phrased items tend to be more difficult than those phrased in a positive way (Dudycha & Carpenter, 1973). If negative item forms are used, emphasize the fact by underlining or using italics. Negative items can be useful, but it is desirable to group them together and to underscore the negative words, such as *not, never,* and *least.* Another useful technique is to end the stem with the words "with one exception; select the exception." For example, "Each of the following men *except one* was president of the United States. Which one was *not*?"

4. *State the problem of the question fully in the stem.* Incomplete stems tend to be more difficult than closed-stem phrasing (Dudycha & Carpenter, 1973).

5. *Ask for the best answer and use terms such as* most *and* primary *if more than one answer is at least partially correct.* One alternative should clearly be best. For example, "The one factor generally considered most important in causing the United States to enter World War II was . . ."

6. *The omissions in incomplete statements should usually occur toward the end of the stem.* Confusion and excessive rereading of the stem can result if a blank appears near the beginning of the stem. Better yet, rephrase the item as a question whenever possible.

7. *The reading and linguistic difficulty of items should be low.* The incidental vocabulary and phrasing used in items should be kept as simple as possible. Incidental or unnecessarily technical terms should be avoided. Consider this example:

III. Lower animals, in contradistinction to *homo sapiens,*
   a) are incapable of any communication.
   b) cannot develop true conditioned responses.
   c) lack adaptive instincts.
   d) do not become objects to themselves.
   e) are independent of the homeostatic principle.

Homo sapiens, conditioned responses, and *homeostatic* may be unnecessarily technical for measuring the objective. *Contradistinction* should be replaced by a simpler word.

8. *Whenever possible, arrange the alternatives in a logical order— order of magnitude, temporal sequence, and so on.*

9. *Avoid regular, recurring patterns of correct responses.* Some examinees are likely to detect them.

10. *Distractors must be plausible and attractive if the item is to measure real understanding.* Distractors must be prepared carefully or they will not be functional. Put yourself in the shoes of the examinees and simulate the likely kinds of errors and misunderstandings. After the item has been administered,

an item analysis (see Chapter 10) should be performed to determine how well the distractors functioned. Unattractive distractors can be replaced.

For example, a teacher of general mathematics in a junior high school might devise the following test item. The various options are designed to reflect different kinds of common errors.

IV. What is the circumference (in inches) of a circle with a radius of 5 inches?
   a) $5 \times 3.14 = 15.7$
   b) $10 \times 3.14 = 31.4$
   c) $5^2 \times 3.14 = 78.5$
   d) $10^2 \times 3.14 = 314$
   e) none of the above

Students who confuse circumference with area ($A = \pi r^2$) might choose option c. Students who confuse diameter with radius might select option a; those who confuse area with circumference might select option c; those who make both errors might choose option d.

Of course, all distractors may not or need not function as planned. The item can still do its job if at least one of the distractors attracts many students who do not deserve credit.

Devising excellent multiple-choice items is a highly creative and challenging process, particularly in the construction of distractors.

11. To the extent possible, *alternatives should be uniform in subject content, form, length, explicitness, and grammatical structure.* In addition, all options should be grammatically consistent with the stem. Inconsistent articles, changes in tense, and the like may introduce intrinsic ambiguity and spoil an otherwise excellent question. An item like the following gives a strong grammatical clue to the correct option:

V. Lewis and Clark were famous for
   a) inventors
   b) exploring the Santa Fe trail.
   c) Indians
   d) the pasteurizing of milk.
   e) the Louisiana Purchase.

The item would be improved by replacing options a, c, d, and e as follows:

   a) inventing the cotton gin.
   c) exploring the northeastern United States.
   d) discovering the pasteurizing process for milk.
   e) exploring the land of the Louisiana Purchase.

The degree of technicality of alternatives should ordinarily be uniform. A flagrant violation will illustrate this difficulty.

VI. An atom is
   a) an amalgam.
   b) a compound.
   c) a mixture.
   d) a molecule.
   e) the basic "building block" of matter, consisting of a nucleus surrounded by electrons in orbits.

Test-wise students will notice immediately that option e is much longer than the other answers. Even without a clear idea of the relationship of atoms to compounds, mixtures, and molecules, they will have little doubt that the correct answer is e because it "stands out" from the others (Chase, 1964). Some experienced item writers occasionally choose to lure students who are test-wise but lack knowledge to a distractor by making it long and elaborate while leaving the correct option short and simple.

The following illustration shows how the degree of understanding required can be increased when options are made more homogeneous:

VII. Engle's law deals with
    a) the coinage of money.   d) marginal utility.
    b) the inevitableness of socialism.   e) family expenditures.
    c) diminishing returns.

VIII. Engel's law deals with family expenditures for
    a) luxuries.   c) clothing.   e) necessaries.
    b) food.   d) rest.

IX. According to Engel's law, family expenditures for food
    a) increase in accordance with the size of the family.
    b) decrease as income increases.
    c) require a smaller percentage of an increasing income.
    d) rise in proportion to income.
    e) vary with the tastes of families.

To respond correctly to item VII, the student must know only that Engel's law deals with family expenditures. For item VIII, the student must know that the specific item of expenditure is food. The maximum degree of discrimination, however, is required in answering item IX, in which more information is given in the stem. Notice that all the options for a given item should have parallel grammatical structure.

12. *The correct response should not occur in a regularly recurring pattern and should occur approximately equally at all response option positions.*

13. *Have three or more options per item* unless doing so requires using implausible options. Five alternatives per item are optimal for many situations, but sometimes more options may be available. The format of many separate answer sheets limits the number of options to five. Fewer options may be desirable for examinees in grade 3 or below.

14. *Use care in the repetition of words or phrases between the stem and the* correct *answer.* It is legitimate and even desirable, however, to incorporate such repetition in the incorrect options. Like all rules, this can be overdone. If all distractors are loaded with irrelevant lengthiness, false technicality, and words from the stem, but the correct response stands out because of its quality and simplicity, test-wise students can select the correct answer without much knowledge about the point being tested. The test constructor must be clever and versatile; he or she should be able to "read the students' minds" in advance (and in retrospect, too, from the item analysis) without allowing his or her intentions to be discernible.

For example, in question X the word *battle* appears in the stem and in the correct option; thus, it provides an irrelevant clue for the test-wise examinee.

X. A decisive battle between United States soldiers and American Indians was the
  a) battle called "Custer's last stand."
  b) fighting at Yorktown.
  c) War of 1812.
  d) storming of the Alamo.

Notice that option c, "War of 1812," is poor since it violates rule 11 (grammatical consistency). The stem specifies a single battle, whereas a war usually involves more than one battle. The test-wise student will ignore option c.

The question might be reworded as follows:

XI. A decisive battle between United States soldiers and American Indians was the
  a) last stand of Custer.   c) Battle of Gettysburg.
  b) fighting at Yorktown.   d) Battle of the Alamo.

Now the word *battle* appears in two incorrect options but not in the correct option, so it may distract test-wise students who do not know the correct answer.

15. *Avoid textbook wording or stereotyped phraseology* (except perhaps in distractors, as discussed earlier). The comprehension and application taxonomy levels require that the question be posed in a fresh context; otherwise, the correct answer can be selected by thoughtless parroting of the textbook.

16. *Avoid items that reveal the answer to another item.* One item should not help the test-wise student detect the answer to another. The items that form the test should be reviewed carefully. When possible, it is helpful to have a competent person review the entire test for overlapping items, grammatical inconsistency, misspellings, and other flaws.

17. *Ordinarily, distractors should not overlap, subsume, or be synonymous with one another.* Consider the following item:

XII. A substance that in its pure form is a good conductor of electricity is
  a) water   c) H_2S
  b) silver   d) H_2O

Since there is only one correct answer, the alert student can eliminate options a and d immediately. The chances of getting undeserved credit for the item are greatly increased.

18. *Avoid specific determiners* such as *always* and *never,* except occasionally to foil test-wise examinees who know that few things are always true or never true. This requires that a word that is usually determining be employed in a nondetermining way part of the time. Options containing "always" should be true about as often as they are false, so that test-wise examinees cannot reject them automatically. Words that are usually specific determiners can be used to increase validity if used judiciously. For example,

XIII. If two parallel forms of a test, each with $r_{xx} = .5$, are combined into a single test,
  *a) the reliability coefficient will always increase.
  b) the mean percent score will probably change considerably.
  c) the test will be too long to be very functional.
  d) its validity coefficient will be approximately doubled.

Notice that the correct answer contains *always,* which ordinarily denotes a distractor. Also, the qualifiers *probably* and *approximately* are included in distractors b and d to make them more attractive to ignorant examinees.

19. *Avoid arranging items in the order in which they were presented in the textbook.* This is especially important for tests on spelling and multiplication facts and other learning tasks in which serial learning is possible. Although test scores are sometimes slightly higher when items are arranged in the order in which they were learned (Norman, 1954; Marso, 1970b), the logical validity of the test is reduced.

20. *Do not include so many items in the test that it becomes a speed rather than a power test.* Thought-provoking and problem-solving items can be time-consuming; items that measure rote knowledge can be answered quickly. If an instructor realizes that too many items have been included in the test for the time allowed, probably the class should be informed that a specified number of the later items will not be scored. Allowing speed of response to be a significant factor influencing test results is a serious threat to the test's validity. Many able students are not speedy test takers.

21. *"None of these" may be a useful last option* for correct-answer items (Williamson and Hopkins, 1967), although its use tends to make items somewhat more difficult (Choppin, 1974). Avoid using it when the keyed response is merely the *best* answer among the responses given rather than the wholly correct or best possible answer. The option saves the test maker's time, since it can be used repeatedly. What answer would you mark for the following item?

XIV. Which word is spelled correctly?
a) Ocurrence
b) Desireable
c) Mispelled
d) Vaccum
e) None of the above

(If you selected option e, give yourself a gold star. Notice how much more knowledge was required than would be the case if you had to identify only one correctly spelled word.) The "none of these" option can introduce intrinsic ambiguity if it is not used carefully. What if option d were changed to "judgement?" Since this spelling of *judgment* is given as an acceptable spelling in most dictionaries, the item would be intrinsically ambiguous.

Also, make sure that "none of these" is sometimes the correct response. It is used rather infrequently by professional item writers, except on math, spelling, and grammar tests, where "correct-answer" rather than "best-answer" options are typical.

22. *"All of the above" or "More than one of the above" options may sometimes be useful.*

XV. If h, k, m, and n are positive numbers, k is greater than m, and n is greater than h, which of the following *can be* true?
1. $n + h = k + m$
2. $k + h = n + m$
3. $k + n = m + h$
a) 1, 2; b) 2 only; c) 3 only; d) two of the above; e) All of the above

Notice that the three equations could be combined in eight ways, producing eight possible options: none (1), any one (3), any two (3), and all (1). The eight alternatives for each such item would yield a slight gain over just five, since the probability of getting the answer correct by chance would be reduced from .20 to .125. A better possibility would be to recast the item into three separate questions.

23. *Paragraph each option,* unless all the options are so brief that they easily fit on a single line. This reduces the time and effort needed to locate the correct answer and the chances of incorrectly reading or mismarking an answer.

24. *Use numerals for items and letters for options.*

25. *Punctuate the options correctly.* If the stem of the item is an incomplete statement, each option is a possible completion of the statement. Therefore, each option should begin with a lower-case letter and be followed by a terminal mark of punctuation (period, question mark, exclamation point). If the stem is a direct question and each option is a sentence that might possibly answer it, begin each option with a capital letter and follow it with a terminal mark of punctuation. If the stem is a question but the options are words or phrases and not complete sentences, begin each option with a capital letter but do not put any mark of punctuation at its end.

There are exceptions to even the best guidelines. But careful consideration of these twenty-five suggestions should help you construct better multiple-choice items. This is no substitute for practice. Practice is invaluable, especially when it is accompanied by the critical reactions of examinees and a measurement specialist, as well as an item analysis.

True–False and Two-Option Items

"If you're smart, you can pass a true or false test without being smart." (Linus in "Peanuts" by Schulz)

The *true-false test,* a form that is very popular with classroom teachers, has been the object of more criticism than any other form of objective test. Ebel (1970a, 1971) has demonstrated that much of the criticism is undeserved and that true–false items are not limited to measuring at the knowledge level of Bloom's taxonomy. Although multiple-choice items tend to be more reliable and valid than true–false items, T–F tests can contain 50% or more items in the same amount of testing time (Frisbie, 1974). Well-constructed T–F tests can compare favorably with multiple-choice tests when using testing time rather than number of items as the basis for comparison (Frisbee, 1973; Ebel, 1971; Irvin, Halpern & Landman, 1980).

The negative-suggestion effect of the true–false item (i.e., the presumably undesirable effect of incorrect statements on students) and the guessing factor are often pointed to as its greatest limitations. The correction formula may provide a fairly satisfactory adjustment for the effect of guessing.

The danger of negative suggestion when pupils read statements that are false has been overstated, but it may not be wise to use true–false tests as pretests when misinformation might be learned, or with young children, who may be more susceptible to misinformation. In such cases it is better to avoid the true–false format; instead of a declarative statement, use a question that can be answered by the two options "yes" or "no."

Several modifications of the true–false test have been proposed, such as having students cross out the part of the statement that is in error. Some researchers (Curtis, Darling, & Sherman, 1943; Wright, 1944) have found that having students correct the wrong statements can increase the reliability of the test. These suggestions add to the labor of scoring and have not been widely accepted. The most obvious ways to improve the true–false test are to *prepare it more carefully* and *make the test longer*. An important and often unrecognized advantage of the true–false test is that more items can be included in the same testing time. To achieve satisfactory reliability, however, more true–false items are required than would ordinarily be necessary with multiple-choice items.

The low regard that many test experts have for true–false items is reflected in their absence from most recent standardized achievement tests. Although this type of item has been overused by classroom teachers, it does have a legitimate use in achievement tests. In some situations it is difficult or impossible to construct more than two plausible responses for a multiple choice item in which one alternative is correct (or true) and the other incorrect. Common examples include the case forms of pronouns (such as *who* vs. *whom*); correct use of singular and plural verbs; confusion of the past tense and past participle; the use of *sit* and *set, lay* and *lie;* and many others. Since true–false items are particularly susceptible to intrinsic ambiguity, it is often preferable to reword declarative statements into questions that can be answered "yes" or "no." Better yet, recast the item into a multiple-choice question with two or more options.

For example, instead of

34. Columbus discovered America in 1492. (T or F)

one could write

35. Columbus discovered America in ____.
   a) 492   b) 1482   c) 1492   d) 1692   e) 1942

or

36. _____ discovered America in **37.** _____.
   a) Magellan   a)   492
   b) Napoleon   b)   1482
   c) Sir Francis Drake c)   1492
   d) Cortez   d)   1692
   e) Columbus   e)   1942

or even

38. _____discovered **39.** _____in **40.** _____
   a) Magellan   a) Africa   a) 492
   b) Napoleon   b) Alaska   b) 1482
   c) Sir Francis Drake   c) America   c) 1492
   d) Cortez   d) Australia   d) 1692
   e) Columbus   e) Toledo   e) 1942

Of course, care is needed to ensure that only one of the 125 possible response patterns is correct.

Illustrations of Two-Choice Fixed-Response Items

california achievement tests, advanced battery[11]

41. (Isn't Aren't) the baskets filled with flowers?   _____ 41

42. I approve of (his him) going.   _____ 42

For each statement given below that is a complete sentence, mark YES; for each that is not, mark NO.

43. When we approach the deserted farmhouse at night.   YES NO 43

44. The mountains resounded with peals of thunder which indicated the storm's fury.   YES NO 44

iowa silent reading tests, new edition, sentence meaning, elementary level[12]

45. Is a dime less in value than a nickel?..................... 45. YES NO

46. Is geography studied in public schools?.................. 46. YES NO

test in english fundamentals, grammar[13]

DIRECTIONS: Classify the italicized words in the sentence below as adjectives or adverbs by placing check marks in the proper columns:

	Adjective	Adverb
47. That was a *silly* remark. 47		
48. Those flowers smell *sweet*. 48		
49. You can *hardly* expect him to wait. 49		

cooperative plane geometry test, revised series Q[14]

DIRECTIONS: Read these statements and mark each one in the parentheses with a plus sign (+) if you think it is always true, or with a zero (0) if you think it is always or sometimes false.

( ) **50.** The diameter of a circle divides the circle into two equal parts.

( ) **51.** If two triangles are similar, their areas are in the same ratio as the medians drawn to corresponding sides.

( ) **52.** All similar polygons are equilateral.

[11] Published by California Test Bureau.

[12] Published by Harcourt Brace Jovanovich.

[13] Published by Ginn.

[14] Published by Cooperative Test Division, Educational Testing Service, Princeton, N.J.

cooperative solid geometry tests[15]

( ) **53.** Any number of planes may be passed through a given straight line.
( ) **54.** Two planes parallel to the same straight line are parallel to each other.
( ) **55.** The square of a diagonal of a cube is three times the square of its edge.

test on everyday problems in science, unit III[16]

( ) **56.** Minerals in our food supply furnish heat and energy to the body.

george washington university english literature test[17]

T F **57.** "Il Penseroso" describes the charms of a merry social life.
T F **58.** "Pilgrim's Progress" is one of the greatest prose allegories in literature.

Suggestions for Constructing True–False Response Items. Preparing excellent fixed-response items requires great skill. The true–false test is generally thought to be one of the easiest to prepare. This ease is more apparent than real. Unusual care must be exercised in wording true–false statements and questions so that the *content* rather than the *form* of the statement determines the response. The test maker's aim should be to phrase the statement so that no unwarranted clues are provided, without needlessly obscuring the meaning. With practice and care, one can attain this balance. The following suggestions may be helpful in constructing true–false tests. Many of the suggestions for constructing multiple-choice tests are also applicable.

1. *Avoid using specific determiners as clues.* It has been found that strongly worded statements are more likely to be false than true, but that moderately worded statements are more likely to be true than false. (As a wit once said, "Every generalization, including this one, is false.") Strongly worded statements often contain *all, always, never, no, none,* or *nothing.* Moderately worded statements often contain qualifying words such as *many, some, sometimes, often, frequently, generally,* and *as a rule.* If one carefully balances the number of true and false statements containing such expressions, these words cease to be specific determiners that afford clues to the answer.

At times one can use specific determiners to increase the validity of an item. For example,

    I. For a given set of test data, the reliability coefficient yielded by Kuder-Richardson formula 21 can never exceed that yielded by K-R formula 20. (T or F)

Test-wise examinees who lack knowledge will tend to answer "false" because of the apparent specific determiner *never.* In other words, because of test-

---

[15] Devised by H. T. Lundholm et al., and published by Cooperative Test Division, Educational Testing Service, Princeton, N.J.
[16] Devised by C. J. Pieper and W. L. Beauchamp, and published by Scott, Foresman.
[17] Published by Center for Psychological Services.

wiseness, fewer ignorant students will select the correct answer. Along the same lines, many ignorant examinees will select "true" to the following item because of the qualifier "usually."

> **II.** Kuder-Richardson 21 reliability estimates are usually larger than K-R20 reliability estimates. (T or F)

2. *Avoid a disproportionate number of either true or false statements.* Several studies have shown that false statements tend to be slightly more valid than true statements because many examinees who do not know the correct answer tend to have an acquiescence response style and mark "true" (Cronbach, 1942). Therefore, it is sometimes suggested that a test should contain more false statements than true ones; Ebel (1965b) suggested that perhaps 60 percent of the items should be false. If this is overdone, however, the validity of the false statements will probably decrease because the "word will get out" to select "false" when in doubt.

3. *Avoid the exact wording of the textbook.* Lifting true statements directly from the textbook or making true statements false by changing a single word or expression emphasizes rote memory rather than understanding.

4. *Avoid trick statements.* These are usually statements that appear to be true but that are really false because of the petty insertion of some inconspicuous word, phrase, or letter.

EXAMPLES:

> **III.** "The Raven" was written by Edgar Allen Poe. [Notice the spelling of *Allan.*]
> **IV.** The Battle of Hastings was fought in 1066 BC [Notice BC]

BETTER:

> **V.** "The Raven" was written by Henry Wadsworth Longfellow.
> **VI.** What famous battle was fought in 1066 AD?
> a) Battle of Bull Run
> b) Battle of Hastings
> c) Battle of Waterloo

5. *Limit each statement to the exact point to be tested.* Do not use two or more stimuli to elicit one response, as in the following partly true, partly false statement: "Poe wrote 'The Gold Bug' and *The Scarlet Letter.*"

6. *Avoid excess use of negative words and phrases.* Such statements introduce intrinsic ambiguity. Knowledgeable students may select the incorrect option because of semantic confusion. An extreme example will graphically illustrate this point:

> **VII.** On true–false tests negative phrases should not be disallowed. (T or F)

7. *Avoid ambiguous words and statements.* With one interpretation certain statements can be true, and with another equally plausible interpretation they can be false. It is impossible to tell what is being measured by intrinsically ambiguous statements that have more than one legitimate interpretation. The statement, "The Aztecs were a backward people," is true if they are

compared with Europeans of the same period, but it is false if they are compared with American Indians of that time.

8. *Avoid complex vocabulary and language and unnecessarily complex sentence structure.* Use simple and concise language. The level of the examinees must be considered in the wording of items. A statement is badly worded if examinees understand the point involved but miss the item because of the language employed. Consider this flagrant violation:

> **VIII.** It is considered good practice to use esoteric, recondite expressions in true–false items. (T or F)

9. *Require the simplest possible method of indicating the response.* When separate answer sheets are not used, let the examinee circle T or F, Yes or No, or underline the correct response.

10. *Use true–false items only for points that lend themselves unambiguously to this kind of item.* Rarely should a major test be composed exclusively of true–false items.

Matching Exercises

A *matching exercise* typically consists of two columns; each stem in the first column is to be paired with an alternative in the second column. Matching exercises that provide more responses than stems are frequently used because they reduce the examinee's chances of guessing successfully. Sometimes the stems in the first column are incomplete sentences, each requiring a word or phrase from the second columnn for its completion. The matching exercise is useful for measuring terminology, knowledge of facts, geography, charts, and diagrams.

Advantages and Limitations of Matching Exercises. Many types of learning involve the association of two things in the learner's mind. Common examples are events and dates, events and persons, events and places, terms and definitions, foreign words and English equivalents, laws and illustrations, rules and examples, authors and their works, and tools and their use. The matching exercise is very convenient for measuring such associations.

Matching items are particularly well adapted to testing in "who, what, where, and when" situations. Their principal limitations are as follows:

1. Matching items are not well adapted to the measurement of understanding as distinguished from mere memory—it is difficult to design a matching exercise that will measure higher-taxonomy-level skills such as the ability to interpret complex relationships.
2. With the possible exception of the true–false test, the matching exercise is the item form that is most likely to include irrelevant clues to the correct response.
3. If they are not skillfully constructed, matching items can be time-consuming and inefficient.

The illustrations and suggestions that follow are designed to overcome the last two of these limitations.

Illustrations of Matching Exercises. Because matching exercises often have too many options (more than 5) for many standard answer sheets, they appear infrequently in current published tests. They are still common in teacher-made tests, however. Following is a "square," 10-by-10, unrevised matching exercise from a social-studies quiz in which we can "learn by undoing."

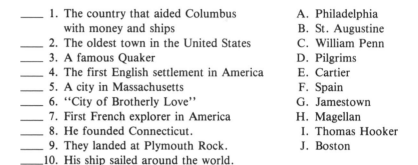

____ 1.	The country that aided Columbus with money and ships	A. Philadelphia
____ 2.	The oldest town in the United States	B. St. Augustine
____ 3.	A famous Quaker	C. William Penn
____ 4.	The first English settlement in America	D. Pilgrims
____ 5.	A city in Massachusetts	E. Cartier
____ 6.	"City of Brotherly Love"	F. Spain
____ 7.	First French explorer in America	G. Jamestown
____ 8.	He founded Connecticut.	H. Magellan
____ 9.	They landed at Plymouth Rock.	I. Thomas Hooker
____10.	His ship sailed around the world.	J. Boston

This material is too heterogeneous for a single matching exercise. Four of the options are names of cities, four are names of persons, one is the name of a country, and one is a plural noun. How much do students have to know about early U.S. history to figure out the correct answers? For item 1, they have only to recognize that Spain is the only country in the list of alternatives. Their choice for item 2 lies among A, B, G, and J. For item 3, they are likely to reject "Cartier" and "Magellan" as not sounding "Quakerish," leaving just C, "William Penn," and I, "Thomas Hooker." Item 4 uses the same four options as item 2, and perhaps "St. Augustine" does not sound like an English name. Item 5 has a nonhistorical ring that is out of context with the other nine items. Item 6 is the fourth and last of the "city" items; it is automatically answerable if one has surmised the correct answers to items 2, 4, and 5. In effect, the "city" questions constitute a 4 x 4 matching exercise that might have better been presented as such, instead of being buried in the 10 x 10 format, which takes more testing time and favors the test-wise.

"Persons" also constitutes an embedded 4 x 4 matching exercise. Item 7 contains the giveaway "French," which points to Cartier, the only French-sounding name among the four. Ignorant but shrewd pupils will probably choose the answer to item 8 between options C and I, because it seems unlikely that Connecticut was founded by a person with a name like Cartier or Magellan. (True, this is a hazardous procedure and requires a little knowledge, but it is the stuff of which test-wiseness is made—the ability to increase the odds of getting credit by using test-taking skills.) Item 9 is ridiculous, for the "They" who landed at Plymouth Rock *must* be the only plural word among the ten alternatives. By the time the average pupil comes to item 10, the fourth person in the list of ten items (it may not have been saved for last), he or she probably feels that cunning is more important than knowledge in getting through this maze. Far better exercises could have been prepared to cover the material.

This 10-item matching exercise appeared in a 40-item social studies test along with 10 three-option multiple-choice items, 10 true–false items, and 10 completion items. It was administered to 33 students who had just completed a unit of instruction on U.S. colonial history. The four teachers who constructed the test claimed that the objectives for the social studies course were (1) to help pupils understand how America developed into a great nation, (2) to teach the children the pertinent facts about the discovery and colonization of our country, and (3) to intensify pupil interest in the workings of democracy. The matching exercise obviously emphasized the second objective.

The results of the item analysis based on the 33 pupils tested are interesting. First the papers were graded for all 40 items. They were then arranged according to total score, from the highest to the lowest (33rd). Then the highest 27 percent (9 papers) and the lowest 27 percent (also 9 papers) were compared for responses to each item. The most discriminating item was number 9, "They landed at Plymouth Rock," which we have already decided could be answered solely from the correspondence of the "They" to the plural "Pilgrims" because these were the only plurals among either the items or the alternatives. The 9 top-scoring pupils on the entire test all marked this item correctly, while the 9 lowest-scoring pupils all marked it incorrectly! It may be that this is the central theme of the unit and that the ablest students would have gotten it right even without the specific determiner, but it is uncomfortable to suspect that the primary determinant of score on the test *might* be verbal ability, reading ability, or test sophistication, not specific knowledge of the topic studied.

The least discriminating of the ten matching items was number 2, "The oldest town in the United States." Only 1 of the 9 in the low group and 3 of the 9 in the high group answered it correctly. The most difficult item on the entire test was number 6, "City of Brotherly Love," which was missed by all 9 in the low group and by 6 in the high group. By looking at the actual options marked, a teacher can to some extent "read the pupils' minds" to give direction for remedial teaching. With just a little direction and practice, the four teachers could devise items that are freer of the faults we noticed.

The following is another type of matching exercise; it was devised as part of a 93-item test for a grade 9 English class of 36 students.

She and Margaret have probably gone to the little grocery store around the cor-
14 15   16   17   18   19   20
ner.

____14. She	A. noun	
____15. Margaret	B. pronoun	
____16. have gone	C. verb	
____17. probably	D. adjective	
____18. little	E. adverb	
____19. grocery	F. preposition	
____20. around		

This is actually a 7 x 6 matching item. Any number of items could be used with the 6 alternatives. On the test itself, 40 items were used, with 15 sentences and a 6-column arrangement for checking the part of speech. Items

16 and 19 were the most discriminating of the 7 shown here, and item 15 was the least discriminating. All items appeared to measure the desired behavior. The most difficult of the 7 items was number 19, which was missed by 11 of the 12 lowest scorers but by only one of the 12 highest scorers. Incidentally, the most discriminating item in the sentence "The *hearty breakfast* was *soon* finished," was the adjective *hearty*. Most of the lowest scorers thought it was an adverb because of the "y" ending—they appeared to be looking more at the form of the word than at its function in the sentence.

A little knowledge can be a dangerous thing, and misapplication of knowledge can sometimes be detected from the item analysis. Consider the following item: "No one but (A. he) (B. him) came to the meeting." Five of the 12 lowest-scoring students chose *he* and missed the item, but nine of the 12 highest scorers missed it. Apparently, the more able students knew that *but* is usually a conjunction and concluded that this is a compound sentence in which *he* is the subject of the verb *came*. The lowest-scoring students, not knowing much about parts of speech, may have based their answer on the sound of the sentence. They were probably used to saying, "This is him," and *him* sounded right in the test sentence. To check this hypothesis, high and low scorers could be questioned about their reasons for marking A or B.

Consider three other examples of matching exercises (Stecklein, 1955). The first goes readily with six-option printed answer sheets when options are lettered.

DIRECTIONS: Famous inventions are listed in the left-hand column below. In the right hand column are names of famous inventors. Place the letter corresponding to the inventor in the space before the invention for which he is famous.

Inventions	*Inventors*
____1. Steam boat	A. Alexander Bell
____2. Cotton gin	B. George Washington Carver
____3. Sewing machine	C. Robert Fulton
____4. Reaper	D. Elias Howe
	E. Cyrus McCormick
	F. Eli Whitney

DIRECTIONS: Quotations from poetry written during the Romantic Period are listed in the column at the left below. In the column at the right, names of famous poets are listed. You are to indicate the author of each of the quotations by writing in the space before the number of the quotation the letter corresponding to the name of the author in the right-hand column.

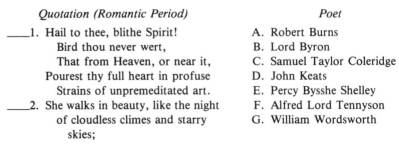

Quotation (Romantic Period)	*Poet*
____1. Hail to thee, blithe Spirit! Bird thou never wert, That from Heaven, or near it, Pourest thy full heart in profuse Strains of unpremeditated art.	A. Robert Burns B. Lord Byron C. Samuel Taylor Coleridge D. John Keats E. Percy Bysshe Shelley
____2. She walks in beauty, like the night of cloudless climes and starry skies;	F. Alfred Lord Tennyson G. William Wordsworth

And all that's best of dark and
bright
meet in her aspect and her eyes.
_____3. My heart leaps up when I behold
a rainbow in the sky;
So was it when my life began;
So is it now I am a man;
So be it when I shall grow old,
or let me die!
_____4. A thing of beauty is a joy forever:
Its loveliness increases; it will never
Pass into nothingness; but still will
keep
A bower quiet for us, and a sleep
Full of sweet dreams, and health,
and quiet breathing.

DIRECTIONS: Three lists are presented below. Famous English authors of plays are listed in the column farthest to the right, names of well-known plays are listed in the center column, and in the column farthest to the left are names of characters in some of these plays. You are to look at the name of the character listed, decide in which play this character appears, and identify the author of this play. Indicate your answers as follows: Place the small alphabet letter corresponding to the play in which the character appears in the first space before the name of the character; place the capital alphabet letter corresponding to the author of this play in the second space before the name of the character. Note that there are more names of plays and authors than there are names of characters, so not all answers will be used.

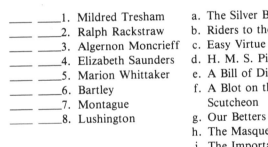

___ ___1. Mildred Tresham	a. The Silver Box	A. John Millington Synge
___ ___2. Ralph Rackstraw	b. Riders to the Sea	B. Clemence Dane
___ ___3. Algernon Moncrieff	c. Easy Virtue	C. Robert Browning
___ ___4. Elizabeth Saunders	d. H. M. S. Pinafore	D. W. Somerset Maugham
___ ___5. Marion Whittaker	e. A Bill of Divorcement	E. Henry Arthur Jones
___ ___6. Bartley	f. A Blot on the Scutcheon	F. Noel Coward
___ ___7. Montague	g. Our Betters	G. Oscar Wilde
___ ___8. Lushington	h. The Masqueraders	H. W. S. Gilbert
	i. The Importance of Being Earnest	I. John Galsworthy

Suggestions for Constructing Matching Exercises. In addition to the suggestions for constructing multiple-choice and true–false items, certain recommendations pertain especially to matching exercises.

1. *Include only homogeneous material in each matching exercise.* Do not mix such dissimilar items as persons and places in a single exercise. We demonstrated in the Colonial America exercise why such heterogeneity is undesirable.

2. *Check each exercise carefully for unwarranted clues to matching*

pairs. For each item ask yourself this question: What is the least amount of information that must be known to select the right response?

3. *Be sure that the students fully understand the rationale for the matching.* May an option be used for more than one item? May the desired response to a given item consist of more than one option? (This is usually an undesirable practice.) Communicate your exact intent to the pupils.

4. *Place items on the left and number them; place options on the right and designate them by letters.* Item numbers should run consecutively throughout the test, but option letters should begin anew with each matching exercise.

5. *Arrange items and options in a systematic order.* If the list consists of numerals or dates, arrange them in order. Option words may be alphabetized to make it easier for the student to locate the desired response.

6. *Place all the items and options for a matching exercise on a single page,* if possible. Turning the page back and forth in search of desired responses is confusing and time-consuming.

7. *Limit a matching exercise to not more than 10–15 items.* Longer lists tend to be too heterogeneous and afford clues for the test-wise; they also require more time per item. If testing time is limited, they can be influenced by clerical speed and accuracy.

Short-Answer Items

The *short-answer* test is an objective test in which each item is in the form of a direct question, a stimulus word or phrase, a specific direction, a specific problem, or an incomplete statement or question. The response must be *supplied* by the pupil rather than merely *identified* from a list of suggested answers supplied by the teacher. This kind of test differs from the essay examination primarily in the degree of structure imposed on the examinees, and the length of the responses. The typical answer to the free-response item is short, usually requiring a single word, number, or phrase. Thus, it is sometimes called a short-answer objective item. Example: "Who developed the 1916 Stanford-Binet Intelligence Scale? _____"

Advantages and Limitations

The short-answer test has the obvious advantage of familiarity and "naturalness." It can eliminate guessing almost completely because the student does not choose among a number of possible options. The short-answer test is particularly valuable for mathematics and the physical sciences, where the stimulus appears in the form of a problem requiring computation. It also has wide application to test situations when it is presented in the form of maps, charts, and diagrams for which the pupil is required to supply, in spaces provided, the names of parts keyed by numbers or letters. The short-answer test may have some advantage over the fixed-response item by increasing long-term retention (Gay, 1980).

A limitation of the short-answer test is that it encourages the measurement of highly specific facts and isolated bits of information. This problem is avoidable if the item writer is ingenious. Also, the scoring must be done by hand and is not always entirely objective. For example, which of the following answers to the item, "Who developed the 1916 Stanford-Binet Intelligence Scale?" is correct: Lewis M. Terman, Lewis Terman, L. M. Terman, Louis Terman, Tarman, Termen, or Tarmen? Probably most teachers will consider any of the first three answers fully correct. Some would penalize the last four for inaccurate spelling, even though the student's intent is clear.

Striking illustrations of scorer unreliability on apparently objective content were provided by the classic studies of Starch and Elliott (1913), who analyzed facsimiles of the same geometry paper marked independently by 116 high school mathematics teachers. The grades given ranged from a low of 28 percent to a high of 92. These differences resulted from partial credit for answers containing certain types of errors, such as clerical or computation errors, spelling errors, and the like. These limitations need not be serious when tests are carefully prepared and are scored with the curricular objectives of geometry clearly in mind.

Illustrations of Short-Answer Items

The following are a few sample short-answer test items taken from published tests.[18]

stone reasoning tests in arithmetic[19]

59. James had 5 cents. He earned 13 cents more and then bought a top for 10 cents. How much money did he have left? Answer: _____

60. How many oranges can I buy for 35 cents when oranges cost 7 cents each? Answer: _____

stones-harry high school achievement test, part II[20]

61. What instrument was designed to draw a circle? _____ 61

62. Write in figures: one thousand seven and four hundredths. _____ 62

cooperative general mathematics tests for college students[21]

63. Eight is what percent of 64?.......................... (   )

64. Write an expression that exceeds M by X................ (   )

65. Solve the formula $V = \dfrac{Bh}{3}$ for h...................... (   )

[18] In the examples of various test items, an effort was made to illustrate a wide variety of formats as well as subject matter and grade level. It is recognized that they are not all of equal merit. Some of the tests referred to are out of print but are needed as illustrations because recent published tests are largely of the multiple-choice variety.

[19] Published by Teachers College Press.

[20] Published by Harcourt Brace Jovanovich.

[21] Published by Cooperative Test Division, Educational Testing Service, Princeton, N.J.

iowa placement examinations, chemistry-training[22]

> **66.** The atomic weight of K is 39; of Cl, 35.5; of O, 16. What is
> the molecular weight of $KClO_3$? _____
>
> **67.** If 7 gm. of iron unite with 4 gm. of sulphur, how many gm.
> of iron sulphide will be produced? _____

tests on everyday problems in science, unit XII[23]

> **68.** What is the pressure in pounds of ordinary air per square
> inch at sea level?.................................... (68) _____

Figures, illustrations, and graphs are often useful test stimuli in social studies, science, and math.

*exercise adapted from a test of academic
progress*[24]

> **69.** Directions: In the sketch below give the names of the chambers of the heart.

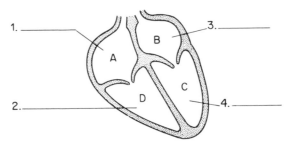

> **70.** Using the letters to represent the chambers in the figure
> above, in what order does the blood circulate through
> the chambers, lungs and body? _____

(This item could be cast into a fixed-response format but in the short-answer format 24 different options are implicit.)

> **71.** Name the three parts of the body of an insect. _____, _____,
> _____

Completion Items

The *completion item,* a special form of the short-answer item, may be defined as a sentence in which certain important words or phrases have been omitted, with blanks inserted for the pupil to fill in. The sentence may contain one or more blanks. The sentences in the test may be disconnected, or they may be organized into a paragraph. Each blank is usually worth one point.

Completion tests have wide applicability. But unless they are prepared

---

[22] Published by Extension Division, State University of Iowa.

[23] Published by Scott, Foresman.

[24] Published by Houghton Mifflin.

with extreme care they are likely to measure rote memory rather than real understanding. Although these limitations cannot be eliminated entirely, they can be greatly reduced, as in the following illustrations.

Illustrations of Completion Tests

test of everyday problems in science, unit XI[25]

72. A pry-pole is an example of a machine called the..... 72 _____

73. A screw is an example of a machine called the........ 73 _____

gregory tests in american history[26]

write your
words and
dates here

74. The man who headed the first expedition to circum-
navigate the globe was........................... 74 _____

75. The "Old Liberty Bell" rang out the decision of Congress to be free from England in the year........... 75 _____

cooperative english test, series 1[27]

76. Write on the lines to the right the contractions—shortened form to represent how the words are naturally spoken—for the seven groups of words underlined in the following sentences. For instance, for do not, you would write don't. You need not copy the sentence, but only the seven contractions.

I have read his story, but I cannot believe _____

that he will get a passing grade on it, _____

for it is not well written and has not _____

a clear-cut plot. The characters are not _____

at all interesting; they are not even human. _____

Suggestions for Constructing Short-Answer Items

The free-response item is one of the most familiar and one of the easiest to prepare. Except in math and science and other problem-solving contexts, the main problem is phrasing the items so that they require responses above the knowledge level.

1. *The direct-question form is often preferable to the statement form.* It is more natural for the pupil and is often easier to phrase.

EXAMPLE: While it circles the sun once, the earth rotates on its axis _____ times.
BETTER: How many times does the earth rotate on its axis while it circles the sun once?
_____

---

[25] Published by Scott, Foresman.
[26] Published by C. A. Gregory Co.
[27] Published by Cooperative Test Division, Educational Testing Service, Princeton, N.J.

2. *The questions should be so worded that the response required is as brief as possible.* This will facilitate objectivity in scoring.

3. *Avoid using textbook wording in phrasing items.* Fresh phrasing will reduce the possibility of correct responses that represent mere meaningless verbal associations; it also will encourage students to "think" as they are reading and studying the book.

4. *The questions should be structured to minimize ambiguity in the correct response; avoid indefinite statements.* This standard is difficult to achieve because pupils are ingenious in reading into questions interpretations that the teacher never intended. When challenged on a history test to "name two ancient sports," one resourceful student answered, "Anthony and Cleopatra." This possibility would not have arisen if the question had taken the form, "What were two popular athletic contests in ancient Greece?" When there is clearly more than one legitimate interpretation of a question, all acceptable replies should be included on the scoring key. Extra care in wording the questions will prevent much of this ambiguity. Care is needed to prevent "frozen subjectivity" in scoring, that is, not giving credit for an equally satisfactory answer just because it is not the keyed answer. If, for example, the answer appears as "2 feet 4 inches," "28 inches" should ordinarily receive full credit. Even "28" without the unit specified should probably receive partial credit.

If they are developed carefully, short-answer questions can measure levels of understanding beyond the knowledge level of Bloom's taxonomy. For example, consider this completion item:

    I. What is the taxonomy level represented by item 69 (on page 260)? (knowledge)
       By item 70 (on page 260)? (comprehension) _____

5. *Omit key words and phrases, rather than trivial details.* If this is not done, the response may be as obvious as the first of the following examples, or as unnecessarily difficult as the second:

    II. Abraham Lincoln was born February ___, 1809. _____
    III. Abraham Lincoln was born in _____ County, Kentucky. _____

6. *Avoid overmutilated statements.* If too many key words are left out, it is impossible to know what meaning was intended. In its present form, it is impossible to tell what the statement in the following example refers to.

EXAMPLE: The (VII) is obtained by dividing the (VIII) by the (IX).

                                   VII. _____
                                  VIII. _____
                                   IX. _____

BETTER: The IQ is obtained by dividing the (X) by the (XI).

                                    X. _____
                                   XI. _____

7. *Avoid grammatical and other clues to the correct answer.*

EXAMPLE: The authors of the first verbal intelligence test were _____

BETTER: The first verbal intelligence test was prepared by _____

BETTER YET: Who prepared the first verbal intelligence test? _____

Whenever the indefinite article is required before a blank, write it in the form *a(n)* so that the examinee must decide whether the correct answer begins with a consonant sound or with a vowel sound.

EXAMPLE: An elementary particle consisting of a charge of negative electricity is called an _____ .

BETTER: An elementary particle consisting of a charge of negative electricity is called a(n) _____ .

Clearly, such words as *proton, coulomb, molecule,* and *meson* could not be used in the first statement. The second statement contains no specific determiner.

The blanks should be made uniform in length. If the blanks vary in length, the pupil has a clue to the length of the correct answer. Even more of a clue is afforded by using a dot or a dash for each letter in the correct word.

8. *Prepare a scoring key that contains all anticipated acceptable answers.* Although it is desirable to have only one "correct" response for each blank, it is not always possible.

The completion item usually is less than fully satisfactory for measuring objectives above the knowledge level, except in the case of problem-solving exercises. Disillusioned writers of completion items may wish to try casting them in multiple-choice form.

Scoring free-response completion items usually requires expert judgment because decisions about the correctness of various answers must be made by the scorer.

Cloze Tests

The cloze[28] test is a relatively recent and promising adaptation and extension of the completion test. It was invented in 1897 by Ebbinghaus, and is sometimes referred to as the "Ebbinghaus completion method" (Buros, 1978). It was presented by Taylor (1953) as a way to measure readability (reading difficulty); later, Taylor (1956) suggested that it could also measure reading comprehension. It is now recognized as having much broader applicability. Cloze tests have had promising validity and reliability results in foreign-language assessment (Aitken, 1977; Jonz, 1976) and a variety of other

---

[28] The term *cloze* was coined by Taylor (1953); its relation to the phrase "reading closure" is evident. *Cloze* refers to an activity in which an examinee fills in a blank. A *modified cloze format* requires the examinee to select the correct words from a set of choices (Pearson & Johnson, 1978).

fields (Anderson, 1974; Bormuth, 1967, 1969; Panackal & Heft, 1978; Buros, 1978).[29]

Representative samples (often selections totaling approximately 250 words) of the subject matter are selected and every fifth word is deleted. The examinee must have enough understanding of the content to supply the missing information from the fragments provided. One cannot ordinarily supply many of the "correct" words if understanding is lacking.

For example, imagine the difficulty a fourth-grader would have with a typical paragraph from the *Encyclopedia Britannica*. An understanding of the general domain and knowledge of the vocabulary at the level at which the selection is written are required to respond successfully to a cloze selection.

A variation of the cloze technique that is probably better for achievement test use (except perhaps on tests designed to measure reading comprehension) is to delete *key* words rather than every fifth word. The following example pertains to test reliability. (Answers are given at the bottom of the page.)

When a test is administered to an ___(1)___ , a score is ___(2)___ . If the examinee had been ___(3)___ on some other test or ___(4)___ , the exact same ___(5)___ probably would not have been earned. The ___(6)___ that would be earned, on the average, if the ___(7)___ had been tested at various times under exactly the same ___(8)___ conditions is called his or her ___(9)___ or ___(10)___ score. Although we can never actually ___(11)___ universe scores, we can be aware of the discrepancy between ___(12)___ scores (which we know) and ___(13)___ scores (which we do not know). This difference, the ___(14)___ score minus the true ___(15)___ , is called error of ___(16)___ .

The ___(17)___ deviation of the ___(18)___ of measurement is the standard error of ___(19)___ (σ_e). About ___(20)___ thirds of the examinees will have obtained ___(21)___ that are within ___(22)___ σ_e of their ___(23)___ scores. Only about one person in twenty will obtain a score that ___(24)___ from his or her universe score by as much as ___(25)___ .

An important advantage of the cloze approach is the simplicity of test development. A teacher can select a representative set of paragraphs from the topics and chapters to be assessed. One can expect a power test to result if there are no more than three to five blanks per minute of testing time.

A practical disadvantage of the cloze approach, as with other short-answer items, is that the scoring has imperfect objectivity and requires more time than the scoring of multiple-choice tests. These can be overcome by utilizing a fixed-response format, which may actually improve reliability and validity (Panackal and Heft, 1978). Item 36 (p. 249) is, in this sense, a type of cloze item, although cloze selections are usually longer, often running to as many as 250 words.

[29] Critical reviews of the cloze procedure by J. C. Anderson, W. B. Elley, and W. L. Smith and references to 400 related articles and studies can be found in Buros, 1978, pp. 1163–78.

Answers to cloze exercise: 1. examinee; 2. obtained, earned; 3. tested, assessed; 4. occasion, time; 5. score; 6. score; 7. person, examinee; 8. testing; 9, 10. true or universe; 11. know, obtain; 12. obtained; 13. universe, true; 14. obtained; 15. score; 16. measurement; 17. standard; 18. errors; 19. measurement; 20. two-; 21. scores; 22. one; 23. universe, true; 24. deviates, varies; 25. $2\sigma_e$.

The modified cloze technique is illustrated in the following items, which are used in the Colorado Needs Assessment, Grade 5 Reading. (The percent of correct answers for blacks, Chicanos, Indians, and whites, respectively, is given in parentheses following each item.)

Select the word that fits best in the blanks of the sentences below:

Hares belong to the same ___(77)___ as rabbits. Hares, however, are usually larger ___(78)___ rabbits. Unlike rabbits, however, their young are ___(79)___ with fur and their eyes open.

77. A) color, *B) family, C) animals
   (70%, 63%, 67%, 77%)
78. A) size, B), important, *C) than
   (44%, 47%, 52%, 64%)
79. *A) born, B) naked, C) grown
   (75%, 71%, 73%, 87%)

In a cave in the mountain, two tiny spotted ___(80)___ were born. They were baby cougars. One day they would be the ___(81)___ hunters in the mountains. But now they were small and ___(82)___ .

80. A) kittens, B) gnats, C) ducklings
   (59%, 61%, 58%, 74%)
81. A) fiercest, B) funniest, C) hungry
   (61%, 52%, 62%, 69%)
82. A) strong, B) cold, C) helpless
   (67%, 61%, 62%, 80%)

Concluding Remarks

Test item writing is a skill and an art; it is assisted by the statistical procedures of item analysis (Chapter 10) and by the evaluative reactions of examinees and people who are knowledgeable in the subject matter and in measurement procedures. As automation becomes more available as an aid in scoring tests, obtaining frequency distributions, item analyses, and determining reliability coefficients and standard errors of measurement, it is important that the heart of the test—its items and exercises—not be neglected by test publishers or teachers. Undue emphasis on mechanical and statistical procedures can lead to undesirable consequences. Too great a preoccupation with indexes of item discrimination, for example, may result in neglect of the item's content validity and its motivational and communication properties. A paragraph in a science test should be acceptable to a subject matter expert, well written, and thought-provoking to the student. An item may discriminate well between high and low scores on a test as a whole and still measure trivia. This situation usually arises when items are not scrutinized for content validity, or when a table of specifications is not used in framing the test. Mastery of measurement concepts is necessary but not sufficient; knowledge of subject matter, sufficient time, and creativity are essential, too. If possible, the items should be thoroughly reviewed by other well-qualified people. Items should be edited, revised, or deleted on the basis of these reviews. This will help compensate for the inevitable limitations of any one person. Further editing for future use results from a detailed item analysis, an important step that is frequently omitted.

In the future, classroom testing may be largely computerized. There are a few experimental situations in which a teacher chooses, from a large pool of items, those that are relevant for the forthcoming test. The computer assembles and numbers the items and even produces a "ditto" or mimeograph master. Considerable experimental work is being done in this area of "tailored," "adaptive," or "computer-assisted individualized" testing, in which an examinee's response to a preliminary set of items is used to select an appropriate set of items to follow (Lord, 1976).

For some time, however, test items and exercises will probably be devised mainly by humans in the current painstaking manner. Therefore, teachers must learn the art of test making or else inferior evaluation measures will result. We have presented the ABCs of test construction. With practice and further study, you should be able to prepare excellent tests.

CHAPTER SUMMARY AND TEST

For this chapter we will use a cloze test as the chapter summary. Each blank should be filled with a single word. We have supplied the more obvious correct answers. (Other synonymous responses should also be credited.)

The most important characteristic of a test __(1)__ is content __(2)__ —does the item __(3)__ the content and process __(4)__ of the domain being __(5)__ ? The process for item __(6)__ should be preceded by a carefully prepared test blueprint or __(7)__ (see Chapter 7) to ensure __(8)__ validity.

Each kind of __(9)__ has unique advantages and __(10)__ . True–false items can be __(11)__ quickly and require less examinee __(12)__ than most other item __(13)__ , but they usually __(14)__ to measure more complex __(15)__ . If not prepared carefully, they often are intrinsically __(16)__ .

An item is intrinsically __(17)__ when people with a thorough __(18)__ of the domain do not __(19)__ on which option is the best __(20)__ ; it results from a fault in the __(21)__ . __(22)__ ambiguity results from an examinee's __(23)__ understanding of the __(24)__ ; it is a fault of the __(25)__ .

Multiple-choice items have the __(26)__ flexibility and potential for measuring __(27)__ . The essential ingredient in their effective __(28)__ is the preparation of attractive __(29)__ . This is also a great practical __(30)__ , because constructing __(31)__ alternatives requires a high level of skill that is developed only with time and __(32)__ .

Matching and short-answer items can measure __(33)__ in an economical manner, although they do not readily lend themselves to measuring comprehension and __(34)__ level objectives (except in math and other problem-solving contexts).

The most important guidelines for item construction may be summarized as follows:

1. Tests should be __(35)__ , not speed measures. Test-taking speed is a response __(36)__ that is not highly __(37)__ with proficiency.

2. The reading level of tests should be kept __(38)__ . The poor reader should be __(39)__ to demonstrate what he or she can __(40)__ in other curricular areas without encountering unnecessary __(41)__ of complex but irrelevant vocabulary and linguistics. Complex, negative, and textbook phrasing should be __(42)__. Direct questions are often __(43)__ to declarative statements.

3. Incorrect response options must be __(44)__ to examinees who lack knowledge and understanding. Skillful test development __(45)__ the odds of selecting the __(46)__ answer on the basis of __(47)__ alone. Options should be __(48)__, homogeneous, and __(49)__ consistent. "Best-answer" items are often superior to __(50)__ items in measuring understanding at the higher levels of Bloom's __(51)__.

ANSWERS TO CHAPTER TEST

1. item, exercise
2. validity
3. represent, sample
4. goals, aims, purposes, objectives
5. assessed, measured, evaluated
6. construction, development, writing
7. specifications
8. content
9. item, test, exercise
10. disadvantages, limitations, drawbacks
11. constructed, developed, built
12. time
13. types
14. fail
15. concepts, objectives
16. ambiguous
17. ambiguous
18. comprehension, understanding
19. agree
20. answer
21. item, exercise, test
22. Extrinsic
23. inadequate, insufficient
24. domain, content, universe, objectives
25. examinee, person, student
26. greatest
27. understanding, concepts
28. use, utilization, implementation
29. distractors, alternatives, options, foils, decoys
30. drawback, disadvantage, obstacle
31. plausible, attractive
32. effort, work, practice
33. knowledge, information, facts
34. application, higher
35. power
36. style, set
37. correlated, related
38. low, easy, simple
39. allowed, able
40. do, perform
41. hurdles, obstacles
42. avoided, minimal, minimized
43. preferable, superior
44. attractive, plausible
45. reduces, minimizes, decreases
46. best, correct, right
47. test-wiseness, test sophistication, guessing
48. plausible, attractive
49. grammatically, logically, linguistically, semantically
50. "correct-answer," "right-answer"
51. taxonomy

IMPORTANT TERMS AND CONCEPTS

option
distractor
free-response items
completion items
short-answer items
recall items
fixed-response items

multiple-choice items
matching exercise
cloze technique
test-wiseness
stem
intrinsic ambiguity
extrinsic ambiguity

specific determiner
power test
speed test
"best-answer" items
tailored testing

ANDERSON, H. R., and E. F. LINDQUIST, rev. David K. Heenan. *Selected test items in world history,* 3rd ed.: Bulletin no. 9. Washington, D.C.: National Council for the Social Studies, 1960.

————, rev. Harriet Stull. *Selected test items in American history:* Bulletin no. 6. Washington, D.C.: National Council for the Social Studies, 1964.

BERG, H. D., ed. Evaluation in social studies. *Thirty-fifth yearbook of the National Council for the Social Studies.* Washington, D.C.: NCSS, 1967.

BLOOM, B. S., J. T. HASTINGS, and G. F. MADAUS. *Handbook on formative and summative evaluation of student learning.* New York: McGraw-Hill, 1971. See special chapters devoted to certain content areas: 13, 15, 16, 17, 18, 19, 20, 21, 22, and 23.

DRESSEL, P. L., ed. *Evaluation in higher education.* Boston: Houghton Mifflin, 1961.

EBEL, R. L. The case for true–false test items. *School Review,* 78 (1970), 373–89.

EDUCATIONAL TESTING SERVICE. *Making your own tests.* Princeton, N.J.: ETS, n.d. A leaflet describing an instructional kit containing three filmstrips, LP records, and related materials.

————. *Multiple-choice questions: A close look.* Princeton, N.J.: ETS, 1963. Reprinted in G. H. Bracht, K. D. Hopkins, and J. C. Stanley, eds. *Perspectives in educational and psychological measurement.* Englewood Cliffs, N.J.: Prentice-Hall, 1972. Selection 15.

ENGELHART, M. D. *Improving classroom testing. What research says to the teacher,* no. 31. Washington, D.C.: National Educational Association, 1964.

GERBERICH, J. R. *Specimen objective test items: A guide to achievement test construction.* New York: D. McKay, 1956.

GERBERICH, J. R., H. A. GREENE, and A. N. JORGENSEN. *Measurement and evaluation in the modern school.* New York: D. McKay, 1962. See chapters on evaluating particular school subjects, such as foreign languages, home economics, physical education, and music.

HEDGES, W. D. *Testing and evaluation for the sciences in the secondary school.* Belmont, Calif.: Wadsworth, 1966.

HENRY, N. B., ed. The measurement of understanding. *Forty-fifth yearbook of the National Society for the Study of Education, Part I.* Chicago: University of Chicago Press, 1946. See chapters on measuring understanding in social studies, science, fine arts, health education, and so on.

KURFMAN, D. *Teacher-made test items in American history:* Bulletin no. 40. Washington, D.C.: National Council for the Social Studies, 1968.

LINDQUIST, E. F., ed. *Educational measurement.* Washington, D.C.: American Council on Education, 1951. See esp. chap. 7, "Writing the test item," by R. L. Ebel.

NATIONAL INSTITUTE OF EDUCATION. *Testing, teaching, and learning.* Washington, D.C., 1979.

PALMER, O. Sense or nonsense? The objective testing of English composition. *English Journal,* 50 (1961), 314–20.

SANDERS, N. M. *Classroom questions: What kinds?* New York: Harper & Row, 1966. Presents item development in terms of Bloom's taxonomy, with many illustrations.

STANLEY, J. C. The ABCs of test construction. *NEA Journal,* 47 (1958), 224–26. Reprinted in J. T. Flynn and H. Garber, eds. *Assessing behavior: Readings in educational and psychological measurement.* Reading, Mass.: Addison-Wesley, 1967.

WEITMAN, M. Item characteristics and long-term retention. *Journal of Educational Measurement,* 2 (1965), 37–47.

WESMAN, A. G. Writing the test item. In R. L. Thorndike, ed., *Educational measurement,* 2nd. ed. Washington, D.C.: American Council on Education, 1971. Chap. 4.

10

Item Analysis for Classroom Tests

If the procedures for test development outlined in Chapters 7, 8, and 9 are followed, the most important quality of an item—*content validity*—will be achieved. This is the *sine qua non* of any good item or test. However, logical relevance is only the first hurdle in the evaluation of test items. An item analysis is needed to indicate the success of the class on each question. Malfunctioning items can also be identified in this way. Whereas the response of one student to an item ordinarily is not sufficient to make a diagnostic decision, the response of a group of students to an individual item can be meaningful and reliable.

It is not uncommon for an item to appear satisfactory, even to an expert, yet be found by the item analysis to be intrinsically ambiguous and to elicit an undesired response pattern from students (Coffman, 1969, p. 14). The immediate purposes of an item analysis are thus to determine the *difficulty* and *discrimination* of each item. When the test is subjected to item analysis, one is almost certain to gain important insights into the examinees' thinking, understanding, and test-taking behavior. The feedback from item analyses should improve an instructor's skills in test construction to a degree that is not otherwise possible (Ebel, 1965b, p. 346). Blessum (1969, p. 5) reported that item analysis feedback to university faculty "resulted in an improvement not only in the quality and fairness of each individual examination, but also in the technical and educational quality of successive tests."

Preparing the Items

In addition to content validity, the two item characteristics on which one desires information are difficulty (the percent of the group tested that answered the question correctly) and discrimination (how well the item distinguishes between the more knowledgeable and the less knowledgeable students). These characteristics can be nearly independent of each other, except that a very easy or very hard item cannot discriminate well. If all students mark the item correctly, it has not distinguished between those who know more and those who know less about the concept. If all students mark an item incorrectly, then the item has little discriminating power for the group—it does not help identify individual differences. But must all items discriminate? What if all the students have mastered the objective? Items on mastery or criterion-referenced tests need not discriminate. If all students respond correctly, so much the better. But this is a realistic expectation only for "training," or knowledge-level, objectives, where there is little implicit generalizability beyond the item itself. For items above the knowledge level, individual differences among examinees are to be expected. Tests with means of 90% or more are unlikely to have many items above the knowledge level of Bloom's taxonomy.

Several different item analysis procedures have been proposed. Some of the more elaborate of these are appropriate for standardized tests or research projects where computerized item analysis programs are available. The following procedure is simple, but adequate for most classroom purposes. It works best with examinations given to large groups but is valuable even for a single class. To minimize response-style effects on teacher-made tests, each student should be strongly encouraged to answer every item. The test length should be such that adequate time is available for nearly everyone to attempt every item.

The items generally should be arranged in ascending order of difficulty, although this is critical only on speeded tests (Brenner, 1964). For a new set of items, this arrangement can be achieved fairly well on a subjective basis; if each item has been administered previously to a similar group, the original difficulty values can be used.

Note that *an item analysis is no substitute for meticulous care in planning, constructing, criticizing, and editing items.* It does supplement those intuitive processes, however, by revealing unsuspected defects or virtues of specific items. The feedback on individual items can also be of instructional value to the teacher in, for example, identifying topics that are in need of review.

The Steps of an Item Analysis

After the test has been given, the papers or answer sheets must be scored. Because test directions usually require the examinee to answer all items, omissions should be few. Each student's score (not corrected for "chance") will be the number of errors (wrong or omitted items) subtracted from the number of items on the test.

1. Order the N papers by score, placing the one with the highest score on top and continuing sequentially until the one with the lowest score is on the bottom.
2. Multiply N, the total number of tests, by 0.27 and round off the result to the nearest whole number;[1] this number is represented by n. If N is 30, n would be 8 (8.1 rounded).
3. Count off the n best papers from the top of the stack. This is the "high" group.
4. Count off the n poorest papers from the bottom of the stack. This is the "low" group.
5. Determine the proportion in the high group (p_H) in which each item was answered correctly by dividing the number of correct answers for the high group by n; that is,

$$p_H = \frac{\text{number of correct answers}}{n}$$

   Repeat the procedure for the low group to obtain p_l for each item.
6. To obtain an item difficulty index, p (that is, the proportion of the total group in which each item was answered correctly[2]) add p_H and p_L and divide by 2:

$$p = \frac{p_H + p_L}{2}$$

   This must be interpreted with the chance level of the item in mind. For example, $p = .5$ for a two-option item that all examinees mark probably indicates little or no knowledge of the point tested.[3]
7. To obtain a measure of item discrimination[4] (i.e., how well this item

---

[1] Henrysson (1971) suggests taking the upper and lower $N/3$ examinees, rather than .27N. Obviously, the smaller the percent used for the upper and lower groups, the greater the differentiation will be. However, the smaller the extreme groups, the less reliable the resulting D-values or item–test correlation coefficients. Kelley (1939) claimed that the optimum point at which these two conditions balance is reached when the upper and lower 27 percent values are used, although D'Agostino and Cureton (1975) contend that 21 percent is slightly better. For classroom use it makes little difference whether 21, 25, 27, or 33 percent is selected. When the item analysis is computerized, all examinees should be used in obtaining item–test correlation coefficients, or other statistics, since economy of time is not an important consideration.

[2] Michael, Haertzka, and Perry (1953) have shown that p-values computed directly, using all examinees, agree closely with the average of p_H and p_L values.

[3] The p-values used in this chapter have not been "corrected for chance." Assuming that all distractors are equally attractive, the proportion of examinees who know the answer (p') can be estimated by

$$p' = p - \frac{1 - p}{A - 1}$$

where A = the number of options for this item. For a procedure that does not assume that the distractors are equally attractive, see Horst's method (Guilford, 1954, pp. 421-22). It is not usually recommended that one correct item difficulty indexes for chance; nevertheless, the chance values for p should be borne in mind when interpreting p-values. If all examinees attempt all items, the p-values expected from chance are 1/A, that is, .50, .33, .25, and .20 for 2-, 3-, 4-, and 5-choice items, respectively.

[4] A standard index of item discrimination is the coefficient of correlation of the examinees' scores on an item with their total scores on the rest of the test. Other indexes have also been suggested (see Henrysson, 1971, and Baker, 1965). The shortcut item analysis method explained here is the D-index for item analysis suggested by Johnson (1951) and popularized by Findley (1956). Its values have been shown to be almost perfectly linearly correlated with biserial coefficients (Bridgman, 1964; Hales, 1972). Engelhart (1965) found D "remarkably effective" in identifying poor items. Mayo (1968) concluded that "from a time-and-motion point of view, D is probably the most economical index to [hand] calculate" (p. 93). The differences in results from using D versus any of the other various measures of item discrimination are "extremely small or nonexistent . . . the selection of an index should be based solely on ease of computation or the need for statistical tests of significance" (Beuchert & Mendoza, 1979, p. 116).

distinguished between the students who understand the content universe of the test well and those who do not), subtract p_L from p_H:

$$D = p_H - p_L$$

It has been shown (Pyrczak, 1973) that the D-values from an item analysis were corroborated by the independent subjective evaluations of item quality. Items that yield a discrimination index of .35 or more are relatively high in discrimination. Those with D-values below .2 are relatively low in discrimination (Ebel, 1954). Items that were miskeyed or are intrinsically ambiguous will tend to have very low or negative D-values; or other options of that item may have higher D-values than the keyed option. These items usually should be double-keyed, since the distinction between the best and next-best options was too fine for the knowledgeable students to discern. Of course, no item should be double-keyed if there is not a logical justification in terms of the concept being measured. This reason for the intrinsic ambiguity may not be readily apparent to the test constructor, but can usually be supplied by high-scoring examinees who did not select the keyed option.

The relationship between item difficulty and *potential* item discrimination is illustrated in Figure 10–1. The potential measurement value of an item is at a maximum when its difficulty level is .5, that is, when only one-half of the examinees are able to answer the item correctly. The figure also shows that there is little opportunity for an item to assess individual differences if it is very easy or very difficult. Note in Figure 10–1 that in the middle range of dif-

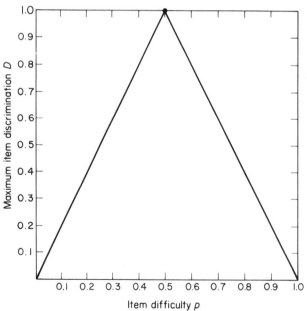

FIGURE 10–1 The relationship between item difficulty (p) and corresponding maximum item discrimination (D).

ficulty (25–75%) all items have the potential for very high discrimination ($D \geq .5$). Of course, an item's being at an appropriate difficulty level does not ensure that it is a good item. The crucial test for an item is whether those who best understand the domain of content (the high scorers on the total test) agree with the keyed answer on the item to a greater extent than those who know least about the subject (the low scorers on the total test). This is the information conveyed by the D-value for the item. The relationship between item difficulty and observed D-values for 120 items is shown in Figure 10-2. The median D-values for the 18 difficult items ($p \leq .25$) and the 23 easy items ($p \geq .75$) are only .10 and .20, respectively, whereas the median D-values for moderately difficult items (p's of .45 to .70) was .36. Notice also that four items on this carefully prepared test (Engelhart, 1965) took away from its measurement value (i.e., had negative D-values). On subsequent versions of the test, these items, as well as others, should be revised or eliminated.

If the mean D-value, $\overline{D}$, on a test is .3, then the mean total score of the high group is .3 or 30% greater than the mean for the low group. In other

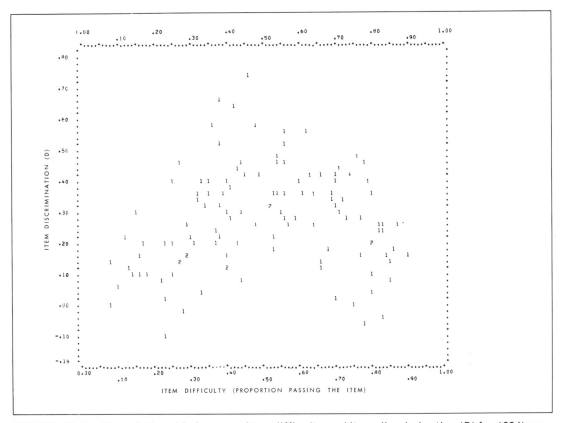

FIGURE 10-2 The relationship between item difficulty and item discrimination (D) for 120 items. (Based on data given by Engelhart, 1965; the authors are grateful to Richard C. Bennet for providing Figure 10-2.)

words, the mean of the high group, $\overline{X}_H$, exceeds the mean of the low group, $\overline{X}_L$, by $.3k$ items, where k is the number of items on a test. For example, on a 50-item test, if $\overline{D}$ is .3, the high group's mean ($\overline{X}_H$) will exceed the low group's mean ($\overline{X}_L$) by 30% or 15 points.

The average D-value, $\overline{D}$, can be used as a quick estimate of a test's standard deviation. The difference between the means of the high and low groups will be about 2.45 standard deviations;[5] that is,

$$kD = \overline{X}_H - \overline{X}_L \doteq 2.45s,$$

where k = the number of items and $\doteq$ means "approximately equal to."

$$s \doteq \frac{\overline{X}_H - \overline{X}_L}{2.45} = \frac{k\overline{D}}{2.45}$$

or, in the preceding example,

$$s \doteq \frac{50(.3)}{2.45} = 6.1 \text{ items}$$

It is usually advantageous to express test scores as percentages. The standard deviation of students' percent scores, $s_{\%}$, is estimated by the formula

$$s_{\%} \doteq \frac{100\overline{D}}{2.45}$$

or, in the preceding example,

$$s_{\%} = \frac{100(.3)}{2.45} = 12.2\%$$

Lower $\overline{D}$-values are associated with lower test reliability.[6] (See Figure 10–3.) Other things being equal, the greater $\overline{D}$ is, the greater are the test's standard deviation and reliability.

---

[5] Kelley (1939) proved that the mean of scores in the tail of a normal distribution is equal to $(y/q)\sigma$, where σ is the standard deviation, q is the proportion of the cases included in the tail, and y is the height of the ordinate of a unit normal distribution at the point of truncation. When the upper 27 percent is chosen for the high group, $q = .27$. From a normal-curve table it can readily be determined that the point of truncation must be .61 standard deviations from the mean, at which point $y = .33$. The mean score of the high group ($\overline{X}_H$) must then equal $(.33/.27)\sigma$ above the mean or, in z-score units, $(.33/.27)(1)$ or 1.225. Correspondingly, the mean of the low group ($\overline{X}_L$) would be -1.225 in z-score units, or a difference in means of 2.45 σ's. The accuracy of this procedure for nonnormal distribution has not been investigated.

[6] The mean D-value, $\overline{D}$, can also be employed to estimate a test's reliability, thereby avoiding the necessity of computing its standard deviation. Kuder-Richardson formulas 20 and 21 become, respectively:

$$r_{KR_{20}} \doteq \frac{k}{k-1}\left[1 - \frac{6\Sigma pq}{(k\overline{D})^2}\right],$$

$$r_{KR_{21}} \doteq \frac{k}{k-1}\left[1 - \frac{6\overline{p}\overline{q}}{k\overline{D}^2}\right],$$

where $\overline{p} = \overline{X}/k$, and $\overline{q} = 1 - \overline{p}$.

Recall that the Kuder-Richardson formula 21 reliability estimate requires the number of items (k) and s. Using our 50-item test and assuming a mean of 40 ($\bar{p} = 40/50 = .8$, $\bar{q} = 1 - \bar{p} = .2$),

$$r_{KR_{21}} = \frac{k}{k-1}\left(1 - \frac{k\bar{p}\bar{q}}{s^2}\right) = \frac{50}{49}\left(1 - \frac{50(.8)(.2)}{(6.1)^2}\right)$$

$$= \frac{50}{49}\left(1 - \frac{8}{37.1}\right) = \frac{50}{49}(.785) = .80.$$

If reliability (r_{XX}) and s are available, the standard error of measurement can also be estimated, using the formula $s_e = s\sqrt{1 - r_{XX}}$. Thus, on the 50-item test with $s = 6.1$ and $r_{XX} = .80$,

$$s_e = 6.1\sqrt{1 - .80} = 2.7$$

or

$$s_{e\%} = s_{\%}\sqrt{1 - r_{XX}} = 12.2\,(.45) = 5.5\%.$$

The direct relationship between item discrimination values and a test's internal-consistency reliability ($r_{KR_{21}}$) is illustrated in Figure 10–3, which depicts the relationship between the mean D-value ($\overline{D}$) and the corresponding $r_{KR_{21}}$ coefficients for tests of 80% difficulty (i.e., $\bar{p} = .8$) and variance lengths. For example, if $\overline{D} = .3$, the estimated values of $r_{KR_{21}}$ are .0, .6, .8, and .9 for

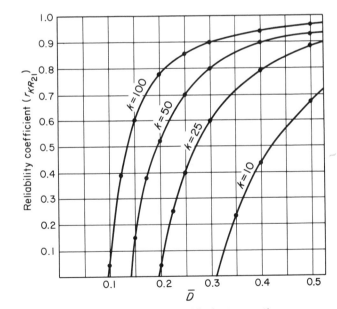

FIGURE 10-3 The relationship between the average D-value, $\overline{D}$, and Kuder-Richardson formula 21 reliability estimates for tests with a mean difficulty of 80% ($\bar{p}$ = .8) with 10, 25, 50, and 100 items.

tests of 10, 25, 50, and 100 items, respectively. Or, read differently, a KR_{21} reliability coefficient of .7 requires 100 items when $\overline{D}$ = .18, 50 items when $\overline{D}$ = .25, 25 items when $\overline{D}$ = .35, but only 10 items when $\overline{D}$ = .52. A 100-item test with $\bar{p}$ = .8 with a mean-item discrimination index of .1 has zero reliability.

Any item whose discrimination is being assessed also contributes a fraction of the total test score—which is the basis for determining the "high" and "low" groups. The degree of internal contamination due to the overlap of item with total test is influenced by test length—the fewer items on the test, the greater the proportion each item contributes to the total score.[7] This factor becomes serious only on very short tests. The following rules of thumb for interpreting item discrimination index values for classroom tests are adapted from Ebel (1965b). These guidelines are relevant only for describing the contribution of an item to a test's reliability.

Index of Discrimination	Item Evaluation
.40 and up	very good item
.30–.39	good item
.20–.29	reasonably good item
.10–.19	marginal item, usually subject to improvement
Below .10	poor item, to be rejected or revised

It should be noted that items with .0 or negative D-values probably were inadvertently miskeyed or else are intrinsically ambiguous. These interpretations are relevant only for the ability of the item to measure individual differences. Criterion-referenced or mastery items often are included in classroom tests for diagnostic or certification purposes and should be retained even if they are answered correctly by almost all students and contribute little or nothing to the measurement of individual differences among the examinees.

An Illustrative Analysis

The four illustrative test items to be discussed were selected from a test given to an introductory measurement class of thirty students. The results of the item analysis are given in Figure 10–4 for items 1, 2, 3, and 4. Only item 1 is stated.

> *Item 1.* "Educational objectives are best determined from the results of objective educational measurements." (T or F*)

Item 1 functioned well from a measurement perspective; it also provided diagnostic feedback to the instructor by indicating a misconception that needed to be clarified for the 37 percent of students (p = .67) who answered the item incorrectly. Item 2 was very easy (p = .88), but it contributed to the test's reliability (D = .25). Item 3 was in the optimal difficulty range, but it

---

[7] Henrysson (1963) presents a procedure that gives an exact correction for this contamination. The refinement should be employed on items in standardized tests, but it is impractical for classroom testing, except at colleges and universities where computerized item analysis procedures may be available.

Item Number	Number of Correct Responses for Groups $(n = 8)$[a]		Proportion of Correct Responses	Item Discrimination $D = p_H - p_L$	Item Difficulty $p = \dfrac{p_H + p_L}{2}$
1	H	7	$p_H = 7/8 = .88$	$(.88 - .38) = .5$	$\dfrac{.88 + .38}{2} = .63$
	L	3	$p_L = 3/8 = .38$		
2	H	8	$p_H = 1.00$	$D = .25$	$p = .88$
	L	6	$p_L = .75$		
3	H	4	$p_H = .5$	$D = .0$	$p = .5$
	L	4	$p_L = .5$		
4	H	2	$p_H = .25$	$D = -.50$	$p = .50$
	L	6	$p_L = .75$		

[a] $n = .27N = .27(30) = 8.1$ (rounded off to 8) students in the "high" group and 8 in the "low" group.

FIGURE 10-4   Item analysis data for 4 items.

failed to discriminate; it may be intrinsically ambiguous and needs to be eliminated or revised. Item 4 is probably miskeyed, or at least is seriously intrinsically ambiguous. The examinees appear to be in a different mental set than the instructor. The item appears to have good measurement potential (note the large D-value) but should be either double-keyed or excluded from the present examination. In its present form it lowers test reliability, and no doubt validity as well. Items like this are frequently found on classroom tests—such items are miskeyed or at least are intrinsically ambiguous. They usually remain unidentified unless an item analysis is performed.

If items 3 and 4 are multiple-choice questions with three or more options, a further analysis is needed to identify the options that are creating the difficulty. For instructors at many colleges and universities, generalized item analysis programs have been developed for the local computer and provide this kind of information to the instructor. This service will probably be available to most secondary-school teachers eventually, but even as a hand operation it can be completed fairly quickly by a teacher or even by a student.

Suppose there were four options to item 3. Consider the following distribution:

DISTRIBUTION OF RESPONSES TO ITEM 3 FOR HIGH- (H) AND LOW- (L) SCORING EXAMINEES

Item	Group	Option					D	p
		A	B*	C	D	Omit		
3	H	0	4	3	0	1	.00	.50
	L	0	4	0	4	0		

* Keyed answer.

Option C deserves scrutiny. It is likely that the distinction between options B and C is too fine; perhaps the distinction has not received adequate instructional emphasis. A study of the item may reveal that both B and C are reasonable and, hence, should be credited as correct. Distractor A probably should be revised for future use, since it was nonfunctional. Option D seems to be an excellent distractor.

Ordinarily, poorly functioning items can be revised by improving the distractors. Sometimes the point tested is not clear or defensible enough to serve as the basis for an item. Some items, such as those for mathematics and science, are much easier to develop than are others, such as those for social studies and literature.

Item 4 appears to have been miskeyed. Only a study of the content of the item can diagnose the reason for its failure.

DISTRIBUTION OF RESPONSES TO ITEM 4 FOR HIGH- (H) AND LOW- (L) SCORING EXAMINEES

		Option					D	p
Item	Group	A	B	C	D*	Omit		
4	H	0	5	1	2	0	−.50	.50
	L	1	1	0	6	0		

* Keyed answer.

Of course, one would not give credit for an incorrect answer such as might be found on an arithmetic test. When the item analysis "faults" an item, the source of the intrinsic ambiguity can usually be identified, particularly if it is discussed with the class. When n is small, one will often obtain peculiar results owing to sampling fluctuations.

Other Examples

The following item was developed by Educational Testing Service (1963, pp. 12–13) and administered to 370 students:

In the following questions you are asked to make inferences from the data which are given you on the map of the imaginary country, Serendip. *The answers in most instances must be probabilities rather than certainties.* The relative size of towns and cities is not shown. To assist you in the location of the places mentioned in the questions, the map is divided into squares lettered vertically from A to E and numbered horizontally from 1 to 5.

5. Which of the following cities would be the best location for a steel mill?
(A) Li (3A), (B) Um (3B), (C) Cot (3D), (D) Dube (4B).

The question requires knowledge of the natural resources used in producing steel and awareness of the importance of transportation facilities in bringing these resources together. It was part of a social-studies test given to high school seniors.

Students who know that iron is the basic raw material of steel and that coal commonly provides the necessary source of heat would proceed to locate deposits of these resources in relation to the cities listed in the question. They

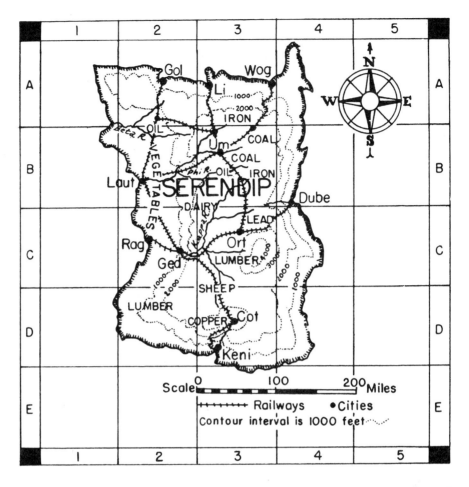

Scale 0   100   200 Miles
+++++ Railways • Cities
Contour interval is 1000 feet

would be able to eliminate "Cot" immediately, since there is no iron or coal in its vicinity, although Cot might be an attractive choice to students who mistakenly think that copper is a basic ingredient of steel. Both "Li" and "Dube" are located reasonably near supplies of iron and therefore might be attractive choices. Um, however, is the more clearly "correct" response, because not only are deposits of iron and coal nearby, but they are more readily transportable by direct railroad routes. Item analysis data for the 370 students are as follows:

EXAMINEE RESPONSE TO ITEM 5

| | | \multicolumn{5}{c|}{Option} | | |
Item	Group	Li A	Um B*	Cot C	Dube D	Omit	D	p
5	H	2	84 $p_H = .84\,^a$	1	6	7	.44	.62
	L	10	40 $p_L = .40^a$	4	9	37		

* Keyed option.
[a] $N = 370$, $n = 100$.

Although the item was rather difficult for the group [it was answered correctly by only 62 percent ($p = .62$) of the examinees], it did discriminate well ($D = .44$). However, some of the discrimination resulted from the fact that 37 percent of the "low" group did not attempt the item. Distractors A, C, and D functioned slightly, but in the right direction. Additional study of the test on which this item appeared revealed that all 7 omits in the "high" group and 29 of the 37 omits in the low group were from students who ran out of time before they had a chance to attempt the item (which appeared near the end of the test). The analysis of this item suggests that there may be a substantial speed element in the test; hence, many examinees with low total scores may not have low map-reading ability but are slow workers who did not have time to respond to many items that they would have been able to answer correctly.

The following item is taken from a writing test administered to 250 college-bound high school students:[8]

In the following question you are given a complete sentence to be rephrased according to the directions which follow it. You should rephrase the sentence mentally to save time, although you may make notes in your test book if you wish.

Below the sentence and its directions are listed words or phrases that may occur in your revised sentence. When you have thought out a good sentence, find in the choices A to E the word or entire phrase that is included in your revised sentence. The word or phrase you choose should be the most accurate and most nearly complete of all the choices given.

Although the directions may require you to change the relationship between parts of the sentence or to make slight changes in meaning in other ways, make only those changes that the directions require; that is, keep the meaning the same, or as nearly the same as the directions permit. If you think that more than one good sentence can be made according to the directions, select the sentence that is most exact, effective, and natural in phrasing and construction.

Sentence: John, shy as he was of girls, still managed to marry one of the most desirable of them.

Directions: Substitute John's shyness for John, shy.

Your rewritten sentence will contain which of the following?

(A) him being married to
(B) himself married to
(C) him from marrying
(D) was himself married to
(E) him to have married

In order to select choice (A), a sentence like John's shyness with girls did not stop him being married to the most desirable of them would have to be used. To make this sentence correct, formal written English demands that the word being be preceded by the possessive pronoun his. Choice (B) presents a sentence similar to Despite John's shyness with girls, he managed to get himself married to one of the most desirable of them. This sentence is wordy and inappropriate in tone (for formal

English). Choice (C), however, yields a sentence on the order of <u>John's</u> <u>shyness with girls did not prevent him from marrying one of the most</u> <u>desirable of them.</u> This retains the meaning of the original sentence and contains no errors in grammar; it is the correct answer. The fourth choice might lead to <u>John's shyness with girls did not keep him single; he</u> <u>was himself married to one of the most desirable of them.</u> This sentence changes the meaning of the original sentence, and it is, at the same time, ambiguous in its own meaning. <u>John's shyness with girls was not a</u> <u>reason for him to have married the most desirable of them,</u> an attempt to use the fifth choice, results in a complete change of meaning. It is therefore unacceptable, even though it is grammatically correct.

EXAMINEES' RESPONSE TO ITEM 6

Item	Group	Option						p	D
		A	B	C*	D	E	Omit		
6	H	3	0	$\begin{array}{c}61\\ p_H = .90^a\end{array}$	1	3	0	.58	.75
	L	5	11	$\begin{array}{c}17\\ p_L = .25^a\end{array}$	14	15	6		

* Keyed option.
[a] $N = 250$, $n = 68$.

The analysis reveals that few of the able students had difficulty with this item, whereas the "low" group had extreme difficulty. Distractors B, D, and E appear excellent, whereas option A made a slightly negative contribution to the item.

More elaborate item analyses, such as the one shown in Table 10-1, are facilitated when a computer is available. The r-values in Table 10-1 are estimates of the item–test (biserial) coefficients of correlation; they convey the same information as the D-values and correlate almost perfectly with them (Bridgman, 1964).

The first column, "Item Number," refers to the number of each question on an 84-question multiple-choice test. Each question includes four possible alternatives; the double columns labeled *A, B, C,* and *D* across the top of the table refer to the number of students selecting that option for each question. Thus, the columns labeled *A* refer to those students who selected alternative A for a given question.

Under each option (A, B, C, D) are two subcolumns, "High" and "Low." "High" refers to those students whose total scores on the test were the highest of all students taking the test. "Low" refers to the students in the low group. Thus, for item 1, the overwhelming majority of both good and poor students (categorized on the basis of overall success on the test) selected answer C; 85 percent of the high scorers and 79 percent of the low scorers selected answer C.

Under the "Total" heading at the far right of the table, the column labeled "Key" indicates the answer that was considered best by the test writers (also given in boldface type). The column labeled p indicates the percent of all

TABLE 10-1

ITEM ANALYSIS OF A FINAL EXAMINATION [a]

Item Number	Percent of High and Low Pupils Responding to Each Option								Total			
	A		B		C		D					
	High	Low	High	Low	High	Low	High	Low	Key	p	r	D
1	01	03	13	17	**85**	**79**	02	02	C	.82	.09	.06
2	**34**	**36**	03	09	55	40	08	15	A	.35	−.02	−.02
3	00	07	01	07	01	05	**98**	**81**	D	.89	.45	.17
4	03	04	**83**	**59**	13	30	01	07	B	.71	.29	.24
5	03	01	17	34	**10**	**04**	69	61	C	.07	.19	.06
6	**79**	**61**	19	31	01	05	01	04	A	.70	.21	.18
7	13	20	**73**	**49**	01	04	14	27	B	.61	.25	.24
8	05	08	01	11	04	43	**89**	**35**	D	.62	.57	.54
9	73	81	**07**	**05**	17	05	03	09	B	.06	.07	.02
10	01	15	**76**	**44**	21	31	02	10	B	.60	.34	.32
.												
.												
81	03	11	66	39	**05**	**13**	24	37	C	.09	−.21	−.08
82	**81**	**39**	01	16	11	27	07	15	A	.60	.44	.42
83	04	26	01	13	03	13	**92**	**44**	D	.68	.56	.48
84	00	07	**71**	**33**	13	31	15	25	B	.52	.38	.38

[a] "High" group consists of the top 27 percent of the pupils in the sample on total test score. "Low" group consists of the bottom 27 percent of the pupils in the sample on total test score.

SOURCE: Reprinted from H. Grobman, *AERA Monograph series in Curriculum Evaluation*, no. 2, *Evaluation activities of curriculum projects* (Chicago: Rand McNally, 1968). By permission of the publisher.

students taking the test who selected the correct answer. For question 1, 82% of the examinees selected option C, the correct answer. Thus, question 1 was very easy for these students.

The last column, *r,* is the biserial correlation (often written as r_{bis}). This is a way of stating statistically the extent to which a question discriminates between the high-scoring students and the low-scoring students on the total test. Thus, for question 1, an r_{bis} of .09 ($D = .06$) indicates that this question did not effectively discriminate between these two groups of students. (Note that $D = .06 = .85-.79$; D and r_{bis} convey the same information.) Question 83, with an r_{bis} of .56, ($D = .48$) was effective in discriminating between good and poor students. Item 81 discriminated negatively. This means that the correct answer was selected more often by the poorer students than by the better students. A majority of the good students selected answer B rather than the correct answer, C. This is an indication of some kind of trouble either with the item or with the curriculum. The problem may be that the question was keyed incorrectly, that is, that the correct answer is B rather than C. Or the question may be intrinsically ambiguous. It may have two correct or equally defensible answers.

The following table presents item analysis data for a science question that was administered to approximately 500 representative sixth- and eleventh-grade students in Colorado. Note that the correlation of each distractor with the total score is given in addition to the item discrimination index for the correct answer. The r's are used in exactly the same way as D's.

Question: Which one of these would happen if you filled a balloon with air and put it in the refrigerator for a while?

6th Grade			11th Grade	
p	r		p	r
.05	−.11	a) The air in the balloon would freeze.	.01	−.02
.14	−.03	b) The balloon would get larger.	.12	−.06
.04	−.11	c) The air in the balloon would get warmer.	.02	−.15
.38	**.30**	*d) The balloon would get smaller.	**.61**	**.46**
.39	−.17	e) The balloon would burst.	.21	−.27
		OMITS	.03	−.40
$(N = 451)$			$(N = 469)$	

Note that only 38% of the sixth-graders selected the correct answer, whereas 61% of the eleventh-graders answered the question correctly. The item discriminated well ($r = .30$) at grade 6, but even better at grade 11. The negative r's for distractors indicate that poorer students selected the distractors more often than better students. Note that distractor a was not attractive —only 5% and 1% of the students selected this option. Note also that e was the most effective distractor at both grade levels; not only was it most attractive (39% and 21%) but it was highest in discrimination as well. The desired pattern is negative r's for distractors and positive r's for the correct option. At grade 11, 3% of the examinees did not answer the question. These examinees probably omitted other questions as well, which helps explain the r of −.40—as expected, students who tend to omit items tend to have lower test scores.

Item Analysis with an External Criterion

When one is developing a test that is going to be used for program evaluation, research, or district-level or state assessment, an external criterion can sometimes be used to evaluate the items', and the test's, validity. This procedure is not often useful for classroom test development.

A useful external criterion for achievement tests is teacher ratings of students' proficiency levels. In the development of items for the Colorado State Assessment, before the tests were administered, classroom teachers were asked to rate the reading ability of their students on a five-point scale. These ratings served as an external criterion with which the responses to the reading items can be correlated. As a group, good readers, as defined by teachers' ratings, should perform better on all items that are validly measuring reading ability. This correlation is an item validity index (r_{ext}) with a stronger indication of quality than the item discrimination index (r)—the latter pertains directly to reliability and only indirectly (and logically) to validity, whereas the correlation of an item to an external criterion is a direct indication of validity.

The results for two items are shown here; the first item (no. 69) is from a reading comprehension test. Only 67% ($p = .67$) of the fifth-grade students were able to make the proper inference from the passage. Notice that those who selected the correct answer, a, also had higher total scores on the reading test ($r = .42$); they were also rated by their teachers as better readers than those who selected the incorrect option ($r_{ext} = .23$). The positive value for item validity makes it difficult to "put down" the item as a "guessing game."

Read this paragraph from the book *Tom Sawyer:*

About noon the next day the boys arrived at the dead tree; they had come for their tools. Tom was impatient to go to the haunted house; Huck was measurably so, also—but suddenly said, "Looky here, Tom, do you know what day it is?"

In the paragraph above we learned that:

69. Tom wanted to go to the haunted house.   a. Yes; b. No

	p	r	r_{ext}
*a. yes	.67	.42	.23
b. no	.28	−.23	−.15
OMITS	.05	−.43	−.19

Illustrative data for an item (no. 86) on a fifth-grade math test are given below. The external criterion was teacher ratings of pupils' math competence. Notice the correspondence between the item discrimination (r) and item validity (r_{ext}) indices. Does it surprise you that only two out of three fifth-grade students can discriminate correctly between these response alternatives? What do you think would have happened if "3 inches" had been an option?

86. About how long is the line drawn below?

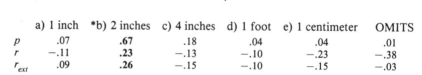

	a) 1 inch	*b) 2 inches	c) 4 inches	d) 1 foot	e) 1 centimeter	OMITS
p	.07	.67	.18	.04	.04	.01
r	−.11	.23	−.13	−.10	−.23	−.38
r_{ext}	.09	.26	−.15	−.10	−.15	−.03

Notice that there is considerable consistency in the pattern of the item discrimination r's and the item validity r_{ext}'s.

There are several other types of external criteria that can be used for certain test validation purposes. The *contrasting groups method* selects two groups that should differ on the measured variable; the performance of the two groups is compared on each item. For example, on the Strong-Campbell Interest Inventory only those items that discriminate between engineers and nonengineers are employed on the engineer scale. One personality inventory eliminated items on which hospitalized mental patients did not differ from nonhospitalized persons.

A scale designed to identify potential school dropouts might administer a pool of items to two groups of persons of high school age who have, and have not, dropped out of school. Items on which the two groups differ have promise as items for identifying potential dropouts. Medley and Klein (1957)

observed 49 classrooms periodically and noted the degree of discipline in the classes. These ratings served as an external criterion that had a significant relationship with the pupils' descriptions of their classes on a self-report inventory.

Summary

The principal purposes of an item analysis are to determine the difficulty and discrimination of each item. Items of moderate difficulty have the *potential* for good item discrimination. The theoretical maximum item discrimination *D*-value (1.0) is possible only when item difficulty is .5. The standard deviation and reliability of a test may be estimated from the mean item discrimination and number of items.

An item analysis—comparing the performance on each item of the most and least successful examinees on the total test—will identify items that are nonfunctional, intrinsically ambiguous, or miskeyed, so they can be revised or thrown out. Usually, not only will this procedure improve the reliability and hence the validity of a particular test, but the experience of studying the students' responses diagnostically will help the instructor both in teaching and in subsequent test construction.

A chain of relationships exists between certain item and test characteristics. Item difficulty affects possible item discrimination, which in turn directly determines the variance and internal-consistency reliability of the test scores. The use of an external criterion (e.g., independent teacher ratings) can be useful in test development for validating items.

For mastery and criterion-referenced testing, high *p*-values and low *D*-values are acceptable. Indeed, $p = 1.0$ (and, hence, $D = .0$) may be the goal. Values of p of 1.0 are unexpected for good items above the knowledge level of Bloom's taxonomy.

IMPORTANT TERMS AND CONCEPTS

item analysis	mean item discrimination ($\overline{D}$)	external criterion
item difficulty (p)	item validity	intrinsic ambiguity
item discrimination (D)		

CHAPTER TEST

1. The most important characteristic of an achievement test item is its
   a) item difficulty, *p,* of .5–.8.
   b) item discrimination, *D,* of .35 or above.
   c) perfect objectivity (scorer agreement).
   d) content validity.
   e) test–retest reliability.

2. The rationale underlying item discrimination *as a basis for judging item quality* is that
   a) item evaluations should be scientific and objective.
   b) as a group, high-scoring examinees know more than low-scoring examinees on all items in the content universe.
   c) high item discrimination indices are impossible with extremely easy or difficult items.

Match the following symbols with the verbal definitions in questions 3–5.

   a) p_H d) $\bar{p}$
   b) p_L e) D
   c) p

3. The proportion of correct answers in the high-scoring group

4. A symbol for the difficulty of an item

5. The average p-value on the test

6. The item discrimination index, D, is
   a) equal to $(p_H + p_L)/2$.
   b) the difference between the proportions of correct responses in the high and low groups.
   c) the average of the percent of correct answers in the high and low groups.
   d) More than one of the above

7. The largest possible value of D is
   a) 0.0   b) 0.5   c) 1.0

8. The maximum value of D occurs when
   a) $p = .05$.   d) $p = .75$.
   b) $p = .25$.   e) $p = 1.0$.
   c) $p = .50$.

9. The empirical relationship between p and D (see Figure 10–2) is
   a) very high and linear.
   b) moderately high and linear.
   c) very high and curvilinear.
   d) moderately high and cuı vilinear.

For a test of 50 items with $\bar{X} = 35$ and $\bar{D} = .25$ (questions 10–13),

10. Estimate s $(s = k\bar{D}/2.45)$.

11. Estimate the $r_{KR_{21}}$. (See p. 275.)

12. Estimate s_e $(s_e = s\sqrt{1 - r_{xx}})$.

13. What are the values of $s_{\%}$ and $s_{e\%}$?

14. Using Figure 10–3, estimate the $r_{KR_{21}}$ reliability for 25-, 50-, and 100-item tests with $\bar{D} = .30$ when $\bar{p} = .8$.

Questions 15–25 are based on the item analysis in Table 10–1.

15. Which item is the easiest?

16. Which item is the most difficult?

Do these items in Table 10–1 (p. 282) suggest possible intrinsic ambiguity and/or double-keying (questions 17–24)?

17. item 1

18. item 2

19. item 3

20. item 4

21. item 5

22. item 9

23. item 10

24. item 81

25. The reliability of the test would increase most if which two items were deleted or double-keyed?

26. If all examinees answer an item correctly, the item could still be serving a significant educational function. (T or F)

27. Which of these requires an external criterion?
   a) Item discrimination indexes
   b) Item difficulty indices
   c) Item validity indices

28. As a general rule, the options on achievement tests that have negative D's
   a) are selected more often by poorer students.
   b) are selected less often by poorer students.
   c) are selected more often by better students.
   d) are correct answers.
   e) More than one of the above

29. Which one of these examples does *not* employ an external criterion for evaluating items on a reading test?
   a) The performance of students in, and not in, remedial reading is compared on each item.
   b) Performance on each item is correlated with teachers' ratings of reading proficiency.
   c) Performance on each item is correlated with semester marks in reading.
   d) Performance on items is correlated with total score on the test.

30. An external criterion is least useful for
   a) the development of a standardized science test
   b) the development of a classroom achievement test
   c) the development of a social-maturity inventory

1. d

2. b

3. a

4. c

5. d

6. b

7. c

8. c

9. d

10. $s = (50)(.25)/2.45 = 5.1$

11. $\bar{p} = 35/50 = .7$, thus

$$r_{KR_{21}} = \frac{50}{49}\left(1 - \frac{50(.7)(.3)}{(5.1)^2}\right)$$

$$= .608$$

12. $s_e = 5.1(.63) = 3.2$

13. 10.2%, 6.4%

14. .40, .70, .85

15. 3, $p = .89$

16. 9, $p = .06$

17. no

18. yes, c

19. no

20. no

21. no

22. yes, c

23. no

24. yes, b

25. 2, 81

26. T

27. c

28. a

29. d

30. b

FOR ADDITIONAL READING

EBEL, R. L. How to improve test quality through item analysis. In *Measuring educational achievement,* 3rd ed. Englewood Cliffs, N.J.: Prentice-Hall, 1979. Chap. 13.

———. The relation of item discrimination to test reliability. *Journal of Educational Measurement,* 4 (1967), 125–28.

ENGELHART, M. D. A comparison of several item discrimination indices. *Journal of Educational Measurement,* 2 (1965), 69–76.

FELDT, L. S., and A. E. HALL. Stability of four item discrimination indices over groups of different average ability. *American Educational Research Journal,* 1 (1964), 35–46.

HENRYSSON, S. Gathering, analyzing, and using data on test items. In R. L. Thorndike, ed., *Educational measurement,* 2nd ed. Washington, D.C.: American Council on Education, 1971. Chap. 5.

LANGE, A., I. J. LEHMANN, and W. A. MEHRENS. Using item analysis to improve tests. *Journal of Educational Measurement,* 2, no. 4 (1967), 65–68.

MYERS, C. T. The relationship between item difficulty and test validity and reliability. *Educational and Psychological Measurement,* 22, no. 3 (1962), 565–71.

11

The Assessment of Affective and Noncognitive Objectives

Cognitive measures assess *maximum* performance (what a person *can do*); affective measures attempt to reflect *typical* performance (what a person *does do or feel*). The objectives for almost any course include statements pertaining to attitudes, appreciation, and interests as well as knowledge and proficiencies. Common affective objectives in education include such phrases as "a positive learner self-concept," "an enjoyment of literature," "an interest in science," and "an acceptance of persons from different cultural and social backgrounds." Many of these aims are assumed to follow naturally from the attainment of cognitive objectives. Successful and unsuccessful academic achievement have positive and negative correlates with students' self-perception (Kifer, 1975; Gadzella & Fournet, 1976). "Human feelings are important both as means and ends in education" (Tyler, 1973, p. 2). As Krathwohl (1965) has stated, "In spite of the lack of explicit formulation . . . nearly all cognitive objectives have an affective component if we search for it" (p. 90).[1] If a child is taught to read but reads only when required to, an extremely important affective educational objective was not achieved.

Although much attention is given to the assessment of cognitive objectives, rarely is any *systematic* effort directed toward the evaluation of affective objectives. Jackson and Lahaderne (1967) and Bauman (1970) found that

[1] Probably the converse also holds: Nearly all affective objectives have a cognitive component.

289

teachers were poor predictors of the affective responses of their students. Tuckman and Lorge (1954) found that a course on the psychology of the adult had little effect on the attitudes of graduate students toward other people, even though such an outcome had frequently been taken for granted. Schon, Hopkins, and Vojir (1980) found that a special unit of instruction did not change students' stereotypes of members of a minority group, even though this was a major objective of the unit. This chapter is concerned with the development and use of affective and certain other noncognitive variables.

Krathwohl and colleagues (1964) produced a handbook and taxonomy designed to stimulate and systematize the assessment of objectives in the affective domain as Bloom's taxonomy had done in the cognitive area.

> The taxonomy, like the periodic table of elements or a check-off shopping list, provides the panorama of objectives. Comparing the range of the present curriculum with the range of possible outcomes may suggest additional goals that might be explored. [Krathwohl, 1965, p. 89]

The degree of *internalization* is proposed as the unifying hierarchical factor underlying the affective taxonomy. Various affective concepts are defined in relation to the internalization hierarchy, as shown in Figure 11–1. The shallowest degree of internalization of feeling is represented by

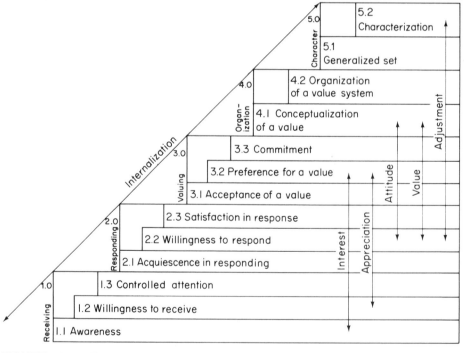

FIGURE 11-1 The range of meaning of common affective terms as defined by the taxonomy of affective educational objectives. (Adapted from Krathwohl et al., 1964.)

awareness; the deepest is represented by *characterization.* Recall that assessment at the higher levels of the cognitive taxonomy is quite difficult to achieve; measuring character and value often poses even greater problems. The affective taxonomy has not had the impact on education that the cognitive taxonomy had. Perhaps this is due partially to the unique assessment problems associated with affective measurement, but the basic impediment is probably ever-present inertia—things at rest remain at rest unless acted on by some external force. We hope that this book may stimulate attempts to assess affective educational objectives in addition to the conventional cognitive outcomes. Krathwohl's taxonomy can be a useful general framework to help organize such assessments.

Cognitive Versus Affective Appraisal

"Who was the third President of the United States?" If you respond, "Thomas Jefferson," you are correct. "Do you like math?" Unlike the preceding question, this one does not have a correct answer that can be designated in advance, because for matters of personal preference the correct (true) answer is not the same for everyone. Rather than offering crude "yes-no" response options, the question could be rephrased so that different degrees of preference or liking can be assessed:

"How well do you like to study math?"
1) Loathe it. 2) Dislike it. 3) Indifferent. 4) Like it. 5) Love it."

The five response categories could then be scored 1, 2, 3, 4, or 5.

Another kind of question partakes of both the knowledge aspect of the President question and the affective nature of the math question. If you ask a student, "Have you read any nonrequired book this semester?" a response of "Yes" may be correct or incorrect. The student either did or did not read such a book, but it may be difficult to verify the statement. The correct answer may not be the ideal answer. *The correct answer to an affective question depends on the person queried; the correct answer to a cognitive question is the same for all respondents.* Note in this example that the implicit affective objective (enjoyment of reading) is inferred from a behavior.

Although attitude scales are the most widely employed means of assessing affective objectives, many other means are used that involve self-reports or reports by others, such as interest inventories, anecdotal records, questionnaires, situational tests, systematic observation, sociometric techniques, interviews, and letters of recommendation.[2] Although their names sound dissimilar, certain common difficulties occur in all such measures. *Situational factors* such as the "set" given to the examinees, the social-desirability response style, and anonymity have a very significant influence on the results of affective measures—far more than they do for ability measures.

---

[2] These and related topics are treated in Chapter 15.

Thurstone Attitude Scales

Ever since the groundbreaking studies by Thurstone at the University of Chicago in 1929, scales have been devised to assess people's attitudes toward a multitude of objects and situations ranging from war to God. Thurstone-type attitude scales have been used to determine the level of employee morale, the effects of movies on attitudes toward crime and toward nationality groups, the effects of social-science courses on student attitudes, and the effects of propaganda on attitudes. Most attitude scales have been developed to answer specific research questions and therefore are not available in a fully standardized form.

Thurstone showed how attitude scales could be constructed for any specified topic, and how to develop items that reveal various degrees of feeling toward the topic or situation. The attitude-toward-movies scale is presented in Figure 11–2. We suggest that you "take" this inventory by responding to the items according to the directions at the top of the figure. After you have completed the scale, determine your score by finding the median scale value (given in parentheses) of all the statements with which you agreed.

What does your score mean? How were the item intensities secured? The higher your score, the more favorable your attitude toward movies; the lower the score, the less favorable. It would be interesting to tabulate the scores of the members of your class (perhaps separately by sex); individuals should remain anonymous. You can make a normative comparison using the absolute meaning of the mean-intensity scores. The scale of intensities is considered to run from 0 through 6. Is the median of the scores in your class approximately $(0 + 6)/2 = 3.0$? How far above or below the median for your class are you?

Thurstone-type attitude scales are developed by giving several hundred persons ("judges") a large number of statements about a topic. Each judge sorts each statement into one of several categories (6 on the movie attitude scale) that range from "extremely favorable" through "neutral" to "extremely unfavorable." Each statement is written on a separate slip of paper. Independently, the judges are asked to rate the intensity of each statement, not the extent to which they agree with it. (This sorting procedure has been described as the method of "equal-appearing intervals," although the judges are not told that the intervals between categories are equal.) Those statements on which there is a consensus among the judges as to intensity rating qualify for the final scale. The attitude scale usually consists of from 20 to 45 statements that spread evenly over the intensity scale, in order to discriminate well among the levels of "favorableness." The intensity scale value of a given statement is the median category of the distribution of the judgments assigned to that statement by the original group of judges (e.g., compare items 4 and 27). The order of these statements is randomized on the final printed form. The examinee is asked to mark those statements with which he or she agrees; his or her score is the median intensity of those statements. The reliability of the scale is then estimated on a sample of subjects. Thurstone-

ATTITUDE TOWARD MOVIES

This is a study of attitudes toward the movies. You will find a number of statements expressing different attitudes toward the movies.

✓ Put a check mark if you agree with the statement.

X Put a cross if you disagree with the statement.

If you simply cannot decide about a statement, mark it with a question mark.

This is not an examination. There are no right or wrong answers to these statements. This is simply an appraisal of people's attitudes toward the movies. Please indicate your own attitude by a check mark (✓) when you agree and by a cross (X) when you disagree.

LIST OF OPINIONS IN THE SCALE

1. (1.5) The movies occupy time that should be spent in more wholesome recreation.
2. (1.3) I am tired of the movies; I have seen too many poor ones.
3. (4.5) The movies are the best civilizing device ever developed.
4. (0.2) Movies are the most important cause of crime.
5. (2.7) Movies are all right but a few of them give the rest a bad name.
6. (2.6) I like to see movies once in a while but they do disappoint you sometimes.
7. (2.9) I think movies are fairly interesting.
8. (2.7) Movies are just a harmless pastime.
9. (1.7) The movies to me are just a way to kill time.
10. (4.0) The influence of the movies is decidedly for good.
11. (3.9) The movies are good, clean entertainment.
12. (3.9) Movies increase one's appreciation of beauty.
13. (1.7) I'd never miss the movies if we didn't have them.
14. (2.4) Sometimes I feel that the movies are desirable and sometimes I doubt it.
15. (0.0) It is a sin to go to the movies.
16. (4.3) There would be very little progress without the movies.
17. (4.3) The movies are the most vital form of art today.
18. (3.6) A movie is the best entertainment that can be obtained cheaply.
19. (3.4) A movie once in a while is a good thing for everybody.
20. (3.4) The movies are one of the few things I can enjoy by myself.
21. (1.3) Going to the movies is a foolish way to spend your money.
22. (1.1) Moving pictures bore me.
23. (0.6) As they now exist movies are wholly bad for children.
24. (0.6) Such a pernicious influence as the movies is bound to weaken the moral fiber of those who attend.
25. (0.3) As a protest against movies we should pledge ourselves never to attend them.
26. (0.1) The movies are the most important single influence for evil.
27. (4.7) The movies are the most powerful influence for good in American life.
28. (2.3) I would go to the movies more often if I were sure of finding something good.
29. (4.1) If I had my choice of anything I wanted to do, I would go to the movies.
30. (2.2) The pleasure people get from the movies just about balances the harm they do.
31. (2.0) I don't find much that is educational in the current films.
32. (1.9) The information that you obtain from the movies is of little value.
33. (1.0) Movies are a bad habit.
34. (3.3) I like the movies as they are because I go to be entertained, not educated.
35. (3.1) On the whole the movies are pretty decent.
36. (0.8) The movies are undermining respect for authority.
37. (2.7) I like to see other people enjoy the movies whether I enjoy them myself or not.
38. (0.3) The movies are to blame for the prevalence of sex offenses.
39. (4.4) The movie is one of the great educational institutions for common people.
40. (0.8) Young people are learning to smoke, drink, and pet from the movies.

The person who has the larger score is more favorably inclined toward the movies than the person with a lower score.

In scoring the attitude scale, we cannot conclude that one score is better or worse than another; we can only say that one person's attitude toward the movies is more or less favorable than another person's. It is purely arbitrary that attitudes unfavorable to the movies have lower scale values than favorable attitudes.

Any individual's attitude is measured by the average or mean scale value of all the statements he checks.

For the purpose of comparing groups, the distributions of attitude in each group can be plotted, and it can then be said whether and how much one group is more favorable to the movies than another group.

FIGURE 11-2 An attitude-toward-movies scale. (Reproduced from L. L. Thurstone, *The measurement of values* [Chicago: University of Chicago Press, 1959], pp. 285–86, by permission of The University of Chicago Press.)

type attitude scales can be constructed for measuring attitudes toward any subject—classical music, collective bargaining, bilingual education, affirmative action, born-again Christians, and so forth. It should be evident that considerable time and effort are required, which limits the use of this kind of scale largely to those areas for which scales are already available. Several extremely useful collections of attitude scales and discussions on many topics have been assembled. These are given along with descriptive annotations in Appendix A.

Likert Scales

There are many types of measures for obtaining information that is pertinent to affective variables. Perhaps the most widely used technique for attitude measurement is the *Likert scale,* on which a statement is followed by the five-response continuum, "strongly agree, agree, undecided, disagree, strongly disagree." Three response categories (e.g., "agree," "uncertain," "disagree") are commonly used with elementary school pupils. More than five categories are occasionally used, although they are usually not worth the extra "responding anxieties" they create for examinees trying to choose between, for example, "very strongly agree" and "strongly agree." The examinee selects the response that best describes his or her reaction to each statement, which are weighted from 1 to 5 when the five-point response continuum is used.

The Education Scale (Rundquist & Sletto, 1936) shown in Figure 11–3 is an example of a Likert scale. Test–retest and split–half reliability estimates of .80 or above are common for this scale.

Another illustrative Likert scale is the Revised Math Attitude Scale (Aiken, 1963) in Figure 11–4. One study reported a test–retest reliability coefficient of .94 for this scale. The scale could easily be adapted for measuring attitudes toward science, typing, reading, or any other curriculum area. Many other examples of attitude scales can be found in Shaw and Wright's (1967) *Scales for the Measurement of Attitudes.*

Likert scales are very flexible and can be constructed more easily than most other types of attitude scales. To generate items, it is often helpful to "role play" and make statements that typify positive and negative attitudes. Ordinarily, items should be a mixture of positive and negative statements to add variety to the scale and reduce the student's tendency to respond perfunctorily. But statements should not be made artifically negative by the addition of *not* or *un-.* As in cognitive assessment, the use of simple language and vocabulary is desirable. The statements should be read aloud if reading may be a problem for some students.

Rating Scales

Rating scales do not differ fundamentally from Likert scales. Instead of using the standard set of response options representing the degree of agreement, rating scales use descriptive terms pertaining to the factor in question.

THE EDUCATION SCALE

READ EACH ITEM CAREFULLY AND UNDERLINE QUICKLY THE
PHRASE WHICH BEST EXPRESSES YOUR FEELING ABOUT THE STATE-
MENT. Wherever possible, let your own personal experience determine your
answer. Do not spend much time on any item. If in doubt, underline the phrase
which seems most nearly to express your present feeling about the statement.
WORK RAPIDLY. Be sure to answer every item.

*1 A man can learn more by working four years than by going to high
school. **Strongly Agree   Agree   Undecided   Disagree   Strongly Disagree**

2 The more education a person has the better he is able to enjoy life.

3 Education helps a person to use his leisure time to better advantage.

4 A good education is a great comfort to a man out of work.

*5 Only subjects like reading, writing, and arithmetic should be taught at
public expense.

*6 Education is no help in getting a job today.

*7 Most young people are getting too much education.

8 A high school education is worth all the time and effort it requires.

9 Our schools encourage an individual to think for himself.

*10 There are too many fads and frills in modern education.

*11 Education only makes a person discontented.

*12 School training is of little help in meeting the problems of real life.

13 Education tends to make an individual less conceited.

14 Solution of the world's problems will come through education.

*15 High school courses are too impractical.

*16 A man is foolish to keep going to school if he can get a job.

17 Savings spent on education are wisely invested.

18 An educated man can advance more rapidly in business and industry.

*19 Parents should not be compelled to send their children to school.

20 Education is more valuable than most people think.

21 A high school education makes a man a better citizen.

*22 Public money spent on education during the past few years could have
been used more wisely for other purposes.

*These are negative items, agreement with which is considered to reflect an unfavorable
attitude. Their weights must be reversed for purposes of scoring. The same response alternatives are used with all items.

FIGURE 11-3 An example of a Likert scale. (Reproduced from E. A. Rundquist and R. F. Sletto, *Personality in the Depression* [Minneapolis: University
of Minnesota Press, 1936], by permission of the publisher. Copyright 1936 by
the University of Minnesota Press.)

REVISED MATH ATTITUDE SCALE

Directions: Please write your name in the upper right hand corner. Each of the statements on this opinionnaire expresses a feeling which a particular person has toward mathematics. You are to express, on a five-point scale, the extent of agreement between the feeling expressed in each statement and your own personal feeling. The five points are: Strongly Disagree (SD), Disagree (D), Undecided (U), Agree (A), Strongly Agree (SA). You are to encircle the letter(s) which best indicates how closely you agree or disagree with the feeling expressed in each statement AS IT CONCERNS YOU.

*1   I am always under a terrible strain in a math class.

     SD   D   U   A   SA

*2   I do not like mathematics, and it scares me to have to take it.
 3   Mathematics is very interesting to me, and I enjoy math courses.
 4   Mathematics is fascinating and fun.
 5   Mathematics makes me feel secure, and at the same time it is stimulating.
*6   My mind goes blank, and I am unable to think clearly when working math.
*7   I feel a sense of insecurity when attempting mathematics.
*8   Mathematics makes me feel uncomfortable, restless, irritable and impatient.
 9   The feeling that I have toward mathematics is a good feeling.
*10 Mathematics makes me feel as though I'm lost in a jungle of numbers and can't find my way out.
 11 Mathematics is something which I enjoy a great deal.
*12 When I hear the word math, I have a feeling of dislike.
*13 I approach math with a feeling of hesitation, resulting from a fear of not being able to do math.
 14 I really like mathematics.
 15 Mathematics is a course in school which I have always enjoyed studying.
*16 It makes me nervous to even think about having to do a math problem.
*17 I have never liked math, and it is my most dreaded subject.
 18 I am happier in a math class than in any other class.
 19 I feel at ease in mathematics, and I like it very much.
 20 I feel a definite positive reaction to mathematics; it's enjoyable

*These are negative items, and must be reversed for purposes of scoring. The same response alternatives are used with all items.

FIGURE 11-4 Another Likert scale. (Reprinted from L. R. Aiken, Jr., *Personality correlates of attitude toward mathematics, Journal of Educational Research,* 1963, 56:576–80, by permission of the author and publisher, Dembar Educational Research Services, Inc.)

An example of a rating scale is the Personality Record (Figure 11–5) used by high schools to send reports to colleges. A teacher or counselor records judgments of the student on eight important factors; all eight represent important educational objectives. Such ratings can be made quickly. If they are consistent across raters, one becomes more confident that the ratings reflect a generalized trait or traits and are not merely a function of the idiosyncracies of a particular student–teacher combination. Special projects (Pardee, 1980) have occasionally used rating scales to monitor students' progress toward noncognitive objectives, using both self-assessments and teacher assessments.

Noncognitive objectives from a different perspective are reflected in students' evaluations of teachers and courses. Rating scales are used at many colleges and universities to help evaluate instruction and teachers. The use of student ratings of instruction below the college level is unfortunately very limited. In a very brief period students can provide much valuable feedback for the teacher. The inventory is sufficiently focused so that if there is a consistently reported weakness, the results have diagnostic and remedial value for the teacher. Research suggests that if teachers would provide opportunity for such simple, straightforward, and systematic pupil feedback, the quality of instruction would improve substantially (Gage, Runkel, & Chatterjee, 1960). Research has shown that student ratings of teachers tend to be reliable (Morrow, 1977; Smith, 1979), to have little relationship to student grades or to a course's difficulty, and to be higher for more experienced teachers (Driscoll & Goodwin, 1979; Remmers, 1963, pp. 367–68; Gillmore, Kane, & Naccarato, 1978). Empirical studies also tend to corroborate the validity of student ratings of teaching effectiveness (McKeachie, Lin & Mann, 1971; Marsh, 1977; Doyle & Whitely, 1974; Kulik & McKeachie, 1975; Aleamoni, 1978; Rotem & Glasman, 1979).

An example of a carefully developed rating scale developed by Ryans (1960) in an extensive study of teacher characteristics is presented in Figure 11–6. (Note the use of bipolar adjectives; the same technique is employed on the semantic-differential scales described in the next section.) With trained raters, interobserver agreement can be quite high (r's of .8 and above). Rating scales like this one can be of value in teacher evaluation and improvement of instruction.

Pictorial response scales are sometimes more effective for assessing attitudes, especially for children. Figure 11–7 illustrates a seven-point rating scale that uses a pictorial response continuum. The stimuli could be "math," "kids at this school," "teachers," "gymnastics," "spinach," "career day," or whatever.

Semantic-Differential Scales

A technique developed by Osgood and his associates (1957) for research on the psychology of meaning, the *semantic-differential scale,* has come to have wide applicability. Concepts are measured and portrayed in three dimensions of meaning, that is, a three-demensional *semantic space.* The dimensions are

Personality Record (Confidential)
(REVISED)

Room................
Grade................

PERSONAL CHARACTERISTICS OF................................

....
Last Name   First Name   Middle Name

School.................. Town or City.................. State..................

The following characterizations are descriptions of behavior. It is recommended that where possible the judgments of a number of the pupil's present teachers be indicated by the use of the following method or by checks:

Example: MOTIVATION

M (5) indicates the most common or modal behavior of the pupil as shown by the agreement of five of the eight teachers reporting. The location of the numerals to the left and right indicates that one teacher considers the pupil *vacillating* and that two teachers consider him *highly motivated*. If preferred, the subject fields or other areas of relationship with the pupil may be used to replace the numerals.

	1		M (5)		2
	√		√ √ √ √		√ √
Example: MOTIVATION	Purposeless	Vacillating	Usually purposeful	Effectively motivated	Highly motivated
1. MOTIVATION	Purposeless	Vacillating	Usually purposeful	Effectively motivated	Highly motivated
2. INDUSTRY	Seldom works even under pressure	Needs constant pressure	Needs occasional prodding	Prepares assigned work regularly	Seeks additional work
3. INITIATIVE	Merely conforms	Seldom initiates	Frequently initiates	Consistently self-reliant	Actively creative
4. INFLUENCE AND LEADERSHIP	Negative	Co-operative but retiring	Sometimes in minor affairs	Contributing in important affairs	Judgment respected—makes things go
5. CONCERN FOR OTHERS	Indifferent	Self-centered	Somewhat socially concerned	Generally concerned	Deeply and actively concerned
6. RESPONSIBILITY	Unreliable	Somewhat dependable	Usually dependable	Conscientious	Assumes much responsibility
7. INTEGRITY	Not dependable	Questionable at times	Generally honest	Reliable, dependable	Consistently trustworthy
8. EMOTIONAL STABILITY	Hyperemotional / Apathetic	Excitable / Unresponsive	Usually well-balanced	Well-balanced	Exceptionally stable

FIGURE 11-5 An illustrative rating scale: the Personality Record. Prepared by a joint committee representing high schools and colleges. (Copyright © 1958, National Association of Secondary School Principals of the NEA; reproduced by permission.)

CLASSROOM OBSERVATION RECORD

TEACHER CHARACTERISTICS STUDY

Teacher_____ No. _____ Sex _____ Class or Subject_____ Date_____

City _____ School_____ Time _____ Observer_____

Pupil Behavior   Remarks:

1.	Apathetic	1	2	3	4	5	6	7	N	Alert
2.	Obstructive	1	2	3	4	5	6	7	N	Responsible
3.	Uncertain	1	2	3	4	5	6	7	N	Confident
4.	Dependent	1	2	3	4	5	6	7	N	Initiating

Teacher Behavior

5.	Partial	1	2	3	4	5	6	7	N	Fair
6.	Autocratic	1	2	3	4	5	6	7	N	Democratic
7.	Aloof	1	2	3	4	5	6	7	N	Responsive
8.	Restricted	1	2	3	4	5	6	7	N	Understanding
9.	Harsh	1	2	3	4	5	6	7	N	Kindly
10.	Dull	1	2	3	4	5	6	7	N	Stimulating
11.	Stereotyped	1	2	3	4	5	6	7	N	Original
12.	Apathetic	1	2	3	4	5	6	7	N	Alert
13.	Unimpressive	1	2	3	4	5	6	7	N	Attractive
14.	Evading	1	2	3	4	5	6	7	N	Responsible
15.	Erratic	1	2	3	4	5	6	7	N	Steady
16.	Excitable	1	2	3	4	5	6	7	N	Poised
17.	Uncertain	1	2	3	4	5	6	7	N	Confident
18.	Disorganized	1	2	3	4	5	6	7	N	Systematic
19.	Inflexible	1	2	3	4	5	6	7	N	Adaptable
20.	Pessimistic	1	2	3	4	5	6	7	N	Optimistic
21.	Immature	1	2	3	4	5	6	7	N	Integrated
22.	Narrow	1	2	3	4	5	6	7	N	Broad

FIGURE 11-6 A rating scale employed by classroom observers. (Reproduced from D. G. Ryans, *Characteristics of teachers* [Washington, D.C.: American Council on Education, 1960], p. 86, by permission of the author and publisher.)

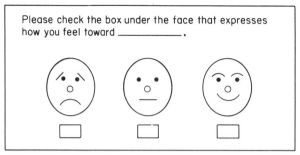

Please check the box under the face that expresses how you feel toward _____ .

FIGURE 11-7 A pictorial response format for assessing attitudes.

evaluation (good–bad), *potency* (strong–weak), and *activity* (fast–slow). Sample directions for the semantic differential are given in Figure 11–8. Each of several concepts (e.g., "Teachers" in Figure 11–9) is followed by a set of 3–15 bipolar adjectives. Osgood recommends that each dimension be measured by at least three separate *scales* that have been empirically shown to be relatively pure measures of that dimension. The "scores" on the bipolar scales for each of the three dimensions are averaged for each concept. The concepts can then be plotted in the three-dimensional semantic space of evaluation, potency, and activity.

The semantic-differential format is illustrated in Figure 11–9. In that figure John Brown has indicated his reaction on each of the nine seven-point scales. His responses are usually "scored" by converting the positions of the check marks into ratings (1–7) using a consistent "low-to-high" direction. For example, the three scales for the activity factors are a, c, and i. On these, the left-most position of scale a (fast–slow) would receive a rating of 7, but the right-most position in scale c would receive that rating. The ratings on the three activity scales in Figure 11–8 are 4, 3, and 5, which are averaged: $(4 + 3 + 5)/3 = 4.0$. The procedure is repeated to obtain the mean (7.0) of the evaluation scales (b, e, h) and the mean (4.7) of the potency scale (d, f, and g).

In actual practice, the major educational concern is with the *value* held by a person for a concept or procedure—whether it is liked, is interesting, and is considered to be useful, valuable, and important. Consequently, most current educational applications of the semantic differential have deviated from the orthodox three-dimensional approach. Scales that have intrinsic relevance for the concept in question are used whether or not they are pure measures of a given dimension. The format is retained, but the semantic-space notion is ignored. The scales are interpreted directly, without averaging. An application at the elementary-school level is shown in Figure 11–10.

Virtually any relevant concept, activity, or person can be studied using the semantic-differential technique: "Geometry," "Reading," "School," "The Ideal Teacher," "Chicanos," "Me," "Most Kids," "Basketball," "Cheating on Tests," and so on. When the integrity of the information is protected, the semantic-differential approach can yield much valuable informa-

SEMANTIC DIFFERENTIAL INSTRUCTIONS

On the following pages there is either a word or an expression in capitalized letters followed by pairs of opposite words underneath the capitalized word or sentence. Between each of the pairs of opposites there are 7 dashes. You are to place a check mark on one of the 7 positions that are between the two opposite words. The check mark should indicate how you feel about the word or concept. Look at the examples below:

EXAMPLE 1:   EDUCATION

Good ✓:___:___:___:___:___:___ Bad
Slow ___:✓:___:___:___:___:___ Fast
Cruel ___:___:___:✓:___:___:___ Kind

In this example EDUCATION is the concept being assessed and the pairs of opposites are Good – Bad, Slow – Fast, and Cruel – Kind. If EDUCATION seemed to you to mean something very Good, you would make a check in position 1 of the Good – Bad scale. If EDUCATION seemed to you to mean something Slow, then you would place your check mark in position 2 of the Slow – Fast scale. And if you feel that EDUCATION means something which is neither Cruel nor Kind, then you would put your check mark in position 4.

In the following example a check has been placed to illustrate how someone would place his check marks if he thought that TEACHERS were very Bad, very Fast, and very Cruel:

EXAMPLE 2:   TEACHERS

Good ___:___:___:___:___:___:✓ Bad
Slow ___:___:___:___:___:___:✓ Fast
Cruel ✓:___:___:___:___:___:___ Kind

On the following pages, place your check marks rapidly. What is wanted is your first impression. This is not a test; the "right" answer is the one that is true for you. Be sure to make only one check mark for each pair of words. Do not skip any pairs of words or pages.

FIGURE 11–8 Sample semantic-differential items and directions.

tion. Very little reading and testing time are required. The semantic differential has been found to yield reasonably reliable information at levels as low as grade 2, but the reliability is greater with older students (Di Vesta and Dick, 1966). The semantic-differential measurement technique has been useful for

TEACHERS

a.	fast	___	___	___	✓	___	___	___	slow
b.	good	✓	___	___	___	___	___	___	bad
c.	passive	___	___	✓	___	___	___	___	active
d.	small	___	___	___	✓	___	___	___	large
e.	worthless	___	___	___	___	___	___	✓	valuable
f.	strong	___	___	✓	___	___	___	___	weak
g.	light	___	___	___	___	✓	___	___	heavy
h.	helpful	✓	___	___	___	___	___	___	not helpful
i.	moving	___	___	✓	___	___	___	___	still

FIGURE 11-9 Responses of one student regarding the concept "teachers," using the semantic-differential technique.

measuring attitudes in a wide spectrum of applications in many fields. Despite its rather brief history, it has become a standard assessment technique. Its chief advantage over Likert scales is ease of construction and administration. Its disadvantages are its lack of flexibility and its greater ambiguity in interpretation—it is easier to interpret responses to direct statements.

Self-Report Inventories

Self-report inventories typically consist of structured questions or statements to which the respondent responds "yes" or "no" or "yes," "?" or "no." Self-report inventories are not fundamentally different from Likert or rating scales. Indeed, the items on self-report inventories often use Likert or rating scale formats. Illustrative items, along with the domain they represent, are the following:

1. I usually wait to the "last minute" before doing my homework. (Study habits)
2. Most teachers care about me as a person. (Attitude toward teachers)
3. Most kids at this school are unfriendly. (Attitude toward peers)
4. I feel guilty because I'm so dumb. (Learner self-concept)

GIVING ORAL REPORTS

worthless	____	____	____	____	____	valuable
interesting	____	____	____	____	____	dull
unpleasant	____	____	____	____	____	pleasant
useless	____	____	____	____	____	useful
easy	____	____	____	____	____	hard

SCIENCE CLASS

interesting	____	____	____	____	____	dull
useless	____	____	____	____	____	useful
easy	____	____	____	____	____	hard
pleasant	____	____	____	____	____	unpleasant
worthless	____	____	____	____	____	valuable

FIGURE 11-10   An example of a semantic-differential measure devised for program evaluation.

Table 11-1 gives sample items from a self-report inventory, the Student Attitude Inventory (Hopkins, Kretke, Martin, & Averill, 1978)[3] together with results from its use as part of a school district's testing program. The percentages of students responding "yes" are given for two grade levels (5 and 11) for two consecutive years (1977 and 1978). Note that at grade 11, means are much less positive than at grade 5, and that there was little change in means between 1977 and 1978.

Notice that the data in Table 11-1 are aggregated—they are reported for all students in the school district. They could also be reported at the school or classroom level. Research indicates that teachers are not good judges of students' attitudes toward school (Khan, 1978). However, pupils' composite descriptions of their classrooms can have considerable validity when the students are anonymous and properly motivated (Medley & Klein, 1957).

Self-report inventories can also be used in the area of study habits and skills. Academic aptitude is of little benefit if it is not nurtured and exercised. Any teacher can point to students who have untapped potential—potential

[3] Items in this inventory are similar to those on the Survey of School Attitudes published by Harcourt Brace Jovanovich in 1975. Related measures of school climate are considered in Chapter 15.

TABLE 11-1

ILLUSTRATIVE ITEMS FROM THE SCHOOL ATTITUDE INVENTORY

Items Pertaining to Attitudes Toward School and Teachers	*Grade*	*1977*[a]	*1978*[a]	*Change*
23. Do you feel that you are really a part of your school?	5	67%	69%	+ 2%
	11	55%	55%	0%
38. Do you think kids should have to go to school even if they don't want to?	5	73%	74%	+ 1%
	11	54%	56%	+ 2%
39. Is going to school important for a happy life?	5	84%	85%	+ 1%
	11	56%	59%	+ 3%
41. Do you often use things you learn in school outside of school?	5	79%	78%	− 1%
	11	75%	77%	+ 2%
42. Do you think that most people who drop out of school before graduation will be sorry someday?	5	85%	87%	+ 2%
	11	80%	81%	+ 1%
22. Do most of your teachers care about what happens to you as a person?	5	70%	69%	− 1%
	11	53%	55%	+ 2%
32. Is there a teacher in your school you would go talk to if you were worried about something?	5	64%	65%	+ 1%
	11	52%	52%	0%
36. Are most teachers friendly?	5	85%	87%	+ 2%
	11	77%	78%	+ 1%
37. Are most teachers helpful?	5	86%	86%	0%
	11	72%	71%	− 1%
Items Pertaining to Educational Aspirations				
27. Do you plan to finish high school?	5	92%	93%	+ 1%
	11	97%	97%	0%
28. Do you plan to go to college?	5	81%	83%	+ 2%
	11	72%	71%	− 1%

[a] Percent responding "yes."

SOURCE: Hopkins, Kretke, Martin, & Averill, 1978.

that is wasted because of poor study habits and motivation. In spite of their obvious importance, however, little *systematic* effort is made in the curriculum to assess, teach, or develop good study skills and habits. When these "survival skills" are lacking, "underachievement" is inevitable. Slansky (1980) found that these skills can be profitably taught to students entering middle school.

A few published study habit inventories are available. One of the most widely used is the Survey of Study Habits and Attitudes (SSHA).[4] The SSHA includes four subtests: (1) Delay Avoidance (e.g., "Daydreaming distracts my attention while I am studying"), (2) Work Methods (e.g., "My teachers criticize my work for being poorly planned or hurriedly written"), (3) Teacher Approval (e.g., "My teachers make their subjects interesting and meaningful to me"), and (4) Educational Acceptance (e.g., "I feel that I would study

[4] Published by the Psychological Corp. Form H is for grades 7–12; Form C is for high school seniors and college students.

harder if I were given more freedom to choose subjects I like"). The items
have been shown to have validity for predicting grades and teachers' ratings
when examinees are motivated to respond truthfully (Goldfried & D'Zurilla,
1973).

Self-concept

> As a man thinketh in his heart, so is he.—*Proverbs 23:7*
>
> Public opinion is a weak tyrant compared with our own private opinion. What a
> man thinks of himself, that it is which determines . . . his fate.
> —Thoreau, *Walden,* 1854

In recent years there has been much interest in the measurement of self-
concept (Shepard, 1979a; Wylie, 1974). One of the most widely used self-
esteem inventories (Coopersmith, 1967), which has been used successfully in
the upper elementary grades and above, as well as with adults, is given in
Figure 11-11. Several studies have produced results that are in exact con-
tradiction to current stereotypes (Trowbridge, 1972; Harms, 1977; Scheirer &
Kraut, 1979), with more positive concepts being reported by blacks than by
whites and by students of lower socioeconomic status than by members of the
middle class.

Q-Sort

A procedure by which one can assess attitudes, interests, and other affective
variables is the *Q-sort technique,* originally developed by Stephenson (1953).
An individual is given a set of cards containing statements, traits, pictures, or
whatever; he or she then sorts them into piles according to their relative standing along a single dimension. The continuum can take many forms: "most
like me" to "least like me," "most important" to "least important," "best"
to "worst," and so forth. The number of cards allowed in each pile is usually
predetermined to approximate a normal frequency distribution.

Students may describe themselves, a course, their interests, their school
principal, and so on. The Q-sort technique has been widely used in counseling
studies in which an individual describes himself or herself with one Q-sort and
resorts the cards to describe his or her ideal self. The sorted piles can then be
correlated to the other methods of assessing attitude that have been discussed.
The content of the Q-sort can be tailor-made to the immediate particular purpose. There are a few standard Q-sorts, the most common of which is the
California Q-set. One hundred descriptive statements are sorted into nine
categories ranging from "extremely characteristic" to "extremely un-
characteristic" of the person. A special feature of this Q-sort set is a description of optimal adjustment, which is consensually based on the judgments of
nine clinical psychologists. This and other examples can be found in Block
(1961).

The major use of the Q-sort technique has been in counseling and

SELF-ESTEEM INVENTORY

Items are answered either "like me" or "unlike me." The high esteem response is indicated in parentheses after each item.

1. I often wish I were someone else. (Unlike me)
2. I find it very hard to talk in front of a group. (Unlike me)
3. There are lots of things about myself I'd change if I could. (Unlike me)
4. I can make up my mind without too much trouble. (Like me)
5. I'm a lot of fun to be with. (Like me)
6. I get upset easily at home. (Unlike me)
7. It takes me a long time to get used to anything new. (Unlike me)
8. I'm popular with people my own age. (Like me)
9. My family expects too much of me. (Unlike me)
10. My family usually considers my feelings. (Like me)
11. I give in very easily. (Unlike me)
12. It's pretty tough to be me. (Unlike me)
13. Things are all mixed up in my life. (Unlike me)
14. Other people usually follow my ideas. (Like me)
15. I have a low opinion of myself. (Unlike me)
16. There are many times when I'd like to leave home. (Unlike me)
17. I often feel upset about the work that I do. (Unlike me)
18. I'm not as nice looking as most people. (Unlike me)
19. If I have something to say, I usually say it. (Like me)
20. My family understands me. (Like me)
21. Most people are better liked than I am. (Unlike me)
22. I usually feel as if my family is pushing me. (Unlike me)
23. I often get discouraged at what I am doing. (Unlike me)
24. Things usually don't bother me. (Like me)

FIGURE 11-11 The Coopersmith self-esteem inventory (Coopersmith, 1967). Copyright 1967 by W. H. Freeman and Company. Reproduced by permission of Stanley Coopersmith.

psychotherapy. For example, Oldridge (1963) used a Q-sort by teachers to ascertain whether the behavior of pupils undergoing counseling was improving more than that of students who were not receiving any treatment. The potential applicability of the Q-sort is much broader. Armitage (1967) used the Q-sort technique to compare the values attached to certain social-studies objectives by "experts" and classroom teachers. Sheldon and Sorenson (1960) used the technique to study changes in the educational philosophy of prospective teachers during their student teaching. The difficulty and time required for administering and scoring the Q-sort, and its focus on a single dimension, reduce its usability for general assessment purposes in comparison to that of the Likert and semantic-differential approaches.

Questionnaires

Sets of questions are frequently used in educational surveys. The questionnaires are usually mimeographed or printed and sent through the mail or administered to "captive" audiences such as groups of students or teachers. The questions may be of any kind that we have discussed in this book. They may begin with background biographical data, such as sex ("Male or Female—check one"), date of birth ("month, day, and year"), and number of years of school completed. The subsequent questions may remain factual ("How many students are enrolled in your classes?" "Which subject do you teach?"), or the instrument may become an opinionnaire, typically of the rating scale or ranking kind. One might, for instance, send the Thurstone-Chave "Attitude Toward Movies" scale to be filled out and returned, but more likely one would select items from previously used inventories (see Appendix A), or use questions of one's own devising.

Questionnaires have all the usual limitations of self-report devices plus some special problems of their own. If they are mailed to individuals to be filled out at whatever times and under whatever circumstances happen to prevail in the home or office of the recipient, the results may vary greatly from one individual to another, depending on the time and care the respondent chooses or is able to give. Some questionnaires will probably be returned with responses made carelessly and perhaps incompletely, unless respondents are in some way wooed into giving the time and care required. Other questionnaires will not be returned unless their receivers are reminded several times. Despite the best efforts of the investigator, there will probably be some people who do not return the questionnaires in a usable condition. These "nonreturners" and "unsatisfactory answerers" are the nonrespondents who bias the generalizations that can legitimately be made from the survey.

Suppose, for example, that we sent out a double postal card to every teacher in your state and asked, "In your opinion, which are better measures of most educational objectives—essay tests or objective tests?" If in two weeks half of the cards have been returned, we would not be in a good position to tabulate and report our results because we would not know which half of the teachers had responded—those who favor essay tests or those who prefer objective tests. We could *assume* that we have secured a representative 50 percent of the teachers, but careful readers of our report might not be willing to permit us that assumption without further justification. It is essential to build in one or two follow-ups into a study plan in order to reduce nonrespondents to as small a percentage as possible. If the initial respondents are compared with the follow-up group(s) we can sometimes get clues as to how the nonrespondents may have answered; that is, we may determine the direction of the bias in our sample. If the percents answering "essay" are

30%, 40%, and 45% for the initial group and the first and second follow-up groups, respectively, we can be reasonably confident that the nonrespondents would be more sympathetic to essay tests than the total group of respondents.

Even with 100 percent returns, however, we would still need to qualify our conclusions. Our figures represent what respondents report feeling, not necessarily how they actually feel. Careless errors, fallible memories, and willful deceptions can discolor findings to some extent. The problems are much greater when the questionnaire includes sensitive attitudinal questions.

Before you attempt to use a questionnaire, additional reading and study pertaining to procedures for administration and development in such sources as Oppenheim (1966) and Appendix A are recommended.

Interviews

Although it is not always recognized as such, the interview is one of the most widely used assessment techniques. What are the purposes of an interview? Interviews are used to assess a wide variety of variables—affective, psychomotor, and cognitive. A few highly select colleges and most medical schools use interviews as a part of their selection process.

Interviews vary in quality as much as interviewers do. Indeed, it is the interviewer who is the yardstick in this assessment procedure. Unplanned and completely unstructured interviews by naive interviewers have few measurement virtues.

Unplanned interviews tend to use up the available time on a few limited topics. Typically, "time runs out" before many important areas have been discussed. The interview has resembled a social exchange more than a procedure for assessing variables that have relevance and predictive validity for the criteria in question.

Untrained interviewers often become too active in the interviewing process and "shape" the interviewee's responses (Bradburn & Sudman, 1979). As in other situations involving human interaction, the "actors" are continually "reading" each other—searching for responses that will be reinforced by the other partner. Especially in contexts in which the interviewer has something the interviewee wants (i.e., controls the reinforcers), as in job or school interview situations, the interviewee is likely to respond to the perceived demand characteristics of the situation. Interviewees are typically in the "set" to supply information that the interviewer wants to hear, rather than the "whole truth and nothing but the truth." The skillful interviewer provides few clues to the "right answers," although the social-desirability set suggests the "right answers" to many questions. "Do you enjoy your work?" "Tell me about your study habits." "Do you have kids?" "Why did you leave your last job?"

The use of the interview as a data-gathering technique in survey research has fewer problems than its use in making a decision about the interview. There is less need for the interviewee to "put his or her best foot forward." But even here the social-desirability response set can contaminate findings unless this incentive is not skillfully disarmed by a competent interviewer and a high level of rapport. In a survey (Edwards, 1957) of the attitudes toward giving cash bonuses to war veterans, a random half of the interviewees were questioned orally and the other half responded anonymously in writing. Those who were questioned orally were much more supportive of the proposition, yet the proportion obtained from those who responded anonymously was much closer to the actual proportion in the referendum. Other studies have shown that interviewees tend to exaggerate their voting frequency, the number possessing library cards, their giving to charity, and other socially desirable behaviors (USDHEW,1977). Interviewers can sometimes insert a few questions designed to assess the social-desirability response tendency (see pp. 310–313) that can help evaluate the validity of respondent answers.

Many studies have shown that the personality and other characteristics of the interviewer can have a profound influence on the responses he or she elicits from interviewees (USDHEW, 1977; Selltiz, Wrightsman, & Cook, 1976, chap. 9). For example, "blue-collar" interviewers elicit more radical opinions than "white-collar" interviewers (USDHEW, 1977). The more the interview is structured, the less the interviewer becomes a factor in determining the responses.

The interview is very much overrated as an assessment procedure. Meehl (1954) found that the simple statistical use of one or two test scores was generally better in predicting or revealing a person's status than judgments made by trained and experienced people via interviews and other informal observational techniques. The popularity of the interview is based more on its face validity than on its demonstrated validity as a method of appraising people. One may ask, "If the interview is such a good method of appraisal, why are there so many poor teachers (and other workers) employed in positions for which they lack the necessary attitudes and skills for effective performance?" The validity of interview "data" is highly dependent on the skill of the interviewer which means in part that the interview will be planned and, to some degree, structured. In essense, the skillful interview is a special instance of systematic observation of a person in a situation in which the interview is providing the stimuli.

Potential users of interviews should consult more comprehensive treatments of the topic such as Selltiz and others (1976, chap. 9) and Kerlinger (1973, chap. 28).

Problems of Affective Measurement

There are four types of problems with affective measurement: (1) fakability, (2) self-deception, (3) semantic problems, and (4) criterion inadequacy.

Fakability

During an interview for a summer position in a music store Carol's reported liking for classical music may differ greatly from what she would tell a close friend. But it is very unlikely that her score on an "ability" test of music vocabulary would be affected much by her desire for employment. For the manager of the music store to learn the true extent of her knowledge, it is only necessary that Carol have enough motivation to take the vocabulary test conscientiously. Even large inducements will not compensate for lack of information about figures and Bach.

Ability tests are keyed a priori; it is not possible to fake a high (or good) score (although of course one could fake a low score, that is, deliberately score poorly on the test). On affective measures one can usually fake in either direction: Carol could tell the music store owner that she prefers classical music and tell her friends that she prefers jazz, when she actually dislikes both forms and prefers country music. A few disguised self-report and other-report devices are fairly resistant to extreme faking; the individual being tested cannot readily ascertain what is being assessed. Properly constructed and administered ability tests yield measures of well-motivated performance; self-report affective devices may more nearly reflect the desire to conform to the special situation, as perceived by the examinee, because such devices do not lend themselves to intrinsic right–wrong scoring. Liking spinach may be "right" for one purpose and "wrong" for another, but the correct spelling of *grandiose* is independent of the context in which the word appears.

Most affective measures require self-reports that are fakable; thus, if the assessment is to be valid, it must be obtained in such a way that there is no incentive to be untruthful. Anonymity is an important ingredient in valid attitude assessment in any situation in which the subject may be rewarded for, or embarrassed by, certain responses. Anonymity precludes the use of the information for individual purposes, but it can still yield feedback that is invaluable to the teacher in assessing the degree to which various affective educational objectives have been achieved. Program and course evaluation measures are typically administered so that the respondent is free from self-jeopardy.

When the identity of the subject is necessary, an honest sharing of one's values, attitudes, interests, and feelings can be expected only when a deep level of rapport and trust has been established between the individual and the users of the information. This was graphically illustrated in a study reported by Cronbach (1970, p. 495) in which a group of industrial workers filled out identical health questionnaires under two conditions. One questionnaire was returned to the company medical department as a preliminary to a medical examination. The other was mailed directly to a research group at a university. Far more symptoms were indicated on the research questionnaire than on the company's, even though an honest report on the latter might facilitate the obtaining of medical help.

The Social-Desirability Response Style

Unless they are dissuaded from doing so, many examinees have a tendency to give a socially desirable impression on self-report inventories; this is sometimes referred to as the "façade" effect. Generally, people tend to act in their own perceived best interest. When it is to one's advantage to "fake bad," a negative façade effect can be expected (Pollaczek, 1952). A draftee who wants a medical discharge may report a staggering array of psychotic symptoms. The giving of socially desirable responses on a self-report inventory does not necessarily indicate deliberate deception by the respondent but, rather, may be an unconscious tendency to "put up a good front." Affective measures can be falsified to some degree no matter how they are constructed (Cronbach, 1970, pp. 495–97), although faking can be reduced and/or assessed by special procedures.

Edwards (1957) developed a special social-desirability (SD) scale that can be embedded in other scales on an inventory in order to assess the magnitude of the effect of this factor on the affective measures. The scale is of value in investigating the extent to which the façade effect contaminates scores on some other measure. If scores on the SD scale correlate highly with scores on another measure, the validity of the measure is suspect. For items on the SD scale, the true answer is almost always different from the "good" (socially desirable) answer.

In the following items from a social-desirability scale designed for children (Crandall, Crandall, & Katkousky, 1965), note that the correct answer is usually socially undesirable:

"I am always respectful of older people"
"I sometimes feel angry when I don't get my way"
"When I make a mistake, I always admit I am wrong"
"I always wash my hands before every meal"

How would you respond to the following ten items, which are taken from the Marlowe-Crowne Social-Desirability Scale?

1. Before voting I thoroughly investigate the qualifications of all the candidates. (T)
2. I never hesitate to go out of my way to help someone in trouble. (T)
3. I like to gossip at times. (F)
4. There have been occasions when I took advantage of someone. (F)
5. I always try to practice what I preach. (T)
6. I sometimes try to get even rather than forgive and forget. (F)
7. When I don't know something I don't at all mind admitting it. (T)
8. I am always courteous, even to people who are disagreeable. (T)
9. There have been times when I was quite jealous of the good fortune of others. (F)
10. I have never deliberately said something that hurt someone's feelings. (T)

If the correct answer for you agreed with the key (the socially desirable answer) on more than two or three of the questions, you are an unusual person. But consider the difference between the set you were in and the set you would be in if you needed a job and these questions were part of the application procedure.

SD items have been implanted in surveys of students' school attitudes to determine whether the more positive school attitudes reported by elementary-school students were partially attributable to a greater (higher mean) SD response (Hopkins, Kretke, Martin, and Averill, 1978). They could not; when responding anonymously only 7–8% of the students gave the SD response.

SD items often have to be adapted to the content at hand. The following are sample SD items that were embedded in a scale designed to measure attitudes toward ethnic minorities:

"I'm always courteous to Mexican-American students even when they are rude."
"All Mexican-American kids are easy to like."

Schon, Hopkins, & Vojir (1980) studied the question of whether a specially designed curriculum improved students' attitudes toward Mexican Americans. The experimental group, which received the special curriculum, might be expected to acquiesce more to the perceived "demand characteristics" of the situation and, hence, report better attitudes than the untreated control group, even if their attitudes were unaffected. This is particularly true if students are not responding anonymously. But if the experimental and control groups do not differ on the SD items but do on the "real" attitude items, the difference has much more credibility.

The *forced-choice item format* can sometimes reduce the influence of the social-desirability set. Items of this type require the respondent to discriminate between two or more alternatives that, ideally, are equally acceptable. A sample forced-choice item follows. Items of this kind attempt to minimize the SD response set by making each choice equally attractive or unattractive.

ABOUT FRIENDS

The forced-choice procedure is widely used on published affective measures (and is discussed further in Chapter 15).

The forced choice can be among more than two alternatives. On the Kuder Vocational Preference Record, for example, the examinee is asked to select the activity that he or she likes most and least among, say, collecting autographs, collecting coins, and collecting butterflies.

Forced-choice measures are much more difficult to develop and interpret than most other types of scales. The forced-choice procedure is more useful on standardized affective measures; it is less useful for locally developed assessment measures.

Self-Deception

A common adjustment phenomenon in human behavior is the tendency to want to like what we see when we look at ourselves. Human defense mechanisms cushion failures, minimize faults, and maximize virtues so that we maintian a sense of personal worth (which, as a consequence, is often exaggerated!). When one is asked questions about oneself, the validity of the responses is vulnerable to the distortions of self-deception. This "blurring" can become a major threat to the validity of self-report measures—people who have the greatest personality problems are those who are the least able to give an accurate self-description. If a man believes himself to be Napoleon, his nonfaked, "honest" responses to personal questions will probably reflect his delusion. The validity of the responses is, of course, another matter. Other than for purposes of school counseling and guidance and psychological case studies, there is rarely a need for assessment of matters that are so sensitive that self-deception becomes a serious problem. There is likely to be little need for self-deceit on attitudes and interests toward educational experiences. People with "a little learning" should resist any temptation to play junior psychiatrist by probing into emotional matters of a very personal nature. Comparing the anonymous responses of groups of persons when evaluating teachers or programs is quite a different matter.

Semantic Problems

On cognitive measures, the alternatives to items are usually categorically different; one of them is the correct or best answer. On affective measures, however, the responses frequently demand differences in degree. Consequently, words like *often, seldom, frequently, usually,* and *sometimes* are required. (See the Mary-Jane forced-choice item on p. 312.) Unfortunately there is considerable variation in the explicit meanings that people attach to such words (Simpson, 1944). When students were asked what percentage frequency of a particular response would correspond to what they "frequently" did, one-fourth of them applied "frequently" only to events occurring at least 80 percent of the time, while another one-fourth indicated that "frequently" could mean a frequency below 40 percent of the time. Similar semantic difficulties occur with other types of terms and expressions. A question such as "Do you find reading interesting?" seems straightforward, but how interesting is interesting? Consider "Do you make friends easily?" How easy is easily? Also, is a friend a casual acquaintance or a very intimate associate? The validity of self-report information is reduced to the extent that the descriptive terms employed do not have uniform meaning across individuals.

Criterion Inadequacy

Definitive criteria against which the validity of the self-report information can be checked are usually either impossible or very difficult to obtain. How is a test of emotional stability or adjustment validated? There is no definitive criterion that will demonstrate the test's validity. Only after many varied and extensive studies would it be possible to establish the construct validity of tests of this kind scientifically. Consequently, one must interpret cautiously the results of published and unpublished affective measures, since only fragmentary data with relevance for validity are available. Occasionally some direct or indirect validity data are available. For example, Shortland and Berger (1970) found that examinees reporting high personal values for honesty, helpfulness, and especially salvation returned the pencils that were loaned to them significantly more frequently than those who reported lower values on these scales.

One is on safer ground when measuring attitudes and interests instead of personality traits. If there seems to be no incentive to fake, and if the nature of the question is not emotionally jeopardizing, the responses have more logical validity and an interpretation can be made with more confidence.

Invasion of Privacy

In the measurement of attitudes, values, personality, and interests, it is important to avoid the invasion of an individual's privacy. The irresponsible use of certain tests and items has resulted in the need for ethical guidelines. (See Reynolds, 1979.) Thorndike and Hagen (1977) offer the following relevant questions to be posed in this regard:

1. *For whose benefit will the information be used?* The information should result in some potential personal and/or social good without undue risk of psychological or physical harm to the individual.
2. *How personal and relevant is the information?* The measures should have established validity if they are to be used in any important decisions.[5] Emotional stability is far more crucial in a pilot than in a janitor. In the past many employers have used personality tests with some "face" validity but little or no criterion-related validity. Topics that are so personal that questions pertaining to them are often considered to be an invasion of privacy include sexual habits (87%), finances (66%), political beliefs (64%), description of spouse's personality (59%), and family background (49%) (Thorndike & Hagen, 1977, p. 612). Cognitive attributes are rarely "personal"—only 9% of the respondents considered IQ to be an invasion of privacy. Obviously, the content and purpose of the query are critical factors in whether the information is "personal" or not. When the respondent's anonymity is protected, many questions can be asked that would otherwise be too personal, threatening, or self-incriminating.

[5] The Equal Employment Opportunities Commission (EEOC) is the federal watchdog that has been created to promote fairness in employee selection. Employers must be able to demonstrate the criterion-related validity of measures used in their selection process.

314

3. *Has "informed consent" been granted?* Has the respondent been told what information will be collected and for what purpose? Does the person understand that he or she may decline to participate? Is the person competent to decide on the appropriateness of participation? Informed consent is required in most medical and psychological research, although the legal provision of *in loco parentis* allows responsible educators to make many decisions for school-related testing of students under their authority if the information sought can be justified as consistent with the mission of the school.

Summary

The appraisal of feelings, interests, and attitudes has been neglected in education, even though affective objectives are implicit, if not explicit, in virtually every educational endeavor. Several techniques have been devised for measuring affect. Common examples are *Thurston, Likert, rating,* and *semantic-differential scales,* and the *Q-sort technique.* Thurstone attitude scales are expensive to construct; a number of them are available (although they are usually somewhat outdated). Likert scales are very flexible and easily constructed. They have a common scale ("strongly agree" to "strongly disagree") for the responses that permits comparison across items. Rating scales are easily constructed and have wide applicability. The semantic differential is a special type of rating scale that requires very little response and administration time. The Q-sort technique, although difficult to administer, facilitates assessment of the degree of relationship (r) between persons or within the same person. Its greatest application has been in personality research, although there are many rich, untapped areas in which it might be used. The interview can be used to assess affective and other variables. Its validity is dependent on the skill of the interviewer. It is highly vulnerable to the social-desirability response set.

Unique assessment problems are encountered in the affective domain: The measures are fakable, vulnerable to self-deception, and usually lacking in definitive external criteria. Forced-choice items and the use of social-desirability scales can help improve the validity of many self-report affective measures. Semantic problems exert great influence on responses to items that reflect differences in degree rather than having a correct answer. Anonymity is usually required for valid evaluative feedback in affective assessment.

IMPORTANT TERMS AND CONCEPTS

affective	semantic differential	social-desirability scale (SD)
Krathwohl taxonomy	Q-sort	forced-choice items
internalization	self-report inventory	self-deception
Thurstone scale	questionnaire	semantic problems
Likert scale	structured interview	criterion inadequacy
rating scale	fakability	

1. Which of these terms do not belong in the affective domaine?
   a) Knowledge   b) Cognitive   c) Attitudes   d) Values
   e) Interests   f) Abilities   g) Aptitudes   h) Appreciations

2. Which of these represents the lowest degree of internalization in the affective domain according to the Krathwohl taxonomy?
   a) Awareness   c) Acceptance
   b) Characterization   d) Commitment

Use the following response options for questions 3–6:
   a) Likert scale   b) Thurstone scale   c) rating scale
              d) semantic differential   e) Q-sort

3. Which of these types of attitude measures requires the most time and effort to develop?

4. Which of the measurement techniques uses the strongly-disagree-to–strongly-agree response continuum?

5. In which does each item carry a designated and variable weight that is used to determine an examinee's total score?

6. Which is often used to obtain a correlation between the "ideal" and the "actual"?

7. Which of the following is the chief limitation in the use of mailed questionnaires for assessing attitudes?
   a) Attitudes cannot be validly measured.
   b) The number of respondents is usually small.
   c) Some respondents do not answer accurately or truthfully.
   d) Attitudes cannot be measured reliably.

8. The tendency of some examinees to give the ideal answer even when it is not accurate is termed
   a) the acquiescence response style.
   b) the gambling response style.
   c) the speed-vs.-accuracy response style.
   d) the social-desirability response style.
   e) the impulse response set.

9. Items that are designed to measure the social-desirability (SD) response style are items
   a) on which the true answer is socially desirable.
   b) on which the true answer is socially undesirable.
   c) designed to measure popularity.
   d) designed to measure desire for social acceptance.

10. Which of the following is *not* an example of an SD item?
   a) I have never intensely disliked anyone.
   b) On occasion I have had doubts about my ability to succeed in life.

c) I've never met a person that I didn't like.

d) I never resent being asked to return a favor.

e) I sometimes regret something I've said or done.

11. If you answered "true" to all five of the statements (a–e) in the previous question,

a) you are a liar.

b) you have deceived yourself.

c) you lack insight into yourself.

d) you need psychotherapy.

e) you're pulling my leg.

f) one or more of the above.

Self-report measures of attitudes and values have four basic drawbacks from the standpoint of validity. Match the following statements (questions 13–16) with the problem indicated.

a) fakability   b) self-deception   c) semantics   d) inadequate criterion

12. The meaning attached to words like *seldom, often, frequently, usually,* and *rarely* is not constant from one person to another.

13. Can you define the behavior of a person with perfect emotional stability?

14. "I'm not lying. I am Jesus Christ."

15. "I knew they would not hire me if they knew I hated kids, so I played games with them on their little test."

16. "I don't care what all my classmates say. I am the most popular girl in the class."

Use Table 11-1 in responding to questions 17–19. If the students responded honestly,

17. students in grade 11 feel that only about one teacher in two cares about what happens to them as people (item 22).   (T or F)

18. student attitudes appear to have changed little between 1977 and 1978.   (T or F)

19. eleventh-graders report less positive attitudes toward school and teachers than fifth-graders do.   (T or F)

20. Compared with skillful interviews, unskilled interviews are more likely to

a) participate more actively in the interview (e.g., do more talking and less listening).

b) sample a broader domain of variables.

c) withhold the "desired answers" to questions from the interviewee.

d) minimize the social-desirability response set.

e) establish a high level of credibility and rapport with the interviewee.

1. a, b, f, g	8. d	15. a
2. a	9. b	16. b
3. b	10. e	17. F
4. a	11. f	18. T
5. b	12. c	19. T
6. e	13. d	20. a
7. c	14. b	

FOR ADDITIONAL READING

ANASTASI, A. Measures of interests, attitudes and values, and other assessment techniques. In *Psychological testing*, 4th ed. New York: Macmillan, 1976. Chaps. 18, 20.

BLOCK, J. *The Q-sort method in personality assessment and psychiatric research.* Springfield, Ill.: Thomas C Thomas, 1961.

BRADBURN, N. M., SUDMAN, S., et al. *Improving interview method and questionnaire design.* San Francisco: Jossey-Bass, 1979.

HENERSON, M. E., L. L. MORRIS, and C. T. FITZ-GIBBON. *How to measure attitudes.* Beverly Hills, Calif.: Sage Publications, 1978.

JOHNSON, O. G., and J. W. BOMMARITO. *Tests and measurement in child development: A handbook.* San Francisco: Jossey-Bass, 1971.

KERLINGER, F. N. *Foundations of behavioral research*, 2nd ed. New York: Holt, Rinehart and Winston, 1973. Chaps. 28, 33, 34. ("Interviews," "Semantic Differential," "Q Methodology").

KRATHWOHL, D. R., B. S. BLOOM, and B. B. MASIA. *Taxonomy of educational objectives: Handbook II, Affective domain.* New York: D. McKay, 1964.

KULIK, J. A., and W. J. MCKEACHIE. The evaluation of teachers in higher education. In F. N. Kerlinger, ed., *Review of Research in Education,* 3 (1975), 210–40, Chap. 7.

LEHRER, B. E., and A. N. HIERONYMOUS. Predicting achievement using intellectual, academic-motivational and selected non-intellectual factors. *Journal of Experimental Education,* 45 (1977), 44–51.

MARSH, H. W. The validity of students' evaluations: Classroom evaluations of instructors independently nominated as best and worst teachers by graduating seniors. *American Educational Research Journal,* 14 (1977), 441–47.

MILLER, D. C. *Handbook of research design and social measurement,* 3rd ed. New York: D. McKay, 1977. Evaluates and reproduces many scales that have been used for measuring morale, job satisfaction, community attitudes, leadership, and other factors.

SCOTT, W. A. Attitude measurement. In G. Lindsey and E. Aronson, eds., *The handbook of social psychology.* Reading, Mass.: Addison-Wesley, 1968. Chap. 11.

SHAW, M. E., and J. M. WRIGHT. *Scales for the measurement of attitudes.* New York: McGraw-Hill, 1967.[6] Reproduces and evaluates numerous attitudes toward various social practices, issues, and institutions, political and religious issues, ethnic groups, and so on.

STERN, G. G. Measuring noncognitive variables in research on teaching. In N. L. Gage, ed., *Handbook of re-*

---

[6] See Appendix A for a more complete annotation of this and other compendiums of published and unpublished affective measures.

search on teaching. Skokie, Ill.: Rand McNally, 1963.

Survey Research Center. *Interviewer's manual.* rev. ed. Ann Arbor: University of Michigan, 1976.

THORNDIKE, R. L., and E. P. HAGEN. Social and political issues in testing. In *Measurement and evaluation in psychology and education.* New York: Wiley, 1977. Chap. 16.

TYLER, R. W. Assessing educational achievement in the affective domain. *NCME Measurement in Education,* 4 (1973), 1–8.

12

Grading and Reporting

The philosopher Michael Scriven (1970) has written,

> Like so many other everyday practices, grading has often seemed too humble to merit the attention of high-powered test and measurement people. My feeling is that it is far more important and in more need of help than anything else they work on. [p. 114]

The process of measurement is only one aspect of evaluation. At regular intervals the quality of students' performance should be conveyed to them and their parents. Converting scores and performance into grades is at best a rather arbitrary process, which is further complicated by public-relations problems in reporting to parents. Frequently these difficulties produce double-talking teachers and confused students and parents.

The conversion of performance data into meaningful ratings of quality has been a hotly debated topic for many decades. Prior to the use of objective tests, marking and grading were usually synonymous and the infallibility of the teacher's judgment was rarely questioned. The classic studies of Johnson (1911) and Starch and Elliot (1912, 1913) revealed the gross subjectivity of teacher-assigned marks even in such clear-cut areas as geometry, initiating a series of controversial innovations in marking that continue to this day. In the 1960s emotional pleas for the abolition of grades were common (Anderson, 1966; Holt, 1968; Glasser, 1969). Such proposals are at least forty-five years old (Dadourian, 1925). In China's "cultural revolution," initiated in 1966, grading was greatly deemphasized to help create a "classless society." But even there the pendulum is now swinging "back to the basics" (Kraft, 1978). In the United States, a recent survey found that both faculty and students believe grading serves several necessary and useful purposes (Chase, 1979b).

Objections to Grades

Four principal allegations are offered as support for the abolition of marking. These allegations have been carefully evaluated by R. L. Thorndike (1969b); the following summary is based largely on his cogent observations.

1. *"Marks are inaccurate and not comparable across instructors, departments, or schools."* There is some truth in this allegation. Personality factors do influence grades (Russell & Wellington, 1955; Hadley, 1954); girls usually do get higher grades than boys of equal ability and achievement (Caldwell & Hartnett, 1967). At most colleges the average grade is the same whether the mean ability of the students is nationally at the 95th percentile or the 5th (Baird & Feister, 1972). Unfortunately, it is unlikely that a teacher's evaluation, whatever its form, can be totally free of some subjectivity. The teacher who gives more F's is the same teacher who would more frequently describe pupils' performance as "unsatisfactory," "inferior," "below acceptable standards," and so on if verbal evaluations were substituted for letter grades. It is naive to assume that a change in symbols from letters to words, percentages, or any other simple substitute would remedy the defects of the conventional system. Indeed, Anderson (1977) found less consistent interpretations of information when it was communicated in verbal form than when it was in numerical form. It is easy to identify imperfections in grading, but it is difficult to propose a satisfactory alternative.

2. *"Marks focus on false and inappropriate objectives and have little relationship to important educational objectives."* This criticism is really directed toward the assessment procedures employed by teachers rather than toward the use of grades. The evaluation procedures employed by many instructors are atrocious, but there is little reason to believe that some other method of *describing* student performance would improve the quality of the evidence on which student evaluations are based. This book has failed in its purpose if the assessment procedures you employ are not more valid as a consequence of your having studied it. The remedy implied in the criticism is not to eliminate formal reporting procedures but to improve the assessment procedures.

3. *"Marks have limited value as a medium of communication between teachers, students and parents."* This allegation is certainly true. To imply that this point justifies the abolition of marks, however, is a *non sequitur*. It should be made clear to students and parents that marks reflect only certain educational factors, primarily cognitive achievement as measured by written tests. Reporting on academic performance of this kind should be only part of

the communication system. The school should employ other means as well for communicating students'. performance such as written comments and parent-teacher conferences.

4. *"Marks are responsible for a variety of detrimental side effects such as anxiety, dishonesty, hostility, and poor mental health; they produce negative attitudes resulting from chronic failure, encourage undesirable value patterns (striving for grades rather than learning), are incompatible with democracy, and so on."* Glasser stated that "the school practice that most produces failure in students is grading" (p. 59) and "grades are also bad because they encourage cheating" (p. 64). The first contention is like claiming that "thermometers produce bad weather"; the second is like saying, "Money is bad because it encourages stealing." As Ebel (1965b, p. 440) pointed out, "There is nothing wrong with encouraging students to work for high marks if the marks are valid measures of achievement."

It is most unfortunate that some students do not read well or have trouble learning arithmetic, but it is erroneous to assume that the cognitive or affective consequences are results of employing letter grades to summarize student performance. Although pupils are not graded on attractiveness, certain unfortunate side effects often accompany peer reactions to social unattractiveness. Poor athletic ability may affect a child's self-concept adversely, but no teacher-given mark is responsible. Any first-grade child is aware of which reading group he or she is in (high, average, low, and so on) and even which students in the group read better; the child knows these facts whether marks are assigned or not. The problem is not marks; it is the perception of inferior performance or failure.

The best creative educational efforts should be directed toward finding methods by which every student can learn effectively. But in any group and on any trait there are always comparisons within the group. For example, the lowest-achieving pupil in a class of gifted pupils is vulnerable to the same detrimental side effects that have been attributed to marks—even though the student receives good marks and would be near the top of a typical class. Avoiding these negative attitudinal side effects would require complete individualization, and probably isolation, of instruction. We are misled if we assume that marks in and of themselves are the culprit. In the final analysis a mark is a judgment of one person's proficiency level by another; it can provide both information and incentive.

It is interesting to note that Jackson and Lahaderne (1967) found that the educational values of teachers distorted their perceptions of pupils' satisfaction with school. A teacher's estimate of a student's satisfaction was more closely related to the student's academic record than to the student's own rating of satisfaction. There was little relationship between scholastic performance and the pupil's rating of satisfaction. Most individuals sooner or later accept their weaknesses and adjust to them, at least to some degree, although exceptions to this generalization are not uncommon.

The problems with grades are many, but to assert that imperfect information and feedback is worse than none at all is to argue for ignorance. Moynihan (1971, p. 4) observed that one of the achievements of democracy, although it seems not much regarded as such today, is the system of grading and sorting individuals so that young persons of talent born to modest or lowly circumstances can be recognized for their worth. (Similarly it provides a means for young persons of social status to demonstrate that they have inherited brains as well as money, as it were.) I have not the least doubt that this system is crude, that it is often cruel, and that it measures only a limited number of things. Yet it measures valid things, by and large. To do away with such systems of accreditation may seem like an egalitarian act, but in fact it would be just the opposite. We would be back to a world in which social connections and privilege count for much more than any of us, I believe, would like. If what you know doesn't count, in the competitions of life, who you know will determine the outcomes.

Grading Tests

Consider the process of assigning grades to tests. Sometimes the grade is given directly, as when an English teacher judges that this is an "A" theme and that is a "C" theme. In the teacher's mind some sort of evaluative process has occurred, a process moderated by his usual standards of grading. The teacher is accustomed to giving certain proportions of A's, B's, and so on. He may be either a "hard" or an "easy" grader compared with other teachers of the same course in the same school. His marks fluctuate to some extent from time to time, of course, but year after year his grades tend to be higher or lower than those of certain other teachers of the same course.

Often teachers give a paper a total point score which is also a percentage mark, as when each of four questions on an essay test is worth up to 25 points. Percentages are used either directly or in the form of letter conversions (e.g., 70–79 = C, 80–89 = B, 90–100 = A). Since the difficulty of a test depends on the questions that happen to be used, and since teachers are not expert judges of such difficulty (nobody is), direct subjective marking usually causes the teacher to grade some tests more leniently than others in order to make the grades come out "right." If percentages are running low, partial credit can be given, unless the questions are wholly objective. If scores are running too high for the teacher's taste, only the most unimpeachable answers can be credited and all the others are counted wrong. If all this adjusting of scoring methods results in a distribution of grades that is different from that desired, the teacher can make the next test easier or harder or adjust the "standards" in order to bring the average grade up or down.

Changing standards so that the percentage grades are "in line" with the letter grades can be confusing to students and is unnecessary. If raw scores on the test are converted to percentages, (to remove the arbitrariness of the number of items or maximum score on the test), teachers can then make the conversion of percentage scores into grades according to their best professional judgment.

No one has ever been able to devise a strategy for making the savage grader more lenient and the easy one more stringent, but a discussion of grading practices and rationale, together with consideration of the distributions of grades assigned by various teachers, might be helpful. If a certain teacher insists year after year that she gets the worst students in her classes, it may be desirable to set up an explicit partitioning of available students at the beginning of the year so that this contention may be shown to be invalid. However, it is difficult, if not impossible, to tighten the grading of the teacher who argues that his lenient grading is indicative of good teaching. (Grading differences among instructors at the college level are probably even greater than they are in high schools and elementary schools.)

Marks and Criterion-Referenced Measures

Individual differences among students are inevitable, regardless of the type of instruction or evaluation measures employed. Even with individualized, mastery learning approaches, students will differ in rate and degree of mastery. As Ebel (1979, p. 240) points out, "The notion that criterion-referenced testing will avoid problems of marking seems to be based on quite unrealistic expectations of uniform achievements in learning by all pupils . . . Programs of mastery learning cannot abolish individual differences in ability, interest, and determination." Students will continue to have strengths and weaknesses irrespective of the instructional strategies employed, and these should be diagnosed and communicated to the students and their parents.

Grading on the Curve

A few schools have set limits on the percent of students who can receive various grades (e.g., not more than 10 percent F's in general mathematics at the end of the year) which all teachers are urged or even required to follow. Such prescriptions are of limited value, since the abilities of students, even in different sections of the same course, can vary considerably. Probably it would be unfair to require the same distribution of grades in both honors mathematics and regular mathematics. A common and often valid complaint against accelerated or honors classes is that the grades of the least "accelerated" students in the special classes often suffer.

The rationale for "grading on the normal curve" was suggested more than fifty years ago by Meyer (1908) after a professor at the University of Missouri flunked his whole class. Meyer found, as have many since (Baird & Feister, 1972; Will, 1976; Goldman, Schmidt, Hewitt, & Fisher, 1974), that grading standards vary considerably among departments and instructors. Grading on the normal curve became popular during the 1920s and 1930s. The most common method was proposed in 1914 by Cajori (Cureton, 1971) and uses 1.5 standard deviations (s) and above for A's (about 7%), $.5s$ to $1.5s$ for B's (about 24%), $-.5s$ to $+.5s$ for C's (about 38%), $-.5s$ to $-1.5s$ for D's (about 24%), and below $-1.5s$ for F's (about 7 percent).

Stripped of its unnecessary complexities, this "grading on the curve" simply amounts to determining in advance approximately what percentage of the class will get A's, B's, and so on. Some amusing and revealing tales are told about how this procedure can miss the mark. On the first day of class a professor of Latin informed the seven students taking his advanced course that he had learned about grading on the curve the previous summer and would use it in this class. As a result, it was certain that one of the seven students would fail the course. As the students left at the close of the class, the poorest student muttered to the other six, "I'm sure to be the one who fails, so I'm dropping the course right now." "But you can't do that," the others exclaimed, "because then one of us would fail." So the six pooled their money and paid the predestined failure to stay in the course and absorb the failing grade.

Another story is similar. During the first few years after World War II, the wives of veterans who were studying at a certain large state university enrolled for the more difficult courses in sufficient numbers to absorb all the failing grades themselves. They simply did little or no work and received F's and D's, while their husbands got grades of C or better with only moderate effort.

Actually, grading on the curve fixes the percent of A's or F's only if the distribution of scores is perfectly normal in shape. If scores are positively skewed, all scores could fall above the point, -1.5 below the mean (i.e., above $z = 1.5$); hence, it is not inevitable that some students will receive a grade of F even when Cajoris' method is employed.

Grading on the curve may be justifiable for, say, the 400 persons enrolled for a required freshman course in psychology. Even then, however, the instructor should have some discretion to weigh the balance of course work and other considerations in determining the final grades.

Parent Conferences

Several substitutes for marking have been proposed; most of them have created additional problems (R. L. Thorndike, 1969, p. 761). Parent–teacher and/or teacher–student conferences have been suggested as a replacement for marks. Conferences have been widely and, in general, effectively used to *supplement* conventional report cards on the elementary-school level. The major disadvantages are the scheduling problem (especially for employed parents) and the time required for conferences. In addition, teachers need some counseling skills; such skills are particularly vital when students are performing below parental expectations. Time and scheduling problems preclude individual conferences at the junior and senior high school levels where departmentalized programs are typical. Some departmentalization and specialization is also now common in the elementary school.

Most schools maintain a cumulative record ("cum folder") of standardized test scores and other information for each student; this record can be useful in parent-teacher conferences. One drawback of most parent conferences is that there is no systematic record of the exchange. A parent-teacher conference report form like that shown in Figure 12-1 overcomes this deficiency. The form illustrates that a parent conference has much in common

```
┌─────────────────────────────────────────────────────────────────────┐
│  Parent-Teacher Conference Report    Teacher  _____       │
│                                                                       │
│  Student  _____           Name of parent  _____     │
│                                                                       │
│  Date  _____                                                     │
│                                      SOCIAL/EMOTIONAL                  │
│  ACADEMIC                               Peer relationships  _____  │
│                                                                       │
│     Reading  _____           Teacher/student  _____   │
│                                                                       │
│     Math  _____              Parent/child  _____     │
│                                                                       │
│     English  _____           Special needs  _____     │
│                                                                       │
│     Social Studies  _____          _____  │
│                                                                       │
│     Science  _____           _____  │
│                                                                       │
│     P. E.  _____                                           │
│                                                                       │
│     Music  _____          WORK HABITS                      │
│                                                                       │
│     Art  _____                Attentiveness  _____     │
│                                                                       │
│  PHYSICAL                                Effort  _____      │
│                                                                       │
│     General Health  _____           Leadership  _____     │
│                                                                       │
│     Vision/Hearing  _____           Neatness  _____     │
│                                                                       │
│     Attendance  _____             Use of time  _____      │
│                                                                       │
│     Health habits (eating, sleeping,     Work style  _____      │
│        grooming)  _____             Interests  _____      │
│                                          Special needs  _____     │
│     _____         _____  │
│                                                                       │
│     Special needs  _____            _____  │
│                                                                       │
│     _____         _____  │
│                                                                       │
│     _____         _____  │
│                                                                       │
│  Teacher comments (parental attitudes, effectiveness of conference,   │
│  suggestions, etc.)  _____  │
│                                                                       │
│  _____  │
│                                                                       │
│  _____  │
└─────────────────────────────────────────────────────────────────────┘
```

FIGURE 12-1   A sample parent-teacher conference report form.

with a structural interview—without guidelines, important gaps will result. It is a checklist in triplicate, with one copy each for the teacher, the parent, and the cum folder.

We emphasize again that it is important to report standardized-test results to students and to their parents. Much valuable information that is of interest to parents and pupils lies buried in files. These results should be used along with teacher evaluations to complete the picture of the student's progress. Reporting to parents must be done skillfully and carefully, with some allowance for error of measurement. But we are convinced that it should be done. Schools have sometimes avoided this responsibility of reporting to parents by contending that "parents will misinterpret scores." This statement, however, says more about deficiencies in the schools than about deficiencies in parents. Many standardized achievement tests provide special interpretive report forms for parents (see p. 398) that can be very helpful in communicating test results.

The following guidelines for effective parent conferences are abridged from suggestions by Gronlund (1974) and Bailard and Strang (1964).

Do's of Parent Conferences

1. Review the student's cumulative record prior to the conference.
2. Assemble samples of the student's work.
3. Use a structured outline like the one in Figure 12–1 to guide the conference.
4. List questions to ask parents and anticipate parents' questions.
5. Be professional and maintain a positive attitude.
6. Be willing to listen; be understanding; encourage two-way communication.
7. Be honest; begin by describing the pupil's strengths.
8. Accept some of the responsibility for problems.
9. Conclude the conference with an overall summary.
10. Keep a succinct written record of the conference, listing problems and suggestions, with a copy for the parents.

Don'ts of Parent Conferences

1. Don't blame parents or put them on the defensive; never argue.
2. Don't make derogatory comments about other teachers, other students, or the school.
3. Don't play amateur psychiatrist.
4. Don't discuss the conference with others, except other school personnel directly involved with the student.
5. Don't do all the talking; skillful professionals are good listeners.

Other Suggestions

Letters from teachers to parents have been proposed in lieu of report cards, but they would require even more teacher time and fail to provide two-way communication. Pupil self-evaluation has been tried, but experimental results have not been satisfactory (Spaights, 1965). Student self-ratings have been found to be consistently higher than corresponding peer ratings (Heywood, 1977). Page (1960) suggested that marks be given by someone other than the teacher; he contends that marking "kills the enjoyment of the class." It is not surprising that proposed substitutes for grades often would relieve the teacher of the unpleasant task of marking. But if the teacher is competent, who is in a better position to evaluate performance? Reassignment of responsibility is the easy answer but is probably not the appropriate solution.

Many pupil report forms currently in use give the teacher an opportunity to make special comments in addition to the formal marks. Burba and Corlis (1963) found that children and parents want report cards with grades. The usefulness of the various substitutes must be evaluated from a realistic perspective. Teachers can hardly be expected to be enthusiastic about any alternative that adds to their already demanding duties.

Roelfs (1955), studying the marking trend from 1925–53, found a decided shift toward letter grades. The National Education Association's national survey (1967) of over 600 school systems found letter or numerical grades used in 80 percent of public schools, except in first grade (73%) and kindergarten (17%). A national survey (Pinchak & Breland, 1974) found that 89% of high schools use letter or percentage grades or a combination of the two. It is apparent that, despite the continuing controversy over marking, the measurement and reporting of student achievement are necessary, and no substantially better or more scientific means of doing so seems likely to appear (Ebel, 1979; Englehart, 1964). However, the validity of the information on which marks are based and, hence, of marks themselves can be increased substantially by improved assessment methods.

The Meaning of Marks

In assigning quarter, semester, and year-end grades for a course, many instructors consider not only achievement as measured by tests but also more subjectively evaluated characteristics such as "effort," punctuality, behavior, and neatness of written work. Usually these noncognitive aspects get much more weight in elementary school than in high school. Often, children who are "working up to capacity" may obtain an excellent mark, even though they are not high achievers, while those who do not seem to be expending "enough" effort receive lower grades despite better achievement. This system is confusing to pupils and parents, especially when a child moves from elementary to junior high school and his or her grades change sharply because the bases for them have changed.

One does not average oranges and bicycles; it is also wise to *keep marks for achievement separate from ratings of study habits and attitudes.* Achievement can be judged from classroom tests and assessments, oral and written work in class, and standardized tests. The meaning of marks is obscured when other aspects of a student's behavior are determiners of marks. Most parents want to know how well their children are doing, how much industry and effort they are giving to the subject, how regular their attendance has been, and so on. Noncognitive factors that are important should be evaluated and reported separately. If both student and parents have an accurate picture of the student's total performance and behavior, they are in a better position to work cooperatively with the schools in developing appropriate educational goals.

The Criterion of Quality

There are several questions pertaining to the criterion to which achievement is referenced: Should it be performed in relation to (1) an absolute standard, (2) student aptitude, (3) individual student growth, or (4) the student's peer group?

Achievement in Relation to an Absolute Standard

In the past an absolute standard percentage was employed, and marks were considered to represent a percentage of complete or perfect mastery. Criterion-referenced measurement is a modern version of this practice. Close scrutiny reveals the "absolute standard" to be rather arbitrary. A poor teacher can give an easy test in which all pupils will score 90 percent or even higher. An excellent teacher can administer a more reliable test and have a class average of 60 percent. Test difficulty is a matter of item construction; it is far from being an absolute standard. On nonobjective evaluations the standard is in the eye of the beholder—in this instance, the teacher. Under scrutiny the absolute standard is usually found to be based on some version of normative performance, as indeed it should be. But this fact is often lost in the heat of rhetoric (e.g., "Kids should be measured against performance standards, not against each other"). The notion of complete mastery of a subject such as English, literature, mathematics, handwriting, or social studies is illusory and should be so identified to prevent erroneous interpretations of performance. Our measurement technology is inadequate to provide grading on a meaningful absolute standard. The most meaningful standard is the normative performance of previous students.

Achievement in Relation to Aptitude

Teachers have no valid basis for estimating aptitude (potential) apart from achievement, except via standardized aptitude and intelligence tests. Different school subjects require a somewhat different set of aptitudes. The technical difficulties in interpreting differences between achievement and aptitude are very complex except when standardized achievement and aptitude tests are employed, and even then there are difficulties (Thorndike, 1963a). Since the more specific course-related objectives are not assessed by them, standardized achievement tests should rarely be used as an exclusive or even the principal basis for assigning marks. Achievement in relation to aptitude is an untenable basis for marking, despite the obvious appeal the idea has for many educators.

Individual Student Growth

The problems of assessing improvement or progress are even more difficult than those associated with contrasting achievement with aptitude (Cronbach and Furby, 1970; Harris, 1963). Even with highly refined instruments, gain or growth scores are usually rather unreliable. When the procedure is attempted on the informal, unsystematic basis available to the teacher, such scores are almost certain to have little validity. If grading were based on growth, it would not take long for "the word" to get out and students would "sandbag" on the pretest.

Achievement in Relation to Peer Achievement

Most marking is a derivative of this model. A child who reads well in the first grade is inferior compared with fifth-graders. The teacher evaluates the child's performance on what can reasonably be expected from a representative group of pupils of the same age. This "phantom" representative group usually turns out to be an imprecise, internal standard developed through the teacher's experience. In most cases the major determiner of the assigned marks is the teacher's perception of the pupil's performance in relation to that of other students in the present class and perhaps recent classes. This "internal standardization" was demonstrated by Aiken (1963) and Baird & Feister (1972), who found that despite substantial changes in the abilities of entering college freshmen, there was no real change in the distribution of assigned marks.

In spite of the lack of a clearly and objectively defined reference group, marks have considerable meaning. This is evidenced by the predictive validity they have for subsequent academic performance. Hicklin (1962) found a correlation of .73 between marks at grade 9 and grade 12. One study (Etaugh, Etaugh, & Hurd, 1972) found that the reliability (year-to-year consistency) of grades in college was in the .50-.70 range. The reliability was found to be less (approximately .40) in graduate school, as might be expected because of the restriction in the range of ability. (See pp. 102–104.) Nell (1963) found that grades in a subject correlated .64 to .81 with performance on the respective subtest of a standardized achievement test battery. High school grades are even better predictors of college grades than standardized intelligence and achievement tests (see, e.g., Hills, 1971, and Richards & Lutz, 1968). In a study by the American College Testing Program (Hoyt & Munday, 1966) of over 100,000 students, the correlation with freshman grades was .58 and .55 for high school marks and composite standardized test scores, respectively. (When both were used, the correlation increased to .65.)

It is true that (1) grading standards differ among teachers, (2) grades tend to be scaled internally for a class regardless of differences in the students' aptitude levels, (3) grades are often contaminated by student deportment, (4) grades often represent crude efforts to mark in relation to aptitude or progress or in relation to an absolute standard, and (5) the anchor points for grades drift with the prevailing winds of fashion (the mean GPA of college students increased .4 between 1960 and 1973, but seems to be leveling off in recent years (see Mehrens and Lehmann, 1975, p. 608). Nonetheless, grades continue to have considerable meaning and predictive validity (Schoenfeldt & Brush, 1975).

A Better Proposal?

If a ranking method were employed, grade inflation would be impossible. This rank in class is essentially the method of reporting success in law school. Many colleges convert GPA to percentile rank in the graduating class to reduce differences in grading leniency among schools. But ranking has its problems too. The seventieth percentile in some classes would be equivalent to the fortieth percentile in others. Most certainly the use of both would be an improvement over the use of either separately. An instructor would send in two performance indicators: the typical grade and the rank in class (which could be converted to a normalized T-score or percentile rank to offset the problems associated with different class sizes). If we knew that an applicant to graduate school had a GPA of 3.1 but a mean T-score of rank in class of 40, we would know he was a below-average student at that institution, indeed, he is in the bottom 20% of his class! The use of both conventional "absolute" marks and relative marks could be especially valuable at the secondary and college levels. Of course, parent conferences and written communication are also strongly recommended whenever practicable.

Assigning Marks

Weighting Components

In arriving at an overall evaluation of student performance, some method must be used to pool the various kinds of information on which the mark is based. The results from tests, homework, and other assignments must be combined in some way. If points on all components are summed, and each component has the same standard deviation, each will correlate about equally with the composite score. Or, equivalently, if each ingredient were converted into a standard score (say, a T-score) and the scores were totaled for each pupil, each factor would be weighted about equally.

Intuitively, it seems as if the maximum possible score on a factor would reflect its influence on the final ordering of the students, but it does not. Consider a science project with 100 possible points. Suppose that each child worked diligently and received 100 points. When these points are added to all the other information on which the grade is to be based, what effect does the project have on the distribution? Every score is increased by 100 points, so the relative standing of each pupil is unchanged. The mean would be increased by 100 points, but the standard score for any pupil on the composite would be unaffected. When scores from various tests, projects, and so on are combined into a total score, each measure contributes to the composite distribution in direct proportion to its standard deviation and to its correlation with the other measures. (See Stanley and Wang, 1970.)

Consider the following data for four components, each of which has a maximum point value of 100:

	Project	Essay Tests	Objective Tests	Homework
Mean	70	70	70	70
Standard deviation	10	20	10	5

If the teacher simply sums each student's points to arrive at a total score on which a final grade will be based, the essay test would tend to have more influence than the other three factors combined, even though each of the four factors might carry an identical number of maximum credits.

When scores are to be totaled, the standard deviations need to be at least approximately in proportion to the desired weights. Fortunately, this can easily be controlled. Recall from Chapter 3 that if every score in a distribution is multiplied by 2, the standard deviation likewise is doubled. If, in this example, you want each factor to be weighted equally, you will multiply the project scores by 2, the objective test by 2, and the homework by 4. Then the standard deviation of the scores on each component will be 20. Or, equivalently, convert all components into T-scores. In actual practice this is too much trouble for busy teachers. But simply being aware of the principle will help you score various projects and assignments that are evaluated subjectively. If the standard deviation on the objective portion of a test is 10 and you desire to weight the essay portion equally, you should scale your scoring of the essays so that the middle two-thirds will fall within roughly a 20-point range, with a total range of about 40 to 60 points (4σ to 6σ).

If each component is converted into a mark before the information is combined, the task of arriving at a final mark is much simpler. Unfortunately, the reliability is decreased because not all the information is used. For instance, students who receive the highest and lowest "B's" on a test are treated equally in this plan. If there are several components to be combined, this loss is not serious. If +'s and −'s are used, the loss will be much less (i.e., there are 15 rather than 5 possible grading categories).

In most instances numerical summation of scores is unnecessary. The teacher can look over the marks of the components and weight them subjectively. Ordinarily one should give some consideration to improvement, especially on the final examination (if it is comprehensive, as it should be). A sequence of grades like A, B, C should be viewed differently from a pattern like C, B, A. The teacher must remember that the final grade in the course should reflect the *extent* to which the student has mastered the course objectives, not *when* they were mastered. Performance on early tests and assignments should usually be weighted less heavily than more current (and inclusive) indicators of terminal mastery level.

Homework and Marking

Ordinarily homework should not have much influence on students' marks, unless they do not do the assignments. Homework should be viewed primarily as an instructional activity, not an activity that has significant implications for evaluation. Students should get help on their homework assignments when they need it, but this help also means that the resulting product is not a good indicator of the student's mastery. If homework carries substantial evaluation credit, some students will become too concerned about having the correct answers, and their success on the assignment may reflect the ability to use resources such as parents and other students rather than mastery of the material.

Number of Categories

The common percentage system of marks has 101 possible categories (0–100). This system still prevails in many countries, and in about one-sixth of American high schools (Pinchak and Breland, 1974). The most common marking system in American schools utilizes 5 categories (A, B, C, D, F), which are expanded to 15 categories if + 's and —'s are used. In elementary schools as few as 3 categories is common (e.g., 0—outstanding; S—satisfactory; N—needs improvement). Some educators favor a two-category pass-fail (P, F) system; that is, a credit–no-credit system. Philosophical and technical measurement issues must be considered in deciding the best number of classifications.

In the late 1960s and early 1970s, colleges and universities began to give students the option of taking a limited number of courses outside their major and minor fields using the pass–fail system. This system is designed to encourage students to broaden their education by exposing themselves to other fields without jeopardizing their academic record. Such a program has logical appeal for increasing the breadth of academic experience, although one study (Warren, 1975) found that this does not in fact happen. As a grading strategy, the system has major defects. Princeton students reported that they tended to study less and learn less in P–F courses than they did in conventionally evaluated courses (Karlins, Kaplan, & Stuart, 1969); the results have been similar at other institutions (Stallings & Smock, 1971; Gold, Reilly, Silberman, & Lehr, 1971).

Ebel (1965b, p. 423) showed that even when the composite on which the marking was based had a reliability of .95, the reliability of the resulting *marks* using a 2-category system would be only .63. If 5 categories were used, the reliability of the corresponding *marks* would be .85; if 15 categories (say, A, B, C, D, F, with + 's and —'s) were used, the reliability would be .94. With fewer categories, one loses all the information that is pertinent to individual differences within category. The severity of any misclassification is much greater as the number of categories is reduced. It is not serious when a student who deserves a B receives a B—, but it is critical when a student who deserves a P receives an F. Reducing the number of categories to two or three clearly compounds the problem of unreliability of marks.

It is unlikely that a widespread move away from the five-category system will occur in the near future, even though the reliability of the marks could be increased slightly with more categories. The marking system recommended by Ebel (1979) has some desirable features. He advocates a modified form of grading on the curve system, with adjustments for the ability level of the students. The two-mark system—"absolute" (e.g., letter grade) and relative (e.g., percentile rank in class)—proposed earlier has advantages, but is practical only with computerized reporting systems. These proposals will probably languish, along with many other attempts to reform the marking system, until enough momentum is generated for a fundamental reform in the marking systems.

Most elementary-school report cards consist of both grades and checklist

BOULDER VALLEY SCHOOL DISTRICT RE-2

SCHOOL		GRADUATION CREDITS	SCHOOL YEAR	HOME ROOM	STUDENT NUMBER	1st PERIOD		2nd PERIOD		3rd PERIOD		4th PERIOD		
						DAYS A	TT	DAYS A	TT	DAYS A	TT	DAYS A	TT	
CENTENNIAL JR. HIGH			79-80	203	258000	2		1						〇

TO THE PARENTS OF	CLASS	SUBJECT	1st QTR		2nd QTR		SEMESTER 1		3rd QTR		4th QTR		SEMESTER 2			TEACHER
			SUBJ	C	SUBJ	C	EXAM	GRADE	SUBJ	C	SUBJ	C	EXAM	GRADE		
HIRTER NANCY L	8	ENGLISH	A	1	A	1	A−	A								TONSO
2530 GLENWOOD		GEOGRAPHY	B+	2	A−	2	A−	A								CLEMENTS
BOULDER, COLORADO 80302		LIFE SCIENCE	C+	2	C	2	C+	C								MACY
		BASIC MATH	A−	2	A	2	C	B								GODDEN
		SPANISH LAB	A	2	A−	2		A								TERRELL
(S) SUBJECT (C) SCHOOL CITIZENSHIP AND		ART	B	2	A	1		A								RICHARDSN
A -SUPERIOR CLASS ATTITUDE		ORCHESTRA	B	2	B+	2		B								FORD
B -VERY GOOD 1.-OUTSTANDING		GIRLS P E	A	2	A	1		A								HOBSON
C -AVERAGE 2.-SATISFACTORY																
D -BELOW AVERAGE 3.-UNSATISFACTORY																
F -FAILING 4.-CONFERENCE REQUESTED																

	GRADE POINT AVERAGE	
I -INCOMPLETE	ACCUM	CURRENT
S -SATISFACTORY	3.42	3.50

SCHOLARSHIP GRADE is an evaluation of the student's achievement and progress in the subject.
CLASS ATTITUDE is an evaluation of the student's RESPECT for authority, property, fellow student and self, and his DEMONSTRATION of self-motivation, responsibility of self and others, cooperation, sportsmanship, punctuality, dependability, honesty, leadership and service.

FIGURE 12-2 A sample report card of an eighth-grade student.

items; some also contain achievement test scores. The trend is toward keeping parents better informed, but as stated earlier, it is important to separate achievement assessment from effort, neatness, citizenship, attendance, and the like. Parents usually want to know both aspects: How the child is achieving in each subject (i.e., cognitive attainments) and how is my child faring in affective and social areas. Is the child using time constructively? Is he or she completing assignments on time? Does the child have good work habits and attitudes?

No single report card is perfect. Each school system must work out its own reporting system to suit the local situation. In many schools computer facilities have simplified and automated reporting procedures. Figure 12-2 illustrates an informative report card (Nancy Hirter's) at the secondary-school level. Some explanatory information is given to the parent on the reverse side of the card. The card gives (1) marks for each subject, (2) associated final-examination grades, (3) citizenship and attitude ratings, and (4) attendance data for each quarter and semester. Nancy's GPA is given for the current grading period (3.50) along with her cumulative GPA (3.42).

Suggestions for Improving Marking and Reporting

After ten years of experimenting with a number of ways to improve marking and reporting practices, Wrinkle (1956), a school principal, listed the twenty-two generalizations which seemed to him to summarize what he and his staff had learned. These suggestions are integrated with those of Gronlund (1974) and listed here. They should give direction for developing an adequate, yet functional, marking and reporting system.

1. The marking and reporting system should be carefully planned and guided by stated objectives, such as school-related motivation; student, parent, and teacher understanding; and home–school cooperation.
2. The reporting system and forms should be developed by students, parents, teachers, and administrators, usually with the aid of a technical expert. This is best done at the district (not school) level to avoid unnecessary and expensive duplication of effort.
3. Informal teacher–student reporting and direct communication should be an ongoing process. Student–teacher conferences should not be a "last resort" and should be encouraged as a normal part of the reporting system.
4. Parent–teacher conferences can be very effective. Released time for teachers is often necessary for this activity to be practicable. It is very difficult to make parent conferences practical for every student at the secondary-school level, but conferences are especially desirable for students whose academic performance begins to decline. Report forms for parent conferences, with copies for each party, are desirable.
5. The reporting system should include feedback on school behavior, attitudes, work habits, and attendance as well as describe performance in school subjects.
6. Marks (often supplemented with explanatory teacher comments) and parent conferences are necessary to fully describe performance at least at the upper elementary and secondary levels. Reporting systems in the primary grades can be less standardized, with greater reliance on parent conferences. Some parents need time to adjust to the reality of their child's abilities.
7. Failing marks are rarely justified or needed in the primary or even upper elementary grades. A failing mark should rarely be given in the elementary or middle school grades.

Summary

Reports of achievement and school behavior are desirable and necessary in education; marks in some form will continue to be needed.

Marks are a means of feedback to students and to their parents; they should be as valid and accurate as possible. Critics of grading have failed to supply superior alternatives.

Although marks have several major defects, they have considerable meaning, reliability, and validity for predicting subsequent academic peformance.

The meaning of marks can be greatly improved if the basis on which they are to be assigned is clearly defined. Great difficulties arise when one attempts to evaluate achievement in relation to aptitude or to evaluate on the basis of improvement. Marks using a standard based on previous normative performance are more defensible than an illusionary absolute standard.

Marks should reflect demonstrated achievement. Other important factors, such as student attitude, effort, and citizenship, should be evaluated and reported independently.

When components are summed into total scores, one needs to be aware that the actual weighting of factors corresponds to the relative size of the standard deviations of the components. Less arithmetic methods of aggregation are usually preferable.

Even when composite scores have very high reliability, the reliability of assigned *marks* decreases (and the severity of errors increases) as the number of categories in the marking system is reduced. The traditional A–F marks with +'s and −'s has an adequate number of categories to accurately describe performance.

Marks should be supplemented with written comments and other means of communication among teacher, student, and parents.

CHAPTER TEST

1. Which of these three methods of reporting test scores is least informative?

    a) Raw scores

    b) Raw scores converted into percent-correct scores

    c) Raw scores converted into percentile ranks

2. Grading on the normal curve, if adhered to rigidly, would *not* keep the mean GPA constant

    a) from class to class.

    b) from year to year.

    c) from grade to grade.

    d) for boys and girls.

3. According to the authors, "grading on the normal curve" is the best method for assigning school marks. (T or F)

4. Marks

    a) are not exactly comparable across instructors.

    b) have little predictive validity.

    c) do not reflect important educational objectives.

    d) are undesirable because they encourage cheating.

    e) are incompatible with democratic ideals.

5. Bob and Bill each correctly answered 60% of the questions on a test. We know that both

    a) are academically dull.

    b) obtained an F on the test.

    c) experienced a sense of failure associated with the test.

    d) were emotionally harmed by the test experience.

    e) none of the above.

6. Parent-teacher conferences are *not*

    a) a useful method of school–home communication.

    b) at all like a two-way interview.

    c) a good way to inform parents about a student's behavior at school.

    d) a quick and easy reporting method.

    e) a good supplement to a standard reporting form.

7. Which one of the following is a recommended practice for parent conferences?

a) Deal with only a single aspect of a child's school behavior.

b) Delve deeply into a child's emotional relationships with his or her parents.

c) Review the student's "cum folder" prior to the conference.

d) Place the responsibility for any difficulty squarely in the home.

e) Cover all aspects of the child's performance before allowing the parents to respond.

8. Which one of the following is the most reasonable basis for assigning grades?

a) A true, absolute standard of performance

b) Growth and improvement

c) Achievement in relation to aptitude

d) Achievement in relation to that of a representative peer group

e) Effort

9. If total, cumulative scores in a class are based on a test, an oral report, and a project, and if each is worth a maximum of 100 points, scores on which one of the following will correlate most highly with the total scores?

	Test	*Oral Report*	*Project*
Mean	80	90	85
S	5	5	10

a) Test

b) Oral Report

c) Project

d) All would correlate equally

10. According to the authors, homework should be weighted heavily in assigning marks. (T or F)

11. In addition to academic performance, it is desirable for report cards to give information on

a) class attitude.

b) attendance.

c) study habits.

d) two of the above.

e) all of the above.

ANSWERS TO CHAPTER TEST

1. a	5. e	9. c
2. d	6. d	10. F
3. F	7. c	11. e
4. a	8. d	

FOR ADDITIONAL READING

CURETON, L. E. The history of grading practices. *NCME Measurement in Education,* 2, no. 4 (May 1971), 1–8.

EBEL, R. L. Marks and marking systems. In *Measuring educational achievement,* 3rd ed. Englewood Cliffs, N.J.: Prentice-Hall, 1979. Chap. 12.

———. Shall we get rid of grades? *NCME Measurement in Education,* 5 (1974), 1–5.

GRONLUND, N. E. *Improving marking and reporting in classroom instruction.* New York: Macmillan, 1974.

PALMER, O. Seven classic ways of grading dishonestly. *English Journal,* 51 (1962), 464–67.

TERWILLIGER, J. S. *Assigning grades to students.* Glenview, Ill.: Scott, Foresman, 1971.

THORNDIKE, R. L. Marks and marking systems. In R. L. Ebel, ed., *Encyclopedia of educational research,* 4th ed. New York: Macmillan, 1969. Reprinted in G. H. Bracht, K. D. Hopkins, and J. C. Stanley, eds., *Perspectives in educational and psychological measurement.* Englewood Cliffs, N.J.: Prentice-Hall, 1972. Selection 17.

THORNDIKE, R. L., and E. P. HAGEN. Marks and marking systems. In *Measurement and evaluation in psychology and education,* 4th ed. New York: Wiley, 1977. Chap. 15.

STANDARDIZED MEASURES

13

Measuring Scholastic Aptitude

Probably the first systematic experimentation concerning individual differences in behavior occurred fortuitously in 1796, when astronomers at Greenwich Observatory were found to differ in the speed with which they could respond to visual stimuli (Cronbach, 1970, p. 197). Four decades later, in 1838, a French physician named Esquirol used various physical and psychological measures in an attempt to assess different degrees of feeblemindedness. (See Goodenough, 1949, pp. 3–5.) He found that language usage was the best indicator of mental level. Unfortunately, Esquirol's work was not widely disseminated or systematically continued; not until a half-century later was the importance of verbal ability as a measure of "intelligence" rediscovered. The use of the term intelligence for these abilities is unfortunate—it is too inclusive. Only a limited portion of the domain of intelligence is represented in these measures. The terms *scholastic aptitude* and *academic aptitude* are more appropriate, since these measures are oriented toward school learning.

The Search for a Valid Measure of Intelligence

Individual differences in mental abilities such as comprehension, problem solving, and analysis—qualities that are usually grouped under the heading of

341

intelligence—were not discovered by modern psychologists; terms like *idiot, genius, bright,* and *dull* have a long history in our language.

Psychology's genuine contribution to the study of intelligence has been that of heightening human understanding of scholastic aptitude, particularly in devising accurate measures of the *degree* of intelligence of an individual. Cronbach (1970, p. 197) observed, "Despite occasional overenthusiasm and misconceptions, . . . the general mental test stands today as the most important technical contribution psychology has made to the practical guidance of human affairs."

Galton and the Study of Human Differences. Coincident with the blossoming of Wundt's experimental psychology laboratory in Leipzig, a slightly different tradition was developing in England under Sir Francis Galton (1822–1911). Although the psychophysicists were interested in determining universal psychological processes and were not interested in the response differences between subjects, Galton was particularly interested in differences among individuals. In Galton's work there is the beginning of a concern for *individual differences* that has been a keystone in the history of psychological and educational testing. From his laboratory of anthropometry, established in London in 1882, came studies of topics such as word association, mental imagery, and the genetic basis of genius. To facilitate his research, Galton invented several statistical devices, including a graphic method for depicting the degree of relationship between two variables such as height and weight. As later refined by Galton's colleague, the statistician Karl Pearson, this device led to the now-classic *coefficient of correlation* discussed in Chapter 4.

Galton also devised the earliest mental tests. He studied individual performance differences on tests of reaction time, memory, and sensory acuity. This tradition of using rather simple "sensory" and "motor" tasks as indicators of intellectual ability was continued by James McKeen Cattell, one of the earliest and best-known American psychologists. Cattell was a product of Wundt's experimental-psychology laboratory at the University of Leipzig. In 1890 he suggested the term *mental test*; he described in detail a series of tests with which he attempted to measure the intelligence of his students at the University of Pennsylvania. Cattell and many of his contemporaries regarded simpler mental and motor processes, such as speed of tapping, reaction time, judgment of time intervals, and keenness of vision and hearing, as indications of what are now called the "higher" mental processes. But because he directed his efforts away from tests of more complex mental processes, his efforts were doomed to failure. At the turn of the century, Seashore (1899) found virtually no relationship between teachers' estimates of general mental ability and children's ability to judge time intervals, judge length of lines, and discriminate loudness and pitch. Shortly thereafter, Bagley (1900) reported that simple motor abilities such as hand strength, trilling a telegraph key, and reaction time bore no relation to a child's actual class standing or to a teacher's judgment of that child. Wissler (1901) was the first to apply Pearson's correlation techniques to test scores. Using Cattell's tests with college students, Wissler found no significant relationship between the tests and college marks (*r*'s of −.09 to .16) and little relationship among the tests *themselves.* Consequently, the attempt to measure intelligence with such tests was all but abandoned.

Binet's Breakthrough. In France incisive work was being done by a French physician named Alfred Binet (1857–1911), the father of modern intelligence testing. As early as 1896 Binet had published a proposal for a series of tests designed to measure children's intellectual capacity. Binet believed that a measure of intelligence must include a range of performances that are normally regarded as intelligent behavior. The test should comprise a series of tasks requiring the ability to reason, make sound judgments, recognize familiar objects, and understand commands; that is, it should call for a variety of mental skills. A child's intelligence would be represented by a summation of his or her scores on each separate task. For Binet, intelligence was a phenomenon requiring many different abilities. Two children might obtain the same total score on his test by scoring quite differently from each other on the subtests.

In 1904 Binet was commissioned by the French Minister of Public Instruction to extend his investigations to determining workable methods of identifying mentally retarded schoolchildren so that they might be given special instruction. He tried and rejected sensory discrimination tasks, size of cranium, handwriting analysis, responses to inkblots, and several other measures. The results appeared in three classic papers, published in 1905 (see Binet and Simon, 1916), in which Binet discussed a number of tasks that he had found useful in approaching the problem. These had been arranged in order of difficulty and then "normed" on a group of normal children at each age level from 3 to 11. By comparing an individual child's performance with the age of children who typically performed likewise, Binet was able to get an indication of the subject's intellectual development; that is, a child's mental age was determined by referring his or her performance to the chronological age at which the average child successfully completed the same tasks. Reports of further investigations and revisions of the original scale appeared in 1908 and 1911. The last version of the scale included such tasks as the following: to earn mental-age credits at the nine-year level a child must give change for 20 cents, define five words at an abstract level, recognize the value of a piece of money, name the months of the year, and understand simple questions such as "When one has missed the train, what must one do?" Similarly, groups of tasks were established as norms for each age level from 3 to 16. Figure 13-1 is a reproduction of the "picture completion" item now presented at the five-year level of the current Stanford-Binet Intelligence Scale. Similar items are included in the Wechsler intelligence scales, which are the most widely used individual intelligence tests.

Later Developments. Binet's method of assessing intelligence met with some criticism but much acclaim. By 1916 his scales had been translated into seven languages and were used in at least twelve countries (Binet & Simon,

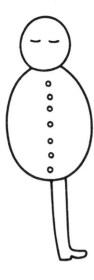

FIGURE 13-1 Picture completion man reproduced from Year V, Test 1, of the 1960 Stanford-Binet Intelligence Scale Record Booklet ([Boston: Houghton Mifflin Company, 1960], by permission of the publisher).

1916). Henry Goddard (1910) appears to have been the first American psychologist to recognize the practical value of Binet's 1908 and 1911 scales; he translated them and, with minor adaptations, tested them at the Vineland Training School for the mentally retarded in New Jersey. In 1911 Kuhlmann published his revision of the Binet scale, extending it downward to the age of three months, considerably below Binet's three-year limit.

It remained for psychologist Lewis M. Terman of Stanford University to make the first thorough revision of the Binet scale. Terman carefully adapted and standardized the scale for use with average, as well as deficient, American children. His scale, known as the Stanford Revision or Stanford-Binet, appeared in 1916 with a comprehensive manual, *The Measurement of Intelligence*. In 1937 and 1960 two further revisions of the Stanford-Binet appeared; the latter was renormed in 1972 (Terman & Merrill, 1937, 1960, 1972). This highly regarded instrument has remained a standard among individual intelligence scales for preschool and school-age children although, as stated earlier, "scholastic aptitude" or "verbal ability" are more descriptive labels than "intelligence." Nevertheless, for the sake of expedience we will use the terms interchangeably.

Performance and Group Tests. Two other distinctly American developments helped make intelligence tests more practical. The early tests had two disadvantages that limited their usefulness: (1) They were highly *verbal,* and (2) the tests were *individual;* that is, only one person could be examined at a time. Reasonably satisfactory solutions were found in 1917, when the pioneering applied psychologists Pintner and Paterson found that the Stanford-Binet was unsatisfactory for deaf children; they overcame this difficulty by developing a series of 15 manipulation or performance tests (which are used only at the preschool levels of the Stanford-Binet). The form board (an intellectual jigsaw puzzle), block design (assembling blocks to copy designs), and other nonlanguage tasks appeared in 1917 as the Pintner-Paterson Performance Scale. In the same year the United States entered World War I and faced the necessity of training a large citizen army with too few commissioned and noncommissioned officers. In this emergency the American Psychological Association offered its services to the War Department. The Binet-type individual intelligence tests not only were unsuitable for recruits who did not speak English but also were far too slowly administered and scored to be used with a large number of soldiers. To deal with this problem, a committee of psychologists headed by Robert M. Yerkes based their efforts on the unpublished work of Arthur S. Otis and prepared the Army Alpha, the first of a long series of group intelligence tests designed for wide use. Thus, the second problem of the early tests, their "one-at-a-time" quality, had been solved; the new group tests could be administered to almost any number of people at a time and scored objectively by clerks.

Nonverbal Tests. It should be noted that the Pintner-Paterson Performance Scale and the Army Alpha group tests each solved but one difficulty at a time. Group tests of the Army Alpha type were generally even more verbal than the individual tests had been. Figure 13-2 is a sample page from the Army Alpha. Notice that the items require reasoning even though the vocabulary is relatively simple. The early performance scales were nonverbal, but they could be administered to only one person at a time. The Army Beta, designed for illiterate and non-English-speaking soldiers, was the first test to combine the group and performance ideas; it also appeared in 1917. Figure 13-3 shows the picture completion portion of the Army Beta; the examinee must identify "what's missing" from each picture.

The Army Alpha and Army Beta proved quite useful. This led to a large number of group "intelligence" tests following the pattern of the Army Alpha that began to be used in schools.

Changing Views of Intelligence Testing

Unfortunately, the determination of children's IQs often became little more than a fashionable fetish without concern for the practical value of such a score or even for the meaning of what was being measured. Several decades of experience with such instruments has resulted in a more realistic perspective on the value of group intelligence tests; it is generally agreed, for example, that verbal, numerical, and reasoning abilities are the major determinants of scores. These abilities are certainly dependent on past learning experiences, though they are influenced less by one's environment than are school-related achievement tests. The value of the tests has been demonstrated by their success in predicting academic performance and occupational level. Group tests of scholastic aptitude have become important working tools for educators; some of the most familiar of these are the California Test of Mental Maturity, the Henmon-Nelson Test of Mental Ability, the Kuhlmann-Anderson Intelligence Tests, the Lorge-Thorndike Intelligence Tests, the Otis-Lennon Mental Ability Tests, the SRA Tests of General Ability (TOGA), the Short Form

SAMPLES
- sky—blue::grass—**table** <u>**green**</u> **warm big**
- fish—swims::man—**paper time** <u>**walks**</u> **girl**
- day—night::white—**red** <u>**black**</u> **clear pure**

In each of the lines below, the first two words are related to each other in some way. What you are to do in each line is to see what the relation is between the first two words, and underline the word in heavy type that is related in the same way to the third word. Begin with No. 1 and mark as many sets as you can before time is called.

1	finger—hand::toe—**box foot doll coat**	1
2	sit—chair::sleep—**book tree bed see**	2
3	skirts—girl::trousers—**boy hat vest coat**	3
4	December—Christmas::November—**month Thanksgiving December early**	4
5	above—top::below—**above bottom sea hang**	5
6	spoon—soup::fork—**knife plate cup meat**	6
7	bird—song::man—**speech woman boy work**	7
8	corn—horse::bread—**daily flour man butter**	8
9	sweet—sugar::sour—**sweet bread man vinegar**	9
10	devil—bad::angel—**Gabriel good face heaven**	10
11	Edison—phonograph::Columbus—**America Washington Spain Ohio**	11
12	cannon—rifle::big—**bullet gun army little**	12
13	engineer—engine::driver—**harness horse passenger man**	13
14	wolf—sheep::cat—**fur kitten dog mouse**	14
15	officer—private::command—**army general obey regiment**	15
16	hunter—gun::fisherman—**fish net bold wet**	16
17	cold—heat::ice—**steam cream frost refrigerator**	17
18	uncle—nephew::aunt—**brother sister niece cousin**	18
19	framework—house::skeleton—**bones skull grace body**	19
20	breeze—cyclone::shower—**bath cloudburst winter spring**	20
21	pitcher—milk::vase—**flowers pitcher table pottery**	21
22	blonde—brunette::light—**house electricity dark girl**	22
23	abundant—cheap::scarce—**costly plentiful common gold**	23
24	polite—impolite::pleasant—**agreeable disagreeable man face**	24
25	mayor—city::general—**private navy army soldier**	25
26	succeed—fail::praise—**lose friend God blame**	26
27	people—house::bees—**thrive sting hive thick**	27
28	peace—happiness::war—**grief fight battle Europe**	28
29	a—b::c—**e b d letter**	29
30	darkness—stillness::light—**moonlight sound sun window**	30
31	complex—simple::hard—**brittle money easy work**	31
32	music—noise::harmonious—**hear accord violin discordant**	32
33	truth—gentleman::lie—**rascal live give falsehood**	33
34	blow—anger::caress—**woman kiss child love**	34
35	square—cube::circle—**line round square sphere**	35
36	mountain—valley::genius—**idiot write think brain**	36
37	clock—time::thermometer—**cold weather temperature mercury**	37
38	fear—anticipation::regret—**vain memory express resist**	38
39	hope—cheer::despair—**grave repair death depression**	39
40	dismal—dark::cheerful—**laugh bright house gloomy**	40

FIGURE 13-2 Test 7 from the Army Alpha. (Reproduced by permission of the National Academy of Sciences.)

FIGURE 13-3 Test 6 from the Army Beta. (Reproduced by permission of the National Academy of Sciences.)

Tests of Academic Aptitude (SFTAA), and the Cognitive Abilities Tests (CAT).

In addition to the tests just listed, there are several tests that yield separate scores for verbal and mathematical abilities that are closely related to the "intelligence" tests but contain items that are more strongly school oriented. Their sole function is to forecast future academic performance—their objective is criterion-related validity, not construct validity, which is required for aptitude measures. Although they are not achievement tests in the strictest sense, they measure students' ability to recognize, understand, and manipulate verbal and mathematical symbols. The Cooperative School and College Ability Test (SCAT), for example, is composed of four parts. The first contains incomplete sentences (each sentence lacks a word, which the student must supply); the second consists of arithmetic computation items; the third is a vocabulary test; and the fourth consists of arithmetic reasoning items. A student's scores on the first and third parts are added together to obtain a verbal score, and his or her scores on the second and fourth parts are summed to obtain a quantitative score. Because these abilities, and those measured by other intelligence or scholastic aptitude tests, are considerably dependent on educational experiences, they are useful in the prediction of scholastic success in most subjects. The two score categories can be considered together or separately, depending on the area of study to be predicted. We would expect the verbal score to be the better indicator of success in the humanities and social studies and the quantitative score to be a superior indicator of success in mathematics and science. The Scholastic Aptitude Test (SAT), a major segment of the College Board's widely administered test program, is an examination of the verbal–quantitative abilities type, as are the aptitude tests of the more advanced Graduate Record Examinations (GRE). Both the SAT and the GRE have substantial predictive validity (Fincher, 1974; Vecchio & Costin, 1977; Conrad et al., 1977; Breland, 1979; ETS, 1980; see Figures 4–11 and 4–15, pp. 97, 101).

The American College Testing Program (ACT) has become a popular alternative to the SAT over the past two decades; both are widely used by colleges as part of their selection process for incoming students.[1] The four ACT tests (English, mathematics, social sciences, and natural sciences) resemble achievement tests more than aptitude tests. The ACT also provides the college with a comprehensive picture of a student's interests and vocational goals. Figure 13–4 is a sample ACT student profile.

The Nature of Intelligence

The Binet scales and their descendants are perhaps the most publicized accomplishments of modern psychology. The term *IQ*, though often misunderstood, is a household word. The practical success of the "IQ test," in its ability to place individuals along a spectrum of scholastic aptitude from dull to bright and in its relationship to school and occupational success, has overshadowed doubt about what the tests were measuring in an exact, psychological sense. Binet continually revised his estimations of the nature of intelligence as determined by his test; he finally characterized intelligence as *inventiveness* dependent on *comprehension* and marked by *purposefulness*

[1] In 1978 the New York Legislature enacted a "truth in testing" law that allows students to receive copies of their SAT, ACT, and other college admissions tests. The U.S. Congress is considering similar federal legislation. Since it costs approximately $100,000 to develop each alternate form of the SAT and several new forms would be required annually, costs to the student will increase dramatically for no obvious advantage. Extensive sets of sample and practice exercises, such as *Taking the SAT,* have long been available.

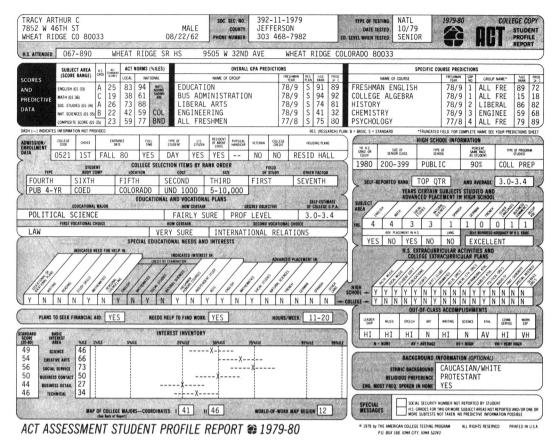

FIGURE 13-4 The ACT Student Profile Report. (Copyright © 1979 by the American Testing Program; reproduced by permission.)

and corrective *judgment* (Binet, 1911). His efforts to define these abilities more exactly or to indicate the specific test behavior that demonstrated them were cut short by his untimely death in 1911.

In 1921 the *Journal of Educational Psychology* published a series of articles by fourteen prominent psychologists, each of whom presented a conception of the nature of "intelligence." Although there was some agreement, it was startling and undeniable that fourteen clearly different conceptions of intelligence emerged. Some of the participants stressed the adaptive nature of intelligence; others saw it as the ability to learn, the ability to think abstractly, or the degree of past learning. This muddle prompted later researchers to propose that since the only intelligence one can discuss objectively is the intelligence that is measured, one should define intelligence as "that which an intelligence test measures" (Peak & Boring, 1926). This so-called operational definition has been a favorite among psychometricians who are wary of theoretical disputes but very impressed with the widespread utility of intelligence tests.

349

E. L. Thorndike (1926) also recognized that "intelligence" is given meaning only by its observable consequences or, as he expressed it, by its "products." The "products" of intelligence are the tasks that an individual is able to complete; the difficulty level of the tasks completed indicates the person's intellectual level. Thorndike therefore envisioned as many different types of intelligence as there are different types of tasks. For his own purposes, however, he felt that the best indicators of what is normally meant by intelligence would be the abilities to supply words to make a statement true and sensible (completion test); solve arithmetic problems; understand single words (vocabulary test); and understand connected discourse, as in oral directions for paragraph reading (directions test).

Some years later a clinical psychologist, David Wechsler, developed an individual intelligence examination especially for adults; Wechsler's test included a verbal and a performance measure of intelligence. First published in 1939 and revised in 1955 as the Wechsler Adult Intelligence Scale (WAIS), this test consists of 11 different subtests (Wechsler, 1958). In 1949 the test was "scaled down" for use with children and named the Wechsler Intelligence Scale for Children (WISC). Revised in 1974, the WISC-R has become the most widely used individual intelligence tests for testing at ages 6–16. In 1967 the scale was further extended downward (and named the Wechsler Preschool and Primary Scale of Intelligence, WPPSI) to allow testing of children in the 4–6-1/2-year age range.

The verbal subtests are Information ("Which month has one extra day during leap year?"); Similarities ("In what way are liberty and justice alike?"); Arithmetic ("A workman earned $36; he was paid $4 an hour. How many hours did he work?"); Vocabulary ("What does compel mean?"); Comprehension ("Why should a promise be kept?"); and Digit Span (repeating a sequence of digits, such as 3–8–9–1–7–4). The nonverbal part is dependent mainly on "performance" or manipulative and visualization skills: Picture Completion ("What is missing in this picture?"); Picture Arrangement (placing cartoon pictures in a correct time sequence); Block Design (reproducing a given design using colored blocks); Object Assembly (puzzles of common objects); Coding (converting numerals into a different set of symbols); and Mazes.

Wechsler feels that it is important to determine an individual's *profile* of abilities. The use of individual subtest profiles for diagnostic purposes is hazardous at best (Hopkins, 1964c). The verbal IQ, performance IQ, and full-scale IQ yielded by the Wechsler scales are much more reliable and useful.

The great psychometrician Louis Thurstone characterized intelligence as a series of distinct abilities. His approach was somewhat different from that of Thorndike or Wechsler, who *assumed* that their individual subtests were pure measures of the designated ability. According to Thurstone, an ability is isolated by giving mental tests to a great number of people and then determining, through a mathematical process known as factor analysis, the lowest number of abilities necessary to explain the correlations among the tests. In his pioneering study Thurstone (1938) isolated six "factors" that accounted for most of the score similarity of 56 different tests given to a group of college students. These were verbal (V), number (N), spatial (S), word fluency (W), memory (M), and reasoning (R). Out of this research came the first of the "multiaptitude" test batteries, the Primary Mental Abilities Tests. Later investigations showed, however, that the number of factors isolated depended considerably on the educational and environmental backgrounds of the subjects tested and on the number and types of tests used in the factor analysis. It was even shown that Thurstone's so-called primary mental abilities correlated positively with each other, which suggests the presence of a still more basic and general mental factor, as had long been argued by the British psychologist Charles Spearman (1927).

Recent thinking among factor analysts about the nature of human intelligence has led to two slightly different ideas. One is represented by Spearman's British tradition of investigation, exemplified by Philip Vernon's (1950) structure of human abilities, in which human mental abilities are arranged in a hierarchy with a broad general factor (*g*) and split into two major "group" factors, one distinguished by verbal and educational abilities (*v: ed*) and the other by practical or performance abilities (*k: m*). Each of these major group factors is then differentiated into more specific factors like Thurstone's verbal, number, and space. These finally break down into factors found in specific types of test. (See Figure 13–5.) Thus, any mental performance can be described as involving percentages of *g, v: ed,* verbal, and others until all the factors needed to account for the performance have been determined. The scheme of Raymond Cattell and John Horn has some similarity to Vernon's structure (Cattell, 1963; Horn, 1967; Horn & Cattell, 1966). Cattell distinguishes between *fluid* and *crystallized* intelligence. Crystallized intelligence is largely a function of environment and is much like the *v: ed* abilities. Fluid intelligence reflects the genetic aspect of intelligence and is more clearly reflected in nonlanguage tasks that are less related to background or previous experience.

The Comprehensive Ability Battery (CAB) (Hakstian & Cattell, 1976) is a recently standardized set of brief tests of twenty ability traits that are

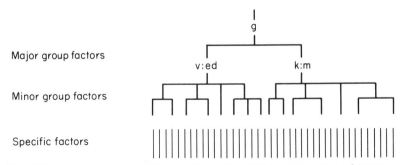

FIGURE 13–5 Diagram illustrating hierarchical structure of human abilities. (Adapted from P. E. Vernon, *The structure of human abilities* [New York: John Wiley & Sons, Inc., 1950], p. 22, by permission of the publisher.)

related to Cattell and Horn's views of intelligence. The CAB has been shown to be useful for predicting academic criteria (Hakstian & Bennet, 1977, 1978).

A two-level theory of mental ability is advocated by Jensen (1968b, 1973a,b). Level I consists of associative learning ability, which is represented in rote learning and rote memory. Level II consists of the higher mental processes of conceptualization, reasoning, and problem solving. Another view of mental organization grows from the Thurstonian tradition of investigation. Its chief advocate is J. P. Guilford (Guilford, 1967, 1968), who devised a theoretical structure-of-intellect model (SI) in which he classifies human mental abilities in three dimensions. The first is defined by the kind of test content confronting the individual—"figural," "symbolic," "semantic," or "behavioral." The second is defined by the types of mental "operations" necessary to deal with the various content forms—"cognition," "memorization," "convergent thinking," "divergent thinking," and "evaluation." The last deals with the outcome or "products" yielded by the various mental operations applied to the various content forms. There are six products: units of information, classes of units, relations between units, systems of information, transformations, and implications. With 4 kinds of content, 5 kinds of operation, and 6 kinds of product involved in mental performance, Guilford postulates 120 (4 × 5 × 6) distinct mental abilities in the SI model. (See Figure 13–6.) Guilford's SI model purports to be sufficiently inclusive to allow for creativity ("divergent thinking") and social intelligence (Hoepfner

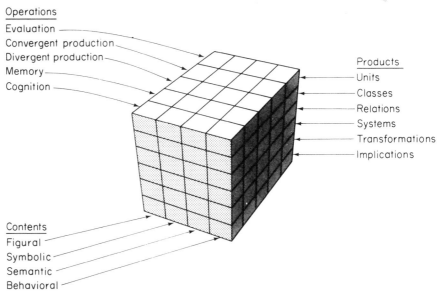

FIGURE 13-6 The theoretical model for Guilford's structure of intellect. (Reproduced from J. P. Guilford, *The structure of intelligence,* in Dean K. Whitla, ed., *Handbook of measurement and assessment in behavioral sciences* [Reading, Mass.: Addison-Wesley, 1968], Fig. 1, p. 220, by permission of the publisher.)

& O'Sullivan, 1968; O'Sullivan & Guilford, 1975). Guilford reports that more than ninety of these abilities have been isolated.

Several authorities have expressed pessimism about the predictive validity of SI tests (Hunt, 1961; Vernon, 1964; McNemar, 1964). Many of the abilities seem to have little practical relevance. Holly & Michael (1972, 1973), however, found that certain of the SI tests combined, had validity at least equal to that of traditional standardized tests for predicting academic performance in high school mathematics.

Perhaps the most important application of factor-analytic studies of mental abilities has been the increasing use of "multiaptitude" test batteries in educational and vocational guidance. These batteries are composed of a series of individual tests built around the findings of factor analysis; to a certain degree each of the general battery's subtests assesses a specific ability. One such battery is the Differential Aptitude Test (DAT) for use with high-school students; the DAT contains seven subtests that measure verbal reasoning, numerical ability, abstract reasoning, space relations, mechanical reasoning, clerical speed and accuracy, and language usage. Although the DAT subtests are not intended to be "pure" measures of single "factors," they provide a profile of an individual's mental strengths and weaknesses that is designed to be more specific, descriptive, and meaningful than an omnibus test of "general mental ability." In addition to the great *descriptive* value of such a test, *prediction* of success or failure in a variety of academic or occupational endeavors can be achieved by isolating the important abilities that are specifically required.

From the preceding discussion it is evident that (1) there are many different ways of conceptualizing intelligence, (2) the nature of intelligence is exceedingly complex and multifaceted, (3) most cognitive abilities are significantly interrelated, and (4) the "final word" on the nature of intelligence is nowhere in sight.

The Development and Measurement of Intelligence

Infant Intelligence Scales

Research findings have revealed that results from infant "intelligence" tests have little predictive validity during the first two years of life. A child's IQ at age 6 can be predicted much better from his or her parents' education (*r* of .5–.6) than from an intelligence test or any other measure taken at 2 years of age or younger (Bayley, 1955). In fact, infant tests have been shown to have virtually no predictive value below 20 months of age (Escalona & Moriarty, 1961; Lewis & McGurk, 1972).

The lack of relationship between IQs or DQs (development quotients) from infant tests and later scores probably occurs because the tests are measuring in different domains. The infant scales must rely primarily on psychomotor responses because of the limited verbal facility of very young children. Yet abstract thinking is best reflected in language. One of the primary uses of infant scales is in the placement of children for adoption. In-

telligence tests should be recognized for what they are—measures that have little or no value below age 2. Knowledge of parents' education, occupational
level, or IQ scores is much more useful in predicting a young child's academic
success than IQs from tests that require little abstract thinking.

At about age 2, the cognitive development of the child is such that a very
crude assessment of intelligence can be made. IQ scores at 24 months correlate
about .4 with IQ scores two years later, .3 with IQ scores at age 6, and only .2
or less with adult IQs (Cavanaugh et al., 1957; Honzik, Macfarlane & Allen,
1948).

Intelligence Growth Curves

Many studies have been conducted to ascertain the sequence and termination
of intellectual growth. Figure 13-7 is based on cross-sectional data from
Wechsler's first (1939) intelligence test and is widely reproduced in
psychological textbooks. The basic flaw in the data results from their cross-
sectional nature, that is, the use of a different sample of persons at each age
level; consequently, variables (besides age) on which they differ, such as formal educational attainment, confound the findings. In the 1958 revision and
restandardization of the Wechsler Bellevue scale, from which the Wechsler
Adult Intelligence Test (WAIS) evolved, the intellectual decline with age was
much less marked than that shown by the 1939 Wechsler-Bellevue data given
in Figure 13-7. This supports the hypothesis that a substantial portion of the
"decline" in Figure 13-7 is not a decline; it simply reflects in large measure
the educational differential and, to some extent, differences in test-taking
speed among the age groups (Lorge, 1952). In several studies (Bayley & Oden,
1955; Droege, Crambert & Henkin, 1963; Owens, 1953, 1966; Schaie &
Strother, 1968; R. L. Thorndike & Gallup, 1944), no loss occurred on verbal
measures, when education was controlled, until around 60 years of age.

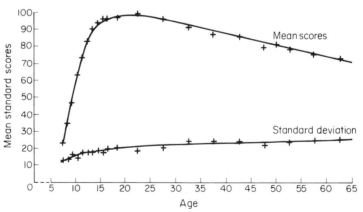

FIGURE 13-7 Changes in full-scale scores of the Wechsler-
Bellevue Form I, ages 7-65. (Reproduced from David Wechsler,
The measurement and appraisal of adult intelligence, 4th ed.
[Baltimore: Williams & Wilkins, 1958], p. 31, by permission of the
author; copyright © 1958 by David Wechsler.)

Measures that require psychomotor responses, visual perception, or an element of speed show considerable decline over the 18–70 age span even with education controlled (Droege, Crambert & Henkin, 1963), but the difference is less than when the education factor is ignored.

Various intellectual functions seem to have different developmental patterns. Thurstone (1955), using cross-sectional data from the Primary Mental Abilities Tests, reported that 80 percent of adult-level perceptual-speed ability was reached by age 12; for spatial abilities the 80 percent point occurred at age 14; for verbal meaning at age 18, but not until age 20 for verbal fluency.

Most studies show a marked tendency for performance on intelligence tests to begin to level off at age 13 or 14. Performance increases little after age 16, although some slight increase in performance occurs until about age 20. The maximum performance on the Wechsler Adult Intelligence Scale is not reached until age 25 (Wechsler, 1958, p. 140). This increase probably reflects the effects of continued education and learning rather than an increase in the capacity to learn (see Horn, 1967; Wechsler, 1958, pp. 202–5; Birren, 1960).

The Reliability of Intelligence Tests

The reliability of *most* tests of scholastic aptitude or intelligence is satisfactory for individual use, but there are several exceptions. Reliability estimates determined by internal-consistency methods or by retesting with an alternate form for a brief interval often exceed .90. Standard errors of measurement (see pp. 119–121) of 3–7 IQ points exist, however, even with reliability coefficients in the .80–.95 range. The relationships between IQ scores on parallel forms *L* and *M* of the Stanford-Binet, shown in Figure 13–8, graphically illustrate the degree of reliability in IQ scores.

IQ Constancy

The constancy of the IQ has been a controversial topic since the "mental quotient" was suggested by Stern and Kuhlmann as early as 1912 as the *ratio* of mental age (MA) to chronological age (CA), multiplied by 100 to remove the decimal point. An examinee's mental age (MA) on a test is the age at which his or her score is the average score. If a 10-year-old correctly answers 38 items on a test, and 38 is the average score at 12.5 years of age, that child has an MA of 12.5 and an IQ of 125:

$$\text{IQ} = 100 \left(\frac{\text{MA}}{\text{CA}} \right) = 100 \, \frac{(12.5)}{10} = 125$$

The *ratio* IQ (i.e., the ratio of MA to CA) was popular until about 1960. Since then it has been largely replaced by the *deviation* IQ, a type of standard score. (See Figure 3–1, p. 58.)

With the ratio IQ, the standard deviation (σ) of the IQs varied considerably from one age to another. Although a σ of 16 was a "typical" value on intelligence tests, the values varied substantially from test to test—even within well-developed tests. Figure 13–9 shows the wide variation in σ's across ages for the two forms of the 1937 Stanford-Binet. This factor would cause

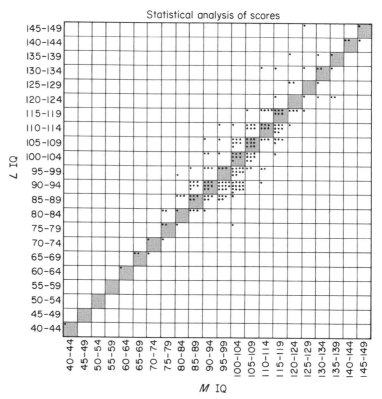

FIGURE 13-8 IQ scores on two forms of the Stanford-Binet obtained by seven-year-old children. (Reproduced from L. M. Terman and M. A. Merrill, *Measuring intelligence* [Boston: Houghton Mifflin Company, 1960], p. 11, by permission of the publisher, Houghton Mifflin Company.)

considerable fluctuation in IQ scores even if IQs correlated perfectly ($r = 1.0$) from one year to the next! For example, as shown in Figure 13-9, a child who consistently remained at the 98th percentile in intelligence would receive ratio IQ scores of 141, 125, and 140 at ages 2½, 6, and 12, respectively—if the child's performance was completely constant relative to that of his or her age peers and the tests correlated perfectly. Users of ratio IQ scores were rarely aware of this "technicality"; hence, many interpretive errors resulted, particularly in the area of "change" in intellectual status. For example, IQs below 70 are often considered to represent mental retardation. However, the percentage of "mental retardation" (on form *L*) would be only 1% at age 6, but 7% at age 12 because of the differences in the values of σ.

The Deviation IQ

The deviation IQ concept was introduced so that the σ's would have a constant value at each age (which would eliminate the aberrant variability of the ratio IQ that is evident in Figure 13-9). The deviation IQ is simply a kind of

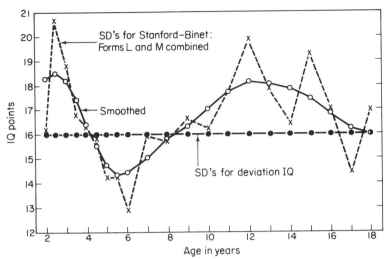

FIGURE 13-9 Fluctuations in the size of standard deviations of conventional (ratio) IQs at different age levels. (Reproduced from S. R. Pinneau, Conventional and deviation IQs for the Stanford-Binet, *Testing Today,* no. 4 [Boston: Houghton Mifflin, n.d.].)

standard score with a mean of 100 and a constant value for the standard deviation (usually 15 or 16) irrespective of age. A constant σ-value of 16 deviation IQs is illustrated in Figure 13-9. A given deviation IQ value represents the same degree of relative intellectual performance for all age levels; there is no vacillation in obtained IQs resulting from scaling artifacts that accompany the use of the ratio IQs. (See Figure 4-1, p. 58.)

For a proper interpretation of results from a scholastic aptitude test, the user must know whether the test employs a ratio or deviation IQ and, if a ratio IQ is used, the value of σ is for each age level. The ratio IQ continues to be employed for several widely used tests, although this practice should soon become a rarity.

Common Variance Versus Score Stability

We have demonstrated that a test must have constant means and standard deviations for each age level if IQ scores are to be stable. Thus, the use of deviation IQs is necessary but not sufficient to obtain a high degree of stability in IQ scores. Correlation coefficients do not necessarily depict score stability. For example, Hopkins and McGuire (1966) found that two intelligence tests correlated very highly ($r = .86$), although the means differed by 8.5 points and the standard deviations differed substantially (16.0 vs. 22.7). That the tests were measuring essentially the same cognitive factors was shown by the high correlation (r, corrected for attenuation,[2] $= .94$); however,

[2] The correction for attenuation is a statistical procedure for estimating the correlation between "true" or universe scores on two measures, that is, what the correlation between them would be if both tests were perfectly reliable. It is useful for estimating the extent to which two

quite different numbers (IQs) were assigned to the same relative level of performance.

In the vast majority of studies of IQ constancy, only the Stanford-Binet test has been involved. The constancy is typically represented by a correlation coefficient. The correlation (stability) coefficient is useful because it depicts predictable variance (r^2 equals predictable variance); nevertheless, it does not explicitly depict IQ constancy. The formula for a correlation coefficient can be written as follows:

$$r_{12} = \frac{\Sigma z_1 z_2}{n}$$

This formula shows that a correlation coefficient is a function of the products of the z-scores for the two measures. Thus, the correlation coefficient between IQ scores at times 1 and 2 is blind to differences resulting from differences in means or standard deviations. Theoretically, two intelligence tests *could* correlate 1.0, yet one could have a mean of 100 and the other a mean of 130! When deviation IQs are used, the IQ stability coefficients are more meaningful, since the means and σ's are the same at every age level—assuming, of course, that the examinees in the standardization group are representative.

Figure 13–10 graphically illustrates the meaning of such coefficients. It depicts the relationship, $r = .8$ (Bloom, 1964, p. 56) of Stanford-Binet deviation IQ's at grade 3 with corresponding IQ scores at grade 12. The coefficient of .8 indicates that the IQ predicted for an examinee at grade 12 will be only eight-tenths (.8) as far from the mean as his or her IQ score at grade 3. As shown in Figure 13–10, pupils who scored 125 in grade 3 tended on the average to score 120 (.8 × 25 = 20) in grade 12. Those examinees who received IQ scores of 80 in grade 3 tended to be only 80 percent as far from the mean (.8 × 20 = 16) at grade 12 and, hence, to have an average IQ of 84.[3]

The accuracy of these predictions is reflected by the standard error of estimate ($\sigma_{2.1}$), which is the standard deviation of actual scores on the criterion (2.1) around the predicted scores:

$$\sigma_{2.1} = \sigma_2 \sqrt{1 - r^2}$$

---

tests measure the same or different factors, after allowance (compensation) has been made for errors of measurement. The formula is

$$r_{1_t 2_t} = \frac{r_{12}}{\sqrt{r_{11} r_{22}}},$$

where $r_{1_t 2_t}$ = the estimated correlation between true scores on measures 1 and 2,

         r_{12} = the obtained correlation between measures 1 and 2, and

      r_{11}, r_{22} = the reliability coefficients of measures 1 and 2, respectively.

In the example noted above, $r_{12} = .861$, $r_{11} = .895$, and $r_{22} = .847$; hence, $r_{1_t 2_t} = .988$. For further information see Nunnally (1978, pp. 237–39) or Lord and Novick (1968, pp. 69–71).

   [3] If the means or standard deviations were not constant for each age, the prediction would have to allow for this by converting the grade 3 score to a z-score (z_1) and multiplying z_1 by r to obtain the predicted z-score (z_2') at grade 12:

$$z_2' = r z_1$$

The z_2' is converted back into the relevant units by multiplying z_2' by σ_2 and adding this value to the mean of the predicted variable ($\overline{X}_2$).

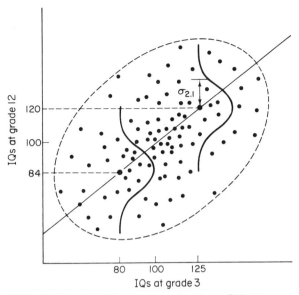

FIGURE 13-10 The relationship ($r = .8$) between deviation IQ scores obtained on the Stanford-Binet (at grades 3 and 12). The distributions of grade 12 IQ scores obtained by examinees who received scores of 80 and 125 at grade 3 are specifically illustrated. (Data from Bloom, 1964, p. 56.)

In the Stanford-Binet example (Figure 13-10), where $\sigma = 16$,

$$\sigma_{2.1} = 16\sqrt{1 - (.8)^2} = 16\sqrt{.36} = 16(.6) = 9.6, \text{ or about 10 points.}$$

The standard error of estimate of 10 shows that even with a substantial degree of stability ($r = .8$), there is still considerable fluctuation in individual scores. The $\sigma_{2.1}$ value of 10 indicates that about one-third of the examinees depicted in Figure 13-10 will have IQs that differ from their *predicted* IQ scores at grade 12 by ten or more points. A .95 confidence interval for a pupil's grade 12 IQ, predicted from the score at grade 3, would be the predicted IQ at grade 12 $\pm 2\sigma_{2.1}$; in other words, it would span a range of more than 40 IQ points! Clearly, a high stability coefficient still allows considerable variation in individual performance. This fact is further illustrated in Figure 13-11, which shows the plot of the actual IQ scores obtained by 354 pupils at grades 5 and 7 on the California Test of Mental Maturity (CTMM). Even though the scores over the two-year period are rather stable ($r = .829$), notice that, of the nine pupils who received IQ scores of 99 at grade 5, one scored 114 at grade 7 and another scored 86, but the grade 7 mean (99.7) differed little from the grade 5 mean (99.0).

As pointed out previously, almost all studies of IQ constancy have been done with individual intelligence tests (usually the Stanford-Binet); only a few studies have employed group tests. Yet group tests are given to all but a very

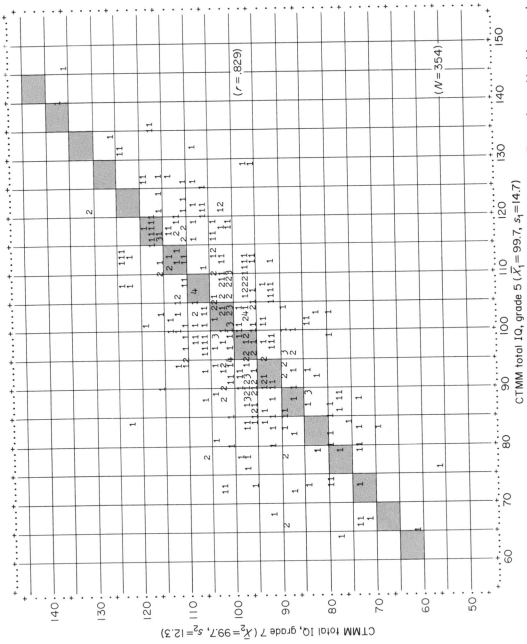

FIGURE 13-11 Scatterplot of IQ scores at grades 5 and 7 for 354 pupils. (Data from Hopkins and Bibelheimer, 1971.)

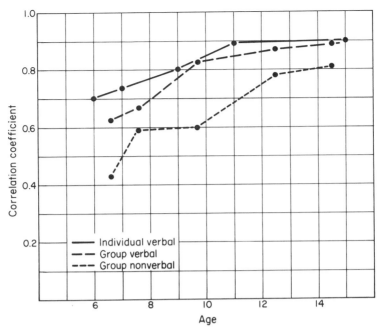

FIGURE 13-12 Correlation coefficients between IQ scores at maturity (age 17, corrected to a common terminal variability) for individual verbal, group verbal, and group nonverbal intelligence tests.

small percentage of students. Figure 13-12 illustrates the typical findings on IQ stabilities with an individual verbal test (the Stanford-Binet; see Bloom, 1964, p. 56), along with corresponding information on *group* verbal and nonverbal intelligence tests. It is evident that IQ scores from individually administered verbal tests are much more stable at younger ages than those from group tests. Whereas IQ scores on individual verbal tests at age 6 correlate about .7 with corresponding IQs at maturity, scores on *group* intelligence tests do not reflect the same degree of stability until 2-3 and 5-6 years later for verbal and nonverbal tests, respectively.

Hopkins and Bracht (1971, 1975) studied IQ constancy and change with group intelligence tests by following a large sample of pupils in grade 1 through elementary, junior high, and high school. Figure 13-13 shows the stability coefficients for verbal and nonverbal IQs. Each line in the figure depicts the correlation of the IQ scores from an initial grade level with scores obtained at subsequent grade levels. For example, the grade 1 verbal IQ (see bottom solid line in Figure 13-13) correlated .51 with grade 2 verbal IQs and .52, .50, .44, and .50 with IQs obtained in grades 4, 7, 9, and 11, respectively. Notice that IQs obtained for students in the primary grades have rather low correlations with their IQ scores in subsequent grades (grade 1 IQs are not even highly related to IQs obtained one year later). Verbal IQs at grade 4 have considerable stability, correlating .81, .79, and .77 with IQs in grades 7, 9,

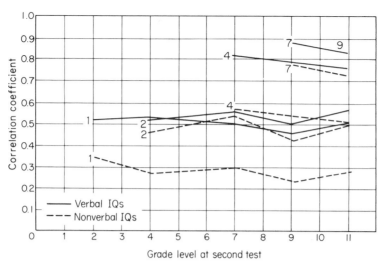

FIGURE 13-13 Graphic representation of stability coefficients for verbal and nonverbal IQs (CIMM used at grades 1, 2, and 4; Lorge-Thorndike at grades 7, 9, and 11.) Grade level of initial testing precedes each line.

and 11, respectively. Figure 13-13 illustrates that nonverbal IQs fluctuated significantly more than verbal IQs and did not show much stability until grade 7. The pattern of results reported in Figure 13-13 is consistent with the results of other groups using different tests (Hopkins & Bibelheimer, 1971; L. E. Tyler, 1958; Magnusson & Backteman, 1978). When verbal and nonverbal IQs are combined in a total IQ score, its stability closely parallels that shown for verbal IQ (stability coefficients average only about .03 higher than the verbal IQs).

The stability of IQ scores expressed directly in IQ units is more informative for most people than stability coefficients. Hopkins and Bracht (1971) found that the *mean* absolute change (+ or −) in total IQ scores from grade 1 to any grade thereafter was 10–12 points. The average absolute difference in grade 2 IQs and IQs from subsequent grades was 9–10 points; grade 4 IQs differ 7–9 points from subsequent IQs, on the average. The mean difference between grade 7 IQs and IQs in grades 9 and 11 was 5–6 points; and grade 9 IQs averaged 5 points different from scores for grade 11. It is important to note that these are *mean* absolute differences; such differences include changes up and down. Recall that the changes are least at the mean and are expected to be progressively greater as scores deviate from the mean. The changes are usually greater when the IQs are obtained on different tests (e.g., Lorge-Thorndike vs. CTMM) than when a different level of the same series is repeated. Mouly and Edgar (1958) compared the IQ scores yielded by four widely used intelligence tests. They found that some tests consistently yielded IQs 5–7 points higher than those yielded by others. This finding shows that degree of IQ change will be even greater across different tests than within the same test.

The standard errors of estimate (standard deviation of obtained IQ scores around the most probable IQ predicted from a prior test; see Figure 13-10) were

1. 12-17 points using grade 1 or grade 2 scores as predictors.
2. 9-12 points using grade 4 scores as predictors.
3. 7-8 points using grade 7 scores for predicting scores in grades 9 and 11.
4. about 7 points in predicting grade 11 IQs from grade 9 IQs.

Several conclusions can be drawn regarding IQ consistency:

1. The stability of IQs from individual verbal tests is fairly high as early as age 5. Infant tests have virtually no validity as predictors of later IQ scores.
2. The stability of IQs from group tests is much less than that of IQs from individual verbal tests until at least 10-12 years of age but becomes comparable thereafter. Accurate long-term predictions cannot be made from group intelligence tests given during the primary grades. IQs from nonverbal group tests tend to be much less stable than those from verbal group tests.
3. Even when there is a high degree of overall stability, the scores of a few individuals will change greatly.
4. Each test varies slightly in the cognitive abilities that are tapped. An IQ score should always be interpreted in terms of the test on which it was obtained.
5. Various intelligence tests differ considerably in IQ stability. For the Primary Mental Abilities Tests, which yield verbal, numerical, spatial, reasoning, and word fluency scores, much less long-term stability is reflected in the spatial and word fluency abilities than in other areas (Meyer & Bending, 1961; L. E. Tyler, 1958).
6. IQ changes are greater when the type of intelligence test used is varied. IQ differences are especially great when the type of test given (verbal vs. nonverbal) is varied. Verbal and nonverbal IQs correlate only .4–.6 at most grade levels (Hopkins & Bibelheimer, 1971; Hopkins & Bracht, 1971).

These conclusions indicate that great care must be taken in interpreting IQs, especially from group tests, which are the only ones available for 95 percent of the students. Scores from group tests given during the primary grades should be viewed only as general indicators of *present* intellectual status. The findings suggest that there are great dangers in disseminating IQ scores to students and parents, who may interpret results with much less tolerance for error and change than is required for a proper evaluation. Certainly, no one has more right to knowledge of a child's abilities than his or her parents, but the information should be given in terms that are meaningful to parents. Perhaps percentile ranks would be more meaningful than IQ scores in this context. Fortunately, many test publishers now provide report forms that interpret a student's performance in terms that both student and parents can understand (See Figures 13-4, 14-9, and 15-2).

Many parents are unaware that intelligence tests tend to measure primarily scholastic aptitude and that many other cognitive abilities that can be legitimately considered to reflect intelligence and special abilities are untapped. For example, Hoepfner and O'Sullivan (1968) found that measures of social intelligence correlated only .3–.4 with scores from conventional intelligence tests.

The Relationship Between IQ and Scholastic Achievement

The data given in Table 13-1 show the relationship between IQs from the Lorge-Thorndike Intelligence Test (LT) and various kinds of academic achievement as measured by the Iowa Tests of Basic Skills (ITBS). At each grade level, each correlation is based on approximately 2,500 pupils from a nationally representative sample. The results illustrate that there is a substantial relationship between achievement in various subject matter areas and measured intelligence. Notice that the degree of relationship tends to increase with grade level. The nonverbal IQs have a consistently lower relationship in every achievement area, but as would be expected, the difference is less in areas that are less verbal (e.g., map or graph reading and arithmetic).

Table 13-2 gives similar information at the high school level for the LT tests and the Tests of Academic Progress (TAP). These findings agree with the typical results from other well-constructed intelligence and achievement tests; they confirm the substantial relationship between measured intelligence and all academic areas of scholastic achievement.

Most authorities feel that current intelligence tests are more aptly described as "scholastic aptitude" tests because they are so highly related to academic performance, although present use suggests that the term *intelligence test* is going to be with us for some time. This reservation is based *not* on the opinion that intelligence tests do not reflect intelligence but on the belief that there are other kinds of intelligence that are not reflected in current tests; the term *intelligence* is too inclusive. It should be clear that intelligence tests reflect abilities that are very important and relevant to educational performance. Wallen (1962) surveyed the research pertaining to IQ scores and

TABLE 13-1

THE RELATIONSHIP BETWEEN VERBAL AND NONVERBAL IQs (LORGE-THORNDIKE) AND STANDARDIZED ACHIEVEMENT TESTS (IOWA TESTS OF BASIC SKILLS) FOR GRADES 3-8 (DATA FROM NORM SAMPLE)

Iowa Tests of Basic Skills	Grade:	*L-T Verbal IQ*						*L-T Nonverbal IQ*					
		3	*4*	*5*	*6*	*7*	*8*	*3*	*4*	*5*	*6*	*7*	*8*
Vocabulary		.71	.75	.77	.78	.80	.82	.56	.62	.62	.62	.64	.65
Reading		.68	.74	.76	.79	.81	.82	.53	.63	.65	.65	.67	.69
Language													
Spelling		.66	.67	.68	.69	.70	.69	.52	.55	.56	.55	.54	.53
Capitalization		.65	.67	.67	.67	.67	.69	.55	.61	.61	.61	.62	.64
Punctuation		.56	.63	.66	.66	.67	.69	.48	.61	.61	.61	.61	.62
Usage		.67	.70	.71	.71	.71	.69	.55	.59	.61	.60	.60	.57
Total		.73	.76	.78	.78	.79	.78	.61	.66	.67	.67	.68	.67
Study Skills													
Maps		.59	.62	.65	.66	.66	.71	.51	.58	.64	.64	.66	.70
Graphs		.63	.65	.66	.66	.69	.70	.56	.62	.62	.63	.68	.68
References		.62	.67	.71	.74	.76	.78	.53	.61	.65	.67	.72	.72
Total		.72	.75	.76	.77	.79	.81	.62	.69	.71	.71	.77	.78
Arithmetic													
Concepts		.65	.70	.71	.71	.72	.75	.61	.67	.69	.69	.71	.72
Problems		.57	.61	.61	.62	.65	.64	.51	.56	.56	.56	.61	.61
Total		.66	.71	.72	.72	.74	.75	.61	.68	.69	.69	.71	.71
Composite		.79	.82	.84	.85	.88	.88	.65	.73	.74	.75	.77	.77
N		2,677	2,757	2,706	2,584	2,605	2,462	2,677	2,757	2,706	2,584	2,605	2,462

SOURCE: Reprinted from *Technical Manual, Lorge-Thorndike Intelligence Tests,* Multilevel Edition by permission of the publisher, Houghton Mifflin Company, Boston.

TABLE 13-2

THE RELATIONSHIP BETWEEN VERBAL AND NONVERBAL IQs (LORGE-THORNDIKE) AND STANDARDIZED ACHIEVEMENT TESTS (TESTS OF ACADEMIC PROGRESS) FOR GRADES 9-12 (DATA FROM NORM SAMPLE)

Tests of Academic Progress	Grade:	L-T Verbal IQ				L-T Nonverbal IQ			
		9	10	11	12	9	10	11	12
Social studies		.81	.81	.81	.83	.66	.64	.62	.61
Composition		.75	.74	.73	.75	.65	.62	.59	.59
Science		.74	.74	.73	.74	.63	.64	.63	.64
Reading		.81	.79	.81	.83	.65	.61	.60	.59
Mathematics		.73	.75	.73	.71	.70	.72	.67	.67
Literature		.79	.79	.81	.84	.63	.60	.59	.60
Composite		.88	.87	.88	.90	.74	.72	.71	.71
N		2,503	2,250	2,174	1,684	2,503	2,250	2,174	1,684

SOURCE: Reprinted from *Technical Manual, Lorge Thorndike Intelligence Tests,* Multilevel Edition by permission of the publisher, Houghton Mifflin Company, Boston.

ability to learn and concluded that "in spite of the not uncommon statement that intelligence tests do not predict ability to learn, the evidence that they do continues to accumulate" (p. 17). Only when the learning tasks are of a primitive, rote type, such as paired-associates tasks, do IQ scores have little relationship with learning behavior. For complex tasks, intelligence tests are substantially related to learning speed and ease (Noble, Noble & Alcock, 1958).

Construct Validity

The appropriate evidence for the validity of intelligence tests is of the construct validity variety. In Chapter 4 (pp. 105-106) we used intelligence tests to illustrate this concept. In a very real sense every bit of information one has on a test may have implications for construct validity; that is, the data respond to the question, "Is the information congruent with theoretical expectations?" IQ constancy has important implications for the construct validity of a given intelligence test. The validity of IQs from infant intelligence tests is rejected because they possess so little consistency with later cognitive performance.

The nature–nurture studies on measured intelligence have an important bearing on the construct validity of IQ scores. If there were no relationship between the IQs of siblings when they are reared apart and a very high relationship between their IQs when they are reared together, we would either revise the theory of intelligence (the proposition that genetic factors play a significant role would have to be eliminated) or reject the validity of the measurements. Either an ingredient in the theory is invalid or else the measurement of the construct must lack validity.

Contrary to indications in much of the popular literature, genetic factors have a strong relationship to IQ (McAskie & Clarke, 1976). Of course, correlation does not necessarily mean causation; much heat and little light has been generated over the nature–nurture issue in intelligence. The question is

TABLE 13-3

CORRELATIONS OF IQ SCORES FOR PEOPLE OF VARIOUS DEGREES OF GENETIC AND ENVIRONMENTAL SIMILARITY

Correlation between	r
Foster parent and child	+.20
Genetically unrelated children, reared together	+.24
First cousins	+.26
Siblings, reared apart	+.47
Siblings, reared together	+.49
Fraternal twins	+.53
Identical twins, reared apart	+.75
Identical twins, reared together	+.87
Grandparent and child	+.27
Parent and child	+.50

exceedingly complex, especially as applied to racial differences (Kempthorne, 1978). Table 13-3 presents the median correlation between IQ scores for varying degrees of genetic similarity. The correlations are generally consistent with theoretical expectations. The correlation between IQ scores of unrelated people reared together is only about .20, but the IQ scores of identical (monozygotic) twins reared apart correlate highly ($r = .75$). In typical environments in the United States and England, genetic factors bear a much stronger general relationship to IQ than environmental factors do (Pezzullo et al., 1972). Of course, for certain individuals or subgroups the environment may have dramatic effects on IQ—as with, for example, brain damage at birth, metabolic types of mental retardation, or extreme environmental deprivation. Although genetic factors are strongly related to academic achievement, that relationship is much less than with intelligence tests (Jensen, 1968b). The achievement scores of unrelated persons reared together are substantially related, and *it is achievement, not intelligence per se, that is socially significant.* The environment tends to have more influence on a student's academic performance than on his or her IQ score. For example, the achievement correlation of identical twins reared apart was .68, whereas that of siblings reared together was much higher—.81.

One can conclude that genetic factors have a strong relationship to measured intelligence. The relationship with scholastic achievement is considerably less. Conversely, the environment has a much stronger relationship with children's academic achievement than with their observed scores on intelligence tests. There is little relationship in measured intelligence among unrelated persons reared together, but there is a substantial relationship (about .5) between their educational achievement levels—about as great as for siblings reared apart.

Intelligence and Occupational Level

The relationship of measured intelligence to occupational level is illustrated in Figure 13-14. There data are based on the testing of approximately 90,000 white recruits during World War II; the Army General Classification Test

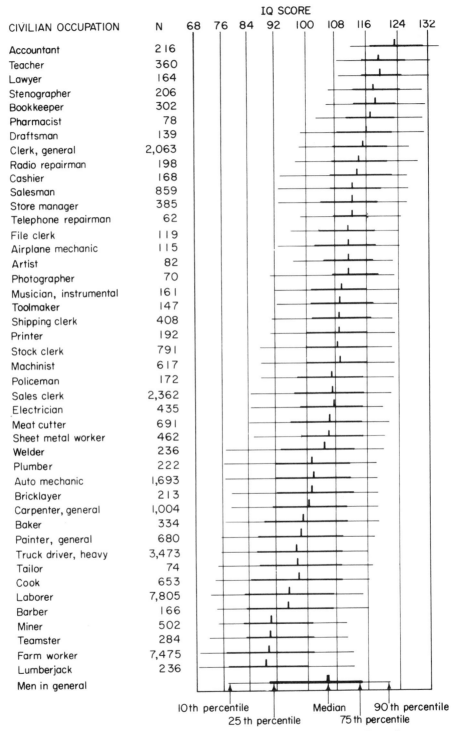

CIVILIAN OCCUPATION	N
Accountant	216
Teacher	360
Lawyer	164
Stenographer	206
Bookkeeper	302
Pharmacist	78
Draftsman	139
Clerk, general	2,063
Radio repairman	198
Cashier	168
Salesman	859
Store manager	385
Telephone repairman	62
File clerk	119
Airplane mechanic	115
Artist	82
Photographer	70
Musician, instrumental	161
Toolmaker	147
Shipping clerk	408
Printer	192
Stock clerk	791
Machinist	617
Policeman	172
Sales clerk	2,362
Electrician	435
Meat cutter	691
Sheet metal worker	462
Welder	236
Plumber	222
Auto mechanic	1,693
Bricklayer	213
Carpenter, general	1,004
Baker	334
Painter, general	680
Truck driver, heavy	3,473
Tailor	74
Cook	653
Laborer	7,805
Barber	166
Miner	502
Teamster	284
Farm worker	7,475
Lumberjack	236
Men in general	

IQ SCORE — 68 76 84 92 100 108 116 124 132

10th percentile   25th percentile   Median   75th percentile   90th percentile

FIGURE 13-14 Scores on the Army General Classification Test for occupational groups converted into deviation IQ equivalents. (Data from Stewart, 1947.)

(AGCT) was given to these recruits. The AGCT uses a standard score system (mean = 100, σ = 20) to describe performance. The scores are similar to IQs, except that the standard deviation is set at 20 rather than 15 or 16. As an aid in interpretation, the median AGCT scores for several different occupations were converted to corresponding IQ equivalents (mean = 100, σ = 16) in Figure 13-14. The variability within each occupation is shown by the bars that extend from the 25th to the 75th percentile in IQ units, and the lines that extend from the 10th to the 90th percentile.

Two important generalizations are apparent from the data given in Figure 13-14. First, *there is a substantial relationship between average mental ability and various occupations.* The median IQ for the highest occupational group was 35 points higher than that for the lowest occupational group. Note that we are talking about *measured intelligence;* the variation in amount of education probably makes the observed differences greater than the true differences in intellectual potential. (Bear in mind that these data are not current. A greater proportion of today's students are remaining in school longer, which could reduce the differences among the means of the various occupational groups.)

On the other hand, if school counseling programs are helping students select vocational plans commensurate with their abilities, some of the very able students who would have become laborers could continue their education and enter a skilled trade or profession. This would make the differences in measured intelligence among the occupations even greater. If there were no change in the occupations entered but simply an increase in the worker's education, the differences among occupational groups shown in Figure 13-14 would be decreased slightly.

Second, *there is a wide range of mental ability within each occupation.* The correlation between occupational level and IQ is much lower than commonly assumed—.3 or less (White, 1976, ETS, 1980b; Jensen, 1980, pp. 43-44). Although the accountants' median was 123, 25 percent of the group scored below an IQ equivalent of 117. Notice that the variability within the occupational groups tends to decrease as the median increases.

There are many bright people in occupations that do not require high mental ability. One-fourth of the lumberjacks scored above the population mean on the test, even though as a group they had the lowest performance.

Multiple-Aptitude Batteries

Although tests that yield a total score and/or separate verbal and nonverbal scores account for the bulk of cognitive aptitude assessment in school testing programs, an increasing use is being made of tests that yield a profile of different aptitudes, especially in vocational guidance. The most popular test battery of this type is the Differential Aptitude Tests (DAT), which yield separate scores on eight somewhat independent aptitudes or abilities: verbal reasoning, numerical ability, abstract reasoning, clerical speed and accuracy, mechanical reasoning, space relations, and language usage (spelling and grammar).

MY APTITUDE TESTS SHOWED I'D MAKE A
GOOD EXECUTIVE, BUT MY I.Q. TESTS SHOWED
I'D BE SMART ENOUGH NOT TO BECOME ONE.

(From *NCME Measurement* News, 19:2)

The basic rationale underlying these tests is that various academic and occupational pursuits require different patterns of aptitude and, hence, a decision in which a profile of aptitudes is available should be more appropriate than a decision based on a single "omnibus" score. This assumption was strongly contested by McNemar (1964). Nevertheless, Figures 13-15 and 13-16 (from the DAT manual) show that the various aptitude tests do have differing degrees of relationship with certain academic and occupational criteria. Notice that some of the differences are counterintuitive; for example, the girls who entered clerical work (Figure 13-15, B) tended to have less clerical ability than the girls who became teachers.

That the separate subtest scores can have substantial validity for certain occupational pursuits is illustrated in Figure 13-17, which shows the relationship between the DAT Space Relations test scores obtained at the beginning of the term and final grades in a watch repair training program. Note that 67% of those with very high DAT scores (80 or above) received A's and none obtained a grade of less than B; whereas no student with a DAT score below 60 received an A grade and many got D's and F's.

Multiple-aptitude tests can provide important information for career

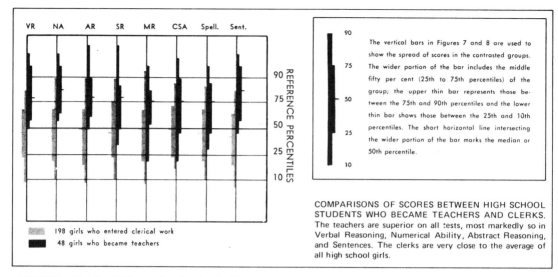

FIGURE 13–15 Differential Aptitude Tests (Forms A and B), scores and subsequent occupations. (Reproduced from G. K. Bennett, H. G. Seashore, and A. G. Wesman, *Differential Aptitude Tests, Forms L and M Fourth Edition Manual* [New York: Psychological Corp.], by permission of the publisher. Copyright © 1966, 1974 by the Psychological Corporation, New York. All rights reserved.)

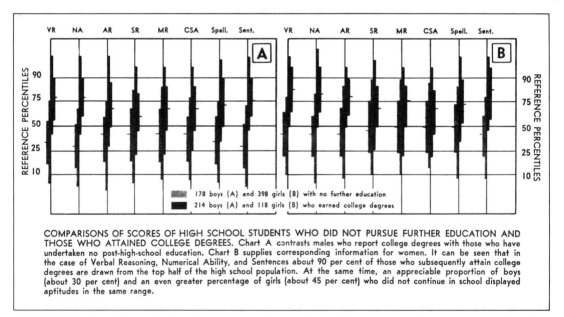

FIGURE 13–16 Differential Aptitude Tests (Forms A and B) scores and subsequent education. (Reproduced from G. K. Bennett, H. G. Seashore, and A. G. Wesman, *Differential Aptitude Tests, Forms L and M Fourth Edition Manual* [New York: Psychological Corp.], by permission of the publisher. Copyright © 1966, 1974 by The Psychological Corporation, New York. All rights reserved.)

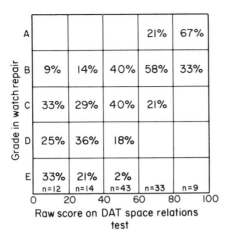

FIGURE 13-17 An expectancy table illustrating the predictive validity of the DAT space relations test for forecasting end-of-course grades for 111 students in the American Institute of Specialized Watch Repair (r = .69).

planning; as McNemar (1964) illustrated, however, their superiority over general scholastic aptitude tests for predicting differential *academic* success is small at best.

The great commonality among the abilities required to succeed in most academic subjects is no doubt a major factor that prevents multiple-aptitude tests from excelling over the omnibus intelligence test in predicting academic success.

Cultural Influences on Test Scores

An examinee's test score reflects all the experiences the individual has had from conception to time of testing, including the effects of the particular genes he or she has inherited. Genetic potential interacts with environmental stimulation (or lack of it) to produce a person who scores high, average, or low on a particular test at a particular time. A child of 5 or even much younger has been exposed to so many strong environmental influences that his or her scores on intelligence tests are almost certainly different to some degree from what they would have been had that child been reared in a different environment (including nutrition and medical care).

"Culture-free" tests are culture free in name only—there are no tests that measure potential or aptitude directly. Intelligence—unlike height and weight, but like all psychological constructs—must be measured indirectly; it must be inferred from intelligent behavior, past and present.

Since environment and culture-free tests cannot be devised, there have been many attempts to develop culture-fair tests. Obviously, it is unfair to judge Jim's intelligence solely from his vocabulary when both of his parents are school dropouts whereas Bob's parents are college graduates. Jim will perform relatively better if the test content is more common to the background of all people is used. Test developers strive, with various degrees of success, to select tasks that will be equally familiar (or equally unfamiliar) to all examinees. This goal is never achieved perfectly, but it is more closely approximated on some tests than many test critics realize. Anti-testing crusaders typically single out and attack a few bad items as if those items are representative (e.g., Hoffman, 1962, 1967a,b).

Contrary to popular opinion, the correlation among students' socioeconomic status (SES) and academic ability is not high (*r*'s are typically .3 or less unless confounded with racial factors—Coleman et al., 1966; White, 1976; Jensen, 1980, p. 43). Note, for example, the great variability *within* the various occupations in Figure 13-14. (Occupation is the major ingredient of SES.) Havinghurst and Neugarten (1975) report that although there is a positive correlation between SES and IQ, more of those who score in the upper 25% on intelligence tests (i.e., IQs above 110) come from "working-class" homes than from the upper and upper-middle classes combined!

Like the authors, you probably know parents who have devoted themselves to giving their children every educational advantage by providing an intellectually enriched environment—educational toys from the crib on, daily reading to the children at the earliest possible age, books and weekly trips to the library, problem-solving puzzles, multisensory–multimethod achievement-oriented preschools, and reward systems tailored to "shape" academic interests and achievements. But many children from this type of experiential background do not become exceptional students—indeed, many are mediocre learners. Obviously, a propitious environment is only one of the important ingredients of superior academic achievement.

Despite its desirability, attempts to produce an intelligence test in which "culturally disadvantaged" people perform as well as those from enriched backgrounds have been largely unsuccessful. A long, major study at the University of Chicago (Eells et al., 1951) resulted in a specially designed test, the Davis-Eells Test of General Intelligence (or Problem-Solving Ability) that did not reduce the differences among the means of the various socioeconomic groups from those reflected in the usual intelligence tests (Ludlow, 1956). Later results with other tests have been similar (Cleary & Hilton, 1968). In a number of studies, greater differences between blacks and whites have been found on nonverbal than on verbal items (Flaugher, 1970).

Mercer (1977) has proposed a System of Multicultural Pluralistic Assessment (SOMPA) that, in effect, uses two sets of norms in assessing each examinee: the national norm group and a comparison group that is similar to the examinee in social and cultural background. The IQ score is "corrected" to depict the examinee's "latent scholastic aptitude." This procedure is based on the tenuous assumption that all differences among social and ethnic groups are the result of unequal environments. Hilliard (National Institue of Education, 1979) has concluded that the SOMPA "appears to have all the weaknesses of the old tests, plus a whole host of new weaknesses all its own, not the least of which is the absence of any construct validity." The SOMPA may be an overreaction to deficiencies in current intelligence tests. (See Gordon, 1975.) Bear in mind that many very high-scoring individuals emerge from impoverished environments and many low-scoring individuals come from enriched environments. Clearly environment is a factor, but not the only factor that affects performance on scholastic aptitude tests.[4] Note in Table 13-3 that the IQs of genetically unrelated children are only slightly correlated with the IQs of their foster parents. Honzik (1957) found that the IQs of adopted children are much more closely related to those of their genetic parents ($r = .4$) than to those of their foster parents ($r \doteq .2$). Similarly, the median r (from 33 studies) of siblings reared apart was $+ .47$, whereas the median r (from 5 studies) of genetically unrelated people reared together is only $+ .24$ (Jensen, 1969).

For many years there has been much discussion about the extent to which culturally disadvantaged persons, especially blacks, tend to score low on intelligence tests because of genetic factors. The "nature versus nurture" argument continues to rage in the United States and elsewhere. If you have plenty of patience and energy, study the pros and cons in Jensen (1968b, 1969, 1980) and subsequent commentaries and critiques (there have been more than 100!).

It seems clear that *within* Caucasian groups intelligence test ability is rather strongly, but by no means completely, a function of heredity. Research on the heritability of intelligence within a black population is very limited.

As a group, culturally disadvantaged tend to score lower on measures of academic aptitude; they also tend to make poorer grades. This is not surprising, because most of the abilities needed to score well on such tests are also required if a student is to do well in class. Many studies (Cleary, 1968; Hills & Stanley, 1970; Kendrick & Thomas, 1970; Stanley & Porter, 1967; Thomas & Stanley, 1969; Stanley, 1971a; Wilson, 1978) have shown that scores on academic aptitude tests predict the college grades of blacks at least as well as they predict those of whites. More often than not, the SAT has been found to overpredict the college GPA of blacks (Breland, 1978) and Mexican Americans (Goldman & Richards, 1974). Whereas high school grades predict college GPA somewhat better than scholastic ability tests among whites, the pattern appears to be reversed for blacks (Thomas & Stanley, 1969).

It is theoretically possible to construct tests that do not discriminate among socioeconomic classes but do predict academic achievement well; however, the many rather fruitless efforts thus far make this seem unlikely unless a fundamentally different method of measuring academic aptitude is discovered.[5]

The U.S. Employment Service has taken steps to improve the assessment of culturally disadvantaged applicants—experimenting with novel tests, improved test orientation and practice, development of nonreading forms of ex-

---

[4] The reader may have read reports of a widely disseminated study by Rosenthal and Jacobson (1968) in which experimenter-induced teacher expectancies are purported to have resulted in significant gains in IQ scores in certain students. The interested reader should consult critical reviews of the study (Snow, 1969; R. L. Thorndike, 1968), which raise some serious questions regarding its validity. Attempts to generate a related effect have not been successful (Fleming & Anttonen, 1970; Gozali & Meyer, 1970; Haberman, 1970; José and Cody, 1971; Mendels & Flanders, 1973; Dusek, 1975; Cooper, 1979). The large increases in IQ scores in the "Milwaukee miracle" are also highly suspect as artifactual. (See Page, 1972.)

[5] The research on using "brain waves" to estimate intelligence is not promising (Fischer et al., 1978).

isting tests, and so on (Jurgensen, 1966). (See also the spring 1976 issue of the *Journal of Educational Measurement,* which is devoted exclusively to "Bias in Selection.") Recently the United States Supreme Court ruled in the Bakke[6] case that it is unconstitutional to base selection decisions on racial quotas.

Tests are not enemies of the culturally disadvantaged. As Anastasi (1968, p. 563) stated, "When social stereotypes and prejudice may distort interpersonal evaluation, tests provide a safeguard against favoritism and arbitrary and capricious decisions." J. A. Fishman and colleagues (1964, p. 139) in "Guidelines for Testing Minority Group Children," also commented, "Without the intervention of standardized tests, many such [bright, nonconforming, and culturally handicapped] children would be stigmatized by the adverse subjective ratings of teachers who tend to reward conformist behavior of middle-class character."

The National Council on Measurement in Education, in its official statement on admissions testing (NCME, 1980), stated, "Although some interpret group differences in performance as bias in a test, it is now recognized among measurement experts that the mere existence of such group differences in performance is not evidence of bias. . . . Few people suggest that differentials in school-related performance could disappear if there were no tests." [p. 5]

Tests should be used as an aid in understanding pupils. No responsible person should fail to take a student's background into consideration in interpreting a test score. The fact that undernourished children weigh less than those who are well fed hardly builds a case for banning scales. In the same vein, Clifford, a black educator, stated that to disparage tests for revealing inequalities is as erroneous as for the residents of Bismark, North Dakota, to condemn the use of thermometers as biased because when it was –11° there it was 73° in Miami, Florida (Clifford & Fishman, 1963, p. 87).

Race Differences in Intelligence (Loehlin, Lindzey, & Spuhler, 1975) is considered to be one of the most objective treatments of ethnic differences on intelligence measures. They offer the following summary (p. 239): Observed mean differences on intelligence–ability tests probably reflect a combination of both (1) inadequacies in the tests and differential environmental conditions, and (2) genetic differences among the groups. The relative weights of these two factors will differ on different tests and with different groups, but regardless of the relative importance of these factors, it seems clear that the

---

[6] Allan Bakke is a Caucasian who was denied admission to the medical school at the University of California at Davis even though his GPA and scores on the admissions test were higher than those of minority students who were admitted. The medical school had set aside 16 of the 100 openings for minorities. Bakke sued the university; the California State Supreme Court ruled in favor of Bakke because his rejection had been racially discriminatory. The U.S. Supreme Court (in a 5 to 4 decision) ruled the medical school had violated the "equal protection" clause of the Constitution because Bakke's rejection was based on a racial quota. The Court did uphold the "affirmative action" principle, indicating that race might legitimately be one element in assessing students for admission, provided that racial quotas are not used. As Jensen (1980, p. 56) noted, "The arguments in such cases will extend far beyond questions of the objective validity of entrance tests and selection procedures. The debate involves fundamental philosophic positions and value judgments in the weighing of one social good against another, as the growing insistence on group rights runs head on into the traditional democratic belief in equality of individual opportunity. These questions of social policy cannot be answered by scientists."

differences among individuals *within* racial–ethnic (and SES) groups are much greater than the average differences *between* such groups.

Several conclusions regarding performance on scholastic aptitude tests as related to SES and race can be stated:

1. There are no direct, pure measures of aptitude; hence, comparisons of native intelligence or the like are equivocal. Whether there are, or are not, differences among different ethnic and racial groups cannot be definitively established or refuted on the basis of current research evidence. At the very least, scores on scholastic aptitude tests represent the examinee's current level of functioning.
2. An enriched environment enhances performance, but a superior environment, compared with an average environment, is not sufficient to produce a bright child. The effects at the other end of the environmental spectrum are greater. An extremely poor environment (lack of school attendance, deaf parents, and the like) can substantially depress intellectual performance.
3. Any responsible interpretation of scholastic aptitude or intelligence tests must take the social and ethnic background of the examinee into account.
4. Scholastic aptitude measures do not generally underpredict the academic achievement of members of ethnic and social minorities (Breland, 1978; Starkman, Butkovich & Murray, 1976). Similar results have been obtained in certain employment and military settings (ETS, 1969; Gordon, 1953).
5. Many of the issues pertaining to the appropriate use of scholastic aptitude tests are inextricably mixed with political and social values and orientations and, as such, do not readily lend themselves to resolution by means of scientific research.

Various General Ability Tests

Many different published tests purport to measure intelligence and cognitive aptitudes. The validity data on many of these are fragmentary and unconvincing. Before selecting a test or using the results from a test, one should read the current critical reviews of that test in the *Mental Measurements Yearbooks (MMY)* edited by Oscar K. Buros, of which the most recent is the eighth, published in 1978.

The representative standardized tests listed here are those that are used most widely. The scores yielded and the ages for which norms are available are also given.

Individual Tests
Stanford-Binet Intelligence Scale (Verbal), ages 2–adult
Wechsler Preschool and Primary Scale of Intelligence (WPPSI) (Verbal and Performance), ages 4–6½
Wechsler Intelligence Scale for Children (WISC-R) (Verbal and Performance), ages 6½–16½
Wechsler Adult Intelligence Scale (WAIS) (Verbal and Performance), ages 16–adult

Group Tests
California Tests of Mental Maturity (CTMM) (Language and Nonlanguage), grades K–adult

Cooperative School and College Ability Tests (SCAT) (Verbal and Quantitative), grades 4–14

Henmon-Nelson Tests of Mental Ability (Verbal and Quantitative), grades 3–14

Kuhlmann-Anderson Intelligence Tests (KA) (Verbal and Quantitative), grades K–12

Lorge-Thorndike Intelligence Tests (LT) (Verbal and Nonverbal), grades 3–adult

Otis-Lennon Mental Ability Tests (Verbal) grades K–adult

Differential Aptitude Tests (DAT) (8 subtests), grades 8–12

Short Form Test of Academic Aptitude (SFTAA) (Language and Nonlanguage), grades 1.5–12

Cognitive Abilities Test (CAT) (Verbal, Quantitative, and Nonverbal), grades K–12

Assessing Creativity

In his 1950 presidential address to the American Psychological Association, Guilford (1950) documented the dearth of attention that psychologists were giving to the study of creativity. His address stimulated interest in the topic, and since that time considerable research effort has been directed toward the definition and assessment of creativity.

Creative thinking is in the *divergent* operation of Guilford's SI model, and he and others have attempted to develop tests of creativity, of which the most common are the Torrence Tests of Creative Thinking and the Wallach and Kogan Creativity Test. Both tests include verbal and visual sections. In these tests examinees are asked how many different uses they can think of for a brick or a tin can; "What would happen if birds could speak the language of man?"; "What might be about to happen in the picture above?"; "Make up a story to fit the title, 'The Lion That Won't Roar' "; "Just suppose that no one ever has to go to school anymore; what would happen?"; "Name all the round things you can think of"; "Name all the ways a potato and a carrot are alike," and so on. Illustrative Torrence items are given in Figure 13–18. Responses are scored by trained scorers according to three criteria: originality, fluency (number of responses), and flexibility (number of different categories of responses).

The creativity tests developed to date have yet to demonstrate their practical value; their predictive validity tends to be low (Hoepfner, 1967). The tests tend to be too unreliable for individual use (Wodtke, 1964; Yamamoto, 1962); test–retest reliabilities tend to be in the .45–.75 range, with a median value of perhaps .65. In addition, many creativity tests do not correlate highly with each other. R. L. Thorndike (1963b) showed that tests of creativity correlate as highly with conventional "convergent" intelligence measures as they do with other "divergent" tests. Performance on creativity measures has much less stability over time than peformance on intelligence tests (Magnusson & Backteman, 1978).

Continued research efforts may refine or develop creativity measures so that they have practical utility, but at present they must be viewed as bold attempts rather than successes in creativity assessment. Tryk (1968, p. 54), in concluding his survey of creativity assessment, stated that "in spite of the re-

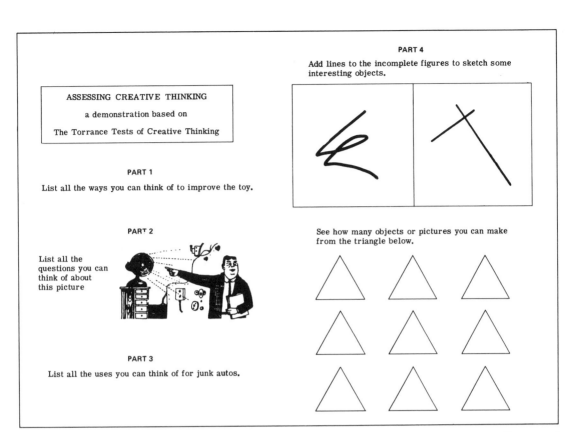

cent upsurge in research, the current status of instruments for assessing creativity is less than satisfactory. Evidence for the validity and reliability of creativity measures fails so far to promote much confidence in their use in assessing specific components of creativity.'' Even Guilford, who stimulated great interest in creativity testing, is leery of some of its developments (Guilford, 1968, p. 251). Crockenberg (1972, p. 40) in her review of creativity tests, wrote, ''Therefore, while it may be eminently reasonable to study the processes that appear to be involved in creativity production, it is conceptually unjustifiable to call these tests 'tests of creativity'.''

Summary

Intelligence measurement became successful shortly after 1900, when Binet employed verbal-reasoning items. There continue to be several theories of intelligence, although it is measured principally by the use of rather heterogeneous collections of verbal or nonverbal items.

The construct validity data for intelligence tests include (1) age differentiation; (2) the considerable stability of IQ scores, (3) the substantial relationship of IQ scores with academic achievement and occupational level; (4) the apparently high relationship of genetic factors with measured intelligence; and (5) the logical content validity of the test items—do they require reasoning, conceptualization, higher-level thought processes, and so forth?

Several conclusions regarding the measurement of scholastic aptitude can be stated:

1. Intelligence tests are best viewed as scholastic aptitude tests; they are heavily oriented toward academic criteria. They tap only a subset, albeit an important one, of the domain of intelligence.
2. Infant intelligence tests have almost no predictive validity.
3. Scholastic aptitude continues to develop until about age 18.
4. Deviation IQ scores are superior to ratio IQ scores because, unlike ratio IQs, their meaning is not obscured by fluctuations in standard deviation across various age levels. Because of the widespread misunderstanding of the IQ, many tests are discontinuing its use. Percentile ranks are less likely to be misinterpreted.
5. A high correlation between intelligence tests indicates that they are measuring common abilities but does not necessarily mean that the tests yield similar IQ scores.
6. High stability coefficients on intelligence tests represent the general consistency in scores, although the scores of some individuals may change dramatically.
7. Individual verbal intelligence tests tend to have greater IQ stability than group verbal tests.
8. IQ scores from verbal tests tend to have more stability than scores from nonverbal tests.
9. Intelligence test scores have a substantial relationship to academic achievement. The relationship tends to increase with grade level and is greater for verbal than for nonverbal tests.
10. There are no truly culture-free or culture-fair tests. Performance and nonverbal tests contain content that is less related to the environment of particular cultures and social classes.
11. Multiple-aptitude tests are widely used in vocational guidance. They are less exclusively academically oriented than general verbal intelligence tests.
12. Available creativity tests should not be viewed as valid measures of creativity.

IMPORTANT TERMS AND CONCEPTS

Scholastic aptitude vs. intelligence
Individual vs. group tests
Performance vs. verbal vs. nonverbal tests
Academic prediction tests (ACT, SAT, GRE)

Stanford-Binet Intelligence Scale
Wechsler Intelligence Scales (WAIS, WISC, WPPSI)
Structure of intellect (SI)
Deviation vs. ratio IQ
Mental age

IQ stability
Standard error of estimate
Multiaptitude battery (DAT)
Creativity tests

1. Intelligence tests are best viewed as
   a) measures of inate cognitive potential.
   b) reading tests.
   c) academic achievement tests.
   d) scholastic aptitude tests.

2. Which of the following types of early intelligence test items was *not* discarded because of lack of construct validity?
   a) Reaction time   b) Picture completion   c) Size of cranium
   d) sensory discrimination

3. Which type of mental ability test was developed first?
   a) Individual verbal   b) Individual performance
   c) Group verbal   d) Group nonverbal

4. Which of the following tests ordinarily is *not* used by colleges for selection decisions?
   a) GRE   b) SAT   c) ACT   d) WAIS

5. If IQ scores are used, which type is preferable?
   a) Deviation IQs   b) Ratio IQs

6. The value of σ is constant at all age levels with
   a) Deviation IQs   b) Ratio IQs

7. On most tests that yield IQ scores, the value of σ is approximately
   a) 9–10.   b) 12–13.   c) 15–16.   d) 18–20.

8. The standard error of measurement, σ_e, in IQ units on most intelligence tests is approximately
   a) 1 point.   b) 3 points.   c) 5 points.   d) 7 points.   e) 9 points.

9. On the Stanford-Binet, σ_e is least at (see Figure 13–8, p. 356)
   a) low IQ values.   b) average IQ values.
   c) high IQ values.   d) very high IQ values.

10. If the correlation between forms 1 and 2 of the ABC IQ test (parallel-form reliability) is .91 and $s = 16$, what is the value (rounded) of the standard error of measurement ($s_e = s\sqrt{1-r_{11}}$)?
    a) 3 points   d) 6 points
    b) 4 points   e) none of the above
    c) 5 points

11. If $r_{12} = 1.0$, which one of the following could not possibly be true?
    a) $\overline{X}_1 = 100$, $\overline{X}_2 = 110$ c) $\sigma_{2.1} = 5.0$
    b) $\sigma_1 = 12$, $\sigma_2 = 15$ d) $\sigma_e = 0.0$

12. Which of the regression-toward-the-mean tendencies is/are evident in Figure 13–11 (p. 360)?
    a) Low scorers at grade 5 tend to obtain higher IQ scores at grade 7.
    b) High scorers at grade 5 tend to obtain higher IQ scores at grade 7.

c) Average scorers at grade 5 tend to obtain higher IQ scores at grade 7.

d) Two of the above   e) All of the above

13. The validity of IQ scores from infant intelligence tests for predicting later IQ scores is

a) almost zero.   b) moderately high.   c) very high.

14. In Figure 13–10 (p. 359), is $\sigma_{2.1}$ another name for the standard error of measurement?

15. IQ scores on which type of test have the greatest degree of stability over several years?

a) Individual verbal tests   c) Group nonverbal tests

b) Group verbal tests

16. IQ scores on which type of test have the least degree of stability over several years?

a) Individual verbal tests   c) Group nonverbal tests

b) Group verbal tests

17. Which of these methods of reporting results of scholastic aptitude tests to students and parents is generally preferable?

a) Percentile ranks   c) Ratio IQs

b) Deviation IQs   d) Mental ages

18. The correlation between IQ scores and achievement is greater

a) in high school than in grades 4–6.

b) in grade 1 than in grade 6.

c) in math than in reading.

d) for nonverbal than for verbal tests.

Among whites, the IQs of which of the following correlate

a) Identical twins, reared apart

b) Siblings, reared together

c) Fraternal twins, reared together

d) Genetically unrelated children, reared together

e) Fraternal twins, reared apart

19. the lowest?

20. the highest?

21. Which of the following is certainly true of standardized intelligence tests?

a) They are direct measures of scholastic aptitude.

b) They reflect only environmental effects.

c) All races and ethnic groups would have exactly the same mean on all aptitude measures if environmental differences were removed.

d) They correlate highly with SES.

e) They are influenced by both hereditary and environmental factors.

22. Which of these statements pertaining to IQ and occupations is *not* correct? (See Figure 13–14, p. 367)
    a) The mean IQ score of blue-collar workers is less than that of white-collar workers.
    b) The mean IQ of individuals in several blue-collar occupations is above 100.
    c) There are very bright individuals in all occupations.
    d) There is great variability within all occupations.
    e) The variability within high-SES occupations is greater than within lower-SES occupations.

23. Using Figure 13–17 (p. 371), if Lola scored 50 on the DAT Space Relations Test, estimate the probability that she will receive a B grade or better in watch repair.
    a) 1.00   c) .40   e) .00
    b) .60   d) .20

24. The demonstrated validity of current creativity tests is
    a) very strong   c) very weak
    b) moderately strong

25. Which one of the following is most closely influenced by school-related achievement?
    a) Individual performance tests   d) Multiple-aptitude
    b) Group verbal tests   test batteries
    c) Group nonverbal tests   e) Creativity tests

ANSWERS TO CHAPTER TEST

1. d	10. c	19. d
2. b	11. c	20. a
3. a	12. a	21. e
4. d	13. a	22. e
5. a	14. no, $\sigma_{2.1} > \sigma_e$	23. c
6. a	15. a	24. c
7. c	16. c	25. b
8. c	17. a	
9. a	18. a	

FOR ADDITIONAL READING

ANASTASI, A. Heredity, environment, and the question "How?" *Psychological Review,* 65, no. 4 (1958), 197–208.

———. Culture fair testing. *Educational Horizons,* 43 (1964), 26–30. Re-printed in G. H. Bracht, K. D. Hopkins, and J. C. Stanley, eds., *Perspectives in educational and psychological measurement.* Englewood Cliffs, N.J.: Prentice-Hall, 1972. Selection 20.

——. Cross-cultural testing. In *Psychological testing,* 4th ed. New York: Macmillan, 1976. Pp. 287–98, 343–48.

CROCKENBERG, S. B. Creativity tests: Boon or boondoggle? *Review of Educational Research,* 42 (1972), 27–48.

CRONBACH, L. J. Heredity, environment, and educational policy. *Harvard Education Review,* 39 (1969), 338–47.

DuBois, P. H. *A history of psychological testing.* Boston: Allyn and Bacon, 1970.

EYSENCK, H. J. *Race, intelligence and education.* London: Maurice Temple Smith, 1971.

GUILFORD, J. P. *The nature of human intelligence.* New York: McGraw-Hill, 1967.

HOPKINS, K. D., and G. H. BRACHT. Ten-year stability of verbal and nonverbal IQ scores. *American Educational Research Journal,* 12 (1975), 469–77.

HORN, J. L. Intelligence—Why it grows, why it declines. *Trans-action,* 5, no. 1 (1967), 23–31.

JENSEN, A. R. *Bias in mental testing.* New York: Free Press, 1980.

LENNON, R. T. Perspective on intelligence testing. *NCME Measurement in Education,* 9 (1978), 1–8.

LOEHLIN, H. C., G. LINDZEY, and J. N. SPUHLER. *Race differences in intelligence.* San Francisco: W. H. Freeman, 1975.

MAGNUSSON, D., and G. BACKTEMAN. Longitudinal stability of person characteristics: Intelligence and creativity. *Applied Psychological Measurement,* 2 (1978), 481–90.

MEHRENS, W. A., and I. J. LEHMANN. *Measurement and evaluation in education and psychology,* 2nd ed. New York: Holt, Rinehart and Winston, 1975. Pp. 407–10, 435–40, 674–80.

McNEMAR, Q. Lost: Our intelligence. Why? *American Psychologist,* 19 (1964), 871–82.

National Council on Measurement in Education. On bias in selection. *Journal of Educational Measurement,* 13 (1976), 1–99.

National Institute of Education. *Testing, teaching, and learning.* Washington, D.C., 1979.

STANLEY, J. C. *Gifted and the creative: A fifty-year perspective.* Baltimore: Johns Hopkins University Press, 1977.

——. Predicting college success of the educationally disadvantaged. *Science,* 171 (1971), 640–47.

TERMAN, L. M. The discovery and encouragement of exceptional talent. *American Psychologist,* 9 (1954), 221–30.

U.S. Civil Service Commission. Uniform guidelines on employee selection procedures. *Federal Register,* 42, no. 251 (1977).

WOODRING, P. Are intelligence tests unfair? *Saturday Review,* April 16, 1966, pp. 79–80.

14

Standardized
Achievement
Tests

In Chapter 7 distinctions were made between standardized and nonstandardized tests. Standardized tests tend to be focused on broader, more general skills and kinds of information that would be included among the educational objectives of most school districts. Since they are ordinarily administered annually (or even less frequently), standardized achievement tests must span a much wider range of content than almost any teacher-constructed test. Teacher-made examinations should be given often to monitor pupil and class progress, to identify the need for remediation, to motivate students, and so on. Teacher-made tests are more specifically focused; they usually reflect only the content of a particular unit or course.

Advantages of Standardized Tests

The norms provided by standardized tests offer a comparison with an external group; such comparison is important for such purposes as quality control, curricular evaluation, academic and vocational counseling, and identifying exceptional students. External comparisons cannot be made readily with nonstandardized tests. Lay people often feel that the average percent correct on a test directly reflects the quality of teaching or learning; they fail to realize that a very poor teacher can construct a test that is so easy and non-discriminating that almost all students will turn in a perfect performance even if they have learned little. On the other hand, an excellent teacher could develop a difficult and discriminating test on which the average score may be only 60 percent or less.

Standardized tests impose more restrictions than teacher-made tests. The prescribed directions, time limits, and other controls of standardized tests demand that the conditions under which the tests are taken be *standard*. Only then is a meaningful basis for evaluating and comparing performance afforded.

Reliability is another point of difference between standardized and locally constructed tests. Standardized tests are usually carefully developed and refined by means of item analysis so that virtually every item functions appropriately. Most intrinsic ambiguity is removed, and implausible distractors are deleted; consequently, the reliability of most standardized tests is (and should be) greater than that of teacher-made tests. Some of the 1,500 standardized achievement tests are not highly reliable, but they are the exception rather than the rule. The number and frequency of teacher-made tests can easily compensate for the lack of high reliability of a single test. Although each of ten weekly quizzes may have a reliability of only .6, the reliability of scores summed over the ten measures would be expected to exceed .90. (See Spearman-Brown formula, p. 126.)

It should be clear that teacher-made and standardized achievement tests are partners rather than competitors. They serve somewhat different purposes and provide complementary information. Both kinds of test are needed for an adequate evaluation of educational achievement by individual students, schools, and school districts.

Aptitude Versus Achievement Tests

Intelligence and aptitude tests are future oriented—their focus is on subsequent performance. Achievement tests are past and present oriented—they register degree of learning or achievement following instruction. Aptitude tests are designed to reflect potential; achievement tests depict present proficiency. A valid musical-aptitude test administered prior to music instruction should predict with some degree of accuracy performance on a music proficiency measure *after* some period of instruction. Aptitude tests attempt to indicate what a person *could learn;* achievement tests represent what a person *has learned*.

In practice this distinction is less clear-cut (Green, 1974). Educational achievement tests predict subsequent achievement better than intelligence tests do (Bracht and Hopkins, 1970b). Intelligence tests reflect a great deal of educational achievement, such as vocabulary; and some achievement tests examine factors that are usually associated with intelligence, such as abstract reasoning and deductive and inductive logic.

Both aptitude and achievement tests reflect developed ability; the primary difference between them is largely in the nature of the test content and its level of generality. An implicit assumption in an achievement test (but not in an aptitude test) is that the examinees have been directly exposed to the content—the universe of content is specifically defined. An achievement test does not indicate how or why the student performs or does not perform, but it does represent his or her level of developed ability.

Anastasi (1976, p. 400) and Cronbach (1970, p. 282) present figures illustrating the concept of an achievement-aptitude continuum. (See Figure 14-1.) Existing tests of developed abilities can be ordered along this continuum. At one extreme are teacher-made tests covering highly specific and even idiosyncratic content. Standardized achievement tests are broader in objectives and content, but are more school-oriented than college admissions tests (ACT, SAT, GRE). Even less achievement oriented are most verbal intelligence tests (e.g., the Stanford-Binet). More general still are performance, nonlanguage, and "culture-fair" tests that may be administered to people who are illiterate or have language restrictions owing to physical or cultural factors.

In support of the continuum in Figure 14-1 are data showing that tests generally correlate most highly with their closest neighbors and progressively less as the separation increases. Some authorities maintain that standardized intelligence and achievement tests correlate so highly that they are essentially parallel forms of measures of the same abilities. Kelley (1927) found (as have others, e.g., Green, 1974) that correlation coefficients between certain achievement and intelligence measures were very high after allowance was made for errors of measurement. (See correcting for attenuation, p. 357.) Kelley consequently warned of the "jangle fallacy," which is committed when one assumes that tests with different labels measure different abilities. He also coined the phrase "jingle fallacy"—assuming that tests with the same labels measure the same functions. For example, one study (Hopkins, Dobson, & Oldridge, 1962) found that a reading vocabulary test correlated as highly with a reading comprehension test as it did with another reading vocabulary test.

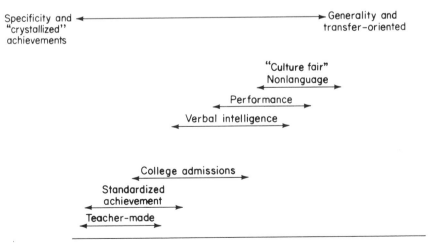

FIGURE 14-1 Spectrum of tests of cognitive abilities.

Another study (Farr & Roelke, 1971) found that a reading comprehension test correlated more highly with teachers' ratings of reading vocabulary than with teachers' ratings of reading comprehension. It is essential that each test establish its own validity.

Figure 14–2 was constructed to illustrate the overlapping variance on

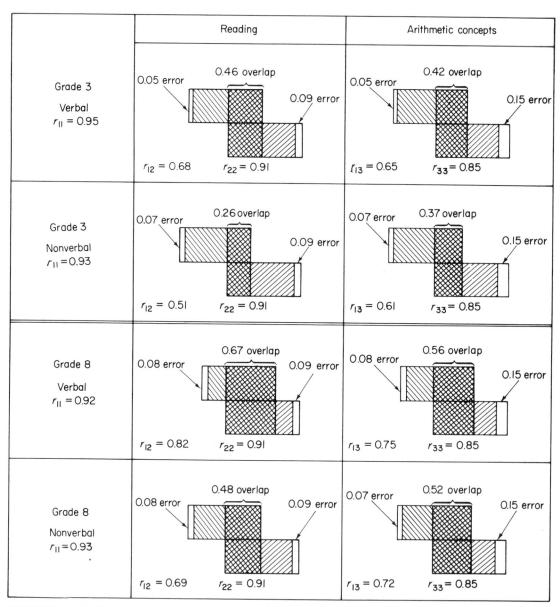

FIGURE 14-2 Degree of overlapping variance on two achievement areas of the Iowa Tests of Basic Skills for both verbal and nonverbal intelligence (Lorge-Thorndike) tests at two grade levels. Diagrams depict data from the technical manuals for the Lorge-Thorndike Intelligence Tests.

well-constructed intelligence and achievement tests. Data are depicted here for two grade levels for verbal and nonverbal intelligence measures. The reliability coefficient of a test indicates what proportion of total variance is true variance, that is, is not error variance. The area depicting true variance is indicated by slanting lines. The crosshatched pattern shows the overlapping variance (r_{12}^2) for each set of tests. For example, the proportions of nonerror variance for the grade 3 verbal intelligence, reading, and arithmetic concepts tests were found to be .95, .91, and .85, respectively. The verbal intelligence test correlated .68 with the reading test; thus, the overlapping (predictable) variance between the two tests was $(.68)^2 = .46$. Forty-six percent of the variance of the verbal intelligence test is true (nonerror) and is not unique to the reading test.

Figures 14–1 and 14–2 illustrate that although there is a substantial relationship between the achievement and scholastic aptitude measures, they have considerable uniqueness. This could also be inferred from our discussion in the preceding chapter; performance on achievement tests is influenced by environmental factors much more than performance on scholastic aptitude measures.

Content Validity

The critical type of validity for achievement tests is content validity, sometimes called content relevance. Does the test reflect the reading or arithmetic objectives at a given grade level? Does the math test reflect the related curriculum? Ideally, the items on an achievement test should be a representative sample of the content and process objectives of a curriculum. If a teacher assumes that the ABC and DEF arithmetic reasoning tests equally reflect arithmetic reasoning objectives and thus are equally valid measures in that school district, he or she is guilty of the "jingle fallacy." Often tests with the same label differ greatly in content, the taxonomy levels represented by their items, degree of speededness, and other important respects. Hopkins and Wilkerson (1965) showed that "parallel" forms within the same standardized achievement test battery can have different content validities for a given curriculum, and that a school district's average on the test might increase or decrease by .2 grade equivalent (GE), depending on the form selected. Publishers of most current standardized achievement tests provide a classification of the skills and content assessed in their tests. (See Figures 4–1 and 4–2, pp. 78, 80–81.) This type of breakdown is especially useful in selecting tests for a particular school or school district.

The pattern of a district's (or a pupil's) results from standardized tests is partially dependent on the test series being used. Several studies (Findley, 1963b; Stake, 1961; Taylor and Crandall, 1962) revealed that a district's average may vary considerably, depending on which test is used. A portion of the disparity is attributable to differential content validity; that is, one test mirrors the district's objectives and instruction more accurately than another. Some of the disparity may result from differences in the definition of grade equivalents (GEs). Some tests use medians; others use means to define GEs.

When distributions are skewed, the mean and median will yield different "averages." In addition, some tests use "modal" norms—norms based only on students who are of the modal or usual age for their grade. When the underage and overage pupils are eliminated from the norm group, the norms become more demanding because more students are nonpromoted than are double promoted, and the former tend to lower the average performance. Another reason for the lack of interchangeability of norms on standardized tests is that the reference groups are never completely comparable. Many school districts refuse to permit publishers to use their pupils for norming purposes; the percent of districts refusing to participate seems to be increasing. For example, in the norming of one educational test, almost one-half of the school districts contacted refused to participate in the test's norming (Hopkins and Sander, 1966). The lack of equivalence in norming populations is one of the chief reasons that it is usually best to select a companion set of intelligence and achievement tests (tests normed on the same students) and to employ the same achievement-test series over several grade levels. Whatever bias there is in the norms is constant for the tests. Thus, the 50th percentile has the same *relative* meaning on all the tests in the companion set, even if perfect norms would yield a somewhat different percentile. For this reason, also, it is advisable to stay with the same achievement battery across grade levels. Otherwise, differences resulting from noncomparable norm groups can appear to be due to ineffective instruction at given grade levels. Tables of comparable scores between various standardized achievement tests have been determined empirically (Jaeger, 1973), but these quickly become outdated because the tests are revised and/or renormed every 5–10 years.

Norming is the weakest link in standardized testing. There are, however, some promising developments on the horizon. Lord (1962a; Lord and Novick, 1968) has developed the theory and procedures by which, through item sampling, only a small portion of testing time is required in the norming process; that is, some students in a class take one short set of items while other students take other sets. Preliminary research on this topic is encouraging (Cook and Stufflebeam, 1967).

Several publishers now furnish normative data for individual items. This information has great value for evaluating the success of a class or district's instruction. Figure 14–3 is an analysis of a class's results on a standardized language arts test. Notice that the percent correct for each item is given for the class and for the national norm group. In the class, 82 percent of the pupils used correct capitalization at the beginning of the sentence, whereas 77 percent of the pupils in the national norm group were correct on that question. Information such as that given in Figure 14–3 can help diagnose instructional and curricular weaknesses of a class, school, or school district and can also serve a quality control function. Often, however, national norms are not the best basis for comparison; norms based on subgroups more like the local system may be preferable. Using the previous year's results as a basis for comparison is often the most useful way to detect trends in performance within a school, district, or state.

Group Item Analysis

Provided by grade for any or all curriculum areas, as specified. The report can be based on grade groups in a school or system.

SRA Achievement Series — Group Item Analysis

BOWIE SCHOOL	WOODSTOCK CITY	IN STATE
DUNN TEACHER OR GROUP	6 GRADE	2 SEM
F TEST LEVEL	4-25-79 DATE TESTED	1 FORM
81213-006 SRA REFERENCE NO	81217 TAPE NO	1 PAGE NO

CODE NO. 7-6695

Column headings for each panel: ITEM NUMBER · GROUP CORRECT RESPONSE · GROUP PERCENT OMIT · GROUP PERCENT CORRECT · *NATIONAL PERCENT CORRECT

READING — VOCABULARY (Literal Meanings / Non Literal Meanings)

Item	Resp.	Omit	Group %	*Nat'l %
1	C	03	68	64
2	B	02	45	50
3	D	05	39	52
4	A	05	75	71
5	C	03	86	80
6	D	02	78	82
7	D	04	62	70
8	C	02	54	68
9	C	03	58	65
10	A	04	47	50
11	B	04	66	70
12	A	02	59	55
13	C	03	72	69
14	D	01	67	66
15	B	02	63	58
16	B	02	76	73
17	C	05	49	62
18	B	05	37	45
19	D	01	88	80
20	A	02	71	83

COMPREHENSION — Grasping Details / Summarizing / Perceiving Relationships

Item	Resp.	Omit	Group %	*Nat'l %
21	B	04	47	50
22	A	04	66	70
23	B	02	59	55
24	C	03	72	69
25	B	01	67	60
26	D	02	63	58
27	D	02	76	73
28	A	04	49	62
29	C	05	37	45
30	C	01	88	80
31	D	03	71	83
32	D	03	68	64
33	A	02	45	50
34	D	05	39	52
35	B	05	75	71
36	C	03	86	80
37	C	02	78	82
38	A	04	62	70
39	A	02	54	68
40	D	03	58	65

COMPREHENSION — Grasping Details / Summarizing / Perceiving Relationships (continued)

Item	Resp.	Omit	Group %	*Nat'l %
11	B	01	88	80
13	D	02	49	62
18	D	02	58	58
24	D	03	72	69
27	D	01	66	70
38	D	04		65
48	B	04	86	70
50	A	03		80
4		05	39	52
12	B	03	68	64
16	B	02	45	50
22	C	05	75	71
34	C	02	78	82
42	A	02	54	68
47	D	04	47	50
1	D	02	59	55
2	A	01	67	60
6	C	02	76	73
8	C	05	37	40
17	C	05	71	83
20	D	05	39	52
21	D	02	78	82
26	D	02	58	65
28	A	02	59	55
30	C	05	37	45
32	B	05	68	64
35	A	03	75	71
39	C	05	75	71
43	B	04	62	70
46	C	05	48	53

COMPREHENSION — Drawing Conclusions / Understanding Author (PAGE 1)

Item	Resp.	Omit	Group %	*Nat'l %
5	D	01	65	64
7	C	03	76	81
9	B	05	49	45
19	B	03	53	52
25	C	03	56	54
29	B	04	73	70
33	D	03	75	68
36	B	05	67	65
37	D	03	70	75
40	C	01	64	68
41	A	06	36	42
45	B	02	51	58
3	B	04	59	66
10	A	03	74	83
14	A	03	69	73
15	D	01	73	69
23	A	02	81	86
31	B	04	49	54
44	A	01	57	60
49	C	02	63	70

*NATIONAL PERCENT RESPONDING CORRECTLY BASED ON SAME GRADE AND SEMESTER AS THIS REPORT

Legend:

A Grade group for whom report is made.
B Teacher's name.
C Test level.
D Curriculum area.
E Item cluster within area.
F Test item number.
G Correct response for item.
H Percent of group omitting item.
I Percent of group who answered item correctly.
J Percent of national grade group who answered item correctly.

All information on these reports is simulated.

FIGURE 14-3 A sample report of class performance on each item of a standardized language arts test, together with national norms for each item. (From the *SRA Achievement Series*. Copyright © 1978, Science Research Associates, Inc. Reprinted by permission of the publisher.)

Some tests provide school norms as well as individual student norms. Figure 14-4 shows the difference in the distributions of school averages and individual pupil scores. Notice that a score of 15 on the test has a percentile rank (PR) of about 76 in the student distribution but a PR of about 99 in terms of school averages; in other words, nearly 27 students in 100 earn a score of 15 or more, whereas only one school in 100 has an average of 15 or more. School norms are less valuable than individual norms, but they can complement the individual information when interpreted properly. The distribution of school *district* means compared to the distribution of pupil scores is very similar to that shown in Figure 14-4 (CSDE, 1977).

Later in this chapter, guidelines are given for selecting standardized tests for a school's testing program. In addition to the logical relevance of the items and other technical considerations, one should appraise the kinds of service available, the time lag between testing and results, and the types of student, class, school and district reports.

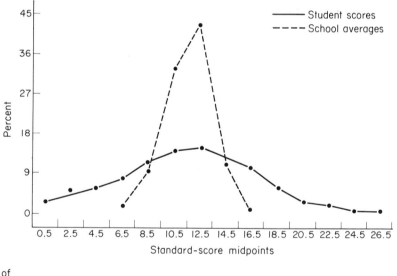

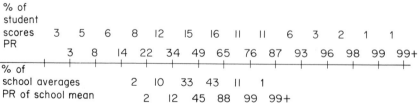

FIGURE 14-4 Differences between school average percentiles and student percentiles. (From the *SRA Test and Guidance Catalog*, © 1973, Science Research Associates, Inc. Reproduced by permission.)

The use of grade-equivalent (GE) norms is the most common method for reporting results on pre-high school standardized achievement tests (Echternacht, 1977). To interpret GE scores properly one must understand how the grade equivalents are established. How can a third-grade child earn a reading score of 8.0 on a test? Interpolation and extrapolation are two procedures used in the determination of grade equivalents.

Suppose that in the standardization process a reading test is given during September to students in grades 4, 5, and 6. The means (or medians) for each grade level are determined; suppose the raw-score means were 24, 40, and 47. (See Figure 14-5.) The respective grade equivalents corresponding to these three scores would be 4.0, 5.0, and 6.0. How does one obtain a GE of 4.5? The difference in the raw-score means of 4.0 and 5.0 is arbitrarily divided into tenths; each tenth corresponds to a GE of 0.1. A raw score of 32 would yield a GE of 4.5. The raw score corresponding to any GE score can be found by reading up from the GE value.

This interpolation procedure assumes a constant rate of growth throughout the year. Empirical studies (Beggs & Hieronymus, 1968; Conklin, Burstein & Kessling, 1979) have demonstrated that this assumption only roughly approximates the true growth curves in various achievement areas. There are such marked discrepancies in arithmetic over the summer (Bernard, 1966) that the same group may average .5 GE less in September than it did the previous June! The same phenomenon, of course, would result whether GE, percentiles, or stanines were used for describing performance. *The safest procedure to prevent interpolation artifacts from contaminating the meaning of scores from standardized achievement tests is to administer the tests during the same period in the school year that was employed in the standardization process.*

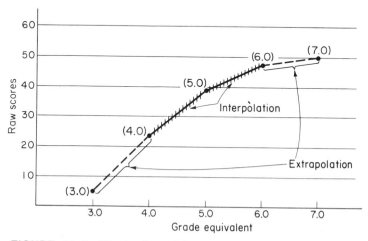

FIGURE 14-5 Illustration of interpolation and extrapolation in establishing grade-equivalent norms.

For some standardized achievement tests the norms were determined empirically at the beginning, middle, and end of the school year, so interpolation artifacts are minimal. Norms for most tests, however, were established from a single administration period during the school year; hence, they must rely more heavily on the validity of the interpolation process.

Extrapolation can result in even greater errors in the interpretation of individual scores. Extrapolation is the most common method for establishing GE values at grade levels outside the range of grades to which the test was actually administered. It is simply a projection of the average performance at some grade levels from the performance of pupils at certain other grade levels. In our interpolation example we gave raw-score means of 24, 40, and 47 for the standardization sample at grades 4.0, 5.0, and 6.0, respectively. This leads one to assume that the mean score at grade 7 would be approximately 50; hence, a score of 50 would receive a GE of 7.0. Similarly, a score of 5 might be predicted to correspond to the average performance at grade 3. Extrapolation is obviously a risky process. As the GE values extend beyond the grades actually sampled during the norming, their credibility is lessened. Figure 14-6 is taken from the technical manual of a widely used standardized achievement battery. Notice that all GE values below 4.6 and above 9.6 were extrapolated;

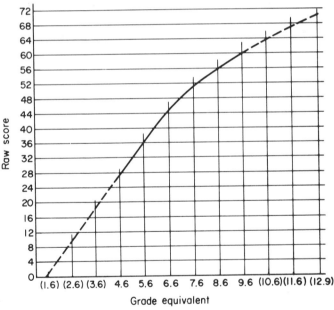

FIGURE 14-6 Grade norm line—social studies. Values below 4.6 and above 9.6 are extrapolations. (From Stanford Achievement Test, Technical Supplement [New York: Harcourt Brace Jovanovich, Inc.], by special permission of the publisher.)

thus, scores below 4.6 and above 9.6 must be interpreted with great caution. Fortunately, there is a tendency in test norming to administer a test above and below the actual grade levels for which it was designed; this procedure provides a much stronger basis for attaching meaning to the GE scores. Even with this procedure, extreme GE scores in relation to a pupil's present grade level must be interpreted with caution. A third-grade pupil and a seventh-grade pupil who received GE scores of 5.0 on an arithmetic test would obtain the same raw score, but they would probably obtain them via different routes and have different arithmetic skills, although one study (Plake & Hoover, 1979) found that the meaning of a GE score is relatively independent of the grade level of the examinee.

A distinct advantage of GE scores is that they help teachers realize the true magnitude of individual differences within a single grade level. Figure 14–7 depicts the actual distribution of performance for grades 2.6–10.6 Note the very large degree of overlap—about one-sixth of third-grade students are performing better than the average student at grade 4. Note also that the variability in achievement increases with each successive grade level. This is true in all achievement areas and is to be expected because the standard deviation of mental ages increases each year until maturity.

Grade equivalents can easily be misinterpreted by parents. "If my third-grade child is reading 4.0, why shouldn't she be promoted to grade 4?" Parents are unaware of the large degree of individual differences within a given grade as shown in Figure 14–7; thus, they do not realize that such a "good" showing on the test will be made by 15 to 20 percent of the pupils in the same third-grade class, or even more in schools where the verbal aptitude is above average. Despite their technical flaws, percentile ranks are probably the preferred method of reporting achievement and aptitude test results to parents.

Another problem with GE scores is that the standard deviations in GE units are not the same for all curricular areas. For example, Table 14–1 shows the standard deviations on the Comprehensive Tests of Basic Skills (CTBS) at grades 3, 5, 7, and 9. Note that these GE scores become more variable with each successive grade. The variability in reading and language tends to be somewhat larger than that in mathematics. If a child in grade 3 (3.0) was at the 98th percentile on all tests of the CTBS, his or her GE scores would vary from about 8.0 for language mechanics to 5.2 for math computation. If the corresponding percentile ranks are reported along with GEs, the chances of misinterpreting them are reduced.

Flanagan (1951, pp. 712–13) summarized the role of GE scores as follows:

> In spite of their many limitations, they [grade equivalents] probably represent the best of available methods for rendering scores "comparable" for elementary school achievement tests. . . . To date the consensus seems to be in favor of the use of grade equivalent scales below grade eight, and some type of [standard score] in high school and college.

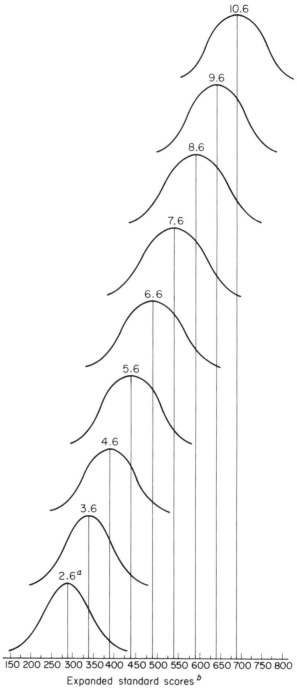

150 200 250 300 350 400 450 500 550 600 650 700 750 800

Expanded standard scores [b]

[a]Test administered during sixth month of school year; grade equivalents of corresponding standard scores are given above the mean of each curve.
[b]Scale employs a mean of 600 and a standard deviation of 100 at grade 10.1

TABLE 14-1

STANDARD DEVIATIONS OF GRADE-EQUIVALENT SCORES ON THE COMPREHENSIVE TESTS OF BASIC SKILLS (CTBS) AT GRADES 3, 5, 7, AND 9 (DATA FROM *CTBS TECHNICAL BULLETIN*)

Test	Grade Level			
	3	5	7	9
Reading Vocabulary	1.6	2.2	2.8	3.0
Reading Comprehension	2.0	2.8	3.2	3.5
Total Reading	1.6	2.4	2.9	3.1
Spelling	2.0	2.9	3.3	3.5
Language Mechanics	2.5	3.4	3.7	3.9
Language Expression	2.4	3.1	3.5	3.7
Total Language	2.2	2.8	3.2	3.5
Mathematics Computation	1.1	2.0	2.8	3.3
Mathematics Concepts	1.8	2.4	2.8	3.2
Mathematics Applications	1.7	2.5	3.0	3.4
Total Mathematics	1.3	2.0	2.7	3.2
Reference Skills	2.0	2.8	3.2	3.4
Science	2.1	2.9	3.2	3.5
Social Studies	1.9	2.8	3.2	3.5
Total Battery	1.6	2.2	2.7	3.0

The lack of continuity in subject matter after grade 8 is a major reason that the logical meaning of GE scores is greatly reduced beyond that grade. There is little growth in certain basic skills during the high school grades; consequently, a small increment in performance often results in a large gain in grade placement units. For example, a raw score of 18 on the Comprehensive Tests of Basic Skills, Language-Mechanics test, corresponds to a GE score of 10.1, but a raw score of 19 corresponds to a GE score of 11.9. This correspondence reflects the smallness of the typical improvement in the eleventh grade of the type of language mechanics measured by this test.

Some standardized tests are accompanied by "expanded standard score scales" that are particularly useful for sequentially evaluating pupil and school growth across several years. These are continuous scales that span several levels of a test. Figure 14-8 illustrates the growth curves of a group and of a student from grade 2 to grade 12. Notice that at grade 8 the student begins to fall behind the class in performance. This type of report is particularly valuable in evaluating the progress of an individual or group.

FIGURE 14-7 (on facing page) An illustration of the great degree of overlap in pupils' achievement performance among grade levels. (Note that approximately one-sixth of grade 2 students [i.e., @ 2.6] received better scores than one-half of grade 3 students [i.e., @ 3.6]. Similarly, approximately one-sixth of grade 3 students received lower scores than one-half of the students in grade 2.) (Reproduced from Technical Memo, Expanded Standard Score Scale used in the CTBS, by permission of the publisher, CTB/McGraw-Hill, Monterey, California.)

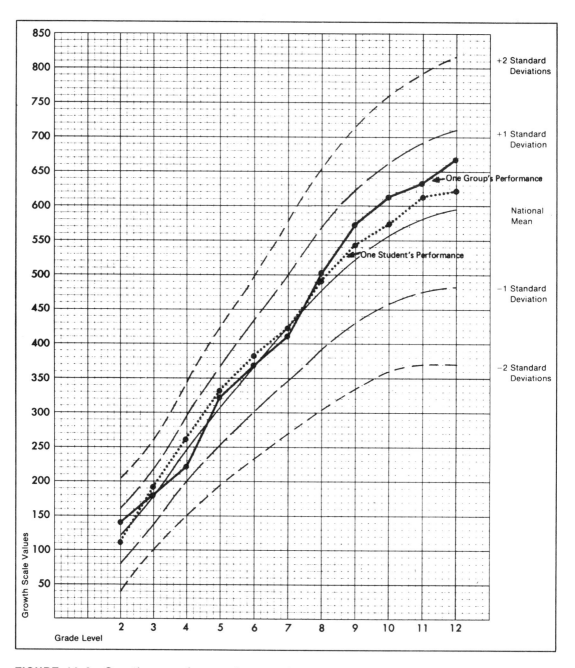

FIGURE 14-8 Growth curves for one class and for one student in the class for grades 2 through 12. Individual growth scale curves allow a student's performance to be compared both in relation to the group's performance and in relation to national performance. (Reproduced by permission of the publisher, Science Research Associates. Copyright by Science Research Associates, Inc.)

One of the chief uses of standardized achievement and intelligence tests is to identify students who need special attention. Dual standardization is very common today—students in the norming population are given both a battery of achievement tests and a scholastic aptitude test. It is then possible to compare a student's achievement with that of pupils at the same grade level and with the same measured scholastic aptitude. The student's "expectancy" or "anticipated achievement" can be approached empirically. This method of identifying underachieving pupils is far superior to that of comparing a student's percentile ranks on an intelligence test with those on an achievement test—a procedure that will always "find" a large proportion of bright students to be "underachieving" and a corresponding proportion of students with low IQs to be achieving "well" in relation to their aptitude. Comparison of percentile ranks fails to acknowledge the universal regression effect (Hopkins, 1969).

Figure 14–9 depicts a standard report form for Ann Roberts, who has taken the Comprehensive Tests of Basic Skills during the first month of grade 5 (5.1). Raw scores (RS), grade equivalents (GE), anticipated achievement grade equivalents (AAGE), and the national percentile ranks corresponding to the raw scores are given for several achievement areas. The profile chart shows the range within which Ann's true score is likely to lie (her score ± one standard error of measurement). This chart helps prevent undue confidence in obtained scores and encourages the viewing of a score as a band rather than as a precise point.

Ann's raw score of 26 on the reading vocabulary test corresponded to a GE score of 5.1 and a percentile rank of 52. The profile chart shows that her *true* percentile rank is probably (68 percent confidence interval) somewhere between 40 and 63. The AAGE of 5.5 is the average score for students of the same age, grade, and SFTAA IQ. The "Difference" column for reading vocabulary is blank, indicating that there is no statistically significant (or reliable) difference between Ann's performance in reading vocabulary and that of other students of the same age, grade, and SFTAA IQ.

Ann had an outstanding performance in spelling (8.4); her obtained GE score was three full grade equivalents above her AAGE. Perhaps she needs to devote more attention to arithmetic, in which she is achieving 1.4 GEs below other students of her age, grade, and scholastic aptitude.

The bottom portion of the CTBS individual test record shows Ann's performance on each item. Her deficiency in arithmetic computation is rather general; she lacks mastery of all basic operations. She appears to be especially lacking in ability to interpret and analyze arithmetic concepts. Ann appears to need a general remedial program in arithmetic. If her IQ had been lower—for example, 80—her arithmetic performance would have been commensurate with her AAGE. If her IQ had been 130, all the AAGE values would have increased substantially.

The report of a student's performance in such a complete and explicit form has become feasible only since computers became part of the test scoring

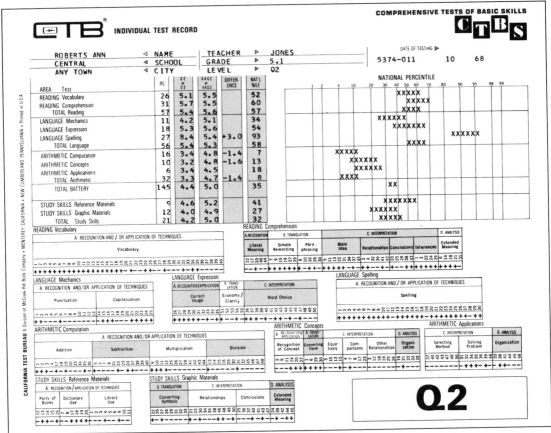

FIGURE 14-9 Sample of individual feedback form used to report the performance of Ann Roberts on a battery of standardized achievement tests. (Reproduced from *Individual Test Record for CTBS* by permission of the publisher, CTB/McGraw-Hill, Monterey, California.)

and reporting process. This kind of report is more valuable than the typical report of the past, which would have given only the student's IQ, GE scores, and, perhaps, corresponding percentile ranks. This kind of test reporting should greatly reduce over- and underinterpretation of standardized-test results.

Test publishers have recently begun to market "criterion-referenced standardized achievement tests." These tests attempt to be diagnostic. Most have no norms to aid in interpreting performance. It is uncertain whether they will provide instructionally functional information for individual pupils; they have all the difficulties of other CRT measures (see pp. 182–187) and also add a considerable expense to testing budgets that typically are already strained. When the items of survey-type achievement tests are classified by objective, as most are, the item-level data can provide a useful "diagnostic" profile at the class, school, or school district level (but not at the pupil level, since there are too few items per objective to keep measurement error from "swamping" the results).

Sampling of the Content Universe

A test cannot have high content validity unless the items are a representative sample of the curricular objectives in skills and content. The upper portion of Figure 14-10 shows that in certain curricular areas, such as reading, there exists a large common core of content, objectives, and sequence of instruction among school districts and states. The lower portion of the figure represents certain other curricular areas, in which there is only a small common core, as in social studies, where there are great differences in content and instructional approaches among states, among school districts, and even among schools within a district. This lack of curricular communality has created severe obstacles to developing highly content-valid standardized tests in these areas. Test developers tend to assess only within the common core of content and objectives; hence, the items are not a representative sample for any school or district—the objectives measured are only a limited subset of the school or district's objectives. This is especially true in social studies, which has the smallest degree of curricular commonality; for example, it is very common in grade 4 to study one's own state, which obviously cannot be included in a na-

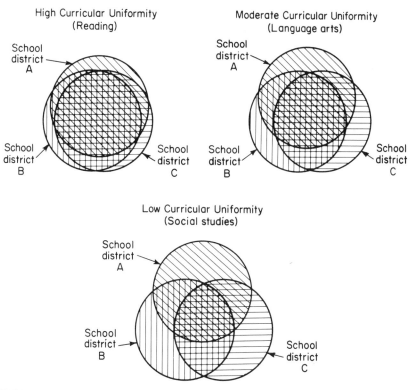

FIGURE 14-10 Graphic illustrations of the "core of curricular commonality" among American elementary schools for curricula with high, moderate, and low uniformity.

tional test. Thus, standardized tests in social studies, and to a lesser extent science and language arts, do not *re-present* the school's curriculum as well as tests in reading and math do. This is the principal reason that standardized reading (and to a lesser extent math) tests have greater content validity than standardized achievement tests in other curricular areas.

Teachers' Ratings as Validation Criteria

The differential validity pattern just described is corroborated when teachers' ratings of students' performance levels are employed as a criterion for validity. When teachers are properly oriented to rate (or rank) the extent to which their students have achieved curricular objectives in reading, the resulting ratings correlate very highly with scores obtained on reliable standardized reading tests. (Obviously, not all standardized tests are good tests.) These correlations often fall in the .8–.9 range, which is extremely high, approaching the parallel-form reliability of the reading test (Hopkins, Dobson & Oldridge, 1962; Farr & Roelke, 1971; Kretke et al., 1976). In other words, in less than an hour the better standardized reading tests can provide an objective assessment that is confirmed by the assessment of a professional based on many hours of careful observation in a wide variety of contexts. Thus, to assert, as some critics have, that multiple-choice tests are only "guessing games," and that the tests have little validity, is in the same breath an indictment of the professional competence of teachers and even of reading specialists (Farr & Roelke, 1971).

Correlations between standardized achievement tests and school marks tend to be substantial (.5–.6), but considerably less than with teachers' ratings of proficiency levels; no doubt because marks are alloyed with grading philosophy, effort, deportment, and other factors that are irrelevant to the purposes of standardized achievement tests.

Using teachers' ratings as a validity criterion, reading tests (especially tests of reading vocabulary) have the greatest validity, followed by math, language arts, science, and social studies tests, in roughly that order. When interpreting the results from standardized achievement tests, either at the pupil level or at the class, school, district, or state level, this factor must be considered—reading and math scores should be taken more seriously than scores in social studies and science.

"Out-of-Level" Testing

A standardized test designed for a particular grade level sometimes is inappropriate in difficulty for a given school, class, or pupil. If the average IQ score of a fourth-grade class is 85 or 90, more valid scores will result if the "out-of-level" test designed for grade 3 is used. When a test is too difficult for a class or a given student, gambling, speed-vs.-accuracy response styles, and chance can result in invalid and misleading scores. A child can often receive a near-average score on a standardized test without even reading the items on the test but, instead, guessing "blindly" on all questions (Hopkins, 1964b; Swan and Hopkins, 1965).

The user of standardized tests must realize that the entire educational story is not represented by the results from those tests. For example, one of the widely used batteries of standardized tests measures the important educational skill of listening. Standardized test data are important, but they are only "fragments of the picture." And there are fewer fragments in certain curricular areas than in others.

Special Problems of Standardized Testing in High School

From elementary school to high school the nature of the curriculum changes radically. In the elementary grades the curriculum is usually quite similar for all the pupils in a school district, but at the high school level considerable "branching" occurs. There is great flexibility even in college-preparatory programs. The common curriculum for all high school students has virtually disappeared, except perhaps in English. This is a major reason for the fact that there is little meaning in grade-equivalent units for most content areas after grade 8 or 9.

Two approaches have been initiated toward solving the problem of standardized testing in the secondary schools. One approach is represented by the widely used Iowa Tests of Educational Development (ITED). The ITED are general education tests. They predict subsequent performance on the College Board examinations and academic success in college quite well. The tests in the ITED battery are the following:

1. Reading Comprehension
2. Reading Vocabulary
3. Language Usage
4. Spelling
5. Mathematics
6. Social Studies
7. Science
8. Uses of Sources

The test titles indicate the general nature of the ITED tests. But this *general* nature is a two-edged sword. The ITED do not presuppose a fixed set of courses for the examinees; nevertheless, the general nature of the examinations severely limits their value for the evaluation of the quality of learning and instruction in specific courses such as Algebra I, American History, or Chemistry.

The second approach to standardized testing at the high school level offers tailor-made tests for specific courses and subjects. These tests are less general and more content oriented than the ITED tests. Examples of such tests are the Nelson Biology Tests, the MLA Cooperative Foreign Language Tests, the Lankton First-Year Algebra Test, the Purdue High School English Test, the Anderson-Fisk Chemistry Test, the Crary American History Test, and the College Entrance Examination Board achievement tests.

The two approaches can be used so that they are mutually complementary. The course-oriented examinations are of greater value in identifying specific weaknesses in a particular curriculum. They offer the teacher or department useful feedback on teaching success because norms on an external reference group are available. The general achievement tests are better as a *general* educational quality control measure, but they are not of great value in identifying specific educational deficiencies in a high school student or a curriculum.

In addition to the tests mentioned earlier, there is a set of standardized subject examinations for college courses that are used primarily to give people who have acquired their education by unconventional means a chance to receive advanced placement and college credit at many colleges. Tests are available in American government, general psychology, geology, Western civilization, English literature, and approximately fifty other subjects. Standardized achievement tests in most college majors—the GRE Advanced Tests—are widely used as one of the criteria for admission to graduate degree programs.

The National Assessment of Educational Progress (NAEP)

The U.S. Office of Education was formed ''for the purpose of collecting such statistics and facts as shall show the condition and progress of education in the several States . . . and of diffusing such information''—Act of Congress, March 2, 1867. Despite that century-old charge, the federal government has collected few meaningful facts on the quality of education in U.S. schools.

In 1964 the Carnegie Corporation and the Ford Foundation were instrumental in the establishment of a committee under the chairmanship of Ralph W. Tyler to explore the feasibility of procedures for securing dependable information that could become a barometer of the progress of education. The committee developed a careful plan to assess achievement at four age levels: 9, following the primary grades; 13, following elementary school; 17, the last age before heavy dropout from school occurs; and young adults. Public, private, and parochial schools are sampled, as well as youth who are not in school at all. Not only are the achievements of the total U.S. population considered, but certain subpopulations in the country can be viewed separately. The sample of 20,000 to 30,000 persons at each age level is broken down by sex, region (northeast, southeast, central, and west), type of community (large city, urban fringe, smaller city, and rural small town), and socioeconomic level. Figure 14–11 presents illustrative findings: comparative data by sex and color for representative 17-year-olds.

Subject Areas Assessed

Selected curricular areas (reading, writing, science, mathematics, social studies, literature, music, art, citizenship, career and occupational development, and related affective variables) are covered by means of a cycling approach; each subject matter field is assessed every three to five years.

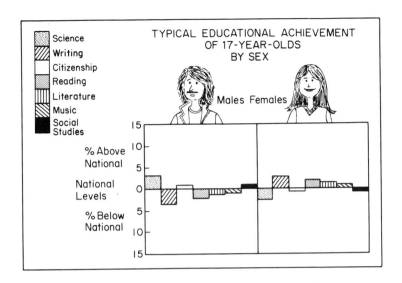

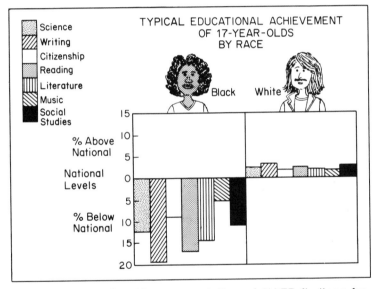

FIGURE 14-11 Graphic representation of NAEP findings for 17-year-olds. (From NAEP, 1975, pp. 16–18.)

Results of the tests are not pinpointed by class, school district, or states in order to prevent any invidious comparisons and pressure to "teach for the tests." Misunderstandings about the use of the findings resulted in considerable controversy during the development of the National Assessment Program.

The assessment reporting plan calls for the withholding of part of the exercises in each subject area so that they may be reused in the next assessment

TABLE 14-2

SAMPLE ITEM AND RESULTS FOR 17-YEAR-OLDS FROM THE NATIONAL ASSESSMENT OF EDUCATIONAL PROGRESS, BY YEAR, REGION, SEX, RACE, AND TYPE OF COMMUNITY

Suppose that a rubber balloon filled with air does not leak and that it is taken from earth to the moon. One can be sure that, on the moon, the balloon will have the same

   (1) size as on earth.
*(2) mass as on earth.
   (3) weight as on earth.
   (4) rate of fall as on earth.
   (5) ability to float as on earth.
   (6) I don't know.

	Percentages of 17-Year-Olds[a] Giving Correct Response			Percent Change	
	'69	'73	'77	'69 to '77	'73 to '77
All 17's	36	27	29	−7	+2
N. East	39	24	32	−7	+8
S. East	28	23	25	−3	+2
Central	32	30	28	−4	−2
West	41	29	31	−10	+2
Male	45	35	37	−8	+2
Female	27	20	21	−6	+1
Black	17	15	12	−5	−3
White	39	30	32	−7	+2
Other	22	16	18	−4	+2
LM[b]	27	20	14	−13	−6
HM[b]	52	35	31	−21	−4
Rural	22	28	30	+8	+2

[a] Refers to all 17-year-olds in school.

[b] In metropolitan areas surrounding cities with over 200,000 population, LM ("low metro") designates communities with the highest proportions of persons on welfare or unemployed while HM ("high metro") designates communities with the highest proportion of persons who are professional or white-collar workers.

cycle for purposes of comparison. The National Assessment Program promises "to provide useful indicators of educational progress."

Sample data for one science question are given in Table 14–2. Note that results are broken down by year, geographic region, sex, race, and type of community.

The NAEP data offer the strongest evidence for the "achievement decline." Notice in Table 14–2 that every subgroup except "Rural" performed better in 1969 than in 1973 or 1977. For the sample item, the downward trend did not continue during the 1973–1977 interval, providing some evidence of a "bottoming out" of the achievement decline (Munday, 1979). The 1978 NAEP results in math, however, continue to show a 1–4% drop from 1973 findings (NAEP, 1979). By and large, the downward trend has been evident in state assessments as well. Many states, following NAEP's lead and the public demand for accountability, have ongoing programs for monitoring student achievement.

It is the exception rather than the rule when a school district invests the time and effort necessary for a sound program of evaluation and testing. The tests selected and used too often depend more on the quality of the publishers' salespeople than on the quality of the product. There is rarely a systematic program to help teachers properly interpret and use the results of the tests. It is not surprising that many teachers question the value of standardized testing.

The Purpose of the Testing Program

It must be acknowledged that tests are only tools and that measurement is always a means to an end, never an end in itself. Thus, the value of any testing program depends on the use made of results. An experienced educator was once heard to say that he had wondered for years what many people did with standard tests after they had been "given." At last he found out. They filed them! Little instructional use is often made of standardized test results above the elementary-school level (Olejnik, 1979).

The initial step in planning a testing program is to make its purposes explicit. The most common purposes include the following:

1. *Quality control and public accountability.* National norms can provide a meaningful reference group for assessing the general level of academic achievement of a school or school district, especially when considered in relation to level of scholastic aptitude and socioeconomic factors. The taxpayers have a right to know the general level of academic achievement in their schools. The achievement trends within the district can also be monitored to determine, for example, whether the district is escaping the achievement decline. Annual reporting of test results can enhance professional credibility and public relations.

2. *Curricular and program evaluation.* Standardized tests can be a useful yardstick for identifying strengths and weaknesses in the curriculum and special programs. For example, parents of Spanish-speaking children in one bilingual program were concerned that the time spent in Spanish instruction might impede their children's progress in English. Comparing the students' test performance to that of similar students at the same school and grade levels for the previous year was useful in this regard.

3. *Individual student assessment and diagnosis.* Standardized tests can serve as an objective measure of the general level of educational attainment of particular pupils. This level of attainment can be compared with that of students of similar aptitude nationwide in order to identify a student's strengths and deficiencies. Achievement trends over grade level can be studied for the student. Other related purposes include grouping, identifying underachievers, identifying the academically talented, and helping students make appropriate educational and vocational choices. Standardized test results should be routinely communicated to the students' parents to help them arrive at a realistic understanding of the child's achievement status and

405

progress. Exemplary schools had a policy of school–home communication and disclosure of relevant information long before the "Buckley Amendment" was passed.[1]

A Cooperative Program

The testing program should be a truly cooperative enterprise. Parents, teachers, and administrators should be made to feel that it is "their" program, as indeed it should be. This is not likely to occur if the principal, superintendent, or research department determines the program and then "hands it down" to the classroom teachers. The entire staff and community should have a voice in determining the purpose of the program and in formulating the plans; they should have the opportunity to participate in it in every way possible from beginning to end. If this is not done, the teachers are not likely to understand the program fully or to appreciate what it is attempting to achieve. It is better to entrust the responsibility of planning the program to a committee representing all interested groups. The success of the program depends largely on cooperative action. An important part of the program is thus conducting a need-assessment survey of parents, students, teachers, administrators, and school board members.

On the basis of the district's needs, a testing program should be proposed, including which curricular areas are to be tested at each grade level. Figure 14-12 represents the testing program of the Boulder Valley School District.

Selecting the Appropriate Test or Tests

After the purposes of the testing program have been determined, the test or tests must be selected. Tests with the same title differ greatly in quality (beware of the "jingle" fallacy).

Criteria for test selection should be established against which available tests will be screened. These criteria should include content validity (including taxonomy levels of items), reliability, recency of norms, representativeness of norms, availability of item-level norms, testing time required, ease of ad-

---

[1] The "Buckley Amendment" (the Family Educational Rights and Privacy Act of 1974 and the Educational Amendments Act of 1974) demands that all educational institutions must, on request, make test results available to students and/or their parents. Specifically, parents are given the right

> to inspect and review any and all official records, files, and data directly related to their children, including all material that is incorporated into each student's cumulative record folder, and intended for school use to be available to parties outside the school or school system, and specifically including, but not necessarily limited to, identifying data, academic work completed, level of achievement (grades, standardized achievement test scores), attendance data, scores on standardized intelligence, aptitude, and psychological tests, interest inventory results, health data, family background information, teacher or counselor ratings and observations, and verified reports of serious or recurrent behavior patterns.

Although the federal government has no direct constitutional authority over educational agencies, the control is exerted indirectly through threats to discontinue federal funds to schools that do not operate according to federal prescriptions.

	Grade level											
	1	2	3	4	5	6	7	8	9	10	11	12
Reading	✓	✓	✓	✓	✓	✓	✓		✓		✓	
Mathematics	✓	✓	✓	✓	✓	✓	✓		✓		✓	
Language Arts			✓	✓	✓	✓	✓		✓		✓	
Science				✓	✓	✓	✓		✓		✓	
Social Studies					✓	✓	✓	✓		✓		✓
Scholastic Aptitude			✓	✓	✓	✓	✓		✓		✓	
*School-Related Attitudes					✓		✓		✓		✓	

*Results on these measures are not reported for individual students.

FIGURE 14-12 An illustrative standardized testing program for a school district. (From Kretke et al., 1976.)

ministration, scoring, co-norming with a comparision scholastic aptitude test, types of converted scores available, articulation across grade levels, costs and reporting aids and services.

Standardized tests differ considerably with respect to technical and nontechnical criteria. In one analysis (Stanley and Hopkins, 1972, p. 420), seven major achievement batteries varied in (1) required testing time (from 161 to 480 minutes), (2) average minutes per subtest (from 16 to 65 minutes), and (3) cost (by a factor of 3 or more).

Locating Available Standardized Tests

Users of standardized tests will find the information contained in Buros' *Tests in Print II* and *The Mental Measurements Yearbooks* (MMY), to be of great value (see Appendix A, p. 464). The breadth of available published measures is indicated by Buros' 8th MMY (1978); Table 14-3 gives the number of tests in each category.

The Mental Measurements Yearbooks present critical reviews on every published test. Unless a test is very new, it has probably been reviewed in the MMYs; usually these reviews are very helpful. In addition to the *Mental Measurements Yearbooks,* the *Journal of Educational Measurement,* the *Personnel and Guidance Journal, Measurement and Evaluation in Guidance, Applied Psychological Measurement,* and several other professional journals publish reviews of new or revised tests.

The MMYs make it easier for a teacher, guidance counselor, or administrator to decide which tests to inspect. One can then send to the publishers for inexpensive "specimen" sets to compare and contrast.

Many aspects determine the suitability of a given test for a given purpose. Test specialists have offered various rating procedures designed to evaluate each of the tests being considered for use so that their characteristics will be considered properly. In this regard, consult *Standards for Educational and Psychological Tests and Manuals* (APA, 1974, or Buros, 1974), produced

TABLE 14-3

THE MENTAL MEASUREMENTS YEARBOOK TEST INDEX AND THE NUMBER OF TESTS IN EACH CATEGORY

MMY Test Index	Number of Entries	MMY Test Index	Number of Entries	MMY Test Index	Number of Entries
Achievement Batteries	37	Miscellaneous	3	Sensory-Motor	11
		Agriculture	1	Motor	3
English	24	Blind	2	Vision	4
Literature	10	Business education	9	Social Studies	8
Spelling	5	Courtship and		Economics	10
Vocabulary	9	Marriage	27	Geography	2
Fine Arts		Driving and Safety		History	11
Art	6	Education	2	Political Science	8
Music	12	Education	47	Sociology	3
Foreign Languages		Health and Physical		Speech and Hearing	4
English	10	Education	9	Hearing	22
French	14	Home Economics	3	Speech	27
German	12	Industrial Arts	2	Vocations	7
Greek	1	Learning Disabilities	33	Careers and Interests	44
Hebrew	2	Listening		Clerical	8
Italian	3	Comprehension	3	Manual Dexterity	11
Latin	3	Philosophy	3		
Russian	6	Psychology	5	Mechanical Ability	6
Spanish	21	Record and Report		Miscellaneous	11
Intelligence		Forms	1	Selection and	
Group	32	Religious Education	4	Rating Forms	4
Individual	29	Socioeconomic Status	1		
Specific	16	Test Programs	12	Specific Vocations	
Mathematics	45	Multi-Aptitude		Accounting	2
Algebra	5	Batteries	12	Business	11
Arithmetic	9	Personality	221	Computer	
Calculus	1	Reading	34	Programming	5
Geometry	2	Diagnostic	32	Dentistry	6
Statistics	1	Miscellaneous	3	Engineering	3
Trigonometry	2	Oral	11	Law	7
		Readiness	16	Medicine	8
		Special Fields	3	Miscellaneous	3
		Speed	1	Nursing	15
		Study Skills	9	Sales	5
		Science	7	Skilled Trades	44
		Biology	6	Supervision	17
		Chemistry	18		
		Miscellaneous	5		
		Physics	6		
		Geology	2		

SOURCE: Buros, 1978.

by a joint committee of the American Psychological Association (APA), the American Educational Research Association (AERA), and the National Council on Measurement in Education (NCME). The recommendations are made under six major headings: "Dissemination of Information," "Interpretation," "Validity," "Reliability," "Administration and Scoring," and "Scales and Norms." Findley's (1963) *Impact and Improvement of School Testing Programs* will probably be even more useful.

Test Administration and Scoring

There are advantages and disadvantages to administering tests in either the fall or the spring. Some pupils are entering the school for the first time, and their status in the group can best be determined by administering tests in the fall. A class roster of results can be reported for the class as a group and, hence, are more conveniently organized for use by the teachers. The teachers then have the entire school year in which to remedy any deficiencies revealed by the tests. Testing in the fall reduces self-imposed pressure on teachers to make a good showing. Since the students in a given classroom have been in several different classes during the previous year, it is less likely that the results will be inappropriately used to evaluate individual teachers. End-of-year testing can encourage some teachers to teach toward the test rather than follow local curriculum guides (Tyler, 1960; Hopkins, 1964a).

On the other hand, administering the tests near the end of the school year makes it possible for the information to serve several purposes. It can aid in making decisions about promotions, educational guidance, and sectioning of grades. It seems likely that an analysis of the errors revealed in spring testing could serve as a basis for remedial teaching in the succeeding grade almost as well as data from fall testing, although sometimes changes may occur during summer vacation. Spring testing has greater value for program and curricular evaluation. A chief drawback of spring testing is that no information is available on students who move into the district during the summer, the period of greatest family mobility.

Test norms are most meaningful if the tests are scheduled during the same month as that in which they were normed, usually October–November and/or April–May. This reduces ambiguities resulting from interpretation. Of course, if norms are to be meaningful, standard administration conditions, directions, and timing must be followed exactly.

In recent years testing in grades 11 and 12 by outside agencies such as the College Board (verbal and quantitative scholastic aptitude, plus as many as three or more achievement tests), the American College Testing Program (four achievement areas), and the National Merit Scholarship Corporation have provided high schools and colleges with a wealth of comparative information about students. This can be used wisely in guidance and selection, in helping the student make thoughtful and satisfying educational and vocational choices. Such information may reduce the need for extensive ability testing at the high school level.

In some states the district's testing program can be integrated with the state's testing program. Figure 14–13 gives illustrative state assessment results for a California school district at four grade levels for three school years in each of the three R's. Results are given in the form of the percent correct (section A), together with the percentile rank of the district's mean in relation to other districts in the state (section B). The margin of error in the district's percentile rank is also given (sections C and D). Note that socioeconomic and other data that are useful in interpreting and evaluating the district's performance are also provided (sections E and F).

PROFILE OF SCHOOL DISTRICT PERFORMANCE
1976-77

California Assessment Program

County—

School District— CALWEST UNIFIED SCHOOL DISTRICT

Grade and Content Area Tested	District Mean Score (A)			State Percentile Rank				Percentile Ranks of the District Mean Score (X) and the Comparison Score Band (0)				
				Of the District Mean Score (B)			Of the Comparison Score Band (C)					
	1974-75	1975-76	1976-77	1974-75	1975-76	1976-77	1976-77	1	25	50	75	99
Grade 2 Reading	76.3	76.4	76.7	79	77	75	61–78			0080		
Grade 3 Reading	87.8	88.4	88.3	73	77	72	60–75			080		
Grade 6 Reading		70.1	70.6		64	68	68–80			800		
Written Expression		67.3	67.9		70	66	66–78			800		
Spelling		66.3	67.2		71	73	63–77			080		
Mathematics		59.9	60.4		63	64	64–81			800		
Grade 12 Reading		65.6	64.5		66	62	63–77		X00			
Written Expression		62.6	62.4		57	64	64–79		800			
Spelling		68.2	68.4		59	62	49–81	08000				
Mathematics		66.9	67.3		56	65	63–82		800			

Background Factors Used to Develop Comparison Score Bands (E)	District Value			State Percentile Rank of District Value		
	1974-75	1975-76	1976-77	1974-75	1975-76	1976-77
Grades 2 and 3						
Entry Level Test	28.69	28.64	28.66	65	68	65
Socioeconomic Index	2.27	2.30	2.30	74	75	75
Percent AFDC	—	6.2	5.1	—	26	23
Percent Bilingual	9.3	8.3	8.8	51	48	49
Pupil Mobility	33.8	37.8	34.5	26	40	46
Grade 6						
Grade 3 Achievement Index		88.0	88.7		74	73
Percent AFDC		5.3	4.5		24	22
Percent Bilingual		8.2	6.9		56	51
Grade 12						
Grade 6 Achievement Index		58.9	66.7		79	68
Percent AFDC		3.5	3.4		22	25

Additional Background Factors (Not Used to Develop Comparison Score Bands) (F)	District Value	State Percentile Rank
Percent minority pupils, total	14.3	50
Percent American Indian	0.2	47
Percent Asian American	3.1	88
Percent Black	1.0	68
Percent Spanish-surnamed	9.7	54
Average class size, elementary	28.5	82
Average class size, high school	28.2	83
Average daily attendance	31,312	99
Assessed valuation per unit of a.d.a.	$15,112	25 U
General purpose tax rate	$4.20	67 U
Expenditures per unit of a.d.a.	$1,129	7 U

FIGURE 14-13 Sample profile of school district performance in a state assessment program. (From *Profiles of School District Performance: A Guide to Interpretation;* reprinted by permission of the California State Department of Education, 1977.)

Interpretation of District Results in Relation to Scholastic Aptitude

Graphic portrayals of test results (see Figure 14–14) are more functional than tables of numbers. The accompanying interpretation of the results is taken from the district's annual testing report (Hopkins, Kretke, Martin, & Averill, 1978).

The results on Total Reading (a composite score averaging scores on two subtests, Reading Vocabulary and Reading Comprehension) for the students in the Boulder Valley School District (BVSD) are given in Figure 14–14. The figure shows the pattern of BVSD reading achievement for grades 1 through 11 in comparison with national averages and with BVSD "expected" scores.

The actual grade levels (year and month) of BVSD students at the time of testing are indicated by the black triangles along the baseline (horizontal axis) of the upper portion of the figure. Testing was done in April, the seventh

410

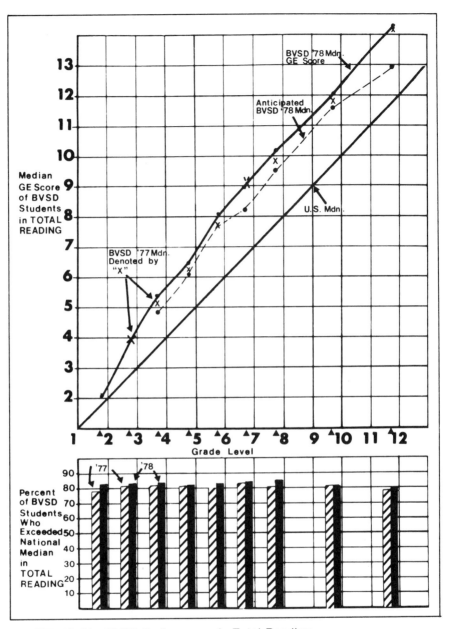

FIGURE 14-14 BVSD Performance in Total Reading.

month of the school year, so the actual grade levels at the time of testing were 1.7, 2.7, 3.7, and so forth, as indicated by the triangles.

Total reading performance in grade-equivalent units is shown on the vertical axis. Grade-equivalent (GE) scores are informative in the elementary grades but have much less meaning in high school.

The 45° diagonal line labeled "U.S. median" in the upper graph of Figure 14–14 represents the median (i.e., the 50th percentile) in the national standardization sample. Scores falling above this line represent a performance better than the average U.S. performance, while scores falling below the U.S. median line are below the U.S. average.

The median (50th percentile) performance of BVSD students at each grade level is shown by the solid, uppermost line. Figure 14–14 shows that the median reading GE score of Boulder Valley first-grade pupils (1.7) was approximately 2.1. Similarly, the median GE scores of BVSD second-graders (2.7) was 4.0; at grade 3 (3.7), the BVSD median GE score was 5.4; and so forth.

Figure 14–14 shows that the levels of reading achievement of BVSD pupils are much higher than those of typical students at the same grade levels nationwide. High achievement is not surprising in view of the fact that BVSD students are well above the national median in academic aptitude. The more important question is, "Are BVSD students doing as well as students across the nation who are comparable in terms of academic aptitude?" Because of the dual norming of the standardized achievement test and a companion academic aptitude measure, the performance of each student can be compared with the performance of similar students throughout the nation on each test. The performance of similar students is termed *anticipated achievement* or *expected achievement*. The anticipated achievement of any student is the average score achieved by students throughout the nation who are of the same sex, age, grade, and academic aptitude. In other words, if Jane Smith is 11.9 years old and is a sixth-grade BSVD student with an aptitude score at the 91st percentile, and has an anticipated GE score in reading of 10.6, then 10.6 is the average reading GE obtained by a nationally representative sample of girls at age 11.9 who obtained an aptitude score at the 91st percentile and were tested in the seventh school month of grade 6. If Jane obtained a GE score of 8.0, her peformance would be below expectation for her, even though her score would be higher than the national average (i.e., 6.7) for sixth-grade students.

Anticipated achievement scores are informative both for interpreting the performance of individual students and for evaluating achievement results for the school district. The dashed line in Figure 14–14 gives the median anticipated achievement grade equivalent (AAGE) in reading for BSVD students. For example, at grade 3.7 the median AAGE score in Total Reading for students throughout the nation who are similar to the median BVSD pupil in grade level, age, sex, and academic aptitude is 4.8. This value is more than a year above the national median of 3.7. The *actual* third-grade BVSD median GE score of 5.4 was six months above the median *anticipated* achievement GE of 4.8.

The performance (median actual GE score) of last year's (1977) BVSD students is shown in Figure 14–14 by the small cross marks, "x." BVSD performance in Total Reading did not differ markedly from 1977 to 1978.

The bar graph in the lower portion of Figure 14–14 permits comparison of the 1977 and 1978 BVSD results from a different perspective. The bars represent the percent of BVSD students who exceed the U.S. median at each grade level at which testing occurred. The solid bars denote the 1978 percentage and the striped bars depict the corresponding 1977 percentage. For example, at grade 7 (actual grade placement of 7.7), 80% of BVSD students exceeded the U.S. median in Total Reading in 1977, whereas the corresponding figure for 1978 was 85%. Note that at every grade level a larger percentage of BVSD students exceeded the U.S. Total Reading median in 1978 than in 1977, although the difference was negligible at grade 9. More than 80% of BVSD students at every grade level exceeded the U.S. median in Total Reading in 1978. Nationwide, one would only expect 50% to exceed the U.S. median.

The overall interpretation of Figure 14-14 can be summarized briefly: Total Reading performance in the Boulder Valley School District is well above the U.S. median. More significant, the BVSD median GE score in "Total Reading" exceeded the median anticipated achievement GE score by 3 or more months (.3 GE) at every grade level for which this comparison could be made. (The companion academic aptitude test, SFTAA, is not given in grades 1 and 2.) In other words, on the average, BVSD students scored somewhat higher in Total Reading than equally bright students in the national norming group. In addition, the Total Reading performance of 1978 BVSD students was slightly higher than that of 1977 BVSD students at corresponding grade levels.

Achievement Stability

Although considerable attention has been given to the issue of IQ stability, the related phenomenon of stability and change in scholastic attainment has been essentially ignored (Bloom, 1964). Do "slow starters" continue to have ignition trouble, or do they "mature" and eventually achieve normally? Are early differences in achievement only a result of age or maturational differences that eventually disappear? Do children who achieve poorly in the early grades continue to be poor achievers? In other words, how stable is academic achievement? Bracht and Hopkins (1970b) studied a large number of children who were given standardized achievement tests during grades 1-7, 9, and 11. They found a high degree of stability and predictability in general academic achievement. The findings indicate that for most pupils success or failure in grade 1 is not likely to represent a temporary pattern or developmental stage. However, a small pecentage of individual pupils may make radical changes in their achievement level, just as some do in IQ.

General academic achievement at the grade 1 level correlates above .6 with general academic achievement ten years later. By grade 3 the relationship is increased to about .75, and by the end of the elementary-school period a further increase to above .8 is observed. Similar results were found by Hilton (1979).

Bias and Achievement Tests

. . . some tests have been viewed as sexually, ethnically, or socioeconomically biased because some groups perform less well on the tests than others. . . . it is now commonly understood among measurement experts that the mere existence of such group differences in performance is not evidence of bias. [NCME, 1980, p. 5]

The question of cultural bias is much different when one is considering achievement tests than when one is dealing with scholastic aptitude tests; the relevant type of validity is content validity, not construct validity. The focus of standardized achievement tests is on course objectives, as illustrated in Figure 14-10. A reading test is biased against a social or ethnic group only if in the items are included that will result in a particular group's having a relatively higher or lower mean than it would have in the content universe of core objectives. Whether there are, or are not, differences among groups is irrelevant to the test's validity. Is the test measuring the intended curricular objectives? Do the items represent the intended content universe? An achievement test is biased if a given cultural or social group would be expected to perform differently on this set of items than it would on a representative set of items. Perhaps certain bilingual students can read in a language other than English better than they can in English; nevertheless, the test in English indicates how well they can. read in English. As Gardner (1978, p. 2) has observed, "Lower scores *alone* on an achievement test do not signify bias. If they did, then every . . . typing test is biased against persons who have never learned to type." No reading expert holds that reading tests are biased against boys because boys perform less well on them than girls.

Efforts to reduce cultural bias on standardized tests are often misguided. Attempting to select items on which ethnic groups do not differ does a great disservice to minority groups. Such "bootstrapping" serves to gloss over or minimize a serious educational problem. The bald reality, as shown by NAEP (NAEP, 1975a; see Figure 14-10) and numerous studies (Okada, Cohen & Mayeske, 1969; Hernandez, 1973; Bradley and Bradley, 1977; Hopkins et al., 1974; NAEP, 1977; Schmeiser & Ferguson, 1978), is that blacks and Mexican Americans are, on the average, well below (.5-1j) the norms in educational achievement. (See Figure 14-11 and Table 14-2). Misdiagnosing this problem and attributing the differences to test bias might make us feel better in the short run, but in the long run it does not serve the best interests of anyone. When the issue is innate aptitude or potential, the degree of cultural bias is moot; not so in the domain of educational achievement, unless the test focuses on content that is less germane to the curriculum of some groups. Bias is most likely on social studies tests and is least likely in reading and math where curricular communality among schools and districts is greatest (see Figure 14-10).

Obviously, the items on achievement tests should not promulgate racial or sex stereotypes; recently developed or revised standardized achievement tests have been careful to avoid this error. (See, e.g., Jensen and Beck, 1979; Wittig and Peterson, 1979.)

Summary

Standardized achievement tests measure important educational objectives, but like any tool, tests can be misused. *The results from standardized tests should be viewed as only one indicator among many of the quality of education within the district.* Standardized achievement batteries are composed of general survey tests. These tests are built around the curricula and objectives that are presumably common to all school districts and students across the nation. *Unique local objectives and content are not represented.* Good standardized measures are unavailable in certain curricular areas (e.g., music, art, and physical education), and these areas are not assessed in school districts' testing programs.

Most high school courses are only indirectly and incidentally sampled by survey-type achievement tests, if they are sampled at all. Little curricular commonality exists among high school students across the nation. Considerable variation in curriculum often exists, even among high schools within the same district, owing to differences in school size and student characteristics. Tests to assess a common core of educational experiences are less feasible at the high school level because of the highly elective nature of high school curricula and the diversity in students' objectives and courses of study. Consequently, *batteries of standardized tests reflect high school curricula only to a very limited extent.* Tests are available for specific high-school (and college) courses but these tests are not widely used. These tests are much less useful as a yardstick of educational quality at the secondary level than at the elementary and middle levels. At the high school level, standardized tests measure what is retained from the earlier grades more than what is learned in high school. The tests are measures of what a student knows or can do at a given point in time, even though the knowledge and skills tested may not be closely related to recent educational experiences. Standardized achievement tests are available for specific high-school (and college) courses, but few courses are so standardized in content that the tests represent the particular emphasis of a given course.

Standardized tests have much more validity in some subject matter fields than others. When there is much uniformity in curricula across school districts and states, the tests have substantial validity. This occurs in subjects with more limited content and a uniform skill sequence. Consequently, *reading and math tests tend to have much higher validity than tests of language arts, science, and social studies,* which are areas in which there is considerable interdistrict and interstate variation in content emphasis and sequencing. Therefore, reading and math results have the greatest validity and significance; the findings in other curricular areas are much less definitive.

Tests should be selected for a district's testing program only after careful study of the content validity of the available tests and batteries. Achievement tests with the same label may differ substantially in what they actually measure (the jingle fallacy). Conversely, tests with differing titles may measure little that is unique (the jangle fallacy).

Standardized achievement tests tend to be more general in scope, more process oriented, and less content oriented than teacher-made tests. The norms on standardized tests usually offer a comparison with a nationally representative sample of students at the same grade levels and in the same courses.

There is no discrete point at which a test measures achievement and no longer measures scholastic aptitude; scholastic aptitude tests are general achievement tests, but they represent an even broader type of achievement than standardized achievement tests do. Although there is considerable overlap between scholastic aptitude and achievement tests, each is usually sufficiently unique to justify its use.

It is generally preferable to use a scholastic aptitude test and an achievement battery that have been standardized on the same students so that aptitude–achievement comparisons can be made with less error.

Presenting normative data for each item—a trend among test publishers —promises to be of much greater value for the evaluation of instruction (or curriculum) for a class, school, or district than reporting only total scores. Item-level data for individual students are less useful and must be interpreted with greater caution.

Grade equivalents are useful units for reporting test results below grade 9 or 10. GE scores should be supplemented by standard scores or percentile ranks. The latter are most useful in reporting to parents. Extrapolation of norms attenuates the meaning that can be attached to GE scores that deviate greatly from a pupil's present grade level. Interpolation of norms also creates serious problems in curricular evaluation; for norms to have their clearest meaning, tests should be administered at the same time in the school year that was used in the norming process.

In the planning of a school testing program, all interested parties should be represented in the decision-making process. The three main purposes of school testing programs are (1) educational quality control and public accountability, (2) curricular and program evaluation, and (3) individual pupil assessment and diagnosis.

Mental Measurements Yearbooks can be very useful in locating and evaluating published measures.

IMPORTANT TERMS AND CONCEPTS

aptitude vs. achievement
crystallized vs. transfer-
   oriented achievement
jingle vs. jangle fallacies
content validity
grade-equivalent (GE) score
school vs. individual norms
interpolation vs. extrapolation
expectancy or anticipated
   achievement

survey vs. diagnostic
   achievement tests
common core content universe
differential content validity
"out-of-level" testing
survey vs. course-specific
   standardized achievement
   tests

National Assessment of
   Educational Progress
   (NAEP)
achievement stability
cultural bias on achievement
   tests
MMY

CHAPTER TEST

1. Using Figure 14–2, which of these conclusions is *not* supported?
   a) The verbal intelligence tests correlated more highly with reading tests than the nonverbal intelligence tests did.
   b) The arithmetic concept tests were less reliable than the reading tests.

c) The nonverbal intelligence tests correlated more highly with the arithmetic concepts than the verbal intelligence tests did.

d) The observed correlation between the intelligence and achievement tests was higher at grade 8 than at grade 3.

2. The influence of the environment on standardized scholastic aptitude and achievement tests, is

a) greater on achievement tests.

b) greater on scholastic aptitude tests.

c) about equal on both types of tests.

d) negligible on both types of tests.

3. On which one of these types of tests is content *least* school related?

a) Verbal intelligence tests

b) Non-language intelligence tests

c) College admission tests

d) Standardized achievement tests

4. The assumption that two tests measure different abilities because one is labeled an intelligence test and the other a test of scholastic aptitude is an example of the

a) jingle fallacy.

b) jangle fallacy.

5. "Reading tests are reading tests, take your pick" illustrates the

a) jingle fallacy.

b) jangle fallacy.

6. Standardized achievement tests do *not* have

a) a standard that defines acceptable performance.

b) a standard time limit.

c) a standard set of directions.

d) norms.

7. Compared to a standardized achievement test, a typical teacher-constructed test tends to

a) be more difficult, if raw scores are converted to percents.

b) have higher reliability.

c) cover large domains of content.

d) allow more flexibility in administration.

8. Compared to aptitude tests, achievement tests tend to

a) be more future oriented.

b) be more transfer oriented.

c) focus on a more clearly defined universe of content.

d) be less able to predict subsequent performance.

9. Which one of these is the major reason that the norms on standardized reading vocabulary tests are not interchangeable?

a) They have different curricular objectives.

b) They have different types of test items.

c) They have noncomparable norm groups.

d) There is a low correlation between the two reading tests.

10. Suppose a school's median on a standardized achievement test is at the 90th percentile using *school norms* (see Figure 14–4). If *individual student norms* are used, the average student would be expected to be

    a) above the 90th percentile in the individual student norms.

    b) at the 90th percentile in the individual student norms.

    c) below the 90th percentile in the individual student norms.

    d) No accurate prediction can be made.

11. In Figure 14–6 the grade-equivalent scores between 4.6 and 9.6 were established using _____ whereas those below 4.6 and above 9.6 utilize the process of _____.

    a) interpolation . . . extrapolation

    b) extrapolation . . . interpolation

12. Which is likely to result in more serious errors in grade-equivalent scores?

    a) Interpolation

    b) Extrapolation

13. Mabel is in the fourth grade and obtained a GE score in math fundamentals of 9.8. Therefore, we know that

    a) she should be promoted to the fifth or sixth grade in mathematics.

    b) she knows more math than most ninth-grade students.

    c) she was very lucky on the test.

    d) she is very advanced in math compared to other fourth-grade students.

14. In reading, which difference in reading ability would probably be greatest? (See Figure 14–7.) The difference between

    a) the median fourth-grade students and the median sixth-grade students.

    b) the 5th and 95th percentiles in grade 5.

    c) GE scores of 5.6 and 7.6.

    d) the 75th percentile in grade 4 and the 25th percentile in grade 6.

15. At which one of these grade levels will the standard deviation in GE scores be greatest?

    a) 2   b) 4   c) 6   d) 8   e) σ will be equal at all grade levels

16. The variability (σ's) of GE scores tends to (see Table 14–1)

    a) increase as grade level increases.

    b) be greater in reading than in math.

    c) (among the separate tests) be least in math computation.

    d) two of the above

    e) all of the above

17. In Figure 14–8, (p. 396)

    a) the group's performance consistently exceeded the national mean at grade 8 and thereafter.

    b) the individual's performance ("One student's performance") consistently exceeded the national mean at grade 8 and thereafter.

    c) the individual's performance falls below the group's performance at grade 8 and thereafter.

d) two of the above

e) all of the above

18. Ann Roberts (see Figure 14–9, p. 398)

a) scored slightly below the national average in reading.

b) scored above "expectancy" in spelling.

c) fell below expectancy in arithmetic.

d) two of the above

e) all of the above

19. The diagnostic value of a survey achievement test is least definitive at the

a) individual student level.

b) class level.

c) school level.

d) district level.

e) state level.

20. Which of these curricular areas has the largest common core of content and objectives?

a) Language arts

b) Science

c) Social studies

d) Math

e) Reading

21. Standardized achievement tests tend to have the least validity in which of these areas?

a) Language arts

b) Science

c) Social studies

d) Math

e) Reading

22. If a fifth-grade class has an average IQ of 90, which of the following standardized reading achievement tests would probably yield the most valid scores for the students? A test designed for a typical class of

a) third-grade students.

b) fourth-grade students.

c) fifth-grade students.

d) sixth-grade students.

23. Standardized achievement tests tend to have greatest content validity and usefulness at the

a) elementary-school level.

b) middle-school level.

c) high school level.

24. Which of these is *not* a standardized test?

a) WISC

b) ITBS

c) NAEP

d) CTBS

25. Using Table 14–2, which of the following conclusions is *not* supported by the data for the nationally representative sample of 17-year-old students on the illustrative item?

    a) Nine percent more of the students answered the item correctly in 1969 than in 1973.

    b) The Northeast showed the greatest decline among geographic regions.

    c) Rural students did not show a decline.

    d) White-collar communities showed a greater decline than inner-city communities.

    e) Blacks' performance declined more than that of whites.

26. A standardized achievement test is certainly culturally biased if

    a) there is a difference among the medians of various cultural groups.

    b) the test is based on a small common core of objectives.

    c) it has a nonrepresentative norm group.

    d) all cultural groups were not represented in its norming.

    e) the differences among the medians of the various cultural groups are relatively greater than they are in the entire content universe.

27. Which one of these is not a common aim of school testing programs?

    a) Evaluation of individual students

    b) Program evaluation

    c) Curricular evaluation

    d) Teacher evaluation

    e) Accountability

28. Which one of these is not a common criterion for the selection of standardized tests for a school testing program?

    a) Content validity

    b) Reliability

    c) Adequacy of norms

    d) Ease of hand scoring

    e) Amount of testing time

29. Which one of these sources provides critical reviews of published tests?

    a) *Tests in Print*

    b) NAEP

    c) MMY

    d) SFTAA

ANSWERS TO CHAPTER TEST

1. c	4. b	7. d
2. a	5. a	8. c
3. b	6. a	9. c

10. c	17. e	24. c
11. a	18. d	25. e
12. b	19. a	26. e
13. d	20. e	27. d
14. b	21. c	28. d
15. d	22. b	29. c
16. e	23. a	

FOR ADDITIONAL READING

AIRASIAN, P. W. A perspective on the uses and misuses of standardized achievement tests. *NCME Measurement in Education,* 10 (1979), 1–12.

AMERICAN PSYCHOLOGICAL ASSOCIATION. *Standards for educational and psychological tests and manuals.* Washington, D.C., 1974.

BADAL, A. W., and E. P. LARSEN. On reporting test results to community groups. *NCME Measurement in Education,* 1 (1970), 1–12.

BEGGS, D. L., and A. N. HIERONYMUS. Uniformity of growth in the basic skills throughout the school year and during the summer. *Journal of Educational Measurement,* 5 (1968), 91–97. Reprinted in G. H. Bracht, K. D. Hopkins, and J. C. Stanley, eds., *Perspectives in educational and psychological measurement.* Englewood Cliffs, N.J.: Prentice-Hall, 1972. Selection 5.

BRACHT, G. H., and K. D. HOPKINS. Stability of general academic achievement. In G. H. Bracht, K. D. Hopkins, and J. C. Stanley, eds., *Perspectives in educational and psychological measurement.* Englewood Cliffs, N.J.: Prentice-Hall, 1972. Selection 25.

BUROS, O. K. Fifty years in testing: Some reminiscences, criticisms, and suggestions. *Educational Researcher,* 6 (1977), 9–15.

———. *The eighth mental measurements yearbook.* Highland Park, N.J.: Gryphon Press, 1978.

COFFMAN, W. E. Achievement tests. In R. L. Ebel, ed., *Encyclopedia of educational research,* 4th ed. New York: Macmillan, 1969. Pp. 7–17.

DYER, H. S. Needed changes to sweeten the impact of testing. *Personnel and Guidance Journal,* 45 (1967), 776–80. Reprinted in G. H. Bracht, K. D. Hopkins, and J. C. Stanley, eds., *Perspectives in educational and psychological measurement.* Englewood Cliffs, N.J.: Prentice-Hall, 1972. Selection 32.

EBEL, R. L. Content standard test scores. *Educational and Psychological Measurement,* 22 (1962), 15–25.

ECHTERNACHT, G. Grade equivalent scores. *NCME Measurement in Education,* 8 (1977), 1–4.

FINDLEY, W. G., ed. The impact and improvement of school testing programs. In *Sixty-second yearbook of the National Society for the Study of Education, Part II.* Chicago: University of Chicago Press, 1963.

GREEN, D. R., ed. *The aptitude–achievement distinction.* Monterey, Calif.: CTB/McGraw-Hill, 1974.

LENNON, R. T., ed. *New directions for testing and measurement: impactive changes on measurement.* San Francisco: Jossey-Bass, 1979.

MILHOLLAND, J. F., ed. *New directions for testing and measurement: insights from large-scale surveys.* San Francisco: Jossey-Bass, 1979.

National Assessment of Educational Progress. *Update on education: A digest of the national assessment of educational progress.* Denver, 1975.

PACE, C. R. *Measuring Outcomes of College.* San Francisco: Jossey-Bass, 1979.

SCHRADER, W. B., ed. *New directions for testing and measurement: mea-*

surement and educational policy. San Francisco: Jossey-Bass, 1979.

SEIBEL, D. W. Measurement of aptitude and achievement. In D. K. Whitla, ed., *Handbook of measurement and assessment in behavioral sciences.* Reading, Mass.: Addison-Wesley, 1968. Chap. 8, pp. 261–314.

STANLEY, J. C., D. P. KEATING, and L. H. FOX, eds. *Mathematical talent: Discovery, description, and development.* Baltimore: The Johns Hopkins University Press, 1974.

STANLEY, J. C., W. C. GEORGE, and C. H. SOLANO, eds. *The gifted and the creative: A fifty-year perspective.* Baltimore: The Johns Hopkins University Press, 1977.

STANLEY, J. C. On educating the gifted. *Educational Researcher,* 9 (1980) 8–13.

WARD, A. W., M. E. BACKMAN, B. W. HALL, and J. L. MAZUR. *Guide for School Testing Programs.* East Lansing, Mich.: National Council on Measurement in Education, n.d.

15

Standard Interest, Personality, and Social Measures

In Chapter 11 we discussed informal methods of affective measurement; there also are many published measures of personal and social characteristics. Their principal use in schools is in vocational counseling, in which interests and personality as well as aptitudes and abilities are important considerations.

Standardized measures of affective characteristics should not be administered by classroom teachers unless they have received special training; the dangers and likelihood of misinterpreting them, especially the personality inventories, are much greater than with standardized ability tests. If teachers have some general understanding of measures of typical performance, however, they can work more effectively with counselors and school psychologists.

Many high school and college students who are anxious to know more about themselves so that they can better define their academic or vocational futures have become familiar with self-report interest inventories. A student wants to know what kind of vocational activities he finds most appealing. Are his scientific interests stronger than his literary interests? Is the pattern of his interests similar to that of school teachers, chemists, automobile mechanics, or forest rangers? These are the kinds of questions that interest inventories can help answer.

The first systematic effort to measure interests appears to have been made in 1915 at the Carnegie Institute of Technology, where James Miner developed a questionnaire to assist students in their vocational choices. Giant steps forward were taken in 1927, when Strong published the first edition of his Vocational Interest Blank (SVIB), and in 1939, when Kuder made available the initial form of the Kuder Preference Record (KPR). Buros (1974) lists fifty-five different published measures of vocational interests, but the Strong and Kuder inventories have dominated the field for many years.

The Strong-Campbell Interest Inventory

The Strong inventory was designed to distinguish men who were successful in a given occupational group from men in general. Strong thought that the interests that are typical of any one occupational group would differ from those of people in general and at least a little from those of any other occupational group. He collected items in which an individual could indicate his interests and preferences in a wide range of activities, as well as what *he himself* considered to be his present abilities. Instead of grouping items in similar-interest clusters, Strong simply gave the test to the members of many different occupational groups. For each group he determined which items were chosen more (or less) frequently than they were by men in general. From these differences he derived *empirically based scoring scales* for each group. Consequently, an individual taking the test can ascertain whether his interests resemble those of artists, architects, printers, morticians, and so on. Scoring scales have been developed for fifty-five occupations, ranging from artist to production manager and from minister to real estate salesman. Strong was not prejudicial in choosing which items would make up each given scale; the *actual* interest choices of the different groups decided the weights of the items for each scale. The success and prestige of the Strong inventory are due to the extensive research involved in its formulation. It has few competitors. It is interesting that Kuder adopted a rather similar scoring approach in the development of his second interest test, the Kuder Occupational Interest Survey (KOIS).

The current version of the Strong inventory, the Strong-Campbell Interest Inventory (SCII), merges the men's and women's forms into a single test. The 124 occupational scales are also integrated into six "occupational themes" based on Holland's (1966, 1973) theory of vocational choice, in which each occupation can be classified as representing one or more of the following themes: realistic, investigative, artistic, social, enterprising, and conventional.

Although examinees are asked to choose between competing activities, most of the 325 items on the SCII require the individual to indicate his or her preference by marking a phrase *D* for "dislike," *I* for "indifferent," or *L* for "like," as in the following three examples (not from the SVIB itself):

Moving a piano	*D*	*I*	*L*
Multiplying one number by another	*D*	*I*	*L*
Purchasing a new automobile	*D*	*I*	*L*

How *should* successful computer programmers, say, respond to "Moving a piano"? We might make a guess that more programmers than people in general would mark it *L,* but only actual data will tell whether they in fact do. Each item is scored once for each occupational scale to which it contributes. Scoring weights are determined by the discrepancies between the markings of the occupational group and the group of people in general. In the computer programmer scale, for example, a $+1$ weight for a response indicates that it occurs more frequently among computer programmers than among people in general, and a -1 weight indicates that it occurs less frequently. Responses that do not differentiate between computer programmers and people in general do not appear on the computer programmer scale, regardless of how frequently they were chosen by computer programmers. An examinee's total raw score on each occupation scale is the sum of the $+1$ and -1 weights of his or her various responses. The raw scores for each scale are converted into *T*-scores (mean $= 50$, $\sigma = 10$). The SCII must be scored separately for each occupation; hence, handscoring is impractical. A list of occupations on which scales have been developed is shown in Figure 15–1. More information regarding the SCII and its use is contained in the "Understanding Your Results" portion of the figure, which is taken from the manual (Campbell, 1974).

The Kuder Interest Inventories

There are three principal Kuder scales, the Kuder Preference Record–Vocational (KPR-V), the Kuder Occupational Interest Survey (KOIS), and the Kuder General Interest Survey (KGIS). The Kuder scales consist of many sets of three phrases of the "You like most to . . ." variety, such as this item:

R. Play a game that requires mental arithmetic
S. Play checkers
T. Work mechanical puzzles

The examinee is to indicate which one of the three activities he or she likes most and which one he or she likes least. This is equivalent to ranking the three activities in order of preference, because obviously the one that is not marked ranks in the middle. Each of the Kuder items has this forced-choice triad (three-part) form.

Empirical keying is employed on the KOIS, as with the SCII. Let us examine the scoring of the sample item for five keys. First, this item does not contribute to the Verification (sincerity vs. faking) scale. Not surprisingly, by empirical scoring you get 1 point on the bank cashier scale if you most like to "Play a game that requires mental arithmetic." You get 1 point on the Librarian scale if you most like to "Play checkers." You get 1 point on the "X-ray Technician" scale if you most like to "Work mechanical puzzles."

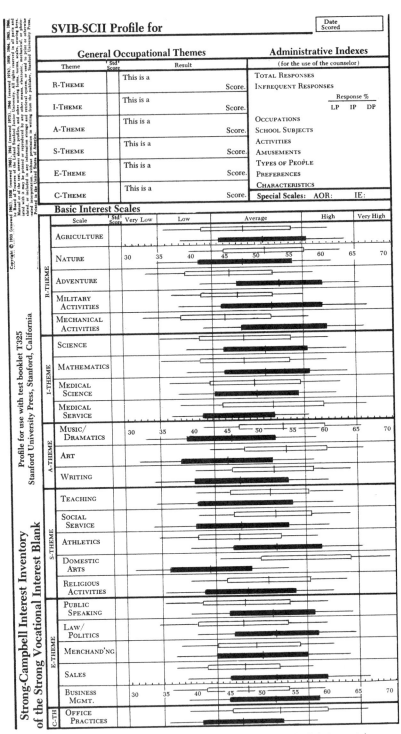

FIGURE 15–1 Report profile on the Strong-Campbell Interest Inventory. (Reprinted from David P. Campbell, *Manual for the Strong-Campbell Interest Inventory Form T325 (merged form) of the Strong Vocational Interest Blank,* 2nd ed., with the permission of the publisher, Stanford University Press. Copyright © 1974, 1977 by the Board of Trustees of the Leland Stanford Junior University.)

Occupational Scales

Code	Scale	Sex Norm
RC	FARMER	m
RC	INSTRUM. ASSEMBL.	f
RCE	VOC. AGRIC. TCHR.	m
REC	DIETITIAN	m
RES	POLICE OFFICER	m
RSE	HWY. PATROL OFF.	m
RE	ARMY OFFICER	f
RS	PHYS. ED. TEACHER	f
R	SKILLED CRAFTS	m
RI	FORESTER	m
RI	RAD. TECH. (X-RAY)	f
RI	MERCH. MAR. OFF.	m
RI	NAVY OFFICER	m
RI	NURSE, REGISTERED	m
RI	VETERINARIAN	m
		(scale: 15 25 45 55)
RIC	CARTOGRAPHER	m
RIC	ARMY OFFICER	m
RIE	AIR FORCE OFFICER	m
RIA	OCCUP. THERAPIST	f
IR	ENGINEER	f
IR	ENGINEER	m
IR	CHEMIST	m
IR	PHYSICAL SCIENTIST	m
IR	MEDICAL TECH.	f
IR	PHARMACIST	f
IR	DENTIST	f
IR	DENTIST	m
		(scale: 15 25 45 55)
IR	DENTAL HYGIENIST	f
IRS	PHYS. THERAPIST	f
IRS	PHYSICIAN	m
IRS	MATH-SCI. TEACHER	m
ICR	MATH-SCI. TEACHER	f
IC	DIETITIAN	f
IRC	MEDICAL TECH.	m
IRC	OPTOMETRIST	m
IRC	COMPUTER PROGR.	f
IRC	COMPUTER PROGR.	m
I	MATHEMATICIAN	f
I	MATHEMATICIAN	m
		(scale: 15 25 45 55)
I	PHYSICIST	f
I	BIOLOGIST	f
I	VETERINARIAN	f
I	OPTOMETRIST	f
I	PHYSICIAN	f
I	SOCIAL SCIENTIST	m
IA	COLLEGE PROFESSOR	f
IA	COLLEGE PROFESSOR	m
IS	SPEECH PATHOL.	f
IS	SPEECH PATHOL.	m
IAS	PSYCHOLOGIST	f
IAS	PSYCHOLOGIST	m
		(scale: 15 25 45 55)
IA	LANGUAGE INTERPR.	f
ARI	ARCHITECT	m
A	ADVERTISING EXEC.	f
A	ARTIST	f
A	ARTIST	m
A	ART TEACHER	f
A	PHOTOGRAPHER	m
A	MUSICIAN	f
A	MUSICIAN	m
A	ENTERTAINER	f
AE	INT. DECORATOR	f

Code	Scale	Sex Norm
AE	INT. DECORATOR	m
AE	ADVERTISING EXEC.	m
A	LANGUAGE TEACHER	f
A	LIBRARIAN	f
A	LIBRARIAN	m
A	REPORTER	f
A	REPORTER	m
AS	ENGLISH TEACHER	f
AS	ENGLISH TEACHER	m
SI	NURSE, REGISTERED	f
SIR	PHYS. THERAPIST	m
SRC	NURSE, LIC. PRACT.	m
S	SOCIAL WORKER	f
S	SOCIAL WORKER	m
S	PRIEST	m
		(scale: 15 25 45 55)
S	DIR., CHRISTIAN ED.	f
SE	YWCA STAFF	f
SIE	MINISTER	m
SEA	ELEM. TEACHER	m
SC	ELEM. TEACHER	f
SCE	SCH. SUPERINTEND.	m
SCE	PUBLIC ADMINISTR.	m
SCE	GUIDANCE COUNS.	m
SER	RECREATION LEADER	f
SEC	RECREATION LEADER	m
SEC	GUIDANCE COUNS.	f
		(scale: 15 25 45 55)
SEC	SOC. SCI. TEACHER	f
SEC	SOC. SCI. TEACHER	m
SEC	PERSONNEL DIR.	m
ESC	DEPT. STORE MGR.	m
ESC	HOME ECON. TCHR.	f
ESA	FLIGHT ATTENDANT	f
ES	CH. OF COMM. EXEC.	m
ES	SALES MANAGER	m
ES	LIFE INS. AGENT	m
E	LIFE INS. AGENT	f
E	LAWYER	f
E	LAWYER	m
		(scale: 15 25 45 55)
EI	COMPUTER SALES	m
EI	INVESTM. FUND MGR.	m
EIC	PHARMACIST	m
EC	BUYER	f
ECS	BUYER	m
ECS	CREDIT MANAGER	m
ECS	FUNERAL DIRECTOR	m
ECR	REALTOR	m
ERC	AGRIBUSINESS MGR.	m
ERC	PURCHASING AGENT	m
ESR	CHIROPRACTOR	m
CE	ACCOUNTANT	m
CE	BANKER	f
		(scale: 15 25 45 55)
CE	BANKER	m
CE	CREDIT MANAGER	f
CE	DEPT. STORE SALES	f
CE	BUSINESS ED. TCHR.	f
CES	BUSINESS ED. TCHR.	m
CSE	EXEC. HOUSEKEEPER	f
C	ACCOUNTANT	f
C	SECRETARY	f
CR	DENTAL ASSISTANT	f
CRI	NURSE, LIC. PRACT.	f
CRE	BEAUTICIAN	f

FIGURE 15-1 (continued)

Understanding Your Results
on the SVIB-SCII

Here are your scores for this interest inventory. They have been calculated from your answer sheet by computer.

First, a caution. There is no magic here. Your answers to the test booklet were used to determine your scores: your results are based on what you said you liked or disliked. The results can give you some useful systematic information about yourself, but you should not expect miracles.

More important, *this test does not measure your abilities*; it can tell you something about the patterns in your interests, and how these compare with those of successful people in many occupations, but the results are based on your *interests*, not your abilities. The results may tell you, for example, that you like the way engineers spend their day; they do *not* tell you whether you have a head for the mathematics involved.

Although most of us know something of our own interests, we're not sure how we compare with other people, especially with people actively engaged in various occupations. We don't know "what it would be like" to be a writer, or salesman, or scientist, or whatever. People using these results are frequently guided to considering occupations they had never given a thought to before.

Men and women, even those in the same occupation, tend to answer some items on the test quite differently. Research has shown that these differences should not be ignored—that separate scales for men and women provide more meaningful results. Generally, the scales for your sex—those marked with the "Sex Norm" corresponding to your sex ("m" or "f")—are more likely to be good predictors for you than scales for the other sex would be. Still, you have been scored on *all* the scales, female and male, so that you can make use of the maximum possible information. In some cases, such as FARMER and SECRETARY, Occupational Scales have not yet been established for both sexes.

Just how accurate the SCII is in predicting future careers is difficult to say. Studies made years later of employed people who completed earlier editions of this form in their high school or college days have shown that about one-half end up in occupations compatible with their profile scores, and most of these like their work. Among those who end up in occupations not compatible with their results, many say they don't like their work, or are doing the job in some unusual manner. In general, profiles with distinct and consistent patterns of high and low scores are better predictors than profiles with scores spread pretty evenly across the middle ranges.

Your answers have been analyzed in three main ways: first, under "General Occupational Themes," for general similarity to six important overall patterns; second, under "Basic Interest Scales," for similarity to clusters of specific activities; third, under "Occupational Scales," for similarity to the interests of men and women in about 100 occupations. The other two groups of data on the profile—in the small blocks labeled "Administrative Indexes" and "Special Scales"—are of interest mainly to your counselor. The first are checks to make certain that you made your marks on the answer sheet clearly and that your answers were processed correctly. The second are scales that have been developed for use in particular settings and require special interpretation; your counselor will discuss them with you.

The Six General Occupational Themes

Psychological research has shown that people can be described or contrasted in a general way by relating them to six overall occupational-interest themes. Your scores for these six themes have been calculated from the answers you gave to the questions in the test booklet. The average person scores about 50 on each theme. If your score on a given theme is a great deal higher, say over 60, you share many of the characteristics of that theme; if your score is low, say below 40, you share very few; and if your score is close to the average, you share some characteristics but not many.

Men and women score somewhat differently on some of these themes, and this difference is taken into account by the printed statement following each score; this statement, which might be, for example, "This is a MODERATELY HIGH score," is based on a comparison between your scores and the average score for your sex. Thus, you can compare your score either with the scores of a combined male-female sample, by noting your numerical score under the column "Std Score," or with the scores of only

the members of your own sex, by noting the phrasing of the printed comment.

Following are descriptions of the "pure," or extreme, types for the six General Occupational Themes. These descriptions are, most emphatically, only generalizations; none will fit any one person exactly, and in fact most people's interests combine all six themes to some degree or other. Even if you have scored quite high on a given theme you will find that some of the statements used to characterize the extreme type of that theme do not apply to you.

R-THEME: Extreme examples here are rugged, robust, practical, physically strong, and frequently aggressive in outlook; such people usually have good physical skills, but sometimes have trouble expressing themselves in words or in communicating their feelings to others. They like to work outdoors, and they like to work with tools, especially large, powerful machines. They prefer to deal with things rather than with ideas or with people. They generally have conventional political and economic opinions, and are usually cool to radical new ideas. They enjoy creating things with their hands and prefer occupations such as mechanic, construction work, fish and wildlife management, laboratory technician, some engineering specialties, some military jobs, agriculture, or the skilled trades. Although no single word can capture the broad meaning of the entire theme, the word REALISTIC has been used to characterize this pattern, thus the term R-THEME.

I-THEME: This theme tends to center around science and scientific activities. Extremes of this type are task-oriented; they are not particularly interested in working around other people. They enjoy solving abstract problems and have a great need to understand the physical world. They prefer to think through problems rather than act them out. Such people enjoy ambiguous challenges and do not like highly structured situations with many rules. They frequently have unconventional values and attitudes and tend to be original and creative, especially in scientific areas. They prefer occupations such as design engineer, biologist, social scientist, research laboratory worker, physicist, technical writer, or meteorologist. The word INVESTIGATIVE is used to summarize this pattern, thus I-THEME.

A-THEME: The extreme type here is artistically oriented, and likes to work in artistic settings where there are many opportunities for self-expression. Such people have little interest in problems that are highly structured or require gross physical strength, preferring those that can be dealt with through self-expression in artistic media. They resemble I-THEME types in preferring to work alone, but have a greater need for individualistic expression, are usually less assertive about their own opinions and capabilities, and are more sensitive and emotional. They score higher on measures of originality than any of the other types. They describe themselves as independent, original, unconventional, expressive, and tense. Vocational choices include artist, author, cartoonist, composer, singer, dramatic coach, poet, actor or actress, and symphony conductor. This is the ARTISTIC theme, or A-THEME.

S-THEME: The pure types here are sociable, responsible, humanistic, and concerned with the welfare of others. They usually express themselves well and get along well with others; they like attention and seek situations allowing them to be at or near the center of the group. They prefer to solve problems by discussions with others, or by arranging or rearranging relationships between others; they have little interest in situations requiring physical exertion or working with machinery. Such people describe themselves as cheerful, popular, achieving, and good leaders. They prefer occupations such as school superintendent, clinical psychologist, high school teacher, marriage counselor, playground director, speech therapist, or vocational counselor. This is the SOCIAL theme, or S-THEME.

E-THEME: The extreme types here have a great facility with words, which they put to effective use in selling, dominating, and leading; frequently they are in sales work. They see themselves as energetic, enthusiastic, adventurous, self-confident, and dominant, and they prefer social tasks where they can assume leadership. They enjoy persuading others to their viewpoints. They are impatient with precise work or work involving long periods of intellectual effort. They like power, status, and material wealth, and enjoy working in expensive settings. Vocational preferences include business executive, buyer, hotel manager, industrial relations consultant, political campaigner, realtor, many kinds of sales work, sports promoter, and television producer. The word ENTERPRISING summarizes this pattern of interests, thus E-THEME.

C-THEME: Extremes of this type prefer the highly ordered activities, both verbal and numerical, that characterize office work. They fit well into large organizations but do not seek leadership; they respond to power and are comfortable working in a well-established chain of command. They dislike ambiguous situations, preferring to know precisely what is expected of them.

FIGURE 15-1 *(continued)*

Such people describe themselves as conventional, stable, well-controlled, and dependable. They have little interest in problems requiring physical skills or intense relationships with others, and are most effective at well-defined tasks. Like the E-THEME type, they value material possessions and status. Vocational preferences are mostly within the business world, and include bank examiner, bank teller, bookkeeper, some accounting jobs, financial analyst, computer operator, inventory controller, tax expert, statistician, and traffic manager. Although, again, one word cannot adequately represent the entire theme, the word CONVENTIONAL more or less summarizes the pattern, hence C-THEME.

These six themes can be arranged in the form of a hexagon, as shown below, in such a way that themes falling *next* to each other (that is, on adjacent corners) are the most similar to each other, whereas those directly *across* the hexagon from each other are the most dissimilar. These similarities and differences among extreme types are useful in interpreting your own scores.

REALISTIC	INVESTIGATIVE
CONVENTIONAL	ARTISTIC
ENTERPRISING	SOCIAL

Few people are "pure" types, scoring high on one theme and low on all the others. Most score high on two, or even three, which means they share some characteristics with each of these; for their career planning, such people should look for an occupational setting that cuts across these patterns.

A few people score low on all six themes; this probably means they have no consistent occupational orientation and would likely be equally comfortable in any of several working environments. But many people, especially young people, score in this manner simply because they haven't had the opportunity to become familiar with a variety of occupational activities.

The Basic Interest Scales

These scales are more or less intermediate between the General Occupational Themes and the Occupational Scales. Each is concerned with one specific area of activity, an area that might partially characterize a General Theme and at the same time be common to a number of occupations. The 23 scales are arranged on the profile in groups corresponding to the strength of their relationships to the six General Themes.

For each scale the level of your score shows how consistently you answered "Like" to the activities in that area. If, for example, you consistently answered "Like" to such items as *Making a speech, Expressing judgments publicly,* and *Be a TV announcer,* then you will have a high score on the PUBLIC SPEAKING scale and you will probably have a higher than average score on the E-THEME. If you consistently answered "Dislike" to these items, you will have a low score on the PUBLIC SPEAKING scale and probably a low score on the E-THEME.

Whether your score is considered high or low depends on how other people answer. On these scales, the average adult scores about 50; if your score for a given scale is substantially higher than that, say about 60, then you have shown more consistent preferences for that kind of activity than the average adult does, and you should look upon that area of activity as an important focus of your interests. The opposite is true for low scores.

As with the other scales, your scores are given both numerically (as a number printed under "Std Score") and graphically (as a mark printed on the grid at the right of the numerical scores).

The differences between the sexes in these areas of interest are also displayed graphically: the open bars indicate the middle 50 percent of female scores, the shaded bars the middle 50 percent of male scores; the extending, thinner lines cover the middle 90 percent of scores; and the mark in the middle is the average.

You might find that your scores on some of the Basic Interest Scales appear to be inconsistent with scores on the corresponding Occupational Scales. This can happen—you might, for example, score high on the MATHEMATICS scale and low on the MATHEMATICIAN scale. Scores of this sort are not errors; they are in fact a useful finding. What they usually mean is that although you have a great liking for the subject matter of an occupation (say, mathematics), you share with people in that occupation (mathematicians) very few of their other likes or dislikes, and you would probably not enjoy the day-to-day life of their working world.

The Occupational Scales

Your score on a given Occupational Scale shows how similar your interests are to the interests of people in that occupation. If you reported the same likes and dislikes as they do, your score will be high and you would probably enjoy working in that occupation or a closely related one. If your likes and dislikes are different from those of the people in the occupation, your score will be low and you would not likely be happy in that kind of work. Remember that the scales for your sex—those marked in the "Sex Norm" column with the sex corresponding to yours—are more likely to be good predictors for you than scales for the other sex would be.

Your score for each scale is printed in numerals and also plotted graphically. Members of an occupation score about 50 on their own scale—that is, female dentists score about 50 on the DENTIST "f" scale, male artists score about 50 on the ARTIST "m" scale, and so forth. If you score high on a particular scale—say 45 or 50—you have many interests in common with the workers in that occupation. The higher your score, the more common interests you have. *But note that on these scales your scores are being compared with those of people working in those occupations;* in the scoring of the General Themes and the Basic Interest Scales you were being compared with "people-in-general." If your score on any of the Occupational Scales is in the "average" range—between 26 and 44—you have responded *in the way people-in-general do.* Scores in this range are therefore of little value in understanding your particular interests, and the profile uses this narrow shaded band to show that such scores should be given little attention.

The Occupational Scales differ from the other scales also in considering your dislikes as well as your likes. If you share the same *dislikes* with the workers in an occupation, you will score moderately high on their scale, even if you don't agree with their *likes.* For example, farmers, artists, and physicists dislike, in general, working with people; if you don't like working with people, you share this attitude with the people in these occupations, and may score fairly high—40, say—on these scales even if you don't like agriculture, art, or science. But a higher score—say 50—reflects an agreement on likes *and* dislikes.

Occupational Groupings

So that the overall pattern of your scores on the Occupational Scales can be better understood, they have been arranged on the profile in six clusters corresponding roughly to the six General Occupational Themes. Within each cluster, occupations expressing more or less similar interests are listed side by side. And because male workers in an occupation sometimes have interests somewhat different from those of female workers in the same occupation, the two scales for that occupation ("m" and "f") may be given on the profile in different groupings.

Just to the left of each Occupational Scale name on the profile are one to three letters indicating the General Themes characteristic of that occupation. These will help you to understand the interest patterns found among the workers in that occupation, and to focus on occupations that might be interesting to you. If you score high on two themes, you should scan the list of Occupational Scales and find any that have the same two theme letters in front of them in any order. If your scores there are also high—as they are likely to be—you should find out more about those occupations, and about related occupations not given on the profile. Your counselor can help you here.

Using Your Scores

Your scores can be used in two main ways: first, to help you understand how your likes and dislikes fit into the world of work; and second, to help you identify problems by pointing out areas where your interests differ substantially from those of people working in occupations that you might be considering. Suppose, for example, that you have your heart set on some field of science, and the results show that you have only a moderate interest in the daily exercise of mathematical skills necessary in that setting. Although this is discouraging to learn, you are at least prepared for the choice between (1) abandoning that field of science as a career objective, (2) trying to increase your enthusiasm for mathematics, and (3) finding some branch of the field that requires less use of mathematics.

You have been scored on a broad range of general interests and specific occupations. But you should not become dead set on one particular occupation where your score is high, at least not at an early age; in the world of work there are many hundreds of specialties and professions. Instead, using these results and your scores on other tests as guides, you should search out as much information as you can *about those occupational areas where your interests and aptitudes are focused.* Ask your librarian for information on jobs in these areas, and talk to people working in these fields. Talk with your counselor, who is especially trained to help you, about your results on this test and other tests, and about your future plans. You should recognize that choosing an occupation is not a single decision, but a series of decisions that will go on for many years; whenever a new decision must be made, you should seek the best possible information about yourself and about the work areas you are considering. Your scores on this inventory should help.

FIGURE 15-1 *(continued)*

You get 1 point on the Pharmaceutical Salesman scale if you *least* like to "Work mechanical puzzles." Thus, these four occupational scales use four of the six possible like-most and like-least responses to the item. Other scales probably use the like-least responses for mental arithmetic and checkers, too.

The chief methodological difference between Strong's approach and Kuder's forced-choice scheme is that the former uses a considerable number of items of the rating scale type that one may mark as one pleases—all *L,* for instance, or all *I*—whereas the Kuder uses a triadic item that may be more resistant to response sets caused by the tendency to prefer one category on a rating scale. Kuder requires, in effect, that the examinee mark exactly 100 "Mosts," one per item, and exactly 100 "Leasts," one per item. Strong does not require the examinee to mark one-third of the 400 items *D,* one-third *I,* and one-third *L,* although he does use some forced-choice items elsewhere in the SCII, which has the advantage over the KOIS of long development and much more research and predictive-validity information.

The KPR-V has probably been used more widely than any other interest inventory. The 168 items include a great variety of activities, and the scoring system determines the examinee's relative preference strength on 10 distinct scales: outdoor, mechanical, computational, scientific, persuasive, artistic, literary, musical, social-service, and clerical. The KPR-V, which can be hand scored, is designed to detect general areas of interest rather than those that are pertinent to a particular occupation. This capacity to detect general areas is considered to be an advantage for high school use but a disadvantage for college use, where more explicit vocational interest differentiation is needed.

Ipsative Versus Normative scales

The Kuder is an *ipsative* rather than a *normative* measure; that is, it shows *relative* intraindividual interests but not absolute degree of interest. Whether Bob has more scientific interest than Bill cannot be ascertained from the Kuder scores; they show only the relative standing of the interest areas *within* each person. The failure to recognize this ipsative property frequently creates consternation for those who attempt to resolve differences in results when an examinee has taken the SCII and the Kuder. In other words, if Jane is a person of many interests, she can be more interested in social work than Mary, even though Mary's greatest vocational interest is in social work; yet social work is not among Jane's greatest interests.

The Kuder General Interest Survey (KGIS) is a downward extension of the KPR-V. Norms are available for grades 6 to 12. Correlations between corresponding KGIS and KPR-V scales are high when allowance is made for their respective reliabilities.

Reliability and Validity of Interest Inventories

For some published interest tests, little or no adequate information is available concerning their validity and reliability. The critical reviews found in Buros' *Mental Measurements Yearbooks* provide invaluable guidance and an important quality control function for prospective users. Our comments will deal exclusively with the Strong and Kuder inventories and may or may not be characteristic of other instruments.

Although internal-consistency reliability estimates are satisfactory evidence of short-term stability in interest profiles, interest measurement over a long period cannot be expected to be stable until interests themselves have crystallized. Consequently, there is considerable fluctuation in the interest profiles of students below age 17 or 18 on the SCII and on the KPR (Crites, 1969). Moderate stability is achieved by college age, and fairly high stability is achieved by the end of the college years (D. P. Campbell, 1966a, b). A stability coefficient of .58 was reported for college freshmen tested 15 years later (Trinkaus, 1954). A 22-year retest correlation of .67 for college seniors was found by D. P. Campbell (1966a, b) for the SVIB. These coefficients are much lower than short-term stability coefficients [e.g., median r of .88 for test–retest r's after one month (Campbell, 1974)].

Fakability

The results of several studies have shown that the Kuder and Strong inventories can be faked (Garry, 1953) and that the "accuracy" of the faked responses is correlated (about .4) with IQ (Durnall, 1954). Thus, efforts to use these measures for selection or employment purposes have not been very successful. Falsification of interest is unlikely in an educational context, however, since there would rarely be a motive for faking. Like other self-report affective measures, its validity depends on removing incentives to prevaricate.

Measured Versus Expressed Interests

Although there is a considerable relationship (r's of about .5) between expressed and measured interests (Frandsen and Sessions, 1953), they are far from interchangeable. Haganah (1953) found that the measured interests agreed with expressed interests about two-thirds of the time for those who claimed business interests, but there was agreement in the science area in only one case in three. Super and Overstreet (1960) found that more than half of a sample of ninth-grade boys wished to enter occupations that appeared inappropriate for them in terms of the intellectual level required.

In Project TALENT, approximately 14,000 representative grade 12 students were asked about their career plans (Flanagan et al., 1962), which were then classified into the broad categories of college–science (31 percent), college–nonscience (19 percent), noncollege–technical (22 percent), and noncollege–nontechnical (29 percent). Five years later a follow-up study was conducted to determine the careers those individuals were pursuing. The percentages of people in each original group who continued in the same broad categories were 31, 56, 51, and 55 percent, respectively. (See Flanagan, 1969, p. 1338.)

Expressed interests are not necessarily less valid than measured interests; in fact, some studies show expressed interests to be the better predictor of ultimate occupation (Flanagan and Cooley, 1966; Wightwick, 1945). Such evidence does not attenuate the validity of measured interest, because many factors other than interest determine one's occupation. For students from the upper social class, where prestige factors limit the "acceptable" occupations that one may pursue, McArthur and Stevens (1955) found that expressed interests predicted better than measured interest; for middle-class subjects, the reverse was true.

The likelihood of being dissatisfied with one's work has been reported (Kuder, 1963) to be much greater for those who choose a line of work that is inconsistent with their measured interests than for those whose occupation and measured interests are consistent, although recent studies have not supported this conclusion. Zytowski (1976), in a 12–19 year follow-up, found that people whose occupations were not consistent with their early interest profiles did not report less job satisfaction than those whose occupations were consistent with their measured interests.

Interests, Abilities, and Grades

Contrary to popular opinion, little relationship exists between abilities and corresponding interests (Darley and Haganah, 1955; Perrone, 1964). Interests are, however, related to perceived abilities (McCall and Moore, 1965), which suggests the need for systematic feedback to students about their performance on standardized tests. Table 15-1 shows the correlations between the KPR-V interests and the various abilities measured by the Differential Aptitude Tests (DAT) for a group of male high school seniors. Although a moderate relationship exists in the mechanical and computational–numerical areas, the other interrelationships are low. Note the r of only .05 between clerical interest and ability.

Interests generally correlate poorly (below .3) with grades in relevant courses or fields (Brokaw, 1956). Even the Academic Orientation (AOR) scale of the SCII has very little relationship (r's in the .1-.3 range) with academic grades (Campbell, 1974, p. 79). Measured interests do predict students'

TABLE 15-1

CORRELATION COEFFICIENTS AMONG VARIOUS INTERESTS (KUDER PREFERENCE RECORD) AND ABILITIES (DIFFERENTIAL APTITUDE TESTS)

	Differential Aptitude Tests							
Kuder Scales	*Verbal*	*Numerical*	*Abstract*	*Space*	*Mechanical*	*Clerical*	*Spelling*	*Sentences*
Mechanical	.13	−.09	.06	.19	.38	−.32	−.28	−.05
Computational	.18	.54	.32	.12	.08	.27	.21	.22
Scientific	.16	.17	.25	.20	.44	−.09	.17	.07
Persuasive	−.05	−.06	−.06	−.15	−.15	.01	.16	.04
Artistic	−.03	−.36	.00	.15	.11	.05	−.18	−.15
Literary	.10	.06	−.28	−.21	−.24	.05	.27	.14
Musical	.02	.28	.12	.12	−.02	.41	−.05	.03
Social Service	−.12	−.14	−.12	−.27	−.37	.00	−.04	−.09
Clerical	−.02	.24	.11	.08	−.12	.05	−.02	.19

SOURCE: Data on 63 twelfth-grade boys, reprinted from G. K. Bennett, H. G. Seashore, and A. G. Wesman, *Differential Aptitude Tests,* Forms *L* and *M,* Fourth Edition Manual (New York: Psychological Corp.), p. A-17, by permission of the publisher. Copyright © 1966, 1974 by The Psychological Corporation, New York. All rights reserved.

ratings of satisfaction with a field of study, but these factors have little relationship to grades (French, 1961).

The educational value of interest measures was illustrated in Berdie's (1955) study, in which the scores on vocational interest tests were shown to be more highly related to the curriculum college students selected than achievement, aptitude, or personality tests; personality tests were the poorest indicator of college major. Many studies have shown that measured interests have validity (Levine and Wallen, 1954; Strong, 1953; Zytowski, 1976) for predicting occupations.

In a review of predictive validity studies on the Strong (Dolliver, Irvin & Bigley, 1972), it was found that the chances are even (1 to 1) that a person will end up in an occupation in which he or she received a high interest score (A). The chances are 8 to 1 *against* a person's ending up in an occupation in which he or she received a very low interest score (C). Results for the KOIS are comparable (Zytowski, 1976).

The limited information on racial difference and interest inventories suggest that this factor is not a serious problem in the assessment of interests (Borgen & Harper, 1973).

The prediction of occupational *success* is somewhat different from the prediction of occupational tenure. In the few studies that have been done in this area, the investigators have reported low positive correlations between measured interests and vocational success. An interest scale that is especially oriented to the skilled and semiskilled occupations is the Minnesota Vocational Interest Inventory (MVII), which follows the SCII approach. Keys have been developed for 21 specific occupations such as truck driver, electrician, and baker. This inventory may have greater value for non-college-bound students with less scholastic aptitude (Hall, 1966) than the SCII and the KOIS.

In interpreting any interest profile, one must remember that (1) the duties of many jobs change with time, (2) many jobs with the same name differ considerably, and (3) there is a wide diversity of activities within most occupations (see D. P. Campbell, 1968a; J. N. McCall, 1965). The "jingle" and "jangle" fallacies are as apparent in job titles as they are in test labels.

In summary, interest tests are of little practical value by themselves, but when considered together with aptitude and achievement patterns they can be a useful aid in helping a student select a career pattern or course of study. A comprehensive report form that gives both ability and interest scores for an examinee, as well as his or her chances of success in various academic and occupational pursuits, is illustrated in Figure 15-2. Its values for self-guidance are obvious.

The Measurement of Personality Variables

Conceptualizing the Human Personality

People have always categorized and evaluated the personalities of their contemporaries. The simplest form of personality evaluation is various *typologies* under which individuals can be classified. The four temperaments of ancient

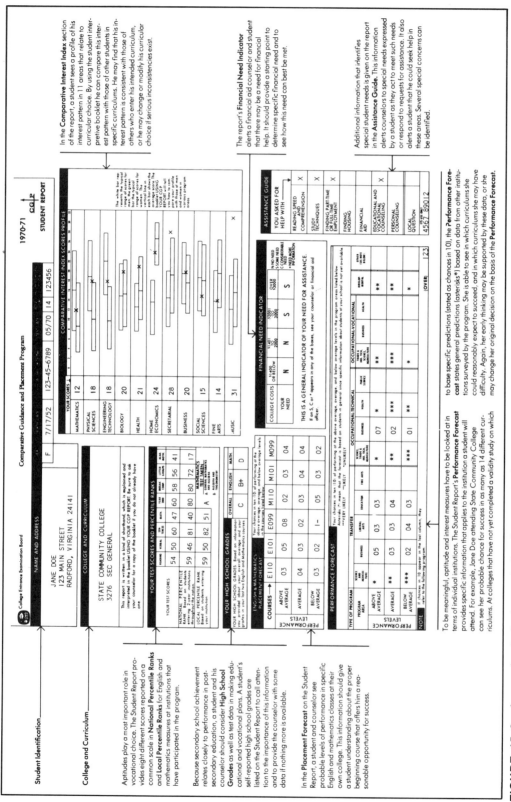

FIGURE 15-2 A sample student report showing results from an ability and interest test, along with performance expectancies on various academic and occupational criteria. (Reproduced from *Twenty-one Years Later: ETS Today*, by permission of the College Entrance Examination Board and the Educational Testing Service.)

times—sanguine, melancholy, phlegmatic, and choleric—made up a classification based on a supposed predominance in an individual of one of the four bodily "humours," or fluids—blood, bile, phlegm, or choler. A typology that is still popular, suggested by the Swiss psychoanalyst C. G. Jung, is introversion–extraversion. Traces of typological psychology remain in personality theory, but more elaborate methods of assessment have been devised in a growing effort to compass the diversity of human personality. Measurement theory has naturally accompanied the development of personality theory. The tests and other evaluative methods used by psychological investigators were constructed for a particular research problem, but there are many "standardized personality tests." Buros (1978) lists 221 published personality tests (see Table 14–3); they are exceeded in number only by achievement tests.

Traits Measured by Direct Observation

In trait assessment by direct observation a sample of behavior that manifests the trait in question is observed and analyzed. In Hartshorne and May's (1928) classic study, the Character Education Inquiry of Yale University, such traits as truthfulness, honesty, and persistence in children were studied by subjecting them to *situational tests* of these traits. Hartshorne and May found that most of the traits investigated depended strongly on the situation; that is, a child might cheat on an examination but not steal pennies.

The wartime Office of Stategic Services (OSS, 1948) was interested in selecting highly qualified men for risky undercover operations. The assessment staff felt that such traits as energy, initiative, effective intelligence, emotional stability, and leadership would be indispensable in this sort of work, so a number of situational tests were devised to measure the degree of these and other attributes. In one situation the subject had to build a five-foot cube of giant Tinkertoys with the aid of two workmen. Unknown to the subject, the two helpers were psychologists who did everything possible to obstruct his progress and belittle him. His reactions under such conditions were later evaluated in terms of the traits being sought. In another trial called the stress interview, the candidate was given a short time to invent a story to cover the fact that he had been caught going through secret governmental papers. In a subsequent third-degree "grilling," his reactions were evaluated again.

Trait Measurement Through Self-Report

Today's personality tests are largely of the paper-and-pencil, self-report variety, in which the examinee is presented with a series of questions describing typical behavior patterns. The score will consist of the number of questions answered in a direction that supposedly displays those traits. Sometimes a self-report test measures only one trait dimension, such as security–insecurity or high anxiety–low anxiety. At other times a test can be devised and scored to measure several traits at once. For example, the California Psychological Inventory (CPI) yields 18 different scores on such traits as sociability, dominance, sense of well-being, self-control, tolerance, and flexibility.

The forerunner of all such devices is the Woodworth Personal Data Sheet; it was devised during World War I to facilitate the psychiatric screening of draftees. It consisted of 116 yes–no questions describing typical symptoms of neurotic behavior. "Normals" averaged about 10 psychoneurotic answers, but those with neurotic complications averaged close to 40 such answers (Franz, 1919). High scorers would be interviewed and evaluated more intensively. The first 36 items from the Woodworth Personal Data Sheet are shown in Figure 15–3. By taking the inventory yourself, you can gain insight into some of the difficulties encountered in assessing personality.

A number of presumably "unidimensional" inventories were developed in the 1920s and 1930s to determine the strength of a variety of personality traits. It remained for psychologist Robert Bernreuter to demonstrate that *one* test could measure a number of personality traits simultaneously. To do this

1. Do you usually feel well and strong?	yes	*no*
2. Do you usually sleep well?	yes	*no*
3. Are you frightened in the middle of the night?	*yes*	no
4. Are you troubled with dreams about your work?	*yes*	no
5. Do you have nightmares?	*yes*	no
6. Do you have too many sexual dreams?	*yes*	no
7. Do you ever walk in your sleep?	*yes*	no
8. Do you ever have the sensation of falling when going to sleep?	*yes*	no
9. Does your heart ever thump in your ears so that you cannot sleep?	*yes*	no
10. Do ideas run through your head so that you cannot sleep?	*yes*	no
11. Do you feel well rested in the morning?	yes	*no*
12. Do your eyes often pain you?	*yes*	no
13. Do things ever seem to swim or get misty before your eyes?	*yes*	no
14. Do you often have the feeling of suffocating?	*yes*	no
15. Do you have continual itching in the face?	*yes*	no
16. Are you bothered much by blushing?	*yes*	no
17. Are you bothered by fluttering of the heart?	*yes*	no
18. Do you feel tired most of the time?	*yes*	no
19. Have you ever had fits of dizziness?	*yes*	no
20. Do you have queer, unpleasant feelings in any part of the body?	*yes*	no
21. Do you ever feel an awful pressure in or about the head?	*yes*	no
22. Do you often have bad pains in any part of the body?	*yes*	no
23. Do you have a great many bad headaches?	*yes*	no
24. Is your head apt to ache on one side?	*yes*	no
25. Have you ever fainted away?	*yes*	no
26. Have you often fainted away?	*yes*	no
27. Have you ever been blind, half-blind, deaf, or dumb for a time?	*yes*	no
28. Have you ever had an arm or leg paralyzed?	*yes*	no
29. Have you ever lost your memory for a time?	*yes*	no
30. Did you have a happy childhood?	yes	*no*
31. Were you happy when 14 to 18 years old?	yes	*no*
32. Were you considered a bad boy?	*yes*	no
33. As a child did you like to play alone better than to play with other children?	*yes*	no
34. Did the other children let you play with them?	yes	*no*
35. Were you shy with other boys?	*yes*	no
36. Did you ever run away from home?	*yes*	no

FIGURE 15–3 The first 36 items of the Woodworth Personal Data Sheet. The "neurotic" response to each item is italicized here, but of course not on the inventory itself. (Reproduced from P. M. Symonds, *Diagnosing personality and conduct* [New York: Century, 1931], p. 175, by permission of Prentice-Hall, Inc.)

he gathered a great number of self-report questions and determined which of them discriminated between high and low scorers on each of four tests, which respectively measured "introversion–extraversion," "ascendance–submission," "neurotic tendency," and "self-sufficiency." He found that a given item might correlate well with more than one of the unidimensional tests; through judicious selection he was able to produce a 125-item test, the responses to which could be variously combined to produce four separate scores, each of which correlated highly with the unidimensional test it was expected to replace.

Further refinement of self-report personality scales was introduced by John C. Flanagan (1935), who maintained that since the four Bernreuter scales showed significant intercorrelation (e.g., people scoring very high on the introversion scale tended to score similarly on the neuroticism scale), the traits could not be called independent, and that, therefore, each separate scale did not necessarily have a precise psychological meaning. Flanagan overcame this difficulty by subjecting the Bernreuter test to a trait or factor analysis. After examining the item correlations, he proposed that only two separate factors are needed to account for the score patterns produced by a great number of individuals. He defined these factors as the self-confident, socially aggressive–self-conscious, emotionally unstable dimension and the sociable–nonsociable dimension. This method of defining personality traits is analogous to the factor-analytic method of determining mental abilities and has become a favorite device for producing multidimensional personality tests. Four of the more prominent tests are the Guilford-Zimmerman Temperament Survey, which yields ten scores on traits such as general activity, ascendance, sociability, emotional stability, and friendliness; Cattell's Sixteen Personality Factor Questionnaire, which yields scores on such trait pairs as aloof–warm, confident–insecure, tough–sensitive, conventional–eccentric, conservative–experimenting; the Edwards Personal Preference Schedule, which yields scores on 15 personality needs—need for achievement, order, autonomy, affiliation, change, aggression, and so on; and the California Psychological Inventory.

A number of things plague those who try to treat self-report personality items the same way they treat ability items. There are, however, technical methods for meeting these problems:

1. A personality inventory (or a parallel form) can be administered to the same individuals after a *short* interval. The correlation between the scores for the first and second times tells how stable they are. If scores fluctuate wildly from one time to another, they cannot be useful for making inferences over time. Many self-report devices can be expected to show considerable fluctuation in scores over a short period because of actual fluctuations in the individual, even when errors of measurement and situationally distorting aspects are small. This is especially true for depression and other mood-related traits.

2. In an attempt to reduce the faking problem, various "lie" and "social-desirability" (see p. 310) scales have been devised for personality inventories. The usual procedure is to insert items to which a particular response very likely indicates intent to deceive, such as "Have you ever deliberately deceived someone?" Since every mortal has done so, a "No" response would be

suspect. If the examinee answers the other social-desirability or lie scale items in like manner, it follows that the answers to the other items are suspect. The examinee either is deliberately distorting the truth to give a favorable impression, is playing games, or is so seriously disturbed that he or she lacks self-insight. Some personality and interest tests have social-desirability items built into them to help identify people who give invalid information either willfully (lying) or because they are deluded.

The MMPI.   The most thoroughly studied paper-and-pencil adjustment inventory is the Minnesota Multiphasic Personality Inventory (MMPI), which first appeared in 1940. Its 550 items are psychiatrically oriented declarative sentences with which the individual either agrees or disagrees. Scores are secured for a number of psychiatric categories (depression, hypochondriasis, schizophrenia, and so on) and for masculine versus feminine interests. The scores are based on empirical keying, as with the Strong. A tremendous amount of research and reanalysis of the MMPI have been done since its appearance. Because the MMPI is a complex instrument, the consequences of misinterpretation can be very serious. Highly trained administrators and interpreters are required. Perhaps more than any other self-report personality test, the MMPI should not be used by school personnel. In the MMPI one's responses are compared with those of various psychiatric groups, which themselves are not defined explicitly enough. Despite the extensive developmental work on this instrument, it has been shown to have no validity for predicting relevant criteria such as success of student teaching (Gough and Pemberton, 1952; Michaelis, 1954) or performance in clinical psychology training (Snyder, 1955). Hathaway and Monachesi (1963), however, found the MMPI to have some slight validity for predicting delinquent behavior among high school students.

Recently a system for scoring and interpreting MMPI profiles by computer has become operational (Dahlstrom, Welsh & Dahlstrom, 1972, 1975). This type of interpretation can be a two-edged sword—it encourages the use of the MMPI by people without the extensive training necessary for its proper clinical use.

Some of the MMPI scales have inadequate reliabilities (some are in the .50s). In addition, the norms are not based on a representative sample of persons. This problem is compounded by the fact that there are substantial social and cultural differences; any MMPI profile must be interpreted in relation to the age, sex, ethnicity, and socioeconomic status of the examinee (Dahlstrom et al., 1972, 1975). The MMPI is a clinical instrument; it should be used by persons with special psychometric and psychological training so that its many limitations and pitfalls can be taken into account.

The CPI.   Whereas the MMPI is oriented toward the abnormal, the California Psychological Inventory (CPI) was developed for use with normal adolescents and adults. The 480 items (true–false) include two scales designed to detect examinees who are "faking good" or "faking bad" (the reverse of social desirability—needed, for example, to identify those who want to be in some special program for the emotionally disturbed, or do not want to be drafted). Most of the scales are based on empirical keying, using peer ratings as criteria. The CPI has been found to have at least some degree of validity for predicting delinquency and dropping out of high school (Megargee, 1972). Test–retest reliability estimates for high school students over a one-year interval average about .67, suggesting the need for considerable caution in individual use of the inventory. As with the MMPI, computerized reporting and interpretation services are available.

The MTAI. The Minnesota Teacher Attitude Inventory (MTAI) has been widely used to study teacher attitudes and has frequently been recommended in selecting prospective teachers (Getzels and Jackson, 1963, p. 517). Each item is empirically weighted on how it discriminated between 100 "superior" and 100 "inferior" teachers (according to principals' ratings) who responded anonymously to many Likert-type items, such as "Without children life would be dull," "Children should be seen and not heard," "A teacher should acknowledge his ignorance of a topic in the presence of his pupils," and so on. Correlations above .4 were reported between MTAI results and the ratings of principals and pupils (Leeds, 1950). A critical flaw that restricts the validity of Leeds' findings for teacher selection or evaluation was that participating teachers responded anonymously; consequently, a "need" or motive to fake was greatly reduced. Rabinowitz (1954) showed that education students have no difficulty simulating the attitudes of permissive or authoritative teachers when motivated to do so. When anonymity was not involved, subsequent studies (Day, 1959; Oelke, 1956; Popham and Trimble, 1960; Sandgren and Schmidt, 1956) generally failed to find any relationship between MTAI scores and teaching success that was great enough to be of any practical value.

A statistically significant relationship between the MTAI and certain criteria has been reported in a few studies, but statistical significance does not ensure practical significance. Popham and Trimble (1960) reported a highly significant difference (.01 level) in MTAI means of 72 "superior" and 72 "inferior" student teachers. This difference represented a correlation (point-biserial)[1] of only .24, which, since both groups were equal in number, indicates that the mean of the "superior" group was .24 standard deviations above the composite mean. Similarly, the inferior group had a mean z-score in the composite distribution of $-.24$. The magnitude of this difference is depicted in Figure 15–4, which shows two normal distributions with a difference in means of $.5\sigma$; this represents a point-biserial correlation of .25. (The ordinary r between the MTAI scores and the ratings of *all* the teachers, including the average ones, is probably considerably less than .24.)

Day (1959) found a predictive validity coefficient of .28 for the MTAI and principals' ratings, but Callis (1953) found coefficients of only .18 and .19 for the same criterion in two other studies.

The MTAI has little apparent promise in teacher selection. In a research

---

[1] A point-biserial correlation coefficent is the appropriate Pearson product–moment correlation coefficient when one of the variables is a true dichotomy.

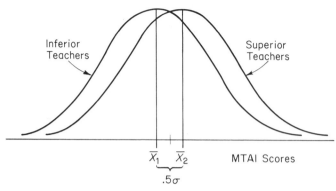

FIGURE 15-4 The magnitude of difference and overlap accompanying a difference in means of .5σ, that is, a point-biserial correlation of .25.

context in which the anonymity of the respondent can be preserved, the MTAI may have some utility, especially as a way to help teacher trainees consider some of their school-related attitudes. For this, however, the empirical scoring system (based on too few cases, anyway) can be abandoned, as Yee and Kriewall (1969) recommended more generally.

Evaluation of Self-report Measures. Self-report personality measures are afflicted with the difficulties of affective assessment described in Chapter 11 (see pp. 309–314) to a greater extent than cognitive or psychomotor tests. They are fakable (Braun and Asta, 1968), although as we have seen several inventories contain scales for detecting the self-deceived or the flagrant prevaricator. The job applicant describes himself or herself much more favorably than the college student (Herzberg, 1954). The difficulty is not reliability but validity; fakers tend to fake consistently (reliably).

Semantic problems and criterion inadequacy are very serious drawbacks to successful self-report personality assessment. Ghiselli and Barthol (1953) surveyed 113 studies in which personality inventories were used for employment selection; they found a median validity coefficient of only .25, which is too low to be of much real practical value for personnel selection.

Current personality inventory scores have generally been of little or no value for predicting future success either in school, on the job, or in personal life. They have more validity for research and evaluation purposes where they often can be administered anonymously.

Projective Techniques

Psychologists have had difficulty making good theoretical sense of a third personality dimension—the "why" or motivational aspect. A *motive* is a psychological state of the individual that is inferred from his or her behavior. Thus, if people begin to eat, the motive is hunger; if they struggle for success, the motive is ambition; if they act uncharitably, the motive is selfishness. One of the founders of modern social psychology, William McDougal (1923), made of list of primary human motives (he called them instincts) that included curiosity, pugnacity, self-assertion, reproduction, and repulsion. Further thought, however, led theorists to believe that such lists of motives really were only *descriptions* of a wide range of human behavior. Rather than explaining anything, they simply provided another way to categorize outwardly similar behaviors. The number of such motives or categories depended solely on the grouping preferences at work. As one critical wag observed, if people twiddle their thumbs, need one infer a thumb-twiddling motive?

This sort of thinking led many psychologists to suggest that, aside from physiological needs such as those for food, air, and rest, the motivation concept should be reformulated. The minimum assumption to be made in explaining human action is that the individual will set goals whose attainment provides satisfaction, pleasure, or gratification. The particular goals of any one person, however, will depend partially on his or her history of rewards and punishments; these in turn probably depend on the value systems of that person's environment—parents, social groups, and general culture. Thus, if a culture reinforces academic success, the behavior leading to such goals will be rewarded and there should be many "educated" individuals.

In this formulation the motive concept differs from the trait concept only in degree of generality. Motives predict behavior in a wide variety of environments; traits refer to more specific responses in highly specified conditions. For our purposes the most important question concerns the measurement of human motives.

The Rorschach and the TAT. Clinical psychologists frequently use two instruments, the Rorschach inkblot test and the Thematic Apperception Test (TAT), or variants of them, in making many of their personality assessments. They are called *projective tests* because a person is expected to project into inkblots or ambiguous pictures his or her needs, wants, desires, aversions, fears, anxieties, and so on. The procedures for administering, scoring, and interpreting the two tests are quite different, but they have in common their ambiguous stimuli—the "nonsensical" inkblots or provocative pictures. The well-known Rorschach inkblot test is the classic measure of this kind. The subject is shown one blot at a time and is asked what he or she sees in it. The examiner notes not only the content of the responses but also such things as use of the whole blot instead of details, injection of movement into the blots, and use of color and white spaces in making a response. Elaborate systems attempt to relate the various perceptual modes to such personality variables as impulsiveness, sensitivity, and emotional stability. Since its appearance in 1921, the Rorschach technique has stimulated much controversial literature; Buros (1978) lists almost 5,000 references pertaining to the Rorschach. Its scientific value as a yardstick of personality, however, is uncertain.

Henry Murray and his associates (1938) proposed that motives are a person's "inner concerns" and that if we learn what those concerns are, we may predict much of that person's behavior. We can learn of the concerns by listening to a person tell spontaneous, imaginative stories in response to pic-

FIGURE 15-5 One of the TAT cards. (Reprinted from Henry Alexander Murray, *Thematic apperception test* [Cambridge, Mass.: Harvard University Press], by permission of the publisher. Copyright 1943 by the President and Fellows of Harvard College.)

ture cues, such as those used in Murray's Thematic Apperception Test (TAT). (See Figure 15–5.) By analyzing the content of a series of these spontaneous, imaginative stories according to well-defined rules, the investigator hopes to identify the presence or absence, as well as the strength, of one or more "motives."

We will not discuss how the TAT or the Rorschach is scored. (There are several scoring procedures.) Much background in the psychology of personality and in clinical psychology is required before one is sufficiently well equipped to attempt to use projective techniques. Most measurement specialists have far less confidence in the validity of projective techniques than many clinical psychologists do. To some of the former, the Rorschach and the TAT rate little higher than the reading of tea leaves. Validity is not well established psychometrically even for the Rorschach and the TAT, much less for newer projective techniques. Perhaps a great part of the reason for their popularity with clinical psychologists rests on what might be called "faith validity" assumed by the users.

Several people have attempted to devise multiple-choice versions of the Rorschach to replace, or at least precede, the much more arduous interview procedure by which the Rorschach is usually administered. An example is the Holtzman Inkblot Technique (Holtzman et al., 1961; Holtzman, 1975). It is not yet known whether the objectively scored projective techniques will be useful.

Guilford (1959, p. 313) reviewed the status of Rorschach validity up to 1959 and concluded that

> in spite of the widespread popularity and use of the Rorschach ink blots, the reliabilities of scores tend to be relatively low, and validities, although quite varied, are generally near zero. This statement regarding validity applies to use of the instrument in discriminating pathological from normal individuals, for diagnosis of more particular pathologies such as anxiety, for indicating degree of maladjustment in the general population, and for predicting academic and vocational success.

Six years later, after reviewing the research on the Rorschach, Jensen (1965, p. 509) concluded that "the rate of scientific progress in clinical psychology might well be measured by the speed and thoroughness with which it gets over the Rorschach." More recently, Peterson (1978, p. 1045), in his MMY review, concluded that "the general lack of predictive validity for the Rorschach raises serious questions about its continued use in clinical practice."

Other Projective Techniques. Another very popular projective technique is the Draw-a-Person Test presented by Machover (1949). The examinee is provided with paper and pencil and asked to draw a person. Next the examinee is asked to draw a person of the sex opposite to that of the person in the first drawing. Every aspect of the drawings is purported to have psychological significance: size, position, order of drawing persons and parts of the body, clothing, shading, omission, background, and so on. Reliability and validity data on such measures are very poor. (See Anastasi, 1976, pp. 574–76.)

Several "copying" measures have become popular in recent years. Most are derivatives of the Bender Visual Motor Gestalt Test shown in Figure 15–6. The subject is asked simply to copy each design. There are several different scoring procedures for this test, but rotation of figures, omission, and distortion are the principal factors in its evaluation (Bender, 1970). "Copying" measurements appear to have some validity for predicting reading failure (DeHirsch et al., 1966) and identifying people with perceptual difficulty and

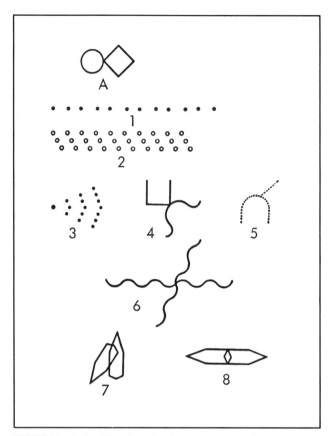

FIGURE 15-6 The Bender Visual Motor Gestalt Test. (Reproduced from Dr. Lauretta Bender, *A Visual Motor Gestalt Test and Its Clinical Use,* American Orthopsychiatric Association, Research Monographs [1938], p. 41, by permission of the author and the American Orthopsychiatric Association, Inc. Copyright 1938 by the American Orthopsychiatric Association, Inc.)

certain types of brain damage. Their value for personality appraisal has not been demonstrated clearly.

An extensive standardization of the Bender-Gestalt was published in 1975 (Koppitz, 1975). Norms are available for ages 5–10. Retest reliabilities over a four-month interval are on the order of .6. Using the Koppitz scoring system, scores correlate moderately to substantially with IQ scores until age 9 or 10, when most normal individuals obtain near-perfect scores. Performance also correlates significantly with academic achievement in the early primary grades.

Evaluation of Projective Techniques. Despite their widespread use by clinical and school psychologists, the validity of projective techniques for personality assessment is equivocal when studies that are vulnerable to criterion contamination are excluded. The status of unstructured projective techniques is essentially the same today as it was when they were critically evaluated by Eysenck (1959, pp. 276–77), who reached the following conclusions:

1. There is no consistent meaningful and testable theory underlying modern projective devices.
2. The actual practice of projective experts frequently contradicts the putative hypotheses on which their tests are built.
3. On the empirical level, there is no indisputable evidence showing any kind of marked relationship between global projective test interpretation by experts and psychiatric diagnosis.
4. There is no evidence of any marked relationship between Rorschach scoring categories combined in any approved statistical fashion into a scale, and diagnostic categories, when the association between the two is tested on a population other than that from which the scale was derived.
5. There is no evidence for the great majority of the postulated relationships between projective test indicators and personality traits.
6. There is no evidence for any marked relationship between projective test indicators of any kind and intellectual qualities and abilities as measured, estimated, or rated independently.
7. There is no evidence for the predictive power of projective techniques with respect to success or failure in a wide variety of fields where personality qualities play an important part.
8. There is no evidence that conscious or unconscious conflicts, attitudes, fears, or fantasies in patients can be diagnosed by means of projective techniques in such a way as to give congruent results with assessments made by psychiatrists independently.
9. There is ample evidence to show that the great majority of studies in the field of projective techniques are inadequately designed, have serious statistical errors in the analysis of the data, and/or are subject to damaging criticisms on the grounds of contamination between test and criterion.

Measuring School and Institutional Climate

In the assessment of educational environments the perceptions of people within the milieu are commonly used. A measure for appraising the organizational climate of schools, the Organizational Climate Description Questionnaire (OCDQ), was devised by Halpin (1966). Teachers and administrators respond to 64 Likert-type items such as "Teachers at this school stay by themselves"; "The morale of teachers is high"; and "The principal goes out of his way to help teachers." The items are grouped into four subtests that describe the group: Disengagement, Hindrance, Esprit, and Intimacy; and four subtests that describe the administration: Aloofness, Production Emphasis, Thrust, and Consideration. Considerable difference among schools is evidenced in the various OCDQ scales (Halpin, 1966, p. 169).

The CFK School Climate profile (Phi Delta Kappa, 1973) is a similar measure but has the advantage of being able to be administered to students and parents in addition to teachers and administrators, thus affording a more comprehensive assessment. Respondents rate each item twice, in terms of "what is" and again in terms of "what should be," so that significant discrepancies can be identified. Preliminary research findings regarding the instrument's reliability and validity are encouraging (Dennis, 1979). For example, Dennis (1979) obtained school climate ratings by administrators, teachers, and students in ten high schools as shown in Figure 15-7. Notice how low the morale appears to be among the teachers and administrators in school C. Notice also that, except in school C, administrators perceived the school climate to be highest and students perceived it to be lowest. The up-and-down profile for administrators tended to be roughly parallel, but to have little correspondence to students' perceptions.

The College Characteristics Index (CCI) is designed to measure the environmental climate of colleges (Stern, 1970). Questions like "There would be a capacity audience for a lecture by an outstanding philosopher or theologian" and "Professors here really care whether students learn" are answered by a representative sample of students. An institutional profile is then constructed using the percent of students subscribing to the statements. The CCI yields scores on thirty subtests, such as Theoretical–Practical Orientation, Conformity, Extracurricular Participation, and Achievement-vs.-Relaxed Pressure. A companion measure oriented toward individuals rather than institutions is the Activities Index (AI). By comparing the respective CCI and AI profiles on the thirty scales, areas of compatibility and dissonance can be identified. A more general form of the CCI, the Organizational Climate Index (OCI), is designed to apply to any organization.

The College and University Environmental Scale (CUES) is a relative of the CCI; it uses students' perceptions to describe the institution in terms of five factors: Practicality, Community, Awareness, Propriety, and Scholarship.

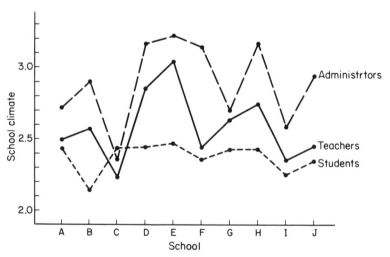

FIGURE 15-7 School climate ratings for ten high schools by administrators, teachers, and students in those schools. (Data from Dennis, 1979.)

The Social Climate Scales (Moos, 1974, 1975) are another measure of ecological climate. They include nine scales that are applicable in a variety of environments, such as a family, a school classroom (e.g., the Classroom Environment Scale; Moos, 1979), or a residence hall. The scales show considerable ability to differentiate and appear to remain quite stable over time.

Climate measures can be useful, especially to administrators and other decision makers, for identifying areas of satisfaction and dissatisfaction, and they can give direction to needed institutional changes. Their reliability and validity is closely tied to the conditions of administration. In most instances anonymity is a critical prerequisite for validity.

Sociometric Techniques

Sociometry is the study of interrelationships among members of a group, that is, its social structure: how each individual is perceived by the group. Sociometry was launched in 1934 with the publication of Moreno's *Who Shall Survive*. Bonney (1960, p. 1319) described the rationale as follows:

> The major assumption underlying sociometric method is that within all groups, such as a school class or teaching staff, in which considerable interaction is allowed, there emerges an informal organization among the members based on varying degrees of positive and negative interpersonal feelings, and that these preferences and aversions are significant factors in the morale and efficiency of this group.

Various techniques that we have discussed, such as Q-sort, semantic differential, or rating scales, can be used to rate others as well as oneself. Special sociometric techniques have been devised for the social appraisal of individuals and groups.

The Sociogram

Teachers may study the social structure of a classroom by asking students to make *meaningful* choices like the following: With which student would you rather study tomorrow's arithmetic lesson? With which three pupils would you rather play at recess? Which two pupils would be the most fun at a party at your home?

A more complex variation is to present the personality sketch of a hypothetical pupil and ask each youngster to name, say, the three members of the class who seem most like the individual described.

We illustrate the sociometric process with actual data from a fourth-grade class that contained 14 girls and 17 boys. The teacher gave each child a dittoed sheet that read as follows:

My three best friends in this class are:
1. My very best friend _____
2. My second best friend _____
3. My third best friend _____

The results are shown in Figure 15–8, where the capital letters from *A* through *N* designate girls and the small letters from *a* through *q* represent boys.

How does one read Figure 15–8? Begin with girl *A*. In *row A* we see that she chose girl *D* as her very best friend, because there is the number 1 at the in-

		Girls Chosen													Boys Chosen															
		A	*B*	*C*	*D*	*E*	*F*	*G*	*H*	*I*	*J*	*K*	*L*	*M*	*N*	*a*	*b*	*c*	*d*	*e*	*f*	*g*	*h*	*i*	*j*	*k*	*l*	*m*	*n*	*o*	*p*	*q*
Girls Chose	*A*			2	1																	3										
	B				2			3															1									
	C	2						3								1																
	D	1		3		2																										
	E		1					2											3													
	F	2			1																			3								
	G	2		3																		1										
	H		1							3	2																					
	I		1		3																		2									
	J					2		1																					3			
	K		2	1															3													
	L						2									1			3													
	M					2										1							3									
	N	1			2	3												ᵃ														
Boys Chose	*a*																					2	1				3					
	b																	1	2						3							
	c	3																1	2													
	d	2																1						3								
	e					2																		1								
	f	3	1													2																
	g															1								2						3		
	h							2															1								3	
	i															2		1						3								
	j															1	2			3												
	k	1		3		2																										
	l						2									1																
	m																2			3						1						
	n																2	1											3			
	o																		3					2		1						
	p															1		3	2													
	q																						1									
1st choice		3	4	1	2			1								5	3	3	1	2	2	1	1		1	1						
2nd choice		4	1	1	1	2	3	2	1	1	1	1				2	3		2	1	2		1	1								
3rd choice		2		3		2	1		2									3	3	2		2		2	1		1	1	1			
Times chosen		9	5	4	3	4	3	3	2	3	1	1				7	6	6	6	5	4	3	2	3	2	1	2	1	1	1		
"Score"		19	14	8	8	6	6	5	5	4	2	2	0	0	0	19	15	12	10	10	10	5	5	4	4	3	2	1	1	1	0	0
		A	*B*	*C*	*D*	*E*	*F*	*G*	*H*	*I*	*J*	*K*	*L*	*M*	*N*	*a*	*b*	*c*	*d*	*e*	*f*	*g*	*h*	*i*	*j*	*k*	*l*	*m*	*n*	*o*	*p*	*q*

FIGURE 15–8 Choices of three best friends by a fourth-grade class of 14 girls and 17 boys.

tersection of row *A* and column *D*. Girl *A* listed girl *C* as her second-best friend. Girl *A* listed boy *c* as her third-best friend.

Who chose girl *A*? Look at *column A,* where you see (from top to bottom) the following numbers: 1 (first choice of girls *D* and *N* and boy *k*), 2 (second choice of girls *C*, *F*, and *G* and boy *d*), and 3 (third choice of boys *c* and *f*). Thus, girl *A* was named by nine pupils—three times as first choice, four times as second choice, and twice as third choice. You will find the numbers 3, 4, and 2 in column *A* of the first three rows below the choices.

In the lower left quadrant of Figure 15–8 you can see that girl *A* was chosen by four boys but no other girl was chosen by more than one boy. You can also determine that no girl chose only boys but boy *k* chose only girls. Did any girl choose boy *k*? No, but *k* was the *first* choice of boy *o*.

If we give 3 points for being chosen as "very best friend," 2 points for "second best friend," and 1 point for "third best friend," the highest scorers are girl *A* and boy *a*, each with 19 points, even though girl *A* was chosen by two more pupils than boy *a*. This happens because boy *a* was chosen as very best friend by five pupils, resulting in 15 points, whereas girl *A* was chosen as very best friend by only three pupils, yielding 9 points. For girl *A,* the computation is $(3 \times 3) + (4 \times 2) + (2 \times 1) = 19$. For boy *a,* it is $(5 \times 3) + (2 \times 2) = 19$.

The lowest scorers, whom nobody chose, are girls *L*, *M*, and *N* and boys *p* and *q*. They may be the fourth- or fifth-best friends of some of the pupils, but they weren't listed as first, second, or third. In Figure 15–8 the girls are arranged in order of total number of points, from *A,* with the most, to *L*, *M*, and *N*, with the least. The boys are arranged in the same way.

Every girl listed three names, but boys *e*, *l*, and *q* did not. Inspect rows *e*, *l*, and *q* to see which choices they omitted. (Do you suppose that fourth-grade boys typically are less careful about such tasks than fourth-grade girls or that some of the boys have fewer close friends than the girls have?)

The 31 very-best-friend choices went to just 15 pupils. How many of these were mutual choices—in which, for example, Mary listed Susan as her very best friend and Susan listed Mary as hers? By examining Figure 15–8 we can see that *A* chose *D* and was chosen by *D*, that *B* chose *f* and was chosen by *f*, that *C* chose *c* but was not chosen by *c*, and so on. The five mutual-first-choice pairs are *AD*, *Bf*, *ag*, *bc*, and *eh*. Fifteen mutual first choices were possible.

It might have been better to ask each pupil to name his or her very best friend and second-best friend *of each sex,* rather than just the three best friends. Girl *E,* for instance, listed girl *B* as her very best friend, but girl *B* listed boy *f* as her very best friend and girl *E* as her second-best friend, probably meaning that girl *E* is her best *girl* friend.

Girl *A,* the most-chosen pupil, has perfect mutuality with all three of her choices. She listed girl *D* as her very best friend, and girl *D* listed her likewise. She chose girl *C* as her second-best friend, and girl *C* reciprocated. She named boy *c* as her third-best friend, and he named her as his third-best friend.

Girl *B*'s three choices all named her as very best friend. Girl *C* listed boy *c* as her very best friend, but he did not choose her at all, instead choosing boys for 1 and 2 and designating her second-best friend, *A,* as his third-best friend.

One could analyze these 89 "chose" and "was chosen by" listings for a long time and uncover a variety of interesting relationships.

The *target diagram* shown in Figure 15-9 is a less common but probably more usable way of depicting sociometric data from groups as large as those found in most classrooms. It portrays the same data as Figure 15-8. Four concentric circles distinguish among the students; roughly one-fourth of them are represented in each of the four areas. Typically, boys are placed in one half,

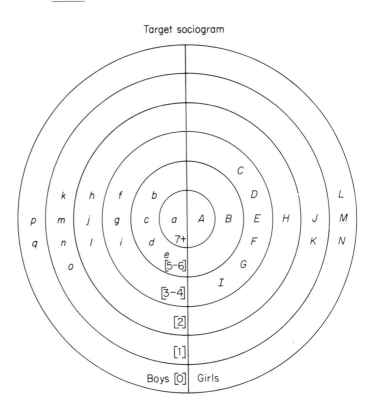

School ___Central___

Teacher ___Williams___

Level or Grade ___5___

Target sociogram

Times chosen	Boys	Girls	Total
7+	1	1	2
5–6	4	1	5
3–4	3	6	9
3–2	3	1	4
5–6	4	2	6
0	2	3	5

FIGURE 15-9 A 'target" sociogram based on data in Figure 15–8.

girls in the other. The *stars* are found near the center, the *isolates* and *fringers* near the periphery.

The "Guess Who" Technique

This technique is one of the simplest methods of obtaining peer judgments. Each student is asked to list the student or students (if any) who match a series of brief descriptions that may include negative as well as positive characteristics. When negative descriptions are included, it is important that the response be optional.

Hartshorne and May (1928) presented this technique as a guessing game for young children; hence its name, the "guess who" technique. Some excellent sample directions are given by Cunningham et al. (1951):

> Below are some word pictures of members of your class. Read each statement and write down the names of the persons whom you think the descriptions fit.
> REMEMBER: One description *may* fit several persons. You may write as many names as you think belong under each.
> The same person may be nominated for more than one description.
> Write "myself" if you think the description fits you.
> If you cannot think of anyone to match a particular description, go on to the next one.
> You will have as much time as you need to finish. Do not hurry.

A series of behavior descriptions follows, such as

> Someone who always seems rather sad, worried, or unhappy.
> Someone who is very friendly, who is nice to everybody.

Torrance (1962) suggested using the "guess who" approach to evaluate different aspects of creative thinking. Sample items include "Who has the most original or unusual ideas?" "Who in your class does the most inventing or developing of new ideas, gadgets, and such?"

The results from an actual "guess who" application in a sixth-grade class are shown in Figure 15-10. The assessment was a part of a case study of student 11, who, because of her maladaptive behavior, had been referred to the school psychologist. The teacher's suspicions were dramatically confirmed by peer judgments obtained by the "guess who" technique. Note that pupil 11 was listed as "not liked" by all but one of her peers. No other student was so identified by even one student. Her one nomination for "best friend" was from her own ballot.

From such a self-portrait of a class, the teacher can identify pupils who most need help. Notice the "quiet" pupils, 15, 18, 22, and 34. Although pupil 15 was perceived as the quietest, he was listed as best friend by two other students; the other three quiet students were not nominated by any peer. Only one of the four received a single identification with "happy" by a peer, whereas each of the four was deemed "unhappy" by at least one peer.

The principal advantage of the "guess who" technique is its usability. It requires only a few minutes to administer and tabulate and can assess several

| | Positive Characteristics (10) | | | | | | | | | | Negative Characteristics (11) | | | | | | | | | | | | |
Pupil No.	Quiet	Most Active in Games	Best Liked	Not Bossy	Polite	Works Well with Others	Happy	Tidy	Takes Care of Things	Best Friend	Restless	Talkative	Silent	Not Liked	Bossy	Not Polite	Does Not Take Care of Things	Unhappy	Untidy	Wastes Time	Does Not Work Well with Others	Sum of Positive Traits	Sum of Negative Traits
1 A.B.		14	2	1		2		1	2							1			1			22	2
2 B.L.							1	1	1						1							3	1
3 B.C.			2		4		1	2	3										1			12	1
4 C.R.							1	1		1					1	1		1		1	2	5
5 E.R.										1	4			6	2	1	2	3	2		0	21
6 B.B.			4	1	1		1										3		1	7	4
7 C.J.								1		1	1			3	1			2	1	1	9
8 E.J.	1	1		2			1	2	2												9	0
9 E.T.				1						1						1	1	2		1	1	6
10 G.P.		2	5	2	2	3	7	2	2	3	2				9					2	28	13
11 H.C.			1				3		1	14	2		34	5	6	22	17	9	15	9	5	133
12 H.S.								1		1	23				5	2	2	2	7	4	2	45
13 H.C.								1	1									1	1	1	2	3
14 J.J.						2															2	0
15 L.J.	13			7	4	1		3	3	2			17					2			33	19
16 M.E.				1	1	1			1					1		1	3	1		4	6
17 M.S.			1		3	1		1	2					2	2		1	1		8	6
18 M.C.	6				3	2		1	1				3				2			13	5
19 M.M.					1		1											1	1	2	2
20 N.R.				1			1	1					1	1			5		3	3	10
21 O.R.					1					1				1						1	2
22 O.S.	6		1	3	6		1	9	2			2		1		1			28	4
23 R.D.				1	8			1	1						1	1	1	10	4
24 R.P.		2	5	1	4	1	2	7					6	1	1					22	8
25 S.M.							1			1	1	2	2			3	1	9
26 S.D.				2		2				3						4	3
27 S.V.		5		1	3	2	1	3	1			1	1		1		2	15	6
28 F.J.			1				1	1		1	1					1	4
29 T.R.		16	15	2	7	4	3		1	4	1					52	1
30 T.K.				1	1	1	2	1					1		5	2
31 T.B.			1	1	2	3	1					1		8	1
32 W.B.			1	2				1		1		3	2
33 M.E.			1	1	2	4	1	2	1		1		1	11	3
34 D.C.	9		3	4	1		10		1	3	17	14
35 A.E.				1	1	1		3	3	1	8
36 B.S.		2	4	1	2	4	1	1	1		1	14	3

Source: Courtesy of Frank Thompson, principal of Hillgrove School, La Puenta, California.
[a] Numbers indicate the frequency with which each student was associated with the "guess who" description by his classmates.

FIGURE 15-10 Results of a typical "guess who" sociometric assessment with a sixth-grade class.[a]

dimensions within a group. The sociogram is limited to a single question—a separate figure or table is required for each item.

Reliability and Validity of Sociometric Data

Gronlund (1955) reported a median test–retest reliability coefficient of .76 for sociometric choices over a four-month interval for elementary-school children. From his extensive study of sociometric literature, Bonney (1960, p. 1321) reported that: "It seems fair to conclude that there is indeed a strong tendency for the members of a group to maintain quite similar sociometric ranks over several weeks or several months. . . ."

Internal-consistency reliability is also evidenced in Figure 15–10; note the high degree of agreement between the independently rated characteristics, "quiet" and "silent." (The classification of "quiet" as a positive characteristic and "silent" as a negative characteristic is obviously inappropriate—they are the same in the minds of the raters.)

The immediate validity of sociometric data appears to be quite satisfactory (Mouton et al., 1955) when certain precautions are taken. The confidentiality of the information must be perceived by the respondent; otherwise, many negative perceptions and interrelationships will not be expressed. A second requirement is that the members of the group must know each other quite well. This requirement reduces the value of sociometric data in large schools in which students change classes each period. Sociometric data have had, and will probably continue to have, their greatest utility at the elementary-school level.

Sociometric techniques should be meaningful to the students and should provide useful data for the teacher. Nothing beneficial can be expected to happen merely because each pupil has been asked, for example, to list his or her three best friends. Responses to this kind of question constitute the starting point from which an ingenious teacher studies the social structure of the classroom and devises ways to help it facilitate his or her teaching. The teacher may try to alter the structure slightly in carefully thought-out ways, such as by forming study groups of low mutuality in the hope that this will permit the "friendless" to make friends. The teacher needs to understand the social psychology of the group rather well in order to do this extensively or radically. It is advisable to proceed with caution.

When properly obtained, according to Bonney (1960, p. 1323), sociometric data have validity for the following classroom uses:

(a) to form subgroups which are composed of persons who have indicated preferences for each other, (b) to study changes in interpersonal relations and in the social structure of a group over a particular time interval, (c) to determine the extent to which students of different racial, religious, and social-class grouping accept each other, (d) to locate individuals and small groups of individuals who are outstanding centers of influence in a particular population in order to utilize their social prestige in the management of the group, and (e) to locate individuals who are isolates or fringers in order to plan some kind of assistance for them so that they may achieve some degree of recognition and feeling of belonging.

Sociometric information can also be useful in parent conferences, in enabling parents to understand better how their child is perceived by classmates.

Appraising Socioeconomic Status

The concept of socioeconomic status (SES) is widely used in education, sociology, and psychology. SES is related to many educational characteristics of pupils, such as achievement motivation, dropping out of school, and academic achievement (although the relationship between SES and academic achievement is only about .3—much less than is commonly assumed [Bryant et al., 1974; White, 1976]). Occupation is an important ingredient of SES; its relationship to intelligence is graphically illustrated in Figure 13–14 (p. 367). Since the concept of SES is so pervasive, it is useful to understand how it is measured, even though it is rarely assessed formally except in research studies.

The methods of assessing SES have evolved largely from sociology and social psychology. Several different SES measures have been devised; all of them employ some combination of the following: educational level, occupational level, kind of residence, amount of income, source of income, and dwelling area.

The Warner-Meeker-Eells Scale

The most widely used SES measure is the Index of Status Characteristics (ISC) (Warner, Meeker, and Eells, 1949), which uses four factors to arrive at an ISC score that is then converted into one of five social classes.

Occupation[2]

1. Professionals and proprietors (such as established physicians, lawyers, certified public accountants, major executives, and "gentlemen" farmers)
2. Minor professionals and proprietors (such as beginning or less successful physicians, lawyers, and so on, and owners of large farms)
3. Semiprofessionals (such as salespeople and cashiers)
4. Skilled workers (such as bookkeepers, factory foremen, sheriffs, and railroad engineers)
5. Medium-skill workers (such as telephone operators, carpenters, plumbers, barbers, and fire fighters)
6. Semiskilled workers (such as taxi and truck drivers, gas station attendants, and waiters)
7. Unskilled workers (such as laborers, miners, and janitors)

Source of Income

1. Inherited wealth
2. Earned wealth

[2] See Bonjean, Hill, and McLemore (1967, pp. 442–48) for a detailed explanation of each category.

3. Profits and professional fees
4. Salary and commissions
5. Wages, determined by an hourly rate
6. Private relief
7. Public relief and nonrespectable income

Housing

1. Excellent houses: very large single-family dwellings surrounded by large land-scaped yards
2. Very good houses, but not as large as those in the first category
3. Good houses, more conventional and less ostentatious than those in the first two categories
4. Average houses, conventional single-family dwellings
5. Fair houses, smaller houses whose condition is not quite as good as that of the houses in category 4
6. Poor, badly run-down houses
7. Very poor houses surrounded by debris

Dwelling Area

1. Very high-status area
2. High-status area
3. Above-average area
4. Average area containing workers' homes
5. Below-average area; close to factories or railroads
6. Low-status area; run-down and semi-slum
7. Very low-status area; slum

Earlier, Warner had included amount of education and amount of income, but since these factors were found to be largely redundant with the four just listed they were eliminated from the scale.

The Index of Status Characteristics (ISC) is arrived at by using the category ratings from the four factors in the following equation:

$$ISC = (4 \times occupation) + (3 \times source\ of\ income) + (3 \times house\ type) + (2 \times dwelling\ area)$$

For example, if one is classified into categories 3, 4, 2, 3 for occupation, source of income, house type, and dwelling area, respectively, one's total ISC score is

$$ISC = (4 \times 3) + (3 \times 4) + (3 \times 2) + (2 \times 3) = 36.$$

A social-class rating as defined by Warner (Warner, Meeker, and Eells, 1949) is then assigned according to the ISC score:

ISC Score	*Social-Class Rating*
12–22	Upper class
23–37	Upper-middle class
38–51	Lower-middle class
52–66	Upper-lower class
67–84	Lower-lower class

Hollingshead's Index

Because of the difficulty and cost of obtaining residential information, other SES scales have been devised that do not require it. One of the most common is Hollingshead's (Hollingshead and Redlich, 1957) Two-Factor Index of Social Position.[3] Hollingshead's scale is popular partially because it is easy to use—the index requires only an occupational scale and an educational scale, each of which is divided into seven levels.

Occupational Scale[4]

1. Major executives of large concerns, major professionals, and proprietors
2. Lesser professionals and proprietors, and business managers
3. Administrative personnel, owners of small business, and minor professionals
4. Clerical and sales workers, and technicians
5. Skilled trades
6. Machine operators and semiskilled workers
7. Unskilled employees

Educational Scale

1. Professionals (master's degree, doctorate, or professional degree)
2. College graduates
3. 1–3 years college or business school
4. High school graduates
5. 10–11 years of schooling
6. 7–9 years of schooling
7. Under 7 years of schooling

A total Index of Social Position (ISP) score is arrived at by using the following equation:

$$ISP = (7 \times \text{occupation rating}) + (4 \times \text{education rating})$$

Thus, a carpenter (5) with nine years of school (6) would have a total ISP score of $(7 \times 5) + (4 \times 6) = 59$. Hollingshead classifies the scores into five priorities, as follows:

Social Class	Scores
I	11–17
II	18–27
III	28–43
IV	44–60
V	61–77

Other SES Scales and Uses

Several similar measures may be found in excellent compendiums by Shaw and Wright (1967); Bonjean, Hill, and McLemore (1967); and Miller (1977), although these devices are not always applicable to nonwhites (Stricker, 1978).

---

[3] Material from the Two-Factor Index of Social Position as it appeared in Bonjean, Hill, and McLemore (1967, pp. 381–85) is included by courtesy of Dr. August B. Hollingshead.

[4] See Bonjean, Hill, and McLemore (1967, pp. 442–48) for a detailed explanation of each category.

The scales have important uses in research studies in which SES may be a relevant variable. For example, Harper (1970) investigated the effects of a cognitive stimulating treatment in relation to pupils' SES level and found that the treatment had different effects for high-SES than for low-SES pupils.

Eckland (1964) found that most male college freshmen of modest academic aptitude persisted to eventual graduation if their parents were of fairly high SES, but were less likely to do so if they were of low SES. Thus, the SES of one's parents has some relationship to one's prospects of educational and life success; however, the relationship is not extremely close. Many people move up or down the SES "ladder"—some of them a great distance.

Summary

The value of standardized interest tests is most apparent for vocational guidance purposes. The major tests of this kind are the Strong-Campbell and Kuder.

During the high school years there is considerable fluctuation in interests, which must be considered in interpreting students' profiles. Measured interests have little relationship to abilities, although they are related to occupational choice and job satisfaction.

Personality assessment is difficult and imprecise with current tests and techniques. Self-report personality inventories are vulnerable to semantic difficulties, self-deception, faking, and criterion inadequacy. Such measures have rarely been shown to yield information of any practical clinical value. Projective techniques are not easily faked, but their unique assessment difficulties greatly limit their usefulness for personality appraisal.

Sociometric techniques can help one understand the status and dynamics of groups such as a class of students. The "guess who" technique is particularly useful, since it yields information on several dimensions and requires little time to administer and tabulate.

Measures of socioeconomic status are often useful in research studies but have limited value for individual or classroom use.

IMPORTANT TERMS AND CONCEPTS

situational test
self-report inventory
empirical keying
social-desirability and lie scales

projective techniques
institutional climate measures
sociometric measures
target diagram

guess-who technique
SES

CHAPTER TEST

1. What are the two principal names associated with the major interest inventories?

2. The scoring of the Strong is based on
a) content validity.

   b) criterion-related validity.
   c) construct validity.

3. Which of the Kuder interest inventories is most similar to the Strong (SCII)?
   a) Kuder General Interest Survey (KGIS)
   b) Kuder Preference Record–Vocational (KPR-V)
   c) Kuder Occupational Interest Survey (KOIS)

4. _____ is to normative as Kuder is to _____ .

5. With an ipsative interest measure
   a) examinees can be compared in absolute degree of interest.
   b) examinees are not forced to choose among options.
   c) an intraindividual interpretation is essential.
   d) percentile ranks can be interpreted in the same way as when a normative measure is used.

6. What is the primary source for obtaining critical reviews of published tests?

7. Which one of the following statements about the stability of interests is true?
   a) Interests are more stable for adolescents than for adults.
   b) Interests at age 17 or 18 correlate substantially with interests 15 or 20 years later.
   c) Interests have virtually no stability until people are in their mid-20s.
   d) Test–retest r's for interest tests of .9 or higher are common for a one-year interval.

8. In order to obtain a valid interest profile, which of the following factors is most important?
   a) Giving the SCVI rather than the KOIS
   b) Admonishing the examinee to answer truthfully
   c) Administering the interest inventory individually rather than in a group
   d) Removing incentives to fake

9. In which of these situations is the validity of a personality inventory *least* suspect?
   a) The inventory is administered to applicants for a job.
   b) The inventory is administered to people who are seeking counseling.
   c) The inventory is taken and scored by the examinee as part of a class assignment and results are reported to the instructor.
   d) The inventory is required by the court as part of a probation decision process.

10. Which of these is the most helpful for detecting prevarication by examinees?
   a) Ipsative scales
   b) Normative scales

c) Social desirability scales

d) Scales based on empirical scoring

11. Measured interests have been shown to be more valid than expressed interests for all groups studied. (T or F)

12. Abilities and corresponding interests (e.g., clerical ability and clerical interest) tend to be

a) very highly correlated.

b) highly correlated.

c) substantially correlated.

d) not highly correlated.

13. Which of these conclusions is most strongly supported by research on interest measurement?

a) People tend to end up in occupations for which they have very high scores.

b) People tend to *not* end up in occupations for which they have very low scores.

c) Options a and b are equally strongly supported.

14. Which of these is more blue-collar oriented and may be a more appropriate interest measure than the Strong for non-college-bound individuals?

a) MVII

b) SCII

c) KOIS

15. In interpreting interest inventories one must bear in mind that

a) there is a wide diversity of activities within most occupations.

b) there is considerable variation among jobs with the same label.

c) the duties of many jobs change with time because of automation and the like.

d) Two of the above

e) All of the above

16. Which of these is *not* a self-report personality inventory?

a) Guilford-Zimmerman Temperament Survey

b) CPI

c) TAT

d) MMPI

17. Which of these is least appropriate for use in schools?

a) MTAI

b) MMPI

c) CPI

d) SCII

18. Criterion-related validity is poorest for

a) personality measures.

b) interest measures.

c) achievement measures.

d) scholastic aptitude measures.

19. Which of these is *not* a serious deficiency for almost all personality inventories?

a) Low internal-consistency reliability coefficients
b) Low criterion-related validity
c) Semantic problems
d) Faking
e) Self-deception

20. One advantage projective techniques have over personality inventories is that projective techniques

a) are more valid.
b) are more reliable.
c) have better norms.
d) are less fakable.

21. Which one of these measures has some validity for detecting perceptual difficulties and correlates with academic performance in the primary grades?

a) Rorschach
b) TAT
c) Draw-a-Person
d) Bender Gestalt

22. Current research supports

a) the validity of the theory underlying most projective techniques.
b) the predictive validity of projective techniques.
c) the relationship between performance on projective techniques and psychiatric diagrams.
d) Two or more of the above
e) None of the above

23. In the sociogram results in Figure 15–8, which children appear to be "isolates" (received no votes)? Which boy chose only girls? Did the two girl "stars" select any boys? Did the two most popular boys select any girls?

24. In the "guess who" results in Figure 15–10, which pupil appears to be most highly regarded by the class? Which two students in the class appear to be having the greatest difficulty with peer acceptance? Which child is the quietest?

25. Of these types of measures, which one tends to have the greatest validity?

a) sociometric techniques.
b) projective techniques.
c) personality inventories.

26. The relationship between students' academic achievement and their socioeconomic status (SES) is

a) very high (.8 +).
b) high (.6–.8).
c) substantial (.4–.6).
d) less than .4.

27. Which one of these is not used in the Hollingshead Two-Factor Index of Social Position?

a) Housing

b) Education

c) Occupation

28. Which of these is a more comprehensive SES measure?

a) Hollingshead's scale

b) The Warner-Meeker-Eells scale

29. On which one of these types of measures are ethnic and racial differences least serious?

a) Interest measures

b) SES measures

c) Achievement measures

d) Intelligence measures

30. In order for measures of organizational climate to have high validity, which one of these factors would be most important?

a) An inventory of 100 questions or more

b) A sample of 100 people or more

c) Up-to-date and representative norms

d) Anonymity for the respondents

ANSWERS TO CHAPTER TEST

1. Kuder, Strong
2. b
3. c
4. Strong, ipsative
5. c
6. Buros' *Mental Measurement Yearbook*
7. b
8. d
9. b
10. c

11. F
12. d
13. b
14. a
15. e
16. c
17. b
18. a
19. a
20. d

21. d
22. e
23. *L, M, N, p, q; k;* yes; no
24. 29; 5 and 11; 15
25. a
26. d
27. a
28. b
29. a
30. d

FOR ADDITIONAL READING

ANASTASI, A. *Psychological testing,* 4th ed. New York: Macmillan, 1976. Chapters 17–20 give a thorough treatment of the topics of personality and interest measurement.

BONJEAN, C. M., R. J. HILL, and S. D. MCLEMORE. *Sociological measurement: An inventory of scales and indices.* San Francisco: Chandler, 1967.

BONNEY, J. M. Sociometric methods. In C. W. Harris, ed., *Encyclopedia of educational research,* 3rd ed. New York: Macmillan, 1960. Pp. 1319–24.

CRITES, J. O. Interests. In R. L. Ebel, ed., *Encyclopedia of educational research,* 4th ed. New York: Macmillan, 1969. Pp. 678–86.

GRONLUND, N. E. *Sociometry in the classroom.* New York: Harper & Row, 1959.

JOHNSON, O. G., and J. W. BOMMARITO. *Tests and measurements in child development: A handbook.* San Francisco: Jossey-Bass, 1971.

JOHNSON, R. W. Test review: Strong-Campbell Interest Inventory. *Measurement and Evaluation in Guidance,* 9 (1977), 40–45.

KERLINGER, F. N. *Foundations of behavioral research,* 2nd ed. New York: Holt, Rinehart and Winston, 1973, chaps. 29–32.

KUDER, G. F. Some principles of interest measurement. *Educational and Psychological Measurement,* 30 (1970), 205–26. Reprinted in G. H. Bracht, K. D. Hopkins, and J. C. Stanley, eds., *Perspectives in educational and psychological measurement.* Englewood Cliffs, N.J.: Prentice-Hall, 1972. Selection 28.

MILLER, D. C. *Handbook of research design and social measurement,* 3rd. ed. New York: Longman, 1977.

MILLER, R. I. *The assessment of college performance: A handbook of techniques and measures for institutional self-evaluation.* San Francisco: Jossey-Bass, 1979.

MOOS, R. H. *Evaluating educational environments: Procedures, measures, findings, and policy implications.* San Francisco: Jossey-Bass, 1979.

SUPER, D. E. Interests. In C. W. Harris, ed., *Encyclopedia of educational research,* 3rd ed. New York: Macmillan, 1960. Pp. 728–33.

WARNER, W. L., M. MEEKER, and K. EELLS. *Social class in America.* Chicago: Science Research Associates, 1949.

APPENDIX A

Resources for the Development and Selection of Measuring Instruments*

AMERICAN ALLIANCE FOR HEALTH, PHYSICAL EDUCATION, AND RECREATION. *Testing for Impaired, Disabled, and Handicapped Individuals.* Washington, D.C.: American Alliance for Health, Physical Education, and Recreation, undated. This monograph contains information about 60 instruments designed for handicapped persons. Types of measures included: motor ability, perceptual-motor development, physical fitness, and developmental profiles.

BEATTY, W. H. *Improving educational assessment and an inventory of measures of affective behavior.* Washington, D.C.: Association for Supervision and Curriculum Development, NEA, 1969. Section II gives a very brief description of approximately 130 instruments classified in eight categories: attitude, creativity, interaction, motivation, personality, readiness, self-concept, and miscellaneous. Instruments are not critically evaluated.

BEERE, C. A. *Women and women's issues: A handbook of tests and measures.* San Francisco: Jossey-Bass, 1979. A handbook designed to help locate suitable instruments for scientifically studying children's sex role behavior, women's attitudes toward marriage and work, men's and women's attitudes toward women's issues, and other related topics.

BONJEAN, C. M., R. J. HILL, and S. D. McLEMORE. *Sociological measurement: An inventory of scales and indices.* San Francisco: Chandler, 1967. Contains bibliographic information on approximately 2,000 sociological scales used in sociological research published between 1954 and 1965. The scales and indexes are divided into 78 conceptual classes; 47 measures that were used or cited more than five times are described in detail. Information in these detailed descriptions includes classification, title, bibliographic information, variables measured, de-

* Descriptions of several of these resources are adapted from Ward and Fetler (1979), Lake, Miles, and Earle (1973), and Miller (1977).

463

velopmental procedures, scoring procedures, validity and reliability data, and a description of the sample with which the measure was used. Copies of some of the instruments are included. Section M of Miller (1977) extends this compendium through 1974.

BORICH, G. D., and S. K. MADDEN. *Evaluating Classroom Instruction: A sourcebook of instruments.* Reading, Mass.: Addison-Wesley, 1977. Describes approximately 175 measures classified using a two-dimensional grid: what is being evaluated (teacher, pupil, or classroom) and by whom it is being evaluated (teacher, pupil, or observer). Instruments are described in terms of type of measure, availability, reliability, validity, norms, and procedures for use. Copies of the instruments are not included, although sample items are provided.

BOYER, E. G., A. SIMON, and G. R. KARAFIN, eds. *Measures of Maturation: An Anthology of Early Childhood Observation Instruments.* Philadelphia: Research for Better Schools, 1973. A three-volume anthology that describes 73 observational systems for recording children's behavior. (See annotation of Simon and Boyer, 1970.)

BUROS, O. K., ed. *Test in print II.* Highland Park, N.J.: Gryphon Press, 1974. Contains 14 major sections: (1) a comprehensive bibliography of all known tests published for use with English-speaking subjects; (2) a classified index to the contents of the test sections of the seven *Mental measurements yearbooks* (MMYs) published to date; (3) a reprinting of the 1974 APA-AERA-NCME *Standards for educational and psychological tests;* (4) comprehensive bibliographies on the construction, use, and validity of certain specific tests through 1971; (5) a classified list of tests that have gone out of print since the 1961 *Tests in print* was published; (6) a cumulative name index for each test, with references; (7) a title index that covers in-print and out-of-print tests, as well as inverted, series, and superseded titles in the MMYs; (8) a name index covering all authors of tests, reviews, excerpts, and references in the MMYs; (9) a publishers' directory with a complete listing of each publisher's test titles; (10) a classified scanning list that describes the population for which each test is intended; (11) identification of foreign tests and journals, with the country of origin in brackets immediately after a test entry or journal; (12) factual statements implying criticism, e.g., "1971 tests identical with 1961 copyrighted tests except for

format," "no manual," etc.; (13) listing of test titles at the foot of each page to permit immediate identification of pages consisting only of references or names; and (14) directions on how to use the book and an expanded table of contents.

BUROS, O. K., ed. *The eighth mental measurements yearbook.* Highland Park, N.J.: Gryphon Press, 1978. Contains critical reviews of virtually all current, commercially available tests (and measurement textbooks) in the fields of education and psychology. Copies of the tests are not included, but publishers are identified. Extensive bibliographies for the tests are provided. See Table 14–3 (p. 408) for a detailed classification of the measures included. Reviews from Volumes 1–7 of the MMY have been completed and published as separate volumes: *Personality Tests and Reviews* (vols. 1, 2), *Reading Tests and Reviews* (vols. 1, 2), *Intelligence Tests and Reviews, Vocational Tests and Reviews, English Tests and Reviews, Foreign Language Tests and Reviews, Science Tests and Reviews,* and *Social Studies Tests and Reviews.*

CATTELL, R. B., and F. WARBURTON. *Objective personality and motivation tests.* Urbana: University of Illinois Press, 1967. The major portion of this volume is a compendium of personality measures. Each measure is described as follows: test title, author's designation and age range of test, administration time, formal structure of test (e.g., ability, performance, opinionnaire, projective, etc.), variables derived from test, techniques for achieving unfakability, theory supporting the test, design (positive and negative features), sample test items, and procedures for administration and scoring. No psychometric data are provided on validity or other technical qualities of the instruments.

CHUN, K., S. COBB, AND J. FRENCH. *Measures for psychological assessment: A guide to 3,000 original sources and their application.* Ann Arbor: University of Michigan, Institute for Social Research, 1975. Developed to provide a comprehensive bibliography on all measures of mental health and related concepts, the volume entries are based on a search of 26 measurement-related journals in psychology and sociology from 1960 to 1970. Information that is relevant to a particular test includes a bibliographic reference to the first source that described the device, the test's title, key words that describe its content, bibliographic data referencing an article or in which the test has been used, and a set of terms indicating the type of information available in the article.

CLARKE, H. *Physical and Motor Tests in the Medford Boys' Growth Study.* Englewood Cliffs, N.J.: Prentice-Hall, 1971. A useful resource for psychomotor and physical measures of physical maturity, physique type, body size, muscular strength and endurance, motor ability, and athletic ability.

COMPTON, C. *A guide to 65 tests for special education.* Belmont, Calif.: Pitman Learning, 1980. Commonly used measures are described and briefly evaluated in the following areas of special education: Academic Achievement (reading, mathematics, language); Perception and Memory (comprehension, auditory, visual and visual-motor); Speech and Language (articulation, language); Gross Motor; Preschool and Kindergarten; Intelligence and Developmental.

COMREY, A. L., T. E. BACKER, and E. M. GLASER. *A sourcebook for mental health measures.* Los Angeles: Human Interaction Research Institute, 1973. Includes 1,100 abstracts of mental-health-related psychological measures classified into 45 categories (e.g., alcoholism, drugs, marriage and divorce, racial attitudes, suicide and death). Each abstract gives title of the measure, source of the measure, author's name and address, and an abstract of 300 words or less providing the following information: purpose of the measure, target population administration time, number of items, types of items, response modes, available reliability and validity data, and findings of the major research application of the measure. Also furnished is information on how to obtain a copy of the measure.

EDUCATIONAL TESTING SERVICE. *Disadvantaged Children and Their First School Experiences: ETS—Head Start Longitudinal Study. Theoretical Considerations and Measurement Strategies.* Princeton, N.J.: Educational Testing Service, 1968. (Also available in ERIC, ED 037486.) ETS maintains an extensive library of over 10,000 measures which serves as an archive of testing materials. On-site access to the test collection is available to qualified persons. Current annotated bibliographies available (with ERIC access numbers) include: Assessing the Attitudes of Young Children (ED 056 086), Language Development Tests (ED 056 082), Measures of Infant Development (ED 058 326), Measures of Social Skills (ED 056 085), School Readiness Measures (ED 056 083), Self-Concept Measures (ED 051 305), (ED 086 737), Tests for Spanish-Speaking Children (ED 056 084).

GOLDMAN, B. A., and J. L. SAUNDERS. *Directory of unpublished experimental measures,* vol. 1. New York: Behavioral Publications, 1974. A very brief description (purpose, number of items, format, source) of 339 unpublished measures classified into achievement (21), adjustment-educational (6), adjustment-psychological (16), adjustment-social (27), aptitude (5), attitudes (22), communication (8), concept meaning (20), creativity (8), development (7), family (9), institutional information (44), interests (10), motivation (7), personality (16), perception (30), preference (11), status (10), trait measurement (22), values (5), and vocational education (34). Instruments are those used in studies published in 29 journals in 1970.

GOLDMAN, B. A., and J. C. BUSCH. *Directory of unpublished experimental measures,* vol. 2. New York: Human Sciences Press, 1979. An extension of the Goldman/Saunders work. Parallels the previous volume in content and organization.

GOODWIN, W. L. and L. A. DRISCOLL. 1980. *Handbook for measurement and evaluation in early childhood education.* San Francisco: Jossey-Bass. Includes a compendium containing detailed yet concise information on measurement concepts, observation procedures, tests and other measures, evaluation designs, and assessment techniques appropriate for preschool levels.

HOEPFNER, R., et al.
   1971. *CSE-ECR Preschool/kindergarten test evaluations.*
   1972. *CSE-RBS Test Evaluations: Tests of Higher-order cognitive, affective, and interpersonal skills.*
   1974. *CSE Secondary School Test Evaluations:* Grades 7 and 8.
   1974. *CSE Secondary School Test Evaluations:* Grades 9 and 10.
   1974. *CSE Secondary School Test Evaluations:* Grades 11 and 12.
   1976. *CSE Elementary School Test Evaluations.*
Los Angeles: UCLA, Center for the Study of Evaluation. Hundreds of published cognitive, affective, and psychomotor instruments are classified into categories and numerically rated in tabular format with respect to approximately 40 characteristics, which are subsets of the four major criteria: measurement validity, examinee

appropriateness, administrative usability, and normed technical excellence. Ratings are useful in identifying measures for more careful review. Tests are keyed to a list of specific educational goals and indexed by goal and test title.

JOHNSON, O. G., et al. *Tests and measurements in child development: Handbooks I and II.* San Francisco: Jossey-Bass, 1971, 1976. A comprehensive guide to noncommercial or unpublished measures in child development covering the age group from birth to 18 and the years 1956–75. Instruments are classified into ten categories. Each description provides the following information: title, author(s), age of subjects for whom the instrument is suitable, variable(s), type of measure, administration and scoring, source from which the tool may be obtained, description of the tool, reliability and validity data, and bibliographic citations.

KEGAN, D. L. *SCALES/RIQS: An inventory of research instruments.* Evanston, Ill., 1970. Contains more than 350 instruments measuring variables that are relevant to organizational theory, stored and retrieved by computer. Information includes author, reference, date, reliability and validity, variables measured, and author comments in 100–150 words. An associated computer file, PROPS/RIQS, is used to retrieve associated empirical studies.

LAKE, D., M. MILES, and R. EARLE. *Measuring human behavior.* New York: Teachers College Press, 1973. Provides systematic reviews of 84 different instruments that meet certain criteria in the following categories: personal variable (38), interpersonal (24), groups (10), and organizational relationships (12). Information provided on each instrument includes title, author, availability, variable measured, format, administration, scoring, development, critique (i.e., psychometric data), general comments (usefulness, cautions, etc.), references, and "uniterms" (key words). The volume also contains reviews of other compendia of instruments.

LYERLY, S. B. *Handbook of psychiatric rating scales.* Rockville, Md.: National Institute of Mental Health, 1973. Contains descriptions of 38 published and unpublished rating scales that are being used or have been used in psychiatric settings with adults and children, as well as some that are general social and vocational adjustment. The basic descriptive format on each scale includes title, source, general description, patients, rater information, source of scale items,

reliability and validity data, and related references. Also included is a listing and brief description of 23 additional scales that have not been used often in recent years but are of historical significance.

MARDELL, C. D. and D. S. GOLDENBERG. *Learning Disabilities/Early Childhood Research Project.* Springfield: Illinois State Office of the Superintendent of Public Instruction, 1972. (Also available in ERIC, ED 082408.) Over 900 instruments for identifying preschool children with potential learning disabilities are evaluated using the criteria of age-appropriateness, administration conditions, cost, and range of behaviors assessed. Critique of 90 instruments are included.

MILLER, D. C. *Handbook of research design and social measurement,* 3rd ed. New York: D. McKay, 1977. Part 4 of the volume describes approximately 50 measures divided into 12 categories: social status; group structure and dynamics; social indicators; organizational structure; organizational effectiveness; community; social participation; leadership in the work organization; morale and job satisfaction; scales of attitudes, values, and norms; family and marriage; and personality measurements. Each review includes title, author, variable(s) measured, description of the measure, where published, reliability and validity data, utility of the measure, and bibliographic data denoting instances of the measure's use in research. In most instances a copy of the measure itself is also included.

MILLER, R. I. *The assessment of college performance: A handbook of techniques and measures for institutional self-evaluation.* San Francisco: Jossey-Bass, 1979. A guide to the task of institution-wide evaluation. The handbook provides the measurement forms needed to appraise institutions. Areas included are faculty, learning, curriculum, administration, financial management, and evaluation. An annotated bibliography of key literature on institutional assessment is provided.

PRICE, J. L. *Handbook of organizational measurement.* Lexington, Mass.: D. C. Heath, 1972. Contains descriptions of measures for 22 concepts relative to organizations. Descriptive information about each measure includes format, definition, data collection procedures, validity, reliability, comments, source of the measure, and further sources of information.

REEDER, L. G., L. RAMACHER, and S. GORELNIK. *Handbook of scales and indices of health behavior.* Pacific Palisades, Calif.: Goodyear, 1976. Focuses on scales and indexes within a defined segment of health services behavior research, i.e., health status, health behavior, health orientations, and utilization of health services. Descriptive information includes author(s); title; major health concept investigated; research design; theoretical framework; research hypotheses and/or questions; model used; conceptualization and operationalization of independent, intervening, and dependent variables; description of population, sample, and analysis units; and major findings and interpretation. Copies of the scales and indexes are also included.

ROBINSON, J. P., R. ATHANASIOU, and K. B. HEAD. *Measures of occupational attitudes and occupational characteristics.* Ann Arbor: University of Michigan, Institute for Social Research, 1969. Provides a systematic review and evaluation of 80 instruments relevant to the study of variables that pertain to occupations. Instruments are classified into categories: general job satisfaction (13), job satisfaction for particular occupations (5), satisfaction with specific job features (8), concepts related to job satisfaction (8), occupational values (7), leadership styles (8), other work-relevant attitudes (10), vocational interest measures (4), and occupational status measures (8). Typical items are provided.

ROBINSON, J. P., J. G. RUSK, and K. B. HEAD. *Measures of Political Attitudes.* Ann Arbor: University of Michigan, Institute for Social Research, Social Research Center, 1968. Approximately 100 measures are classified by domain assessed: liberalism–conservatism (17), democratic principles (6), domestic government policies (5), racial and ethnic attitudes (13), international affairs (12), hostility-related national attitudes (11), community-based political attitudes (6), political information (4), political participation (7), attitudes toward political process (14), and miscellaneous (9). Instruments are described in 300–500 words in terms of sample used, reliability, validity, source, administration, and results and comments. Copies of instruments are included.

ROBINSON, J. P., and P. SHAVER. *Measures of social psychological attitudes,* rev. ed. Ann Arbor: University of Michigan, 1973. Approximately 100 scales are reviewed in 300–500 words under the headings of self-esteem, alienation anomia,

authoritarianism/dogmatism, socio-political values, attitudes toward people, religious attitudes, and methodological scales (e.g., social desirability).

SHAW, M. E., and J. M. WRIGHT. *Scales for the measurement of attitudes.* New York: McGraw-Hill, 1967. In addition to chapters on the nature of attitudes and methods of scale construction, includes descriptions of 176 attitude scales that deal with social issues and practices, international issues, abstract concepts, political and religious attitudes, ethnic and national groups, significant others, and social institutions. Descriptive material about each scale includes title, description, subjects, response mode, reliability and validity, and comments on strengths and/or weaknesses. An exhibit of each instrument accompanies the description. Evaluative comments on the adequacy of the scales are presented.

SIMON, A., and E. G. BOYER. *Mirrors for behavior: An anthology of observation instruments,* 14 vols. Philadelphia: Research for Better Schools, 1970. Approximately 100 "systems" and instruments for measuring variables in the school setting via observation are described; most pertain specifically to classroom observation. A given system is classified with respect to content focus [affective, cognitive, psychomotor (body movement), activity, content, sociological structure, and physical environment], coding units used (e.g., time unit, speaker change), collecting and coding methods (video/audio required, number of observers), setting focus (classroom vs. nonclassroom, counseling, group dynamics, subject matter), population observed (teacher, pupil, family, small group, counselor, administrator), number of subjects observed, and purpose of observation (research, feedback, evaluation). Abstracts of each instrument/system are contained in a "summary" volume.

STRAUSS, M. A. *Family measurement techniques: Abstracts of published instruments, 1935-1965.* Minneapolis: University of Minnesota Press, 1969. Educational, psychological, and sociological professional journal literature from 1935 to 1965 was searched; 319 family behavior measures were classified into adolescent, child, family, parent, premarital, and spousal categories and described in this volume. Each abstract contains the following material on the measure described: author, title, variables measured, instrument description, a sample item, validity data, sample size, sampling method, sample characteristics, reliability, norms, administration and scoring, availability, and references. Evaluative comments are few but can be found elsewhere (Straus, 1964; Mussen, 1960).

THOMAS, H. "Psychological Assessment Instruments for Use with Human Infants." *Merrill-Palmer Quarterly,* 1970, 16, 179–223, Review of 9 instruments, together with related research: variables assessed, format, administration procedures, test content, standardization procedures, and validity.

WALKER, D. K. *Socioemotional measures for preschool and kindergarten children.* San Francisco: Jossey-Bass, 1973. Lists and describes 143 commercial and noncommercial, published and unpublished, measures that focus on the social and emotional behavioral areas of children aged 3 to 6. The measures are divided into six categories—attitudes, general personality and emotional adjustment, interests or preferences, personality or behavior traits, self-concept, and social skills or competency. For each measure, Walker provides title, author(s), age range of appropriate respondents, measurement technique involved, sources in which measure is described, where measure can be obtained, administration and scoring information, norms, reliability, and validity data.

WARD, M. J., and M. E. FETLER. *Instruments for use in nursing education research.* Boulder, Colo.: Western Interstate Commission for Higher Education, 1979. Descriptions, brief critiques of approximately 75 previously unpublished instruments used in nursing education research. Approximately 50 published instruments are also described.

WARD, M. J., C. LINDEMAN, and D. BLOCH, eds. *Instruments for measuring nursing and other health care variables: Psychosocial and physiological.* Washington, D.C.: Government Printing Office, 1978. Contains descriptions of 138 instruments for measuring psychosocial variables and 19 pieces of apparatus for measuring human physiological variables. Headings for descriptions of psychosocial instruments include title, author(s), variables measured, nature and content, administration and scoring, development (rationale, source of items, procedure for development), reliability and validity, use in research, comments, references, sources of additional information, and copyright information. Copies of 133 of the instruments are included. The headings for the physiological instrument descriptions are title, variable(s), parameters, research application, description, and comments. Indexed by author, title, and key concepts.

WYLIE, R. C. *The self concept: A review of methodological considerations and measuring instruments.* Lincoln: University of Nebraska Press, 1974. This comprehensive volume extends and updates the author's previous work: *The self concept: A critical survey of pertinent research* (1961, same publisher). A critical analysis of conceptual and theoretical issues in the measurement of self-concept, self-regard, self-acceptance, and related constructs. Widely used instruments of many formats (Q-sort, questionnaires, rating scales, adjective checklists) are evaluated.

Other Resources

Psychological Abstracts gives a brief summary of current articles relative to educational and psychological tests. Relevant articles tend to be classified under such headings as "Psychometrics and Statistics," "Test Construction and Validation," "Educational Psychology," and "Applied Psychology." It is also possible to obtain a computer search of articles indexed by key terms.

Education Index deals with the general field of education but organizes material by topic (e.g., ability tests, educational measurement, and mental tests).

The Educational Resources Information Clearinghouse (ERIC) for tests and measurements at the Educational Testing Service assembles literature on selected tests and measurement issues. Access is through usual ERIC channels. Abstracts can be found in *Resources in education;* computer searches are also possible. The *Test collection bulletin* lists acquisitions to the Educational Testing Service Test Collection, an extensive library of standardized tests and assessment devices.

Periodicals that are useful in applied educational and psychological measurement include *Educational and Psychological Measurement, Journal of Educational Measurement, Applied Psychological Measurement, Measurement and Evaluation in Guidance, The Testing Digest,* and *New Directions for Testing and Measurement*. Occasional articles in *Psychological Bulletin, Review of Educational Research, Annual Review of Psychology, Annual Review of Research in Education, Evaluation Review,* and *Evaluation Studies Review Annual* pertain to measurement and assessment.

APPENDIX B

Major Publishers of Standardized Tests

The following list includes the most significant test publishers, as indicated by Buros' (1974) *Tests in print II*. The number of tests published is given in parentheses following each entry.

ADDISON-WESLEY PUBLISHING COMPANY, 2725 Sand Hill Rd., Menlo Park, Calif. 94025 (89)

AMERICAN COLLEGE TESTING PROGRAM, P.O. Box 168, Iowa City, Iowa 52240 (33).

AMERICAN GUIDANCE SERVICES, INC., Publishers Bldg., Circle Pines, Maine (39).

AUSTRALIAN COUNCIL FOR EDUCATIONAL RESEARCH, P.O. Box 210, Hawthorn, Victoria, 3122 Australia (47).

BOBBS-MERRILL COMPANY, INC., 4300 East 62nd St., Indianapolis, Ind. 46268 (69).

COLLEGE BOARD, 888 Seventh Ave., New York, N.Y. 10019 (111).

CONSULTING PSYCHOLOGISTS PRESS, INC., 577 College Ave., Palo Alto, Calif. 94306 (51).

CTB/McGRAW-HILL, Del Monte Research Park, Monterey, Calif. 93940 (39).

EDUCATIONAL TESTING SERVICE, Princeton, N.J. 08540 (130).

HARCOURT BRACE JOVANOVICH, INC., 757 Third Ave., New York, N.Y. 10017 (64).

HODDER & STROUGHTON EDUCATIONAL, P.O. Box 702, Dunton Green, Sevenoaks, Kent TN13 2YD, England (33).

HOUGHTON MIFFLIN COMPANY, 1 Beacon St., Boston, Mass. 02107 (46).

470

HUMAN SCIENCES RESEARCH COUNCIL, Private Bag 41, Pretoria, Republic of South Africa (30).

INSTITUTE FOR PERSONALITY & ABILITY TESTING, 1602 Coronado Dr., Champaign, Ill. 61820 (15).

NATIONAL INSTITUTE FOR PERSONNEL RESEARCH, P.O. Box 10319, Johannesburg, Republic of South Africa (31).

NATIONAL OCCUPATIONAL COMPETENCY TESTING INSTITUTE, 45 Colvin Ave., Albany, N.Y. 12206 (25).

NFER PUBLISHING COMPANY, 2 Jennings Bldgs., Thames Ave., Windsor Berks SL4 1QS England (49). (Formerly Ginn & Co.)

PSYCHOLOGICAL CORPORATION, 707 Third Ave., New York, N.Y. 10017 (94).

PSYCHOMETRIC AFFILIATES, Box 3167, Munster, Ind. 46321 (101).

SCIENCE RESEARCH ASSOCIATES, INC., 155 N. Wacker Dr., Chicago, Ill. 60606 (75).

SHERIDAN PSYCHOLOGICAL SERVICES, P.O. Box 6101, Orange, Calif. 92667 (36).

STOELTING CO., 1350 So. Kostner Ave., Chicago, Ill. 60623 (22).

WESTERN PSYCHOLOGICAL SERVICES, 12031 Wilshire Blvd., Los Angeles, Calif. 90025 (98).

Bibliography

ABBOT, R. D., and D. PERKINS. 1978. Development and construct validity of a set of student rating-of-instruction items. *Educational and Psychological Measurement,* 38:1069–75.

ABRAMOWITZ, S., and A. I. LAW. 1978. The California High School Proficiency Exam: A study of student choice. *AERA 1978 Annual Meeting: Abstracts of Papers.* Washington, D.C.: AERA.

ABRAMSON, T. 1969. The influence of examiner race on first-grade and kindergarten subjects' Peabody Picture Vocabulary Test scores. *Journal of Educational Measurement,* 6:241–46.

ACE, M. C., and DAWIS, R. V. 1973. Item structure as a determinant of item difficulty in verbal analogies. *Educational and Psychological Measurement,* 33:143–49.

AIKEN, L. R., JR. 1963. The grading behavior of a college faculty. *Educational and Psychological Measurement,* 23:319–22.

AIRASIAN, P. W. 1979. A perspective on the uses and misuses of standardized achievement tests. *NCME measurement in education,* 10:1–12.

AIRASIAN, P. W., and G. F. MADAUS. 1972. Criterion-referenced testing in the classroom. *NCME measurement in education,* 3:1–8.

AITKEN, K. 1977. Using cloze procedure as an overall language proficiency test. *TESOL Quarterly,* 11:59–67.

ALDERMAN, D. L. and D. E. POWERS. 1980. *The effects of special preparation on SAT-Verbal Scores. American Educational Research Journal,* 17:239–51.

ALEAMONI, L. 1978. Development and factorial validation of the Arizona counsel instructor evaluation questionnaire. *Educational and Psychological Measurement,* 38:1063–67.

ALKER, H. A., CARLSON, J. A., and HERMAN, M. G. 1969. Multiple-choice questions and students' characteristics. *Journal of Educational Psychology,* 60:231–43.

ALLISON, D. E. 1970. Test anxiety, stress, and intelligence-test peformance. *Canadian Journal of Behavioral Science,* 2:26–37.

472

THE AMERICAN COLLEGE. 1978. *Test wiseness: Test-taking skills for adults.* New York: McGraw-Hill.

AMERICAN ALLIANCE FOR HEALTH, PHYSICAL EDUCATION, AND RECREATION. (undated). *Testing for Impaired, Disabled, and Handicapped Individuals,* Washington, D.C.: American Alliance for Health, Physical Education, and Recreation.

AMERICAN COLLEGE TESTING PROGRAM. 1973. *Technical Report for the ACT Assessment Program.* Iowa City.

AMERICAN PERSONNEL AND GUIDANCE ASSOCIATION. 1972. The responsible use of tests: A position paper of AMEG, APGA, and NCME. *Measurement and Evaluation in Guidance,* 5:385–88.

AMERICAN PSYCHOLOGICAL ASSOCIATION. 1974. *Standards for educational and psychological tests and manuals.* Washington, D.C.

AMMONS, MARGARET. 1969. Objectives and outcomes. In R. L. Ebel, ed., *Encyclopedia of educational research,* 4th ed. New York: Macmillan. Pp. 908–14.

ANASTASI, A. 1958. Heredity, environment, and the question "How?" *Psychological Review,* 65:197–208.

———. 1968, 1976. *Psychological testing,* 3rd and 4th ed. New York: Macmillan.

ANDERSON, B. L. 1972. Sex differences in variability on standardized intelligence and aptitude tests. Masters thesis, University of Colorado.

———. 1977. Differences in teacher's judgment policies for varying numbers of verbal and numerical clues. *Organizational Behavior and Human Performance,* 19:68–88.

ANDERSON, J. H. 1974. Cloze measures as indices of achievement comparison when learning from extended prose. *Journal of Educational Measurement,* 11:83–92.

ANDERSON, R. 1970. Comments on Professor Gagné's paper entitled "Instructional variables and learning outcomes." In M. C. Wittrock and D. E. Wiley, eds., *The evaluation of instruction.* New York: Holt, Rinehart and Winston.

ANDERSON, R. D. 1967. Has the objective been attained? *Science and Children,* 5:33–36.

ANDERSON, R. H. 1966. The importance and purposes of reporting. *National Elementary School Principal,* 45:6–11.

ANDERSON, S. B. 1952. Sequence in multiple choice item opinions. *Journal of Educational Psychology,* 43:364–68.

ANGOFF, W. H. 1971. Scales, norms, and equivalent scores. In R. L. Thorndike, ed., *Educational measurement,* 2nd ed. Washington, D.C.: American Council on Education. Chap. 15.

ARMITAGE, J. H. 1967. *Analysis of citizenship goals in social studies instruction.* Doctoral dissertation, University of Colorado. University Microfilms, no. 68–10,601. *Dissertation Abstracts,* 29:396-A, 397-A (August 1968).

ARMSTRONG, R. J., and R. F. MOONEY. 1969. Confidence testing: Is it reliable? Paper read at the annual meeting of the National Council on Measurement in Education, Los Angeles, February.

ASHBURN, R. R. 1938. An experiment in the essay-type question. *Journal of Experimental Education,* 7:1–3.

ASTIN, A. W. 1970. *Predicting academic performance in college.* New York: Free Press.

AYRES, L. P. 1918. History and present status of educational measurements. *Seventeenth yearbook of the National Society for the Study of Education, Part II.* Bloomington, Ill.: Public School Publishing.

BAGLEY, W. C. 1900. On the correlation of mental and motor ability in school children. *American Journal of Psychology,* 12:193–205.

BAILARD, V. and R. STRANG. 1964. *Parent-teacher conferences.* New York: McGraw-Hill.

BAILEY, R. L. 1977. The test of standard written English: Another look. *Measurement and Evaluation in Guidance,* 10:70–74.

BAIRD, L. L., and W. J. FEISTER. 1972. Grading standards: The relation of changes in average student ability to the average grades awarded. *American Educational Research Journal,* 9:431–42.

BAJTELSMIT, J. 1977. Test-wiseness and systematic desensitization programs for increasing adult test-taking skills. *Journal of Educational Measurement,* 14:335–42.

BAKER, F. B. 1965. Origins of the item parameters X_{50} and beta as a modern item analysis technique. *Journal of Educational Measurement,* 2:167–80.

BARCH, A. M. 1957. The relation of departure time and retention to academic achievement. *Journal of Educational Psychology,* 48:352–58.

BAUER, D. H. 1973. Error sources in aptitude and achievement test scores: A review and recommendation. *Measurement and Evaluation in Guidance.* Selection 6, pp. 5–43.

BAYLEY, N. 1955. On the growth of intelligence. *American Psychologist,* 10:805–17.

———, and M. H. ODEN. 1955. The maintenance of intellectual ability in gifted adults. *Journal of Gerontology,* 10:91–107.

BEATON, A. E., T. L. HILTON, and W. B. SCHRADER. 1977. *Changes in the verbal abilities of high school seniors, college entrants, and SAT candidates between 1960 and 1972.* Princeton, N.J.: Educational Testing Service.

BECK, M. D. 1974. Achievement test reliability as a function of pupil-response procedures. *Journal of Educational Measurement,* 11:109–14.

BEERE, C. A. 1979. *Women and women's issues: A handbook of tests and measures.* San Francisco: Jossey-Bass.

BEESON, R. O. 1973. Immediate knowledge of results and test performance. *Journal of Educational Research,* 66:224–26.

BEGGS, D. L., and A. N. HIERONYMUS. 1968. Uniformity of growth in the basic skills throughout the school year and during the summer. *Journal of Educational Measurement,* 5:91–97. Reprinted in G. H. Bracht, K. D. Hopkins, and J. C. Stanley, eds. 1972. *Perspectives in educational and psychological measurement.* Englewood Cliffs, N.J.: Prentice-Hall. Selection 5.

BENDER, L. 1970. Use of the Visual Motor Gestalt Test in the diagnosis of learning disabilities. *Journal of Special Education,* 4:29–39.

BENNETT, G. K., and J. E. DOPPELT. 1956. Item difficulty and speed of response. *Educational and Psychological Measurement,* 16:494–96.

———, H. G. SEASHORE, and A. G. WESMAN. 1974. *Differential Aptitude Tests,* 5th ed. Manual, Forms M and L. New York: Psychological Corp.

BERDIE, R. F. 1955. Aptitude, achievement, interest, and personality tests: A longitudinal comparison. *Journal of Applied Psychology,* 39:103–14.

BERG, H. D. 1958. Suggestions for increasing the thought content of objective test items. Mimeographed, 9 pp.

———. 1961. Evaluation in social science. In P. L. Dressel, ed., *Evaluation in higher education.* Boston: Houghton Mifflin. Chap. 4.

BERGEN, F. H., and G. T. HARPER. 1973. Predictive validity of measured vocational interests with black and white college men. *Measurement and Evaluation in Guidance,* 6:19–27.

BERGLUND, G. W. 1969. Effect of knowledge of results on retention. *Psychology in Schools,* 6, 420–21.

BERK, R. A. 1980. *Criterion-referenced measurement: The state of the art.* Baltimore: Johns Hopkins Press.

BERNARD, J. 1966. Achievement test norms and time of year of testing. *Psychology in Schools,* 3:273–75.

BEUCHERT A. K., and J. L. MENDOZA. 1979. A Monte Carlo comparison of ten item discrimination indices. *Journal of Educational Measurement,* 16:109–18.

BINET, A. 1911. *Les idées modernes sur les enfants.* Paris: Flammarion.

———, and T. SIMON. 1916. *The development of intelligence in children.* Translated by Elizabeth S. Kite. Baltimore: Williams & Wilkins.

BIRD, D. E. 1953. Teaching listening comprehension. *Journal of Communication,* 3:127–30.

BIRREN, J. E. 1960. Psychological aspects of aging. In P. R. Farnsworth, ed., *Annual Review of Psychology,* vol. 11. Palo Alto: Annual Reviews. Pp. 161–98.

BLESSUM, W. T. 1969. *Annual Report 1968–1969, Medical Computer Facility.* Irvine: University of California, Irvine, California College of Medicine.

BLOCK, J. 1961. *The Q-sort method in personality assessment and psychiatric research.* Springfield, Ill.: Charles C Thomas.

BLOCK, J. H., ed. 1971. *Mastery learning: Theory and practice.* New York: Holt, Rinehart and Winston.

BLOOM, B. S. 1956. The 1955 normative study of the tests of general educational development. *School Review,* 64:110–24.

———. 1961. Quality control in education. In *Tomorrow's teaching.* Oklahoma City: Frontiers of Science Foundation. Pp. 54–61.

474

——. 1964. *Stability and change in human characteristics.* New York: Wiley.

——, M. D. ENGLEHART, G. J. FURST, W. H. HILL, and D. R. KRATHWOHL. 1956. *Taxonomy of educational objectives* (subtitle: The classification of educational goals): *Handbook I, The cognitive domain.* New York: David McKay Company, Inc.

——, J. T. HASTINGS, and G. F. MADAUS. 1971. *Handbook on formative and summative evaluation of student learning.* New York: McGraw-Hill.

BOAG, A. K., and M. NEILD. 1962. The influence of the time factor on the scores of the Triggs Diagnostic Reading Test as reflected in the performance of secondary school pupils grouped according to ability. *Journal of Educational Research,* 55:181–83.

BOERSMA, W. C. 1967. The effectiveness of the evaluative criteria as a stimulus for school improvement in eleven Michigan high schools. Doctoral dissertation, University of Michigan, 184 pp.

BOYER, E. G., A. SIMON, and G. R. KARAFIN, eds. 1973. *Measures of Maturation: An Anthology of Early Childhood Observation Instruments.* Philadelphia: Research for Better Schools.

BRADBURN, N. M., S. SUDMAN, et al. 1979. *Improving interview method and questionnaire design.* San Francisco: Jossey-Bass.

BRASKAMP, L. A., D. CAULLEY, and F. COSTIN. 1979. Student ratings and instructor self-ratings and their relationship to student achievement. *American Educational Research Journal,* 16:295–306.

BONJEAN, C. M., R. J. HILL, and S. D. McLEMORE. 1967. *Sociological measurement: An inventory of scales and indices.* San Francisco: Chandler Publishing.

BONNEY, M. E. 1960. Sociometric methods. In C. W. Harris, ed., *Encyclopedia of educational research,* 3rd ed. New York: Macmillan. Pp. 1319–24.

BORGEN, F. H., and G. T. HARPER. 1973. Predictive validity of measured vocational interests with black and white college men. *Measurement and Evaluation in Guidance,* 6:19–27.

BORMUTH, J. R. 1967. Comparable cloze and multiple-choice comprehension test scores. *Journal of Reading,* 10:291–99.

——. 1968. Cloze test readability: Criterion reference scores. *Journal of Educational Measurement,* 5:189–96.

——. 1969. Factor validity of cloze tests as measures of reading comprehension ability. *Reading Research Quarterly,* 4:358–65.

BRACHT, G. H. 1967. The comparative values of objective and essay testing in undergraduate education: Implications for valid assessment of instruction. Unpublished master's thesis, University of Colorado.

——, and K. D. HOPKINS. 1968. Comparative validities of essay and objective tests. Research Paper no. 20. Boulder: University of Colorado, Laboratory of Educational Research.

——. 1970a. The commonality of essay and objective tests of academic achievement. *Educational and Psychological Measurement,* 30:359–64.

——. 1970b. *Stability of general academic achievement.* Paper presented at the annual meeting of the National Council on Measurement in Education, Minneapolis, March. Reprinted in G. H. Bracht, K. D. Hopkins, and J. C. Stanley, eds. 1972. *Perspectives in educational and psychological measurement.* Englewood Cliffs, N.J.: Prentice-Hall. Selection 25.

BRADLEY, L. A., and G. W. BRADLEY. 1977. The academic achievement of black students in desegregated schools: A critical review. *Review of Educational Research,* 47:399–450.

BRAUN, J. R., and P. ASTA. 1968. Effects of faking instructions on sales motivation inventory scores. *Journal of Educational Measurement,* 5:339–40.

BRELAND, H. M. 1978. *Population validity and college entrance measures.* Princeton, N.J.: Educational Testing Service.

——. 1979. *Population validity and college entrance measures.* Princeton, N.J.: College Board Publications.

——, and J. L. GAYNOR. 1979. A comparison of direct and indirect assessments of writing skill. *Journal of Educational Measurement,* 16:119–28.

BRENNER, M. H. 1964. Test difficulty reliability and discrimination as functions of item difficulty order. *Journal of Applied Psychology,* 48:98–100.

BRICKMAN, W. W. 1961. Ethics, examinations and education. *School and Society,* 89:412–15.

BRIDGMAN, C. S. 1964. The relation of the upper-lower item discrimination index, *D,* to the bivariate normal correlation coefficient. *Educational and Psychological Measurement,* 24:85–90.

BROKAW, L. D. 1956. Technical school validity of the Airman Activity Inventory. *AFPTRC Development Report,* 56–109.

BRYANT, E. C., E. GLASER, M. H. HANSEN, and A. KIRSCH. 1974. *Association between educational outcomes and background variables: A review of selected literature.* National Assessment of Educational Progress.

BUNDA, M. A., and J. R. SANDERS, eds. 1979. *Practice and problems in competency-based measurement.* National Council on Measurement in Education.

BURACK, B. 1961. Have you checked machine scoring error lately? *Vocational Guidance Quarterly,* 9:191–93.

BURBA, D. V., and W. S. CORLISS. 1963. *A study of the results of a questionnaire concerning attitudes of children toward report cards.* Birmingham, unpublished.

BUROS, O. K., ed. 1938, 1941, 1949, 1953, 1959, 1965, 1972, 1978. *The mental measurements yearbook* (first through eighth). Highland Park, N.J.: Gryphon Press.

———. 1974. *Tests in print II.* Highland Park, N.J.: Gryphon Press.

BUROS, O. K. 1977. Fifty years in testing: Some reminiscences, criticisms, and suggestions. *Educational Researcher,* 6:9–15.

BURR, W. L. 1963. Empirical relationships among modes of testing, modes of instruction and reading levels in sixth-grade social studies. *Journal of Experimental Education,* 31:433–35.

BURTON, N. W. 1978. Societal standards. *Journal of Educational Measurement,* 15:263–71.

———. 1980. Stability of the national assessment scoring methods. *Journal of Educational Measurement,* 17:95–106.

BUSHWAY, A., and W. R. NASH. 1977. School cheating behavior. *Review of Educational Research,* 47:623–32.

CALDWELL, E., and R. HARTNETT. 1967. Sex bias in college grading. *Journal of Educational Measurement,* 4:129–32.

CALIFORNIA STATE DEPARTMENT OF EDUCATION. 1977. *Profiles of school performance: A guide to interpretation.* Sacramento.

CALLENBACH, C. 1973. The effects of instruction and practice in content-independent test-taking techniques upon the standardized reading test scores of selected second-grade students. *Journal of Educational Measurement,* 10:25–30.

CALLIS, R. 1953. The efficiency of the Minnesota Teacher Attitude Inventory for predicting interpersonal relations in the classroom. *Journal of Applied Psychology,* 37:82–85.

CAMPBELL, D. P. 1966a. Stability of interests within an occupation over 30 years. *Journal of Applied Psychology,* 50:51–56.

———. 1966b. Stability of vocational interests within occupations over long time spans. *Personnel and Guidance Journal,* 44:1012–19.

———. 1968a. Changing patterns of interests within the American society. *Measurement and Evaluation in Guidance,* 1:36–49.

———. 1968b. The Strong Vocational Interest Blank: 1927–1967. In P. McReynolds, ed., *Advances in psychological assessment,* vol. 1. Palo Alto, Calif.: Science and Behavior Books. Pp. 105–30.

———. 1974. *Manual for the Strong-Campbell Interest Inventory.* Stanford, Calif.: Stanford University Press.

CAMPBELL, D. T. 1969. Reforms as experiments. *American Psychologist,* 24:409–29.

———, and D. W. FISKE. 1959. Convergent and discriminant validation by the multitrait-multimethod matrix. *Psychological Bulletin,* 56:81–105.

CAMPBELL, J. T., T. L. HILTON, and B. PITCHER. 1967. *Effects of repeating on test scores of the Graduate Record Examinations.* Graduate Record Examinations Special Report 67–1. Princeton, N.J.: Educational Testing Service.

CATTELL, R. B. 1963. Theory of fluid and crystallized intelligence: A critical experiment. *Journal of Educational Psychology,* 54:1–22.

———, and F. WARBURTON, 1967. *Objective personality and motivation tests.* Urbana: University of Illinois Press.

CAVANAUGH, M. C., I. COHEN, D. DUNPHY, E. A. RINGWALL, and I. D. GOLDBERG. 1957. Prediction from the Cattell Infant Intelligence Scale. *Journal of Consulting Psychology,* 21:33–37.

CHADWICK, E. 1864. Statistics of educational results. *Museum,* 3:480–84.

CHAMBERS, A. C., K. D. HOPKINS, and B. R. HOPKINS. 1972. Anxiety, physiologically and psychologically measured: Its effects on mental test performance. *Psychology in the Schools,* 9:198–206.

CHANDLER, T. A., and W. J. HUNTER. 1976. Effects of testing conditions on self-concept measurement. *Measurement and Evaluation in Guidance,* 8:240–44.

CHASE, C. I. 1964. Relative length of options and response set in multiple choice items. *Educational and Psychological Measurement,* 24:861–66.

——. 1968. The impact of some obvious variables on essay test scores. *Journal of Educational Measurement,* 5:315–18.

——. 1979a. The impact of achievement expectations and handwriting quality on scoring essay tests. *Journal of Educational Measurement,* 16:39–42.

——. 1979b. Students and faculty view the grading system. Paper presented at the annual meeting of the National Council on Measurement in Education, San Francisco, April.

CHAUNCEY, H., and J. E. DOBBIN. 1963. *Testing: Its place in education today.* New York: Harper & Row.

CHAUNCEY, H., and T. L. HILTON. 1965. Are aptitude tests valid for the highly able? *Science,* 148:1297–1304.

CHOPPIN, B. H. 1974. *The correction for guessing on objective tests.* IEA Monograph Studies, no. 4. Stockholm.

CHUN, K., S. COBB, and J. FRENCH. 1975. *Measures for psychological assessment: A guide to 3,000 original sources and their application.* Ann Arbor: University of Michigan, Institute for Social Research.

CHURCHILL, W. D., and S. E. SMITH. 1966. The relationship of the 1960 Revised Stanford-Binet Intelligence Scale to intelligence and achievement test scores over a three-year period. *Educational and Psychological Measurement,* 26:1015–20.

CLARK, C. A. 1968. The use of separate answer sheets in testing slow-learning pupils. *Journal of Educational Measurement,* 5:61–64.

CLARK, D. C. 1972. *Using instructional objectives in teaching.* Glenview, Ill.: Scott, Foresman.

CLARKE, H. 1971. *Physical and Motor Tests in the Medford Boys' Growth Study.* Englewood Cliffs, N.J.: Prentice-Hall.

CLEARY, T. A. 1968. Test bias: Prediction of grades of Negro and white students in integrated colleges. *Journal of Educational Measurement,* 5:115–24.

——, and T. L. HILTON. 1968. An investigation of item bias. *Educational and Psychological Measurement,* 28:61–75.

CLIFFORD, P. I., and J. A. FISHMAN. 1963. The impact of testing programs on college preparation and attendance. In *The impact and improvement of school testing programs.* LXII yearbook, National Society for the Study of Education.

COCHRAN, R. E., and C. C. WEIDEMANN. 1934. "Explain" essay vs. word answer fact test. *Phi Delta Kappan,* 17:59–61, 75.

——. 1937. A study of special types of tests. *Phi Delta Kappan,* 19:113–15, 131.

COFFMAN, W. E. 1969. Achievement tests. In R. L. Ebel, ed., *Encyclopedia of educational research,* 4th ed. New York: Macmillan.

——. 1971. Essay examinations. In R. L. Thorndike, ed., *Educational measurement,* 2nd ed. Washington, D.C.: American Council on Education. Chap. 10.

——. 1972. On the reliability of ratings of essay examinations. *NCME Measurement in Education,* 3:1–7.

——. 1974. A moratorium? What kind? *NCME Measurement in Education,* 5: no. 2.

——, COLEMAN, W., and E. E. CURETON. 1954. Intelligence and achievement: The "jangle fallacy" again. *Educational and Psychological Measurement,* 14:347–51.

COFFMAN, W. E., and D. KURFMAN. 1968. A comparison of two methods of reading essay examinations. *American Educational Research Journal,* 5:99–107.

COLEMAN, J. S., et al. 1966. *The equality of educational opportunity.* Washington, D.C.: U.S. Department of Health, Education and Welfare, Office of Education.

COLLER, A. R. 1971. *Self-Concept Measures: An Annotated Bibliography.* Princeton, N.J.: Educational Testing Service.

CONKLIN, J. E., L. BURSTEIN, and J. W. KEESLING. 1979. The effects of date of testing and method of interpolation on the use of standardized test scores in the validation of large-scale educational programs. *Journal of Educational Measurement,* 16:239–46.

COLLEGE ENTRANCE EXAMINATION BOARD. 1968. *Effects of coaching on Scholastic Aptitude Test.* Princeton, N.J.

———. 1975. *The Test of Standard Written English: A preliminary report.* Princeton, N.J.

———. 1977. *On further examination.* New York.

COLLET, L. S. 1971. Elimination scoring: An empirical evaluation. *Journal of Educational Measurement,* 8:209–14.

COMPTON, A. 1980. *A guide to 65 tests for special education.* Belmont, Calif.: Pitman Learning.

COMREY, A. S., T. E. BACKER, and E. M. GLASER. 1973. *A sourcebook for mental health measures.* Los Angeles: Human Interaction Research Institute.

CONRAD, L., D. TRISMEN, and R. MILLER, eds. 1977. *Graduate Record Examinations technical manual.* Princeton, N.J.: Educational Testing Service.

COOK, D. L. 1955. An investigation of three aspects of free response and choice type tests at the college level. Doctoral dissertation, State University of Iowa. 377 pp.

———, and D. L. STUFFLEBEAM. 1967. Estimating test norms from variable size item and examinee samples. *Journal of Educational Measurement,* 4:27–33.

COOPER, H. M. 1979. Pygmalion grows up: A model for teacher expectation communication and performance influence. *Review of Educational Research,* 49:389–410.

COOPERSMITH, S. 1967. *The antecedents of self-esteem.* San Francisco: W. H. Freeman.

COPELAND, D. A. 1972. Should chemistry students change answers on multiple choice tests? *Journal of Chemical Education,* 49:258.

CORNEHLSEN, V. H. 1965. Cheating attitudes and practices in a suburban high school. *Journal of the National Association of Women Deans and Counselors,* 28:106–9.

CREAGER, J. A. 1965. *Predicting doctorate attainment with GRE and other variables.* Technical Report no. 25. Washington, D.C.: National Academy of Sciences–National Research Council, Office of Scientific Personnel.

CRITES, J. O. 1969. Interests. In R. L. Ebel, ed., *Encyclopedia of educational research,* 4th ed. New York: Macmillan. Pp. 678–86.

CROCKENBERG, S. B. 1972. Creativity tests: Boon or boondoggle? *Review of Educational Research,* 42:27–48.

CROCKER, L., and J. BENSON. 1976. Achievement, guessing, and risk-taking under norm referenced and criterion referenced testing conditions. *American Educational Research Journal,* 13:207–15.

CRONBACH, L. J. 1942. Studies of acquiescence as a factor in true–false tests. *Journal of Educational Psychology,* 33:401–15.

———. 1946. Response sets and test validity. *Educational and Psychological measurement,* 6:475–94.

———. 1950. Further evidence on response sets and test design. *Educational and Psychological Measurement,* 10:3–31.

———. 1951. Coefficient alpha and the internal structure of tests. *Psychometrika,* 16:297–334.

———. 1969a. Heredity, environment, and educational policy. *Harvard Educational Review,* 39:338–47.

———. 1969b. Validation of educational measures. *Proceedings of the 1969 Invitational Conference on Testing Problems.* Princeton, N.J.: Educational Testing Service. Pp. 35–52. Reprinted in G. H. Bracht, K. D. Hopkins, and J. C. Stanley, eds. 1972. *Perspectives in educational and psychological measurement.* Englewood Cliffs, N.J.: Prentice-Hall. Selection 9.

———. 1970. *Essentials of psychological testing,* 3rd ed. New York: Harper & Row.

———. 1971. Test validation. In R. L. Thorndike, ed., *Educational measurement,* 2nd ed. Washington, D.C.: American Council on Education. Chap. 14.

——, and H. AZUMA. 1962. Internal-consistency reliability formulas applied to randomly sampled single-factor tests: An empirical comparison. *Educational and Psychological Measurement,* 22:645–65.

——, and L. FURBY. 1970. How we should measure change—or should we? *Psychological Bulletin,* 74(1):68–80.

——, and P. E. MEEHL, 1955. Construct validity in psychological tests. *Psychological Bulletin,* 52:281–302.

CROSS, L., and R. FRARY. 1977. An empirical test of Lord's theoretical results regarding formula scoring of multiple-choice tests. *Journal of Educational Measurement,* 17:313–22.

CUNNINGHAM, R., et al. 1951. *Group behavior of boys and girls.* New York: Columbia University Press.

CURETON, E. E. 1969. Measurement theory. In R. L. Ebel, ed., *Encyclopedia of educational research,* 4th ed. New York: Macmillan. Pp. 785–804.

CURETON, L. E. 1971. The history of grading practices. *NCME Measurement in Education,* 2, no. 4:1–8.

CURTIS, F. D., W. C. DARLING, and N. H. SHERMAN. 1943. A study of the relative values of two modifications of the true–false test. *Journal of Educational Research,* 36:517–27.

CURTIS, H. A., and R. P. KROPP. 1961. A comparison of scores obtained by administering a test normally and visually. *Journal of Experimental Education,* 29:249–60.

DADOURIAN, H. M. 1925. Are examinations worth the price? *School and Society,* 21:442–43.

D'AGOSTINO, R. B., and E. E. CURETON. 1975. The 27 percent rule revisited. *Educational and Psychological Measurement,* 25:41–50.

DAHLSTROM, W. G., G. S. WELSH, and L. E. DAHLSTROM. 1972. *An MMPI handbook.* Vol 1, *Clinical interpretation.* Minneapolis: University of Minnesota Press.

——. 1975. *An MMPI handbook.* Vol. 2, *Research developments and applications.* Minneapolis: University of Minnesota Press.

DARLEY, J. G., and T. HAGANAH. 1955. *Vocational interest measurement: Theory and practice.* Minneapolis: University of Minnesota Press.

DAVIDSON, W. M., and J. B. CARROLL. 1945. Speed and level components in time-limit scores: A factor analysis. *Educational and Psychological Measurement,* 1945, 5:411–27.

DAVIS, F. B. 1951. Item selection techniques. In E. F. Lindquist, ed., *Educational measurement.* Washington, D.C.: American Council on Education.

DAY, H. P. 1959. A study of predictive validity of the MTAI. *Journal of Educational Research,* 53:37–38.

DEHIRSCH, K., J. J. JANSKY, and W. S. LANGFORD. 1966. *Predicting reading failure.* New York: Harper & Row.

DE LANDSHEERE, V. 1977. On defining educational objectives. In *Evaluation in Education: International Progress,* 1:2, Elmsford, N.Y.: Pergamon Press.

DENNIS, P. 1979. An assessment of the validity and reliability of the CFK Ltd. School Climate Profile. Doctoral dissertation, University of Colorado.

DIAMOND, J. J. 1975. A preliminary study of the reliability and validity of a scoring procedure based upon confidence and partial information. *Journal of Educational Measurement,* 12: 129–34.

——, and W. J. EVANS. 1973. The correction for guessing. *Review of Educational Research,* 43:181–92.

DIEDERICH, P. B. 1964. *Short-cut statistics for teacher-made tests.* Princeton: Educational Testing Service, Evaluation and Advisory Service Series, no. 5, p. 19.

DISTEFANO, P., and S. VALENCIA. 1980. The effects of syntactic maturity on comprehension of graded reading passages. *Teaching English,* in press.

DIVESTA, F. J., and W. DICK. 1966. The test–retest reliability of children's ratings on the semantic differential. *Educational and Psychological Measurement,* 26:605–16.

DIZNEY, H. F., P. R. MERRIFIELD, and O. L. DAVIS, JR. 1966. Effects of answer-sheet format on arithmetic test scores. *Educational and Psychological Measurement,* 26:491–93.

DOLLIVER, R. H., J. A. IRVIN, and S. E. BIGLEY. 1972. Twelve-year follow-up of the Strong Vocational Interest Blank. *Journal of Counseling Psychology,* 19:212–17.

DOYLE, K. O., and S. E. WHITELY. 1974. Student ratings as criteria for effective teaching. *American Educational Research Journal,* 11:259–74.

DRESSEL, P. L., and J. SCHMIDT. 1951. *An evaluation of the tests for general educational development.* Washington, D.C.: American Council on Education.

DRISCOLL, L. A., and W. L. GOODWIN. 1979. The effects of varying information about use and disposition of results on university students' evaluation of faculty and courses. *American Educational Research Journal,* 16:25–37.

DROEGE, R. C., A. C. CRAMBERT, and J. B. HENKIN. 1963. Relationship between G.A.T.B. aptitude scores and age for adults. *Personnel and Guidance Journal,* 41:502–8.

DUBOIS, P. H. 1966. A test-dominated society: China, 1115 B.C.–1905 A.D. In A. Anastasi, ed., *Testing problems in perspective.* Washington, D.C.: American Council on Education. Pp. 29–38.

DUDYCHA, A. L. and J. B. CARPENTER. 1973. Effects of item format on item discrimination and difficulty. *Journal of Applied Psychology,* 58:11–121.

DUNCAN, A. J. 1947. Some comments on the Army General Classification Test. *Journal of Applied Psychology,* 31:143–49.

DURNALL, E. J., JR. 1954. Falsification of interest patterns on the Kuder preference record. *Journal of Educational Psychology,* 45:240–43.

DUROST, W. N. 1954. Present progress and needed improvements in school evaluation programs. *Educational and Psychological Measurement,* 14:247–54.

DUSEK, J. B. 1975. Do teachers bias children's learning? *Review of Educational Research,* 45:661–84.

DYER, H. S. 1977. Criticisms of testing: How mean is the median? *NCME Measurement in Education,* 8, no. 3.

DUNNETTE, M. D. 1963. Critics of psychological tests: Basic assumptions: How good? *Psychology in the Schools,* 1:63–69.

EBEL, R. L. 1954. Procedures for the analysis of classroom tests. *Educational and Psychological Measurement,* 14:352–64.

———. 1956. Obtaining and reporting evidence on content validity. *Educational and Psychological Measurement,* 16:269–82.

———. 1960. Some tests of competence in educational measurement. *The seventeenth yearbook of the National Council on Measurements Used in Education.* Ames, Iowa: National Council on Measurements Used in Education. Pp. 93–104.

———. 1961a. Improving the competence of teachers in educational measurement. *Clearing House,* 36:67–71.

———. 1961b. Standardized achievement tests: Uses and limitations. *National Elementary School Principal,* 40:29–32.

———. 1965a. Confidence weighting and test reliability. *Journal of Educational Measurement,* 2:49–57.

———. 1965b, 1979. *Measuring educational achievement,* 2nd and 3rd eds. Englewood Cliffs, N.J.: Prentice-Hall.

———. 1968. The value of internal consistency in classroom examinations. *Journal of Educational Measurement,* 5:71–73.

———. 1970a. The case for true–false test items. *School Review,* 78:373–89.

———. 1970b. Some limitations of criterion-referenced measurment. In G. H. Bracht, K. D. Hopkins, and J. C. Stanley, eds. 1972. *Perspectives in educational and psychological measurement.* Englewood Cliffs, N.J.: Prentice-Hall. Selection 14.

———. 1971. How to write true–false test items. *Educational and Psychological Measurement,* 31:417–26.

———. 1972. Some limitations of criterion-referenced measurement. In G. H. Bracht, K. D. Hopkins, and J. C. Stanley, eds. 1972. *Perspectives in educational and psychological measurement.* Englewood Cliffs, N.J.: Prentice-Hall. Selection 14.

———. 1974. Shall we get rid of grades? *NCME Measurement in Education,* 5:1–5.

———. 1976. The paradox of educational testing. *NCME Measurement in Education,* 7, no. 4.

———. 1978. The case for norm-referenced measurements. *Educational Researcher,* 7:3–5.

ECHTERNACHT, G. 1977. Grade equivalent scores. *NCME Measurement in Education,* 8, no. 2:1–4.

ECKLAND, B. K. 1964. College dropouts who came back. *Harvard Educational Review,* 34:404–20.

EDUCATIONAL POLICIES COMMISSION. 1961. *The central purpose of American education.* Washington, D.C.: National Education Association.

EDUCATIONAL TESTING SERVICE. 1960. *A description of the College Board Scholastic Aptitude Test.* Princeton, N.J.

———. 1961. Judges disagree on qualities that characterize good writing. *ETS Developments,* 9:2.

———. 1963. *Multiple choice questions: A close look.* Princeton, N.J. Reprinted in G. H. Bracht, K. D. Hopkins, and J. C. Stanley, eds. 1972. *Perspectives in educational and psychological measurement.* Englewood Cliffs, N.J.: Prentice-Hall. Selection 15.

———. 1969. Bias in selection tests and criteria studies by ETS and U.S. Civil Service. *ETS Developments,* 17:2.

———. 1980a. *Test use and validity.* Princeton, N.J.

———. 1980b. *Test scores and family income.* Princeton, N.J.

EDWARDS, A. L. 1957. *The social desirability variability in personality assessment and research.* New York: Dryden Press.

EELLS, K., et al. 1951. *Intelligence and cultural differences.* Chicago: University of Chicago Press.

EISS, A. F., and M. B. HARBECK. 1969. *Behavioral objectives in the affective domain.* Washington, D.C.: National Education Association.

ENGELHART, M. D. 1964. *Improving classroom testing: What research says to the teacher.* Booklet no. 31. Washington D.C.: National Education Association.

———. 1965. A comparison of several item discrimination indices. *Journal of Educational Measurement,* 2:69–76.

ESCALONA, S. K., and A. MORIARTY. 1961. Prediction of school age intelligence from infant tests. *Child Development,* 32:597–605.

ETAUGH, A. F., C. F. ETAUGH, and D. HURD. 1972. Reliability of college grades and grade point averages: Some implications for predicting academic performance. *Educational and Psychological Measurement,* 32:1045–1105.

EYSENCK, H. J. 1959. Rorschach review. In O. K. Buros, ed., *The fifth mental measurements yearbook.* Highland Park, N.J.: Gryphon Press. Pp. 276–78.

———. 1971. *Race, intelligence and education.* London: Maurice Temple Smith.

FAIRBROTHER, R. 1975. The reliability of teachers' judgments of the abilities being tested by multiple choice items. *Educational Research,* 17: 202–10.

FARGO, G. A., D. C. CROWELL, M. H. NOYES, R. Y. FUCHIGAMI, J. M. GORDON, and P. DUNN-RANKIN. 1967. Comparability of group television and individual administration of the Peabody Picture Vocabulary Test: Implications for screening. *Journal of Educational Psychology,* 58:137–40.

FARLEY, E. J., C. E. WEINHOLD, and A. P. CRABTREE. 1967. *High school certification through the G.E.D. tests.* New York: Holt, Rinehart and Winston.

FARR, R., and P. ROELKE. 1971. Measuring subskills of reading: Intercorrelations between standardized reading tests, teachers' ratings, and reading specialists' ratings. *Journal of Educational Measurement,* 8:27–32.

FELDHUSEN, J. F. 1964. Student perceptions of frequent quizzes and post-mortem discussions of tests. *Journal of Educational Measurement,* 1:51–54.

FINCHER, C. 1974. An evaluation of the SAT. *Review of Educational Research,* 44:293–306.

FINDLEY, W. G. 1956. Rationale for evaluation of item discrimination statistics. *Educational and Psychological Measurement,* 16:175–80.

FINDLEY, W. G., ed. 1963a. The impact and improvement of school testing programs. *Sixty-second yearbook of the National Society for the Study of Education, Part II.* Chicago: University of Chicago Press.

———. 1963b. Purpose of school testing programs and their efficient development. In W. G. Findley, ed., 1963a, pp. 1–27.

FINLEY, C. J. 1963. A comparison of the California Achievement Test, Metropolitan Achievement Test and Iowa Test of Basic Skills. *California Journal of Educational Research,* 14 (March): 79–88

FISCHER, D. G., D. HUNT, and B. S. RANDHAWA. 1978. Empirical validity of Ertl's brain-wave analyzer. *Educational and Psychological Measurement,* 38:1017–30.

FISHMAN, J. A., et al. 1964. Guidelines for testing minority group children. *Journal of Social Issues,* 20:127–45.

FLANAGAN, J. C. 1935. *Factor analysis in the study of personality.* Stanford, Calif.: Stanford University Press.

———. 1937. A proposed procedure for increasing the efficiency of objective tests. *Journal of Educational Psychology,* 28:17–21.

———. 1951a. Units, scores, and norms. In E. F. Lindquist, ed., *Educational measurement.* Washington, D.C.: American Council on Education.

———. 1951b. The use of comprehensive rationales in test development. *Educational and Psychological Measurement,* 11:151–55.

———. 1952. The effectiveness of short methods for calculating correlation coefficients. *Psychological Bulletin,* 49:342–48.

———. 1969. Student characteristics: Elementary and secondary. In R. L. Ebel, ed., *Encyclopedia of educational research,* 4th ed. New York: Macmillan. Pp. 1330–39.

———, and W. W. COOLEY. 1966. *Project Talent: One-year follow-up studies.* Pittsburgh: University of Pittsburgh Press.

———, et al., 1962. *Design for a study of American youth.* Vol. 1, *The talents of American youth.* Boston: Houghton Mifflin.

FLAUGHER, R. L. 1970. *Testing practices, minority groups, and higher education.* Princeton, N.J.: Educational Testing Service.

———, M. H. MAHONEY, and R. B. MESSING. 1967. *Credit by examination for college-level studies: An annotated bibliography.* New York: College Entrance Examination Board.

FLEMING, E. S., and R. G. ANTTONEN. 1970. Teacher expectancy or my fair lady. In John Pilder, ed., *Abstracts/One: 1970 Annual Meeting Paper Session.* Washington, D.C.: American Educational Research Association. P. 66.

FLESCH, R. 1948. A new readability yardstick. *Journal of Applied Psychology,* 34:384–90.

FOOTE, R., and C. BELINKY. 1972. It pays to switch? Consequences of changing answers on multiple-choice examinations. *Psychological Reports,* 31:667–73.

FRANDSEN, A. N., and A. D. SESSIONS. 1953. Interests and school achievement. *Educational and Psychological Measurement,* 13:94–101.

FRANKEL, E. 1960. Effects of growth, practice, and coaching on Scholastic Aptitude Test scores. *Personnel and Guidance Journal,* 38:713–19.

FRANZ, S. I. 1919. *Handbook of mental examination methods.* New York: Macmillan.

FRARY, R. B., L. H. CROSS, and S. R. LOWRY. 1977. Random guessing, correction for guessing, and reliability of multiple-choice test scores. *Journal of Experimental Education,* 46:9–15.

FRENCH, J. W. 1961. Aptitude and interest score patterns related to satisfaction with college major field. *Educational and Psychological Measurement,* 21:287–94.

———. 1962. Effect of anxiety on verbal and mathematical examination scores. *Educational and Psychological Measurement,* 22:553–64.

FRISBEE, D. A. 1973. Multiple-choice versus true-false: A comparison of reliabilities and concurrent validities. *Journal of Educational Measurement,* 10:297–304.

FRY, E. B. 1976. A readability formula that saves time. *Journal of Reading,* 11:513–16.

———. 1977. Fry's readability graph: Clarification, validity, and extension to level 17. *Journal of Reading,* 21:242–52.

FORSYTH, R. A. and K. F. SPRATT. 1980. Measuring problem solving ability in mathematics with multiple-choice items: The effect of item format. *Journal of Educational Measurement,* 17:31–44.

FURST, E. J., and P. J. ROELFS. 1979. Validation of the Graduate Record Examinations and the Miller Analogies test in a doctoral program in education. *Educational and Psychological Measurement,* 39:147–52.

GADZELLA, B. M., and G. P. FOURNET. 1976. Differences between high and low achievers on self-perception. *Journal of Experimental Education,* 44:44–48.

GAFFNEY, R. F., and T. O. MAGUIRE. 1971. Use of optically scored test answer sheets with young children. *Journal of Educational Measurement,* 8:103–6.

GAGE, N. L., P. J. RUNKEL, and B. B. CHATTERJEE. 1960. *Equilibrium theory and behavior change: An experiment in feedback from pupils to teachers.* Urbana: Bureau of Educational Research, University of Illinois. (Mimeographed.)

GARBER, H. 1967. The digital computer simulates human rating behavior. In J. T. Flynn and H. Garber, *Assessing behavior: Readings in educational and psychological measurement.* Reading, Mass.: Addison-Wesley.

GARDNER, E. F. 1978. Bias. *NCME Measurement News,* 21:2.

GARLOCK, J., R. S. DOLLARHIDE, and K. D. HOPKINS. 1965. Comparability of scores on the Wide Range and the Gilmore Oral Reading Tests. *California Journal of Educational Research,* 16:54–57.

GARRY, R. 1953. Individual differences in ability to fake vocational interests. *Journal of Applied Psychology,* 37:33–37.

GAY, L. R. 1980. The comparative effects of multiple-choice versus short-answer tests on retention. *Journal of Educational Measurement,* 17:45–50.

GETZELS, J. W., and P. W. JACKSON. 1963. The teacher's personality and characteristics. In N. L. Gage, ed., *Handbook of research on teaching.* Skokie, Ill.: Rand McNally. Pp. 506–82.

GHISELLI, E. E., and R. P. BARTHOL. 1953. The validity of personality inventories in the selection of employees. *Journal of Applied Psychology,* 37:18–20.

GILLMORE, G. M., M. T. KANE, and R. W. NACCARATO. 1978. The generalizability of student ratings of instruction. *Journal of Educational Measurement,* 15:1–14.

GILMAN, D. A., and P. FERRY. 1972. Increasing test reliability through self-scoring procedures. *Journal of Educational Measurement,* 9:205–8.

GLASER, R. 1963. Instructional technology and the measurement of learning outcomes: Some questions. *American Psychologist,* 18:519–21.

——, and A. J. NITKO. 1971. Measurement in learning and instruction. In R. L. Thorndike, ed., *Educational measurement,* 2nd ed. Washington, D.C.: American Council on Education. Chap. 17.

GLASS, G. V 1975. A paradox about excellence of schools and the people in them. *Educational Researcher,* 4:9–12.

——. 1978a. Standards and criteria. *Journal of Educational Measurement,* 15:237–61.

——. 1978b. Minimum competence and incompetency. *The Educational Forum.* 42:139–44.

——. 1978c. Mathew Arnold and minimal competency. *The Educational Forum.* 42:139–44.

——, and J. C. STANLEY. 1970. *Statistical methods in education and psychology.* Englewood Cliffs, N.J.: Prentice-Hall.

——, and K. D. HOPKINS, 1982. *Statistical methods in education and psychology,* 2nd ed. Englewood Cliffs, N.J.: Prentice-Hall.

——, and D. E. WILEY. 1964. Formula scoring and test reliability. *Journal of Educational Measurement,* 1:43–47.

GLASSER, W. 1969. *Schools without failure.* New York: Harper & Row.

GODDARD, H. H. 1910. A measuring scale for intelligence. *The Training School,* 6:146–55.

GODSHALK, F. I., F. SWINEFORD, W. E. COFFMAN, and EDUCATIONAL TESTING SERVICE. 1966. *The measurement of writing ability.* New York: College Entrance Examination Board.

GOLD, R. M., A. REILLY, R. SILBERMAN, and R. LEHR. 1971. Academic achievement declines under pass–fail grading. *Journal of Experimental Education,* 39:17–21.

GOLDMAN, B. A., and J. L. SAUNDERS. 1974. *Directory of unpublished experimental measures,* vol. 1. New York: Behavioral Publications.

GOLDMAN, R. D., and R. RICHARDS. 1974. The SAT prediction of grades for Mexican-American students versus Anglo-American students at the University of California, Riverside. *Journal of Educational Measurement,* 11:129–36.

GOLDMAN, R. D., D. E. SCHMIDT, B. N. HEWITT, and R. FISHER. 1974. Grading practices in different major fields. *American Educational Research Journal,* 11:343–57.

GOLDMAN, R. D., and R. E. SLAUGHTER. 1976. Why college grade point average is difficult to predict. *Journal of Educational Psychology,* 68:9–14.

GOLDRIED, D. M., and T. D'ZURILLA. 1973. Prediction of academic competence by means of the Survey of Study Habits and Attitudes. *Journal of Educational Psychology,* 64:116–22.

GOODENOUGH, F. L. 1949. *Mental testing.* New York: Holt, Rinehart and Winston.

GOODWIN, W. L. 1966. Effect of selected methodological conditions on dependent measures taken after classroom experimentation. *Journal of Educational Psychology,* 57:350–58.

GOODWIN, W. L. and L. A. DRISCOLL. 1980. *Handbook for measurement and evaluation in early childhood education.* San Francisco: Jossey-Bass.

GORDON, M. A. 1953. A study of the applicability of the same minimum qualifying scores for technical schools to white males, WAF, and Negro males. Technical Report 53–54. San Antonio, Texas: Lackland Air Force Base, Human Resources Research Center.

GORDON, R. A. 1975. Examining labelling theory: The case of mental retardation. In W. R. Gove, ed., *The labelling of deviance: Evaluating a perspective.* New York: Halsted Press. Chap. 4.

GOSLIN, D. A. 1967. *Teachers and testing.* New York: Russell Sage.

GOUGH, H. G., and W. H. PEMBERTON. 1952. Personality characteristics related to success in practice teaching. *Journal of Applied Psychology,* 36:307–9.

GOZALI, J., and E. L. MEYER. 1970. The influence of the teacher expectancy phenomenon on the academic performance of educable mentally retarded pupils in special classes. *Journal of Special Education,* 4:417–24.

GRAFF, K. 1965. The high school equivalency program. *Vocational Guidance Quarterly,* 13:297–99.

GRANICH, L. A. 1931. A technique for experimenting on guessing in objective tests. *Journal of Educational Psychology,* 22:145–56.

GREEN, D. R. 1974. *The aptitude–achievement distinction.* Monterey, Calif.: CTB/McGraw-Hill.

GREENE, K. B. 1928. The influence of specialized training on tests of general intelligence. *The 27th yearbook, National Society for the Study of Education, Part I.* Pp. 421–28.

GROBMAN, H. 1968. *Evaluation activities of curriculum projects.* AERA Monograph Series in Curriculum Evaluation, no. 2. Chicago: Rand McNally. P. 93.

GRONLUND, N. E. 1955. The relative stability of classroom social status with unweighted and weighted sociometric choices. *Journal of Educational Psychology,* 46:345–54.

———. 1974. *Improving marking and reporting in classroom instruction.* New York: Macmillan.

GUILFORD, J. P. 1950. Creativity. *American Psychologist,* 14:469–79.

———. 1954. *Psychometric methods,* 2nd ed. New York: McGraw-Hill.

———. 1959. *Personality.* New York: McGraw-Hill.

———. 1965. *Fundamental statistics in psychology and education,* 4th ed. New York: McGraw-Hill.

———. 1967. *The nature of human intelligence.* New York: McGraw-Hill.

———. 1968. The structure of intelligence. In D. K. Whitla, ed., *Handbook of measurement and assessment in behavioral sciences.* Reading, Mass.: Addison-Wesley. Chap. 7.

———, and J. I. LACEY, eds. 1947. *Printed classification tests. Army Air Forces aviation psychology research program reports, Report 5.* Washington, D.C.: U.S. Government Printing Office.

GULLICKSON, A., and K. D. HOPKINS. 1976. Interval estimation of correlation coefficients corrected for restriction of range. *Educational and Psychological Measurement,* 36:9–25.

GUSTAV, A. 1963. Response set in objective achievement tests. *Journal of Psychology,* 56:421–27.

HABERMAN, M. 1970. The relationship of bogus expectations to success in student teaching (or, Pygmalion's illegitimate son). In *Abstracts/One: 1970 Annual Meeting Paper Sessions.* Washington, D.C.: American Educational Research Association. P. 66. Critique session: "The Pygmalion effect: A teacher's expectations," John L. Hayman, chair.

HADLEY, S. T. 1954. A school mark—Fact or fancy? *Educational Administration and Supervision,* 40:305–12.

HAGANAH, T. 1953. *A normative study of the revised Strong Vocational Interest Blank for Men.* Doctoral dissertation, University of Minnesota.

HAKSTIAN, A. R. 1971. The effect on study methods and test performance of objective and essay examinations. *Journal of Educational Research,* 64:319–24.

———, and R. W. BENNET. 1977. Validity studies using the comprehensive ability battery (CAB): I. Academic achievement criteria. *Educational and Psychological Measurement,* 37:425–37.

———. 1978. Validity studies using the Comprehensive Ability Battery (CAB):II. Relationships with the DAT and GATB. *Educational and Psychological Measurement,* 38:1003–15.

HAKSTIAN, A. R., and R. B. CATTELL. 1976. *Manual for the comprehensive ability battery (CAB), 1976 edition.* Champaign, Ill.: Institute for Personality and Ability Testing.

HAKSTIAN, A. R., and W. KANSUP. 1975. A comparison of several methods of assessing partial knowledge in multiple-choice tests: II. Testing procedures. *Journal of Educational Measurement,* 12:231–40.

HALES, L. W. 1972. Method of obtaining the index of discrimination for item selection: A comparative study. *Educational and Psychological Measurement,* 32:929–37.

———, and E. TOKAR. 1975. The effect of the quality of preceding responses on the grades assigned to subsequent responses to an essay question. *Journal of Educational Measurement,* 12:115–18.

HALL, D. W. 1966. The Minnesota Vocational Interest Inventory. *Journal of Educational Measurement,* 3:337–41.

HALPIN, A. W. 1966. *Theory and research in administration.* New York: Macmillan.

HAMBLETON, R. K. 1978. Criterion-referenced testing and measurement: A review of technical issues and developments. *Review of Educational Research,* 4:1–48.

———, and D. R. EIGNOR. 1978. Guidelines for evaluating criterion-referenced tests and test manuals. *Journal of Educational Measurement,* 15:321–27.

HAMBLETON, R. K., H. S. SWAMINATHAN, J. ALGINA, and D. B. COULSON. 1978. Criterion-referenced testing and measurement: A review of technical issues and developments. *Review of Educational Research,* 48:1–48.

HAMBLETON, R. K., H. S. SWAMINATHAN, L. L. COOK, D. R. EIGNOR, and J. A. GIFFORD. 1978. Developments in latent trait theory: Models, technical issues, and applications. *Review of Educational Research,* 48:467–510.

HAMBLETON, R. K., and R. E. TRAUB, 1974. The effects of item order on test performance and stress. *Journal of Experimental Education,* 43:40–46.

HAMILTON, C. H. 1950. Bias and error in multiple-choice tests. *Psychometrika,* 15:151–68.

HANNA, G. S. 1975. Incremental reliability and validity of multiple-choice tests with an answer-until-correct procedure. *Journal of Educational Measurement,* 12:175–78.

———, and OWENS, R. E. 1973. Incremental validity of confidence weighting of items. *California Journal of Educational Research,* 24:165–68.

HARCLEROAD, F. F. 1974. The tangled web. *NCME Measurement in Education,* 5, no. 1.

HARMS, N. C. 1977. Relationships among learner self-concept, locus of control, and ethnic group membership. Doctoral dissertation, University of Colorado.

HARNISCHFEGER, A., and D. E. WILEY. 1976. Achievement test scores drop. So what? *Educational Researcher,* 5:5–12.

HARPER, H. E. 1970. *The identification of socioeconomic differences and their effect on the teaching of readiness for "new math concepts" in the kindergarten.* Final Report: Project no. 9-H-004. Washington, D.C.: U.S. Department of Health, Education and Welfare, Office of Education, Bureau of Research.

HARRIS, C. W., ed. 1963. *Problems in measuring change.* Madison: University of Wisconsin Press.

HARTSHORNE, H., and M. A. MAY. 1928. *Studies in deceit.* New York: Macmillan.

HASHIMOTO, JUJI. 1959. Test no yokoku koka ni tsuite (The effect of announcement of the coming test). *Japanese Journal of Eduational Psychology,* 6:217–22, 265.

HATHAWAY, S. R., and E. D. MONACHESI. 1963. *Adolescent personality and behavior.* Minneapolis: University of Minnesota Press.

HAVINGHURST, R. J., and B. C. NEUGARTEN. 1975. *Society and education,* 4th ed. Boston: Allyn and Bacon.

HAWKES, H. E., E. F. LINDQUIST, and C. R. MANN. 1936. *The construction and use of achievement examinations.* Boston: Houghton Mifflin.

HAYWARD, P. 1967. A comparison of test performance on three answer sheet formats. *Educational and Psychological Measurement,* 27: 997–1004.

HEDGES, W. D. 1966. *Testing and evaluation for the secondary school.* Belmont, Calif.: Wadsworth.

HENERSON, M. E., L. L. MORRIS, and C. T. FITZ-GIBBON. 1978. *How to measure attitudes.* Beverly Hills, Calif.: Sage Publications.

HENRYSSON, S. 1963. Correction of item-total correlations in item analysis. *Psychometrika,* 28:211–18.

———. 1971. Gathering, analyzing, and using data on test items. In R. L. Thorndike, ed., *Educational measurement,* 2nd ed. Washington, D.C.: American Council on Education. Chap. 5.

HENSLEY, H., and R. A. DAVIS. 1952. What high-school teachers think and do about their examinations. *Educational Administration and Supervision,* 38:219–28.

HERNANDEZ, N. G. 1973. Variables affecting achievement of middle school Mexican-Americans. *Review of Educational Research,* 43:1–40.

HERZBERG, F. 1954. Temperament measures in industrial selection. *Journal of Applied Psychology,* 38:81–84.

HEYWOOD, J. 1977. *Assessment in higher education.* New York: Wiley.

HICKLIN, N. J. 1962. A study of long-range techniques for predicting patterns of scholastic behavior. Unpublished Ph.D. thesis, University of Chicago.

HILL, W. H., and P. L. DRESSEL. 1961. The objectives of instruction. In P. L. Dressel, ed., *Evaluation in higher education.* Boston: Houghton Mifflin. Chap. 2.

HILLS, J. R. 1971. Use of measurement in selection and placement. In R. L. Thorndike, ed., *Educational measurement,* 2nd ed. Washington, D.C.: American Council on Education. Chap. 19.

———, and STANLEY. 1970. Easier test improves prediction of black students' college grades. *Journal of Negro Education,* 39:320–24.

HILTON, T. L. 1979. ETS study of academic prediction and growth. In J. E. Milholland, ed., *New directions for testing and measurement.* San Francisco: Jossey-Bass.

HOEPFNER, R. 1967. Review of the Torrance Tests of Creative Thinking. *Journal of Educational Measurement,* 4:191–92.

———, and M. O'SULLIVAN. 1968. Social intelligence and IQ. *Educational and Psychological Measurement,* 28:339–44.

HOEPFNER, R., et al. 1976. *CSE elementary school test evaluation.* Los Angeles: UCLA, Center for the Study of Evaluation.

HOFFMANN, B. 1962. *The tyranny of testing.* New York: Crowell-Collier and Macmillan.

———. 1967a. Psychometric scientism. *Phi Delta Kappan,* 48:381–86.

———. 1967b. Multiple-choice tests. *Physics Education,* 2:247–51.

HOFFMAN, L. W., and R. LIPPITT. 1960. The measurement of family life variables. In P. H. Mussen, ed., *Handbook of research methods in child development.* New York: Wiley, 1960. Pp. 945–1014.

HOFFMAN, R. A., and E. W. ZIEGLER. 1978. The use of a standard language test to identify college students with deficient writing skills. *Measurement and Evaluation in Guidance,* 11:159–61.

HOGAN, T. P., and C. MISHLER. 1980. Relationship between essay tests and objective tests of language skills for elementary school students. *Journal of Educational Measurement,* 17:219–28.

HOLLAND, J. L. 1966. *The psychology of vocational choice: A theory of personality types and model environments.* Waltham, Mass.: Blaisdell.

———. 1973. *Making vocational choices: A theory of careers.* Englewood Cliffs, N.J.: Prentice-Hall.

HOLLINGSHEAD, A. B., and F. C. REDLICH. 1957. *Two factor index of social position.* New Haven, Conn.: Published by the authors.

HOLLY, K. A., and W. B. MICHAEL. 1972. The relationship of structure-of-intellect factor abilities to performance in high school modern algebra. *Educational and Psychological Measurement,* 32:447–50.

———. 1973. Comparative validities and testing times for composites of structure-of-intellect tests and previous mathematics grades. *Educational and Psychological Measurement,* 33: 915–19.

HOLT, J. 1968. *How children fail.* New York: Pitman.

HOLTZMAN, W. H. 1975. New developments in Holtzman Inkblot technique. In P. Mc-Reynolds, ed., *Advances in psychological assessment,* vol. 3. San Francisco: Jossey-Bass.

———, et al. 1961. *Inkblot perception and personality—Holtzman technique.* Austin: University of Texas Press.

HONZIK, M. P. 1957. Developmental studies of parent–child resemblance in intelligence. *Child Development,* 28:215–28.

———, J. W. MACFARLANE, and L. ALLEN. 1948. The stability of mental test performance between two and eighteen years. *Journal of Experimental Education,* 17:309–24.

HOPKINS, K. D. 1964a. Evaluating pupil achievement: A critical look at provincial and standardized testing. *The British Columbia Fourth School Principals' Conference,* 107–13.

———. 1964b. Extrinsic reliability: Estimating and attenuating variance from response styles, chance, and other irrelevant sources. *Educational and Psychological Measurement,* 24: 271–81. Reprinted in G. H. Bracht, K. D. Hopkins, and J. C. Stanley, eds. 1972. *Perspectives in educational and psychological measurement.* Englewood Cliffs, N.J.: Prentice-Hall. Selection 10.

———. 1964c. An empirical analysis of the efficacy of the WISC in the diagnosis of organicity of children of normal intelligence. *Journal of Genetic Psychology,* 105:163–72.

———. 1965. The readability of standardized achievement tests for the elementary school. M.S. thesis, University of Southern California, Los Angeles.

———. 1969. Regression and the matching fallacy in quasi-experimental research. *Journal of Special Education,* 3:329–36.

———, and M. BIBELHEIMER. 1971. Five-year stability IQ's from language and nonlanguage group tests. *Child Development,* 42:645–49.

HOPKINS, K. D., and G. H. BRACHT. 1971. The stability and change of language and non-language IQ Scores. Final Report, Project no. O-H-O24. Washington, D.C.: U.S. Department of Health, Education and Welfare, Office of Education, Bureau of Research.

———. 1975. Ten-year stability of verbal and non-verbal I.Q. scores. *American Educational Research Journal,* 12:469–77.

HOPKINS, K. D., J. C. DOBSON, and O. A. OLDRIDGE. 1962. The concurrent and congruent validities of the Wide Range Achievement Test. *Educational and Psychological Measurement,* 22:791–93.

HOPKINS, K. D., and G. V GLASS. 1978. *Basic statistics for the behavioral sciences.* Englewood Cliffs, N.J.: Prentice-Hall.

HOPKINS, K. D., and B. R. HOPKINS. 1964. Intraindividual and interindividual positional preference response styles in ability tests. *Educational and Psychological Measurement,* 24:801–5.

HOPKINS, K. D., G. L. KRETKE, N. C. HARMS, R. M. GABRIEL, D. L. PHILLIPS, C. RODRIGUEZ, and M. AVERILL. 1974. *A technical report on the Colorado needs-assessment program, spring 1973.* Boulder: University of Colorado, Laboratory of Educational Research.

HOPKINS, K. D., G. KRETKE, L. MARTIN, and M. AVERILL. 1978, 1979. *District testing report.* Boulder, Colo.: Boulder Valley School District.

HOPKINS, K. D., D. W. LEFEVER, and B. R. HOPKINS. 1967. TV vs. teacher administration of standardized tests: Comparability of scores. *Journal of Educational Measurement,* 4:35–40.

HOPKINS, K. D., and L. McGUIRE. 1966. Mental measurement of the blind: The validity of the Wechsler Intelligence Scale for Children. *International Journal for Education of the Blind,* 15:65–73.

HOPKINS, K. D., and D. L. SANDER. 1966. Review of the Academic Ability Test. *Journal of Educational Measurement,* 3:81–83.

HOPKINS, K. D., and E. G. SITKIE. 1969. Predicting grade one reading performance: Intelligence vs. reading readiness tests. *Journal of Experimental Education,* 37:31–33.

487

HOPKINS, K. D., and C. J. WILKERSON. 1965. Differential content validity: The California Spelling Test, an illustrative example. *Educational and Psychological Measurement,* 25: 413–19.

HORN, J. L. 1966. Some characteristics of classroom examinations. *Journal of Educational Measurement,* 3:293–95.

———. 1967. Intelligence—why it grows, why it declines. *Trans-action,* 5:23–31.

———, and R. B. CATTELL. 1966. Refinement and test of the theory of fluid and crystallized general intelligence. *Journal of Educational Psychology,* 57:253–70.

HOYT, D. P., and L. A. MUNDAY. 1966. *Your college freshmen.* Iowa City: American College Testing Program.

HUGHES, D. C., B. KEATING, and B. F. TUCK. 1980. The influence of context position and scoring method on essay scoring. *Journal of Educational Measurement,* 17:131–36.

HUNKINS, F. P. 1969. Effects of analysis and evaluation questions on various levels of achievement. *Journal of Experimental Education,* 38:45–58.

HUNT, J. McV. 1961. *Intelligence and experience.* New York: Ronald.

HUSÉN, T. 1951. Undersökningar rörande sambanden mellan somatiska föhållanden och intellektuell prestationsformága. *Särtryck ur Tidskrift i militär Hälsovård,* 76:41–74.

INGLE, R. B., and G. DE AMICO. 1969. The effect of physical conditions of the test room on standardized achievement test scores. *Journal of Educational Measurement,* 6:237–40.

IRVIN, L. K., A. S. HALPERN, and J. T. LANDMAN. 1980. Assessment of retarded student achievement with standardized true–false and multiple-choice tests. *Journal of Educational Measurement,* 17:51–58.

JACKSON, P. W., and H. M. LAHADERNE. 1967. Scholastic success and attitude toward school in a population of sixth graders. *Journal of Educational Psychology,* 58:15–18.

JACKSON, R. A. 1955. Guessing and test performance. *Educational and Psychological Measurement,* 15:74–79.

JACOBS, J. N., and J. L. FELIX. 1968. Testing the educational and psychological development of preadolescent children—Ages 6–12. *Review of Educational Research,* 38:19–29.

JACOBS, S. S. 1968. Bias in the keying of standardized tests: A reexamination. *Journal of Educational Measurement,* 5:335–36.

———. 1972. Answer changing on objective tests: Some implications for test validity. *Educational and Psychological Measurement,* 32:1039–44.

JAEGER, R. M., and C. K. TITTLE. 1979. *Minimum competency achievement testing.* American Educational Research Association: Washington, D.C..

JENKINS, W. L. 1946. A short-cut method for σ and r. *Educational and Psychological Measurement,* 6:533–36.

JENSEN, A. R. 1965. Review of the Rorschach. In O. K. Buros, ed., *The sixth mental measurements yearbook.* Highland Park, N.J.: Gryphon Press. Reprinted in G. H. Bracht, K. D. Hopkins, and J. C. Stanley, eds. 1972. *Perspectives in educational and psychological measurement.* Englewood Cliffs, N.J.: Prentice-Hall. Selection 30.

———. 1968a. Another look at culture-fair testing. In Thomas A. Shellhammer, chr., *Measures for educational planning.* Seventeenth annual western regional conference on testing problems. Princeton, N.J.: Educational Testing Service. Pp. 50–104.

———. 1968b. Social class, race, and genetics: Implications for education. *American Educational Research Journal,* 5:1–42.

———. 1969. How much can we boost IQ and scholastic achievement? *Harvard Educational Review,* 39:1–123. Reprinted in G. H. Bracht, K. D. Hopkins, and J. C. Stanley, eds. 1972. *Perspectives in educational and psychological measurement.* Englewood Cliffs, N.J.: Prentice-Hall. Selection 19.

———. 1973a. *Genetics and education.* New York: Harper & Row.

———. 1973b. *Educability and group differences.* New York: Harper & Row.

———. 1980. *Bias in mental testing.* New York: The Free Press.

———, and J. A. SCHMITT. 1970. The influence of test title on test response. *Journal of Educational Measurement,* 7:241–46.

JENSEN, M., and M. D. BECK. 1979. Gender balance analysis on the Metropolitan Achievement Tests, 1978 edition. *Measurement and Evaluation in Guidance,* 12:25–34.

JESSELL, J. C., and W. L. SULLINS. 1975. The effect of keyed response sequencing of multiple choice items on performance and reliability. *Journal of Educational Measurement,* 12:45–48.

JOHNSON, A. P. 1951. Notes on a suggested index of item validity. *Journal of Educational Psychology,* 42:499–504.

JOHNSON, F. W. 1911. A study of high school grades. *School Review,* 19:13–24.

JOHNSON, O. G. 1976. *Tests and measurements in child development: Handbooks I and II.* San Francisco: Jossey-Bass.

——, and J. W. BOMMARITO. 1971. *Tests and measurements in child development: A handbook.* San Francisco: Jossey-Bass.

JOHNSON, R. W. 1977. Test review: Strong-Campbell Interest Inventory. *Measurement and Evaluation in Guidance,* 9:40–45.

JONZ, J. 1976. Improving on the basic egg: The M-C cloze. *Language Learning,* 26:255–65.

JORGENSON, G. W. 1975. An analysis of teacher judgments of reading level. *American Educational Research Journal,* 12:67–75.

JOSÉ, J., and J. J. CODY. 1971. Teacher-pupil interaction as it relates to attempted changes in teacher expectancy of academic ability and achievement. *American Educational Research Journal,* 8:39–50.

JURGENSEN, C. E. 1966. Advisory panel appraises suitability of USES testing. *Industrial Psychologist,* 1966, 4:41–44.

JURS, S., and K. D. HOPKINS. 1971. Jenkins' shortcut standard deviation: Its accuracy with nonnormal distributions. Paper presented to the National Council on Measurement in Education, New York.

KAHN, S. B. 1968. The relative magnitude of speed and power in SCAT. *Journal of Educational Measurement,* 5:327–30.

——. 1978. A comparative study of assessing children's school-related attitudes. *Journal of Educational Measurement,* 15:59–66.

KAISER, H. F. 1958. A modified stanine scale. *Journal of Experimental Education,* 26:261.

KANE, M., and J. MALONEY. 1978. The effect of guessing on item reliability under answer-until-correct scoring. *Applied Psychological Measurement,* 2:41–49.

KARLINS, J. K., M. KAPLAN, and W. STUART. 1969. Academic attitudes and performance as a function of a differential grading system: An evaluation of Princeton's pass-fail system. *Journal of Experimental Education,* 37:38–50.

KELLEY, T. L. 1927. *Interpretation of educational measurements.* New York: World.

——. 1939. The selection of upper and lower groups for the validation of test items. *Journal of Educational Psychology,* 30:17–24.

KEMPTHORNE, O. 1978. Logical, epistemological and statistical aspects of nature–nurture data interpretation. *Biometrics,* 34:1–23.

KENDRICK, S. A., and C. L. THOMAS. 1970. Education for socially disadvantaged children: Transition from school to college. *Review of Educational Research,* 40:151–79.

KERLINGER, F. N. 1973. *Foundations of behavioral research,* 2nd ed. New York: Holt, Rinehart and Winston.

KEYSOR, R. E., and D. D. WILLIAMS. 1977. The effect of "test wiseness" on professional school screening test scores. *NCME Measurement News,* 20:9.

KHOURY, B. V., ed. 1978. *1978–79 guide for the use of the Graduate Record Examinations.* Princeton, N.J.: Educational Testing Service.

KIFER, E. 1975. Relationship between academic achievement and personality characteristics: A quasi-longitudinal study. *American Educational Research Journal,* 12:191–210.

KIRKLAND, M. D. 1971. The effects of tests on students and schools. *Review of Educational Research,* 41:303–50.

KLARE, G. R. 1975. Assessing readability. *Reading Research Quarterly,* 10:62–102.

KLEIN, S. P., and F. M. HART. 1968. The nature of essay grades in law school. Research Bulletin 68-6. Princeton, N.J.: Educational Testing Service.

KLEINKE, D. 1979. Systematic errors in approximations to the standard error of measurement and reliability. *Applied psychological measurement,* 3:161–64.

KLUGMAN, S. F. 1944. The effect of money incentive versus praise upon the reliability and obtained scores of the revised Stanford-Binet test. *Journal of General Psychology*, 30:255–69.

KNAPP, R. R. 1960. The effects of time limits on the intelligence test performance of Mexican and American subjects. *Journal of Educational Psychology*, 51:14–20.

KOEHLER, R. A. 1971. A comparison of the validities of conventional choice testing and various confidence marking procedures. *Journal of Educational Measurement*, 8:297–303.

———. 1974. Overconfidence on probabilistic tests. *Journal of Educational Measurement*, 11:101–8.

KOPPITZ, E. M. 1975. *The Bender Gestalt Test for young children: Research and application, 1963–1973.* New York: Grune & Stratton.

KRAFT, R. S. 1978. Inside Chinese education. *School and University Review*, 8:4–8.

KRATHWOHL, D. R. 1965. Stating objectives appropriately for program, for curriculum, and for instructional materials development. *Journal of Teacher Education*, 16:83–92.

———, and D. PAYNE. 1971. Defining and assessing educational objectives. In R. L. Thorndike, ed., *Educational measurement*, 2nd ed. Washington, D.C.: American Council on Education. Chap. 2.

KRATHWOHL, D. R., et al. 1964. *Taxonomy of educational objectives: Handbook II, Affective domain.* New York: D. McKay.

KREIT, L. H. 1968. The effects of test-taking practice on pupil test performance. *American Educational Research Journal*, 5:616–25.

KROPP, R. P., H. W. STOKER, and W. L. BASHAW. 1966. *The construction and validation of tests of the cognitive processes as described in the taxonomy of educational objectives.* Cooperative Research Project no. 2117. Washington, D.C.: U.S. Department of Health, Education and Welfare, Office of Education.

KRUEGER, W. C. F. 1929. The effect of overlearning on retention. *Journal of Experimental Psychology*, 12:71–78.

KUDER, G. F. 1963. A rationale for evaluating interests. *Educational and Psychological Measurement*, 23:3–12.

———, and M. W. RICHARDSON. 1937. The theory of the estimation of test reliability. *Psychometrika*, 2:151–60.

KULIK, J. A., and W. J. MCKEACHIE. 1975. The evaluation of teachers in higher education. In F. N. Kerlinger, ed., *Review of research in education*, vol. 3. Chap. 7, pp. 210–40.

LA FAVE, L. 1964. Essay tests can be standardized. *Science*, 146:171.

———. 1966. Essay vs. multiple-choice: Which test is preferable? *Psychology in the Schools*, 3:65–69.

LAKE, D., M. MILES, and R. EARLE. 1973. *Measuring human behavior.* New York: Teachers College Press.

LAVIN, D. E. 1967. *The prediction of academic performance.* New York: Wiley.

LEEDS, C. H. 1950. A scale for measuring teacher-pupil attitudes and teacher-pupil rapport. *Psychological Monographs*, 64 (6, whole no. 312).

LEHRER, B. E., and A. N. HIERONYMOUS. 1977. Predicting achievement using intellectual, academic-motivational and selected non-intellectual factors. *Journal of Experimental Education*, 45:44–51.

LENNON, R. T. 1978. Perspective on intelligence testing. *NCME Measurement in Education*, 9:1–8.

———, ed. 1979. *New Directions for Testing and Measurement: Impactive Changes on Measurement.* San Francisco: Jossey-Bass.

LEVINE, P. R., and R. WALLEN. 1954. Adolescent vocational interests and later occupation. *Journal of Applied Psychology*, 38:428–31.

LEVINE, R. S., and W. H. ANGOFF. 1958. *The effects of practice and growth on scores on the Scholastic Aptitude Test.* Statistical Report 58-6. Princeton, N.J.: Educational Testing Service.

LEWIS, M., and H. MCGURK. 1972. Evaluation of infant intelligence. *Science*, 178:1174–77.

LINDQUIST, E. F. 1944. The use of tests of accreditation of military experience and in the educational placement of war veterans. *Educational Record*, 25:357–76.

LITTLE, E., and J. CREASER. 1966. Uncertain responses on multiple-choice examinations. *Psychological Reports*, 18:801–2.

LIVINGSTON, S. A. 1972. Criterion-referenced applications of classical test theory. *Journal of Educational Measurement,* 9:13–26.

LOEHLIN, H. C., G. LINDZEY, and J. N. SPUHLER. 1975. *Race differences in intelligence.* San Francisco: W. H. Freeman.

LORD. F. M. 1952. The relation of the reliability of multiple-choice tests to the distribution of item difficulties. *Psychometrika,* 17:181–94.

———. 1955. A survey of observed test-score distribution with respect to skewness and kurtosis. *Educational and Psychological Measurement,* 15:383–89.

———. 1956. A study of speed factors in tests and academic grades. *Psychometrika,* 21:31–50.

———. 1959a. Test norms and sampling theory. *Journal of Experimental Education,* 27:247–63.

———. 1959b. Tests of the same length do have the same standard error of measurement. *Educational and Psychological Measurement.* 19: 233–39.

———. 1962. Estimating norms by item-sampling. *Educational and Psychological measurement,* 22:259–67.

———. 1963. Formula scoring and validity. *Educational and Psychological Measurement,* 23: 663–72.

———. 1971a. The self-scoring flexilevel test. *Journal of Educational Measurement,* 8:147–51.

———. 1971b. A theoretical study of the measurement effectiveness of flexilevel tests. *Educational and Psychological Measurement,* 31: 805–14.

———. 1975. Formula scoring and number-right scoring. *Journal of Educational Measurement,* 12:7–12.

———. 1976. Invited discussion. In *Proceedings of the first conference on computerized adoptive testing.* Washington, D.C.: U.S. Civil Service Commission.

———, and M. R. NOVICK. 1968. *Statistical theories of mental test scores.* Reading, Mass.: Addison-Wesley.

LORGE, I. 1952. Speed of response as a factor in mental "decline" with age. In R. G. Kuhlen and G. G. Thompson, eds. *Psychological studies of human development.* Englewood Cliffs, N.J.: Prentice-Hall. Pp. 173–79.

LOYD, B. H., and H. D. HOOVER. 1980. Vertical equating using the Rasch model. *Journal of Educational Measurement,* 17:179–94.

LUDLOW, H. G. 1956. Some recent research on the Davis-Eells games. *School and Society,* 84: 146–48.

LYERLY, S. B. 1973. *Handbook of psychiatric rating scales.* Rockville, Md.: National Institute of Mental Health.

LYMAN, H. B. 1978. *Test scores and what they mean.* Englewood Cliffs, N.J.: Prentice-Hall.

LYNCH, D. O., and B. C. SMITH. 1975. Item response changes: Effects on test scores. *Measurement and Evaluation in Guidance,* 7:220–24.

McARTHUR, C., and L. B. STEVENS. 1955. The validation of expressed interests as compared with inventoried interests: A fourteen-year follow-up. *Journal of Applied Psychology,* 39:184–89.

McASKIE, M., and A. M. CLARKE. 1976. Parent-offspring resemblances in intelligence: Theories and evidence. *British Journal of Psychology,* 67:243–73.

McCALL, J. N. 1965. Trends in the measurement of vocational interest. *Review of Educational Research,* 35:53–62.

———, and G. D. MOORE. 1965. Do interest inventories measure estimated abilities? *Personnel and Guidance Journal,* 43:1034–37.

McDOUGAL, W. 1923. *An introduction to social psychology,* 15th ed. Boston: John W. Luce.

McGUIRE, C. 1963. Research in the process approach to the construction and analysis of medical examinations. *The twentieth yearbook of the National Council on Measurement in Education.* Pp. 7–16.

McKEACHIE, W. J., YI-GUANG LIN, and W. MANN. 1971. Student ratings of teacher effectiveness: Validation Studies. *American Educational Research Journal,* 8:435–45.

McMILLAN, J. H. 1977. The effect of effort and feedback on the formation of student attitudes. *American Educational Research Journal,* 14:317–30.

McMORRIS, R. F. 1971. Evidence on the quality of several approximations for commonly used measurement statistics. Paper presented to the

National Council on Measurement in Education, New York.

McNAMARA, W. J., and E. WEITZMAN. 1945. The effect of choice placement on the difficulty of multiple-choice questions. *Journal of Educational Psychology,* 36:103–13.

McNEMAR, Q. 1964. Lost: our intelligence. Why? *American Psychologist,* 19:871–82.

MACHOVER, K. 1949. *Personality projection in the drawing of the human figure: A method of personality investigation.* Springfield, Ill.: Charles C Thomas.

MADAUS, G. F. and J. T. McDONAGH, 1979. Minimum competency testing: Unexamined assumptions and unexplored negative outcomes. In R. T. Lennon, ed., *New Directions for Testing and Measurement: Impactive Changes on Measurement.* San Francisco: Jossey-Bass.

MAGNUSSON, D., and G. BACKTEMAN. 1978. Longitudinal stability of person characteristics: Intelligence and creativity. *Applied Psychological Measurement,* 2:481–90.

MAGUIRE, T. O. 1973. Semantic differential for structuring attitudes. *American Educational Research Journal,* 10:295–306.

MANN, H. 1845. Report of the annual examining committee of the Boston grammar and writing schools. *Common School Journal,* 7:326–36.

MARCUS, A. 1963. The effect of correct response location on the difficulty level of multiple-choice questions. *Journal of Applied Psychology,* 47:48–51.

MARDELL, C. D., and D. S. GOLDENBERG. 1972. *Learning Disabilities/Early Childhood Research Project.* Springfield: Illinois State Office of the Superintendent of Public Instruction. (Also available in ERIC, ED 082408.)

MARKHAM, L. R. 1976. Influences of handwriting quality on teacher evaluation of written work. *American Educational Research Journal,* 13:277–84.

MARSH, H. W. 1977. The validity of students' evaluations: Classroom evaluations of instructors independently nominated as best and worst teachers by graduating seniors. *American Educational Research Journal,* 14:441–47.

MARSHALL, J. C. 1967. Composition errors and essay examination grades re-examined. *American Educational Research Journal,* 4:375–85.

———, and J. M. POWERS. 1969. Writing readability, composition errors, and essay grades. University of Missouri–St. Louis. Paper presented at the annual meeting of the National Council on Measurement in Education, Los Angeles, February 6–8.

MARSO, R. N. 1970. Test item arrangement, testing time and performance. *Journal of Educational Measurement,* 7:113–18.

MASLING, J. 1959. The effects of warm and cold interaction on the administration and scoring of an intelligence test. *Journal of Consulting Psychology,* 23:336–41.

MASON, G. P., and R. E. ODEH. 1968. A short-cut formula for standard deviation. *Journal of Educational Measurement,* 5:319–20.

MAYO, S. T. 1967. *Pre-service preparation of teachers in educational measurement.* Final report. Chicago: Loyola University.

———. 1968. The methodology and technology of educational and psychological testing. *Review of Educational Research,* 38:92–101.

———. 1970. Mastery learning and mastery testing. *Measurement in Education: A series of special reports of the National Council on Measurement in Education,* 1.

MEDLEY, D. M., and A. A. KLEIN. 1957. Measuring classroom behavior with a pupil reaction inventory. *Elementary School Journal,* 57:315–19.

MEEHL, P. E. 1954. *Clinical versus statistical prediction: A theoretical analysis and a review of the evidence.* Minneapolis: University of Minnesota Press.

MEGARGEE, E. I. 1972. *The California Psychological Inventory Handbook.* San Francisco: Jossey-Bass.

MEHRENS, W. A. 1974. Evaluators, educators, and the publics: A détente? *NCME Measurement in Education,* 5, no. 3.

———, and R. L. EBEL. 1979. Some comments on criterion-referenced and norm-referenced achievement tests. *NCME Measurement in Education,* 10, no. 1.

MEHRENS, W. A., and I. J. LEHMANN. 1975. *Measurement and evaluation in education and psychology,* 2nd ed. New York: Holt, Rinehart and Winston.

MENDELS, G. E., and J. P. FLANDERS. 1973. Teachers'

expectations and pupil performance. *American Educational Research Journal*, 10:203–12.

MERCER, J. 1977. *System of multicultural pluralistic assessment (SOMPA)*. New York: Psychological Corp.

METFESSEL, N. S., and G. SAX. 1957. Response set patterns in published instructors' manuals in education and psychology. *California Journal of Educational Research*, 8:195–97.

————. 1958. Systematic biases in the keying of correct responses on certain standardized tests. *Educational and Psychological Measurement*, 18:58–62.

MEYER, M. 1908. The grading of students. *Science*, 27:243–50.

MEYER, W. J., and A. W. BENDIG. 1961. A longitudinal study of the Primary Mental Abilities Test. *Journal of Educational Psychology*, 52:50–60.

MICHAEL, J. J. 1968a. The reliability of a multiple-choice examination under various test-taking instructions. *Journal of Educational Measurement*, 5:307–14.

————. 1968b. Structure of intellect theory and the validity of achievement examinations. *Educational and Psychological Measurement*, 28:1141–49.

————, and W. B. MICHAEL. 1969. The relationship of performance on objective achievement examinations to the order in which students complete them. *Educational and Psychological Measurement*, 29:511–13.

MICHAEL, W. B., F. HAERTZKA, and N. C. PERRY. 1953. Errors in estimates of item difficulty obtained from use of extreme groups on a criterion variable. *Educational and Psychological Measurement*, 13:601–6.

MICHAEL, W. B., T. COOPER, P. SHAFFER, and E. WALLIS. 1980. A comparison of the reliability and validity of ratings of student performance on essay examinations by professors of English and by professors in other disciplines. *Educational and Psychological Measurement*, 40:183–95.

MICHAELIS, J. U. 1954. The prediction of success in student teaching from personality and attitude inventories. *University of California Public Education*, 11:415–81.

MILHOLLAND, J. E., ed. 1979. *New Directions for Testing and Measurement: Insights from Large-Scale Surveys*, San Francisco: Jossey-Bass.

MILLER, D. C. 1977. *Handbook of research design and social measurement*, 3rd ed. New York: D. McKay.

MILLER, R. I. 1979. *The assessment of college performance: A handbook of techniques and measures for institutional self-evaluation*. San Francisco: Jossey-Bass.

MILLER, W. G., H. SNOWMAN, and T. O'HARA. 1979. Application of alternative statistical techniques to examine the hierarchical ordering in Bloom's taxonomy. *American Educational Research Journal*, 16:241–48.

MILLMAN, J. 1961. Multiple-choice test item construction rules. Ithaca, N.Y.: Cornell University Press. Mimeographed, 7 pp.

————. 1974. Criterion-referenced measurement. In W. J. Popham, ed., *Evaluation in education: Current applications*. Berkeley, Calif.: McCutchan.

————, C. H. BISHOP, and R. EBEL. 1965. An analysis of test-wiseness. *Educational and Psychological Measurement*, 25:707–26.

MILLMAN, J., and W. PAUK. 1969. *How to take tests*. New York: McGraw-Hill.

MIYAZAKI, I. 1976. *China's examination hell: The civil service examinations of imperial China*. Translated by C. Schirokauer. New York and Tokyo: Weatherhill.

MOLLENKOPF, W. G. 1960. Time limits and the behavior of test takers. *Educational and Psychological Measurement*, 20:223–30.

MONROE, W. S., and R. E. CARTER. 1923. *The use of different types of thought questions in secondary schools and their relative difficulty for students*. Bulletin no. 14. Urbana: University of Illinois, Bureau of Educational Research.

MOORE, J. C., R. E. SCHUTZ, and R. L. BAKER. 1966. The application of a self-instructional technique to develop a test-taking strategy. *American Educational Research Journal*, 3:13–17.

MOOS, R. H. 1974. *The social climate scales: An overview*. Palo Alto, Calif.: Consulting Psychologists Press.

————. 1975. Assessment and impact of social climate. In P. McReynolds, ed., *Advances in psychological assessment*, vol. 3. San Francisco: Jossey-Bass. Chap. 1.

———. 1979. *Evaluating educational environments. Procedures, measures, findings, and policy implications.* San Francisco: Jossey-Bass.

MORRIS, L. L., and C. T. FITZ-GIBBON. 1978. *How to measure achievement.* Beverly Hills, Calif.: Sage Publications.

MORROW, J. R. 1976. The effects of response position and item simplicity on the factorial structure of teacher evaluations. Doctoral dissertation, University of Colorado.

———. 1977. Some statistics regarding the reliability and validity of student ratings of teachers. *The Research Quarterly,* 48:372–75.

MOULY, G. J., and SR. MARY EDGAR, R.S.M. 1958. Equivalence of IQ's for four group intelligence tests. *Personnel and Guidance Journal,* 36 (May): 623–26.

MOUTON, J. S., et al. 1955. The validity of sociometric responses. *Sociometry,* 18:7–48.

MOYNIHAN, P. 1971. Seek parity of educational achievement, Moynihan urges. *Report on Educational Research* (March 3), 3(5):4.

MUELLER, D. J., and A. SHWEDEL. 1975. Some correlates of net gain from answer changing on objective test items. *Journal of Educational Measurement,* 12:251–54.

MUELLER, D. J., and V. WASSER. 1977. Implications of changing answers on objective test items. *Journal of Educational Measurement,* 14:9–14.

MULLER, D., E. CALHOUN, and R. ORLING. 1972. Test reliability as a function of answer sheet mode. *Journal of Educational Measurement,* 9:321–24.

MUNDAY, L. A. 1979. Changing test scores, especially since 1970. *Phi Delta Kappan,* 61:496–99.

Murphy, G. 1949. *Historical introduction to modern psychology,* rev. ed. New York: Harcourt Brace Jovanovich.

MURRAY, H. A., et al. 1938. *Explorations in personality.* New York: Oxford University Press.

MYERS, C. T. 1960. Symposium: The effects of time limits on test scores. *Educational and Psychological Measurement,* 20:221–22.

NATIONAL ASSESSMENT OF EDUCATIONAL PROGRESS. 1975. *Update on education.* Denver, Colo.

———. 1976. Minimal competency tests. *NAEP Newsletter,* 9.

———. 1977a. Hispanic youths "consistently" below contemporaries in education achievement. *NAEP Newsletter,* 10:1–6.

———. 1977b. Essay task: A woman's place is (where?). *NAEP Newsletter,* 10:1–8.

———. 1979. Math achievement is plus and minus. *NAEP Newsletter,* 12, no. 5.

NATIONAL COUNCIL ON MEASUREMENT IN EDUCATION. 1976. On bias in selection. *Journal of Educational Measurement,* 13:1–99.

———. 1980. NCME statement on educational admissions testing. *NCME Measurement News,* 23:4–6.

NATIONAL EDUCATION ASSOCIATION. 1967. National Education Association report to parents. *NEA Research Bulletin,* 45:51–53.

NATIONAL INSTITUTE OF EDUCATION. 1979. *Testing, teaching and learning.* Washington, D.C.: NIE.

NELL, W. 1963. A comparative investigation of teacher assigned grades and academic achievement in the Aztec Junior High, New Mexico. In Society for the Study of Education, *Educational Research Bulletin.* Pp. 15–16.

NILSSON, I. 1975. The occurrence of test-wiseness and the possibility of inducing it via instruction. *Educational Reports UMEA,* no. 8.

NOBLE, C. E., J. L. NOBLE, and W. T. ALCOCK. 1958. Prediction of individual differences in human trial-and-error learning. *Perceptual and Motor Skills,* 8:151–72.

NORMAN, R. D. 1954. The effects of a forward-retention set on an objective achievement test presented forwards or backwards. *Educational and Psychological Measurement,* 14:487–98.

NOVICK, M. R., and C. LEWIS. 1967. Coefficient alpha and the reliability of composite measurements. *Psychometrika,* 32:1–13.

NUNNALLY, J. C. 1979. *Psychometric theory, 2nd ed.* New York: McGraw-Hill.

OAKLAND, T. 1977. *Psychological and educational assessment of minority children.* New York: Bruner/Mazel Publishers.

OELKE, M. C. 1956. A study of student teachers' attitudes toward children. *Journal of Educational Psychology,* 47:193–96.

OKADA, T., W. M. COHEN, and G. W. MAYESKE. 1969. *Growth in achievement for different racial, regional and socio-economic groupings of students.* Washington, D.C.: U.S. Department of Health, Education and Welfare, Office of Education, Office of Program Planning and Evaluation, Division of Elementary and Secondary Programs.

OLDRIDGE, O. A. 1963. *An experimental study of two guidance emphases in the elementary school.* Doctoral dissertation, University of Southern California. University Microfilms, no. 63-5061. *Dissertation Abstracts,* 24:632-33 (August 1963).

OLEJNIK, S. 1979. Standardized achievement testing program viewed from the perspective of the non-measurement specialist. *NCME Measurement News,* 22:27.

OPPENHEIM, A. N. 1966. Questionnaire design and attitude measurement. New York: Basic Books.

OSGOOD, C. E., G. J. SUCI, and P. H. TANNENBAUM. 1957. *The measurement of meaning.* Urbana: University of Illinois.

OSS ASSESSMENT STAFF. 1948. *Assessment of men: Selection of personnel for the Office of Strategic Services.* New York: Rinehart.

OSTERLUND, B. L., and K. CHENEY. 1978. A holistic essay-reading composite as a criterion for the validity of the test of standard written English. *Measurement and Evaluation in Guidance,* 11:155-58.

O'SULLIVAN, M., and J. P. GUILFORD. 1975. Six factors of behavioral cognition: Understanding other people. *Journal of Educational Measurement,* 12:255-72.

OWENS, T. R., and D. L. STUFFLEBEAM. 1969. An experimental comparison of item sampling and examinee sampling for estimating test norms. Paper presented at the annual meeting of the National Council on Measurement in Education, Los Angeles, February 6-8.

OWENS, W. A. 1953. Age and mental abilities: A longitudinal study. *Genetic Psychology Monographs,* 48:3-54.

———. 1966. Age and mental abilities: A second adult follow-up. *Journal of Educational Psychology,* 57:311-25.

PACE, C. R. 1979. *Measuring outcomes of college.* San Francisco: Jossey-Bass.

PAGE, A. 1960. To grade or retrograde. *College English,* 21:213-16.

———. 1963. Socrates on cheating. *Liberal Education,* 49:193-97.

PAGE, E. B. 1958. Teacher comments and student performance: A seventy-four classroom experiment in school motivation. *Journal of Educational Psychology,* 49:173-81.

———. 1966. The imminence of grading essays by computer. *Phi Delta Kappan,* 47:238-43.

———. 1972. Miracle in Milwaukee: Raising the IQ. *Educational Research,* 1:8-16.

———. 1973. Educational values for measurement technology: Some theory and data. In W.E. Coffman, ed., *Frontiers of educational measurement and information-1973.* Boston: Houghton Mifflin.

PAGE, E. G., and T. F. BREEN. 1973. Educational values for measurement technology: Some theory and data. In W. E. Coffman, ed., *Frontiers of educational measurement and information systems.* Proceedings of the Invitational Conference on the Occasion of the Dedication of the Lindquist Center for Measurement. Boston: Houghton Mifflin.

PALMER, O. 1962. Seven classic ways of grading dishonestly. *English Journal,* 51:464-67.

PANACKAL, A. A., and C. S. HEFT. 1978. Cloze technique and multiple choice technique: Reliability and validity. *Educational and Psychological Measurement,* 38:917-32.

PASCALE, P. J. 1974. Changing answers on multiple-choice achievement tests. *Measurement and Evaluation in Guidance,* 6:236-38.

PAYNE, D. A. 1963. A note on skewness and internal consistency reliability estimates. *Journal of Experimental Education,* 32(1):43-46.

PEAK, H., and E. G. BORING. 1926. The factor of speed in intelligence. *Journal of Experimental Psychology,* 9:71.

PEARSON, P. D., and D. D. JOHNSON. 1978. *Teaching reading comprehension.* New York: Holt, Rinehart and Winston.

PERRONE, P. A. 1964. Factors influencing high school seniors' occupational preference. *Personnel and Guidance Journal,* 42:976-80.

PETERS, F. R. 1956. Measurement of informal educational achievement by the GED tests. *School Review,* 64:227–32.

PETERSON, R. A. 1978. Review of the Rorschach. In O. K. Buros, ed., *The eighth mental measurements yearbook.* Highland Park, N.J.: Gryphon Press. Pp. 1042–45.

PEZZULLO, T. R., E. E. THORSEN, and G. F. MADAUS. 1972. The heritability of Jensen's level I and II and divergent thing. *American Educational Research Journal,* 9:539–46.

PHI DELTA KAPPA. 1973. *School climate improvement.*

PHILLIPS, B. N. 1971. School stress as a factor in children's responses to tests and testing. *Journal of Educational Measurement,* 8:21–26.

———, and G. WEATHERS. 1958. Analysis of errors in scoring standardized tests. *Educational and Psychological Measurement,* 18:563–67.

PIDGEON, D. A., and A. YATES. 1957. Experimental inquiries into the use of essay-type English papers. *British Journal of Educational Psychology,* 27:37–47.

PIKE, L. W. 1978. *Short-term instruction, test-wiseness, and the scholastic aptitude test: A literature review with research recommendations.* Research Bulletin RB-78-2. Princeton, N.J.: Educational Testing Service.

PINCHAK, B. M., and H. M. BRELAND. 1974. Grading practices in American high schools: National longitudinal study of high school class of 1972. *Educational Digest,* 39:21–23.

PIPPERT, R. 1966. Final note on the changed answer myth. *Clearinghouse,* 38:165–66.

PLAKE, B. S. and H. D. HOOVER. 1979. The comparability of equal raw scores obtained from in-level and out-of-level testing. *Journal of Educational Measurement,* 16:271–78.

PLUMLEE, L. B. 1964. Estimating means and standard deviations from partial data—an empirical check on Lord's item sampling technique. *Educational and Psychological Measurement,* 24:623–30.

POLLACZEK, P. P. 1952. A study of malingering on the CVS abbreviated individual intelligence scale. *Journal of Clinical Psychology,* 8:75–81.

POOLE, R. L. 1972. Characteristics of the taxonomy of educational objectives: Cognitive domain: A replication. *Psychology in the Schools,* 9:83–88.

POPHAM, W. J. 1978a. The case for criterion-referenced measurement. *Educational Research,* 7:6–10.

———. 1978b. *Criterion-referenced measurement.* Englewood Cliffs, N.J.: Prentice-Hall.

———, and T. R. HUSSEK. 1969. Implications of criterion-referenced measurement. *Journal of Educational Measurement,* 6:1–10. Reprinted in G. H. Bracht, K. D. Hopkins, and J. C. Stanley, eds. 1972. *Perspectives in educational and psychological measurement.* Englewood Cliffs, N.J.: Prentice-Hall. Selection 13.

POPHAM, W. J., and R. R. TRIMBLE. 1960. The Minnesota Teacher Attitude Inventory as an index of general teaching competence. *Educational and Psychological Measurement,* 20: 509–72.

POWERS, D. E. and D. L. ALDERMAN. 1979. *The use, acceptance, and impact of "Taking the SAT"—a test familiarization booklet.* Princeton: Educational Testing Service.

PRESSLEY, M. M. 1976. Inflation hits the campuses. *Wall Street Journal,* January 21.

PRICE, J. L. 1972. *Handbook of organizational measurement.* Lexington, Mass.: D. C. Heath.

PYRCZAK, F. 1973. Validity of the discrimination index as a measure of item quality. *Journal of Educational Measurement,* 10:227–31.

QUIRK, T. J., B. J. WITTEN, and S. F. WEINBERG. 1973. Review of studies of the concurrent and predictive validity of the National Teacher Examinations. *Review of Educational Research,* 43:89–113.

RABINOWITZ, F. M. 1970. Characteristic sequential dependencies in multiple-choice situations. *Psychological Bulletin,* 74:141–48.

RABINOWITZ, W. 1954. The fakability of the Minnesota Teacher Attitude Inventory. *Educational and Psychological Measurement,* 14:657–64.

RADER, N. 1980. An evaluation of an experiential education program. Ph.D. thesis, University of Colorado.

RAMOS, R. A., and J. STERN. 1973. Item behaviour associated with changes in the number of alternatives in multiple-choice items. *Journal of Educational Measurement,* 10:305–10.

REEDER, L. G., L. RAMACHER, and S. GORELNIK. 1976. *Handbook of scales and indices of health behavior.* Pacific Palisades, Calif.: Goodyear.

REILING, E., and R. TAYLOR. 1972. A new approach to the problem of changing initial responses to multiple-choice questions. *Journal of Educational Measurement,* 9:67–70.

REMMERS, H. H. 1963. Rating methods in research on teaching. In N. L. Gage, ed., *Handbook of research on teaching.* Skokie, Ill.: Rand McNally & Company, Chap. 7.

RENTZ, R. R., and C. C. RENTZ. 1979. Does the Rasch model really work? A discussion for practitioners. *NCME Measurement in Education,* 10:1–11.

REYNOLDS, P. D. 1979. *Ethical dilemmas and social science research: An analysis of moral issues confronting investigators in research using human participants.* San Francisco: Jossey-Bass.

RICHARDS, J. M., JR., and S. W. LUTZ. 1968. Predicting student accomplishment in college from the ACT assessment. *Journal of Educational Measurement,* 5:17–29.

ROBINSON, J. P., R. ATHANASIOU, and K. B. HEAD. 1969. *Measures of occupational attitudes and occupational characteristics.* Ann Arbor: University of Michigan, Institute for Social Research.

ROBINSON, J. P., and P. SHAVER. 1973. *Measures of social psychological attitudes.* Ann Arbor: University of Michigan, Institute of Social Research.

ROBINSON, J. P., et al. 1968. *Measures of political attitudes.* Ann Arbor: University of Michigan.

RODGER, A. G. 1936. The application of six group intelligence tests to the same children, and the effects of practice. *British Journal of Educational Psychology,* 6:291–305.

ROELFS, R. M. 1955. Trends in junior high school progress reporting. *Journal of Educational Research,* 49:241–49.

ROEMER, R. E. 1965. Nine-year validity study of predictors of medical school success. *Journal of Educational Research,* 59:183–85.

ROSENTHAL, R., and L. JACOBSON. 1968. *Pygmalion in the classroom: Teacher expectation and pupils' intellectual development.* New York: Holt, Rinehart and Winston. Reviewed by Richard E. Snow in *Contemporary Psychology,* 14 (1969): 197–99.

ROTEM, A., and N. S. GLASMAN. 1979. On the effectiveness of students' evaluative feedback to university instructors. *Review of Educational Research,* 49:497–511.

RUEBUSH, B. K. 1963. Anxiety. In the Yearbook Committee and Associated Contributors, H. W. Stevenson, J. Kagan, and C. Spiker, eds., *Child psychology: The sixty-second yearbook of the National Society for the Study of Education.* Chicago: University of Chicago Press.

RULON, P. J. 1939. A simplified procedure for determining the reliability of a test by split halves. *Harvard Educational Review,* 9:99–103.

RUNDQUIST, E. A., and B. F. SLETTO. 1936. *Personality in the depression.* Minneapolis: University of Minnesota Press.

RUSSELL, I. L., and A. T. WELLINGTON. 1955. Personality: Does it influence teachers' marks? *Journal of Educational Research,* 48:561–64.

RYANS, D. G. 1960. *Characteristics of teachers.* Washington, D.C.: American Council on Education.

SABERS, D. L., and R. D. KLAUSMEIER. 1971. Accuracy of short-cut estimates for standard deviation. *Journal of Educational Measurement,* 8, 335–39.

SANDERS, N. M. 1966. *Classroom questions: What kinds?* New York: Harper & Row.

SANDGREN, D. L., and L. G. SCHMIDT. 1956. Does practice teaching change attitudes toward teaching? *Journal of Educational Research,* 49: 673–80.

SARASON, S. S., G. MANDLER, and P. G. CRAIGHILL. 1952. The effect of differential instructions on anxiety and learning. *Journal of Abnormal and Social Psychology,* 47:561–65.

SARASON, S. B., et al. 1960. *Anxiety in elementary school children.* New York: Wiley.

SARNACKI, R. E. 1979. An examination of test-wiseness in the cognitive test domain. *Review of Educational Research,* 49:252–79.

SAX, G., and A. CARR. 1962. An investigation of response set on altered parallel forms. *Educational and Psychological Measurement,* 22: 371–76.

SAX, G., and L. S. COLLET. 1968. The effects of differing instructions and guessing formulas on reliability and validity. *Educational and Psychological Measurement,* 28:1127–36.

SAX, G., and T. R. CROMACK. 1966. The effects of various forms of item arrangements on test performance. *Journal of Educational Measurement,* 3:309–11.

SAX, G., and M. READE. 1964. Achievement as a function of test difficulty level. *American Educational Research Journal,* 1:22–25.

SCANNELL, D. P., and J. C. MARSHALL. 1966. The effect of selected composition errors on grades assigned to essay examinations. *American Educational Research Journal,* 3:125–30.

SCHAIE, K. W., and C. R. STROTHER. 1968. A cross-sequential study of age changes in cognitive behavior. *Psychological Bulletin,* 70:671–80.

SCHEIRER, M. A., and R. E. KRAUT. 1979. Increasing educational achievement via self-concept change. *Review of Educational Research,* 49:131–50.

SCHMEISER, C. B., and R. L. FERGUSON. 1978. Performance of black and white students on test materials containing content based on black and white cultures. *Journal of Educational Measurement,* 15:193–200.

SCHOENFELDT, L. F., and D. H. BRUSH. 1975. Patterns of college grades across curricular areas: Some implications for GPA as a criterion. *American Educational Research Journal.* 12:313–21.

SCHON, I., K. D. HOPKINS, and C. VOJIR. 1980. The effects of special curricular study of Mexican culture on Anglo and Mexican-American students' perceptions of Mexican-Americans. Paper presented to the American Educational Research Association, Boston, March, 1980.

SCHRADER, W. B., ed. 1979. *New Directions for Testing and Measurement: Measurement and Educational Policy.* San Francisco: Jossey-Bass.

SCHULTZ, M. K., and W. H. ANGOFF, 1956. The development of new scales for the aptitude and advanced tests of the Graduate Record Examinations. *Journal of Educational Psychology.* 47:285–94.

SCHUMACHER, C. F., and H. H. GEE. 1961. The relationship between initial and retest scores on the Medical College Admission Test. *Journal of Medical Education,* 36:129–33.

SCHWARZ, J. C. 1967. A new procedure for administering objective tests to large classes. *Journal of Educational Measurement,* 4:167–68.

SCOTT, W. A. 1968. Attitude measurement. In G. Lindsey and E. Aronson, eds., *The handbook of social psychology.* Reading, Mass.: Addison-Wesley. Chap. 11.

SCRIVEN, M. 1970. Discussion. *Proceedings of the 1969 Invitational Conference on Testing Problems.* Princeton, N.J.: Educational Testing Service. Pp. 112–17.

SEASHORE, C. E. 1899. Some psychological statistics. *University of Iowa Studies in Psychology,* 2:1–84.

SELLTIZ, C., L. S. WRIGHTSMAN, and S. W. COOK. 1976. *Research methods in social relations,* 3rd ed. New York: Holt, Rinehart and Winston.

SHANKER, A. 1977. AFT position paper on testing. *American Education,* 62:15.

SHAW, M. E., and J. M. WRIGHT. 1967. *Scales for the measurement of attitudes.* New York: McGraw-Hill.

SHELDON, M. S., and A. G. SORENSON. 1960. On the use of Q-techniques in educational evaluation and research. *Journal of Experimental Education,* 29:143–51.

SHEPARD, L. A. 1976. Setting standards and living with them. *Florida Journal of Educational Research,* 18:28–32.

———. 1979a. Self-acceptance: The evaluative component of the self-concept construct. *American Educational Research Journal,* 16:139–60.

———. 1979b. Setting standards. In M. A. Bunda and J. R. Sanders, eds., *Practices and problems in competency-based measurement.* Washington, D.C.: National Council on Measurement in Education.

———. 1979c. Norm-referenced vs. criterion-referenced tests. *Educational Horizons,* 58:26–32.

———. 1980. Technical issues in minimum competency testing. *Review of Research in Education,* 8: in press. Itasca, Ill.: Peacock.

———, and K. D. HOPKINS. 1977. Regression and the matching fallacy in quasi-experimental research. *National Association for Business Teachers Education Review,* 4:11–15.

SHEPHERD, E. M. 1929. The effect of the quality of penmanship on grades. *Journal of Educational Research,* 19:102–5.

SHERRIFFS, A. C., and D. S. BOOMER. 1954. Who is

penalized by the penalty for guessing? *Journal of Educational Psychology*, 45:81–90.

SHOEMAKER, D. M. 1975. Toward a framework for achievement testing. *Review of Educational Research*, 45:127–47.

SHORTLAND, R. L., and W. G. BERGER. 1970. Behavioral validation of several values. *Journal of Applied Psychology*, 54:433–35.

SILVERSTEIN, A. B., P. J. MOHAN, R. E. FRANKEN, and D. E. RHONE. 1964. Test anxiety and intellectual performance in mentally retarded school children. *Child Development*, 35:1137–46.

SIMON, A., and E. G. BOYER, eds. 1974. *Mirrors for behavior III: An anthology of observation instruments*. Philadelphia: Research for Better Schools.

SIMPSON, R. H. 1944. The specific meanings of certain terms indicating different degrees of frequency. *Quarterly Journal of Speech*, 30:328–30.

SINICK, D. 1956. Encouragement, anxiety, and test performance. *Journal of Applied Psychology*, 40:315–18.

SLAKTER, M. J. 1967. Risk taking on objective examinations. *American Educational Research Journal*, 4:31–43.

———. 1968. The penalty for not guessing. *Journal of Educational Measurement*, 5:141–44.

———. 1969. Generality of risk taking on objective examinations. *Educational and Psychological Measurement*, 29:115–28.

———, R. A. KOEHLER, and S. H. HAMPTON. 1970. Grade level, sex, and selected aspects of test-wiseness. *Journal of Educational Measurement*, 7:119–22.

SLANSKY, J. A. 1979. The effectiveness of study skills instruction for seventh graders. Ed.D. thesis, University of Colorado.

SLATER, R. D. 1964. The equivalency of IBM mark-sense answer cards and IBM answer sheets when used as answer formats for a precisely-timed test of mental ability. *Journal of Educational Research*, 57:545–47.

SLINDE, J. A., and R. L. LINN. 1978. An exploration of the adequacy of the Rasch model for the problem of vertical equating. *Journal of Educational Measurement*, 15:23–36.

———. 1979. A note on vertical equating via the Rasch model for groups of quite different ability and tests of quite different difficulty. *Journal of Educational Measurement*, 16:159–65.

SMITH, A., and J. C. MOORE. 1976. The effects of changing answers on scores of non-test-sophisticated examinees. *Measurement and Evaluation in Guidance*, 8:252–56.

SMITH, M., K. P. WHITE, and R. H. COOP. 1979. The effect of item type on the consequences of changing answers on multiple choice tests. *Journal of Educational Measurement*, 16:203–8.

SMITH, P. L. 1979. The generalizability of student ratings of courses: Asking the right questions. *Journal of Educational Measurement*, 16:77–88.

SNOW, R. E. 1969. Unfinished pygmalion, review of Rosenthal and Jacobson's *Pygmalion in the classroom*. *Contemporary Psychology*, 14:197–99.

SNYDER, W. U. 1955. The personality of clinical students. *Journal of Counseling Psychology*, 2:47–52.

SODERQUIST, H. 1936. A new method of weighting scores in a true-false test. *Journal of Educational Research*, 30:290–92.

SPAIGHTS, E. 1965. Accuracy of self-estimation of junior high school students. *Journal of Educational Research*, 58:416–19.

SPEARMAN, C. 1927. *The abilities of man*. New York: Macmillan.

STAFFORD, R. E. 1971. The speededness quotient: A new descriptive statistic for tests. *Journal of Educational Measurement*, 8:275–77.

STAKE, R. E. 1961. "Overestimation" of achievement with the California Achievement Test. *Educational and Psychological Measurement*, 21:59–62.

———, and D. D. SJOGREN. 1964. Activity level and learning effectiveness. NDEA Title VII, Project no. 753. Lincoln: University of Nebraska.

STALLINGS, W. M., and H. R. SMOCK. 1971. The pass–fail grading option at a state university: A five semester evaluation. *Journal of Educational Measurement*, 8:153–60.

STALNAKER, J. M. 1936. The problem of the English examination. *Educational Record*, 17 (Suppl. no. 10): 41.

———. 1961. Research in the National Merit

Scholarship program. *Journal of Counseling Psychology,* 8:268–71.

STANLEY, J. C. 1954. Psychological correction for chance. *Journal of Experimental Education,* 22:297–98.

———. 1957. K-R 20 as the stepped-up mean item intercorrelation. *Yearbook of the National Council on Measurements Used in Education,* 14:78–92.

———. 1960. College studies and college life in Belgium. *College Board Review,* 40:10–14.

———. 1971a. Predicting college success of the educationally disadvantaged. *Science,* 171: 640–47.

———. 1971b. Reliability. In R. L. Thorndike, ed., *Educational measurement,* 2nd ed. Washington D.C.: American Council on Education. Chap. 13.

———. 1971c. Reliability of test scores and other measurements. In L. C. Deighton, ed., *The encyclopedia of education.* New York: Macmillan. Reprinted in G. H. Bracht, K. D. Hopkins, and J. C. Stanley, eds. 1972. *Perspectives in educational and psychological measurement.* Englewood Cliffs, N.J.: Prentice-Hall. Selection 6.

———. 1977. The gifted and the creative: A fifty-year perspective. Baltimore: Johns Hopkins University Press.

———. 1980 On educating the gifted. *Educational Researcher,* 9:8–13.

———, and E. Y. BEEMAN. 1956. Interaction of major field of study with kind of test. *Psychological Reports,* 2:333–36.

———, and D. L. BOLTON. 1957. A review of Bloom's *Taxonomy of educational objectives. Educational and Psychological Measurement,* 17: 631–34.

———, and K. D. HOPKINS. 1972. *Educational and psychological measurement and evaluation.* Englewood Cliffs, N.J.: Prentice-Hall.

———, D. P. KEATING, and L. H. FOX, eds. 1974. *Mathematical talent: Discovery, description, and development.* Baltimore: The Johns Hopkins University Press.

———, W. C. GEORGE, and C. H. SOLANO, eds. 1977. *The gifted and the creative: A fifty-year perspective.* Baltimore: The Johns Hopkins University Press.

———, and A. C. PORTER. 1967. Correlation of Scholastic Aptitude Test score with college grades for Negroes versus whites. *Journal of Educational Measurement,* 4:199–218.

———, and M. D. WANG. 1970. Weighting test items and test-item options, an overview of the analytical and empirical literature. *Educational and Psychological Measurement,* 30:21–35.

STARCH, D., and E. C. ELLIOT. 1912. Reliability of grading high school work in English. *Scholastic Review,* 20:442–57.

———. 1913. Reliability of grading high school work in mathematics. *Scholastic Review,* 21: 254–59.

STARKMAN, S., C. BUTKOVICH, and T. MURRAY. 1976. The relationship among measures of cognitive development, learning proficiency, academic achievement, and IQ for seventh grade, low socioeconomic status black males. *Journal of Experimental Education,* 45:52–56.

STEININGER, M., R. E. JOHNSON, and D. K. KIRTS. 1964. Cheating on college examinations as a function of situationally aroused anxiety and hostility. *Journal of Educational Psychology,* 55:317–24.

STEPHENSON, W. 1953. *The study of behavior: Q-technique and its methodology.* Chicago: University of Chicago Press.

STERN, G. G. 1963. Measuring noncognitive variables in research on teaching. In N. L. Gage, ed., *Handbook of research on teaching.* Skokie, Ill.: Rand McNally. Chap. 9.

———. 1970. *People in context: Measuring person–environment congruence in education and industry.* New York: Wiley.

STEVENSON, H. W. 1961. Social reinforcement with children as a function of CA, sex of examiner, and sex of subject. *Journal of Abnormal and Social Psychology,* 63:147–54.

STEWART, N. 1947. AGCT scores of Army personnel grouped by occupation. *Occupations,* 26:5–41.

STOREY, A. G. 1968. The versatile multiple-choice item. *Journal of Educational Research,* 62: 169–72.

STRANG, H. R. 1977. The effects of technical and unfamiliar options upon guessing on multiple choice test items. *Journal of Educational Measurement,* 14:253–60.

——, and J. O. RUST. 1973. The effects of immediate knowledge of results and task definition on multiple-choice answering. *Journal of Experimental Education,* 42:77–80.

STRAUSS, M. A. 1969. *Family measurement techniques: Abstracts of published instruments, 1935–1965.* Minneapolis: University of Minnesota Press.

——. 1964. Measuring families. In H. T. Christensen, ed., *Handbook of marriage and the family.* Chicago: Rand McNally. Pp. 335–400.

STRICKER, L. J. 1978. *Indexes of social stratification: What do they measure?* Research Bulletin 78-14. Princeton, N.J.: Educational Testing Service.

STRONG, E. K., JR. 1953. Validity of occupational choice. *Educational and Psychological measurement,* 13:110–21.

SUPER, D. E., ed. 1958. *The use of multifactor tests in guidance.* Washington, D.C.: American Personnel and Guidance Association.

——, W. F. BRAASCH, and J. B. SHAY. 1947. The effect of distractions on test results. *Journal of Education Psychology,* 38:373–77.

——, and P. L. OVERSTREET. 1960. *The vocational maturity of ninth grade boys.* New York: Columbia University, Teachers College.

SURVEY RESEARCH CENTER. 1976. *Interviewer's manual,* rev. ed. Ann Arbor: University of Michigan.

SWAN, R. J., and K. D. HOPKINS. 1965. An investigation of theoretical and empirical chance scores on selected standardized group tests. *California Journal of Educational Research,* 16:34–41.

SWINEFORD, F. 1938. The measurement of a personality trait. *Journal of Educational Psychology,* 29:295–300.

——. 1941. Analysis of a personality trait. *Journal of Educational Psychology,* 32:438–44.

——, and P. M. MILLER. 1953. Effects of directions regarding guessing on item statistics of a multiple-choice vocabulary test. *Journal of Educational Psychology,* 44:129–39.

TANUR, J. M., F. MOSTELLER, W. H. KRUSKAL, R. F. LINK, R. S. PIETERS, G. R. RISING, and E. L. LEHMANN. 1978. *Statistics: A guide to the unknown,* 2nd ed. San Francisco: Holden-Day.

TATE, M. W. 1948. Individual differences in speed of response in mental test materials of varying degrees of difficulty. *Educational and Psychological Measurement,* 8:353–74.

TAYLOR, E. A., and J. H. CRANDALL. 1962. A study of the "norm-equivalence" of certain tests approved for the California state testing program. *California Journal of Educational Research,* 13:186–92.

TAYLOR, W. L. 1953. Cloze procedure: A new tool for measuring readability. *Journalism Quarterly,* 30:415–33.

——. 1956. Recent developments in the cloze procedure. *Journalism Quarterly,* 33:42–48.

TERMAN, L. M. 1954. The discovery and encouragement of exceptional talent. *American Psychologist,* 9:221–30.

——, and M. A. MERRILL. 1937. *Measuring intelligence.* Boston: Houghton Mifflin.

——. 1960. *Stanford-Binet Intelligence Scale.* Boston: Houghton Mifflin.

——. 1972. *Stanford-Binet Intelligence Scale: Manual for third revision.* Boston: Houghton Mifflin.

TERWILLIGER, J. S. 1971. *Assigning grades to students.* Glenview, Ill.: Scott, Foresman.

THACKER, A. J., and R. E. WILLIAMS. 1974. The relationship of the graduate record examination to grade point average and success in graduate school. *Educational and Psychological Measurement,* 34:939–44.

THOMAS, C. L., and J. C. STANLEY. 1969. Effectiveness of high school grades for predicting college grades of black students: A review and discussion. *Journal of Educational Measurement,* 6:203–15.

THOMAS, H. 1970. Psychological assessment instruments for use with human infants. *Merrill-Palmer Quarterly,* 16:179–223.

THORNDIKE, E. L. 1910. *Handwriting.* New York: Columbia University, Teachers College, Bureau of Publications.

——. 1918. The nature, purposes, and general methods of measurements of educational products. In *The seventh yearbook of the National Society for the Study of Education, Part II.* P. 16.

——. 1926. *The measurement of intelligence.* New York: Columbia University, Teachers College.

THORNDIKE, R. L. 1949. *Personnel selection.* New York: Wiley.

——. 1951. Reliability. In E. F. Lindquist, ed., *Educational measurement.* Washington, D.C.: American Council on Education.

——. 1963a. The concepts of over- and under-achievement. New York: Columbia University, Teachers College, Bureau of Publications.

——. 1963b. Some methodological issues in the study of creativity. In *Proceedings of the 1962 Invitational Conference on Testing Problems.* Princeton, N.J.: Educational Testing Service. Reprinted in G. H. Bracht, K. D. Hopkins, and J. C. Stanley, eds. 1972. *Perspectives in educational and psychological measurement.* Englewood Cliffs, N.J.: Prentice-Hall. Selection 21.

——. 1968. Review of Rosenthal and Jacobson's *Pygmalion in the classroom. American Educational Research Journal,* 5:708–11.

——. 1969. Marks and marking systems. In R. L. Ebel, ed., *Encyclopedia of educational research,* 4th ed. New York: Macmillan. Pp. 759–66. Reprinted in G. H. Bracht, K. D. Hopkins, and J. C. Stanley, eds. 1972. *Perspectives in educational and psychological measurement.* Englewood Cliffs, N.J.: Prentice-Hall. Selection 17.

——, and G. A. GALLUP. 1944. Verbal intelligence of the American adult. *Journal of General Psychology,* 30:75–85.

THORNDIKE, R. L., and E. HAGEN. 1974. *Technical manual: Cognitive Abilities Test.* New York: Houghton Mifflin.

——. 1977. *Measurement and evaluation in psychology and education,* 4th ed. New York: Wiley.

THURSTONE, L. L. 1938. Primary mental abilities. *Psychometric Monographs,* 1.

——. 1955. The differential growth of mental abilities. Paper no. 14. University of North Carolina, Psychometric Laboratory.

TIME MAGAZINE, 1979. Tests on trial in Florida. July 30, p. 66.

TINKELMAN, S. N. 1971. Planning the objective test. In R. L. Thorndike, ed., *Educational measurement,* 2nd ed. Washington, D.C.: American Council on Education.

TOLLEFSON, N. 1978. Effect of item-difficulty arrangement and state anxiety on achievement test performance. In *AERA 1978 annual meeting abstracts of papers.* Washington D.C.: American Educational Research Association.

TORRANCE, E. P. 1962. Guiding creative talent. Englewood Cliffs, N.J.: Prentice-Hall.

TRAUB, R. E., and R. K. HAMBLETON. 1972. The effect of scoring instructions and degree of speededness on the validity and reliability of multiple-choice tests. *Educational and Psychological Measurement,* 32:737–58.

TRAUB, R. E., R. K. HAMBLETON, and B. SINGH. 1968. Effects of promised reward and threatened penalty on performance of a multiple-choice vocabulary test. Unpublished manuscript, The Ontario Institute for Studies in Education.

TRENTHAM, L. L. 1975. The effect of distractions on sixth-grade students in a testing situation. *Journal of Educational Measurement,* 12:13–18.

TRINKAUS, W. K. 1954. The permanence of vocational interests of college freshmen. *Educational and Psychological Measurement,* 14:641–46.

TROWBRIDGE, N. 1972. Self-concept and socio-economic status in elementary group membership among public school students. *American Educational Research Journal,* 9:525–37.

TUCKMAN, J., and I. LORGE. 1954. The influence of changed directions on stereotypes about aging: Before and after instruction. *Educational and Psychological Measurement,* 14:128–32.

TUINMAN, J. J., R. FARR, and B. E. BLANTON. 1972. Increases in test scores as a function of material rewards. *Journal of Educational Measurement,* 9:215–23.

TYLER, L. E. 1956. The GED tests—Friends or foes? *California Journal of Educational Research,* 3:66–71.

——. 1958. The stability of patterns of primary mental abilities among grade school children. *Educational and Psychological Measurement,* 18:769–74.

TYLER, R. W. 1960. What testing does to teachers and students. *The 1959 Invitational Conference on Testing Problems.* Princeton, N.J.: Educational Testing Service.

——. 1973. Assessing educational achievement in the affective domain. *NCME Measurement in Education,* 4:1–8.

——, and R. M. Wolf, eds. 1974. *Crucial issues in testing.* Berkeley, Calif.: McCutchan.

Underwood, B. J. 1964. Laboratory studies of verbal learning. In E. R. Hilgard, ed., *Theories of learning and instruction, the sixty-third yearbook of the National Society for the Study of Education.* Chicago: University of Chicago Press.

U.S. Civil Service Commission. 1977. Uniform guidelines on employee selection procedures. *Federal Register,* 42, no. 251.

Vallance, T. R. 1947. A comparison of essay and objective examination as learning experience. *Journal of Educational Research,* 41:279–88.

Veal, S. R., and E. F. Biesbrock. 1971. Primary essay tests. *Journal of Educational Measurement,* 8:45–46.

Vecchio, R., and F. Costin. 1977. Predicting teacher effectiveness from graduate admissions predictors. *American Educational Research Journal,* 14:169–76.

Vernon, P. E. 1950. *The structure of human abilities.* London: Methuen.

——. 1954. Symposium on the effect of coaching and practice in intelligence tests. *British Journal of Educational Psychology,* 24:57–63.

——. 1962. The determinants of reading comprehension. *Educational and Psychological Measurement,* 22:269–86.

——. 1964. Creativity and intelligence. *Journal of Educational Research,* 6:163–69.

Votaw, D. F. 1936. The effect of "do not guess" directions on the validity of true-false and multiple-choice tests. *Journal of Educational Psychology.* 27:699–704.

Wahlstrom, M., and F. J. Boersma. 1968. The influence of test-wiseness upon achievement. *Educational and Psychological Measurement,* 28:413–20.

Walberg, H. J. 1967. Scholastic aptitude, the National Teacher Examinations, and teaching success. *Journal of Educational Research,* 61:129–31.

Walker, D. K. 1973. *Socioemotional measures for preschool and kindergarten children.* San Francisco: Jossey-Bass.

Walker, H. M. 1929. *Studies in the history of statistical method.* Baltimore: Williams & Wilkins.

——. 1950. Statistical understandings every teacher needs. *High School Journal,* 33:30–36.

Wallen, N. E. 1962. Development and application of tests of general mental ability. *Review of Educational Research,* 32:15–24.

Wang, M. D., and J. C. Stanley. 1970. Differential weighting: A review of methods and empirical studies. *Review of Educational Research,* 40:663–705.

Wanlop, K., and A. R. Hakstian. 1975. A comparison of several methods of assessing partial knowledge in multiple-choice tests: I. Scoring procedures. *Journal of Educational Measurement,* 12:219–30.

Ward, A. W., M. E. Backman, B. W. Hall, and J. L. Mazur. 1976. *Guide for school testing programs.* East Lansing, Mich.: National Council on Measurement in Education.

Ward, M. J., and C. A. Lindeman. n.d. *Instruments for measuring nursing practice and other health care variables,* vols. 1 and 2. Washington, D.C.: Government Printing Office.

Ward, M. J., C. Lindeman, and D. Bloch, eds. 1978. *Instruments for measuring nursing and other health care variables: Psychological and physiological.* Washington, D.C.: Government Printing Office.

Warner, W. L., M. Meeker, and K. Eells. 1949. *Social class in America.* Chicago: Science Research Associates.

Warren, G. R. 1975. The continuing controversy over grades. T. M. Report 51, ERIC Clearinghouse on Tests, Measurements, and Evaluation. Princeton, N.J.: Educational Testing Service.

Ward, W. C., N. Frederiksen, and S. B. Carlson. 1980. Construct validity of free-response and machine-scorable forms of a test. *Journal of Educational Measurement,* 17:11–30.

Waters, L. K. 1967. Effect of perceived scoring formula on some aspects of test performance. *Educational and Psychological Measurement,* 27:1005–10.

Wechsler, D. 1958. *The measurement and appraisal of adult intelligence,* 4th ed. Baltimore: Williams & Wilkins.

——. 1974. *Manual for the Wechsler Intelligence Scale for Children–Revised.* New York: Psychological Corp.

WEIDEMANN, C. C. 1933. Written examination procedures. *Phi Delta Kappan,* 16:78–83.

———. 1941. Review of essay test studies. *Journal of Higher Education,* 12:41–44.

WEISS, D. J. 1976. *Computerised ability testing 1972–1975.* University of Minnesota, Psychometric Methods Program.

WEISS, R. A. 1961. *The effects of practicing a test: A review of the literature.* Research Memorandum 61-12. Princeton, N.J.: Educational Testing Service.

WEITZMAN, E., and W. J. McNAMARA. 1946. Apt use of the inept choice in multiple-choice testing. *Journal of Educational Research,* 39:517–22.

WEVRICK, L. 1962. Response set in a multiple-choice test. *Educational and Psychological Measurement,* 22:533–38.

WHITCOMB, M. A. 1958. The IBM answer sheet as a major source of variance on highly speeded tests. *Educational and Psychological Measurement,* 18:757–59.

WHITE, E. E. 1886. *The elements of pedagogy.* New York: American Book Company.

WHITE, H. B. 1932. Testing as an aid to learning. *Educational Administration and Supervision,* 18:41–46.

WHITE, K. R. 1976. *The relationship between socioeconomic status and academic achievement.* Doctoral dissertation, University of Colorado.

WHITELY, S. E., and R. V. DAWIS. 1974. The nature of objectivity with the Rasch model. *Journal of Educational Measurement,* 11:163–78.

WIGHTWICK, M. I. 1945. *Vocational interest patterns.* Contributions to Education, no. 900. New York: Columbia University, Teachers College.

WILBUR, P. H. 1970. Positional responses set among high school students on multiple choice examinations. *Journal of Educational Measurement,* 7:161–63.

WILEY, D. E., J. R. COLLINS, and G. V. GLASS. 1970. *Sources of variation in multiple-choice test performance.* Research Paper 37. Boulder: University of Colorado, Laboratory of Educational Research.

WILL, G. F. 1976. D is for dodo. *Newsweek.* February 9, p. 84.

WILLIAMS, R. G., and J. E. WARE. 1976. Validity of student ratings of instruction under different incentive conditions. *Journal of Educational Psychology,* 68:48–56.

WILLIAMSON, M. L., and K. D. HOPKINS. 1967. The use of "none-of-these" versus homogeneous alternatives on multiple-choice tests: Experimental reliability and validity comparisons. *Journal of Educational Measurement,* 4:53–58.

WILSON, K. M. 1978. *Predicting the long-term performance in college of minority and nonminority students.* Research Bulletin RB-78-6. Princeton, N.J.: Educational Testing Service.

WISEMAN, S. and S. WRIGLEY. 1958. Essay-reliability: the effect of choice of essay-title. *Educational and Psychological Measurement,* 18: 129–38.

WISSLER, C. 1901. The correlation of mental and physical tests. *Psychological Review, Monograph Supplements,* 8 (16). 62 pp.

WITTIG, M. E., and A. C. PETERSEN, eds. 1979. *Sex-related differences in cognitive functioning: Developmental issues.* A volume in the Academic Press Series in Cognition and Perception. New York: Academic Press.

WODTKE, K. H. 1964. Some data on the reliability and validity of creativity tests at the elementary school level. *Educational and Psychological Measurement,* 24:399–408.

WOMER, F. B., and N. K. WAHI. 1969. Test use. In R. L. Ebel, ed., *Encyclopedia of educational research,* 4th ed. New York: Macmillan. Pp. 1461–69.

WOOD, R. 1976. Inhibiting blind guessing: The effect of instructions. *Journal of Educational Measurement,* 13:297–307.

———. 1977. Multiple choice: A state of the art report. *Evaluation in Education,* 1:191–280.

WOODRING, P. 1966. Are intelligence tests unfair? *Saturday Review.* April 16, pp. 79–80.

WRIGHT, W. H. E. 1944. The modified true–false item applied to testing in chemistry. *School Science and Mathematics,* 44:637–39.

WRINKLE, W. L. 1956. *Improving marking and reporting practices in elementary and secondary schools.* New York: Holt, Rinehart and Winston, Inc.

WYLIE, R. C. 1974. *The self-concept: A review of methodological considerations and measure-*

ment instruments. Lincoln: University of Nebraska Press.

YAMAMOTO, K. 1962. A study of the relationships between creative thinking abilities of fifth-grade teachers and academic achievement. Doctoral dissertation, University of Minnesota, Minneapolis.

———, and H. F. DIZNEY. 1965. Effects of three sets of test instructions on scores on an intelligence scale. *Educational and Psychological Measurement,* 25:87–94.

YATES, A. J., et al. 1953, 1954. Symposium on the effects of coaching and practice in intelligence tests. *British Journal of Educational Psychology,* 23:147–54; 24:1–8, 57–63.

YEE, A. H., and T. KRIEWALL. 1969. A new logical scoring key for the Minnesota Teacher Attitude Inventory. *Journal of Educational Measurement,* 6:11–14.

ZASTROW, C. H. 1970. Cheating among college graduate students. *Journal of Educational Research,* 64:157–60.

ZILLER, R. C. 1957. A measure of the gambling response set in objective tests. *Psychometrika,* 22:289–92.

ZONTINE, P. L., H. C. RICHARDS, and H. R. STRANG. 1972. Effect of contingent reinforcement on Peabody Picture Vocabulary Test performance. *Psychological Reports,* 31:615–22.

ZYTOWSKI, D. G. 1976. Predictive validity of the Kuder Occupational Interest Survey: A 12- to 19-year follow-up. *Journal of Counseling Psychology,* 23:221–33.

Name Index

Subject Index